RACING POST RACING & FOOTBALL OUT

FOOTBALL ANNUAL 2018 2019

Editor *Dan Sait*

Assistant Editor *Joe Champion*

Contributors *Dan Childs, Michael Cox, Steve Davies, Alex Deacon, Liam Flin, Glenn Jeffreys, Mark Langdon, Chris Mann, James Milton, Kevin Pullein, Andrew Wilsher*

Data editor *Paul Charlton*

Cover design *Jay Vincent*

Published in 2018 by Racing Post Books,
27 Kingfisher Court, Hambridge Road, Newbury, Berkshire, RG14 5SJ

ISBN 978-1-910497-54-8
ISSN 977-1753-334-605

Printed and bound in Great Britain by Buxton Press

CONTENTS

Ladbrokes

9/2
LIVERPOOL TO WIN
THE PREMIER LEAGUE 18/19

PREMIER LEAGUE OUTRIGHT

MAN CITY	4/6	NEWCASTLE	500/1
LIVERPOOL	9/2	SOUTHAMPTON	500/1
MAN UTD	6/1	WEST HAM	500/1
CHELSEA	9/1	BOURNEMOUTH	750/1
TOTTENHAM	11/1	BURNLEY	750/1
ARSENAL	25/1	BRIGHTON	1000/1
WOLVES	100/1	CARDIFF	1000/1
EVERTON	200/1	FULHAM	1000/1
LEICESTER	200/1	HUDDERSFIELD	1000/1
CRYSTAL PALACE	500/1	WATFORD	1000/1

Each-way 1/3 the odds a place 1-2

EDITOR'S INTRODUCTION

A one-horse race in the Premier League, the same old club retaining the Champions League and England slipping out of the World Cup at the first sight of a serious opponent – how on earth did 2017-18 manage to make such a sumptuous silk purse out of a sow's ear of ingredients?

Pep Guardiola's Manchester City wowed us with attacking play and creative genius. Giddy talk of quadruples is almost always premature, but in City's case it felt justified – this was a side who looked destined for immortality. They may still be.

Real Madrid spluttered in Europe, teasing with an air of vulnerability before ruthlessly cutting rivals down with uncontainable brilliance. Cristiano Ronaldo's stunning overhead kick looked a goal for the ages, but was usurped within weeks by Gareth Bale's act of genius in a Champions League showpiece that had everything – a truly fitting finale to a competition in which caution was thrown to the wind to rain goals and glory.

To cap it all, a World Cup to reignite our love affair with the international game. The trophy went to deserving victors across the channel, but for once England supporters felt like winners. Their team may not have been the best in Russia, far from it, but it was once again *their* team. For so long the relationship had looked irreparably toxic, but four weeks in Russia has changed all that – England fans are free to dream.

Trophies may never follow, but if last season reminded us of anything, it is that football is still at its best when played with vigour and watched with a smile. For fans of the beautiful game, 2017-18 really was the season that football came home.

Dan Sait

Pep put any doubts to bed but future may yet be Red

1 Pep Guardiola is pretty good

The knives were out for Pep Guardiola after a trophyless first season at the Etihad, but those who called him Fraudiola were left eating their words as the former Barcelona and Bayern boss bounced back in stunning style.

Manchester City were all class as they won the League Cup and Premier League, the latter by 19 points from neighbours United with 106 goals and 100 points in the process.

Records tumbled as City destroyed most of their opponents with Kevin De Bruyne particularly impressive with his range of midfield passing.

Of course, Guardiola is helped by possessing a big budget but the signings still have to come off and goalkeeper Ederson added a new dimension to City's approach, not only producing super saves but starting off attacks with his feet.

Guardiola proved his coaching prowess as he improved the likes of Raheem Sterling and Leroy Sane, while who would have thought Fabian Delph could be so good as a left-back? That's the real genius of Guardiola.

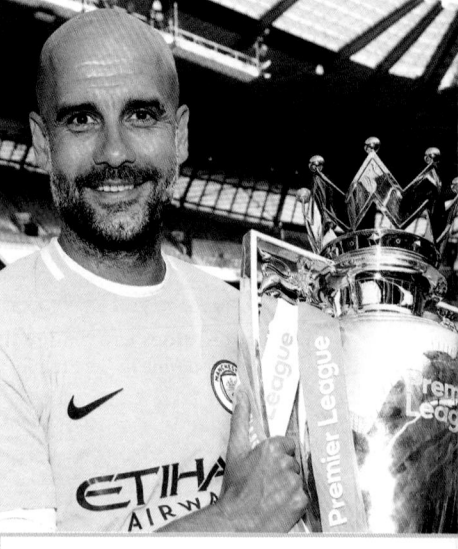

2 Joyless Jose needs to ditch negative approach

Most of Europe's top teams are committed to attacking football – the Champions League goals record duly fell last season – but one man refuses to get involved in such gung-ho battles.

United ground their way to second in the Premier League but it was mainly joyless stuff from Jose Mourinho's side, who must change to get close to winning the title.

Man City have set a benchmark of 100 points and even if they drop back slightly United will have to play to win every match, even the difficult away fixtures that Mourinho usually aims to draw.

3 Liverpool getting closer to silverware

Jurgen Klopp can't seem to take that final step with Liverpool but they are getting closer and the Champions League runners-up were better than their eventual fourth-placed finish in the Premier League suggests.

Don't forget they were seen as favourites to win at Old Trafford – that is a mark of the respect shown to them by bookmakers – and beating City three times is further evidence of Klopp improving the Merseysiders.

Virgil van Dijk's arrival in January helped them defensively and the front three of Mohamed Salah, Roberto Firmino and Sadio Mane should be just as devastating next season.

4 Promoted sides can bridge the gap

For the third time in the Premier League and the first time since 2012 all three promoted sides – Brighton, Huddersfield and Newcastle – stayed in the top flight.

That suggests the gap from the second tier to the bottom end of the Premier League is narrowing and Wolves and Fulham should be able to adjust. It will be tougher for Cardiff, but if Huddersfield can do it, why not the Bluebirds?

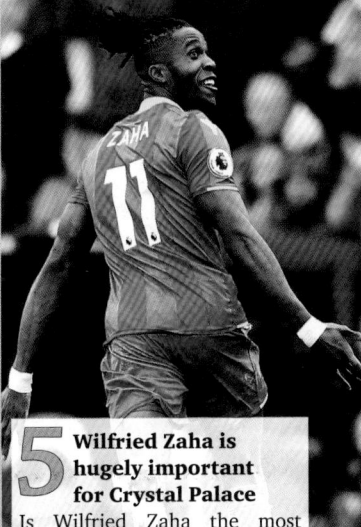

5 Wilfried Zaha is hugely important for Crystal Palace

Is Wilfried Zaha the most important individual to any side in the Premier League?

The twinkle-toed Eagles wide man failed to start ten league matches last season and Palace lost the lot. He simply has to remain at Selhurst Park.

Magical Manchester City, au revoir Arsene and the story of an Egyptian king

Nick Berry's 'Every Loser Wins' always strikes me as an encouraging anthem for punters, but football managers can also take solace from the 1986 hit. Take Frank de Boer, for example. Football is a results business, as we're so often told, so when your first seven games in charge end 0-3, 0-1, 0-2, 0-1, 0-1, 0-5 and 0-4, your long-term job prospects don't look great.

But De Boer's stunning losing start at Crystal Palace meant the 16-1 shot stylishly won the Premier League sack race, joining an illustrious list of former champions including Alain Perrin, Iain Dowie, Paul Hart and Jose Mourinho.

By the time De Boer was shown De Door, the title race was effectively over with Manchester City opening their legs and showing their class.

Pep Guardiola's entertainers won 18 of their first 20 league matches and there were few worries for anyone who backed them at 6-4 to be the division's top goalscorers – their first eight outings included two 5-0 wins, a 6-0 drubbing of Watford and a 7-2 thumping of Stoke.

City's hopes of completing an unbeaten campaign came to an end with a pulsating 4-3 defeat at Liverpool in January. Given the two teams' swashbuckling approaches, that outcome should have gone off favourite in the correct-score market.

Pep's men finished the campaign with 106 goals and 100 points – 19 more than second-placed Manchester United, who had a funny old season.

On expected-goals data, Mourinho's side should have finished midway down League One and they lost away to all three promoted clubs before being beaten at home by relegated West Brom in a 20-1 shock.

The Baggies had been 33-1 to finish bottom but even a lively team-bonding trip to Barcelona with Alan Pardew couldn't help them avoid the wooden spoon.

With Huddersfield, 4-6 ante-post relegation favourites, gamely staying up, Swansea (9-4) and Stoke (7-1) joined West Brom in the bottom three although 25-1 Southampton gave their relegation backers a tremendous run for their money.

Tottenham's Harry Kane was exposed as a two-season wonder, with a pathetic tally of 30 league goals leaving him two short of 66-1 Golden Boot winner Mohamed Salah.

The Egyptian and his Liverpool pals enjoyed a wonderful run to the Champions League final. The Reds, 22-1 to rule Europe at the start of the competition, lost 3-1 to Real Madrid as Sergio Ramos ran amok and Zinedine Zidane resigned in protest at Gareth Bale scoring a better Champions League final volley than his own against Bayer Leverkusen.

Arsenal gave Arsene Wenger the perfect send-off with a Europa League semi-final defeat to Atletico Madrid in which they missed loads of chances and allowed Diego Costa to score the decisive goal. It's what Arsene would have wanted …

New Gunners boss Unai Emery will be keen to avoid Burnley in this term's Europa League. The Clarets landed odds of 14-1 in an opening-weekend win at Chelsea and ended up seventh, in a photo-finish with champions

Benjamin Mendy attempts to strum a tune on the Premier League trophy

City in the Premier League handicap.

The Citizens thumped Arsenal in the League Cup final while the FA Cup final produced an amazing story with 50,000-1 shots Blyth Spartans beating Royal Engineers 6-5. Just kidding, Chelsea won 1-0 against Manchester United – and there's absolutely no shame in admitting you've already forgotten that game.

Celtic hacked up in Scotland, as did Wolves in the Championship under Nuno 'what does he know about English football?' Espirito Santo. Neil 'what doesn't he know about English football?' Warnock guided Cardiff to automatic promotion with Fulham pipping John Terry's Aston Villa in the playoff final.

At the other end of the table, Sunderland completed back-to-back relegations – a 16-1 chance when it all kicked off last August.

The Black Cats' pre-season campaign ended with a 5-0 friendly defeat at home to Celtic and it was all downhill from there – at least until the final day when they thumped champions Wolves 3-0. You're only as good as your last game.

Lancashire hotpots Wigan and Blackburn won automatic promotion in League One, but spare a thought for Shrewsbury, 40-1 ante-post outsiders of 24 to go up. They finished third before losing to a 103rd-minute goal against Rotherham in the playoff final.

And down in League Two, champions Accrington proved it is possible to win the league title without spending £100m on full-backs. There you go, Pep – that's your mission for 2018-19.

Past results not always the definitive pointer for future events

T he race is not always to the swift or the battle to the strong, but that is the way to bet. So wrote Damon Runyon. Bettors in Runyon's stories usually lost more money than they won.

The first part of Runyon's sentence comes from the Bible. Ecclesiastes chapter nine verse 11 says: "The race is not to the swift or the battle to the strong, nor does food come to the wise or wealth to the brilliant or favour to the learned; but time and chance happen to them all."

Any bettor outside of a Runyon story who hears those words ought to nod their head in recognition.

Life is often at least a bit strange. Logic leads us to expect one thing then we get another. Why? One of the reasons is that our expectations develop from our experience and our experience can be misleading. What we saw might not have been all that was going on.

For every Premier League game last season I noted the number of goals scored by each team and the number and location of their attempts. In games that were not drawn this is what I found. Three out of four winners scored an unusually high number of goals for the number and position of their attempts. Three out of four losers scored an unusually low number of goals for the number and

Graham Taylor understood that winning teams aren't always as strong as some might think

position of their attempts.

In half of all games that were not drawn both things happened: the winners scored an abnormally large number of goals and the losers scored an abnormally small number of goals. Winners usually played better than losers, but usually they enjoyed good fortune as well.

The score tells us something about the performances of the teams, the quality and quantity of their scoring opportunities tell us something else – but not everything else. Sometimes a team's build-up play deserved a different reward: more and better chances,

Germany who then lost to South Korea.

Over a large number of games results become a less unreliable proxy for ability. Usually by then good and bad luck have mostly cancelled out. But not always. Some teams will have stacked up a lot more of one than the other.

Teams with really good results, more often than not, have enjoyed a surfeit of good fortune. They have a lot of ability but not as much as their results suggest. Teams with really bad results, more often than not, have suffered a surfeit of bad fortune. They have little ability but not as little as their results suggest.

One of the few people to understand these things was former England manager Graham Taylor. He said: "When you are winning you are rarely as good as people say you are, and when you are losing you are rarely as bad as people say you are."

Bettors like to back teams who have been getting fine results up until now. Punters collectively have a good day when those teams win. Bookmakers collectively have a good day when those teams draw or lose. Bookmakers, as a group, have more good days than bad. Punters, as a group, have more bad days than good. This must mean that teams with fine previous results win their next game less often than most bettors imagine. What else can it mean?

Thucydides was a historian in ancient Greece. He was born about 2,500 years ago and may have lived at the same time as the author of Ecclesiastes.

Thucydides wrote: "If Sparta was to become desolate, any antiquarian judging merely from its ruins would be inclined to regard the tale of Spartan domination as an idle myth, for the city is a mere collection of villages after the old fashion of Greece, and has none of those splendid public buildings and temples which characterise Athens, and whose remains, in the case of the latter city, would be so marvellous as to lead the superficial observer into an exaggerated estimate of Athenian power."

What we can see of the past does not tell us everything that went on in the past.

or fewer and worse. And sometimes a team's performance was unusual for them, either unusually good or unusually bad.

All of these things could tell us bits about the ability of a team. Often we notice only the score. So we form impressions of teams that are less accurate than they could be.

How inaccurate can past results be as a guide to future results? Think back to the group stage of the World Cup. Japan beat Colombia who then beat Poland who then beat Japan. Mexico beat Germany who then beat Sweden who then beat Mexico. South Korea lost to Sweden who then lost to

Melting pot of managerial heavyweights set to serve up a tactical masterclass

The Premier League has become the ultimate battleground for the world's greatest managers and 2018-19 may feature the most fascinating tactical battle the division has seen. Last season's top four are still coached by Pep Guardiola, Jose Mourinho, Mauricio Pochettino and Jurgen Klopp. Now, there are two new names to add to the mix: Chelsea coach Maurizio Sarri and new Arsenal manager Unai Emery.

Both rank among the most fascinating tacticians in Europe and should bring an extra dimension to the battle for the top four.

The appointment of Sarri is as intriguing as it was belated – he was appointed just three weeks before Chelsea's trip to Wembley for the Community Shield – and Chelsea will surely not be entirely ready for the start of the new campaign, particularly with Sarri among the most demanding of managers.

Sarri's Napoli side were extraordinary. While they failed to dethrone Juventus, Sarri revolutionised the club after an unexciting Rafael Benitez regime, introducing a remarkable brand of pass-and-move football reminiscent of Guardiola's Barcelona side.

The commitment to possession play was striking, particularly how Napoli's defenders would tease opponents with their possession play, provoking a press, before suddenly cutting through the opposition lines at pace.

Building that type of approach requires patience, not something you associate with Chelsea, and there's a sense that Sarri could be another Andre Villas-Boas,.

Crucially, Sarri has brought Jorginho with him and the his intelligent distribution from the holding role was a key feature of Sarri's Napoli. Jorginho is likely to dovetail with N'Golo Kante, providing the creativity to complement Kante's energy.

In fact, Chelsea and Arsenal could be undergoing something of a role reversal.

Whereas Emery appreciated the requirement to state his belief in possession football at his Emirates unveiling, in truth he's a pragmatic coach who appreciates positional discipline and tactical flexibility, rather than focusing on aesthetics in the manner of Arsene Wenger.

There is, however, a similarity to Chelsea in the sense that Arsenal have recruited a holding midfielder, Lucas Torreira, who should command possession play in a similar mould to Jorginho at Chelsea. Torreira impressed for Uruguay at the World Cup with his mixture of tenacity and technicality and should ensure Arsenal's passing tempo is considerably higher than last season.

Emery's other purchases seem relatively unspectacular. Goalkeeper Bernd Leno is steady but nothing more, full-back Stephan Lichtsteiner is 34, and centre-back Sokratis Papastathopoulos is vulnerable to speed.

But they provide competition for places in defensive roles and Arsenal's improvement up front should come from Emery's work on the training ground. Henrikh Mkhitaryan, Mesut Ozil, Pierre-Emerick Aubameyang and Alexdandre Lacazette is a fearsome attacking unit, and Emery's ability to incorporate elements of 4-2-3-1 and 4-3-3 into his approach could work excellently.

Two other top clubs have also recruited new midfielders. Manchester United's Fred, signed from Shakhtar Donestk, is an

energetic all-rounder likely to be fielded in a box-to-box role, perhaps with Paul Pogba also afforded license to break forward, leaving Nemanja Matic sitting just behind. Fred is more adventurous than Chelsea's Jorginho or Arsenal's Torreira, and should bring extra urgency to United's attacking play.

It's Liverpool, however, who have made the most impressive signings. The arrival of Naby Keita provides Klopp with a brilliant all-round midfielder who, on his day, boasts the ball-winning ability of Kante and the ball-playing ability of Jorginho, almost a one-man midfield by himself. The recruitment of Monaco's Fabinho, who is capable of playing either as a right-back or a box-to-box midfielder, adds yet more mobility and pressing quality to Klopp's side. Liverpool should be set for a serious title challenge.

Pochettino's Tottenham have, as ever, been more reserved in the transfer market, but their improvement is likely to come from internal improvement – this remains the youngest squad among the big six and Pochettino believes there's more to come.

Guardiola's City, meanwhile, lost out on Jorginho. Riyad Mahrez is an exciting addition and while some will question whether his purchase was strictly necessary, ultimately Guardiola had only four options – Leroy Sane, Sergio Aguero, Gabriel Jesus and Raheem Sterling – for his front three.

Mahrez's natural role is on the right, but he might be the type of player Guardiola deploys as a false nine, too. Guardiola rarely moves from one season to the next without a significant tactical change.

Indeed, a decisive tactical tweak might be crucial in staying ahead of the chasing pack as City's major contenders are likely to have improved since last season.

No-one has retained the Premier League title in the last decade. For Guardiola to break that pattern he might need to come up with something special amid competition from a host of highly skilled tacticians.

ASK THE JURY

Mark Langdon
RP Football Editor

Last season's best bet?
Cristiano Ronaldo winning the Champions League Golden Boot. He seems obsessed with personal awards which always makes him one to follow in the top goalscorer heats.

And what was your head-in-hands betting moment?
Luton picked up the each-way money but I was counting the title winnings a long, long way from home. They were miles clear and easily the best side in League Two. I'm still gutted.

How will the Premier League title race shape up?
Presumably Manchester City will win it, but perhaps not with as much ease as last season. The interesting one for me is the betting without City – I'd be against Manchester United.

And who wins the other three English leagues?
Middlesbrough for the second tier. They're a solid side who just made a slow start last term. Lincoln look like improvers in League Two and I find League One a head-scratcher. Maybe take a look at Southend and Rochdale at big each-way odds.

A dark horse for 2018-19...
Fulham are third-favourites to be relegated, but that looks bonkers. They excelled in the Championship and signing Jean Michael Seri shows intent.

Your betting golden rule...
The league table does lie so look beyond results.

Best bet for 2018-19?
Mansfield's spending power makes them top-seven bankers in League Two – they're 11-10.

Dan Childs
Racing Post tipster

Last season's best bet?
An each-way bet on Marseille to win the Europa League. They took advantage of a kind draw to land the place money despite losing the final against Atletico.

And what was your head-in-hands betting moment?
Northampton were having a tough time in League One but I fancied them to turn things around against Bristol Rovers in October. They lost 6-0 at home.

How will the Premier League title race shape up?
Manchester City look streets ahead of the competition but it will be tough for them to reach 100 points again. Another second place beckons for United while Tottenham and Liverpool could fill the other Champions League spots.

And who wins the other three English leagues?
Stoke, Sunderland and MK Dons.

A dark horse for 2018-19...
Leeds have the potential to improve. Extra investment has boosted their budget, giving them a better chance of challenging at the top end.

Your betting golden rule...
Be flexible from week to week. Football is a game of fine margins and it doesn't take much – perhaps the return of a key player – to turn a below-par team into an above-par side.

Best bet for 2018-19?
Sunderland can punch their weight by winning the League One title at 3-1. They have some exciting young players and new manager Jack Ross is used to success.

Steve Davies
Scotland expert

Last season's best bet?
Man City to win the Premier League? Pah, that was obvious! City on the handicap was, however, far more fruitful. The gulf between the best and the rest just gets bigger.

And what was your head-in-hands betting moment?
Would have been nice to have got a run – rather than relegation – from my League One each-way fancy, MK Dons.

How will the Premier League title race shape up?
Manchester City will win it again. From United again. Liverpool third and you can throw a blanket over the three London sides. So pretty much 2017-18 revisited.

And who wins the other three English leagues?
Aston Villa, Charlton and Northampton.

A dark horse for 2018-19...
Fulham are a huge price to finish in the top half. Such a progressive side and up against so many average teams, they can make the top ten.

Your betting golden rule...
The points gulf in final tables is far bigger than the handicap quotes would have you believe. If you fancy a short-priced divisional winner, it makes sense to back them at much fancier odds on the handicap.

Best bet for 2018-19?
Norwich to be relegated from the Championship. They signed off last term going backwards – three wins in 16 games – and with key men flying the nest, the Canaries look vulnerable.

Joe Champion
European expert

Last season's best bet?
Real Madrid to win the Champions League when they drew PSG in the last 16. Los Blancos virtually halved in price after that victory before getting the job done in Kiev.

And what was your head-in-hands betting moment?
I advised Mohamed Salah for Premier League top goalscorer at the start of last season, didn't have a penny on, and watched in horror as he claimed the Golden Boot in style.

How will the Premier League title race shape up?
Manchester City are going to take some catching and I fail to see how the chasing pack can close such a significant gap. The battle for second looks much more interesting although I still expect Manchester United to follow their city rivals home.

And who wins the other three English leagues?
Leeds, Sunderland, MK Dons.

A dark horse for 2018-19...
Everyone is talking about Wolves but it wouldn't be the biggest surprise were Fulham to register a top-ten finish.

Your betting golden rule...
Absorb as much information as you can. There's so much great stuff being written and produced which can help to make betting profitable.

Best bet for 2018-19?
Monaco without PSG in Ligue 1. Leonardo Jardim has done a marvellous job there and looks like staying for another season. They can continue to get closest to the dominant Parisians.

Dan Sait
RFO Football Editor

Last season's best bet?
Fulham's promotion was a relief after a year of antepost near-misses, but the World Cup was a money-spinner. The correct-score system I devised for the Outlook enjoyed a 50.89% return on investment and has serious potential. I'll be looking to fine-tune it during 2018-19.

And what was your head-in-hands betting moment?
Bolton scoring twice in the last five minutes of their final match to keep themselves up. Made for great radio but made a real mess of my antepost portfolio.

How will the Premier League title race shape up?
City will be hard to stop but Liverpool have made some big signings. At the prices I'd rather take Spurs and Arsenal to finish in the top four over Man United and Chelsea, who look too short at 4-11 and 8-11.

And who wins the other three English leagues?
West Brom, Sunderland, Lincoln.

A dark horse for 2018-19...
I'm not sure Nottingham Forest still count given the money coming in for them, but Sheffield Wednesday should improve after a poor 2017-18.

Your betting golden rule...
When you get something wrong, admit it, adapt and move on. We all make mistakes but learning from them is vital.

Best bet for 2018-19?
Rotherham to be relegated. It's only 5-4 but should be odds-on. They're out of their depth in the Championship so 4-1 for them to finish bottom looks tasty, too.

Colin Miles
Ladbrokes trader

Best result for Ladbrokes last season?
Accrington beating Luton to the League Two title was an important result for us. We were starting to sweat on Manchester City going unbeaten, but in the end their title win was a decent result.

And what was the worst?
Wolves winning the Championship was a bad result as punters were keen to be with them after their impressive start.

How will the Premier League title race shape up?
Manchester City are a class apart. I fancy Manchester United to pip Liverpool to second this season with Tottenham finishing fourth as I think Chelsea may get off to a slow start while Maurizio Sarri implements his style at Stamford Bridge.

And who wins the other three English leagues?
Stoke, Luton and Lincoln.

A dark horse for 2017-18...
Plymouth really impressed me in the second half of last season and they could mount a challenge for a top-six finish in League One this term.

Your betting golden rule...
Bet with your head and not your heart, so I refrain from getting involved with the team that I support.

Best bet for 2017-18?
Luton to be promoted from League One. They have an ambitious manager who is always looking to strengthen his squad.

Premier League winner

	bet365	Betfair	Coral	Hills	Lads	Skybet
Man City	8-13	8-13	4-6	8-13	4-6	2-3
Liverpool	9-2	9-2	9-2	9-2	9-2	9-2
Man Utd	13-2	6	6	7	6	7
Chelsea	14	11	9	14	9	12
Tottenham	16	13	11	14	11	12
Arsenal	20	20	25	25	25	25
Everton	250	100	200	200	200	250
Wolves	250	200	100	150	100	250
Leicester	300	200	200	200	200	250
West Ham	300	500	500	500	500	500
Southampton	500	500	500	500	500	500
Crystal Palace	750	500	500	500	500	750
Newcastle	750	500	500	500	500	750
Bournemouth	1000	500	750	750	750	1000
Brighton	1000	500	1000	1000	1000	1000
Burnley	750	500	750	750	750	1000
Watford	1000	500	1000	1000	1000	1000
Fulham	1000	500	1000	1000	1000	1500
Huddersfield	1500	500	1000	1000	1000	1500
Cardiff	2000	500	1000	1500	1000	2000

Win or each-way

Premier League relegation

	bet365	Betfair	Coral	Hills	Lads	Skybet
Cardiff	8-11	4-6	4-5	4-5	4-5	2-3
Huddersfield	6-5	11-10	6-5	5-4	6-5	6-5
Fulham	6-4	8-5	13-8	13-8	13-8	15-8
Brighton	2	8-5	2	9-4	2	9-4
Watford	2	17-10	15-8	2	15-8	7-4
Burnley	4	7-2	7-2	7-2	7-2	10-3
Bournemouth	5	9-2	9-2	9-2	9-2	5
Newcastle	6	5	5	5	5	5
Crystal Palace	11-2	5	6	5	6	5
Southampton	7	15-2	7	8	7	8
Wolves	6	11-2	7	13-2	7	9
West Ham	6	6	6	7	6	9
Leicester	14	14	14	12	14	12
Everton	33	35	33	33	33	33
Arsenal	500	500	500	100	500	500
Chelsea	250	500	500	250	500	500
Tottenham	1000	500	1000	500	1000	1000
Liverpool	2000	500	1000	500	1000	2000
Man Utd	2000	500	1000	500	1000	2000
Man City	4000	500	2500	1000	2500	5000

Win only

Premier League top-four finish

	bet365	Betfair	Coral	Hills	Lads	Skybet
Man City	1-16	1-25	1-20	1-16	1-20	1-25
Liverpool	1-4	1-6	2-9	1-6	2-9	2-7
Man Utd	2-7	1-6	2-7	2-7	2-7	4-11
Chelsea	4-6	8-11	4-6	4-6	4-6	8-11
Tottenham	4-5	4-5	4-5	4-5	4-5	8-11
Arsenal	2	7-4	2	9-4	2	3-2
Everton	20	20	16	20	16	14
Leicester	33	33	33	25	33	33
Wolves	40	33	25	16	25	33
West Ham	40	50	50	40	50	40
Southampton	50	66	50	33	50	50
Crystal Palace	66	80	66	50	66	80
Newcastle	66	100	66	80	66	100
Bournemouth	100	100	100	100	100	80
Burnley	150	100	100	100	100	200
Watford	150	150	150	150	150	200
Brighton	150	150	150	150	150	250
Huddersfield	200	200	200	150	200	250
Cardiff	300	250	250	150	250	500
Fulham	150	150	200	150	200	500

Win only

Premier League top-half finish

	bet365	Betfair	Coral	Hills	Lads	Skybet
Man City	-	-	-	-	-	-
Liverpool	-	-	-	-	-	-
Man Utd	-	-	-	-	-	-
Chelsea	-	-	-	-	-	1-100
Tottenham	-	-	-	-	-	1-100
Arsenal	1-200	1-100	1-200	1-200	1-200	1-33
Everton	1-3	1-4	1-3	1-4	1-3	2-5
Leicester	8-11	8-11	4-6	8-11	4-6	10-11
Wolves	6-5	10-11	11-10	11-10	11-10	11-10
Southampton	11-8	6-5	11-8	11-8	11-8	5-4
West Ham	5-4	6-4	11-10	5-6	11-10	6-5
Crystal Palace	9-4	15-8	11-5	9-4	11-5	2
Newcastle	9-4	15-8	11-5	2	11-5	2
Bournemouth	5-2	15-8	9-4	5-2	9-4	15-8
Burnley	4	3	4	4	4	3
Brighton	11-2	5	5	5	5	9-2
Watford	11-2	5	5	11-2	5	11-2
Fulham	11-2	5	5	5	5	11-2
Huddersfield	7	8	7	9	7	8
Cardiff	12	12	12	12	12	16

Win only

PREMIER LEAGUE ODDS, NEWS, REVIEWS, TIPS & BIG MATCH ANALYSIS

SOCCERBASE.COM

Championship winner

	bet365	Betfair	Coral	Hills	Lads	Skybet
Stoke	5	11-2	11-2	6	11-2	9-2
West Brom	8	7	8	8	8	7
Middlesbrough	9	8	8	8	8	9
Nottm Forest	10	9	10	10	10	10
Leeds	12	11	10	11	10	10
Swansea	12	10	10	11	10	11
Aston Villa	12	14	14	8	14	12
Derby	14	16	16	14	14	16
Brentford	16	12	16	16	16	14
Norwich	20	25	25	20	25	22
Sheffield Utd	20	20	18	25	20	22
Sheffield Wed	33	30	20	16	20	28
Preston	33	25	20	25	25	28
Wigan	40	40	33	25	33	33
Birmingham	33	40	33	33	33	40
Blackburn	50	50	33	40	33	40
Millwall	50	33	33	33	33	50
Hull	66	33	33	50	33	40
Reading	50	66	50	66	50	50
QPR	40	40	40	50	40	40
Ipswich	66	66	50	66	50	66
Bolton	200	100	80	80	80	100
Rotherham	200	150	80	80	80	150
Bristol City	33	33	25	25	25	25

Win or each-way

Championship relegation

	bet365	Betfair	Coral	Hills	Lads	Skybet
Rotherham	11-10	6-5	6-5	5-4	6-5	6-5
Bolton	1	5-4	5-4	11-10	5-4	3-2
Ipswich	3	12-5	11-4	5-2	11-4	11-4
Hull	7-2	6	9-2	4	9-2	4
Reading	4	9-2	4	10-3	4	4
QPR	9-2	5	4	4	4	11-2
Blackburn	9-2	9-2	9-2	5	9-2	11-2
Birmingham	8	5	5	5	5	5
Aston Villa	9	9	7	9	7	8
Millwall	9-2	9	6	9	6	5
Wigan	5	6	7	9	7	13-2
Bristol City	12	9	9	8	9	15-2
Norwich	12	9	10	9	10	11
Preston	9	10	9	12	9	8
Sheffield Utd	14	12	10	9	10	11
Sheffield Wed	10	9	11	14	11	8
Brentford	20	20	16	12	16	18
Derby	16	16	16	16	16	14
Leeds	20	12	16	14	16	18
Nottm Forest	25	16	14	14	14	18
Swansea	40	25	25	33	25	22
West Brom	40	40	33	33	33	33
Middlesbrough	50	33	33	40	33	40
Stoke	66	50	40	40	40	50

Win only

League One winner

	bet365	Betfair	Coral	Hills	Lads	Skybet
Sunderland	3	3	3	11-4	3	3
Barnsley	8	8	8	8	8	8
Charlton	12	10	12	12	11	10
Portsmouth	14	10	12	12	14	12
Luton	16	14	14	14	12	14
Peterborough	14	14	16	16	14	14
Scunthorpe	16	12	14	14	12	12
Plymouth	20	20	18	25	18	22
Coventry	20	20	20	20	20	20
Bradford	25	20	25	25	25	25
Oxford	16	25	25	25	25	22
Bristol Rovers	25	20	20	25	25	28
Southend	25	25	20	25	25	28
Burton	20	16	25	25	25	25
Fleetwood	20	20	33	33	33	33
Shrewsbury	25	20	20	20	20	33
Doncaster	33	25	25	33	25	33
Rochdale	40	25	33	33	33	33
Blackpool	40	25	33	33	25	33
Wimbledon	40	40	40	40	40	50
Walsall	50	66	50	50	50	100
Gillingham	66	80	50	66	50	100
Wycombe	100	66	66	66	66	150
Accrington	100	100	66	80	66	200

Win or each-way

League One relegation

	bet365	Betfair	Coral	Hills	Lads	Skybet
Accrington	5-4	6-5	5-4	6-5	5-4	6-5
Wycombe	11-8	13-10	5-4	11-8	5-4	3-2
Gillingham	15-8	7-4	7-4	11-8	7-4	7-4
Walsall	2	7-4	7-4	7-4	7-4	7-4
Wimbledon	5-2	12-5	9-4	2	9-4	3
Blackpool	5-2	12-5	10-3	7-2	10-3	10-3
Rochdale	3	3	7-2	9-2	7-2	4
Southend	5	5	5	4	5	5
Fleetwood	9-2	9-2	7-2	7-2	7-2	9-2
Bradford	7	5	5	11-2	5	4
Bristol Rovers	9-2	6	6	7	6	11-2
Coventry	6	5	6	7	6	6
Doncaster	9-2	7-2	9-2	7-2	9-2	9-2
Plymouth	7	6	6	13-2	6	13-2
Shrewsbury	5	6	11-2	6	11-2	4
Burton	8	15-2	7	10	7	5
Oxford	10	6	8	13-2	8	13-2
Peterborough	10	10	10	12	10	9
Scunthorpe	10	10	12	10	12	11
Charlton	16	16	16	16	16	12
Portsmouth	14	14	14	16	14	14
Luton	10	8	12	12	12	12
Barnsley	20	20	20	20	20	18
Sunderland	40	25	33	20	33	28

Win only

League Two winner

	bet365	Betfair	Coral	Hills	Lads	Skybet
MK Dons	6	6	6	13-2	6	13-2
Notts County	6	9	6	7	6	11-2
Lincoln	10	8	9	8	9	10
Mansfield	10	9	10	10	10	9
Northampton	12	10	12	12	12	12
Swindon	12	12	11	12	12	14
Bury	14	8	14	14	14	12
Oldham	20	9	16	16	16	22
Colchester	20	25	20	20	20	22
Carlisle	25	20	20	20	20	25
Exeter	25	16	20	20	20	25
Cambridge	25	25	20	20	20	25
Port Vale	20	25	20	25	25	33
Tranmere	25	16	20	20	18	20
Grimsby	40	40	33	33	33	33
Cheltenham	33	25	25	33	25	40
Crewe	33	33	33	40	33	40
Newport	40	40	25	33	33	33
Stevenage	40	33	33	33	25	40
Forest Green	40	33	40	40	40	40
Crawley	40	25	40	50	40	50
Macclesfield	66	50	50	50	50	100
Yeovil	66	50	66	66	66	100
Morecambe	100	50	66	66	66	150

Win or each-way

League Two relegation

	bet365	Betfair	Coral	Hills	Lads	Skybet
Morecambe	5-2	12-5	5-2	5-2	5-2	5-2
Macclesfield	7-2	7-2	7-2	7-2	7-2	4
Yeovil	7-2	3	3	10-3	3	7-2
Crawley	8	6	6	7	6	5
Crewe	8	15-2	7	7	7	8
Forest Green	8	15-2	7	7	7	13-2
Newport C	6	15-2	8	7	8	8
Cheltenham	8	8	9	9	9	9
Grimsby	7	15-2	7	7	7	10
Stevenage	8	15-2	8	7	8	15-2
Cambridge	12	12	12	12	12	14
Carlisle	14	12	12	12	12	12
Tranmere	14	12	12	14	12	14
Exeter	10	12	14	14	14	12
Port Vale	16	10	12	11	12	9
Oldham	8	12	14	14	14	12
Colchester	20	16	16	14	16	16
Bury Town	12	20	20	22	20	25
Northampton	33	25	25	20	25	25
Swindon	33	25	25	33	25	22
Lincoln	33	25	33	40	33	28
Mansfield	50	33	33	33	33	28
Notts County	50	33	40	25	40	33
MK Dons	100	40	50	40	50	40

Win only

National League winner

	bet365	Betfair	Coral	Hills	Lads	Skybet
Salford City	9-4	11-5	9-4	9-4	9-4	9-4
Chesterfield	8	7	8	7	8	7
Barnet	12	13	14	12	14	11
Fylde	14	14	14	14	14	14
Leyton Orient	14	14	12	12	12	12
Aldershot	16	14	16	16	16	14
Boreham	16	16	20	20	20	18
Ebbsfleet	16	14	20	20	20	18
Wrexham	16	14	20	14	20	14
Dover	25	25	25	25	25	25
Hartlepool	25	20	20	20	20	20
Sutton Utd	20	18	25	20	25	18
Bromley	33	25	25	33	25	25
Eastleigh	40	40	25	40	25	33
Halifax	40	33	40	40	40	40
Harrogate	40	33	40	33	40	40
Havant & W	33	33	40		40	33
Dagenham	40	16	50	20	50	20
Maidenhead	25	33	40	50	40	33
Maidstone	50	33	40	50	40	33
Barrow	66	66	66	33	66	50
Braintree	66	40	66	50	66	40
Gateshead	80	50	66	50	66	40
Solihull	100	66	100	80	100	40

Win or each-way

FA Cup winner

	bet365	Betfair	Coral	Hills	Lads	Skybet
Man City	4	7-2	4	7-2	4	4
Man Utd	6	13-2	11-2	13-2	11-2	5
Chelsea	7	13-2	7	11-2	7	13-2
Liverpool	6	6	11-2	7	11-2	7
Arsenal	8	9	8	9	8	8
Tottenham	8	7	7	9	7	7
Everton	20	25	20	20	20	20
Leicester	25	25	20	25	20	25
Wolves	33	33	33	25	33	33
West Ham	33	33	33	33	33	33
Newcastle	50	40	50	40	50	33
Southampton	50	50	33	50	33	33
Bournemouth	66	50	50	50	50	50
Burnley	66	33	66	40	66	40
Crystal Palace	50	33	50	50	50	33
Watford	50	50	50	50	50	50
Brighton	66	66	66	66	66	66
Fulham	66	66	66	66	66	66
Huddersfield	80	66	66	50	66	66
Cardiff	80	100	100	66	100	80
Middlesbrough	100	100	66	80	66	100
Stoke	100	100	66	50	66	80
West Brom	100	100	66	66	66	80
Aston Villa	150	100	150	80	150	66

Others available. Win or each-way. See bookmakers for details

Scottish Premiership winner

	bet365	Betfair	Coral	Hills	Lads	Skybet
Celtic	1-10	1-10	1-12	1-10	1-10	1-10
Rangers	8	8	8	7	7	8
Aberdeen	20	20	20	20	18	22
Hibernian	50	66	66	66	80	66
Kilmarnock	500	350	300	250	300	250
Hearts	200	200	200	200	200	500
Motherwell	1000	1000	1000	1000	1000	1000
Dundee	1500	2000	1000	1000	1000	2500
St Johnstone	2000	2000	1000	1000	1000	2500
Hamilton	2500	2500	1000	1000	1000	5000
Livingston	2500	2500	1000	1000	1000	5000
St Mirren	2500	2500	1000	1000	1000	5000

Win or each-way

Scottish Championship winner

	bet365	Betfair	Coral	Hills	Lads	Skybet
Dundee Utd	3	11-4	11-4	3	11-4	11-4
Ross County	3	11-4	11-4	3	11-4	3
Partick	10-3	11-4	3	3	3	10-3
Inverness	7	7	7	6	7	7
Dunfermline	10	10	8	10	8	10
Falkirk	10	10	10	10	10	9
Morton	16	20	20	20	20	20
Queen of Sth	25	25	20	25	20	25
Ayr	66	50	33	66	33	50
Alloa	80	90	100	66	100	80

Win or each-way

Scottish League One winner

	bet365	Betfair	Coral	Hills	Lads	Skybet
Dumbarton	2	7-4	7-4	7-4	7-4	7-4
Raith Rovers	13-8	9-5	15-8	2	15-8	2
Airdrie	8	7	7	7	7	6
Arbroath	12	10	8	9	8	10
Brechin	10	12	12	12	12	12
Stranraer	16	16	14	16	14	16
East Fife	20	16	20	20	20	16
Forfar	33	25	16	25	16	20
Montrose	25	33	33	25	33	28
Stenh'semuir	50	40	40	40	40	40

Win or each-way

Scottish League Two winner

	bet365	Betfair	Coral	Hills	Lads	Skybet
Peterhead	13-8	21-10	7-4	6-4	7-4	7-4
Clyde	7-4	11-4	5-2	11-4	5-2	11-4
Stirling	10	8	9	9	9	9
Edinburgh City	10	17-2	10		10	10
Queens Park	12	8	9	9	9	10
Elgin	14	17-2	9	10	9	10
Annan	16	14	14	14	14	16
Cowdenbeath	33	25	20	20	20	20
Berwick	40	25	25	28	25	25
Albion Rovers	50	18	16	20	16	20

Win or each-way

Champions League winner

	bet365	Betfair	Coral	Hills	Lads	Skybet
Man City	11-2	11-2	5	11-2	5	6
Juventus	7	7	7	13-2	7	7
Barcelona	5	13-2	6	13-2	6	6
Real Madrid	13-2	7	6	7	6	7
Paris St-G	13-2	8	6	8	6	7
Bayern	13-2	8	7	15-2	7	7
Liverpool	14	12	14	12	14	14
Atl Madrid	14	14	14	14	14	16
Man Utd	14	18	14	14	14	14
Tottenham	25	22	25	25	25	20
Napoli	40	25	33	20	40	25
Dortmund	40	40	50	40	40	33
Roma	40	50	50	40	50	50
Inter	50	50	66	40	66	50
Valencia	66	66	50	66	50	50
Monaco	80	100	50	100	50	80
Porto	100	66	80	100	80	80
Schalke	66		66	66	66	55
Benfica	150	100	150	125	150	100
Lyon	66	100	66	80	66	100
Hoffenheim	150	100	80	100	80	80
Shakhtar	150	200	100	200	100	150
Galatasaray	200	150	150	125	150	150
Ajax	250	200	250	200	250	250
Fenerbahce	250	250	250	125	250	250
CSKA	200	250	200	250	200	250
Dynamo Kiev	250	200	250	200	250	200
PSV	200	250	150	200	150	200
Basel	500	750	50	250	500	750
Lok. Moscow	200	300	200	500	200	250
Salzburg	500	200	250	250	250	200
Celtic	1000	750	500	250	500	1500

Others available. Win or each-way. See bookmakers for details

Europa League winner

	bet365	Betfair	Betfred	Betway	Hills	Skybet
Chelsea	7	-	6	7	6	7
Arsenal	9	-	7	9	7	9
Sevilla	16	-	16	16	14	16
Lazio	20	-	16	16	20	16
Leverkusen	20	-	16	20	20	20
Marseille	20	-	12	20	14	20
RB Leipzig	20	-	20	25	16	20
Villarreal	25	-	16	20	20	20
Real Betis	33	-	25	25	25	25
Frankfurt	40	-	33	33	33	33
Feyenoord	50	-	33	50	33	33
Sporting	66	-	40	33	33	25
Bordeaux	50	-	50	50	66	66
Burnley	66	-	125	100	100	80
Rangers	250		150	150	125	100
Hibernian	500		150	200	100	100

Others available. Win or each-way. See bookmakers for details

July 2018

Tue-Wed 10-11	Champions League first qualifying round, first leg
Thursday 12	Europa League first qualifying round, first leg
Saturday 14	Scottish League Cup group stage, matchday one
Tue-Wed 17-18	Champions League first qualifying round, second leg
	Scottish League Cup group stage, matchday two
Thursday 19	Europa League first qualifying round, second leg
Saturday 21	Scottish League Cup group stage, matchday three
Monday 23	Champions League third qualifying round draw
	Europa League third qualifying round draw
Tue-Wed 24-25	Champions League second qualifying round, first leg
	Scottish League Cup group stage, matchday four
Thursday 26	Europa League second qualifying round, first leg
Saturday 28	Scottish League Cup group stage, matchday five
Tuesday 31	Champions League second qualifying round, second leg

August 2018

Wednesday 1	Champions League second qualifying round, second leg
Thursday 2	Europa League second qualifying round, second leg
Friday 3	Start of Football League season
Saturday 4	Start of National League season
	Start of Scottish Football League season
Sunday 5	FA Community Shield
	Chelsea v Manchester City
Monday 6	Champions League playoff round draw
	Europa League playoff round draw
Tue-Wed 7-8	Champions League third qualifying round, first leg
Thursday 9	Europa League third qualifying round, first leg
Friday 10	Start of Dutch Eredivisie season
Saturday 11	Start of Premier League season
	Start of French Ligue 1 season
	Start of Portuguese Primeira Liga season
	FA Cup extra preliminary round
	Scottish Cup first preliminary round
Tuesday 14	Champions League third qualifying round, second leg
Tue-Wed 14-15	League Cup first round
	Scottish Challenge Cup first round
Wednesday 15	Uefa Super Cup, Tallinn
	Real Madrid v Atletico Madrid
Thursday 16	Europa League third qualifying round, second leg
Saturday 18	Scottish League Cup last 16
	Start of Spanish La Liga season
Sunday 19	Start of Italian Serie A season
Tue-Wed 21-22	Champions League playoff round, first leg
Thursday 23	Europa League playoff round, first legxc
Friday 24	Start of German Bundesliga season
Saturday 25	FA Cup preliminary round
Tue-Wed 28-29	Champions League playoff round, second leg
	League Cup second round
Thursday 30	Champions League group stage draw
	Europa League playoff round, second leg
Friday 31	Europa League group stage draw

September 2018

Saturday 1	Scottish Cup second preliminary round
	FA Vase first qualifying round
Tue-Wed 4-5	EFL Trophy group stage, matchday one

Thursday 6	Uefa Nations League matchday one
	Wales v Ireland
Friday 7	Uefa Nations League matchday one
Saturday 8	Uefa Nations League matchday one
	England v Spain
	Northern Ireland v Bosnia
	FA Cup first qualifying round
	Scottish Challenge Cup second round
Sunday 9	Uefa Nations League matchday two
	Denmark v Wales
Monday 10	Uefa Nations League matchday two
	Scotland v Albania
Tuesday 11	Uefa Nations League matchday two
Saturday 15	FA Vase second qualifying round
Tue-Wed 18-29	Champions League group stage, matchday one
Thursday 20	Europa League group stage, matchday one
Saturday 22	FA Cup second qualifying round
	Scottish Cup first round
Tue-Wed 25-26	League Cup third round
	Scottish League Cup quarter-finals

October 2018

Tue-Wed 2-3	Champions League group stage, matchday two
Thursday 4	Europa League group stage, matchday two
Saturday 6	FA Cup third qualifying round
Tue-Wed 9-10	EFL Trophy group stage, matchday two
Thursday 11	Uefa Nations League matchday three
	Israel v Scotland
Friday 12	Uefa Nations League matchday three
	Croatia v England
	Austria v Northern Ireland
Saturday 13	Uefa Nations League matchday three
	Ireland v Denmark
	FA Trophy preliminary round
	FA Vase first round
	Scottish Challenge Cup third round
Sunday 14	Uefa Nations League matchday four
	Spain v England
Monday 15	Uefa Nations League matchday four
	Bosnia v Northern Ireland
Tuesday 16	Uefa Nations League matchday four
	Ireland v Wales
Saturday 20	FA Cup fourth qualifying round
	Scottish Cup second round
Tue-Wed 23-24	Champions League group stage, matchday three
Thursday 25	Europa League group stage, matchday three
Saturday 27	Scottish League Cup semi-finals
	FA Trophy first qualifying round
Tue-Wed 30-31	League Cup fourth round

November 2018

Saturday 3	FA Vase second round
Tue-Wed 6-7	Champions League group stage, matchday four
Thursday 8	Europa League group stage, matchday four
Saturday 10	FA Cup first round
	FA Trophy second qualifying round
Tue-Wed 13-14	EFL Trophy group stage, matchday three

Thursday 15	Uefa Nations League matchday five
Friday 16	Uefa Nations League matchday five
	Wales v Denmark
Saturday 17	Uefa Nations League matchday five
	Albania v Scotland
	Scottish Challenge Cup quarter-final
Sunday 18	Uefa Nations League matchday six
	England v Croatia
	Northern Ireland v Austria
Monday 19	Uefa Nations League matchday six
	Denmark v Ireland
Tuesday 20	Uefa Nations League matchday six
	Scotland v Israel
Saturday 24	FA Trophy third qualifying round
	Scottish Cup third round
Tue-Wed 27-28	Champions League group stage, matchday five
Thursday 29	Europa League group stage, matchday five

December 2018

Saturday 1	FA Cup second round
	FA Vase third round
Sunday 2	Scottish League Cup final
Tue-Wed 4-5	EFL Trophy last 32
Tue-Wed 11-12	Champions League group stage, matchday six
Wednesday 12	Fifa Club World Cup begins, *United Arab Emirates*
Thursday 13	Europa League group stage, matchday six
Saturday 15	FA Trophy first round
Monday 17	Champions League last 16 draw
	Europa League last 32 draw
Tue-Wed 18-19	League Cup quarter-finals
Saturday 22	Fifa Club World Cup final, *Abu Dhabi*

January 2019

Saturday 5	FA Cup third round
	FA Vase fourth round
Tue-Wed 8-9	League Cup semi-final, first leg
	EFL Trophy last 16
Saturday 12	FA Trophy second round
Saturday 19	Scottish Cup fourth round
Tue-Wed 22-23	League Cup semi-final, second leg
	EFL Trophy quarter-final
Saturday 26	FA Cup fourth round

February 2019

Saturday 2	FA Trophy third round
	FA Vase fifth round
Saturday 9	Scottish Cup fifth round
Tue-Wed 12-13	Champions League last 16, first leg
Thursday 14	Europa League last 32, first leg
Saturday 16	FA Cup fifth round
	Scottish Challenge Cup semi-final
Tue-Wed 19-20	Champions League last 16, first leg
Thursday 21	Europa League last 32, second leg
Friday 22	Europa League last 16 draw
Saturday 23	FA Trophy fourth round
	FA Vase sixth round
Sunday 24	League Cup final
Tue-Wed 26-27	EFL Trophy semi-final

March 2019

Saturday 2	Scottish Cup quarter-finals
Tue-Wed 5-6	Champions League last 16, second leg
Thursday 7	Europa League last 16, first leg
Tue-Wed 12-13	Champions League last 16, second leg
Thursday 14	Europa League last 16, second leg
Friday 15	Champions League quarter-final draw
	Europa League quarter-final draw
Saturday 16	FA Cup quarter-final
	FA Trophy semi-final, first leg
	FA Vase semi-final, first leg
Saturday 23	FA Trophy semi-final, second leg
	FA Vase semi-final, second leg
	Scottish Challenge Cup final
Sunday 31	EFL Trophy final

April 2019

Sat-Sun 6-7	FA Cup semi-finals
Tue-Wed 9-10	Champions League quarter-final, first leg
Thursday 11	Europa League quarter-final, first leg
Sat-Sun 13-14	Scottish Cup semi-finals
Tue-Wed 16-17	Champions League quarter-final, second leg
Thursday 18	Europa League quarter-final, second leg
Friday 19	Champions League semi-final draw
	Europa League semi-final draw
Sat-Sun 13-14	Scottish Premiership splits
Saturday 27	National League season ends
Tuesday 30	Champions League semi-final, first leg

May 2019

Wednesday 1	Champions League semi-final, first leg
Thursday 2	Europa League semi-final, first leg
Saturday 4	Scottish Championship, League One, League Two seasons end
Sunday 5	Football League season ends
Tue-Wed 7-8	Champions League semi-final, second leg
Wednesday 8	Scottish Premiership playoffs begin
Thursday 9	Europa League semi-final, second leg
Saturday 11	National League Premier playoff final *(date to be confirmed)*
	National League North & South playoff finals *(dates TBC)*
Saturday 18	FA Cup final
Sunday 19	Premier League season ends
	FA Trophy final
	FA Vase final
	Scottish Premiership season ends
Thursday 23	Scottish Premiership playoff final, first leg
Saturday 25	League Two playoff final
	Scottish Cup final
Sunday 26	League One playoff final
	Scottish Premiership playoff final, second leg
Monday 27	Championship playoff final
Wednesday 29	Europa League final, *Baku*

June 2019

Saturday 1	Champions League final, *Madrid*
Wed-Sun 5-9	Uefa Nations League finals

PREMIER LEAGUE

Record-breaking Citizens unlikely to lose grip on their Premier League crown

C ritics of Manchester City will argue that it takes more than one season to define a great team but the Citizens' Premier League dominance is only just beginning and they look solid favourites to defend their title, writes Dan Childs. The frightening thing about City is that they could improve further. Pep Guardiola is eyeing multiple trophies and will be keen to address the issues which contributed to a Champions League defeat to Liverpool.

City had their problems against the Reds, who defeated them three times in four matches last season, but no other team dared to go toe-to-toe with Guardiola's side.

They look to improve their squad in every transfer window, but City are already strong in all areas and the best is yet to come from Leroy Sane and Gabriel Jesus. Getting close to the champions will be a costly business.

Manchester United should spend big but will have to get better value for money than was the case when they bought Alexis Sanchez from Arsenal. The highly-paid Chilean made little impact at Old Trafford, scoring three goals in 18 games.

Paul Pogba blew hot and cold while the most consistent of last summer's buys was Nemanja Matic, who had a solid campaign.

However, with further reinforcements United have a good chance of improving on their 81-point tally, making them strong candidates to be best of the rest.

Tottenham could post a top-three finish for the fourth-successive campaign. Mauricio Pochettino has built a talented young squad and the core group of players are likely to stay for at least one more year as they prepare to move into their new stadium. Spurs had their problems at Wembley and there is scope for them to get better results at the new arena.

A top-four finish is also on the cards for Liverpool, although talk of a possible title challenge looks fanciful despite some stunning individual performances.

The Reds' points tally (75) was one fewer than the season before when they didn't have Mohamed Salah on board as they continued to drop points against lesser teams, sharing the spoils in seven home games.

Chelsea are going through another summer of upheaval with Maurizio Sarri replacing Antonio Conte. They are likely to switch from a back three to Sarri's favoured back four and should be more attack-minded.

Napoli gained a reputation for attractive football under Sarri but ended the campaign without a major trophy while the Italian inherits a team which has been up and down in recent seasons. He will need time and new players to implement his ideas and an instant improvement is far from guaranteed.

Arsenal are used to stability but the winds of change are blowing through the Emirates with Unai Emery replacing Arsene Wenger.

Emery won the Europa League three times with Sevilla and his love affair with the competition may need to continue if Arsenal are to qualify for the Champions League. Arsenal are in need of major surgery but the new signings may take time to gel.

Recommendations

Man City to win Premier League, 4-6
Tottenham top-four finish, 4-5
West Ham top-half finish, 6-4
Southampton bottom-half finish, 8-13
Southampton to be relegated, 8-1
Huddersfield to be relegated, 5-4

Key to the data

The table next to every team profile shows head-to-head data for every side they will have to play in the league this season.

1 Every team the club will play in the league in the order they finished last season

2 Results of last season's league meetings **W** win **D** draw **L** loss. Where there was more than one league meeting, the latest is at the right. Regular season only

3 Head-to-head results over the last six seasons at the club's own ground. **P** games played **W** wins **D** draws **L** losses **OV** games with over 2.5 total goals **UN** games with under 2.5 total goals **BS** games in which both teams scored **CS** number of clean sheets for the home side

4 Promoted and relegated teams shown in fawn in the order in which they finished last season

5 League finishes over the last three seasons

6 Over and under 2.5 and both sides to score stats, including rank in club's division last season. The bar chart shows, horizontally, from top to bottom and rounded to the nearest 5 per cent, the division high, the profiled club and the division low

Leading scorers Numbers in brackets show first goals then 'any-time' goals

			2017-18		Last six seasons at home							
			H	A	P	W	D	L	OV	UN	BS	CS
1 Man City					0	0	3	2	1	1	0
2 Man United **3**			L	L	1	0	2	2	1	2	0
Tottenham			L	L	3	0	1	2	2	1	2	1
Liverpool			L	L	3	1	0	2	3	0	2	0
Chelsea			L	W	3	0	0	3	2	1	2	0
Arsenal			L	L	3	1	1	1	2	1	2	0
Burnley			W		3	1	1	1	2	2	2	0
Everton			L	L	3	2	1	0	2	1	2	1
Leicester			D		4	1	2	1	0	4	1	2
Newcastle			W		2	0	1	1	1	1	1	0
Crystal Palace			D	D	3	0	2	1	1	2	1	1
Bournemouth												
West Ham			D		3	1	1	1	3	0	3	0
Watford			W		5	1	3	1	1	4	3	1
Brighton			W		3	2	1	0	2	1	3	0
Huddersfield			L		3	2	1	0	2	1	2	1
Southampton			L		3	1	1	1	2	1	2	1
4 Wolves					1	1	0	0	1	0	1	0
Cardiff					1	1	0	0	0	1	1	0
Fulham					1	1	0	0	0	1	0	1

5

Season	Division	Pos	P	W	D	L	F	A	GD	Pts
2017-18	Premier League	12	38	11	11	16	45	61	-16	44
2016-17	Premier League	9	38	12	10	16	55	61	-12	46
2015-16	Premier League	16	38	11	9	18	45	67	-22	42

6 Over/Under 66%/34% 3rd   Both score 58%/42% 2nd

ARSENAL

Nickname: The Gunners
Colours: Red and white
Ground: Emirates Stadium
Tel: 020-7619-5000

Capacity: 60,432
www.arsenal.com

Unai Emery won three consecutive Europa League titles with Seville and his strong record in the competition could be a major bonus for Arsenal as they seek to retrieve Champions League status.

The Gunners' aim is to break back into the top four but, given the strength of their rivals and lack of a massive transfer war chest, that looks like a long-term project.

Arsenal's 63-point tally last season was their lowest since 1995 and their defensive record (51 goals conceded) was the worst among the top seven.

Defender Laurent Koscielny (Achilles) will miss the start of the season although experienced Swiss right-back Stephan Lichtsteiner has joined on a free transfer.

Arsenal's midfield struggled in away games last season and it will be tricky for them to improve on sixth place.

Longest run without a loss: 7
Longest run without a win: 3
Highest/lowest league position: 4/7
Clean sheets: 13
Yellow cards: 57 **Red cards:** 2
Average attendance: 48,166
Players used: 30
Leading scorer: A Lacazette 14 (4,12)

2017-18	H	A	P	W	D	L	OV	UN	BS	CS

2017-18			Last six seasons at home							
	H	A	P	W	D	L	OV	UN	BS	CS
Man City	L	L	6	1	3	2	4	2	4	0
Man United	L	L	6	2	2	2	3	3	3	3
Tottenham	W	L	6	3	3	0	1	5	4	2
Liverpool	D	L	6	2	3	1	4	2	4	2
Chelsea	D	D	6	1	3	2	3	3	2	3
Arsenal										
Burnley	W	W	3	3	0	0	3	0	1	2
Everton	W	W	6	4	2	0	3	3	4	2
Leicester	W	L	4	4	0	0	3	1	3	1
Newcastle	W	L	5	5	0	0	3	2	2	3
Crystal Palace	W	W	5	4	1	0	2	3	3	2
Bournemouth	W	L	3	3	0	0	2	1	1	2
West Ham	W	D	6	5	0	1	5	1	3	2
Watford	W	L	3	2	0	1	3	0	1	2
Brighton	W	L	1	1	0	0	0	1	0	1
Huddersfield	W	W	1	1	0	0	1	0	0	1
Southampton	W	D	6	5	1	0	3	3	3	3
Wolves	-	-	-	-	-	-	-	-	-	-
Cardiff			1	1	0	0	0	1	0	1
Fulham			2	1	1	0	1	1	1	1

Season	Division	Pos	P	W	D	L	F	A	GD	Pts
2017-18	Premier League	6	38	19	6	13	74	51	+23	63
2016-17	Premier League	5	38	23	6	9	77	44	+33	75
2015-16	Premier League	2	38	20	11	7	65	36	+29	71

Over/Under 68%/32% 2nd

Both score 55%/45% 5th

Key stat: Arsenal lost 11 Premier League away games last season. Only Watford, Brighton and West Brom were defeated more times on their travels

2017-18 Premier League appearances

	P	G	Y	R
P Aubameyang	12 (1)	10	-	-
H Bellerin	34 (1)	2	5	-
P Cech	34	0	1	-
C Chambers	10 (2)	0	1	-
F Coquelin	1 (6)	0	-	-
Eddie Nketiah	0 (3)	0	-	-
M Elneny	11 (2)	0	3	1
O Giroud	1 (15)	4	-	-
R Holding	9 (3)	0	3	-
A Iwobi	22 (4)	3	1	-
S Kolasinac	25 (2)	2	3	-
L Koscielny	25	2	4	-
A Lacazette	26 (6)	14	1	-
A Maitland-Niles	8 (7)	0	1	-
K Mavropanos	3	0	-	1
P Mertesacker	4 (2)	1	-	-
H Mkhitaryan	9 (2)	2	-	-
N Monreal	26 (2)	5	3	-
S Mustafi	25 (2)	3	6	-
R Nelson	2 (1)	0	-	-
D Ospina	4 (1)	0	-	-

	P	G	Y	R
A Ox-Chamberlain	3	0	-	-
M Ozil	24 (2)	4	4	-
A Ramsey	21 (3)	7	-	-
A Sanchez	17 (2)	7	4	-
T Walcott	0 (6)	0	-	-
D Welbeck	12 (16)	5	1	-
J Willock	1 (1)	0	-	-
J Wilshere	12 (8)	1	6	-
G Xhaka	37 (1)	1	10	-

Arsenal fans said farewell to Arsene Wenger

BOURNEMOUTH

Nickname: The Cherries
Colours: Red and black
Ground: Dean Court   **Capacity:** 11,700
Tel: 0344-576-1910   www.afcb.co.uk

Eddie Howe is the longest-serving manager in the Premier League but cannot afford to rest on his laurels if he is going to extend Bournemouth's top-flight status for another year.

The Cherries have played some excellent football over the last three seasons but their ongoing defensive problems are a concern.

They have shipped more than 60 league goals in each of the last three campaigns and remain unconvincing despite a club-record purchase of Nathan Ake.

Barring a change of approach, Howe's side must score freely to paper over the defensive cracks but none of their strikers reached double figures last term.

Bournemouth finished 11 points clear of the drop last term, but the league looks stronger and the Cherries could be at risk.

Longest run without a loss: 7
Longest run without a win: 8
Highest/lowest league position: 9/19
Clean sheets: 6
Yellow cards: 56 **Red cards:** 1
Average attendance: 24,658
Players used: 22
Leading scorer: C Wilson 8 (2,6) J King 8 (2,8)

	2017-18		Last six seasons at home							
	H	A	P	W	D	L	OV	UN	BS	CS
Man City	L	L	3	0	0	3	2	1	1	0
Man United	L	L	3	1	0	2	2	1	2	0
Tottenham	L	L	3	0	1	2	2	1	2	1
Liverpool	L	L	3	1	0	2	3	0	2	0
Chelsea	L	W	3	0	0	3	2	1	2	0
Arsenal	W	L	3	1	1	1	2	1	2	0
Burnley	L	W	3	1	1	1	2	1	3	0
Everton	W	L	3	2	1	0	2	1	2	1
Leicester	D	D	4	1	2	1	0	4	1	2
Newcastle	D	W	2	0	1	1	1	1	1	0
Crystal Palace	D	D	3	0	2	1	1	2	1	1
Bournemouth										
West Ham	D	D	3	1	1	1	3	0	3	0
Watford	L	D	5	1	3	1	1	4	3	1
Brighton	W	D	3	2	1	0	2	1	3	0
Huddersfield	W	L	3	2	1	0	2	1	2	1
Southampton	D	L	3	1	1	1	1	2	2	1
Wolves			1	1	0	0	1	0	1	0
Cardiff			1	1	0	0	1	0	1	0
Fulham			1	1	0	0	0	1	0	1

Season	Division	Pos	P	W	D	L	F	A	GD	Pts
2017-18	Premier League	12	38	11	11	16	45	61	-16	44
2016-17	Premier League	9	38	12	10	16	55	67	-12	46
2015-16	Premier League	16	38	11	9	18	45	67	-22	42

Over/Under 66%/34% 3rd   **Both score** 58%/42% 2nd

Key stat: Bournemouth have kept two clean sheets in their last league matches

2017-18 Premier League appearances

	P	G	Y	R		P	G	Y	R
B Afobe	5 (12)	0	-	-	A Surman	20 (5)	2 ∎	2	-
N Ake	37 (1)	2 ∎	5	-	C Wilson	23 (5)	8 ∎∎∎∎∎∎	-	-
H Arter	11 (2)	1 ∎	4	-					
A Begovic	38	0	2	-					
L Cook	25 (4)	0	5	-					
S Cook	31 (3)	2 ∎	5	-					
C Daniels	34 (1)	1 ∎	-	-					
J Defoe	11 (13)	4 ∎∎∎	1	-					
S Francis	31 (1)	0	9	1					
R Fraser	23 (3)	5 ∎∎∎∎	-	-					
D Gosling	21 (7)	2 ∎	8	-					
E Hyndman	1	0	-	-					
J Ibe	22 (10)	2 ∎	1	-					
J King	27 (6)	8 ∎∎∎∎∎∎	3	-					
T Mings	3 (1)	0	1	-					
L Mousset	4 (19)	2 ∎	1	-					
M Pugh	11 (9)	0	2	-					
J Simpson	1	0	-	-					
A Smith	22 (5)	1 ∎	6	-					
J Stanislas	17 (2)	5 ∎∎∎∎	1	-					

Callum Wilson (left) scored eight for the Cherries

BRIGHTON

Nickname: The Seagulls
Colours: Blue and white
Ground: Amex Stadium
Tel: 0344 324 6282

Capacity: 30,750
www.seagulls.co.uk

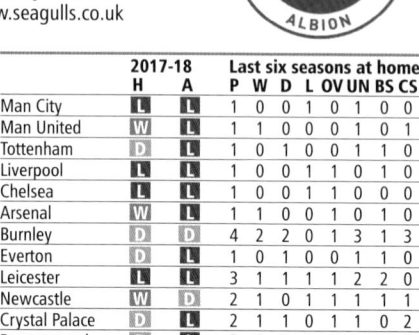

Brighton have progressed every season since appointing Chris Hughton in December 2014 and can build on last term's respectable 15th-placed finish.

Staying up is the only concern for newly-promoted clubs and the Seagulls did an excellent job, finishing seven points above the drop zone.

They played some of their best football in the run-in – drawing 1-1 at home to Tottenham and winning 1-0 at home to Manchester United – and have strengthened their squad over the summer.

Brighton had the best home record among the bottom-half teams, but paid the price for being too cautious on their travels. A few tweaks could enhance their away performances and help them climb further up the table.

Longest run without a loss: 5
Longest run without a win: 7
Highest/lowest league position: 8/16
Clean sheets: 10
Yellow cards: 54 **Red cards:** 2
Average attendance: 34,169
Players used: 24
Leading scorer: G Murray 12 (5,10)

	2017-18 H	2017-18 A	Last six seasons at home P	W	D	L	OV	UN	BS	CS
Man City	L	L	1	0	0	1	0	1	0	0
Man United	W	L	1	1	0	0	0	1	0	1
Tottenham	D	L	1	0	1	0	0	1	1	0
Liverpool	L	L	1	0	0	1	1	0	1	0
Chelsea	L	L	1	0	0	1	1	0	0	0
Arsenal	W	L	1	1	0	0	1	0	1	0
Burnley	D	D	4	2	2	0	1	3	1	3
Everton	D	L	1	0	1	0	0	1	1	0
Leicester	L	L	3	1	1	1	1	2	2	0
Newcastle	W	D	2	1	0	1	1	1	1	1
Crystal Palace	D	L	2	1	1	0	1	1	0	2
Bournemouth	D	L	3	0	2	1	1	2	2	0
West Ham	W	W	1	1	0	0	1	0	1	0
Watford	W	D	4	1	1	2	1	3	2	1
Brighton										
Huddersfield	D	L	6	3	3	0	2	4	3	3
Southampton	D	D	1	0	1	0	0	1	1	0
Wolves			4	2	1	1	0	4	1	2
Cardiff			4	1	3	0	0	4	2	2
Fulham			3	2	0	1	3	0	2	1

Season	Division	Pos	P	W	D	L	F	A	GD	Pts
2017-18	Premier League	15	38	9	13	16	34	54	-20	40
2016-17	Championship	2	46	28	9	9	74	40	+34	93
2015-16	Championship	3	46	24	17	5	72	42	+30	89

Over/Under 34%/66% 20th

Both score 42%/58% 16th

Key stat: Brighton were unbeaten at home to the bottom-half teams last season

2017-18 Premier League appearances

	P	G	Y	R
S Baldock	0 (2)	0	-	-
G Bong	25	0	2	-
I Brown	4 (9)	0	-	-
Bruno	23 (2)	0	3	-
S Duffy	37	0	8	-
L Dunk	38	1	7	-
C Goldson	2 (1)	0	1	-
P Gross	35 (3)	7	2	-
T Hemed	9 (7)	2	-	-
U Hunemeier	0 (1)	0	-	-
J Izquierdo	23 (9)	5	2	-
B Kayal	8 (11)	0	2	-
A Knockaert	27 (6)	3	4	1
J Locadia	3 (3)	1	-	-
S March	18 (18)	1	3	-
J Murphy	1 (3)	0	-	-
G Murray	25 (10)	12	9	-
D Propper	35	0	2	1
L Rosenior	1 (2)	0	-	-
M Ryan	38	0	-	-
M Schelotto	15 (5)	0	3	-

	P	G	Y	R
D Stephens	36	0	6	-
M Suttner	13 (1)	0	-	-
L Ulloa	2 (8)	1	-	-

Brighton enjoyed their Premier League bow

BURNLEY

Nickname: The Clarets
Colours: Claret and blue
Ground: Turf Moor **Capacity:** 21,800
Tel: 01282-446800 www.burnleyfootballclub.com

Sean Dyche has done an amazing job at Burnley but there are fine lines between success and failure in the Premier League and the 2018-19 campaign could be a tough one for the Clarets.

Securing European football was a fantastic achievement. However, depending on the outcome of Europa League qualification, it may lead to an increase in fixtures and place added strain on a fairly small squad.

Dyche wants to prioritise the Premier League but the supporters and the players are understandably excited about the prospect of playing in Europe and it may become a distraction.

Burnley are slowly adding quality to the group but a lot of their emphasis is on hard work and organisation. If the focus slips, it could pose a problem.

Longest run without a loss: 6
Longest run without a win: 11
Highest/lowest league position: 5/9
Clean sheets: 12
Yellow cards: 65 **Red cards:** 0
Average attendance: 29,159
Players used: 24
Leading scorer: C Wood 10 (4,9)

	2017-18 H	A	Last six seasons at home P	W	D	L	OV	UN	BS	CS
Man City	D	L	3	1	1	1	1	2	2	1
Man United	L	D	3	0	1	2	0	3	0	1
Tottenham	L	D	3	0	1	2	1	2	0	1
Liverpool	L	D	3	1	0	2	1	2	1	1
Chelsea	L	W	3	0	1	2	2	1	3	0
Arsenal	L	L	3	0	0	3	0	3	0	0
Burnley										
Everton	W	W	3	2	0	1	3	0	3	0
Leicester	W	L	5	2	0	3	1	4	1	1
Newcastle	W	D	2	1	1	0	0	2	1	1
Crystal Palace	W	L	4	3	0	1	2	2	2	2
Bournemouth	L	W	3	1	1	1	2	1	3	0
West Ham	D	W	3	0	1	2	2	1	3	0
Watford	W	W	4	2	2	0	0	4	1	3
Brighton	D	D	4	0	3	1	1	3	2	2
Huddersfield	D	D	4	2	1	1	2	2	2	1
Southampton	D	W	3	2	1	0	0	3	1	2
Wolves			2	1	1	0	0	2	1	1
Cardiff			2	0	2	0	0	2	1	1
Fulham			1	1	0	0	1	0	1	0

Season	Division	Pos	P	W	D	L	F	A	GD	Pts
2017-18	Premier League	7	38	14	12	12	36	39	-3	54
2016-17	Premier League	16	38	11	7	20	39	55	-16	40
2015-16	Championship	1	46	26	15	5	72	35	+37	93

Over/Under 37%/63% 17th **Both score** 45%/55% 14th

Key stat: Burnley scored 36 league goals last season – the lowest tally among the top 14 clubs

2017-18 Premier League appearances

	P	G		Y	R
S Arfield	15 (3)	2		3	-
P Bardsley	13	0		5	-
A Barnes	21 (15)	9		10	-
R Brady	15	1		3	-
J Cork	38	2		7	-
S Defour	24	1		6	-
J Gudmundsson	32 (3)	2		2	-
T Heaton	4	0		-	-
J Hendrick	29 (5)	2		1	-
A Lennon	13 (1)	0		2	-
K Long	16	1		1	-
M Lowton	25 (1)	0		1	-
D McNeil	0 (1)	0		-	-
B Mee	29	0		5	-
G Nkoudou Mbida	2 (6)	0		1	-
N Pope	34 (1)	0		3	-
J Tarkowski	31	0		5	-
C Taylor	10 (1)	0		3	-
S Vokes	7 (23)	4		3	-
J Walters	0 (3)	0		-	-
S Ward	28	1		1	-

	P	G		Y	R
N Wells	0 (9)	0		-	-
A Westwood	12 (7)	0		2	-
C Wood	20 (4)	10		1	-

Sean Dyche continues to do a fine job at Burnley

CARDIFF

Nickname: The Bluebirds
Colours: Red
Ground: Cardiff City Stadium
Tel: 0845-365-1115

Capacity: 33,280
www.cardiffcityfc.co.uk

Neil Warnock achieved a minor miracle by steering Cardiff to automatic promotion, but he faces an even bigger challenge this season with the Welsh side rated among the favourites to be relegated.

Cardiff play a physical, high-tempo style of football which is ideally suited to the Championship. It can also work in the Premier League, as has been demonstrated by Sean Dyche at Burnley, but Cardiff need better players if they are to cope with the step up in class.

Even in the second tier they lacked quality in attack. Winger Callum Paterson – formerly a right-back – was their top scorer with ten league goals while centre-back Sean Morrison notched seven.

Cardiff's budget will be among the smallest in the Premier League and they must recruit wisely if they are to survive.

Longest run without a loss: 13
Longest run without a win: 4
Highest/lowest league position: 1/4
Clean sheets: 19
Yellow cards: 82 **Red cards:** 1
Average attendance: 19,013
Players used: 32
Leading scorer: C Paterson 10 (5,9)

	2017-18		Last six seasons at home							
	H	A	P	W	D	L	OV	UN	BS	CS
Man City			1	1	0	0	1	0	1	0
Man United			1	0	1	0	1	0	1	0
Tottenham			1	0	0	1	0	1	0	0
Liverpool			1	0	0	1	1	0	1	0
Chelsea			1	0	0	1	1	0	1	0
Arsenal			1	0	0	1	1	0	0	0
Burnley			2	1	1	0	2	0	1	1
Everton			1	0	1	0	0	1	0	1
Leicester			1	0	1	0	1	0	1	0
Newcastle			2	0	0	2	1	1	1	0
Crystal Palace			2	1	0	1	2	0	1	0
Bournemouth			1	0	1	0	0	1	1	0
West Ham			1	0	0	1	1	0	0	0
Watford			2	1	0	1	2	0	2	0
Brighton			4	1	2	1	1	3	1	2
Huddersfield			4	4	0	0	2	2	2	2
Southampton			1	0	0	1	1	0	0	0
Wolves	**L**	**W**	5	3	0	2	2	3	2	1
Cardiff										
Fulham	**L**	**D**	5	2	2	1	3	2	4	1

Season	Division	Pos	P	W	D	L	F	A	GD	Pts
2017-18	Championship	2	46	27	9	10	69	39	+30	90
2016-17	Championship	12	46	17	11	18	60	61	-1	62
2015-16	Championship	8	46	17	17	12	56	51	+5	68

Over/Under 43%/57% 18th   **Both score** 46%/54% 17th

Key stat: Cardiff have lost one of their last ten home fixtures

---

2017-18 Championship appearances

	P	G	Y	R
S Bamba	43 (3)	4	7	-
J Bennett	38	1	7	-
O Bogle	4 (6)	3	1	1
C Bryson	19 (3)	2	4	-
M Connolly	4	0	2	-
L Damour	18 (9)	0	5	-
B Ecuele Manga	35 (3)	0	4	-
N Etheridge	45	0	1	-
L Feeney	4 (11)	0	1	-
F Gounongbe	0 (3)	0	1	-
M Grujic	12 (1)	1	5	-
A Gunnarsson	17 (3)	1	3	-
G Halford	2 (10)	0	3	-
K Harris	1 (2)	0	-	-
R Healey	1 (2)	0	-	-
D Hoilett	44 (2)	9	2	-
M Kennedy	0 (1)	0	-	-
G Madine	5 (8)	0	1	-
N Mendez-Laing	33 (5)	6	1	-
S Morrison	38 (1)	7	5	-
B Murphy	1	0	-	-
C Paterson	23 (9)	10	4	-

	P	G	Y	R
L Peltier	27 (3)	0	11	-
A Pilkington	1 (7)	3	1	-
J Ralls	37	7	8	-
A Richards	5 (1)	0	2	-
L Tomlin	5 (8)	1	2	-
A Traore	4 (1)	1	3	-
J Ward	2 (2)	0	1	-
D Ward	6 (12)	4	-	-
Y Wildschut	3 (7)	0	-	-
K Zohore	30 (6)	9	-	-

Cardiff surprised many by securing promotion

CHELSEA

Nickname: The Blues
Colours: Blue
Ground: Stamford Bridge **Capacity:** 42,055
Tel: 0371-811-1955 www.chelseafc.com

The recent trend with Chelsea has been to follow up a poor season with an outstanding campaign, but last season's fifth place may not be easy to improve on.

Roman Abramovich has been the Blues' driving force since buying the club in 2003, but his commitment may be on the wane after failing to renew his UK visa.

Chelsea's plans to build a new stadium are on hold and there are question marks over how much Abramovich will invest in improvements to the playing squad.

Champions League football is off the agenda for a second time in three seasons and the Blues cannot afford to take the Europa League lightly.

They have fallen a long way behind the Manchester clubs and it may be easier to win the Europa League than to climb above Tottenham and Liverpool.

Longest run without a loss: 8
Longest run without a win: 2
Highest/lowest league position: 2/5
Clean sheets: 16
Yellow cards: 45 **Red cards:** 4
Average attendance: 39,347
Players used: 26
Leading scorer: E Hazard 12 (3,8)

	2017-18		Last six seasons at home							
	H	A	P	W	D	L	OV	UN	BS	CS
Man City	L	L	6	2	2	2	3	3	3	1
Man United	W	L	6	4	1	1	3	3	3	3
Tottenham	L	W	6	3	2	1	6	0	4	2
Liverpool	W	D	6	2	2	2	3	3	5	1
Chelsea										
Arsenal	D	D	6	5	1	0	3	3	2	4
Burnley	L	W	3	1	1	1	2	1	2	1
Everton	W	D	6	5	1	0	3	3	2	4
Leicester	D	W	4	2	2	0	1	3	1	3
Newcastle	W	L	5	5	0	0	3	2	2	3
Crystal Palace	W	L	5	3	0	2	4	1	4	1
Bournemouth	L	W	3	1	0	2	2	1	0	1
West Ham	D	L	6	3	3	0	2	4	3	3
Watford	W	L	3	2	1	0	3	0	3	0
Brighton	W	W	1	1	0	0	0	1	0	1
Huddersfield	D	W	1	0	1	0	0	1	1	0
Southampton	W	W	6	3	2	1	4	2	5	1
Wolves			-	-	-	-	-	-	-	-
Cardiff			1	1	0	0	1	0	1	0
Fulham			2	1	1	0	0	2	0	2

Season	Division	Pos	P	W	D	L	F	A	GD	Pts
2017-18	Premier League	5	38	21	7	10	62	38	+24	70
2016-17	Premier League	1	38	30	3	5	85	33	+52	93
2015-16	Premier League	10	38	12	14	12	59	53	+6	50

Over/Under 55%/45% 7th **Both score** 45%/55% 14th

Key stat: Chelsea suffered four home league defeats last season – the most of the big six and the same as 15th-placed Brighton

2017-18 Premier League appearances

	P	G		Y	R
M Alonso	33	7	▍▍▍▍	6	-
E Ampadu	0 (1)	0		-	-
C Azpilicueta	37	2	▌	1	-
T Bakayoko	24 (5)	2	▌	4	▉
R Barkley	2	0		-	-
M Batshuayi	3 (9)	2	▌	-	-
J Boga	1	0		-	-
W Caballero	3	0		-	-
G Cahill	24 (3)	0		1	▉
C Musonda	0 (3)	0		-	-
A Christensen	23 (4)	0		-	-
T Courtois	35	0		2	-
D Drinkwater	5 (7)	1	▌	-	-
Emerson	3 (2)	0		-	-
C Fabregas	25 (7)	2	▌	6	▉
O Giroud	6 (8)	3	▍▍▍	-	-
E Hazard	28 (6)	12	▍▍▍▍▍▍▍	2	-
C Hudson-Odoi	0 (2)	0		-	-
N Kante	34	1	▌	3	-
D Luiz	9 (1)	1	▌	4	▉
A Morata	24 (7)	11	▍▍▍▍▍▍	7	-

	P	G		Y	R
V Moses	25 (3)	3	▍▍	3	-
Pedro	17 (14)	4	▍▍▍	1	-
A Rudiger	25 (2)	2	▌	4	-
Willian	20 (16)	6	▍▍▍▍	1	-
D Zappacosta	12 (10)	1	▌	-	-

Chelsea beat Man United in the FA Cup final

CRYSTAL PALACE

Nickname: The Eagles
Colours: Red and blue
Ground: Selhurst Park
Tel: 020-8768-6000

Capacity: 25,456
www.cpfc.co.uk

Roy Hodgson did a remarkable job by lifting Crystal Palace from bottom to 11th and may take them even higher in his first full season with the club.

Palace were in desperate trouble when Hodgson arrived – pointless and goalless and struggling to find a way forward without injured attackers Christian Benteke and Wilfried Zaha.

Benteke's return from injury made little difference but Zaha was instrumental in turning their season around. They also improved defensively and a lot of that was down to Hodgson's work on the training ground.

The Eagles have a habit of finishing the season well before dropping their standards three months later, but Palace can aim for seventh spot if they get their summer planning right.

Longest run without a loss: 8
Longest run without a win: 7
Highest/lowest league position: 11/20
Clean sheets: 9
Yellow cards: 72 **Red cards:** 0
Average attendance: 31,168
Players used: 28
Leading scorer: L Milivojevic 10 (3,10)

	2017-18 H	A	Last six seasons at home P	W	D	L	OV	UN	BS	CS
Man City	D	L	5	1	1	3	2	3	2	1
Man United	L	L	5	0	1	4	3	2	3	1
Tottenham	L	L	5	1	0	4	2	3	2	0
Liverpool	L	L	5	1	1	3	5	0	5	0
Chelsea	W	L	5	2	0	3	3	2	2	1
Arsenal	L	L	5	1	0	4	4	1	3	1
Burnley	W	L	4	2	1	1	1	3	1	2
Everton	D	L	5	0	3	2	1	4	1	2
Leicester	W	W	5	2	2	1	3	2	2	2
Newcastle	D	L	4	1	2	1	2	2	3	0
Crystal Palace										
Bournemouth	D	D	3	0	2	1	2	1	3	0
West Ham	D	D	5	1	1	3	3	2	3	1
Watford	W	D	4	2	0	2	3	1	3	1
Brighton	W	D	2	2	0	0	2	0	1	1
Huddersfield	L	W	2	0	1	1	1	1	1	0
Southampton	L	W	5	2	0	3	2	3	1	2
Wolves			1	1	0	0	1	0	1	0
Cardiff			2	2	0	0	1	1	1	1
Fulham			1	0	0	1	1	0	1	0

Season	Division	Pos	P	W	D	L	F	A	GD	Pts
2017-18	Premier League	11	38	11	11	16	45	55	-10	44
2016-17	Premier League	14	38	12	5	21	50	63	-13	41
2015-16	Premier League	15	38	11	9	18	39	51	-12	42

Over/Under 55%/45% 7th   **Both score** 50%/50% 9th

Key stat: In four of the last five seasons, Crystal Palace have accumulated fewer than 20 points at the half-way stage

2017-18 Premier League appearances

	P G		Y	R
C Benteke	24 (7)	3	6	-
Y Cabaye	28 (3)	0	7	-
S Dann	16 (1)	1	4	-
D Delaney	1 (1)	0	-	-
T Fosu-Mensah	17 (4)	0	2	-
W Hennessey	27	0	1	-
S Kaikai	0 (1)	0	-	-
M Kelly	12 (3)	0	1	-
F Ladapo	0 (1)	0	-	-
Lee Chung-Yong	1 (6)	0	-	-
R Loftus-Cheek	21 (3)	2	1	-
L Lumeka	0 (1)	0	-	-
J McArthur	27 (6)	5	5	-
L Milivojevic	35 (1)	10	8	-
P N'Diaye Souare	0 (1)	0	-	-
J Puncheon	6 (4)	0	5	-
J Riedewald	4 (8)	0	-	-
M Sakho	18 (1)	1	1	-
B Sako	4 (12)	3	-	-
J Schlupp	21 (3)	0	3	-
A Sorloth	4	0	-	-

	P G		Y	R
J Speroni	11	0	-	-
J Tomkins	27 (1)	3	8	-
A Wan-Bissaka	35 (1)	2	3	-
A Wan-Bissaka	7	0	1	-
J Ward	19	0	4	-
W Zaha	28 (1)	9	5	-
P Van Aanholt	25 (3)	5	7	-

Wilfried Zaha lit up Crystal Palace's season

EVERTON

Nickname: The Toffees
Colours: Blue and white
Ground: Goodison Park **Capacity:** 39,572
Tel: 0151-530-5300 www.evertonfc.com

Everton's lengthy pursuit of Marco Silva was concluded nine months after they first targeted the Portuguese manager and they may need to show further patience if they are to realise their long-held ambition of challenging the big six.

Silva made a great start at Watford last season but was sacked after the Hornets slipped to within just four points of the drop zone.

His teams play attractive football and that has not gone unnoticed by Everton, who are seeking a change from the direct tactics employed by Sam Allardyce.

Everton rose from 13th to eighth under Allardyce, but the idea that he somehow saved them from relegation is overplayed.

They are probably the biggest club outside of the top six and seventh place is a realistic target.

Longest run without a loss: 7
Longest run without a win: 6
Highest/lowest league position: 8/19
Clean sheets: 10
Yellow cards: 53 **Red cards:** 3
Average attendance: 38,197
Players used: 30
Leading scorer: W Rooney 10 (5,8)

	2017-18 H	2017-18 A	P	W	D	L	OV	UN	BS	CS
								Last six seasons at home		
Man City	L	D	6	2	1	3	3	3	3	2
Man United	L	L	6	3	1	2	2	4	1	3
Tottenham	L	L	6	1	3	2	2	4	3	1
Liverpool	D	D	6	0	5	1	2	4	3	2
Chelsea	D	D	6	2	1	3	4	2	3	2
Arsenal	L	L	6	2	2	2	4	2	4	1
Burnley	L	L	3	2	0	1	1	2	1	1
Everton										
Leicester	W	L	4	2	1	1	4	0	4	0
Newcastle	W	W	5	4	1	0	4	1	2	3
Crystal Palace	W	D	5	1	2	2	3	2	5	0
Bournemouth	W	L	3	3	0	0	3	0	3	0
West Ham	W	L	6	5	0	1	3	3	2	4
Watford	W	L	3	2	1	0	2	1	2	1
Brighton	W	D	1	1	0	0	0	1	0	1
Huddersfield	W	W	1	1	0	0	0	1	0	1
Southampton	D	L	6	4	2	0	3	3	4	2
Wolves			-	-	-	-	-	-	-	-
Cardiff			1	1	0	0	1	0	1	0
Fulham			2	2	0	0	1	1	1	1

Season	Division	Pos	P	W	D	L	F	A	GD	Pts
2017-18	Premier League	8	38	13	10	15	44	58	-14	49
2016-17	Premier League	7	38	17	10	11	62	44	+18	61
2015-16	Premier League	11	38	11	14	13	59	55	+4	47

Over/Under 47%/53% 12th   **Both score** 53%/47% 7th

Key stat: Everton conceded 58 league goals last season – the highest since the 2000-01 campaign

2017-18 Premier League appearances

	P	G	Y	R
L Baines	22	2	1	-
B Baningime	1 (7)	0	1	-
M Besic	0 (2)	0	-	-
Y Bolasie	11 (5)	1	-	-
D Calvert-Lewin	18 (14)	4	4	-
S Coleman	12	0	-	-
T Davies	20 (13)	2	7	-
R Funes Mori	1 (3)	0	1	-
I Gueye	32 (1)	2	7	1
M Holgate	13 (2)	0	3	-
P Jagielka	23 (2)	0	2	-
M Keane	29 (1)	0	3	-
J Kenny	17 (2)	0	2	-
D Klaassen	3 (4)	0	-	-
A Lennon	9 (6)	0	-	-
A Lookman	1 (6)	0	-	-
E Mangala	2	0	-	-
C Martina	20 (1)	0	1	-
J McCarthy	3 (1)	0	-	-
K Mirallas	2 (3)	0	1	-
O Niasse	10 (12)	8	2	-
J Pickford	38	0	-	-

	P	G	Y	R
S Ramirez	3 (5)	0	-	-
W Rooney	27 (4)	10	5	-
M Schneiderlin	24 (6)	0	5	1
G Sigurdsson	25 (2)	4	2	-
C Tosun	12 (2)	5	-	-
N Vlasic	7 (5)	0	-	-
T Walcott	13 (1)	3	2	-
A Williams	20 (4)	1	3	1

Jordan Pickford joined Everton last summer

FULHAM

Nickname: The Cottagers
Colours: White and black
Ground: Craven Cottage
Tel: 0843-208-1222

Capacity: 26,600
www.fulhamfc.com

Three of the last four Championship playoff winners have slipped straight back down, but Huddersfield bucked the trend and Fulham will hope to follow their lead.

The Cottagers played some of the best football in the second tier and were outstanding after the turn of the year, collecting 52 points from a possible 63.

Going up gives them a better chance of keeping their best players – although highly-rated defender Ryan Fredericks has departed for West Ham.

Fulham are facing a step up in class and need to address defensive weaknesses having conceded 46 league goals last season – the highest among the top five.

Loanee Aleksandr Mitrovic starred from January onwards but they cannot afford to wait until the next winter window if they are to prosper in the Premier League.

Longest run without a loss: 23
Longest run without a win: 6
Highest/lowest league position: 3/17
Clean sheets: 15
Yellow cards: 77 **Red cards:** 3
Average attendance: 19,787
Players used: 28
Leading scorer: R Sessegnon 15 (4,10)

	2017-18		Last six seasons at home							
	H	A	P	W	D	L	OV	UN	BS	CS
Man City			2	0	0	2	2	0	2	0
Man United			2	0	0	2	1	1	1	0
Tottenham			2	0	0	2	2	0	1	0
Liverpool			2	0	0	2	2	0	2	0
Chelsea			2	0	0	2	2	0	1	0
Arsenal			2	0	0	2	1	1	1	0
Burnley			1	0	0	1	1	0	1	0
Everton			2	0	1	1	2	0	2	0
Leicester			-	-	-	-	-	-	-	-
Newcastle			3	3	0	0	1	2	1	2
Crystal Palace			1	0	1	0	1	0	1	0
Bournemouth			1	0	0	1	1	0	1	0
West Ham			2	2	0	0	2	0	2	0
Watford			1	0	0	1	1	0	0	0
Brighton			3	0	0	3	2	1	2	0
Huddersfield			3	2	1	0	2	1	2	1
Southampton			2	0	1	1	1	1	1	0
Wolves	W	L	4	1	0	3	2	2	1	1
Cardiff	D	W	5	1	3	1	3	2	5	0
Fulham										

Season	Division	Pos	P	W	D	L	F	A	GD	Pts
2017-18	Championship	3	46	25	13	8	79	46	+33	88
2016-17	Championship	6	46	22	14	10	85	57	+28	80
2015-16	Championship	20	46	12	15	19	66	79	-13	51

Over/Under 46%/54% 16th   **Both score** 59%/41% 2nd

Key stat: Fulham have not lost any of their last 15 home league fixtures

2017-18 Championship appearances

	P	G	Y	R
S Aluko	4	-	-	-
F Ayite	24 (5)	4	2	-
M Bettinelli	29	-	6	-
D Button	20	-	2	-
T Cairney	33 (4)	6	3	-
C Christie	1 (5)	-	-	-
I Cisse	2 (4)	-	-	-
L De la Torre	0 (5)	-	-	-
M Djalo	0 (2)	-	-	-
T Edun	1 (1)	-	-	-
R Fonte	16 (11)	3	2	-
R Fredericks	47	-	10	-
J Graham	0 (3)	-	-	-
S Johansen	46 (2)	8	12	-
T Kalas	29 (6)	-	-	1
A Kamara	10 (22)	7	7	1
N Kebano	10 (17)	3	1	-
K McDonald	45	3	11	-
A Mitrovic	18 (2)	12	3	-
Y Mollo	2 (4)	-	1	-
O Norwood	22 (17)	5	6	-
D Odoi	33 (8)	2	7	2

	P	G	Y	R
O Ojo	18 (4)	4	3	-
L Piazon	14 (9)	5	1	-
Rafa	0 (3)	-	-	-
T Ream	47	1	2	-
R Sessegnon	48 (1)	15	2	-
M Targett	20 (1)	1	3	-

Fulham were promoted as playoff winners

HUDDERSFIELD

Nickname: The Terriers
Colours: Blue and white
Ground: John Smith's Stadium   **Capacity:** 24,500
Tel: 01484 484112   www.htafc.com

Fighting against the odds is something Huddersfield relished in their first Premier League season but the 2018-19 campaign may prove even tougher.

Having a year of extra Premier League funding is an advantage for the Terriers, who will have opportunities to add extra quality to their squad, but they may still find it difficult to recruit the players necessary to transform them into a stable, mid-table outfit.

Huddersfield's problems are in attack – despite spending £11.5 million on centre-forward Steve Mounie last summer, they were the joint-lowest scorers in the league with 28 goals.

David Wagner is an impressive manager who gets the best out of meagre resources but Huddersfield will be at great risk unless they can add goals to the side.

Longest run without a loss: 4
Longest run without a win: 8
Highest/lowest league position: 10/19
Clean sheets: 10
Yellow cards: 64 **Red cards:** 3
Average attendance: 30,129
Players used: 25
Leading scorer: S Mounie 7 (1,5)

	2017-18		Last six seasons at home							
	H	A	P	W	D	L	OV	UN	BS	CS
Man City	L	D	1	0	0	1	1	0	1	0
Man United	W	L	1	1	0	0	1	0	1	0
Tottenham	L	L	1	0	0	1	1	0	0	0
Liverpool	L	L	1	0	0	1	1	0	0	0
Chelsea	L	D	1	0	0	1	1	0	1	0
Arsenal	L	L	1	0	0	1	0	1	0	0
Burnley	D	D	4	2	1	1	2	2	2	2
Everton	L	L	1	0	0	1	1	0	1	0
Leicester	D	L	3	0	1	2	0	3	1	0
Newcastle	W	L	2	1	0	1	1	1	1	1
Crystal Palace	L	W	2	1	0	1	0	2	0	1
Bournemouth	W	L	3	2	0	1	3	0	2	0
West Ham	L	L	1	0	0	1	1	0	1	0
Watford	W	W	4	2	0	2	3	1	3	1
Brighton	W	D	6	2	3	1	2	4	5	1
Huddersfield										
Southampton	D	D	1	0	1	0	0	1	0	1
Wolves			4	3	0	1	2	2	2	2
Cardiff			4	0	2	2	2	2	1	2
Fulham			3	0	1	2	1	2	2	0

Season	Division	Pos	P	W	D	L	F	A	GD	Pts
2017-18	Premier League	16	38	9	10	19	28	58	-30	37
2016-17	Championship	5	46	25	6	15	56	58	-2	81
2015-16	Championship	19	46	13	12	21	59	70	-11	51

Over/Under 37%/63% 17th   **Both score** 32%/68% 20th

Key stat: Huddersfield have scored three goals in their last ten league fixtures

2017-18 Premier League appearances

	P	G	Y	R		P	G	Y	R
P Billing	8 (8)	0	3	-	T Smith	21 (3)	0	7	-
M Cranie	2 (1)	0	-	-	D Whitehead	0 (4)	0	-	-
L Depoitre	18 (15)	6	1	-	D Williams	11 (9)	0	2	-
F Hadergjonaj	19 (4)	0	3	-	R Van La Parra	26 (7)	3	3	1
M Hefele	0 (2)	0	1	-					
J Hogg	29 (1)	0	9	1					
T Ince	27 (6)	2	-	-					
M Jorgensen	38	0	6	-					
E Kachunga	17 (2)	1	1	-					
T Kongolo	11 (2)	0	-	-					
J Lolley	2 (4)	1	1	-					
J Lossl	38	0	1	-					
C Lowe	19 (4)	0	1	-					
S Malone	12 (10)	0	3	-					
A Mooy	34 (2)	4	5	-					
S Mounie	21 (7)	7	2	-					
K Palmer	1 (3)	0	2	-					
A Pritchard	12 (2)	1	1	-					
C Quaner	13 (13)	0	4	-					
A Sabiri	2 (3)	0	1	-					
C Schindler	37	0	7	1					

David Wagner's team stayed up against the odds

LEICESTER

Nickname: The Foxes
Colours: Blue
Ground: King Power Stadium **Capacity:** 32,315
Tel: 0344-815-5000 www.lcfc.co.uk

Memories of Leicester's stunning 2015-16 title triumph are starting to fade but the Foxes can post their highest finish since those heady days in 2018-19.

Expectations have risen at the King Power and their ninth-place finish last season was seen as a disappointment, prompting calls for the removal of manager Claude Puel. With a little more realism, he might be allowed to build on his good work and establish Leicester as the top team outside of the big six.

They were the league's seventh-highest scorers last term but had issues to resolve at the back, shipping 60 goals – four more than relegated Swansea and West Brom.

Jonny Evans has been brought in to stiffen up the back four as the Foxes target seventh place and a decent run in the cups.

Longest run without a loss: 5
Longest run without a win: 6
Highest/lowest league position: 7/18
Clean sheets: 9
Yellow cards: 56 **Red cards:** 5
Average attendance: 34,655
Players used: 27
Leading scorer: J Vardy 20 (7,18)

	2017-18		Last six seasons at home							
	H	A	P	W	D	L	OV	UN	BS	CS
Man City	L	L	4	1	1	2	1	3	1	1
Man United	D	L	4	1	2	1	3	1	3	0
Tottenham	W	L	4	1	1	2	3	1	4	0
Liverpool	L	L	4	2	0	2	3	1	3	1
Chelsea	L	D	4	1	0	3	4	0	3	0
Arsenal	W	L	4	1	2	1	2	2	3	1
Burnley	W	L	5	3	2	0	3	2	3	2
Everton	W	L	4	2	1	1	2	2	2	1
Leicester										
Newcastle	L	W	3	2	0	1	2	1	1	2
Crystal Palace	L	L	5	2	0	3	3	2	2	1
Bournemouth	D	D	4	1	3	0	1	3	3	1
West Ham	L	D	4	2	1	1	2	2	2	1
Watford	W	L	5	3	1	1	4	1	3	2
Brighton	W	W	3	2	0	1	1	2	1	2
Huddersfield	W	D	3	3	0	0	3	0	2	1
Southampton	D	W	4	2	2	0	0	4	0	4
Wolves			1	1	0	0	1	0	1	0
Cardiff			1	0	0	1	0	1	0	0
Fulham			-	-	-	-	-	-	-	-

Season	Division	Pos	P	W	D	L	F	A	GD	Pts
2017-18	Premier League	9	38	12	11	15	56	60	-4	47
2016-17	Premier League	12	38	12	8	18	48	63	-15	44
2015-16	Premier League	1	38	23	12	3	68	36	+32	81

Over/Under 55%/45% 7th **Both score** 63%/37% 1st

Key stat: Leicester's away games last season featured 69 goals – the highest in the division

2017-18 Premier League appearances

	P	G	Y	R		P	G	Y	R
A Silva	9 (3)	0	3	-	S Okazaki	17 (10)	6	2	-
M Albrighton	30 (4)	2	5	1	K Schmeichel	33	0	3	-
D Amartey	6 (2)	0	1	1	D Simpson	27 (1)	0	4	-
H Barnes	0 (3)	0	-	-	I Slimani	2 (10)	1	-	-
Y Benalouane	1	0	-	-	L Ulloa	0 (4)	0	-	-
B Chilwell	20 (4)	0	2	1	J Vardy	37	20	3	-
H Choudhury	4 (4)	0	1	-					
F Diabate	5 (9)	0	1	-					
A Dragovic	7 (4)	0	2	-					
C Fuchs	21 (4)	0	1	-					
D Gray	17 (18)	3	2	-					
B Hamer	3 (1)	0	-	-					
V Iborra	17 (2)	3	-	-					
K Iheanacho	7 (14)	3	2	-					
E Jakupovic	2	0	-	-					
M James	11 (2)	0	2	-					
A King	5 (6)	1	1	-					
H Maguire	38	2	7	-					
R Mahrez	34 (2)	12	2	-					
W Morgan	32	0	4	-					
O Ndidi	33	0	8	2					

Jamie Vardy hit 20 league goals for Leicester

LIVERPOOL

Nickname: The Reds
Colours: Red
Ground: Anfield **Capacity:** 54,074
Tel: 0151-264-2500 www.liverpoolfc.com

Jurgen Klopp has led Liverpool to consecutive fourth-place finishes but may struggle to lift the Anfield outfit any higher next season.

Few teams can match the entertainment consistently served up by the free-scoring Reds but they still have a habit of dropping points against the top flight's lesser lights.

Liverpool drew eight matches against teams from outside of the big six and half of those were at Anfield.

Offensively, they benefited hugely from Mohamed Salah's stellar first season at the club and there seems no reason why the Egyptian should not continue to thrive.

However, Liverpool conceded 38 goals – the highest of the top-four clubs – and while the signings of Alisson and Fabinho will help shore things up, it may take time to mould the Reds into title contenders.

Longest run without a loss: 14
Longest run without a win: 3
Highest/lowest league position: 2/8
Clean sheets: 17
Yellow cards: 44 **Red cards:** 1
Average attendance: 45,088
Players used: 27
Leading scorer: M Salah 32 (9,24)

	2017-18		Last six seasons at home							
	H	A	P	W	D	L	OV	UN	BS	CS
Man City	W	L	6	5	1	0	5	1	4	2
Man United	D	L	6	1	2	3	2	4	2	3
Tottenham	D	L	6	4	2	0	4	2	4	2
Liverpool										
Chelsea	D	L	6	0	4	2	2	4	5	0
Arsenal	W	D	6	3	2	1	5	1	4	1
Burnley	D	W	3	2	1	0	1	2	2	1
Everton	D	D	6	3	3	0	3	3	3	3
Leicester	W	W	4	3	1	0	3	1	3	1
Newcastle	W	D	5	3	2	0	2	3	3	2
Crystal Palace	W	W	5	2	0	3	4	1	4	1
Bournemouth	W	W	3	2	1	0	2	1	1	2
West Ham	W	W	6	3	2	1	4	2	3	2
Watford	W	D	3	3	0	0	2	1	1	2
Brighton	W	W	1	1	0	0	1	0	0	1
Huddersfield	W	W	1	1	0	0	1	0	0	1
Southampton	W	W	6	3	2	1	2	4	2	3
Wolves			-	-	-	-	-	-	-	-
Cardiff			1	1	0	0	1	0	1	0
Fulham			2	2	0	0	2	0	0	2

Season	Division	Pos	P	W	D	L	F	A	GD	Pts
2017-18	Premier League	4	38	21	12	5	84	38	+46	75
2016-17	Premier League	4	38	22	10	6	78	42	+36	76
2015-16	Premier League	8	38	16	12	10	63	50	+13	60

Over/Under 66%/34% 3rd **Both score** 47%/53% 12th

Key stat: Liverpool are unbeaten in their last 21 Premier League home matches

2017-18 Premier League appearances

	P	G	Y	R
T Alexander-Arnold	18 (1)	1	3	-
E Can	24 (2)	3	8	-
N Clyne	2 (1)	0	1	-
P Coutinho	13 (1)	7	-	-
J Gomez	21 (2)	0	3	-
M Grujic	0 (3)	0	-	-
J Henderson	25 (2)	1	1	-
D Ings	3 (5)	1	-	-
Karius	19	0	1	-
R Klavan	16 (3)	1	-	-
A Lallana	1 (11)	0	1	-
D Lovren	24 (5)	2	4	-
S Mane	28 (1)	10	3	1
J Matip	22 (3)	1	3	-
S Mignolet	19	0	3	-
J Milner	16 (16)	0	3	-
A Moreno Perez	14 (2)	0	1	-
D Origi	0 (1)	0	-	-
A Ox-Chamberlain	14 (18)	3	3	-
R Firmino	32 (5)	15	1	-
A Robertson	22	1	2	-

	P	G	Y	R
M Salah	34 (2)	32	1	-
D Solanke	5 (16)	1	-	-
D Sturridge	5 (4)	2	-	-
G Wijnaldum	27 (6)	1	1	-
B Woodburn	0 (1)	0	-	-
V van Dijk	15	0	1	-

Mo Salah won the Premier League Golden Boot

MANCHESTER CITY

Nickname: The Citizens
Colours: Sky blue and white
Ground: Etihad Stadium **Capacity:** 55,097
Tel: 0161-444-1894 www.mcfc.co.uk

History was made last season as Manchester City amassed 100 points and scored 106 goals and Pep Guardiola was right to say that those standards will be tough to repeat.

However, City could dominate English football for years to come and it is hard to see them dropping to a level which would allow their rivals to pose a meaningful challenge this season.

They are always looking to strengthen and the Champions League will be a priority, given the disappointment of their quarter-final exit against Liverpool.

David Silva and Fernandinho are getting towards the stage in their careers where their talents may start to fade, but the majority of City's squad are the right side of 30 and some of the players have scope for further improvement.

Longest run without a loss: 22
Longest run without a win: 1
Highest/lowest league position: 1/1
Clean sheets: 18
Yellow cards: 61 **Red cards:** 2
Average attendance: 44,648
Players used: 25
Leading scorer: S Aguero 21 (6,13)

	2017-18 H	A	Last six seasons at home P	W	D	L	OV	UN	BS	CS
Man City										
Man United	L	W	6	2	1	3	3	3	3	2
Tottenham	W	W	6	4	1	1	6	0	5	1
Liverpool	W	L	6	3	2	1	5	1	5	1
Chelsea	W	W	6	3	1	2	2	4	2	3
Arsenal	W	W	6	3	2	1	4	2	5	0
Burnley	W	D	3	2	1	0	3	0	2	1
Everton	D	W	6	2	4	0	1	5	4	2
Leicester	W	W	4	3	0	1	3	1	3	1
Newcastle	W	W	5	5	0	0	5	0	2	3
Crystal Palace	W	D	5	5	0	0	4	1	0	5
Bournemouth	W	W	3	3	0	0	3	0	1	2
West Ham	W	W	6	5	0	1	4	2	4	2
Watford	W	W	3	3	0	0	1	2	1	2
Brighton	W	W	1	1	0	0	1	0	1	0
Huddersfield	D	W	1	0	1	0	0	1	0	1
Southampton	W	W	6	5	1	0	4	2	5	1
Wolves	-	-	-	-	-	-	-	-	-	-
Cardiff			1	1	0	0	1	0	1	0
Fulham			2	2	0	0	1	1	0	2

Season	Division	Pos	P	W	D	L	F	A	GD	Pts
2017-18	Premier League	1	38	32	4	2	106	27	+79	100
2016-17	Premier League	3	38	23	9	6	80	39	+41	78
2015-16	Premier League	4	38	19	9	10	71	41	+30	66

Over/Under 71%/29% 1st **Both score** 53%/47% 7th

Key stat: Manchester City have scored three or more goals in 13 of their last 18 home league games

2017-18 Premier League appearances

	P	G		Y	R
S Aguero	22 (3)	21		2	-
C Bravo	2 (1)	0		-	-
Danilo	13 (10)	3		2	-
K De Bruyne	36 (1)	8		2	-
F Delph	21 (1)	1		2	-
B Diaz	0 (5)	0		-	-
Ederson Moraes	36	0		1	-
Fernandinho	33 (1)	5		7	-
P Foden	0 (5)	0		-	-
Gabriel Jesus	19 (10)	13		6	-
I Gundogan	15 (15)	4		3	-
V Kompany	17	1		6	-
A Laporte	9	0		1	-
E Mangala	4 (5)	0		-	-
B Mendy	4 (3)	0		2	-
L Nmecha	0 (2)	0		-	-
N Otamendi	33 (1)	4		9	-
L Sane	27 (5)	10		4	-
D Silva	28 (1)	9		5	-
B Silva	15 (20)	6		-	-
R Sterling	29 (4)	18		4	1

	P	G		Y	R
J Stones	16 (2)	0		-	-
Y Toure	1 (9)	0		1	-
K Walker	32	0		3	1
A Zinchenko	6 (2)	0		1	-

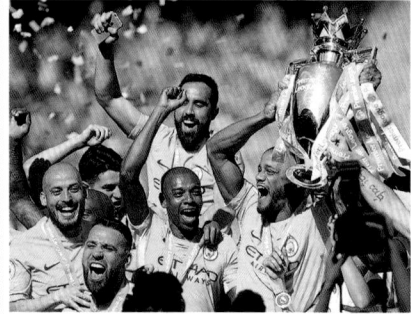

Man City regained the Premier League title

MANCHESTER UNITED

Nickname: The Red Devils
Colours: Red and white
Ground: Old Trafford
Tel: 0161-868-8000

Capacity: 75,643
www.manutd.com

Jose Mourinho signed for Manchester United to win the biggest prizes but has fallen short so far and further disappointment looks on the cards.

The Portuguese manager steered United to second place last term, but they were 19 points adrift of Man City and it's hard to see how they can bridge the gap.

Mourinho spent big on Paul Pogba and Alexis Sanchez but neither has come close to justifying the massive outlay.

Nemanja Matic and Romelu Lukaku have done better, yet it is questionable whether either would get into City's side.

Mourinho can point to an improvement in the points tally (81) and the league position (second) since taking charge at Old Trafford. However, they are still miles behind their rivals and another second place may be the best they can hope for.

Longest run without a loss: 8
Longest run without a win: 3
Highest/lowest league position: 2/3
Clean sheets: 19
Yellow cards: 64 **Red cards:** 1
Average attendance: 55,562
Players used: 27
Leading scorer: R Lukaku 16 (6,15)

	2017-18		Last six seasons at home							
	H	A	P	W	D	L	OV	UN	BS	CS
Man City	L	W	6	1	1	4	5	1	4	1
Man United										
Tottenham	W	L	6	4	0	2	3	3	2	4
Liverpool	W	D	6	4	1	1	5	1	4	1
Chelsea	W	L	6	2	3	1	1	5	2	3
Arsenal	W	W	6	4	2	0	3	3	5	1
Burnley	D	W	3	1	2	0	2	1	2	1
Everton	W	W	6	4	1	1	2	4	2	3
Leicester	W	D	4	3	1	0	2	2	3	1
Newcastle	W	L	5	3	1	1	3	2	3	1
Crystal Palace	W	W	5	5	0	0	1	4	0	5
Bournemouth	W	W	3	2	1	0	1	2	2	1
West Ham	W	D	6	4	2	0	3	3	3	3
Watford	W	W	3	3	0	0	3	0	3	0
Brighton	W	L	1	1	0	0	0	1	0	1
Huddersfield	W	L	1	1	0	0	0	1	0	1
Southampton	D	W	6	2	2	2	1	5	2	2
Wolves	-	-	-	-	-	-	-	-	-	-
Cardiff			1	1	0	0	0	1	0	1
Fulham			2	1	1	0	2	0	2	0

Season	Division	Pos	P	W	D	L	F	A	GD	Pts
2017-18	Premier League	2	38	25	6	7	68	28	+40	81
2016-17	Premier League	6	38	18	15	5	54	29	+25	69
2015-16	Premier League	5	38	19	9	10	49	35	+14	66

Over/Under 50%/50% 11th   **Both score** 37%/63% 19th

Key stat: Manchester United have scored more than two goals just once in their last 17 home fixtures

2017-18 Premier League appearances

	P	G	Y	R
E Bailly	11 (2)	1	2	-
D Blind	4 (3)	0	-	-
M Carrick	1 (1)	0	-	-
M Darmian	5 (3)	0	-	-
M Fellaini	5 (11)	4	1	-
A Herrera	13 (13)	0	5	-
Z Ibrahimovic	1 (4)	0	-	-
P Jones	23	0	2	-
V Lindelof	13 (4)	0	1	-
J Lingard	20 (13)	8	2	-
R Lukaku	33 (1)	16	4	-
A Martial	18 (12)	9	1	-
J Mata	23 (5)	3	1	-
N Matic	35 (1)	1	6	-
S McTominay	7 (6)	0	2	-
H Mkhitaryan	11 (4)	1	2	-
P Pogba	25 (2)	6	5	1
M Rashford	17 (18)	7	3	-
M Rojo	8 (1)	0	6	-
S Romero	1	0	-	-
A Sanchez	12	2	1	-
L Shaw	8 (3)	0	2	-

	P	G	Y	R
C Smalling	28 (1)	4	4	-
A Tuanzebe	0 (1)	0	-	-
L Valencia	31	3	7	-
A Young	28 (2)	2	7	-
D De Gea	37	0	-	-

Jose Mourinho's tactics were often criticised

NEWCASTLE

Nickname: The Magpies
Colours: Black and white
Ground: St James' Park
Tel: 0844-372-1892

Capacity: 52,354
www.nufc.co.uk

Newcastle performed the best of the newly-promoted clubs last season, finishing tenth, but are going to need an influx of talented players to kick on and get close to the big six.

Rafa Benitez did a magnificent job last season despite getting little financial backing from owner Mike Ashley and the Magpies had the best defensive record among the teams outside the top seven.

Centre-back Jamaal Lascelles impressed and goalkeeper Martin Dubravka excelled on loan from Sparta Prague and has since made a permanent switch to Tyneside.

However, Newcastle lacked quality in attacking areas with eight-goal striker Ayoze Perez topping their scoring charts.

They will need to recruit better players up front or run the risk of being drawn into a relegation scrap.

Longest run without a loss: 4
Longest run without a win: 9
Highest/lowest league position: 6/18
Clean sheets: 9
Yellow cards: 53 **Red cards:** 2
Average attendance: 44,563
Players used: 27
Leading scorer: Ayoze Perez 8 (2,7)

	2017-18		Last six seasons at home							
	H	A	P	W	D	L	OV	UN	BS	CS
Man City	L	L	5	0	1	4	1	4	2	0
Man United	W	L	5	1	1	3	3	2	1	1
Tottenham	L	L	5	2	0	3	4	1	3	0
Liverpool	D	L	5	2	2	1	2	3	2	2
Chelsea	W	L	5	4	1	0	4	1	3	2
Arsenal	W	L	5	1	0	4	2	3	2	0
Burnley	D	L	2	0	2	0	1	1	2	0
Everton	L	L	5	1	0	4	3	2	2	0
Leicester	L	W	3	1	0	2	2	1	1	1
Newcastle										
Crystal Palace	W	D	4	3	1	0	1	3	1	3
Bournemouth	L	D	2	0	0	2	1	1	1	0
West Ham	W	W	5	3	1	1	2	3	1	3
Watford	L	L	2	0	0	2	2	0	1	0
Brighton	D	L	2	1	1	0	0	2	0	2
Huddersfield	W	L	2	1	0	1	1	1	1	1
Southampton	W	D	5	2	2	1	4	1	4	1
Wolves			1	0	0	1	0	1	0	0
Cardiff			2	2	0	0	2	0	1	1
Fulham			3	2	0	1	1	2	1	2

Season	Division	Pos	P	W	D	L	F	A	GD	Pts
2017-18	Premier League	10	38	12	8	18	39	47	-8	44
2016-17	Championship	1	46	29	7	10	85	40	+45	94
2015-16	Premier League	18	38	9	10	19	44	65	-21	37

Over/Under 42%/58% 14th   **Both score** 42%/58% 16th

Key stat: Newcastle have lost one of their last ten home fixtures

2017-18 Premier League appearances

	P	G	Y	R
R Aarons	1 (3)	0	-	-
C Atsu	19 (9)	2	1	-
A Perez	28 (8)	8	3	-
C Clark	19 (1)	2	3	-
K Darlow	10	0	-	-
M Diame	23 (8)	2	3	-
M Dubravka	12	0	-	-
P Dummett	19 (1)	0	1	-
R Elliot	16	0	-	-
J Gamez	1 (1)	0	-	-
D Gayle	23 (12)	6	3	-
M Haidara	0 (1)	0	-	-
I Hayden	15 (11)	1	7	-
J Manquillo	20 (1)	0	2	-
Joselu	19 (11)	4	2	-
Kenedy	13	2	1	-
J Lascelles	32 (1)	3	5	-
F Lejeune	24	0	3	-
C Mbemba	7 (2)	0	-	-
M Merino	14 (10)	1	4	-
A Mitrovic	0 (6)	1	-	-
J Murphy	13 (12)	1	-	-

	P	G	Y	R
M Ritchie	32 (3)	3	6	-
H Saivet	1	1	-	-
J Shelvey	25 (5)	1	3	2
I Slimani	1 (3)	0	1	-
D Yedlin	31 (3)	0	5	-

Captain Jamaal Lascelles starred for Newcastle

SOUTHAMPTON

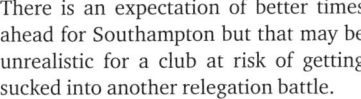

Nickname: The Saints
Colours: Red and white
Ground: St Mary's Stadium **Capacity:** 32,505
Tel: 0845-688-9448 www.saintsfc.co.uk

There is an expectation of better times ahead for Southampton but that may be unrealistic for a club at risk of getting sucked into another relegation battle.

Saints finished the season strongly but their 36-point total was the lowest of any surviving club since 2013-14.

Mark Hughes has a lot of problems to fix, including a defence which has largely struggled since the January sale of Virgil Van Dijk to Liverpool.

Offensively they are too reliant on the injury-prone Charlie Austin and they seem to have lost the golden touch which they once had in the transfer market.

Last season's big-money buys Mario Lemina and Guido Carillo have failed to sparkle and Saints will have to recruit a lot better if they are to avoid another season of struggle.

Longest run without a loss: 4
Longest run without a win: 12
Highest/lowest league position: 10/18
Clean sheets: 8
Yellow cards: 64 **Red cards:** 2
Average attendance: 33,884
Players used: 26
Leading scorer: C Austin 7 (2,6)

	2017-18		Last six seasons at home							
	H	A	P	W	D	L	OV	UN	BS	CS
Man City	L	L	6	2	1	3	4	2	3	0
Man United	L	D	6	0	2	4	3	3	4	1
Tottenham	D	L	6	0	2	4	4	2	5	0
Liverpool	L	L	6	2	1	3	3	3	2	1
Chelsea	L	L	6	1	1	4	4	2	4	0
Arsenal	D	L	6	2	3	1	2	4	3	2
Burnley	L	D	3	2	0	1	1	2	1	1
Everton	W	D	6	4	1	1	3	3	1	4
Leicester	L	D	4	2	1	1	3	1	2	2
Newcastle	D	L	5	4	1	0	4	1	2	3
Crystal Palace	L	W	5	4	0	1	3	2	3	2
Bournemouth	W	D	3	2	1	0	1	2	1	2
West Ham	W	L	6	2	3	1	2	4	3	3
Watford	L	D	3	1	1	1	0	3	1	1
Brighton	D	D	1	0	1	0	0	1	1	0
Huddersfield	D	D	1	0	1	0	0	1	1	0
Southampton										
Wolves			-	-	-	-	-	-	-	-
Cardiff			1	0	0	1	0	1	0	0
Fulham			2	1	1	0	1	1	1	1

Season	Division	Pos	P	W	D	L	F	A	GD	Pts
2017-18	Premier League	17	38	7	15	16	37	56	-19	36
2016-17	Premier League	8	38	12	10	16	41	48	-7	46
2015-16	Premier League	6	38	18	9	11	59	41	+18	63

Over/Under 42%/58% 14th **Both score** 55%/45% 5th

Key stat: Southampton's tally of four home wins last season was the second lowest in the top flight

2017-18 Premier League appearances

	P	G		Y	R
C Austin	10 (14)	7	▌▌▌▌▌	2	-
J Bednarek	5	1	▌	1	-
R Bertrand	35	0		2	-
S Boufal	11 (15)	2	▌▌	1	-
G Carrillo	5 (2)	0		-	-
S Davis	17 (6)	3	▌▌▌	-	-
F Forster	20	0		-	-
M Gabbiadini	11 (17)	5	▌▌▌▌▌	2	-
W Hoedt	28	0		7	-
P Hojbjerg	19 (4)	0		6	-
M Lemina	20 (5)	1	▌	2	-
S Long	15 (15)	2	▌▌	6	-
A McCarthy	18	0		2	-
S McQueen	1 (6)	0		-	-
M Obafemi	0 (1)	0		-	-
J Pied	2	0		-	-
N Redmond	22 (9)	1	▌	3	-
O Romeu	34	1	▌	11	-
J Sims	1 (5)	0		-	-
C Soares	32	0		3	-
J Stephens	22	2	▌▌	6	1

	P	G		Y	R
D Tadic	34 (2)	6	▌▌▌▌▌	4	-
M Targett	2	0		-	-
J Ward-Prowse	20 (10)	3	▌▌▌	3	-
M Yoshida	23 (1)	2	▌▌	3	1
V Van Dijk	11 (1)	0		-	-

Southampton celebrated last-gasp survival

TOTTENHAM

Nickname: Spurs
Colours: White and navy blue
Ground: Wembley/Tottenham Stadium
Tel: 0344-499-5000
Capacity: 90,000/62,062
www.tottenhamhotspur.com

Mauricio Pochettino has steered Tottenham to three successive top-four finishes and can keep them entrenched in the Champions League qualifying slots.

Spurs have to settle into their new stadium but are likely to find it easier there than at Wembley, where they had a mixed campaign. Tottenham chalked up 43 points at Wembley, ten fewer than the 53-point total reached in the final season at White Hart Lane.

Performing better at home could make a big difference because Tottenham's away points total last season (34) was the joint-second best.

Financially, Spurs cannot compete with the Manchester clubs. But Pochettino has signed a contract extension, the core of the squad remain, and they should continue to be a force among the big six.

Longest run without a loss: 14
Longest run without a win: 4
Highest/lowest league position: 3/7
Clean sheets: 16
Yellow cards: 51 **Red cards:** 2
Average attendance: 43,256
Players used: 25
Leading scorer: H Kane 30 (10,19)

	2017-18		Last six seasons at home							
	H	A	P	W	D	L	OV	UN	BS	CS
Man City	L	L	6	3	0	3	4	2	4	1
Man United	W	L	6	3	3	0	3	3	3	3
Tottenham										
Liverpool	W	D	6	2	2	2	4	2	3	1
Chelsea	L	W	6	2	2	2	3	3	4	2
Arsenal	W	L	6	4	1	1	3	3	3	2
Burnley	D	W	3	2	1	0	2	1	3	0
Everton	W	W	6	4	2	0	4	2	3	3
Leicester	W	L	4	2	1	1	2	2	3	0
Newcastle	W	W	5	2	0	3	3	2	3	1
Crystal Palace	W	W	5	4	1	0	0	5	0	5
Bournemouth	W	W	3	3	0	0	2	1	0	3
West Ham	D	W	6	3	2	1	5	1	5	0
Watford	W	D	3	3	0	0	1	2	0	3
Brighton	W	D	1	1	0	0	0	1	0	1
Huddersfield	W	W	1	1	0	0	0	1	0	1
Southampton	W	D	6	5	0	1	4	2	4	2
Wolves	-	-	-	-	-	-	-	-	-	-
Cardiff			1	1	0	0	0	1	0	1
Fulham			2	1	0	1	1	1	1	0

Season	Division	Pos	P	W	D	L	F	A	GD	Pts
2017-18	Premier League	3	38	23	8	7	74	36	+38	77
2016-17	Premier League	2	38	26	8	4	86	26	+60	86
2015-16	Premier League	3	38	19	13	6	69	35	+34	70

Over/Under 45%/55% 13th

Both score 50%/50% 9th

Key stat: Tottenham have won ten of their last 11 domestic home games

2017-18 Premier League appearances

	P	G	Y	R		P	G	Y	R
T Alderweireld	13 (1)	0	3	-	M Vorm	1	0	-	-
D Alli	34 (2)	9	7	-	K Walker-Peters	2 (1)	0	-	-
S Aurier	16 (1)	2	2	1	V Wanyama	8 (10)	1	2	-
B Davies	26 (3)	2	3	-	H Winks	9 (7)	0	-	-
M Dembele	21 (7)	0	6	-					
E Dier	32 (2)	0	4	-					
C Eriksen	37	10	-	-					
P Gazzaniga	1	0	-	-					
Heung-Min Son	27 (10)	12	-	-					
V Janssen	0 (1)	0	-	-					
H Kane	35 (2)	30	5	-					
E Lamela	7 (18)	2	4	-					
F Llorente	1 (15)	1	1	-					
H Lloris	36	0	1	-					
Lucas Moura	2 (4)	0	1	-					
G Nkoudou Mbida	0 (1)	0	-	-					
D Rose	9 (1)	0	4	-					
D Sanchez	29 (2)	0	1	1					
M Sissoko	15 (18)	1	3	-					
K Trippier	21 (3)	0	1	-					
J Vertonghen	36	0	4	-					

Harry Kane was just pipped to the Golden Boot

WATFORD

Nickname: The Hornets
Colours: Yellow and red
Ground: Vicarage Road **Capacity:** 21,438
Tel: 01923-49600 www.watfordfc.co.uk

Watford have posted unremarkable finishes of 13th, 17th and 14th since returning to the Premier League but have never been dragged into a major relegation battle and their existence as a stable top-flight club can continue.

The Hornets had injury problems last season – they topped the table of minutes lost through injury – and were adversely affected when Everton stepped up their pursuit of manager Marco Silva.

A downturn in results led to Silva's dismissal but his replacement, Javi Gracia, steadied the ship and remains at the helm.

There will be plenty of ins and outs but the club continues to benefit hugely from the Pozzo scouting network, which unearths a steady stream of gems.

Given better luck on the injury front, Watford may rise a little higher.

Longest run without a loss: 4
Longest run without a win: 7
Highest/lowest league position: 4/13
Clean sheets: 9
Yellow cards: 64 **Red cards:** 4
Average attendance: 28,769
Players used: 29
Leading scorer: A Doucoure 7 (1,7)

	2017-18		Last six seasons at home							
	H	A	P	W	D	L	OV	UN	BS	CS
Man City	L	L	3	0	0	3	3	0	1	0
Man United	L	L	3	1	0	2	3	0	3	0
Tottenham	D	L	3	0	1	2	2	1	3	0
Liverpool	D	L	3	1	1	1	2	1	1	1
Chelsea	W	L	3	1	1	1	2	1	2	1
Arsenal	W	L	3	1	0	2	3	0	2	0
Burnley	L	L	4	1	2	1	3	1	4	0
Everton	W	L	3	2	1	0	1	2	2	1
Leicester	W	L	5	3	0	2	4	1	3	0
Newcastle	W	W	2	2	0	0	2	0	2	0
Crystal Palace	D	L	4	0	3	1	1	3	2	1
Bournemouth	D	W	5	1	4	0	3	2	4	1
West Ham	W	L	3	2	1	0	0	3	1	2
Watford										
Brighton	D	L	4	1	2	1	0	4	1	2
Huddersfield	L	L	4	2	0	2	4	0	3	1
Southampton	D	W	3	0	2	1	2	1	2	1
Wolves			2	1	0	1	1	1	1	0
Cardiff			2	0	1	1	0	2	0	1
Fulham			1	1	0	0	0	1	0	1

Season	Division	Pos	P	W	D	L	F	A	GD	Pts
2017-18	Premier League	14	38	11	8	19	44	64	-20	41
2016-17	Premier League	17	38	11	7	20	40	68	-28	40
2015-16	Premier League	13	38	12	9	17	40	50	-10	45

Over/Under 55%/45% 7th **Both score** 47%/53% 12th

Key stat: All of Watford's last 15 goals have been scored at Vicarage Road

2017-18 Premier League appearances

	P	G	Y	R
N Amrabat	3	0	-	-
M Britos	10 (2)	1	3	1
E Capoue	18 (5)	1	3	-
A Carrillo	16 (12)	1	2	-
C Cathcart	5 (2)	0	1	-
N Chalobah	5 (1)	0	1	-
T Cleverley	22 (1)	1	2	1
T Deeney	20 (9)	5	1	1
G Deulofeu	5 (2)	1	-	-
A Doucoure	37	7	10	-
H Gomes	24	0	-	-
A Gray	16 (15)	5	1	-
J Holebas	26 (2)	0	7	-
W Hughes	11 (4)	2	-	-
D Janmaat	21 (2)	3	3	-
C Kabasele	27 (1)	2	5	-
Y Kaboul	2	0	-	-
O Karnezis	14 (1)	0	-	-
Kiko	19 (4)	1	2	-
D Lukebakio	0 (1)	0	-	-
A Mariappa	24 (4)	0	4	-
S Okaka	3 (12)	1	2	-

	P	G	Y	R
R Pereyra	18 (14)	5	3	-
S Prodl	17 (4)	0	5	-
Richarlison	32 (6)	5	4	-
J Sinclair	0 (4)	0	-	-
M Wague	5 (1)	1	-	-
B Watson	6 (2)	0	1	-
M Zeegelaar	12	0	4	1

Richarlison was a big hit at Vicarage Road

WEST HAM

Nickname: The Hammers/Irons
Colours: Claret and blue
Ground: London Stadium   **Capacity:** 57,000
Tel: 0333-030-1966   www.whufc.com

West Ham were delighted to appoint Manuel Pellegrini and are likely to progress under the Chilean, who led Manchester City to the Premier League title in 2013-14.

Pellegrini must quickly reacquaint himself with the division, which has grown in strength during his absence.

West Ham have posted successive bottom-half finishes since moving to the London Stadium and were flirting with relegation last season until David Moyes rode to the rescue.

Moyes can count himself a little unlucky to have lost his job but the appointment of Pellegrini shows ambition.

Several strong signings come as a positive signing for the Hammers, who look candidates for a top-half finish, but Manuel Lanzini's knee injury is a blow.

Longest run without a loss: 6
Longest run without a win: 8
Highest/lowest league position: 11/19
Clean sheets: 10
Yellow cards: 74 **Red cards:** 2
Average attendance: 46,278
Players used: 27
Leading scorer: M Arnautovic 11 (2,9)

	2017-18		Last six seasons at home							
	H	A	P	W	D	L	OV	UN	BS	CS
Man City	L	L	6	1	2	3	5	1	4	1
Man United	D	L	6	1	3	2	2	4	3	1
Tottenham	L	D	6	3	0	3	2	4	2	3
Liverpool	L	L	6	2	0	4	5	1	4	1
Chelsea	W	D	6	3	0	3	4	2	3	1
Arsenal	D	L	6	0	2	4	5	1	5	1
Burnley	L	D	3	2	0	1	1	2	0	2
Everton	W	L	6	1	2	3	4	2	5	1
Leicester	D	W	4	1	1	2	2	2	3	1
Newcastle	L	L	5	2	1	2	2	3	2	3
Crystal Palace	D	D	5	1	2	2	3	2	3	1
Bournemouth	D	D	3	1	1	1	1	2	2	1
West Ham										
Watford	W	L	3	2	0	1	2	1	2	1
Brighton	L	L	1	0	0	1	1	0	0	0
Huddersfield	W	W	1	1	0	0	0	1	0	1
Southampton	W	L	6	4	0	2	6	0	4	1
Wolves			-	-	-	-	-	-	-	-
Cardiff			1	1	0	0	0	1	0	1
Fulham			2	2	0	0	2	0	0	2

Season	Division	Pos	P	W	D	L	F	A	GD	Pts
2017-18	Premier League	13	38	10	12	16	48	68	-20	42
2016-17	Premier League	11	38	12	9	17	47	64	-17	45
2015-16	Premier League	7	38	16	14	8	65	51	+14	62

Over/Under 58%/42% 5th   **Both score** 58%/42% 2nd

Key stat: West Ham have not finished lower than 13th since winning promotion in 2011-12

2017-18 Premier League appearances

	P	G	Y	R
Adrian	19	0	2	-
M Antonio	16 (5)	3 ▮▮▮	1	-
M Arnautovic	28 (3)	11 ▮▮▮▮▮▮▮▮▮▮▮	5	1
A Ayew	9 (9)	3 ▮▮▮	2	-
S Byram	2 (3)	0	1	-
A Carroll	7 (9)	3 ▮▮▮	6	1
J Collins	12 (1)	1 ▮	3	-
A Cresswell	35 (1)	1 ▮	7	-
J Cullen	0 (2)	0	-	-
P Evra	3 (2)	0	-	-
E Fernandes	9 (5)	0	1	-
J Fonte	8	0	-	-
J Hart	19	0	-	-
J Hernandez	16 (12)	8 ▮▮▮▮▮▮▮▮	3	-
J Hugill	0 (3)	0	-	-
Joao Mario	12 (1)	2 ▮▮	-	-
C Kouyate	32 (1)	2 ▮▮	5	-
M Lanzini	23 (4)	5 ▮▮▮▮	4	-
A Masuaku	21 (6)	0	5	-
M Noble	28 (1)	4 ▮▮▮	6	-
P Obiang	18 (3)	2 ▮▮	3	-

	P	G	Y	R
A Ogbonna	32	1 ▮	3	-
R Oxford	0 (1)	0	-	-
W Reid	17	0	5	-
D Rice	15 (11)	0	1	-
D Sakho	0 (14)	2 ▮▮	2	-
P Zabaleta	37	0	9	-

West Ham had to work hard to avoid relegation

WOLVES

Nickname: Wolves
Colours: Gold and black
Ground: Molineux **Capacity:** 31,700
Tel: 0871-222-2220 www.wolves.co.uk

Few teams have won promotion to the Premier League as impressively as big-spending Wolves, who finished top of the Championship on 99 points.

Wolves have the core of a decent top-flight team but, like every other promoted side, they need to adjust to a higher standard of football.

Fosun International are ambitious owners but they will be operating in a competitive environment alongside clubs who have benefited from several seasons of Premier League TV money.

Nuno Espirito Santo is an impressive manager and with one or two sensible additions his team should have no problems avoiding a relegation battle.

However, expectations of a push for Europa League qualification may prove wide of the mark.

Longest run without a loss: 13
Longest run without a win: 3
Highest/lowest league position: 1/3
Clean sheets: 24
Yellow cards: 71 **Red cards:** 4
Average attendance: 22,915
Players used: 31
Leading scorer: Diogo Jota 17 (7,16)

	2017-18		Last six seasons at home							
	H	A	P	W	D	L	OV	UN	BS	CS
Man City	-	-	-	-	-	-	-	-	-	-
Man United	-	-	-	-	-	-	-	-	-	-
Tottenham	-	-	-	-	-	-	-	-	-	-
Liverpool	-	-	-	-	-	-	-	-	-	-
Chelsea	-	-	-	-	-	-	-	-	-	-
Arsenal	-	-	-	-	-	-	-	-	-	-
Burnley			2	0	1	1	1	1	1	1
Everton	-	-	-	-	-	-	-	-	-	-
Leicester			1	1	0	0	1	0	1	0
Newcastle			1	0	0	1	0	1	0	0
Crystal Palace			1	0	0	1	1	0	1	0
Bournemouth			1	0	0	1	1	0	1	0
West Ham	-	-	-	-	-	-	-	-	-	-
Watford			2	0	2	0	1	1	2	0
Brighton			4	0	3	1	1	3	2	1
Huddersfield			4	1	0	3	3	1	2	1
Southampton	-	-	-	-	-	-	-	-	-	-
Wolves										
Cardiff	L	W	5	2	0	3	4	1	4	1
Fulham	W	L	4	3	1	0	3	1	2	2

Season	Division	Pos	P	W	D	L	F	A	GD	Pts
2017-18	Championship	1	46	30	9	7	82	39	+43	99
2016-17	Championship	15	46	16	10	20	54	58	-4	58
2015-16	Championship	14	46	14	16	16	53	58	-5	58

Over/Under 52%/48% 5th **Both score** 39%/61% 23rd

Key stat: Wolves are unbeaten in their last nine home fixtures

---

2017-18 Championship appearances

	P	G	Y	R
B Afobe	7 (9)	6	-	-
D Batth	15 (1)	1	3	1
R Bennett	27 (2)	1	7	-
W Boly	36	3	2	-
H Burgoyne	0 (1)	0	-	-
O Buur	0 (1)	1	-	-
I Cavaleiro	31 (11)	9	4	-
C Coady	45	1	4	1
H Costa	21 (15)	5	2	-
S Deslandes	0 (1)	0	-	-
N Dicko	0 (5)	1	-	-
Diogo Jota	43 (1)	17	9	-
M Doherty	45	4	3	1
B Douglas	38 (1)	5	6	-
D Edwards	1 (2)	0	5	1
B Enobakhare	5 (16)	1	-	-
M Gibbs-White	1 (12)	0	-	-
K Hause	0 (1)	0	-	-
Leo Bonatini	29 (14)	12	-	-
B Marshall	1 (5)	0	1	-
R Miranda	16 (1)	0	2	-
A N'Diaye	13 (20)	3	4	-

	P	G	Y	R
R Neves	42	6	12	1
W Norris	1	0	-	-
J Price	0 (5)	0	-	-
Rafa Mir	0 (2)	0	-	-
C Ronan	0 (3)	0	-	-
J Ruddy	45	0	1	-
R Saiss	37 (5)	4	11	-
R Vinagre	8 (1)	1	-	-

Wolves dominated last season's Championship

Premier League stats 2017-18

Key Points in all tables (except the league table) do not include any deductions imposed by the league. **POS H A** Overall league position, rank from home games only, rank from away games only **Sup** Average match supremacy **GFA** Goals For Average **GAA** Goals Against Average **PGA** Points Gained Average

			Premier League 2017-18		Home					Away						
Pos	H	A		P	W	D	L	F	A	W	D	L	F	A	GD	Pts
1	1	1	Man City (CL)	38	16	2	1	61	14	16	2	1	45	13	79	100
2	3	3	Man Utd (CL)	38	15	2	2	38	9	10	4	5	30	19	40	81
3	5	2	Tottenham (CL)	38	13	4	2	40	16	10	4	5	34	20	38	77
4	4	5	Liverpool (CL)	38	12	7	0	45	10	9	5	5	39	28	46	75
5	6	4	Chelsea (EL)	38	11	4	4	30	16	10	3	6	32	22	24	70
6	2	11	Arsenal (EL)	38	15	2	2	54	20	4	4	11	20	31	23	63
7	14	6	Burnley (EL)	38	7	5	7	16	17	7	7	5	20	22	-3	54
8	7	14	Everton	38	10	4	5	28	22	3	6	10	16	36	-14	49
9	10	7	Leicester	38	7	6	6	25	22	5	5	9	31	38	-4	47
10	9	12	Newcastle	38	8	4	7	21	17	4	4	11	18	30	-8	44
11	13	9	Crystal Palace	38	7	5	7	29	27	4	6	9	16	28	-10	44
12	15	8	Bournemouth	38	7	5	7	26	30	4	6	9	19	31	-16	44
13	11	13	West Ham	38	7	6	6	24	26	3	6	10	24	42	-20	42
14	12	15	Watford	38	7	6	6	27	31	4	2	13	17	33	-20	41
15	8	20	Brighton	38	7	8	4	24	25	2	5	12	10	29	-20	40
16	16	16	Huddersfield	38	6	5	8	16	25	3	5	11	12	33	-30	37
17	19	10	Southampton	38	4	7	8	20	26	3	8	8	17	30	-19	36
18	17	19	Swansea (R)	38	6	3	10	17	24	2	6	11	11	32	-28	33
19	18	18	Stoke (R)	38	5	5	9	20	30	2	7	10	15	38	-33	33
20	20	17	West Brom (R)	38	3	9	7	21	29	3	4	12	10	27	-25	31

Best attack

		GF	GFA
1	Man City	106	2.79
2	Liverpool	84	2.21
3	Tottenham	74	1.95
4	Arsenal	74	1.95
5	Man Utd	68	1.79
6	Chelsea	62	1.63
7	Leicester	56	1.47
8	West Ham	48	1.26
9	Crystal Palace	45	1.18
10	Bournemouth	45	1.18
11	Everton	44	1.16
12	Watford	44	1.16
13	Newcastle	39	1.03
14	Southampton	37	0.97
15	Burnley	36	0.95
16	Stoke	35	0.92
17	Brighton	34	0.89
18	West Brom	31	0.82
19	Huddersfield	28	0.74
20	Swansea	28	0.74

Best defence

		GA	GAA
1	Man City	27	0.71
2	Man Utd	28	0.74
3	Tottenham	36	0.95
4	Liverpool	38	1
5	Chelsea	38	1
6	Burnley	39	1.03
7	Newcastle	47	1.24
8	Arsenal	51	1.34
9	Brighton	54	1.42
10	Crystal Palace	55	1.45
11	Southampton	56	1.47
12	Swansea	56	1.47
13	West Brom	56	1.47
14	Everton	58	1.53
15	Huddersfield	58	1.53
16	Leicester	60	1.58
17	Bournemouth	61	1.61
18	Watford	64	1.68
19	West Ham	68	1.79
20	Stoke	68	1.79

Top scorers

	Team	Goals scored	
M Salah	Liverpool	32	▮▮▮▮▮▮▮▮▮▮▮▮▮▮▮▮
H Kane	Tottenham	30	▮▮▮▮▮▮▮▮▮▮▮▮▮▮▮
S Aguero	Man City	21	▮▮▮▮▮▮▮▮▮▮▮
J Vardy	Leicester	20	▮▮▮▮▮▮▮▮▮▮
R Sterling	Man City	18	▮▮▮▮▮▮▮▮▮
R Lukaku	Man Utd	16	▮▮▮▮▮▮▮▮
R Firmino	Liverpool	15	▮▮▮▮▮▮▮
A Lacazette	Arsenal	14	▮▮▮▮▮▮▮
G Jesus	Man City	13	▮▮▮▮▮▮
E Hazard	Chelsea	12	▮▮▮▮▮▮
S Heung-Min	Tottenham	12	▮▮▮▮▮▮
R Mahrez	Leicester	12	▮▮▮▮▮▮
G Murray	Brighton	12	▮▮▮▮▮▮
M Arnautovic	West Ham	11	▮▮▮▮▮
A Morata	Chelsea	11	▮▮▮▮▮
P Aubameyang	Arsenal	10	▮▮▮▮▮
C Eriksen	Tottenham	10	▮▮▮▮▮
S Mane	Liverpool	10	▮▮▮▮▮
L Milivojevic	C Palace	10	▮▮▮▮▮
W Rooney	Everton	10	▮▮▮▮▮
L Sane	ManCity	10	▮▮▮▮▮
C Wood	Burnley	10	▮▮▮▮▮

Over 2.5 goals

	H	A	%
Man City	16	11	71%
Arsenal	15	11	68%
Bournemouth	13	12	66%
Liverpool	11	14	66%
Stoke, West Ham			58%

Under 2.5 goals

	H	A	%
Brighton	11	14	66%
Burnley	13	11	63%
Huddersfield	12	12	63%
Swansea	12	12	63%
Newcastle, So'ton, WBA			58%

Both to score

	H	A	%
Leicester	10	14	63%
Bournemouth	12	10	58%
Stoke	11	11	58%
West Ham	10	12	58%
Arsenal, Southampton			55%

Both not to score

	H	A	%
Huddersfield	12	14	68%
Man United	13	11	63%
Swansea	12	11	61%
Brighton	8	14	58%
Newcastle	13	9	58%

Premier League results 2017-18

	Arsenal	Bournemouth	Brighton	Burnley	Chelsea	Crystal Palace	Everton	Huddersfield	Leicester	Liverpool	Man City	Man United	Newcastle	Southampton	Stoke	Swansea	Tottenham	Watford	West Brom	West Ham
Arsenal		3-0	2-0	5-0	2-2	4-1	5-1	5-0	4-3	3-3	0-3	1-3	1-0	3-2	3-0	2-1	2-0	3-0	2-0	4-1
Bournemouth	2-1		2-1	1-2	0-1	2-2	2-1	4-0	0-0	0-4	1-2	0-2	2-2	1-1	2-1	1-0	1-4	0-2	2-1	3-3
Brighton	2-1	2-2		0-0	0-4	0-0	1-1	1-1	0-2	1-5	0-2	1-0	1-0	1-1	2-2	4-1	1-1	1-0	3-1	3-1
Burnley	0-1	1-2	0-0		1-2	1-0	2-1	0-0	2-1	1-2	1-1	0-1	1-0	1-1	1-0	2-0	0-3	1-0	0-1	1-1
Chelsea	0-0	0-3	2-0	2-3		2-1	2-0	1-1	0-0	1-0	0-1	1-0	3-1	1-0	5-0	1-0	1-3	4-2	3-0	1-1
Crystal Palace	2-3	2-2	3-2	1-0	2-1		2-2	0-3	5-0	1-2	0-0	2-3	1-1	0-1	2-1	0-2	0-1	2-1	2-0	2-2
Everton	2-5	2-1	2-0	0-1	0-0	3-1		2-0	2-1	0-0	1-3	0-2	1-0	1-1	1-0	3-1	0-3	3-2	1-1	4-0
Huddersfield	0-1	4-1	2-0	0-0	1-3	0-2	0-2		1-1	0-3	1-2	2-1	1-0	0-0	1-1	0-0	0-4	1-0	1-0	1-4
Leicester	3-1	1-1	2-0	1-0	1-2	0-3	2-0	3-0		2-3	0-2	2-2	1-2	0-0	1-1	1-1	2-1	2-0	1-1	0-2
Liverpool	4-0	3-0	4-0	1-1	1-1	1-0	1-1	3-0	2-1		4-3	0-0	2-0	3-0	0-0	5-0	2-2	5-0	0-0	4-1
Man City	3-1	4-0	3-1	3-0	1-0	5-0	1-1	0-0	5-1	5-0		2-3	3-1	2-1	7-2	5-0	4-1	3-1	3-0	2-1
Man United	2-1	1-0	1-0	2-2	2-1	4-0	4-0	2-0	2-0	2-1	1-2		4-1	0-0	3-0	2-0	1-0	1-0	0-1	4-0
Newcastle	2-1	0-1	0-0	1-1	3-0	1-0	0-1	1-0	2-3	1-1	0-1	1-0		3-0	2-1	1-1	0-2	0-3	0-1	3-0
Southampton	1-1	2-1	1-1	0-1	2-3	1-2	4-1	1-1	1-4	0-2	0-1	0-1	2-2		0-0	0-0	1-1	0-2	1-0	3-2
Stoke	1-0	1-2	1-1	1-1	0-4	1-2	1-2	2-0	2-2	0-3	0-2	2-2	0-1	2-1		2-1	1-2	0-0	3-1	0-3
Swansea	3-1	0-0	0-1	1-0	0-1	1-1	1-1	2-0	1-2	1-0	0-4	0-4	0-1	0-1	1-2		0-2	1-2	1-0	4-1
Tottenham	1-0	1-0	2-0	1-1	1-2	1-0	4-0	2-0	5-4	4-1	1-3	2-0	1-0	5-2	5-1	0-0		2-0	1-1	1-1
Watford	2-1	2-2	0-0	1-2	4-1	0-0	1-0	1-4	2-1	3-3	0-6	2-4	2-1	2-2	0-1	1-2	1-1		1-0	2-0
West Brom	1-1	1-0	2-0	1-2	0-4	0-0	0-0	1-2	1-4	2-2	2-3	1-2	2-2	2-3	1-1	1-1	1-0	2-2		0-0
West Ham	0-0	1-1	0-3	0-3	1-0	1-1	3-1	2-0	1-1	1-4	1-4	0-0	2-3	3-0	1-1	1-0	2-3	2-0	2-1	

Record when first to score

		P	W	D	L	F	A	Sup	PGA	Pts
1	Man Utd	21	21	0	0	47	6	1.95	3	63
2	Man City	31	29	1	1	98	20	2.52	2.8	88
3	Tottenham	22	20	2	0	48	9	1.77	2.8	62
4	Chelsea	22	19	1	2	47	14	1.50	2.6	58
5	Liverpool	25	19	6	0	74	19	2.20	2.5	63
6	Burnley	16	12	3	1	26	13	0.81	2.4	39
7	Arsenal	22	16	2	4	54	19	1.59	2.3	50
8	Everton	14	10	2	2	22	11	0.79	2.3	32
9	Huddersfield	13	9	3	1	21	8	1.00	2.3	30
10	Brighton	15	9	5	1	25	14	0.73	2.1	32
11	West Ham	15	9	4	2	31	14	1.13	2.1	31
12	Leicester	17	10	4	3	33	18	0.88	2	34
13	Newcastle	17	10	4	3	28	18	0.59	2	34
14	Watford	16	9	3	4	30	18	0.75	1.9	30
15	Crystal Palace	13	7	4	2	25	16	0.69	1.9	25
16	Bournemouth	13	6	4	3	21	15	0.46	1.7	22
17	Swansea	11	6	1	4	18	14	0.36	1.7	19
18	Southampton	15	6	6	3	23	18	0.33	1.6	24
19	West Brom	17	6	7	4	22	21	0.06	1.5	25
20	Stoke	13	5	5	3	20	20	0.00	1.5	20

Record when keeping a clean sheet

		P	W	D	F	Sup	PGA	Pts
1	Tottenham	16	15	1	31	1.94	2.9	46
2	Man City	18	16	2	48	2.67	2.8	50
3	Newcastle	9	8	1	14	1.56	2.8	25
4	Man Utd	19	16	3	35	1.84	2.7	51
5	Arsenal	13	11	2	28	2.15	2.7	35
6	Chelsea	16	13	3	30	1.88	2.6	42
7	Liverpool	17	13	4	42	2.47	2.5	43
8	Everton	10	7	3	13	1.30	2.4	24
9	West Ham	10	7	3	14	1.40	2.4	24
10	Burnley	12	8	4	11	0.92	2.3	28
11	Watford	9	6	3	11	1.22	2.3	21
12	Leicester	9	6	3	12	1.33	2.3	21
13	Bournemouth	6	4	2	9	1.50	2.3	14
14	West Brom	10	6	4	7	0.70	2.2	22
15	Swansea	9	5	4	7	0.78	2.1	19
16	Crystal Palace	9	5	4	13	1.44	2.1	19
17	Brighton	10	5	5	7	0.70	2	20
18	Huddersfield	10	5	5	8	0.80	2	20
19	Stoke	6	3	3	4	0.67	2	12
20	Southampton	8	3	5	3	0.38	1.8	14

Moore's magic touch can help send Baggies back up as second-tier champions

N one of the three sides relegated into the Championship were truly out of their depth in the top flight and all three could have survived but for a little more competence in the boardroom or dugout, writes Dan Sait. Whether that says more about the untapped potential in Stoke, West Brom or Swansea or simply highlights the lack of quality in the bottom half of the Premier League is open to debate, but all three can aim high.

Swansea may struggle to hit their targets, though, as a squad weakened by years of outgoings doesn't look suited to the grind of the second tier. New manager Graham Potter could well prove a fine addition to the English game after seven years impressing in Sweden, but it would be no surprise if the bedding-in process took some time.

Stoke have obvious chances as market leaders, but the dressing room suffered from disharmony last season and the squad needs plenty of work. Appointing Gary Rowett could go either way – he would have been a perfect replacement for Tony Pulis in 2013, but the squad is less suited to direct, physical football after five years under Mark Hughes and the current Stoke crop are hardly the die-for-the-shirt crew of yesteryear.

Rowett can, of course, still make it work if he hits the ground running, but there's precious little juice in the Potters' price.

West Brom look a better bet. Darren Moore didn't lose any of his five meaningful games as caretaker – beating Spurs and Man United and drawing with Liverpool – and while interim success doesn't always translate into the full-time position, Moore's early tenure suggests he has the inspiration and savvy required to get the best from his squad.

There have been some issues, with three players failing to show up in pre-season, but all three are set to move on leaving Moore to focus on promotion rather than in-fighting.

The Baggies boss has funds to replace any key men lost and at 9-1 for the title West Brom look an attractive prospect.

Joining them in the top flight could be a Middlesbrough side who improved in the second half of the season after Pulis took over. While their football won't endear Boro to the neutrals, it could get them back up.

The rest of the top-six battle is wide open. Stoke will be up there but are too short. And while Nottingham Forest look a team going places, there is little value in their price.

Instead, try Sheffield Wednesday at tasty odds. The Owls are nowhere near as weak as last season's injury-affected results suggest and it won't take much for them to improve.

At the other end, Bolton's escape last term will surely prove a mere stay of execution for a threadbare squad while Rotherham look out of their depth – they finished 28 points adrift of safety in 2017 and came back up 17 points behind second-placed Blackburn.

QPR are the pick of the perennial strugglers to join them in League One, with Rangers under huge financial pressure and facing increasing discontent in the stands.

Recommendations

West Brom to win Championship, 8-1
Middlesbrough to be promoted, 3-1
Sheffield Wednesday top-six, 7-2
Bolton/Rotherham relegation double, 9-2
QPR to be relegated, 11-2

West Brom striker Jay Rodriguez could make hay in the Championship

ASTON VILLA

Nickname: The Villans
Colours: Claret and blue
Ground: Villa Park (42,790)
Tel: 0121-327-2299   www.avfc.co.uk

Playoff final failure is always tough, but it could have massive implications for Villa.

With the Premier League millions now not forthcoming, Tony Xia's gamble has backfired spectacularly and if he is unable to find, or release, new investment a firesale of star players seems inevitable.

Four of the playoff final team were now-returned loanees – including keeper Sam Johnstone – while John Terry has left and key men such as Jack Grealish and James Chester look set to follow.

Longest run without win/loss: 5/8
High/low league position: 3/14
Clean sheets: 20 **Yellows:** 6 **Reds:** 2
Avg attendance: 27,123 **Players used:** 30
Leading scorer: A Adomah 14 (7,11)
Key stat: Aston Villa failed to score in nearly a quarter of their league games last season (11 of 46)

	2017-18 H	A	Last six seasons at home P	W	D	L	OV	UN	BS	CS
Swansea			4	1	1	2	1	3	2	1
Stoke			4	0	1	3	2	2	2	1
West Brom			4	2	1	1	2	2	3	0
Aston Villa										
Middlesbrough	D	W	1	0	1	0	0	1	0	1
Derby	D	L	2	1	1	0	0	2	1	1
Preston	D	W	2	0	2	0	1	1	2	0
Millwall	D	L	1	0	1	0	0	1	0	1
Brentford	D	L	2	0	2	0	0	2	1	1
Sheffield United	D	W	1	0	1	0	1	0	1	0
Bristol City	W	D	2	2	0	0	1	1	0	2
Ipswich	W	W	2	1	0	1	0	2	0	1
Leeds	W	D	2	1	1	0	0	2	1	1
Norwich	W	L	5	4	1	0	2	3	3	2
Sheffield Wed	L	W	2	1	0	1	1	1	1	1
QPR	L	W	4	2	1	1	3	1	3	1
Nottm Forest	W	W	2	1	1	0	2	0	2	0
Hull	D	D	3	2	1	0	2	1	3	0
Birmingham	W	D	2	2	0	0	0	2	0	2
Reading	W	L	3	2	0	1	2	1	1	2
Bolton	W	L	1	1	0	0	0	1	0	1
Wigan			2	1	0	1	1	0	1	
Blackburn			1	1	0	0	1	0	1	0
Rotherham			1	1	0	0	1	0	0	1

Season	Division	Pos	P	W	D	L	F	A	GD	Pts
2017-18	Championship	4	46	24	11	11	72	42	+30	83
2016-17	Championship	13	46	16	14	16	47	48	-1	62
2015-16	Premier League	20	38	3	8	27	27	76	-49	17

Over/Under 48%/52% 12th   **Both score** 43%/57% 18th

BIRMINGHAM

Nickname: Blues
Colours: Blue
Ground: St Andrew's (30,009)
Tel: 0121-772-0101   www.bcfc.com

Garry Monk became Birmingham's fifth permanent manager in 15 months upon his March appointment and the club sorely needs a period of stability in the dugout to help them progress.

But Monk looks a good fit and he spent the summer bringing a bit of focus to a chaotic recruitment process and trying to implement a more professional approach.

However, he starts from a low base as Blues have avoided relegation on only the final day in three of the last five seasons.

Longest run without win/loss: 7/4
High/low league position: 19/24
Clean sheets: 10 **Yellows:** 80 **Reds:** 6
Avg attendance: 20,438 **Players used:** 32
Leading scorer: S Gallagher 6 (1,6)
Key stat: Birmingham's points-per-game average rose from 0.86 to 1.45 after Garry Monk arrived at St Andrew's

	2017-18 H	A	Last six seasons at home P	W	D	L	OV	UN	BS	CS
Swansea			-	-	-	-	-	-	-	-
Stoke			-	-	-	-	-	-	-	-
West Brom			-	-	-	-	-	-	-	-
Aston Villa	D	L	2	0	2	0	0	2	1	1
Middlesbrough	L	L	5	1	3	1	3	2	4	0
Derby	L	D	6	1	2	3	5	1	4	0
Preston	L	D	3	0	2	1	3	0	3	0
Millwall	L	L	4	1	1	2	1	3	1	1
Brentford	L	L	4	2	0	2	2	2	2	1
Sheffield United	W	D	1	1	0	0	1	0	1	0
Bristol City	W	L	4	4	0	0	2	2	2	2
Ipswich	W	L	6	3	2	1	3	3	3	2
Leeds	W	L	6	2	1	3	3	3	4	2
Norwich	L	L	3	1	1	1	1	2	0	2
Sheffield Wed	W	W	6	3	1	2	3	3	3	2
QPR	L	L	4	1	0	3	3	1	3	0
Nottm Forest	W	L	6	3	2	1	2	4	2	3
Hull	W	L	3	2	0	1	2	1	1	2
Birmingham										
Reading	L	W	5	2	0	3	3	2	3	0
Bolton	D	W	5	2	1	2	2	3	2	2
Wigan			3	1	0	2	1	2	1	0
Blackburn			5	1	3	1	2	3	3	2
Rotherham			3	2	0	1	2	1	2	0

Season	Division	Pos	P	W	D	L	F	A	GD	Pts
2017-18	Championship	19	46	13	7	26	38	68	-30	46
2016-17	Championship	19	46	13	14	19	45	64	-19	53
2015-16	Championship	10	46	16	15	15	53	49	+4	63

Over/Under 35%/65% 24th   **Both score** 39%/61% 23rd

BLACKBURN

Nickname: Rovers
Colours: Blue and white
Ground: Ewood Park (31,367)
Tel: 01254-372-001   www.rovers.co.uk

Blackburn were always likely candidates to bounce straight back from League One as a solid second-tier squad would never have been relegated in 2017 had they been competently led from the dugout.

Tony Mowbray is a steady hand on the tiller and while Rovers landed with a bump in the third tier, losing their first two games, they went on to lose only four more of their subsequent 44 matches.

A club known for its chaotic nature may have finally turned the corner.

Longest run without win/loss: 2/18
High/low league position: 1/11
Clean sheets: 17 **Yellows:** 72 **Reds:** 3
Avg attendance: 11,007 **Players used:** 29
Leading scorer: B Dack 18 (7,15)
Key stat: After losing two of their first three home games, Rovers went unbeaten in the following 20, winning 14

	2017-18 H	2017-18 A	Last six seasons at home P	W	D	L	OV	UN	BS	CS
Swansea			-	-	-	-	-	-	-	-
Stoke			-	-	-	-	-	-	-	-
West Brom			-	-	-	-	-	-	-	-
Aston Villa	1	1	0	0	0	1	0	1		
Middlesbrough	4	2	1	1	2	2	2	2		
Derby	5	2	2	1	1	4	2	3		
Preston	2	0	1	1	2	0	2	0		
Millwall	3	2	0	1	1	2	1	1		
Brentford	3	1	1	1	2	1	3	0		
Sheffield United			-	-	-	-	-	-	-	-
Bristol City	3	1	2	0	1	2	2	1		
Ipswich	5	4	1	0	1	4	1	4		
Leeds	5	2	1	2	3	2	3	2		
Norwich	2	0	0	2	2	0	2	0		
Sheffield Wed	5	1	2	2	2	3	2	2		
QPR	3	2	1	0	0	3	1	2		
Nottm Forest	5	2	2	1	3	2	2	2		
Hull	2	1	0	1	0	2	0	1		
Birmingham	5	2	2	1	1	4	3	2		
Reading	4	2	1	1	3	1	3	1		
Bolton	4	2	1	1	2	2	2	2		
Wigan	D	D	4	3	1	0	3	1	3	1
Blackburn										
Rotherham	W	D	4	4	0	0	2	2	2	2

Season	Division	Pos	P	W	D	L	F	A	GD	Pts
2017-18	League One	2	46	28	12	6	82	40	+42	96
2016-17	Championship	22	46	12	15	19	53	65	-12	51
2015-16	Championship	15	46	13	16	17	46	46	0	55

Over/Under 52%/48% 4th   **Both score** 54%/46% 7th

BOLTON

Nickname: The Trotters
Colours: White and blue
Ground: Macron Stadium (28,723)
Tel: 01204-673-673   www.bwfc.co.uk

The greatest of great escapes saw all the results go their way on the final day, but Bolton certainly did their bit in dramatic fashion, scoring two goals in the final five minutes to beat Nottingham Forest 3-2 and thus secure survival.

It was an extraordinary achievement as Phil Parkinson was operating under a transfer embargo last summer and had to sell top scorer Gary Madine in January.

However, funds remain tight at the club and another tough battle awaits.

Longest run without win/loss: 11/7
High/low league position: 19/24
Clean sheets: 9 **Yellows:** 99 **Reds:** 2
Avg attendance: 17,972 **Players used:** 30
Leading scorer: G Madine 10 (6,9)
Key stat: Only relegated Burton had a worse goal difference than Bolton's -35 last season

	2017-18 H	2017-18 A	Last six seasons at home P	W	D	L	OV	UN	BS	CS
Swansea			-	-	-	-	-	-	-	-
Stoke			-	-	-	-	-	-	-	-
West Brom			-	-	-	-	-	-	-	-
Aston Villa	W	L	1	1	0	0	0	1	0	1
Middlesbrough	L	L	5	1	1	3	5	0	4	0
Derby	L	L	5	1	2	2	2	3	2	2
Preston	L	D	2	0	0	2	2	0	2	0
Millwall	L	D	5	3	1	1	1	4	2	2
Brentford	L	L	3	1	1	1	2	1	2	0
Sheffield United	L	W	2	1	0	1	0	2	0	1
Bristol City	W	L	3	2	1	0	1	2	1	2
Ipswich	D	L	5	0	4	1	2	3	4	1
Leeds	L	L	5	0	3	2	2	3	4	0
Norwich	W	D	2	1	0	1	2	0	2	0
Sheffield Wed	W	D	5	1	3	1	1	4	2	2
QPR	D	L	3	0	2	1	0	3	2	0
Nottm Forest	W	L	5	1	4	0	3	2	5	0
Hull	W	L	3	3	0	0	1	2	1	2
Birmingham	L	D	5	1	1	3	2	3	2	0
Reading	D	D	4	0	3	1	1	3	3	0
Bolton										
Wigan			2	1	1	0	1	1	2	0
Blackburn			4	4	0	0	2	2	1	3
Rotherham			2	2	0	0	2	0	2	0

Season	Division	Pos	P	W	D	L	F	A	GD	Pts
2017-18	Championship	21	46	10	13	23	39	74	-35	43
2016-17	League One	2	46	25	11	10	68	36	+32	86
2015-16	Championship	24	46	5	15	26	41	81	-40	30

Over/Under 39%/61% 20th   **Both score** 43%/57% 18th

BRENTFORD

Nickname: The Bees
Colours: Red
Ground: Griffin Park (12,573)
Tel: 0208-847-2511   www.brentfordfc.co.uk

Operating on one of the tightest second-tier budgets and having lost key men last summer, Dean Smith deserves credit for guiding Brentford to a fourth-consecutive top-ten finish in the Championship.

A slow start was expected and the Bees took just three points from their first seven games, but they settled to go nine games unbeaten, winning five. And while Brentford never seriously troubled the top six, their passing football doesn't look out of place at the top end of the table.

Longest run without win/loss: 8/9
High/low league position: 8/22
Clean sheets: 15 **Yellows:** 68 **Reds:** 3
Avg attendance: 14,914 **Players used:** 28
Leading scorer: N Maupay 12 (4,12)
Key stat: Brentford lost just three home games last term, but drew a league-high 11 matches in front of their own supporters

	2017-18 H	A	Last six seasons at home P	W	D	L	OV	UN	BS	CS
Swansea	-	-	-	-	-	-	-	-	-	-
Stoke	-	-	-	-	-	-	-	-	-	-
West Brom	-	-	-	-	-	-	-	-	-	-
Aston Villa	W	D	2	2	0	0	2	0	1	1
Middlesbrough	D	D	3	0	1	2	0	3	1	0
Derby	D	L	4	2	1	1	3	1	3	1
Preston	D	W	5	4	1	0	2	3	2	3
Millwall	W	L	2	1	1	0	1	1	1	1
Brentford										
Sheffield United	D	L	3	2	1	0	1	2	2	1
Bristol City	D	W	4	2	2	0	2	2	3	1
Ipswich	W	L	4	2	1	1	2	2	2	2
Leeds	W	L	4	3	1	0	1	3	2	2
Norwich	L	W	3	0	1	2	1	2	0	1
Sheffield Wed	W	L	4	1	2	1	1	3	2	2
QPR	W	D	3	3	0	0	2	1	2	1
Nottm Forest	L	W	4	2	1	1	3	1	3	1
Hull	D	L	2	0	1	1	0	2	1	0
Birmingham	W	W	4	1	1	2	2	2	2	1
Reading	D	W	4	2	1	1	3	1	4	0
Bolton	W	W	3	2	1	0	2	1	2	1
Wigan			2	1	1	0	1	1	0	2
Blackburn			3	1	0	2	2	1	2	0
Rotherham			4	3	0	1	2	2	2	1

Season	Division	Pos	P	W	D	L	F	A	GD	Pts
2017-18	Championship	9	46	18	15	13	62	52	+10	69
2016-17	Championship	10	46	18	10	18	75	65	+10	64
2015-16	Championship	9	46	19	8	19	72	67	+5	65

Over/Under 39%/61% 20th   **Both score** 48%/52% 14th

BRISTOL CITY

Nickname: The Robins
Colours: Red and white
Ground: Ashton Gate (27,000)
Tel: 0117-963-0600   www.bcfc.co.uk

A poor end to a promising season left a dull sheen on City's campaign, but they still improved their league position for a fourth-successive year to finish 11th.

The Robins also enjoyed a fantastic run to the League Cup semi-finals, claiming the scalps of Man United and three other top-flight clubs before losing to Man City.

Falling short of the playoffs hurt, but City were decent against the top six and if Lee Johnson gets his signings right a fluent side can take another step forward.

Longest run without win/loss: 5/10
High/low league position: 3/11
Clean sheets: 14 **Yellows:** 82 **Reds:** 4
Avg attendance: 19,895 **Players used:** 30
Leading scorer: B Reid 19 (6,16)
Key stat: A different City player has finished in the top four of the scoring charts in each of City's three seasons back in the Championship

	2017-18 H	A	Last six seasons at home P	W	D	L	OV	UN	BS	CS
Swansea	-	-	-	-	-	-	-	-	-	-
Stoke	-	-	-	-	-	-	-	-	-	-
West Brom	-	-	-	-	-	-	-	-	-	-
Aston Villa	D	L	2	1	1	0	1	1	2	0
Middlesbrough	W	L	3	3	0	0	1	2	1	2
Derby	W	D	4	1	1	2	2	2	3	0
Preston	L	L	5	0	1	4	3	2	4	0
Millwall	D	L	2	0	2	0	0	2	1	1
Brentford	L	D	4	0	0	4	2	2	2	0
Sheffield United	L	W	3	0	0	3	2	1	2	0
Bristol City										
Ipswich	W	W	4	4	0	0	2	2	2	2
Leeds	L	D	4	1	1	2	3	1	2	1
Norwich	L	D	2	0	1	1	0	2	1	0
Sheffield Wed	W	D	4	2	2	0	3	1	3	1
QPR	W	D	3	2	1	0	1	2	2	1
Nottm Forest	W	D	4	4	0	0	2	2	2	2
Hull	D	W	3	0	2	1	2	1	3	0
Birmingham	W	L	4	1	1	2	1	3	1	1
Reading	W	W	3	1	0	2	1	2	1	1
Bolton	W	L	3	2	0	1	2	1	1	2
Wigan			1	1	0	0	1	0	1	0
Blackburn			3	1	0	2	1	2	1	1
Rotherham			3	1	1	1	1	2	2	1

Season	Division	Pos	P	W	D	L	F	A	GD	Pts
2017-18	Championship	11	46	17	16	13	67	58	+9	67
2016-17	Championship	17	46	15	9	22	60	66	-6	54
2015-16	Championship	18	46	13	13	20	54	71	-17	52

Over/Under 54%/46% 4th   **Both score** 54%/46% 7th

DERBY

Nickname: The Rams
Colours: White and black
Ground: Pride Park Stadium (33,597)
Tel: 0871-472-1884   www.dcfc.co.uk

Derby were back to their old selves last season – teasing fans with the promise of promotion but falling agonisingly short.

And their playoff failure could signal an end to Derby challenging with the big boys as owner Mel Morris seems eager to cut the wage bill and reduce investment.

It is understood that Derby are willing to cash in on player of the season Matej Vydra and they accepted compensation from Stoke for Gary Rowett. Rookie manager Frank Lampard takes his place.

Longest run without win/loss: 8/12
High/low league position: 2/16
Clean sheets: 19 **Yellows:** 74 **Reds:** 2
Avg attendance: 24,058 **Players used:** 27
Leading scorer: M Vydra 21 (9,18)
Key stat: Frank Lampard is Derby's sixth manager in three years

	2017-18 H	A	Last six seasons at home P	W	D	L	OV	UN	BS	CS
Swansea	-	-	-	-	-	-	-	-	-	-
Stoke	-	-	-	-	-	-	-	-	-	-
West Brom	-	-	-	-	-	-	-	-	-	-
Aston Villa	W	D	2	1	1	0	0	2	0	2
Middlesbrough	L	W	5	2	1	2	3	2	4	0
Derby										
Preston	W	W	3	1	2	0	0	3	1	2
Millwall	W	D	4	2	1	1	1	3	0	3
Brentford	W	D	4	2	2	0	1	3	1	3
Sheffield United	D	L	1	0	1	0	0	1	1	0
Bristol City	D	L	4	2	2	0	3	1	1	3
Ipswich	L	W	6	0	2	4	1	5	2	0
Leeds	D	W	6	4	1	1	4	2	4	2
Norwich	D	W	3	1	2	0	1	2	2	1
Sheffield Wed	W	L	6	4	2	0	3	3	3	3
QPR	W	D	4	4	0	0	0	4	0	4
Nottm Forest	W	D	6	4	1	1	3	3	2	4
Hull	W	D	3	2	0	1	3	0	1	2
Birmingham	D	W	6	2	3	1	3	3	4	1
Reading	L	D	5	1	1	3	4	1	4	0
Bolton	W	W	5	3	2	0	3	2	3	2
Wigan			3	0	1	2	1	2	1	1
Blackburn			5	2	2	1	1	4	3	2
Rotherham			3	3	0	0	2	1	0	3

Season	Division	Pos	P	W	D	L	F	A	GD	Pts
2017-18	Championship	6	46	20	15	11	70	48	+22	75
2016-17	Championship	9	46	18	13	15	54	50	+4	67
2015-16	Championship	5	46	21	15	10	66	43	+23	78

Over/Under 48%/52% 12th   **Both score** 50%/50% 11th

HULL

Nickname: The Tigers
Colours: Amber and black
Ground: KCOM Stadium (25,450)
Tel: 0870-837-0003   www.hullcityafc.net

The Leonid Slutsky experiment failed spectacularly – he won just four of his 20 games – and Hull spent most of 2017-18 looking to avoid consecutive relegations.

Replacement Nigel Adkins hardly set the KC alight, winning his first game but then failing to win any of the next nine, and he has plenty to prove after poor spells at Reading and Sheffield United.

Key players have been allowed to leave, but at least owner Assem Allam has brought in a few decent replacements.

Longest run without win/loss: 9/4
High/low league position: 14/22
Clean sheets: 12 **Yellows:** 84 **Reds:** 2
Avg attendance: 17,749 **Players used:** 29
Leading scorer: J Bowen 14 (3,13)
Key stat: Hull's points-per-game ratio only rose from 0.95 under Leonid Slutsky to 1.15 under Nigel Adkins

	2017-18 H	A	Last six seasons at home P	W	D	L	OV	UN	BS	CS
Swansea			3	2	0	1	1	2	1	1
Stoke			3	0	2	1	0	3	1	1
West Brom			3	1	2	0	0	3	1	2
Aston Villa	D	D	3	1	2	0	0	3	0	3
Middlesbrough	L	L	4	3	0	1	3	1	2	2
Derby	D	L	3	1	1	1	1	2	1	1
Preston	L	L	2	1	0	1	1	1	1	1
Millwall	L	D	2	1	0	1	2	0	2	0
Brentford	W	D	2	2	0	0	1	1	1	1
Sheffield United	W	L	1	1	0	0	0	1	0	1
Bristol City	L	D	3	1	1	1	2	1	1	2
Ipswich	D	W	3	2	1	0	3	0	2	1
Leeds	D	L	3	1	2	0	1	2	1	2
Norwich	W	D	2	2	0	0	1	1	1	1
Sheffield Wed	L	D	3	0	1	2	1	2	1	1
QPR	W	L	3	2	1	0	2	1	2	1
Nottm Forest	L	W	3	0	1	2	2	1	3	0
Hull										
Birmingham	W	L	3	3	0	0	2	1	2	1
Reading	D	D	2	1	1	0	1	1	1	1
Bolton	W	W	3	3	0	0	2	1	1	2
Wigan			-	-	-	-	-	-	-	-
Blackburn			2	1	1	0	0	2	1	1
Rotherham			1	1	0	0	1	0	1	0

Season	Division	Pos	P	W	D	L	F	A	GD	Pts
2017-18	Championship	18	46	11	16	19	70	70	0	49
2016-17	Premier League	18	38	9	7	22	37	80	-43	34
2015-16	Championship	4	46	24	11	11	69	35	+34	83

Over/Under 57%/43% 1st   **Both score** 57%/43% 5th

IPSWICH

Nickname: Town/Tractor Boys
Colours: Blue and white
Ground: Portman Road (30,311)
Tel: 01473-400-500   www.itfc.co.uk

By his own admission, 2016-17 was a poor campaign for Mick McCarthy at Ipswich and 2017-18 was hardly a thriller with Town bumping around in mid-table and playing some pretty uninspiring football.

However, he was operating under a tight budget and while McCarthy's playing style may be open to criticism, he overachieved in terms of league position.

Successor Paul Hurst arrives at a club with decent building blocks in place, but making any great strides will be tough.

Longest run without win/loss: 6/4
High/low league position: 5/14
Clean sheets: 14 **Yellows:** 89 **Reds:** 2
Avg attendance: 18,129 **Players used:** 35
Leading scorer: M Waghorn 16 (5,13)
Key stat: Ipswich had a W0 D1 L9 record against the top five but a W8 D2 L0 record against the bottom five

	2017-18 H	A	Last six seasons at home P	W	D	L	OV	UN	BS	CS
Swansea	-	-	-	-	-	-	-	-	-	-
Stoke	-	-	-	-	-	-	-	-	-	-
West Brom	-	-	-	-	-	-	-	-	-	-
Aston Villa	L	L	2	0	1	1	1	1	0	1
Middlesbrough	D	L	5	3	1	1	3	2	2	2
Derby	L	W	6	1	0	5	4	2	3	0
Preston	W	W	3	2	1	0	1	2	1	2
Millwall	D	W	4	3	1	0	3	1	1	3
Brentford	W	L	4	1	2	1	1	3	3	1
Sheffield United	D	L	1	0	1	0	0	1	0	1
Bristol City	L	L	4	1	2	1	3	1	4	0
Ipswich										
Leeds	W	L	6	4	1	1	4	2	4	2
Norwich	L	D	3	0	1	2	0	3	1	0
Sheffield Wed	D	W	6	3	1	2	5	1	4	0
QPR	D	L	4	2	1	1	3	1	2	2
Nottm Forest	W	L	6	4	1	1	3	3	4	1
Hull	L	D	3	0	0	3	2	1	1	0
Birmingham	W	L	6	4	2	0	2	4	4	2
Reading	W	W	5	3	1	1	2	3	2	2
Bolton	W	D	5	5	0	0	0	5	0	5
Wigan			3	1	1	1	2	1	1	2
Blackburn			5	3	2	0	2	3	4	1
Rotherham			3	1	1	1	1	2	1	1

Season	Division	Pos	P	W	D	L	F	A	GD	Pts
2017-18	Championship	12	46	17	9	20	57	60	-3	60
2016-17	Championship	16	46	13	16	17	48	58	-10	55
2015-16	Championship	7	46	18	15	13	53	51	+2	69

Over/Under 46%/54% 16th   **Both score** 41%/59% 21st

LEEDS

Nickname: United
Colours: White
Ground: Elland Road (37,890)
Tel: 0871-334-1919   www.leedsunited.com

For all their history Leeds now look the epitome a of mid-table Championship side, finishing between seventh and 15th for the last eight seasons and boasting a wage bill on a par with Bristol City.

They did briefly threaten to meet lofty expectations, staying in the top six into the new year, but as soon as United dropped off manager Thomas Christiansen found himself hoofed out of the hot seat.

Marcelo Bielsa looks a fine replacement, but he has struggled in recent jobs.

Longest run without win/loss: 9/7
High/low league position: 1/14
Clean sheets: 14 **Yellows:** 87 **Reds:** 7
Avg attendance: 25,833 **Players used:** 32
Leading scorer: K Roofe 11 (4,9)
Key stat: Marcelo Bielsa is Leeds's tenth permanent manager in four years

	2017-18 H	A	Last six seasons at home P	W	D	L	OV	UN	BS	CS
Swansea	-	-	-	-	-	-	-	-	-	-
Stoke	-	-	-	-	-	-	-	-	-	-
West Brom	-	-	-	-	-	-	-	-	-	-
Aston Villa	D	L	2	1	1	0	0	2	1	1
Middlesbrough	W	L	5	4	1	0	3	2	3	2
Derby	L	D	6	2	2	2	3	3	4	2
Preston	D	L	3	2	1	0	1	2	0	3
Millwall	L	L	4	3	0	1	2	2	2	2
Brentford	W	L	4	2	1	1	0	4	1	2
Sheffield United	L	L	1	0	0	1	1	0	1	0
Bristol City	D	W	4	3	1	0	2	2	2	2
Ipswich	W	L	6	4	1	1	2	4	3	2
Leeds										
Norwich	W	L	3	1	1	1	1	2	1	1
Sheffield Wed	L	L	6	2	3	1	2	4	5	1
QPR	W	W	4	1	2	1	0	4	1	2
Nottm Forest	D	W	6	2	2	2	1	5	1	3
Hull	W	D	3	2	0	1	2	1	2	1
Birmingham	W	L	6	1	3	2	4	2	2	2
Reading	L	D	5	2	1	2	2	3	2	2
Bolton	W	W	5	4	0	1	3	2	3	2
Wigan			3	1	1	1	0	3	1	1
Blackburn			5	1	1	3	4	1	3	0
Rotherham			3	1	1	1	1	2	0	2

Season	Division	Pos	P	W	D	L	F	A	GD	Pts
2017-18	Championship	13	46	17	9	20	59	64	-5	60
2016-17	Championship	7	46	22	9	15	61	47	+14	75
2015-16	Championship	13	46	14	17	15	50	58	-8	59

Over/Under 57%/43% 1st   **Both score** 50%/50% 11th

MIDDLESBROUGH

Nickname: Boro
Colours: Red and white
Ground: Riverside Stadium (33,746)
Tel: 0844-499-6789   www.mfc.co.uk

Garry Monk's Boro had been struggling to impose themselves after dropping into the second tier, beating the lesser sides but losing to potential promotion rivals.

With the team slipping into mid-table and Christmas approaching, Steve Gibson replaced Monk with Tony Pulis, who promptly Pulisised Boro, making them solid but hardly great entertainers.

It nearly worked, but a lack of ambition saw Boro fall short in the playoffs as they bowed out tamely to Aston Villa.

Longest run without win/loss: 5/6
High/low league position: 5/13
Clean sheets: 16 **Yellows:** 82 **Reds:** 5
Avg attendance: 23,068 **Players used:** 28
Leading scorer: B Assombalonga 15 (all)
Key stat: Middlesbrough managed just one win in 12 meetings with fellow top-six rivals in the regular season and playoffs, losing eight

	2017-18		Last six seasons at home							
	H	A	P	W	D	L	OV	UN	BS	CS
Swansea			1	1	0	0	1	0	0	1
Stoke			1	0	1	0	0	1	1	0
West Brom			1	0	1	0	0	1	1	0
Aston Villa	L	D	1	0	0	1	0	1	0	0
Middlesbrough										
Derby	L	W	5	3	1	1	2	3	1	3
Preston	D	W	2	1	1	0	0	2	0	2
Millwall	W	L	4	2	0	2	3	1	2	2
Brentford	D	D	3	2	1	0	3	0	2	1
Sheffield United	W	L	1	1	0	0	0	1	0	1
Bristol City	W	L	3	1	0	2	2	1	2	0
Ipswich	W	D	5	4	1	0	1	4	1	4
Leeds	W	L	5	3	1	1	2	3	0	4
Norwich	L	L	2	1	0	1	1	1	0	1
Sheffield Wed	D	W	5	2	2	1	2	3	3	2
QPR	W	W	3	2	0	1	2	1	2	1
Nottm Forest	W	L	5	3	1	1	1	4	1	3
Hull	W	W	4	4	0	0	1	3	1	3
Birmingham	W	W	5	3	1	1	1	4	1	3
Reading	W	W	4	3	0	1	3	1	2	1
Bolton	W	W	5	5	0	0	2	3	1	4
Wigan			2	1	1	0	0	2	0	2
Blackburn			4	1	3	0	0	4	2	2
Rotherham			2	2	0	0	0	2	0	2

Season	Division	Pos	P	W	D	L	F	A	GD	Pts
2017-18	Championship	5	46	22	10	14	67	45	+22	76
2016-17	Premier League	19	38	5	13	20	27	53	-26	28
2015-16	Championship	2	46	26	11	9	63	31	+32	89

Over/Under 50%/50% 10th   **Both score** 48%/52% 14th

MILLWALL

Nickname: The Lions
Colours: Blue and white
Ground: The Den (20,146)
Tel: 020-7232-1222   www.millwallfc.co.uk

Millwall outperformed expectations in impressive fashion last season, going off as fourth favourites for relegation but finishing just three points off the playoffs.

Fans favourite Neil Harris has hardly put a foot wrong in three years at the helm, twice guiding Millwall to the League One playoffs and also leading the club on a thrilling FA Cup run.

A tight budget is likely to limit further progress, but Harris has made his team a tough nut to crack home and away.

Longest run without win/loss: 6/17
High/low league position: 6/19
Clean sheets: 19 **Yellows:** 79 **Reds:** 4
Avg attendance: 16,690 **Players used:** 24
Lead scorers: G Saville 10 (3,8) L Gregory 10 (4,10)
Key stat: Millwall rose from 17th to eighth in the second half of 2017-18, going 17 unbeaten from January 13 to April 14 and winning 11

	2017-18		Last six seasons at home							
	H	A	P	W	D	L	OV	UN	BS	CS
Swansea			-	-	-	-	-	-	-	-
Stoke			-	-	-	-	-	-	-	-
West Brom			-	-	-	-	-	-	-	-
Aston Villa	W	D	1	1	0	0	0	1	0	1
Middlesbrough	W	L	4	2	0	2	3	1	3	0
Derby	D	L	4	1	2	1	3	1	3	1
Preston	D	D	1	0	1	0	0	1	1	0
Millwall										
Brentford	W	L	2	1	0	1	1	1	1	1
Sheffield United	W	D	3	3	0	0	2	1	2	1
Bristol City	W	D	2	2	0	0	1	1	1	1
Ipswich	L	D	4	1	1	2	2	2	2	2
Leeds	W	W	4	4	0	0	0	4	0	4
Norwich	W	L	2	1	0	1	2	0	1	1
Sheffield Wed	W	L	4	1	1	2	3	1	4	0
QPR	W	D	2	1	1	0	1	1	1	1
Nottm Forest	W	L	4	1	2	1	1	3	1	2
Hull	D	W	2	0	1	1	0	2	0	1
Birmingham	W	W	4	1	1	2	3	1	3	1
Reading	W	W	3	1	1	1	2	1	1	1
Bolton	D	W	5	1	2	2	1	4	3	0
Wigan			3	2	1	0	1	2	1	2
Blackburn			3	0	2	1	3	0	3	0
Rotherham			1	0	0	1	0	1	0	0

Season	Division	Pos	P	W	D	L	F	A	GD	Pts
2017-18	Championship	8	46	19	15	12	56	45	+11	72
2016-17	League One	6	46	20	13	13	66	57	+9	73
2015-16	League One	4	46	24	9	13	73	49	+24	81

Over/Under 37%/63% 23rd   **Both score** 41%/59% 21st

NORWICH

Nickname: The Canaries
Colours: Yellow and green
Ground: Carrow Road (27,244)
Tel: 01603-760-760   www.canaries.co.uk

A Norwich team fancied for promotion regressed under Daniel Farke, scoring just 49 goals – down from 85 in 2016-17 – and winning 15 matches to finish 15 points adrift of the top six.

Farke has worked hard in the transfer market to address the lack of goal threat but the loss of player of the year James Maddison to Leicester won't help.

More signings are likely to arrive but the disruption could result in a slow start for a Canaries side with a lot to work on.

Longest run without win/loss: 7/8
High/low league position: 8/16
Clean sheets: 15 **Yellows:** 90 **Reds:** 1
Avg attendance: 22,741 **Players used:** 28
Leading scorer: J Maddison 14 (6,12)
Key stat: Only Birmingham and relegated Sunderland and Burton scored fewer goals on home soil than Norwich last term

	2017-18 H	A	Last six seasons at home P	W	D	L	OV	UN	BS	CS
Swansea			3	1	2	0	1	2	2	1
Stoke			3	1	2	0	0	3	2	1
West Brom			3	1	0	2	1	2	0	1
Aston Villa	W	L	5	3	0	2	2	3	2	2
Middlesbrough	W	W	2	1	0	1	0	2	0	1
Derby	L	D	3	1	1	1	2	1	2	1
Preston	D	D	2	0	1	1	0	2	1	0
Millwall	W	L	2	2	0	0	2	0	2	0
Brentford	L	W	3	1	0	2	3	0	2	1
Sheffield United	L	W	1	0	0	1	1	0	1	0
Bristol City	D	W	2	1	1	0	0	2	0	2
Ipswich	D	W	3	1	2	0	0	3	2	1
Leeds	W	L	3	1	1	1	2	1	3	0
Norwich										
Sheffield Wed	W	L	3	2	1	0	1	2	1	2
QPR	W	L	3	2	1	0	1	2	1	2
Nottm Forest	D	L	3	2	1	0	2	1	2	1
Hull	D	L	2	1	1	0	0	2	1	1
Birmingham	W	W	3	2	1	0	1	2	1	2
Reading	W	W	4	3	0	1	4	0	4	0
Bolton	D	L	2	1	1	0	1	1	1	1
Wigan			3	2	0	1	2	1	2	0
Blackburn			2	1	1	0	2	0	2	0
Rotherham			2	1	1	0	1	1	2	0

Season	Division	Pos	P	W	D	L	F	A	GD	Pts
2017-18	Championship	14	46	15	15	16	49	60	-11	60
2016-17	Championship	8	46	20	10	16	85	69	+16	70
2015-16	Premier League	19	38	9	7	22	39	67	-28	34

Over/Under 39%/61% 20th   **Both score** 54%/46% 7th

NOTTINGHAM FOREST

Nickname: Forest
Colours: Red and white
Ground: City Ground (30,602)
Tel: 0115-982-4444 www.nottinghamforest.co.uk

Reliable lawyers could be as important to Forest as good players with owner Evangelos Marinakis never far from trouble, but his desire to turn Forest into a serious force looks genuine enough.

He wrote off a £40m loan, is spending big – with a link to agent Jorge Mendes returning some classy signings – and has won fans over with reduced ticket prices.

Manager Aitor Karanka has the pieces in place to emulate his 2016 promotion success in the Middlesbrough dugout.

Longest run without win/loss: 6/7
High/low league position: 8/17
Clean sheets: 13 **Yellows:** 95 **Reds:** 1
Avg attendance: 21,368 **Players used:** 35
Leading scorer: K Dowell 9 (2,7)
Key stat: The average age of Forest's 13 most used players last term was 25 years and four months, with seven of them 23 or younger

	2017-18 H	A	Last six seasons at home P	W	D	L	OV	UN	BS	CS
Swansea			-	-	-	-	-	-	-	-
Stoke			-	-	-	-	-	-	-	-
West Brom			-	-	-	-	-	-	-	-
Aston Villa	L	L	2	1	0	1	1	1	1	0
Middlesbrough	W	L	5	2	2	1	4	1	4	1
Derby	D	L	6	2	3	1	1	5	2	3
Preston	L	D	3	1	1	1	2	1	1	1
Millwall	W	L	4	1	0	3	2	2	2	1
Brentford	L	W	4	0	0	4	3	1	2	0
Sheffield United	W	D	1	1	0	0	1	0	1	0
Bristol City	D	L	4	2	1	1	1	3	1	3
Ipswich	W	L	6	3	3	0	3	3	3	3
Leeds	L	D	6	3	2	1	3	3	5	0
Norwich	W	D	3	2	0	1	2	1	2	1
Sheffield Wed	L	L	6	1	1	4	4	2	2	1
QPR	W	W	4	2	2	0	1	3	1	3
Nottm Forest										
Hull	L	W	3	0	0	3	1	2	1	0
Birmingham	W	L	6	3	2	1	4	2	5	1
Reading	D	L	5	3	1	1	4	1	4	1
Bolton	W	L	5	4	1	0	4	1	3	2
Wigan			3	2	0	1	3	0	2	1
Blackburn			5	1	2	2	2	3	3	1
Rotherham			3	3	0	0	1	2	1	2

Season	Division	Pos	P	W	D	L	F	A	GD	Pts
2017-18	Championship	17	46	15	8	23	51	65	-14	53
2016-17	Championship	21	46	14	9	23	62	72	-10	51
2015-16	Championship	16	46	13	16	17	43	47	-4	55

Over/Under 48%/52% 12th   **Both score** 43%/57% 18th

PRESTON

Nickname: The Lilywhites/North End
Colours: White and navy blue
Ground: Deepdale (23,404)
Tel: 0344-856-1964   www.pnefc.co.uk

A late surge nearly saw Preston sneak into the top six, but a final day victory for Derby denied them a shot at the playoffs.

That North End even entered the discussion is testament to how well the team is being run – their budget places Preston closer to League One than the top six – and Alex Neil did well to build on foundations laid by Simon Grayson.

Taking North End a step further is a big ask given the lack of real attacking class, but they remain a very well-drilled side.

Longest run without win/loss: 7/9
High/low league position: 4/14
Clean sheets: 15 **Yellows:** 11 **Reds:** 5
Avg attendance: 16,520 **Players used:** 28
Leading scorer: S Maguire 10 (2,9)
Key stat: Only promoted Wolves and Fulham had better away records than Preston last term

	2017-18		Last six seasons at home							
	H	A	P	W	D	L	OV	UN	BS	CS
Swansea	-	-	-	-	-	-	-	-	-	-
Stoke	-	-	-	-	-	-	-	-	-	-
West Brom	-	-	-	-	-	-	-	-	-	-
Aston Villa	L	D	2	1	0	1	0	2	0	1
Middlesbrough	L	D	2	0	1	1	1	1	1	1
Derby	L	L	3	0	0	3	1	2	1	0
Preston										
Millwall	D	D	1	0	1	0	0	1	0	1
Brentford	L	D	5	1	1	3	4	1	4	0
Sheffield United	W	W	4	1	2	1	0	4	1	2
Bristol City	W	W	5	3	2	0	2	3	3	2
Ipswich	L	L	3	0	1	2	1	2	2	0
Leeds	W	D	3	1	1	1	2	1	3	0
Norwich	D	D	2	0	1	1	1	1	1	1
Sheffield Wed	W	L	3	2	1	0	0	3	1	2
QPR	W	W	3	2	1	0	1	2	2	1
Nottm Forest	D	W	3	1	2	0	0	3	2	1
Hull	W	W	2	2	0	0	1	1	1	1
Birmingham	D	W	3	1	2	0	1	2	3	0
Reading	W	L	3	3	0	0	1	2	0	3
Bolton	D	W	2	0	2	0	0	2	0	2
Wigan			1	1	0	0	0	1	0	1
Blackburn			2	1	0	1	2	0	2	0
Rotherham			3	1	2	0	2	1	3	0

Season	Division	Pos	P	W	D	L	F	A	GD	Pts
2017-18	Championship	7	46	19	16	11	57	46	+11	73
2016-17	Championship	11	46	16	14	16	64	63	+1	62
2015-16	Championship	11	46	15	17	14	45	45	0	62

Over/Under 43%/57% 18th   **Both score** 54%/46% 7th

QPR

Nickname: The R's
Colours: Blue and white
Ground: Loftus Road (19,148)
Tel: 020-8743-0262   www.qpr.co.uk

QPR have been playing with fire for years and with a £40m Financial Fair Play fine to pay and parachute payments coming to an end, there's little suggestion that the purse-strings are set to be loosened.

Incoming manager Steve McClaren admitted he took the job without knowing what sort of squad he'd be left with and the early signs aren't promising – a team who struggled defensively have lost Nedum Onuoha, Jack Robinson and highly-rated goalkeeper Alex Smithies.

Longest run without win/loss: 7/4
High/low league position: 11/19
Clean sheets: 7 **Yellows:** 86 **Reds:** 5
Avg attendance: 17,177 **Players used:** 31
Leading scorer: M Smith 11 (2,11)
Key stat: QPR were solid at home last season, but only Birmingham and Bolton had worse away records

	2017-18		Last six seasons at home							
	H	A	P	W	D	L	OV	UN	BS	CS
Swansea			2	0	1	1	1	1	1	0
Stoke			2	0	1	1	1	1	1	0
West Brom			2	1	0	1	2	0	2	0
Aston Villa	L	W	4	1	1	2	1	3	2	1
Middlesbrough	L	L	3	1	0	2	2	1	1	1
Derby	D	L	4	2	1	1	1	3	2	1
Preston	L	L	3	0	1	2	1	2	1	1
Millwall	D	L	2	0	2	0	1	1	2	0
Brentford	D	L	3	1	1	1	2	1	1	1
Sheffield United	W	L	1	1	0	0	0	1	0	1
Bristol City	D	L	3	2	1	0	0	3	1	2
Ipswich	W	D	4	4	0	0	2	2	2	2
Leeds	L	L	4	2	1	1	2	2	2	2
Norwich	W	D	3	2	1	0	2	1	2	1
Sheffield Wed	W	D	4	2	1	1	3	1	3	1
QPR										
Nottm Forest	L	L	4	2	0	2	3	1	3	1
Hull	W	L	3	1	0	2	2	1	2	0
Birmingham	W	W	4	3	1	0	1	3	2	2
Reading	W	L	5	1	3	1	4	4	4	1
Bolton	W	D	3	3	0	0	2	1	2	1
Wigan			3	2	1	0	1	2	2	1
Blackburn			3	0	3	0	1	2	2	1
Rotherham			2	2	0	0	2	0	2	0

Season	Division	Pos	P	W	D	L	F	A	GD	Pts
2017-18	Championship	16	46	15	11	20	58	70	-12	56
2016-17	Championship	18	46	15	8	23	52	66	-14	53
2015-16	Championship	12	46	14	18	14	54	54	0	60

Over/Under 57%/43% 1st   **Both score** 63%/37% 1st

READING

Nickname: The Royals
Colours: Blue and white
Ground: Madejski Stadium (24,161)
Tel: 0118 968-1100   www.readingfc.co.uk

After mounting one of the more unlikely promotion challenges in 2016-17, Reading slipped back last term to repeat their 2014 and 2015 relegation scraps.

For spells they looked in serious danger of the drop and Jaap Stam was sacked with the Royals just three points above relegation with eight games remaining.

Replacement Paul Clement got the two wins that saw Reading over the line, but it was far from convincing and it looks a big job getting the club to fulfil its potential.

Longest run without win/loss: 9/5
High/low league position: 14/20
Clean sheets: 8 **Yellows:** 82 **Reds:** 5
Avg attendance: 18,345 **Players used:** 28
Leading scorer: M Barrow 10 (3,9)
Key stat: Reading managed just three wins against top-half sides in 2017-18

	2017-18 H	A	Last six seasons at home P	W	D	L	OV	UN	BS	CS
Swansea			1	0	1	0	0	1	0	1
Stoke			1	0	1	0	0	1	1	0
West Brom			1	1	0	0	1	0	1	0
Aston Villa	W	L	3	1	0	2	3	0	3	0
Middlesbrough	L	L	4	2	1	1	0	4	0	3
Derby	D	W	5	0	3	2	2	3	2	1
Preston	W	L	3	2	0	1	1	2	1	2
Millwall	L	L	3	1	1	1	1	2	2	0
Brentford	L	D	4	1	0	3	2	2	2	0
Sheffield United	L	L	1	0	0	1	0	1	0	0
Bristol City	L	L	3	2	0	1	1	2	1	1
Ipswich	L	L	5	4	0	1	4	1	3	1
Leeds	D	W	5	2	2	1	1	4	1	3
Norwich	L	L	4	2	1	1	3	1	3	1
Sheffield Wed	D	L	5	2	2	1	1	4	2	2
QPR	W	L	5	1	2	2	0	5	1	2
Nottm Forest	W	D	5	3	1	1	3	2	3	1
Hull	D	D	2	0	1	1	1	1	2	0
Birmingham	L	W	5	1	1	3	0	5	0	2
Reading										
Bolton	D	D	4	2	2	0	2	2	3	1
Wigan			4	1	0	3	2	2	1	1
Blackburn			4	2	1	1	1	3	1	2
Rotherham			3	3	0	0	2	1	1	2

Season	Division	Pos	P	W	D	L	F	A	GD	Pts
2017-18	Championship	20	46	10	14	22	48	70	-22	44
2016-17	Championship	3	46	26	7	13	68	64	+4	85
2015-16	Championship	17	46	13	13	20	52	59	-7	52

Over/Under 48%/52% 12th   **Both score** 50%/50% 11th

ROTHERHAM

Nickname: The Millers
Colours: Red and white
Ground: New York Stadium (12,021)
Tel: 08444 140733   www.themillers.co.uk

A playoff final extra-time winner sealed the clean sweep as all three relegated sides bounced back up, but Rotherham's return was far from straightforward.

While they were deserving Wembley victors the Millers were miles off the top two – finishing 17 points back – and spent half the season outside the top six, conceding three goals on six occasions.

Paul Warne did a fair job stabilising things after a dire 2016-17, but they're punching above their weight at this level.

Longest run without win/loss: 7/14
High/low league position: 4/13
Clean sheets: 15 **Yellows:** 76 **Reds:** 4
Avg attendance: 8,013 **Players used:** 26
Leading scorer: K Moore 13 (3,9)
Key stat: Rotherham managed just two points from 23 away games in their last season in the Championship

	2017-18 H	A	Last six seasons at home P	W	D	L	OV	UN	BS	CS
Swansea			-	-	-	-	-	-	-	-
Stoke			-	-	-	-	-	-	-	-
West Brom			-	-	-	-	-	-	-	-
Aston Villa			1	0	0	1	0	1	0	0
Middlesbrough			2	1	0	1	1	1	0	1
Derby			3	0	3	0	2	1	3	0
Preston			3	0	2	1	1	2	1	2
Millwall			1	1	0	0	1	0	1	0
Brentford			4	3	0	1	2	2	1	2
Sheffield United			1	1	0	0	1	0	1	0
Bristol City			3	2	1	0	3	0	2	1
Ipswich			3	2	0	1	2	1	1	2
Leeds			3	2	0	1	3	0	3	0
Norwich			2	1	1	0	1	1	2	0
Sheffield Wed			3	0	0	3	2	1	2	0
QPR			2	1	0	1	1	1	0	1
Nottm Forest			3	0	3	0	1	2	1	2
Hull			1	1	0	0	0	1	0	1
Birmingham			3	0	2	1	0	3	1	1
Reading			3	1	1	1	1	2	2	0
Bolton			2	2	0	0	2	0	1	1
Wigan	L	D	3	1	0	2	3	0	3	0
Blackburn	D	L	4	1	2	1	0	4	2	1
Rotherham										

Season	Division	Pos	P	W	D	L	F	A	GD	Pts
2017-18	League One	4	46	24	7	15	73	53	+20	79
2016-17	Championship	24	46	5	8	33	40	98	-58	23
2015-16	Championship	21	46	13	10	23	53	71	-18	49

Over/Under 50%/50% 9th   **Both score** 54%/46% 7th

SHEFFIELD UNITED

Nickname: The Blades
Colours: Red and white
Ground: Bramall Lane (32,702)
Tel: 0114-253-720   www.sufc.co.uk

A dream start back in the second tier had Blades fans dreaming of consecutive promotions and they were top after 14 games having beaten the likes of Wolves, Derby and rivals Sheffield Wednesday.

But the impetus generated from the 2017 promotion party finally wore off and United settled into a perfectly respectable tenth-placed finish.

A lack of harmony between co-owners Musa'ad bin Abdulaziz and Kevin McCabe is a concern but there are funds available.

Longest run without win/loss: 6/5
High/low league position: 1/11
Clean sheets: 10 **Yellows:** 83 **Reds:** 4
Avg attendance: 23,852 **Players used:** 30
Leading scorer: L Clarke 19 (5,12)
Key stat: United won 12 of their first 17 games last term, but just eight more of their remaining 29

	2017-18		Last six seasons at home							
---	H	A	P	W	D	L	OV	UN	BS	CS
Swansea	-	-	-	-	-	-	-	-	-	-
Stoke	-	-	-	-	-	-	-	-	-	-
West Brom	-	-	-	-	-	-	-	-	-	-
Aston Villa	L	D	1	0	0	1	0	1	0	0
Middlesbrough	W	L	1	1	0	0	1	0	1	0
Derby	W	D	1	1	0	0	1	0	1	0
Preston	L	L	4	1	1	2	1	3	1	1
Millwall	D	L	3	1	1	1	1	2	2	1
Brentford	W	D	3	1	2	0	1	2	1	2
Sheffield United										
Bristol City	L	W	3	1	0	2	3	0	2	1
Ipswich	W	D	1	1	0	0	0	1	0	1
Leeds	W	W	1	1	0	0	1	0	1	0
Norwich	L	W	1	0	0	1	0	1	0	0
Sheffield Wed	D	W	1	0	1	0	0	1	0	1
QPR	W	L	1	1	0	0	1	0	1	0
Nottm Forest	D	L	1	0	1	0	0	1	0	1
Hull	W	L	1	1	0	0	1	0	1	0
Birmingham	D	L	1	0	1	0	0	1	1	0
Reading	W	W	1	1	0	0	1	0	1	0
Bolton	L	W	2	1	0	1	0	2	0	1
Wigan			1	0	0	1	0	1	0	0
Blackburn	-	-	-	-	-	-	-	-	-	-
Rotherham	L		1	1	0	0	0	1	0	1

Season	Division	Pos	P	W	D	L	F	A	GD	Pts
2017-18	Championship	10	46	20	9	17	62	55	+7	69
2016-17	League One	1	46	30	10	6	92	47	+45	100
2015-16	League One	11	46	18	12	16	64	59	+5	66

Over/Under 50%/50% 10th   **Both score** 54%/46% 7th

SHEFFIELD WED

Nickname: The Owls
Colours: Blue and white
Ground: Hillsborough (39,732)
Tel: 03700-20-1867   www.swfc.co.uk

A team fancied for a title charge failed to hint at even a top-six challenge, sitting between 11th and 18th from November.

However, the Owls' season was greatly disrupted by a succession of injuries to key men and it was no surprise that they struggled to put together a run of form.

That didn't save Carlos Carvalhal, who was sacked at the halfway stage with the team in 15th, and while results picked up under Jos Luhukay he was helped by so many key men returning to full fitness.

Longest run without win/loss: 7/7
High/low league position: 9/17
Clean sheets: 12 **Yellows:** 77 **Reds:** 5
Avg attendance: 23,769 **Players used:** 35
Leading scorer: A Nuhiu 11 (4,7)
Key stat: Sheffield Wednesday's best run of form came in the final ten games, with the Owls putting together a W6 D2 L2 record

	2017-18		Last six seasons at home							
---	H	A	P	W	D	L	OV	UN	BS	CS
Swansea	-	-	-	-	-	-	-	-	-	-
Stoke	-	-	-	-	-	-	-	-	-	-
West Brom	-	-	-	-	-	-	-	-	-	-
Aston Villa	L	W	2	1	0	1	1	1	1	1
Middlesbrough	L	D	5	3	0	2	2	3	2	3
Derby	W	L	6	2	3	1	2	4	2	3
Preston	W	L	3	3	0	0	3	0	3	0
Millwall	W	L	4	2	2	0	3	1	4	0
Brentford	W	L	4	3	0	1	3	1	2	2
Sheffield United	L	D	1	0	0	1	1	0	1	0
Bristol City	D	L	4	2	1	1	2	2	2	2
Ipswich	L	D	6	0	4	2	2	4	6	0
Leeds	W	W	6	3	1	2	3	3	2	3
Norwich	W	L	3	2	1	0	2	1	2	1
Sheffield Wed										
QPR	D	L	4	2	2	0	1	3	2	2
Nottm Forest	W	W	6	3	0	3	2	4	2	1
Hull	D	W	3	0	2	1	1	2	2	0
Birmingham	L	L	6	4	1	1	5	1	3	3
Reading	W	D	5	3	1	1	2	3	2	2
Bolton	D	L	5	1	1	3	4	1	5	0
Wigan			3	2	0	1	3	0	2	0
Blackburn			5	3	1	1	5	0	5	0
Rotherham			3	1	1	1	0	3	0	2

Season	Division	Pos	P	W	D	L	F	A	GD	Pts
2017-18	Championship	15	46	14	15	17	59	60	-1	57
2016-17	Championship	4	46	24	9	13	60	45	+15	81
2015-16	Championship	6	46	19	17	10	66	45	+21	74

Over/Under 52%/48% 5th   **Both score** 57%/43% 5th

STOKE

Nickname: The Potters
Colours: Red and white
Ground: bet365 Stadium (30,089)
Tel: 01782-367-598   www.stokecityfc.com

By the owners' own admission, a major overhaul is needed after a shambolic end to Stoke's ten-year stay in the top flight.

Mark Hughes was sacked in January and while few supporters mourned his departure the Potters were at least still two places above the drop at that stage.

Replacement Paul Lambert won just one of his 14 meaningful games in charge so his departure was no surprise, but it could take time for Gary Rowett to rebuild a fractured, unbalanced squad.

Longest run without win/loss: 13/3
High/low league position: 13/20
Clean sheets: 6 **Yellows:** 62 **Reds:** 1
Avg attendance: 32,771 **Players used:** 30
Leading scorer: X Shaqiri 8 (4,8)
Key stat: Stoke dropped 12 points from winning positions in just 15 games under Paul Lambert

	2017-18 H	A	Last six seasons at home P	W	D	L	OV	UN	BS	CS
Swansea	W	W	6	4	2	0	4	2	5	1
Stoke										
West Brom	W	D	6	2	3	1	1	5	2	3
Aston Villa			4	2	0	2	3	1	3	0
Middlesbrough			1	1	0	0	0	1	0	1
Derby			-	-	-	-	-	-	-	-
Preston			-	-	-	-	-	-	-	-
Millwall			-	-	-	-	-	-	-	-
Brentford			-	-	-	-	-	-	-	-
Sheffield United			-	-	-	-	-	-	-	-
Bristol City			-	-	-	-	-	-	-	-
Ipswich			-	-	-	-	-	-	-	-
Leeds			-	-	-	-	-	-	-	-
Norwich			3	2	0	1	1	2	1	1
Sheffield Wed			-	-	-	-	-	-	-	-
QPR			2	2	0	0	1	1	1	1
Nottm Forest			-	-	-	-	-	-	-	-
Hull			3	3	0	0	1	2	1	2
Birmingham			-	-	-	-	-	-	-	-
Reading			1	1	0	0	1	0	1	0
Bolton			-	-	-	-	-	-	-	-
Wigan			1	0	1	0	1	0	1	0
Blackburn			-	-	-	-	-	-	-	-
Rotherham			-	-	-	-	-	-	-	-

Season	Division	Pos	P	W	D	L	F	A	GD	Pts
2017-18	Premier League	19	38	7	12	19	35	68	-33	33
2016-17	Premier League	13	38	11	11	16	41	56	-15	44
2015-16	Premier League	9	38	14	9	15	41	55	-14	51

Over/Under 58%/42% 5th   **Both score** 58%/42% 2nd

SWANSEA

Nickname: The Swans
Colours: White
Ground: Liberty Stadium (20,592)
Tel: 01792-616-600   www.swanseacity.net

Carlos Carvalhal looked to be the saviour, taking over with Swansea bottom after 20 games and leading them on a run of five wins – including defeats of Liverpool and Arsenal – and three draws in ten games.

However, a lack of quality in the squad eventually told, with Swansea taking three points from their final nine games to finish three points adrift of safety.

Repeatedly selling star men has cost them, but the appointment of in-demand manager Graham Potter looks sensible.

Longest run without win/loss: 9/5
High/low league position: 13/20
Clean sheets: 9 **Yellows:** 51 **Reds:** 1
Avg attendance: 28,970 **Players used:** 26
Leading scorer: J Ayew 7 (1,7)
Key stat: Swansea managed just 103 shots on target last season – a divisional low and just 2.7 per match

	2017-18 H	A	Last six seasons at home P	W	D	L	OV	UN	BS	CS
Swansea										
Stoke	L	L	6	3	1	2	3	3	3	2
West Brom	W	D	6	5	0	1	4	2	3	3
Aston Villa			4	3	1	0	2	2	2	2
Middlesbrough			1	0	1	0	0	1	0	1
Derby			-	-	-	-	-	-	-	-
Preston			-	-	-	-	-	-	-	-
Millwall			-	-	-	-	-	-	-	-
Brentford			-	-	-	-	-	-	-	-
Sheffield United			-	-	-	-	-	-	-	-
Bristol City			-	-	-	-	-	-	-	-
Ipswich			-	-	-	-	-	-	-	-
Leeds			-	-	-	-	-	-	-	-
Norwich			3	2	0	1	2	1	1	2
Sheffield Wed			-	-	-	-	-	-	-	-
QPR			2	2	0	0	1	1	1	1
Nottm Forest			-	-	-	-	-	-	-	-
Hull			3	1	1	1	1	2	2	0
Birmingham			-	-	-	-	-	-	-	-
Reading			1	0	1	0	1	0	1	0
Bolton			-	-	-	-	-	-	-	-
Wigan			1	1	0	0	1	0	1	0
Blackburn			-	-	-	-	-	-	-	-
Rotherham			-	-	-	-	-	-	-	-

Season	Division	Pos	P	W	D	L	F	A	GD	Pts
2017-18	Premier League	18	38	8	9	21	28	56	-28	33
2016-17	Premier League	15	38	12	5	21	45	70	-25	41
2015-16	Premier League	12	38	12	11	15	42	52	-10	47

Over/Under 37%/63% 17th   **Both score** 39%/61% 18th

WEST BROM

WEST BROM

Nickname: The Baggies/Albion
Colours: Navy blue and white
Ground: The Hawthorns (26,852)
Tel: 0871-271-1100   www.wba.co.uk

Poor decisions in the boardroom, dugout and in Barcelona taxi-ranks sent Albion down after eight top-flight seasons.

Tony Pulis was sacked with West Brom just above the drop zone, but his dour football did at least bring security and Alan Pardew was a dreadful replacement.

Murmurs of discontent soon surfaced and the Baggies were ten points adrift of safety by the time Pardew was sacked.

Darren Moore inspired an impressive late rally but it arrived far too late.

Longest run without win/loss: 20/5
High/low league position: 10/20
Clean sheets: 10 **Yellows:** 73 **Reds:** 1
Avg attendance: 30,781 **Players used:** 24
Leading scorer: J Rondon 7 (3,7) J Rodriguez 7 (5,7)
Key stat: West Brom beat Man United, Spurs and Newcastle under Moore in their final six games and drew with Liverpool and Swansea

	2017-18		Last six seasons at home							
	H	A	P	W	D	L	OV	UN	BS	CS
Swansea	D	L	6	3	2	1	2	4	4	1
Stoke	D	L	6	3	1	2	2	4	3	2
West Brom										
Aston Villa			4	1	3	0	2	2	2	2
Middlesbrough			1	0	1	0	0	1	0	1
Derby			-	-	-	-	-	-	-	-
Preston			-	-	-	-	-	-	-	-
Millwall			-	-	-	-	-	-	-	-
Brentford			-	-	-	-	-	-	-	-
Sheffield United			-	-	-	-	-	-	-	-
Bristol City			-	-	-	-	-	-	-	-
Ipswich			-	-	-	-	-	-	-	-
Leeds			-	-	-	-	-	-	-	-
Norwich			3	1	0	2	1	2	1	0
Sheffield Wed			-	-	-	-	-	-	-	-
QPR			2	1	0	1	2	0	2	0
Nottm Forest			-	-	-	-	-	-	-	-
Hull			3	2	1	0	1	2	2	1
Birmingham			-	-	-	-	-	-	-	-
Reading			1	1	0	0	0	1	0	1
Bolton			-	-	-	-	-	-	-	-
Wigan			1	0	0	1	1	0	1	0
Blackburn			-	-	-	-	-	-	-	-
Rotherham			-	-	-	-	-	-	-	-

Season	Division	Pos	P	W	D	L	F	A	GD	Pts
2017-18	Premier League	20	38	6	13	19	31	56	-25	31
2016-17	Premier League	10	38	12	9	17	43	51	-8	45
2015-16	Premier League	14	38	10	13	15	34	48	-14	43

Over/Under 42%/58% 14th   **Both score** 50%/50% 9th

WIGAN

Nickname: The Latics
Colours: Blue and white
Ground: DW Stadium (25,138)
Tel: 01942-774-000   www.wiganlatics.co.uk

Following the pain of relegation, Wigan's 2017-18 couldn't have been any brighter.

Incoming manager Paul Cook led his team to six wins in their first eight League One games and they never looked likely to miss out on automatic promotion, even if there was a backlog of games due to a stunning FA Cup run that saw them dump out quadruple-chasing Manchester City.

The task now is to avoid a repeat of 2016-17 when relegation followed a third-tier title, but Wigan look on the up.

Longest run without win/loss: 2/11
High/low league position: 1/5
Clean sheets: 27 **Yellows:** 74 **Reds:** 3
Avg attendance: 8,698 **Players used:** 27
Leading scorer: W Grigg 19 (8,14)
Key stat: Wigan won just two of their 11 home games against fellow top-half League One opponents last term

	2017-18		Last six seasons at home							
	H	A	P	W	D	L	OV	UN	BS	CS
Swansea			1	0	0	1	1	0	1	0
Stoke			1	0	1	0	1	0	1	0
West Brom			1	0	0	1	1	0	1	0
Aston Villa			2	0	1	1	1	1	1	0
Middlesbrough			2	0	2	0	1	1	2	0
Derby			3	0	0	3	1	2	1	0
Preston			1	0	1	0	1	0	1	0
Millwall			3	0	2	1	1	2	1	1
Brentford			2	1	1	0	1	1	1	1
Sheffield United			1	0	1	0	1	0	1	0
Bristol City			1	0	0	1	0	1	0	0
Ipswich			3	1	0	2	2	1	2	1
Leeds			3	1	1	1	0	3	1	1
Norwich			3	1	1	1	2	1	1	1
Sheffield Wed			3	1	0	2	0	3	0	1
QPR			3	0	2	1	1	2	1	1
Nottm Forest			3	1	2	0	1	2	1	2
Hull			-	-	-	-	-	-	-	-
Birmingham			3	1	2	0	1	2	1	2
Reading			4	2	1	1	4	0	2	1
Bolton			2	1	1	0	1	1	2	0
Wigan										
Blackburn	D	D	4	2	2	0	2	2	2	2
Rotherham	D	W	3	1	1	1	2	1	2	1

Season	Division	Pos	P	W	D	L	F	A	GD	Pts
2017-18	League One	1	46	29	11	6	89	29	+60	98
2016-17	Championship	23	46	10	12	24	40	57	-17	42
2015-16	League One	1	46	24	15	7	82	45	+37	87

Over/Under 48%/52% 13th   **Both score** 37%/63% 24th

Championship stats 2017-18
Key Points in all tables (except the league table) do not include any deductions imposed by the league.
POS H A Overall league position, rank from home games only, rank from away games only **Sup** Average match supremacy **GFA** Goals For Average **GAA** Goals Against Average **PGA** Points Gained Average

Championship 2017-18			Home					Away						
Pos	H	A		P	W	D	L	F	A	W	D	L	F	A	GD	Pts
1	1	1	Wolves (P)	46	16	5	2	47	18	14	4	5	35	21	43	99
2	2	4	Cardiff (P)	46	16	4	3	40	16	11	5	7	29	23	30	90
3	4	2	Fulham (P)	46	13	8	2	40	17	12	5	6	39	29	33	88
4	3	5	Aston Villa	46	14	7	2	42	19	10	4	9	30	23	30	83
5	5	7	Middlesbrough	46	14	3	6	33	17	8	7	8	34	28	22	76
6	7	6	Derby	46	12	5	6	41	22	8	10	5	29	26	22	75
7	13	3	Preston	46	9	8	6	27	22	10	8	5	30	24	11	73
8	6	9	Millwall	46	12	7	4	33	21	7	8	8	23	24	11	72
9	11	8	Brentford	46	9	11	3	37	24	9	4	10	25	28	10	69
10	8	11	Sheff Utd	46	12	5	6	33	20	8	4	11	29	35	7	69
11	10	10	Bristol City	46	11	6	6	41	28	6	10	7	26	30	9	67
12	14	13	Ipswich	46	9	6	8	29	27	8	3	12	28	33	-3	60
13	12	15	Leeds	46	10	6	7	32	27	7	3	13	27	37	-5	60
14	17	12	Norwich	46	8	8	7	25	25	7	7	9	24	35	-11	60
15	18	14	Sheff Wed	46	8	7	8	37	31	6	8	9	22	29	-1	57
16	9	22	QPR	46	12	5	6	38	31	3	6	14	20	39	-12	56
17	15	20	Nottm Forest	46	10	3	10	25	27	5	5	13	26	38	-14	53
18	20	19	Hull	46	7	8	8	41	32	4	8	11	29	38	0	49
19	16	23	Birmingham	46	10	3	10	21	24	3	4	16	17	44	-30	46
20	22	18	Reading	46	5	8	10	25	35	5	6	12	23	35	-22	44
21	19	24	Bolton	46	9	4	10	25	33	1	9	13	14	41	-35	43
22	21	21	Barnsley (R)	46	5	9	9	25	32	4	5	14	23	40	-24	41
23	23	16	Burton (R)	46	4	5	14	19	43	6	6	11	19	38	-43	41
24	24	17	Sunderland (R)	46	3	7	13	23	39	4	9	10	29	41	-28	37

Best attack

		GF	GFA
1	Wolves	82	1.78
2	Fulham	79	1.72
3	Aston Villa	72	1.57
4	Derby	70	1.52
5	Hull	70	1.52
6	Cardiff	69	1.5
7	Middlesbrough	67	1.46
8	Bristol City	67	1.46
9	Sheff Utd	62	1.35
10	Brentford	62	1.35
11	Leeds	59	1.28
12	Sheff Wed	59	1.28
13	QPR	58	1.26
14	Preston	57	1.24
15	Ipswich	57	1.24
16	Millwall	56	1.22
17	Sunderland	52	1.13
18	Nottm Forest	51	1.11
19	Norwich	49	1.07
20	Reading	48	1.04
21	Barnsley	48	1.04
22	Bolton	39	0.85
23	Birmingham	38	0.83
24	Burton	38	0.83

Best defence

		GA	GAA
1	Wolves	39	0.85
2	Cardiff	39	0.85
3	Aston Villa	42	0.91
4	Middlesbrough	45	0.98
5	Millwall	45	0.98
6	Fulham	46	1
7	Preston	46	1
8	Derby	48	1.04
9	Brentford	52	1.13
10	Sheff Utd	55	1.2
11	Bristol City	58	1.26
12	Norwich	60	1.3
13	Ipswich	60	1.3
14	Sheff Wed	60	1.3
15	Leeds	64	1.39
16	Nottm Forest	65	1.41
17	Birmingham	68	1.48
18	QPR	70	1.52
19	Hull	70	1.52
20	Reading	70	1.52
21	Barnsley	72	1.57
22	Bolton	74	1.61
23	Sunderland	80	1.74
24	Burton	81	1.76

Top scorers

	Team	Goals scored
M Vydra	Derby	21 ▬▬▬▬▬▬▬▬▬▬▬
L Grabban	Aston Villa	20 ▬▬▬▬▬▬▬▬▬▬
L Clarke	Sheff Utd	19 ▬▬▬▬▬▬▬▬▬
B Reid	Bristol City	19 ▬▬▬▬▬▬▬▬▬
Diogo Jota	Wolves	17 ▬▬▬▬▬▬▬▬
M Waghorn	Ipswich	16 ▬▬▬▬▬▬▬
B Assombalonga	Middlesbrough	15 ▬▬▬▬▬▬▬
R Sessegnon	Fulham	15 ▬▬▬▬▬▬▬

Over 2.5 goals

	H	A	%
Hull	14	12	57%
Leeds	12	14	57%
QPR	15	11	57%
Bristol City	13	12	54%
Barnsley, Burton, Sheff Wed, Sunderland, Wolves			52%

Under 2.5 goals

	H	A	%
Birmingham	15	15	65%
Millwall	14	15	63%
Bolton	12	16	61%
Brentford	14	14	61%
Norwich	14	14	61%
Cardiff, Preston			57%

Both to score

	H	A	%
QPR	16	13	63%
Barnsley	12	15	59%
Fulham	12	15	59%
Sunderland	13	14	59%
Hull	14	12	57%

Both not to score

	H	A	%
Birmingham	16	12	61%
Wolves	13	15	61%
Ipswich	16	11	59%
Millwall	12	15	59%
Villa, Bolton, Forest			57%

Championship results 2017-18

	Aston Villa	Barnsley	Birmingham	Bolton	Brentford	Bristol City	Burton	Cardiff	Derby	Fulham	Hull	Ipswich	Leeds	Middlesbrough	Millwall	Norwich	Nottm Forest	Preston	QPR	Reading	Sheffield Utd	Sheffield Wed	Sunderland	Wolves
Aston Villa		3-1	2-0	1-0	0-0	5-0	3-2	1-0	1-1	2-1	1-1	2-0	1-0	0-0	0-0	4-2	2-1	1-1	1-3	3-0	2-2	1-2	2-1	4-1
Barnsley	0-3		2-0	2-2	2-0	2-2	1-2	0-1	0-3	1-3	0-1	1-2	0-2	2-2	0-2	1-1	2-1	0-0	1-1	1-1	3-2	1-1	3-0	0-0
Birmingham	0-0	0-2		0-0	0-2	2-1	1-1	1-0	0-3	3-1	3-0	1-0	1-0	0-1	0-1	0-2	1-0	1-3	1-2	0-2	2-1	1-0	3-1	0-1
Bolton	1-0	3-1	0-1		0-3	1-0	0-1	2-0	1-2	1-1	1-0	1-1	2-3	0-3	0-2	2-1	3-2	1-3	1-1	2-2	0-1	2-1	1-0	0-4
Brentford	2-1	0-0	5-0	2-0		2-2	1-1	1-3	1-1	3-1	1-1	1-0	3-1	1-1	1-0	0-1	3-4	1-1	2-1	1-1	1-1	2-0	3-3	0-0
Bristol City	1-1	3-1	3-1	2-0	0-1		0-0	2-1	4-1	1-1	5-5	1-0	0-3	2-1	0-0	0-1	2-1	1-2	2-0	2-0	2-3	4-0	3-3	1-2
Burton	0-4	2-4	2-1	2-0	0-2	0-0		0-1	3-1	2-1	0-5	1-2	1-2	1-1	0-1	0-0	0-0	1-2	1-3	1-3	1-3	1-1	0-2	0-4
Cardiff	3-0	2-1	3-2	2-0	2-0	1-0	3-1		0-0	2-4	1-0	3-1	3-1	1-0	0-0	3-1	2-1	0-1	2-1	0-0	2-0	1-1	4-0	0-1
Derby	2-0	4-1	1-1	3-0	3-0	0-0	1-0	3-1		1-2	5-0	0-1	2-2	1-2	3-0	1-1	2-0	1-0	2-0	2-4	1-1	2-0	1-4	0-2
Fulham	2-0	2-1	1-0	1-1	1-1	0-2	6-0	1-1	1-1		2-1	4-1	2-0	1-1	1-0	2-2	2-2	1-0	3-0	0-1	2-1	2-0	2-1	0-2
Hull	0-0	1-1	6-1	4-0	3-2	2-3	4-1	0-2	0-0	2-2		2-2	0-0	1-3	1-2	4-3	2-3	1-2	4-0	0-0	1-0	0-1	1-1	2-3
Ipswich	0-4	1-0	1-0	2-0	2-0	1-3	0-0	0-1	1-2	0-2	0-3		1-0	2-2	2-2	0-1	4-2	3-0	0-0	2-0	0-0	2-2	5-2	0-1
Leeds	1-1	2-1	2-0	2-1	1-0	2-2	5-0	1-4	1-2	0-0	1-0	3-2		2-1	3-4	1-0	0-0	0-0	2-0	0-1	1-2	1-1	1-1	0-3
Middlesbrough	0-1	3-1	2-0	2-0	2-2	2-1	2-0	0-1	0-3	0-1	3-1	2-0	3-0		2-0	0-1	2-0	0-0	3-2	2-1	1-0	0-0	1-0	1-2
Millwall	1-0	1-3	2-0	1-1	1-0	2-0	0-1	1-1	0-0	0-3	0-0	3-4	1-0	2-1		4-0	2-0	1-1	1-0	2-1	3-1	2-1	1-1	2-2
Norwich	3-1	1-1	1-0	0-0	1-2	0-0	0-0	0-2	1-2	0-2	1-1	1-1	2-1	1-0	2-1		0-0	1-1	2-0	3-2	1-2	3-1	1-3	0-2
Nottm Forest	0-1	3-0	2-1	3-2	0-1	0-0	2-0	0-2	0-0	1-3	0-2	2-1	0-2	2-1	1-0	1-0		0-3	4-0	1-1	2-1	0-3	0-1	1-2
Preston	0-2	1-1	1-1	0-0	2-3	2-1	2-1	3-0	0-1	1-2	2-1	0-1	3-1	2-3	0-0	0-0	1-1		1-0	1-0	1-0	2-2	1-1	1-1
QPR	1-2	1-0	3-1	2-0	2-2	1-1	0-0	2-1	1-1	1-2	2-1	0-1	3-1	2-3	0-0	2-2	4-1	2-5		1-2	2-0	4-2	1-0	2-1
Reading	2-1	3-0	0-2	1-1	0-1	0-1	1-2	2-2	3-3	1-1	1-1	0-4	2-2	0-2	0-2	1-2	3-1	1-0	1-0		1-3	0-0	2-2	0-2
Sheffield Utd	0-1	1-0	1-1	0-1	1-0	1-2	2-0	1-1	3-1	4-5	4-1	1-0	2-1	2-1	1-1	0-1	0-0	0-1	2-1	2-1		0-3	3-0	2-0
Sheffield Wed	2-4	1-1	1-3	1-1	2-1	0-0	0-3	0-0	2-0	0-1	2-2	1-2	3-0	1-2	2-1	5-1	3-1	4-1	1-1	3-0	2-4		1-1	0-1
Sunderland	0-3	0-1	1-1	3-3	0-2	1-2	1-2	1-2	1-1	1-0	1-0	0-2	0-2	3-3	2-2	1-1	0-1	0-2	1-1	1-3	1-2	1-3		3-0
Wolves	2-0	2-1	2-0	5-1	3-0	3-3	3-1	1-2	2-0	2-0	2-2	1-0	4-1	1-0	1-0	2-2	0-2	3-2	2-1	3-0	3-0	0-0	0-0	

Record when first to score

		P	W	D	L	F	A	Sup	PGA	Pts
1	Middlesbrough	20	19	1	0	43	8	1.75	2.9	58
2	Wolves	32	29	3	0	72	16	1.75	2.8	90
3	Aston Villa	24	22	2	0	58	14	1.83	2.8	68
4	Nottm Forest	13	12	1	0	30	9	1.62	2.8	37
5	Cardiff	27	24	1	2	55	18	1.37	2.7	73
6	Fulham	30	21	8	1	53	18	1.17	2.4	71
7	Sheff Utd	25	19	3	3	50	26	0.96	2.4	60
8	Leeds	21	16	2	3	42	18	1.14	2.4	50
9	Preston	20	14	6	0	31	12	0.95	2.4	48
10	Norwich	16	12	2	2	25	12	0.81	2.4	38
11	Derby	26	18	7	1	54	17	1.42	2.3	61
12	Millwall	24	17	5	2	41	20	0.88	2.3	56
13	Ipswich	20	14	4	2	40	18	1.10	2.3	46
14	Bristol City	22	15	4	3	45	23	1.00	2.2	49
15	Bolton	16	10	5	1	26	16	0.63	2.2	35
16	Burton	12	8	2	2	20	12	0.67	2.2	26
17	Brentford	27	17	6	4	48	25	0.85	2.1	57
18	Reading	18	10	7	1	30	17	0.72	2.1	37
19	Birmingham	17	11	3	3	26	16	0.59	2.1	36
20	Sheff Wed	22	13	5	4	44	23	0.95	2	44
21	QPR	18	11	3	4	35	21	0.78	2	36
22	Barnsley	17	9	6	2	33	20	0.76	1.9	33
23	Hull	19	10	5	4	53	29	1.26	1.8	35
24	Sunderland	17	7	8	2	29	18	0.65	1.7	29

Record when keeping a clean sheet

		P	W	D	F	Sup	PGA	Pts
1	Fulham	15	14	1	29	1.93	2.9	43
2	Wolves	24	20	4	41	1.71	2.7	64
3	Sunderland	6	5	1	8	1.33	2.7	16
4	Cardiff	19	15	4	26	1.37	2.6	49
5	Middlesbrough	16	13	3	26	1.63	2.6	42
6	Brentford	15	12	3	23	1.53	2.6	39
7	Ipswich	14	11	3	20	1.43	2.6	36
8	Birmingham	10	8	2	11	1.10	2.6	26
9	Aston Villa	20	15	5	34	1.70	2.5	50
10	Derby	19	14	5	34	1.79	2.5	47
11	Millwall	19	13	6	22	1.16	2.4	45
12	Leeds	14	10	4	21	1.50	2.4	34
13	Sheff Utd	10	7	3	11	1.10	2.4	24
14	QPR	7	5	2	7	1.00	2.4	17
15	Bolton	9	6	3	7	0.78	2.3	21
16	Reading	8	5	3	8	1.00	2.3	18
17	Barnsley	8	5	3	10	1.25	2.3	18
18	Preston	15	9	6	14	0.93	2.2	33
19	Norwich	15	9	6	11	0.73	2.2	33
20	Hull	12	7	5	20	1.67	2.2	26
21	Nottm Forest	13	7	6	14	1.08	2.1	27
22	Bristol City	14	7	7	14	1.00	2	28
23	Sheff Wed	12	6	6	13	1.08	2	24
24	Burton	11	4	7	7	0.64	1.7	19

Lack of competition from relegated sides bolsters Bradford's bid for success

There are reasons to oppose all three sides who have dropped down from the Championship in League One's race for promotion, writes Liam Flin. Relegated duo Sunderland and Barnsley head the market for the 2018-19 title but neither they nor Burton, who are a much bigger price, are enticing options. Punters may instead want to target those with experience of England's turbulent third tier and Bradford are the pick of the bunch.

The Bantams are heading into their sixth consecutive League One campaign having reached the playoffs in two of their last three seasons, and they look overpriced to top the table this time around.

Bradford floundered under Simon Grayson in the latter part of last season, with 12 defeats in their final 23 matches causing the wheels to come off their promotion push. New boss Michael Collins, although inexperienced at this level, looks an excellent fit. He has coached at U18 level for the club and the time taken to appoint him permanently suggests the owners were meticulous in their recruitment strategy.

City have snapped up midfielder Hope Akpan in addition to Northampton shot-stopper Richard O'Donnell, Josh Wright and Anthony O'Connor this summer while Charlie Wyke remains an ever-present threat in the final third. If Bradford can rediscover the form they showed in the early stages of last season, they will be a danger to all.

Jack Ross was successful with St Mirren and was a sensible long-term appointment by Sunderland but it's hard to see the squad gelling quickly following a mass player exodus. Burton were consistently poor at both ends of the pitch last term and are rightfully a big price, while Barnsley have allowed key players to leave in Andy Yiadom and Matty Pearson.

Accrington and Wycombe head the relegation market but it has been six years since a newly-promoted side experienced the drop in their first season in League One.

Walsall finished two places above the relegation zone in 2017-18 and have since lost last term's top scorer Erhun Oztumer to Bolton. They won just twice after Dean Keates took charge in March and he remains an unconvincing figure in the Saddlers' dugout. New signing Zeli Ismail barely featured for Bury last season and is unlikely to alter Walsall's chances of survival.

Gillingham also look in danger, finishing 17th and 20th in their last two seasons.

An overreliance on Tom Eaves, who netted just over a third of their league goals last term, highlights a lack of attacking options and they too could struggle.

Luton have returned to League One and could be set for back-to-back promotions. They turned Kenilworth Road into a fortress last term, losing just four games there, and their lethal front-line oozes confidence. They have bolstered what was League Two's joint-best defence with the signings of Barnsley's Pearson and Sonny Bradley while Andrew Shinnie has made his loan permanent.

Recommendations

Bradford to win (each-way), 28-1
Luton to be promoted, 6-1
Walsall to be relegated, 2-1
Gillingham to be relegated, 15-8

Charlie Wyke leads the line for Bradford

ACCRINGTON

Nickname: Stanley
Colours: Red
Ground: Crown Ground (5,057)
Tel: 01254-356-950   accringtonstanley.co.uk

Last season will be fondly remembered by Accrington Stanley who, for the first time in their history, secured promotion from England's fourth tier.

A Boxing Day defeat to Carlisle left John Coleman's side outside the playoff places but 18 wins in their final 23 matches propelled the club to the League Two title. The goalscoring heroics of player of the season Billy Kee coupled with a big-game mentality made Stanley one of the success stories of the season.

Longest run without win/loss: 4/15
High/low league position: 1/7
Clean sheets: 19 **Yellows:** 73 **Reds:** 3
Avg attendance: 3,335 **Players used:** 31
Leading scorer: B Kee 25 (10,23)
Key stat: Accrington did not fall below ninth position all season in League Two

	2017-18 H	A	Last six seasons at home P	W	D	L	OV	UN	BS	CS
Barnsley	-	-	-	-	-	-	-	-	-	-
Burton		3	1	1	1	1	2	1	1
Sunderland	-	-	-	-	-	-	-	-	-	-
Shrewsbury		1	0	0	1	1	0	1	0
Scunthorpe		1	0	0	1	1	0	1	0
Charlton	-	-	-	-	-	-	-	-	-	-
Plymouth		5	2	2	1	1	4	3	1
Portsmouth		4	1	2	1	2	2	3	1
Peterborough	-	-	-	-	-	-	-	-	-	-
Southend		3	0	2	1	0	3	2	0
Bradford		1	0	1	0	0	1	1	0
Blackpool		1	1	0	0	1	0	1	0
Bristol Rovers		3	3	0	0	1	2	1	2
Fleetwood Town		2	1	0	1	1	0	0	1
Doncaster		1	1	0	0	1	0	1	0
Oxford		4	1	1	2	2	2	1	2
Gillingham		1	0	1	0	0	1	1	0
AFC Wimbledon		4	3	0	1	3	1	2	2
Walsall	-	-	-	-	-	-	-	-	-	-
Rochdale		2	0	0	2	2	0	2	0
Accrington									
Luton	L	W	4	0	2	2	2	2	3	0
Wycombe	W	W	6	1	4	1	1	5	4	1
Coventry	W	W	1	1	0	0	0	1	0	1

Season	Division	Pos	P	W	D	L	F	A	GD	Pts
2017-18	League Two	1	46	29	6	11	76	46	+30	93
2016-17	League Two	13	46	17	14	15	59	56	+3	65
2015-16	League Two	4	46	24	13	9	74	48	+26	85

Over/Under 52%/48% 7th   **Both score** 50%/50% 19th

AFC WIMBLEDON

Nickname: The Dons
Colours: Blue and yellow
Ground: Cherry Red Records Stadium (4,850)
Tel: 0208-547-3528   afcwimbledon.co.uk

Wimbledon were staring down the barrel of relegation until an end-of-season run of seven matches unbeaten kept Neal Ardley's side afloat.

No League One club used fewer players last term than the Dons (25), who placed faith in mainstays such as Cody McDonald, Lyle Taylor and skipper Barry Fuller. Wimbledon suffered uninspiring defeats against Bury and Northampton but managed to beat bigger sides when it counted most.

Longest run without win/loss: 4/7
High/low league position: 16/23
Clean sheets: 12 **Yellows:** 67 **Reds:** 2
Avg attendance: 6,105 **Players used:** 25
Leading scorer: L Taylor 14 (5,11)
Key stat: Wimbledon only did the double over two sides in League One last term

	2017-18 H	A	Last six seasons at home P	W	D	L	OV	UN	BS	CS
Barnsley	-	-	-	-	-	-	-	-	-	-
Burton		3	2	1	0	2	1	2	1
Sunderland	-	-	-	-	-	-	-	-	-	-
Shrewsbury	L	L	3	0	2	1	1	2	2	0
Scunthorpe	D	D	3	1	1	1	2	1	3	0
Charlton	W	L	2	1	0	0	2	1	1	1
Plymouth	L	L	5	0	3	2	0	5	2	1
Portsmouth	L	L	4	2	0	2	1	3	0	2
Peterborough	D	D	2	0	2	0	1	1	1	1
Southend	W	L	5	1	1	3	1	4	0	2
Bradford	W	W	3	2	0	1	3	0	3	0
Blackpool	W	L	1	1	0	0	0	1	0	1
Bristol Rovers	W	W	5	2	2	1	1	4	1	3
Fleetwood Town	L	L	4	2	1	1	2	2	2	1
Doncaster	W	D	1	1	0	0	0	1	0	1
Oxford	W	L	6	2	1	3	4	2	3	1
Gillingham	D	D	3	1	1	1	0	3	1	1
AFC Wimbledon									
Walsall	L	W	2	1	0	1	1	1	1	1
Rochdale	D	D	4	1	1	2	3	1	2	1
Accrington		4	1	2	1	2	2	3	1
Luton		2	2	0	0	2	0	2	0
Wycombe		4	1	3	0	1	3	2	2
Coventry		1	0	1	0	0	1	1	0

Season	Division	Pos	P	W	D	L	F	A	GD	Pts
2017-18	League One	18	46	13	14	19	47	58	-11	53
2016-17	League One	15	46	13	18	15	52	55	-3	57
2015-16	League Two	7	46	21	12	13	64	50	+14	75

Over/Under 39%/61% 20th   **Both score** 43%/57% 23rd

BARNSLEY

Nickname: Tykes
Colours: Red and white
Ground: Oakwell (23,009)
Tel: 01226-211-211   barnsleyfc.co.uk

A 4-1 defeat away to Derby on the last day of the Championship season sealed a second relegation in five years for Barnsley.

Sunderland were the only team in the Championship to win fewer matches than the Tykes, who were victorious in just two of their final 13 games in 2017-18.

They had chances to secure survival but often lacked composure when hitting the front, winning just nine out of 17 matches in which they led.

Longest run without win/loss: 10/4
High/low league position: 16/22
Clean sheets: 8 **Yellows:** 74 **Reds:** 2
Avg attendance: 16,735 **Players used:** 35
Leading scorer: T Bradshaw 9 (5,8) O McBurnie 9 (3,8)
Key stat: Barnsley won three of their four games against the other relegated sides

	2017-18 H	2017-18 A	P	W	D	L	OV	UN	BS	CS
Barnsley										
Burton	L	W	3	1	1	1	1	2	2	1
Sunderland	W	W	1	1	0	0	1	0	0	1
Shrewsbury			1	0	0	1	1	0	1	0
Scunthorpe			2	0	1	1	1	1	1	1
Charlton			2	0	1	1	2	0	1	0
Plymouth			-	-	-	-	-	-	-	-
Portsmouth			-	-	-	-	-	-	-	-
Peterborough			3	1	1	1	0	3	1	1
Southend			1	0	0	1	0	1	0	0
Bradford			2	1	1	0	1	1	1	1
Blackpool			3	2	1	0	1	2	2	1
Bristol Rovers			-	-	-	-	-	-	-	-
Fleetwood Town			2	0	0	2	1	1	1	0
Doncaster			3	1	2	0	0	3	1	2
Oxford			-	-	-	-	-	-	-	-
Gillingham			2	2	0	0	1	1	1	1
AFC Wimbledon			-	-	-	-	-	-	-	-
Walsall			2	1	0	1	1	1	0	1
Rochdale			2	2	0	0	2	0	1	1
Accrington			-	-	-	-	-	-	-	-
Luton			-	-	-	-	-	-	-	-
Wycombe			-	-	-	-	-	-	-	-
Coventry			2	2	0	0	0	2	0	2

Season	Division	Pos	P	W	D	L	F	A	GD	Pts
2017-18	Championship	22	46	9	14	23	48	72	-24	41
2016-17	Championship	14	46	15	13	18	64	67	-3	58
2015-16	League One	6	46	22	8	16	70	54	+16	74

Over/Under 52%/48% 5th   **Both score** 59%/41% 2nd

BLACKPOOL

Nickname: The Seasiders
Colours: Tangerine and white
Ground: Bloomfield Road (17,338)
Tel: 01253-685000   blackpoolfc.co.uk

Following promotion from League Two in 2016-17, last term was a season of consolidation for Blackpool in the third tier.

The Seasiders floated in the mid-table positions for much of the campaign and no side used more players throughout the season than Blackpool's 30 as Gary Bowyer struggled to find his best XI.

Results were not dismal, however, as the club lost the fewest games of any team outside of the division's top six.

Longest run without win/loss: 8/7
High/low league position: 3/19
Clean sheets: 14 **Yellows:** 59 **Reds:** 0
Avg attendance: 5,919 **Players used:** 30
Leading scorer: K Vassell 11 (8,10)
Key stat: Blackpool finished top of the fair play table last term as they went the whole campaign without picking up a red card

	2017-18 H	2017-18 A	P	W	D	L	OV	UN	BS	CS
Barnsley			3	1	1	1	1	2	2	1
Burton			1	0	0	1	1	0	1	0
Sunderland			-	-	-	-	-	-	-	-
Shrewsbury	D	L	2	0	1	1	1	1	2	0
Scunthorpe	L	D	2	1	0	1	2	0	1	1
Charlton	W	D	4	1	0	3	2	2	0	1
Plymouth	D	W	2	0	1	1	1	1	1	0
Portsmouth	L	W	2	1	0	1	2	0	2	0
Peterborough	D		3	1	1	1	0	3	1	1
Southend	D	L	2	1	1	0	0	2	1	1
Bradford	D	L	2	1	0	1	1	1	0	1
Blackpool										
Bristol Rovers	D	L	1	0	1	0	0	1	0	1
Fleetwood Town	W	D	2	2	0	0	1	1	1	1
Doncaster	L	D	4	1	1	2	2	2	3	0
Oxford	W	L	1	1	0	0	1	0	1	0
Gillingham	D	W	2	1	1	0	0	2	1	1
AFC Wimbledon	W	L	1	1	0	0	0	1	0	1
Walsall	D	D	2	0	1	1	2	0	1	0
Rochdale	D	W	2	0	1	0	2	0	1	0
Accrington			1	0	1	0	0	1	0	1
Luton			1	0	1	0	1	0	1	0
Wycombe			1	0	1	0	1	0	1	0
Coventry			1	0	0	1	0	1	0	0

Season	Division	Pos	P	W	D	L	F	A	GD	Pts
2017-18	League One	12	46	15	15	16	60	55	+5	60
2016-17	League Two	7	46	18	16	12	69	46	+23	70
2015-16	League One	22	46	12	10	24	40	63	-23	46

Over/Under 50%/50% 9th   **Both score** 57%/43% 5th

BRADFORD

Nickname: The Bantams
Colours: Claret and amber
Ground: Valley Parade (25,136)
Tel: 0871-978-1911   bradfordcityfc.co.uk

Bradford were among the favourites for the title at the start of the campaign after losing the 2016-17 League One playoff final to Millwall, but it was a dismal end to the season which cost them promotion.

Charlie Wyke finished as top scorer with 15 goals and the team were in the mix for a playoff spot until their season petered out in January with just three wins in their final 20 matches. Manager Simon Grayson parted ways with the Bantams at the end of the campaign.

Longest run without win/loss: 10/6
High/low league position: 3/13
Clean sheets: 9 **Yellows:** 72 **Reds:** 4
Avg attendance: 13,387 **Players used:** 35
Leading scorer: C Wyke 15 (7,12)
Key stat: Bradford lost just one of their opening nine matches in League One last term, winning six

	2017-18 H	A	P	W	D	L	OV	UN	BS	CS
Barnsley			2	1	0	1	0	2	0	1
Burton			2	2	0	0	0	2	0	2
Sunderland	-	-	-	-	-	-	-	-	-	-
Shrewsbury	D	W	4	2	2	0	1	3	2	2
Scunthorpe	L	D	4	1	2	1	1	3	2	2
Charlton	L	D	2	0	1	1	0	2	0	1
Plymouth	L	L	2	1	0	1	0	2	0	1
Portsmouth	W	W	1	1	0	0	1	0	1	0
Peterborough	L	W	5	2	0	3	1	4	1	2
Southend	L	W	4	1	2	1	1	3	2	1
Bradford										
Blackpool	W	L	2	2	0	0	1	1	1	1
Bristol Rovers	W	L	3	2	1	0	2	1	3	0
Fleetwood Town	L	W	5	3	1	1	4	1	3	1
Doncaster	W	L	3	2	0	1	2	1	2	1
Oxford	W	D	3	2	0	1	2	1	2	1
Gillingham	W	W	6	1	3	2	2	4	4	1
AFC Wimbledon	L	L	3	2	0	1	3	0	1	1
Walsall	D	D	5	2	2	1	1	4	2	2
Rochdale	W	D	5	2	1	2	5	0	4	1
Accrington			1	1	0	0	1	0	1	0
Luton	-	-	-	-	-	-	-	-	-	-
Wycombe			1	1	0	0	0	1	0	1
Coventry			4	2	2	0	3	1	3	1

Season	Division	Pos	P	W	D	L	F	A	GD	Pts
2017-18	League One	11	46	18	9	19	57	67	-10	63
2016-17	League One	5	46	20	19	7	62	43	+19	79
2015-16	League One	5	46	23	11	12	55	40	+15	80

Over/Under 50%/50% 9th   **Both score** 54%/46% 7th

BRISTOL ROVERS

Nickname: The Pirates/The Gas
Colours: Blue and white
Ground: Memorial Stadium (12,296)
Tel: 01179-096-648   bristolrovers.co.uk

It was slow and steady from Bristol Rovers in their second season in League One since promotion in 2016.

No team salvaged more points from trailing positions (26) in League One than Rovers last term.

The presence of long-serving Darrell Clarke in the dugout coupled with the second-oldest squad in the division made them one of the more settled groups in the division, while an EFL Cup third-round tie was arguably the highlight.

Longest run without win/loss: 7/6
High/low league position: 9/18
Clean sheets: 7 **Yellows:** 66 **Reds:** 4
Avg attendance: 8,454 **Players used:** 31
Leading scorer: E Harrison 12 (2,11)
Key stat: Bristol's first 23 matches of the season did not feature a single draw

	2017-18 H	A	P	W	D	L	OV	UN	BS	CS
Barnsley	-	-	-	-	-	-	-	-	-	-
Burton			2	2	0	0	1	1	0	2
Sunderland	-	-	-	-	-	-	-	-	-	-
Shrewsbury	L	L	2	1	0	1	1	1	1	1
Scunthorpe	D	L	3	0	3	0	0	3	2	1
Charlton	D	L	2	0	1	1	1	1	2	0
Plymouth	W	L	4	3	1	0	3	1	4	0
Portsmouth	W	L	3	2	0	1	2	1	2	1
Peterborough	L	D	2	0	0	2	2	0	2	0
Southend	W	D	4	2	1	1	2	2	1	3
Bradford	W	L	3	1	2	0	2	1	3	0
Blackpool	W	D	1	1	0	0	1	0	1	0
Bristol Rovers										
Fleetwood Town	W	L	4	2	1	1	3	1	3	1
Doncaster	L	W	1	0	0	1	0	1	0	0
Oxford	L	W	5	1	1	3	1	4	2	0
Gillingham	D	L	3	1	1	1	1	2	2	0
AFC Wimbledon	L	L	5	4	0	1	3	2	2	3
Walsall	W	D	2	1	1	0	1	1	2	0
Rochdale	W	L	4	2	1	1	4	0	4	0
Accrington			3	0	0	3	0	3	0	0
Luton			1	1	0	0	0	1	0	1
Wycombe			3	2	0	1	1	2	0	2
Coventry			1	1	0	0	1	0	1	0

Season	Division	Pos	P	W	D	L	F	A	GD	Pts
2017-18	League One	13	46	16	11	19	60	66	-6	59
2016-17	League One	10	46	18	12	16	68	70	-2	66
2015-16	League Two	3	46	26	7	13	77	46	+31	85

Over/Under 54%/46% 3rd   **Both score** 61%/39% 3rd

BURTON

Nickname: The Brewers
Colours: Yellow and black
Ground: Pirelli Stadium (6,912)
Tel: 01283-565938 burtonalbionfc.co.uk

The 2017-18 season was one to forget for Burton supporters.

After losing their opening three league matches, the Brewers failed to rise above 19th in the Championship and were consistently poor at both ends of the pitch.

No side shipped more than Burton's 81 goals and no team netted fewer than their tally of 38. Birmingham were the only club to lose more games and Albion were rightfully consigned to the drop.

Longest run without win/loss: 9/3
High/low league position: 19/24
Clean sheets: 11 **Yellows:** 68 **Reds:** 2
Avg attendance: 12,739 **Players used:** 31
Leading scorer: L Dyer 7 (2,7)
Key stat: Burton suffered the biggest home and away defeats in the Championship last term – 0-5 hosting Hull and 6-0 at Fulham

	2017-18		Last six seasons at home							
	H	A	P	W	D	L	OV	UN	BS	CS
Barnsley	L	W	3	0	2	1	1	2	1	2
Burton										
Sunderland	L	W	1	0	0	1	0	1	0	0
Shrewsbury			2	1	0	1	1	1	1	1
Scunthorpe			2	1	1	0	2	0	2	0
Charlton			-	-	-	-	-	-	-	-
Plymouth			3	2	1	0	0	3	1	2
Portsmouth			2	1	0	1	1	1	1	1
Peterborough			1	1	0	0	1	0	1	0
Southend			4	3	0	1	1	3	1	2
Bradford			2	2	0	0	1	1	1	1
Blackpool			1	1	0	0	0	1	0	1
Bristol Rovers			2	1	1	0	0	2	1	1
Fleetwood Town			3	1	0	2	2	1	2	0
Doncaster			1	0	1	0	1	0	1	0
Oxford			3	2	0	1	1	2	0	2
Gillingham			2	2	0	0	2	0	2	0
AFC Wimbledon			3	1	2	0	1	2	2	1
Walsall			1	0	1	0	0	1	0	1
Rochdale			3	3	0	0	1	2	1	2
Accrington			3	3	0	0	2	1	1	2
Luton			1	1	0	0	0	1	0	1
Wycombe			3	3	0	0	0	3	0	3
Coventry			1	0	0	1	0	1	0	0

Season	Division	Pos	P	W	D	L	F	A	GD	Pts
2017-18	Championship	23	46	10	11	25	38	81	-43	41
2016-17	Championship	20	46	13	13	20	49	63	-14	52
2015-16	League One	2	46	25	10	11	57	37	+20	85

Over/Under 52%/48% 5th **Both score** 48%/52% 14th

CHARLTON

Nickname: Addicks
Colours: Red and white
Ground: The Valley (27,111)
Tel: 020-8333-4000 cafc.co.uk

One win in eight matches across February and March put the Addicks' playoff hopes in jeopardy, but the appointment of Lee Bowyer, who replaced Karl Robinson, sparked a late surge of six wins from ten matches as they secured sixth spot before losing to Shrewsbury in the semi-finals.

Charlton's season was nonetheless steady, with the club occupying the top nine positions after matchday two and conceding just 51 goals – their best defensive display since 2011-12.

Longest run without win/loss: 8/9
High/low league position: 3/9
Clean sheets: 14 **Yellows:** 80 **Reds:** 1
Avg attendance: 9,558 **Players used:** 33
Leading scorer: J Magennis 10 (4,10)
Key stat: Five of Charlton's final six games were settled by a 1-0 scoreline

	2017-18		Last six seasons at home							
	H	A	P	W	D	L	OV	UN	BS	CS
Barnsley			2	0	0	2	1	1	1	0
Burton			-	-	-	-	-	-	-	-
Sunderland			-	-	-	-	-	-	-	-
Shrewsbury	L	W	2	1	0	1	1	1	0	1
Scunthorpe	L	L	2	1	0	1	1	1	1	0
Charlton										
Plymouth	W	L	1	1	0	0	0	1	0	1
Portsmouth	L	W	1	0	0	1	0	1	0	0
Peterborough	D	L	3	1	1	1	1	2	1	1
Southend	W	L	2	2	0	0	2	0	2	0
Bradford	D	W	2	0	2	0	2	2	2	0
Blackpool	D	L	4	1	3	0	2	2	3	1
Bristol Rovers	W	D	2	2	0	0	1	1	1	1
Fleetwood Town	D	W	2	0	2	0	0	2	1	1
Doncaster	W	D	2	2	0	0	2	0	2	0
Oxford	L	D	2	0	0	2	1	1	1	0
Gillingham	L	L	2	1	0	1	2	0	1	1
AFC Wimbledon	W	L	2	1	0	1	1	1	1	1
Walsall	W	D	2	1	1	0	1	1	2	0
Rochdale	W	L	2	1	0	1	1	1	1	0
Accrington			-	-	-	-	-	-	-	-
Luton			-	-	-	-	-	-	-	-
Wycombe			-	-	-	-	-	-	-	-
Coventry			1	1	0	0	1	0	0	1

Season	Division	Pos	P	W	D	L	F	A	GD	Pts
2017-18	League One	6	46	20	11	15	58	51	+7	71
2016-17	League One	13	46	14	18	14	60	53	+7	60
2015-16	Championship	22	46	9	13	24	40	80	-40	40

Over/Under 37%/63% 23rd **Both score** 46%/54% 18th

COVENTRY

Nickname: The Sky Blues
Colours: Sky blue
Ground: Ricoh Arena (32,609)
Tel: 024-7699-1987   ccfc.co.uk

Not only did last season see the Sky Blues record their first top-seven finish since 1989 but they also secured promotion to League One via the playoffs with a 3-1 victory over Exeter in the final.

Mark Robins' men failed to string together more than three successive wins all season but the second-best defensive record coupled with the league's top scorer Marc McNulty, who netted 23 goals, propelled them into the playoff places and beyond.

Longest run without win/loss: 4/7
High/low league position: 3/10
Clean sheets: 16 **Yellows:** 71 **Reds:** 2
Avg attendance: 7,233 **Players used:** 29
Leading scorer: M McNulty 23 (8,16)
Key stat: Coventry won more of their matches without McNulty (63 per cent) than with him (48 per cent) last term

	2017-18		Last six seasons at home							
	H	A	P	W	D	L	OV	UN	BS	CS
Barnsley			2	1	1	0	2	0	2	0
Burton			1	0	0	1	0	1	0	0
Sunderland			-	-	-	-	-	-	-	-
Shrewsbury			4	1	2	1	1	3	0	3
Scunthorpe			4	0	1	3	2	2	3	0
Charlton			1	0	1	0	0	1	1	0
Plymouth			-	-	-	-	-	-	-	-
Portsmouth			1	0	1	0	0	1	1	0
Peterborough			4	4	0	0	3	1	3	1
Southend			2	0	1	1	1	1	1	0
Bradford			4	1	2	1	0	4	1	2
Blackpool			1	0	1	0	0	1	0	1
Bristol Rovers			1	1	0	0	0	1	0	1
Fleetwood Town			3	0	1	2	1	2	2	0
Doncaster			3	1	1	1	2	1	2	1
Oxford			1	1	0	0	1	0	1	0
Gillingham			4	4	0	0	3	1	3	1
AFC Wimbledon			1	0	1	0	1	0	1	0
Walsall			5	3	2	0	2	3	3	2
Rochdale			3	1	1	1	2	1	1	1
Accrington	L	L	1	0	0	1	0	1	0	0
Luton	D	W	1	0	1	0	1	0	1	0
Wycombe	W	W	1	1	0	0	1	0	1	0
Coventry										

Season	Division	Pos	P	W	D	L	F	A	GD	Pts
2017-18	League Two	6	46	22	9	15	64	47	+17	75
2016-17	League One	23	46	9	12	25	37	68	-31	39
2015-16	League One	8	46	19	12	15	67	49	+18	69

Over/Under 43%/57% 19th   **Both score** 46%/54% 24th

DONCASTER

Nickname: Rovers
Colours: Red and white
Ground: Keepmoat Stadium (15,231)
Tel: 01302-764-664   doncasterroversfc.co.uk

It was a season of two halves for Doncaster following their promotion to England's third tier. Ten of their 16 defeats came in the first 23 matches last term and Rovers finished the campaign with the second-most stalemates in the division and a goal difference of zero.

John Marquis was far and away their best player of the campaign, netting at crucial times in victories at Blackburn and MK Dons, but he often lacked support in the final third.

Longest run without win/loss: 8/8
High/low league position: 10/19
Clean sheets: 14 **Yellows:** 63 **Reds:** 0
Avg attendance: 7,864 **Players used:** 28
Leading scorer: J Marquis 14 (5,12)
Key stat: Doncaster failed to score in each of their final six league matches last season

	2017-18		Last six seasons at home							
	H	A	P	W	D	L	OV	UN	BS	CS
Barnsley			3	2	1	0	2	1	2	1
Burton			1	0	1	0	0	1	0	1
Sunderland			-	-	-	-	-	-	-	-
Shrewsbury	L	D	3	1	0	2	1	2	1	1
Scunthorpe	L	D	4	2	0	2	2	2	1	1
Charlton	D	L	2	1	1	0	1	1	1	1
Plymouth	D	W	2	0	1	1	0	2	1	0
Portsmouth	W	D	3	2	1	0	2	1	3	0
Peterborough	D	D	3	0	1	2	1	2	1	1
Southend	W	D	2	1	1	0	1	1	1	1
Bradford	W	L	3	1	0	2	1	2	0	1
Blackpool	D	W	4	0	1	3	2	2	2	0
Bristol Rovers	L		1	0	0	1	1	0	1	0
Fleetwood Town	W	D	3	2	1	0	1	2	0	3
Doncaster										
Oxford	L	L	1	0	0	1	0	1	0	0
Gillingham	D	D	3	0	2	1	2	1	2	1
AFC Wimbledon	D	L	1	0	1	0	0	1	0	1
Walsall	L	L	4	0	0	4	3	1	2	0
Rochdale	W	L	3	1	1	1	0	3	1	1
Accrington			1	0	1	0	1	0	1	0
Luton			1	0	1	0	0	1	1	0
Wycombe			1	0	1	0	1	0	1	0
Coventry			3	2	0	1	1	2	1	2

Season	Division	Pos	P	W	D	L	F	A	GD	Pts
2017-18	League One	15	46	13	17	16	52	52	0	56
2016-17	League Two	3	46	25	10	11	85	55	+30	85
2015-16	League One	21	46	11	13	22	48	64	-16	46

Over/Under 43%/57% 17th   **Both score** 46%/54% 18th

FLEETWOOD TOWN

Nickname: The Cod Army
Colours: Red and white
Ground: Highbury Stadium (5,327)
Tel: 01253-775080   fleetwoodtownfc.com

Having reached the playoff semi-finals in the 2016-17 campaign, Fleetwood stumbled to a 14th-placed finish in the league last year in a season of managerial mayhem.

Following four consecutive defeats in February, Uwe Rosler was dismissed, with John Sheridan replacing him in the dugout until the end of the season.

Despite an eight-game unbeaten run including four wins and five clean sheets, Sheridan did not extend his stay.

Longest run without win/loss: 9/7
High/low league position: 7/21
Clean sheets: 15 **Yellows:** 66 **Reds:** 4
Avg attendance: 5,260 **Players used:** 28
Leading scorer: D Cole 10 (3,9)
Key stat: Fleetwood lost the most league matches (21) of the sides not to be relegated last season

	2017-18 H	A	Last six seasons at home P	W	D	L	OV	UN	BS	CS
Barnsley			2	0	1	1	0	2	0	1
Burton			3	1	0	2	3	0	1	1
Sunderland			-	-	-	-	-	-	-	-
Shrewsbury	L	L	3	1	1	1	2	1	1	2
Scunthorpe	L	D	5	1	2	2	4	1	4	0
Charlton	L	D	2	0	1	1	2	0	2	0
Plymouth	D	W	3	1	1	1	2	1	1	1
Portsmouth	L	L	2	1	0	1	2	0	2	0
Peterborough	L	L	4	2	1	1	1	3	2	2
Southend	L	W	5	0	4	1	1	4	4	1
Bradford	L	W	5	1	2	2	3	2	4	0
Blackpool	D	L	2	0	2	0	0	2	0	2
Bristol Rovers	W	L	4	3	0	1	3	1	2	1
Fleetwood Town										
Doncaster	D	L	3	1	2	0	1	2	1	2
Oxford	W	W	4	3	1	0	1	3	1	3
Gillingham	L	L	5	3	1	1	3	2	3	1
AFC Wimbledon	W	W	4	1	3	0	0	4	1	3
Walsall	W	L	4	2	0	2	1	3	1	1
Rochdale	D	W	6	1	4	1	2	4	2	3
Accrington			2	1	0	1	2	0	2	0
Luton			-	-	-	-	-	-	-	-
Wycombe			2	1	0	1	0	2	0	1
Coventry			3	1	0	2	0	3	0	1

Season	Division	Pos	P	W	D	L	F	A	GD	Pts
2017-18	League One	14	46	16	9	21	59	68	-9	57
2016-17	League One	4	46	23	13	10	64	43	+21	82
2015-16	League One	19	46	12	15	19	52	56	-4	51

Over/Under 52%/48% 4th   **Both score** 52%/48% 12th

GILLINGHAM

Nickname: The Gills
Colours: Blue and white
Ground: Priestfield Stadium (11,582)
Tel: 01634-300-000 gillinghamfootballclub.com

The Gills finished four places above the drop zone last season after picking up just one win from their opening nine matches.

That woeful run of form cost Adrian Pennock his job but even the managerial switch could not improve the club's poor home record.

Gillingham sat in the relegation places on home form, but ranked eighth in the away standings as they won just five matches at the Priestfield Stadium.

Longest run without win/loss: 9/8
High/low league position: 10/23
Clean sheets: 10 **Yellows:** 75 **Reds:** 5
Avg attendance: 6,672 **Players used:** 30
Leading scorer: T Eaves 17 (2,12)
Key stat: Gillingham won just one of their final ten games last season

	2017-18 H	A	Last six seasons at home P	W	D	L	OV	UN	BS	CS
Barnsley			2	1	0	1	1	1	1	0
Burton			2	1	0	1	2	0	1	0
Sunderland			-	-	-	-	-	-	-	-
Shrewsbury	L	D	4	0	2	2	2	2	4	0
Scunthorpe	D	W	4	2	1	1	3	1	2	1
Charlton	W	W	2	1	1	0	0	2	1	1
Plymouth	W	L	2	2	0	0	2	0	2	0
Portsmouth	L	W	1	0	0	1	0	1	0	0
Peterborough	D	W	5	2	2	1	3	2	4	0
Southend	D	L	4	2	2	0	2	2	3	1
Bradford	L	L	6	3	1	2	2	4	2	2
Blackpool	L	D	2	1	0	1	2	0	1	0
Bristol Rovers	W	D	3	3	0	0	3	0	2	1
Fleetwood Town	W	W	5	2	1	2	4	1	4	0
Doncaster	D	D	3	1	2	0	0	3	1	2
Oxford	W	L	3	0	1	2	0	3	1	0
Gillingham										
AFC Wimbledon	D	D	3	0	3	0	3	0	3	0
Walsall	D	W	5	0	4	1	2	3	3	2
Rochdale	W	L	5	4	0	1	3	2	2	3
Accrington			1	1	0	0	0	1	0	1
Luton			-	-	-	-	-	-	-	-
Wycombe			1	0	0	1	0	1	0	0
Coventry			4	3	1	0	3	1	3	1

Season	Division	Pos	P	W	D	L	F	A	GD	Pts
2017-18	League One	17	46	13	17	16	50	55	-5	56
2016-17	League One	20	46	12	14	20	59	79	-20	50
2015-16	League One	9	46	19	12	15	71	56	+15	69

Over/Under 43%/57% 17th   **Both score** 54%/46% 7th

LUTON

Nickname: The Hatters
Colours: White and black
Ground: Kenilworth Road (10,300)
Tel: 01582-411-622   lutontown.co.uk

Luton set the tone for their promotion season with an 8-2 annihilation of Yeovil on the opening day of the League Two campaign.

The Hatters secured second spot and finished as top scorers with 94 goals, the highest tally from a side in the division since 2010.

They lost fewer games (eight) than any other team and had the joint-best defensive record as they made amends for a 2016-17 playoff semi-final defeat.

Longest run without win/loss: 5/9
High/low league position: 1/5
Clean sheets: 18 **Yellows:** 89 **Reds:** 8
Avg attendance: 6,708 **Players used:** 27
Leading scorer: D Hylton 21 (4,16)
Key stat: Every home game for Luton featured a goal last season

	2017-18 H	A	P	W	D	L	OV	UN	BS	CS
Barnsley			-	-	-	-	-	-	-	-
Burton			1	0	0	1	0	1	0	0
Sunderland			-	-	-	-	-	-	-	-
Shrewsbury			1	0	1	0	0	1	0	1
Scunthorpe			-	-	-	-	-	-	-	-
Charlton			-	-	-	-	-	-	-	-
Plymouth			3	0	1	2	1	2	2	0
Portsmouth			3	0	1	2	2	1	3	0
Peterborough			-	-	-	-	-	-	-	-
Southend			1	1	0	0	0	1	0	1
Bradford			-	-	-	-	-	-	-	-
Blackpool			1	1	0	0	0	1	0	1
Bristol Rovers			1	0	0	1	0	1	0	0
Fleetwood Town			-	-	-	-	-	-	-	-
Doncaster			1	1	0	0	1	0	1	0
Oxford			2	1	1	0	1	1	1	1
Gillingham			-	-	-	-	-	-	-	-
AFC Wimbledon			2	1	0	1	0	2	0	1
Walsall			-	-	-	-	-	-	-	-
Rochdale			-	-	-	-	-	-	-	-
Accrington	L	W	4	2	0	2	1	3	1	2
Luton										
Wycombe	L	W	4	1	0	3	3	1	3	0
Coventry	L		1	0	0	1	0	1	0	0

Season	Division	Pos	P	W	D	L	F	A	GD	Pts
2017-18	League Two	2	46	25	13	8	94	46	+48	88
2016-17	League Two	4	46	20	17	9	70	43	+27	77
2015-16	League Two	11	46	19	9	18	63	61	+2	66

Over/Under 57%/43% 4th   **Both score** 50%/50% 19th

OXFORD UNITED

Nickname: The U's
Colours: Yellow
Ground: The Kassam Stadium (12,573)
Tel: 01865-337500   oufc.co.uk

Three managers – Pep Clotet, caretaker Derek Fazackerley and Karl Robinson – oversaw a disappointing season for Oxford United.

They pushed for promotion in 2016-17, ultimately finishing eighth, but failed to make the top half last year as consistency evaded them.

The U's appeared to struggle with the extra expectation last term and won just two of their eight games against the four relegated teams in League One.

Longest run without win/loss: 5/5
High/low league position: 6/17
Clean sheets: 13 **Yellows:** 69 **Reds:** 2
Avg attendance: 8,077 **Players used:** 30
Leading scorer: J Henry 10 (3,10) W Thomas 10 (4,10)
Key stat: Oxford suffered the biggest home defeat of any side in League One last season as they lost 7-0 against Wigan

	2017-18 H	A	P	W	D	L	OV	UN	BS	CS
Barnsley			-	-	-	-	-	-	-	-
Burton			3	0	1	2	1	2	2	0
Sunderland			-	-	-	-	-	-	-	-
Shrewsbury	D	L	3	1	1	1	0	3	1	1
Scunthorpe	D	L	3	1	1	1	1	2	2	0
Charlton	D	W	2	0	2	0	0	2	0	0
Plymouth	L	W	5	2	1	2	2	3	2	2
Portsmouth	W	L	4	1	2	1	1	3	1	2
Peterborough	W	W	2	2	0	0	2	0	2	0
Southend	W	D	5	2	0	3	1	4	1	2
Bradford		D	3	1	1	1	1	2	1	1
Blackpool	W	L	1	1	0	0	0	1	0	1
Bristol Rovers	L	W	5	0	0	5	2	3	2	0
Fleetwood Town	L	L	4	0	0	4	2	2	2	0
Doncaster	W	W	1	1	0	0	0	1	0	1
Oxford										
Gillingham	W	D	3	2	1	0	1	2	0	3
AFC Wimbledon	W	L	6	4	1	1	4	2	3	3
Walsall	L	L	2	0	1	1	1	1	1	1
Rochdale	W	D	4	3	1	0	2	2	2	2
Accrington			4	2	0	2	4	0	3	1
Luton			2	0	1	1	1	1	2	0
Wycombe			4	1	1	2	3	1	2	1
Coventry			1	1	0	0	0	1	0	0

Season	Division	Pos	P	W	D	L	F	A	GD	Pts
2017-18	League One	16	46	15	11	20	61	66	-5	56
2016-17	League One	8	46	20	9	17	65	52	+13	69
2015-16	League Two	2	46	24	14	8	84	41	+43	86

Over/Under 57%/43% 1st   **Both score** 54%/46% 7th

PETERBOROUGH

Nickname: The Posh
Colours: Blue
Ground: London Road (15,314)
Tel: 01733-563 947   theposh.com

Home to the league's top scorer Jack Marriott and leading assist maker Marcus Maddison, Peterborough's shortcomings were not going forward but in a defence that leaked more goals (60) than relegation-threatened Wimbledon (55) and Rochdale (57).

Steve Evans replaced Grant McCann in February after one win in eight matches but a poor end to the campaign condemned Posh to a sixth-successive season in League One.

Longest run without win/loss: 5/7
High/low league position: 2/11
Clean sheets: 9 **Yellows:** 76 **Reds:** 5
Avg attendance: 6,770 **Players used:** 25
Leading scorer: J Marriott 27 (8,22)
Key stat: Peterborough finished their campaign with five defeats in their last six games

	2017-18 H	A	Last six seasons at home P	W	D	L	OV	UN	BS	CS
Barnsley			3	3	0	0	3	0	3	0
Burton			1	0	0	1	0	1	0	0
Sunderland			-	-	-	-	-	-	-	-
Shrewsbury	W	L	4	3	1	0	1	3	2	2
Scunthorpe	D	L	4	0	1	3	2	2	2	0
Charlton	W	D	3	2	1	0	2	1	2	1
Plymouth	W	L	1	1	0	0	1	0	1	0
Portsmouth	W	L	1	1	0	0	1	0	1	0
Peterborough										
Southend	L	D	3	0	1	2	1	2	1	1
Bradford	L	W	5	2	0	3	3	2	2	1
Blackpool	L	D	3	1	0	2	2	1	2	0
Bristol Rovers	D	W	2	1	1	0	1	1	2	0
Fleetwood Town	W	W	4	3	0	1	2	2	2	2
Doncaster	D	D	3	1	2	0	1	2	1	2
Oxford	L	L	2	0	0	2	2	0	2	0
Gillingham	L	D	5	1	2	2	1	4	3	1
AFC Wimbledon	D	D	2	0	1	1	0	2	1	0
Walsall	W	D	5	1	4	0	1	4	3	2
Rochdale	L	L	4	2	0	2	3	1	3	0
Accrington			-	-	-	-	-	-	-	-
Luton			-	-	-	-	-	-	-	-
Wycombe			-	-	-	-	-	-	-	-
Coventry			4	2	1	1	1	3	2	1

Season	Division	Pos	P	W	D	L	F	A	GD	Pts
2017-18	League One	9	46	17	13	16	68	60	+8	64
2016-17	League One	11	46	17	11	18	62	62	0	62
2015-16	League One	13	46	19	6	21	82	73	+9	63

Over/Under 52%/48% 4th   **Both score** 65%/35% 1st

PLYMOUTH

Nickname: The Pilgrims
Colours: Green and white
Ground: Home Park (20,922)
Tel: 01752-562 561   pafc.co.uk

After winning just one of their opening 14 matches, few would have thought Plymouth would survive relegation, let alone push for a Championship return.

The Pilgrims went on a remarkable run of ten wins, three draws and one defeat in 14 matches between December and mid-February to propel them from bottom to sixth in the table.

Argyle failed to hold onto a playoff spot but finished in the highest position of the promoted sides.

Longest run without win/loss: 12/8
High/low league position: 5/24
Clean sheets: 13 **Yellows:** 56 **Reds:** 6
Avg attendance: 9,128 **Players used:** 33
Leading scorer: G Carey 14 (4,13)
Key stat: No team scored more goals from midfield than Plymouth (32) in League One last season

	2017-18 H	A	Last six seasons at home P	W	D	L	OV	UN	BS	CS
Barnsley			-	-	-	-	-	-	-	-
Burton			3	0	1	2	1	2	2	0
Sunderland			-	-	-	-	-	-	-	-
Shrewsbury	D	W	2	1	1	0	0	2	1	1
Scunthorpe	L	L	2	0	0	2	1	1	0	0
Charlton	W	L	1	1	0	0	0	1	0	1
Plymouth										
Portsmouth	D	L	5	1	3	1	3	2	3	2
Peterborough	W	L	1	1	0	0	1	0	1	0
Southend	W	D	4	2	2	0	1	3	2	2
Bradford	W	W	2	1	1	0	0	2	0	2
Blackpool	L	D	2	0	0	2	2	0	1	0
Bristol Rovers	W	L	4	2	2	0	1	3	3	1
Fleetwood Town	L	D	3	1	0	2	2	1	2	0
Doncaster	L	D	2	1	0	1	1	1	0	1
Oxford	L	W	5	0	1	4	3	2	2	0
Gillingham	W	L	2	1	1	0	2	0	2	0
AFC Wimbledon	W	W	5	1	1	3	4	1	5	0
Walsall	W	L	1	1	0	0	0	1	0	1
Rochdale	D	D	3	2	1	0	1	2	2	1
Accrington			5	2	2	1	0	5	0	4
Luton			3	0	0	3	1	2	0	0
Wycombe			5	0	1	4	2	3	1	0
Coventry			-	-	-	-	-	-	-	-

Season	Division	Pos	P	W	D	L	F	A	GD	Pts
2017-18	League One	7	46	19	11	16	58	59	-1	68
2016-17	League Two	2	46	26	9	11	71	46	+25	87
2015-16	League Two	5	46	24	9	13	72	46	+26	81

Over/Under 46%/54% 16th   **Both score** 52%/48% 12th

PORTSMOUTH

Nickname: Pompey
Colours: Blue and white
Ground: Fratton Park (20,688)
Tel: 023-9273-4129   portsmouthfc.co.uk

Brett Pitman's tally of 24 league goals was the second highest in League One last term but an over-reliance on the forward cost Portsmouth a higher finish.

Pompey had fewer goalscorers than any other side in England's third tier (ten) and scored the fewest goals in the division's top ten. The south coast club finished five points adrift of the playoff places and lost three of their last four matches, including a 1-0 defeat to relegated Bury in their final away game.

Longest run without win/loss: 5/6
High/low league position: 6/15
Clean sheets: 14 **Yellows:** 63 **Reds:** 6
Avg attendance: 13,160 **Players used:** 31
Leading scorer: B Pitman 24 (8,16)
Key stat: Portmouth's squad had the youngest average age in the division at 24

	2017-18 H	2017-18 A	P	W	D	L	OV	UN	BS	CS
Barnsley	-	-	-	-	-	-	-	-	-	-
Burton			2	0	2	0	0	2	1	1
Sunderland	-	-	-	-	-	-	-	-	-	-
Shrewsbury	L	L	3	1	0	2	1	2	1	0
Scunthorpe	D	L	3	1	1	1	2	1	3	0
Charlton	L	W	1	0	0	1	0	1	0	0
Plymouth	W	D	5	2	2	1	3	2	4	1
Portsmouth										
Peterborough	W	L	1	1	0	0	0	1	0	1
Southend	W	L	3	1	0	2	2	1	2	1
Bradford	L	L	1	0	0	1	0	1	0	0
Blackpool	L	W	2	1	0	1	0	2	0	1
Bristol Rovers	W	L	3	3	0	0	3	0	2	1
Fleetwood Town	W	W	2	1	0	1	1	1	1	0
Doncaster	D	L	3	0	1	2	2	1	2	0
Oxford	W	L	4	1	1	2	2	2	1	2
Gillingham	L	W	1	0	0	1	0	1	0	0
AFC Wimbledon	W	W	4	2	1	1	3	1	3	2
Walsall	D	W	2	0	1	1	1	1	2	0
Rochdale	W	D	2	2	0	0	1	1	0	2
Accrington			4	2	1	1	3	1	1	3
Luton			3	2	1	0	0	3	0	3
Wycombe			4	2	2	0	3	1	4	0
Coventry			1	1	0	0	0	1	0	1

Season	Division	Pos	P	W	D	L	F	A	GD	Pts
2017-18	League One	8	46	20	6	20	57	56	+1	66
2016-17	League Two	1	46	26	9	11	79	40	+39	87
2015-16	League Two	6	46	21	15	10	75	44	+31	78

Over/Under 48%/52% 13th   **Both score** 46%/54% 18th

ROCHDALE

Nickname: The Dale
Colours: Blue and black
Ground: Spotland Stadium (9,961)
Tel: 0844-826-1907   rochdaleafc.co.uk

Rochdale ended a point above the drop zone as they followed a top-half finish in 2016-17 with a relegation-threatened 2017-18 campaign.

It was a lack of ruthlessness that cost Dale as they struggled to see games out. No team drew more matches than Keith Hill's men last term and they won just 11 of the 24 games which they led.

They did, however, concede the fewest goals among the division's bottom six as an end-of-season surge secured survival.

Longest run without win/loss: 7/4
High/low league position: 17/24
Clean sheets: 17 **Yellows:** 66 **Reds:** 3
Avg attendance: 5,585 **Players used:** 33
Leading scorer: I Henderson 13 (4,10)
Key stat: Rochdale just lost two of their final 11 matches

	2017-18 H	2017-18 A	P	W	D	L	OV	UN	BS	CS
Barnsley			2	1	0	1	1	1	0	1
Burton			3	1	1	1	1	2	2	0
Sunderland	-	-	-	-	-	-	-	-	-	-
Shrewsbury	W	L	3	3	0	0	3	0	3	0
Scunthorpe	D	D	5	3	1	1	4	1	4	0
Charlton	W	L	2	1	1	0	1	1	1	1
Plymouth	D	D	3	2	1	0	1	2	1	2
Portsmouth	D	L	2	1	1	0	2	0	1	1
Peterborough	W	W	4	2	0	2	1	3	1	2
Southend	D	D	5	3	1	1	4	1	2	2
Bradford	D	L	5	0	3	2	1	4	3	1
Blackpool	L	D	2	1	0	1	2	0	1	1
Bristol Rovers	W	L	4	3	1	0	1	3	1	3
Fleetwood Town	L	D	6	2	1	3	2	4	2	2
Doncaster	W	L	3	1	1	3	0	3	0	0
Oxford	D	L	4	2	1	1	2	2	0	3
Gillingham	W	L	5	2	3	0	2	3	4	1
AFC Wimbledon	D	D	4	0	2	2	1	3	3	0
Walsall	D	W	4	2	1	1	3	1	2	2
Rochdale										
Accrington			2	1	0	1	2	0	1	0
Luton	-	-	-	-	-	-	-	-	-	-
Wycombe			2	2	0	0	2	0	2	0
Coventry			3	2	1	0	0	3	0	3

Season	Division	Pos	P	W	D	L	F	A	GD	Pts
2017-18	League One	20	46	11	18	17	49	57	-8	51
2016-17	League One	9	46	19	12	15	71	62	+9	69
2015-16	League One	10	46	19	12	15	68	61	+7	69

Over/Under 39%/61% 20th   **Both score** 48%/52% 16th

Nickname: The Iron
Colours: Claret and blue
Ground: Glanford Park (9,088)
Tel: 01724-848 077   scunthorpe-united.co.uk

It was another year of heartache for Scunthorpe as they lost a playoff semi-final for a second-consecutive season.

Graham Alexander was dismissed in March after the Iron won just once in 13 matches, with Nick Daws taking charge as caretaker to steer them towards a fifth-placed finish. Daws then took the position on a permanent basis.

The Iron tended to struggle in big games, recording just two wins against the rest of the top six.

Longest run without win/loss: 10/8
High/low league position: 3/11
Clean sheets: 15 **Yellows:** 67 **Reds:** 2
Avg attendance: 6,154 **Players used:** 30
Leading scorer: J Morris 11 (5,9)
Key stat: Scunthopre topped the form table for the final six matches of the season, winning four and drawing two

	2017-18 H	2017-18 A	P	W	D	L	OV	UN	BS	CS
Barnsley			2	1	0	1	0	2	0	1
Burton			2	2	0	0	0	2	0	2
Sunderland			-	-	-	-	-	-	-	-
Shrewsbury	L	L	4	1	1	2	2	2	2	1
Scunthorpe										
Charlton	W	W	2	1	1	0	0	2	0	2
Plymouth	W	W	2	2	0	0	0	2	0	2
Portsmouth	W	D	3	3	0	0	2	1	2	1
Peterborough	W	D	4	2	1	1	2	2	2	1
Southend	W	L	4	3	1	0	3	1	2	2
Bradford	D	W	4	1	2	1	1	3	3	0
Blackpool	D	W	2	0	1	1	0	2	0	1
Bristol Rovers	W	D	3	2	1	0	1	2	2	1
Fleetwood Town	D	W	5	1	2	2	0	5	1	2
Doncaster	D	W	4	1	1	2	2	2	3	1
Oxford	W	D	3	2	1	0	0	3	1	2
Gillingham	L	D	4	2	1	1	3	1	2	2
AFC Wimbledon	D	D	3	0	2	1	1	2	2	1
Walsall	W	L	5	2	2	1	1	4	2	2
Rochdale	D	D	5	3	2	0	3	2	4	1
Accrington			1	0	0	1	0	1	0	0
Luton			-	-	-	-	-	-	-	-
Wycombe			1	0	1	0	0	1	0	1
Coventry			4	3	0	1	3	1	3	1

Season	Division	Pos	P	W	D	L	F	A	GD	Pts
2017-18	League One	5	46	19	17	10	65	50	+15	74
2016-17	League One	3	46	24	10	12	80	54	+26	82
2015-16	League One	7	46	21	11	14	60	47	+13	74

Over/Under 39%/61% 20th   **Both score** 57%/43% 5th

Nickname: The Shrews
Colours: Blue and amber
Ground: Greenhous Meadow (9,875)
Tel: 01743-289177   shrewsburytown.com

Shrewsbury's campaign was so impressive that it earned manager Paul Hurst a switch to Championship outfit Ipswich Town.

The Shrews finished third in the league but went on to lose the playoff final against Rotherham in extra-time.

Only champions Wigan conceded fewer goals than Salop, who managed to keep Charlton quiet in both legs in the playoffs and started their league season unbeaten in 15 matches.

Longest run without win/loss: 3/15
High/low league position: 1/3
Clean sheets: 16 **Yellows:** 65 **Reds:** 4
Avg attendance: 6,821 **Players used:** 26
Leading scorer: S Payne 11 (4,11)
Key stat: Shrewsbury occupied top spot in League One at the close of a total 15 match days

	2017-18 H	2017-18 A	P	W	D	L	OV	UN	BS	CS
Barnsley			1	0	0	1	1	0	0	0
Burton			2	1	0	1	0	2	0	1
Sunderland			-	-	-	-	-	-	-	-
Shrewsbury										
Scunthorpe	W	W	4	1	1	2	1	3	1	1
Charlton	L	W	2	1	0	1	1	1	1	0
Plymouth	L	D	2	0	0	2	1	1	1	0
Portsmouth	W	W	3	3	0	0	2	1	2	1
Peterborough	W	L	4	1	1	2	3	1	4	0
Southend	W	D	4	2	1	1	1	3	2	2
Bradford	L	D	4	2	1	1	1	3	2	1
Blackpool	W	D	2	2	0	0	0	2	0	2
Bristol Rovers	W	W	2	2	0	0	1	1	0	2
Fleetwood Town	W	W	3	1	1	1	0	3	1	1
Doncaster	D	W	3	0	1	2	3	0	3	0
Oxford	W	W	3	3	0	0	1	2	1	2
Gillingham	D	W	4	1	2	1	2	2	3	1
AFC Wimbledon	W	W	3	3	0	0	1	2	1	2
Walsall	W	D	5	2	1	2	1	4	2	2
Rochdale	W	L	3	3	0	0	1	2	1	2
Accrington			1	1	0	0	1	0	0	1
Luton			1	1	0	0	0	1	0	1
Wycombe			1	0	1	0	0	1	0	1
Coventry			4	2	2	0	2	2	3	1

Season	Division	Pos	P	W	D	L	F	A	GD	Pts
2017-18	League One	3	46	25	12	9	60	39	+21	87
2016-17	League One	18	46	13	12	21	46	63	-17	51
2015-16	League One	20	46	13	11	22	58	79	-21	50

Over/Under 35%/65% 24th   **Both score** 52%/48% 12th

SOUTHEND

Nickname: The Shrimpers
Colours: Blue
Ground: Roots Hall (12,392)
Tel: 01702-304-050   southendunited.co.uk

Southend failed to string together more than three-successive victories last season and lost away from home to eight of the nine sides above them in the final standings.

Four-consecutive defeats in January ended Phil Brown's five-year run in the Shrimpers' dugout, with Chris Powell taking his place. United had one of the oldest squads in the division and struggled up front, with Simon Cox finishing top scorer on just ten goals.

Longest run without win/loss: 7/5
High/low league position: 9/20
Clean sheets: 15 **Yellows:** 67 **Reds:** 3
Avg attendance: 7,357 **Players used:** 30
Leading scorer: S Cox 10 (4,8)
Key stat: After switching from Brown to Powell as manager, Southend's average points per game increased from 0.6 to 2.6

	2017-18		Last six seasons at home							
	H	A	P	W	D	L	OV	UN	BS	CS
Barnsley			1	1	0	0	1	0	1	0
Burton			4	2	1	1	1	3	1	2
Sunderland			-	-	-	-	-	-	-	-
Shrewsbury	L	L	4	1	1	2	1	3	2	1
Scunthorpe	W	L	4	3	0	1	3	1	3	0
Charlton	W	L	2	1	1	0	1	1	2	0
Plymouth	D	L	4	1	2	1	0	4	1	2
Portsmouth	W	L	3	3	0	0	2	1	2	1
Peterborough	D	W	3	1	2	0	1	2	3	0
Southend										
Bradford	L	W	4	1	1	2	3	1	2	1
Blackpool	W	D	2	2	0	0	1	1	1	1
Bristol Rovers	D	L	4	0	4	0	0	4	2	2
Fleetwood Town	L	W	5	1	2	2	2	3	3	1
Doncaster	D	L	2	0	1	1	1	1	0	1
Oxford	D	L	5	3	2	0	2	3	3	2
Gillingham	W	D	4	1	1	2	2	2	2	1
AFC Wimbledon	W	L	5	2	0	3	2	3	1	2
Walsall	L	W	3	1	0	2	2	1	1	0
Rochdale	D	D	5	2	3	0	3	2	4	1
Accrington			3	1	0	2	1	2	1	1
Luton			1	1	0	0	0	1	0	1
Wycombe			3	1	2	0	1	2	2	1
Coventry			2	2	0	0	2	0	1	1

Season	Division	Pos	P	W	D	L	F	A	GD	Pts
2017-18	League One	10	46	17	12	17	58	62	-4	63
2016-17	League One	7	46	20	12	14	70	53	+17	72
2015-16	League One	15	46	16	11	19	58	64	-6	59

Over/Under 52%/48% 4th   **Both score** 46%/54% 18th

SUNDERLAND

Nickname: Mackems/Black Cats
Colours: Red and white
Ground: Stadium of Light (49,000)
Tel: 0371-911-1200   safc.com

Sunderland's points tally of 37 was the highest of a bottom-placed Championship side since 2014, but their relegation to the third tier was justified.

The Mackems went through two permanent managers in Simon Grayson and Chris Coleman and struggled to get going after one win in their first 18 league matches. Key players Jermain Defoe and Jordan Pickford left at the start of the season and the Black Cats failed to restore any squad cohesion.

Longest run without win/loss: 16/3
High/low league position: 21/24
Clean sheets: 6 **Yellows:** 92 **Reds:** 6
Avg attendance: 24,212 **Players used:** 37
Leading scorer: L Grabban 12 (2,9)
Key stat: Sunderland won just three league games at the Stadium of Light last term

	2017-18		Last six seasons at home							
	H	A	P	W	D	L	OV	UN	BS	CS
Barnsley	L	L	1	0	0	1	0	1	0	0
Burton	L	W	1	0	0	1	1	0	1	0
Sunderland										
Shrewsbury			-	-	-	-	-	-	-	-
Scunthorpe			-	-	-	-	-	-	-	-
Charlton			-	-	-	-	-	-	-	-
Plymouth			-	-	-	-	-	-	-	-
Portsmouth			-	-	-	-	-	-	-	-
Peterborough			-	-	-	-	-	-	-	-
Southend			-	-	-	-	-	-	-	-
Bradford			-	-	-	-	-	-	-	-
Blackpool			-	-	-	-	-	-	-	-
Bristol Rovers			-	-	-	-	-	-	-	-
Fleetwood Town			-	-	-	-	-	-	-	-
Doncaster			-	-	-	-	-	-	-	-
Oxford			-	-	-	-	-	-	-	-
Gillingham			-	-	-	-	-	-	-	-
AFC Wimbledon			-	-	-	-	-	-	-	-
Walsall			-	-	-	-	-	-	-	-
Rochdale			-	-	-	-	-	-	-	-
Accrington			-	-	-	-	-	-	-	-
Luton			-	-	-	-	-	-	-	-
Wycombe			-	-	-	-	-	-	-	-
Coventry			-	-	-	-	-	-	-	-

Season	Division	Pos	P	W	D	L	F	A	GD	Pts
2017-18	Championship	24	46	7	16	23	52	80	-28	37
2016-17	Premier League	20	38	6	6	26	29	69	-40	24
2015-16	Premier League	17	38	9	12	17	48	62	-14	39

Over/Under 52%/48% 5th   **Both score** 59%/41% 2nd

LEAGUE ONE

WALSALL

Nickname: The Saddlers
Colours: Red and white
Ground: Banks's Stadium (11,300)
Tel: 01922-622-791   saddlers.co.uk

Walsall's 19th-placed finish was the lowest position they had occupied since the opening day and the Saddlers were on course for mid-table prior to a collapse in the second half of the season.

Dean Keates replaced Jon Whitney in mid-March but struggled to push the club up the table.

They lost nine of their final 14 games, but slender victories in vital games ag relegation rivals Bury and Northampton guided the Midlands outfit to safety.

Longest run without win/loss: 5/4
High/low league position: 11/19
Clean sheets: 8 **Yellows:** 55 **Reds:** 1
Avg attendance: 6,080 **Players used:** 28
Leading scorer: E Oztumer 15 (7,12)
Key stat: No team scored more first-half goals than Walsall last season

| | 2017-18 | | Last six seasons at home | | | | | | | |
	H	A	P	W	D	L	OV	UN	BS	CS
Barnsley			2	1	0	1	2	0	2	0
Burton			1	1	0	0	0	1	0	1
Sunderland			-	-	-	-	-	-	-	-
Shrewsbury	D	L	5	4	1	0	3	2	4	1
Scunthorpe	W	L	5	1	1	3	3	2	3	2
Charlton	D	L	2	0	1	1	2	0	2	0
Plymouth	W	L	1	1	0	0	1	0	1	0
Portsmouth	L	D	2	1	0	1	0	2	0	1
Peterborough	D	L	5	3	2	0	0	5	1	4
Southend	L	W	3	1	1	1	0	3	0	2
Bradford	D	D	5	1	3	1	2	3	3	1
Blackpool	D	D	2	0	2	0	0	2	2	0
Bristol Rovers	D	L	2	1	1	0	1	1	1	1
Fleetwood Town	W	L	4	3	0	1	2	2	2	1
Doncaster	W	W	4	3	0	1	3	1	1	2
Oxford	W	W	2	1	1	0	1	1	2	0
Gillingham	L	D	5	1	2	2	2	3	4	0
AFC Wimbledon	L	W	2	1	0	1	2	0	2	0
Walsall										
Rochdale	L	D	4	1	0	3	3	1	1	0
Accrington			-	-	-	-	-	-	-	-
Luton			-	-	-	-	-	-	-	-
Wycombe			-	-	-	-	-	-	-	-
Coventry			5	2	1	2	2	3	2	1

Season	Division	Pos	P	W	D	L	F	A	GD	Pts
2017-18	League One	19	46	13	13	20	53	66	-13	52
2016-17	League One	14	46	14	16	16	51	58	-7	58
2015-16	League One	3	46	24	12	10	71	49	+22	84

Over/Under 50%/50% 9th   **Both score** 59%/41% 4th

WYCOMBE

Nickname: The Chairboys
Colours: Sky and navy blue
Ground: Adams Park (10,000)
Tel: 01494-472-100   wwfc.com

Wycombe were the second-top scorers in League Two and also shipped the most goals in the top eight last term so it was no surprise to see them secure promotion in dramatic fashion.

Trailing 1-0 to Chesterfield on the penultimate weekend, Wycombe fought back to win 2-1 as they sealed a return to League One after a six-year absence.

Adebayo Akinfenwa netted 17 league goals for Wycombe, who lost just three of their last 20 matches to seal promotion.

Longest run without win/loss: 5/8
High/low league position: 2/12
Clean sheets: 14 **Yellows:** 81 **Reds:** 1
Avg attendance: 4,346 **Players used:** 29
Leading scorer: A Akinfenwa 17 (8,14)
Key stat: Wycombe topped the League Two away table last season, with 12 wins from 23 matches on the road

| | 2017-18 | | Last six seasons at home | | | | | | | |
	H	A	P	W	D	L	OV	UN	BS	CS
Barnsley			-	-	-	-	-	-	-	-
Burton			3	1	0	2	3	0	2	1
Sunderland			-	-	-	-	-	-	-	-
Shrewsbury			1	1	0	0	0	1	0	1
Scunthorpe			1	0	1	0	0	1	1	0
Charlton			-	-	-	-	-	-	-	-
Plymouth			5	0	2	3	1	4	3	0
Portsmouth			4	1	2	1	1	3	1	2
Peterborough			-	-	-	-	-	-	-	-
Southend			3	2	0	1	3	0	3	0
Bradford			1	0	0	1	1	0	0	0
Blackpool			1	0	1	0	0	1	0	1
Bristol Rovers			3	2	0	1	1	2	1	2
Fleetwood Town			2	1	1	0	0	2	1	1
Doncaster			1	1	0	0	1	0	1	0
Oxford			4	1	0	3	3	1	3	0
Gillingham			1	0	0	1	0	1	0	0
AFC Wimbledon			4	1	0	3	2	2	1	1
Walsall			-	-	-	-	-	-	-	-
Rochdale			2	0	0	2	1	1	1	0
Accrington	L	L	6	0	3	3	2	4	2	1
Luton	L	W	4	0	2	2	1	3	3	0
Wycombe										
Coventry	L	L	1	0	0	1	0	1	0	0

Season	Division	Pos	P	W	D	L	F	A	GD	Pts
2017-18	League Two	3	46	24	12	10	79	60	+19	84
2016-17	League Two	9	46	19	12	15	58	53	+5	69
2015-16	League Two	13	46	17	13	16	45	44	+1	64

Over/Under 61%/39% 2nd   **Both score** 61%/39% 2nd

League One stats 2017-18
Key Points in all tables (except the league table) do not include any deductions imposed by the league.
POS H A Overall league position, rank from home games only, rank from away games only **Sup** Average match supremacy **GFA** Goals For Average **GAA** Goals Against Average **PGA** Points Gained Average

LEAGUE ONE

League One 2017-18				Home					Away						
Pos	H	A		P	W	D	L	F	A	W	D	L	F	A	GD	Pts
1	3	1	Wigan (P)	46	13	8	2	37	11	16	3	4	52	18	60	98
2	1	2	Blackburn (P)	46	15	6	2	46	20	13	6	4	36	20	42	96
3	4	3	Shrewsbury	46	14	4	5	32	17	11	8	4	28	22	21	87
4	2	7	Rotherham (P)	46	15	3	5	45	23	9	4	10	28	30	20	79
5	12	4	Scunthorpe	46	9	8	6	28	23	10	9	4	37	27	15	74
6	10	5	Charlton	46	11	6	6	31	24	9	5	9	27	27	7	71
7	6	12	Plymouth	46	13	3	7	37	30	6	8	9	21	29	-1	68
8	8	10	Portsmouth	46	12	3	8	33	21	8	3	12	24	35	1	66
9	7	14	Peterborough	46	12	4	7	37	26	5	9	9	31	34	8	64
10	5	21	Southend	46	12	7	4	38	21	5	5	13	20	41	-4	63
11	15	6	Bradford	46	9	4	10	28	32	9	5	9	29	35	-10	63
12	11	13	Blackpool	46	9	8	6	37	29	6	7	10	23	26	5	60
13	9	19	Bristol Rovers	46	11	6	6	38	30	5	5	13	22	36	-6	59
14	20	9	Fleetwood	46	7	6	10	32	35	9	3	11	27	33	-9	57
15	16	11	Doncaster	46	7	9	7	30	25	6	8	9	22	27	0	56
16	13	16	Oxford	46	9	6	8	34	32	6	5	12	27	34	-5	56
17	21	8	Gillingham	46	5	11	7	26	26	8	6	9	24	29	-5	56
18	19	15	AFC Wimbledon	46	8	6	9	25	30	5	8	10	22	28	-11	53
19	14	22	Walsall	46	9	6	8	30	31	4	7	12	23	35	-13	52
20	17	17	Rochdale	46	6	12	5	24	24	5	6	12	25	33	-8	51
21	18	20	Oldham (R)	46	8	6	9	31	33	3	11	9	27	42	-17	50
22	23	18	Northampton (R)	46	7	5	11	20	35	5	6	12	23	42	-34	47
23	22	23	MK Dons (R)	46	6	8	9	24	30	5	4	14	19	39	-26	45
24	24	24	Bury (R)	46	7	4	12	20	30	1	8	14	21	41	-30	36

Best attack

		GF	GFA
1	Wigan	89	1.93
2	Blackburn	82	1.78
3	Rotherham	73	1.59
4	Peterborough	68	1.48
5	Scunthorpe	65	1.41
6	Oxford Utd	61	1.33
7	Shrewsbury	60	1.3
8	Blackpool	60	1.3
9	Bristol Rovers	60	1.3
10	Fleetwood	59	1.28
11	Charlton	58	1.26
12	Plymouth	58	1.26
13	Southend	58	1.26
14	Oldham	58	1.26
15	Portsmouth	57	1.24
16	Bradford	57	1.24
17	Walsall	53	1.15
18	Doncaster	52	1.13
19	Gillingham	50	1.09
20	Rochdale	49	1.07
21	Wimbledon	47	1.02
22	Northampton	43	0.93
23	MK Dons	43	0.93
24	Bury	41	0.89

Best defence

		GA	GAA
1	Wigan	29	0.63
2	Shrewsbury	39	0.85
3	Blackburn	40	0.87
4	Scunthorpe	50	1.09
5	Charlton	51	1.11
6	Doncaster	52	1.13
7	Rotherham	53	1.15
8	Blackpool	55	1.2
9	Gillingham	55	1.2
10	Portsmouth	56	1.22
11	Rochdale	57	1.24
12	Wimbledon	58	1.26
13	Plymouth	59	1.28
14	Peterborough	60	1.3
15	Southend	62	1.35
16	Bristol Rovers	66	1.43
17	Oxford Utd	66	1.43
18	Walsall	66	1.43
19	Bradford	67	1.46
20	Fleetwood	68	1.48
21	MK Dons	69	1.5
22	Bury	71	1.54
23	Oldham	75	1.63
24	Northampton	77	1.67

Top scorers

	Team	Goals scored
J Marriott	Peterborough	27 ▐▐▐▐▐▐▐▐▐▐▐▐▐▐▐▐▐▐▐▐▐▐▐▐▐▐▐
B Pitman	Portsmouth	24 ▐▐▐▐▐▐▐▐▐▐▐▐▐▐▐▐▐▐▐▐▐▐▐▐
W Grigg	Wigan	19 ▐▐▐▐▐▐▐▐▐▐▐▐▐▐▐▐▐▐▐
B Dack	Blackburn	18 ▐▐▐▐▐▐▐▐▐▐▐▐▐▐▐▐▐▐
T Eaves	Gillingham	17 ▐▐▐▐▐▐▐▐▐▐▐▐▐▐▐▐▐
E Oztumer	Walsall	15 ▐▐▐▐▐▐▐▐▐▐▐▐▐▐▐
N Powell	Wigan	15 ▐▐▐▐▐▐▐▐▐▐▐▐▐▐▐
C Wyke	Bradford	15 ▐▐▐▐▐▐▐▐▐▐▐▐▐▐▐

Over 2.5 goals

	H	A	%
Oldham	12	14	57%
Oxford Utd	14	12	57%
Bristol Rovers	14	11	54%
Blackburn, Fleetwood, S'thend, N'hampton, Peterboro'			52%

Under 2.5 goals

	H	A	%
Shrewsbury	17	13	65%
Charlton	13	16	63%
Wimbledon	13	15	61%
Rochdale	15	13	61%
Scunthorpe	15	13	61%

Both to score

	H	A	%
Peterborough	13	17	65%
Oldham	15	14	63%
Bristol Rovers	19	9	61%
Walsall	13	14	59%
Blackpool	16	10	57%
Scunthorpe	13	13	57%

Both not to score

	H	A	%
Wigan		17	12	63%
Wimbledon	13	13	57%
Doncaster	12	13	54%
Portsmouth	13	12	54%
Southend	10	15	54%
Bury, Charlton			54%

League One results 2017-18

	AFC Wimbledon	Blackburn	Blackpool	Bradford	Bristol Rovers	Bury	Charlton	Doncaster	Fleetwood	Gillingham	MK Dons	Northampton	Oldham	Oxford Utd	Peterborough	Plymouth	Portsmouth	Rochdale	Rotherham	Scunthorpe	Shrewsbury	Southend	Walsall	Wigan
AFC Wimbledon		0-3	2-0	2-1	1-0	2-2	1-0	2-0	0-1	1-1	0-2	1-3	2-2	2-1	2-2	0-1	0-2	0-0	3-1	1-1	0-1	2-0	1-2	0-4
Blackburn	0-1		3-0	2-0	2-1	2-0	2-0	1-3	2-2	1-0	4-1	1-1	2-2	2-1	3-1	1-1	3-0	2-0	2-0	2-2	3-1	1-0	3-1	2-2
Blackpool	1-0	2-4		5-0	0-0	2-1	1-0	1-2	2-1	1-1	1-0	3-0	2-1	3-1	1-1	2-2	2-3	0-0	1-2	2-3	1-1	1-1	2-2	1-3
Bradford	0-4	0-1	2-1		3-1	2-2	0-1	2-0	0-3	1-0	2-0	1-2	1-1	3-2	1-3	0-1	3-1	4-3	1-0	1-2	0-0	0-2	1-1	0-1
Bristol Rovers	1-3	1-1	3-1	3-1		2-1	1-1	0-1	3-1	1-1	2-0	1-1	2-3	0-1	1-4	2-1	2-1	3-2	2-1	1-1	1-2	3-0	2-1	1-1
Bury	2-1	0-3	1-1	3-1	2-3		0-1	0-1	0-2	2-3	2-2	3-0	0-1	0-0	1-0	0-2	0-3	0-1	1-0	0-0	1-0	0-0	1-0	0-2
Charlton	1-0	1-0	1-1	1-1	1-0	1-1		1-0	0-0	1-2	2-2	4-1	1-0	2-3	2-2	2-0	0-1	2-1	3-1	0-1	0-2	2-1	1-0	3-3
Doncaster	0-0	0-1	3-3	2-0	1-3	3-3	1-1		3-0	0-0	2-1	3-0	1-1	0-1	0-0	1-1	2-1	2-0	1-1	0-1	1-2	4-1	0-3	0-1
Fleetwood	2-0	1-2	0-0	1-2	2-0	3-2	1-3	0-0		0-2	1-1	2-0	2-2	2-0	2-3	1-1	1-2	2-2	2-0	2-3	1-2	2-4	2-0	0-4
Gillingham	2-2	0-0	0-3	0-1	4-1	1-1	1-0	0-0	2-1		1-2	1-2	0-0	1-1	1-1	5-2	0-1	2-1	0-1	0-0	1-2	3-3	0-0	1-1
MK Dons	0-0	1-2	0-0	1-4	0-1	2-1	1-2	1-2	1-0	1-0		0-0	4-4	1-1	1-0	0-1	1-2	3-2	3-2	0-2	1-1	1-1	1-1	0-1
Northampton	0-1	1-1	1-0	0-1	0-6	0-0	0-4	1-0	0-1	1-2	2-1		2-2	0-0	1-4	2-0	3-1	0-1	0-3	0-3	1-1	3-1	2-1	0-1
Oldham	0-0	1-0	2-1	2-1	1-1	2-1	3-4	0-0	1-2	1-1	1-0	5-1		0-2	3-2	1-2	0-2	3-1	1-1	2-3	1-2	0-3	1-1	0-2
Oxford Utd	3-0	2-4	1-0	2-2	1-2	1-2	1-1	1-0	0-1	3-0	3-1	1-2	0-0		2-1	0-1	3-0	2-1	3-3	1-1	1-1	2-0	1-2	0-7
Peterborough	1-1	2-3	0-1	1-3	1-3	3-0	4-1	1-1	2-0	0-1	2-0	2-0	1-4	2-1		2-1	0-1	2-1	2-2	1-0	0-1	2-1	3-2	
Plymouth	4-2	2-0	1-3	1-0	3-2	3-0	2-0	0-3	1-2	2-1	0-1	2-0	4-1	0-4	2-1		0-0	1-1	2-1	0-4	1-1	4-0	1-0	1-3
Portsmouth	2-1	1-2	0-2	0-1	3-0	1-0	0-1	2-2	4-1	1-3	2-0	3-1	1-2	3-0	2-0	1-0		2-0	0-1	1-1	0-1	1-0	1-1	2-1
Rochdale	1-1	0-3	1-2	1-1	1-0	0-0	1-0	2-1	0-2	3-0	0-0	2-2	0-0	0-0	2-0	1-1	3-3		0-1	1-1	3-1	0-0	1-1	1-4
Rotherham	2-0	1-1	1-0	2-0	2-0	3-2	0-2	2-1	3-2	1-3	2-1	1-0	5-1	3-1	1-1	1-1	1-0	0-1		2-0	1-2	5-0	5-1	1-3
Scunthorpe	1-1	0-1	0-0	1-1	1-0	1-0	2-0	1-1	1-1	1-3	2-2	2-2	0-2	1-0	2-1	2-0	2-0	1-1	1-2		1-2	3-1	1-0	1-2
Shrewsbury	1-0	1-1	1-0	0-1	4-0	1-1	0-2	2-2	1-0	1-1	0-1	1-0	1-0	3-2	3-1	1-2	2-0	3-2	0-1	2-0		1-0	2-0	1-0
Southend	1-0	2-1	2-1	1-2	0-0	1-0	3-1	0-0	1-2	4-0	4-0	2-2	2-0	1-1	1-1	1-1	3-1	0-0	2-0	3-2	1-2		0-3	3-1
Walsall	2-3	1-2	1-1	3-3	0-0	1-0	2-2	4-2	4-2	0-1	1-0	1-0	2-1	2-1	1-1	2-1	0-1	0-3	1-2	1-0	1-1	0-1		0-3
Wigan	1-1	0-0	0-2	1-2	3-0	4-1	0-0	3-0	2-0	2-0	5-1	1-0	3-0	0-0	1-0	1-1	1-0	0-0	3-3	0-0	3-0	2-0		

Record when first to score

		P	W	D	L	F	A	Sup	PGA	Pts
1	Wigan	30	27	2	1	73	9	2.13	2.8	83
2	Blackburn	30	25	5	0	65	21	1.47	2.7	80
3	Gillingham	12	10	2	0	25	8	1.42	2.7	32
4	Portsmouth	21	18	1	2	38	15	1.10	2.6	55
5	Shrewsbury	29	22	5	2	44	20	0.83	2.4	71
6	Charlton	26	19	6	1	49	23	1.00	2.4	63
7	Rotherham	26	20	3	3	56	20	1.38	2.4	63
8	Southend	24	16	6	2	45	22	0.96	2.3	54
9	Scunthorpe	24	16	6	2	41	18	0.96	2.3	54
10	Plymouth	23	15	7	1	42	19	1.00	2.3	52
11	Oxford Utd	17	12	3	2	31	9	1.29	2.3	39
12	Bradford	25	17	5	3	47	29	0.72	2.2	56
13	Blackpool	20	14	2	4	40	20	1.00	2.2	44
14	Wimbledon	20	12	8	0	37	19	0.90	2.2	44
15	Northampton	17	11	5	1	32	19	0.76	2.2	38
16	Oldham	16	10	5	1	36	22	0.88	2.2	35
17	Fleetwood	23	16	1	6	42	23	0.83	2.1	49
18	Bury	10	6	3	1	15	9	0.60	2.1	21
19	Peterborough	25	14	5	6	49	29	0.80	1.9	47
20	Walsall	21	11	7	3	33	21	0.57	1.9	40
21	Doncaster	19	10	6	3	32	17	0.79	1.9	36
22	MK Dons	16	9	3	4	18	13	0.31	1.9	30
23	Bristol Rovers	16	8	6	2	31	16	0.94	1.9	30
24	Rochdale	21	9	6	6	33	26	0.33	1.6	33

Record when keeping a clean sheet

		P	W	D	F	Sup	PGA	Pts
1	Rotherham	15	14	1	26	1.73	2.9	43
2	Portsmouth	14	13	1	22	1.57	2.9	40
3	Blackburn	17	15	2	30	1.76	2.8	47
4	Shrewsbury	16	14	2	21	1.31	2.8	44
5	Bradford	9	8	1	10	1.11	2.8	25
6	Scunthorpe	15	13	2	22	1.47	2.7	41
7	Charlton	14	12	2	18	1.29	2.7	38
8	Plymouth	13	11	2	19	1.46	2.7	35
9	Wigan	27	22	5	51	1.89	2.6	71
10	Fleetwood	15	12	3	22	1.47	2.6	39
11	Peterborough	9	7	2	14	1.56	2.6	23
12	Oxford Utd	13	10	3	21	1.62	2.5	33
13	Walsall	8	6	2	10	1.25	2.5	20
14	Southend	15	10	5	21	1.40	2.3	35
15	Blackpool	14	9	5	19	1.36	2.3	32
16	Wimbledon	12	8	4	14	1.17	2.3	28
17	MK Dons	11	7	4	9	0.82	2.3	25
18	Rochdale	17	9	8	15	0.88	2.1	35
19	Bristol Rovers	7	4	3	12	1.71	2.1	15
20	Doncaster	14	7	7	15	1.07	2	28
21	Bury	8	4	4	6	0.75	2	16
22	Northampton	6	3	3	4	0.67	2	12
23	Gillingham	10	4	6	5	0.50	1.8	18
24	Oldham	8	3	5	4	0.50	1.8	14

Lincoln can put playoff heartbreak behind them with bold title challenge

Accrington were shock 33-1 winners of League Two last season but punters are advised to look much further up the betting for potential title candidates this season, with two teams worth backing in the outright market, writes Mark Langdon. All the summer money has been for Notts County and, alongside MK Dons, they are seen as the strongest challengers, but Lincoln and Mansfield appear better bets.

Lincoln enjoyed an excellent first season back in the Football League, finishing seventh, and that was despite becoming slightly distracted by a first ever trip to Wembley which culminated in lifting the Checkatrade Trophy, beating Shrewsbury in the final.

There was to be no double as the Imps fell short in the playoffs but Danny Cowley's direct side look primed for another strong challenge, aided by the cash from that Wembley visit and the season previous when Lincoln reached the FA Cup quarter-finals.

Losing Alex Woodyard to Peterborough was a blow but they have made a number of decent signings, including the arrival of target-man John Akinde from Barnet. There should be more to come and Cowley knows the non-league game better than most, bringing in Boreham Wood duo Grant Smith and Bruno Andrade to boost the numbers.

Mansfield were ante-post favourites this time last year following an ambitious summer spending spree but the Stags failed to even make the playoffs as the disruption of losing manager Steve Evans to Peterborough proved too big a handicap to overcome.

David Flitcroft has now had the summer to work with the squad and they look strong in the final third with Tyler Walker, Craig Davies and Otis Khan among the new arrivals.

Khan, a class act on the wing for Yeovil, has turned down League One clubs to go to Field Mill so this looks a club with a hefty budget.

MK Dons are a big club with an astonishing stadium for this level and they look to have made a sound managerial appointment with the capture of Paul Tisdale from Exeter.

Ryan Harley is one of the headline signings, but Tisdale is not a man usually in a hurry so he may take his time to get everything spot on for a club that had totally lost its way.

Notts County are making serious moves in the transfer market with Andy Kellett, David Vaughan, Kristian Dennis, Kane Hemmings and Enzio Boldewijn among the summer arrivals. However, the value prices for the Magpies may have already been snapped up.

Last year we tipped Accrington at juicy prices for promotion but there is nobody standing out this time and it should be dominated by those towards the top end with the likes of Northampton booked in for a playoff spot behind the front four in the betting.

In the relegation betting, it may pay to remember Grimsby were in horrendous trouble until the final couple of weeks of the season. The controversial coaching appointment of Michael Jolley worked wonders but that seems to have been way over-factored into the market.

Recommendations

Lincoln to win League Two, 10-1 (general)
Mansfield to win League Two, 10-1 (general)
Grimsby to be relegated, 10-1 (Skybet)

Lincoln City can build on last season's EFL Trophy success

BURY

Nickname: The Shakers
Colours: White and blue
Ground: Gigg Lane (11,840)
Tel: 0161-764-4881   buryfc.co.uk

A summer of investment saw expectations rise at Gigg Lane but Bury knew their fate early, winning one of their opening nine matches and twice suffering seven-straight League One defeats.

Manager Lee Clark was sacked, replaced by Ryan Lowe, who was then replaced by Chris Lucketti before Lowe saw out the campaign. Jermaine Beckford's season-ending injury did not help Bury's fight against relegation but they did at least finish with three draws and a win.

Longest run without win/loss: 10/5
High/low league position: 19/24
Clean sheets: 8 **Yellows:** 67 **Reds:** 4
Avg attendance: 5,828 **Players used:** 41
Leading scorer: G Miller 8 (2,8) J Beckford 8 (2,8)
Key stat: Bury won one away league match last season

| | 2017-18 | | Last six seasons at home | | | | | | | |
	H	A	P	W	D	L	OV	UN	BS	CS
Oldham	D	L	4	0	2	2	1	3	2	0
Northampton	L	D	4	2	1	1	3	1	3	1
MK Dons	L	L	3	0	1	2	1	2	1	1
Bury										
Exeter			2	1	1	0	0	2	1	1
Notts County			1	0	0	1	0	1	0	0
Lincoln			-	-	-	-	-	-	-	-
Mansfield			2	1	1	0	0	2	0	2
Swindon			3	1	1	1	1	2	1	1
Carlisle			2	1	1	0	1	1	2	0
Newport County			2	0	1	1	1	1	1	1
Cambridge Utd			1	1	0	0	0	1	0	1
Colchester			2	1	0	1	2	0	2	0
Crawley Town			1	0	0	1	0	1	0	0
Crewe			2	0	2	0	1	1	1	1
Stevenage			2	2	0	0	1	1	1	1
Cheltenham			2	1	0	1	1	1	1	0
Grimsby			-	-	-	-	-	-	-	-
Yeovil			1	1	0	0	1	0	1	0
Port Vale			2	2	0	0	1	1	1	1
Forest Green			-	-	-	-	-	-	-	-
Morecambe			2	0	0	2	1	1	1	0
Macclesfield			-	-	-	-	-	-	-	-
Tranmere			2	1	0	1	0	2	0	1

Season	Division	Pos	P	W	D	L	F	A	GD	Pts
2017-18	League One	24	46	8	12	26	41	71	-30	36
2016-17	League One	19	46	13	11	22	61	73	-12	50
2015-16	League One	14	46	16	12	18	56	73	-17	60

Over/Under 48%/52% 13th   **Both score** 46%/54% 18th

CAMBRIDGE UTD

Nickname: The U's
Colours: Yellow and black
Ground: Abbey Stadium (8,127)
Tel: 01223-566500   cambridge-united.co.uk

There were not many Cambridge fans shedding tears when Shaun Derry was sacked in February after a dour campaign where United never looked like gaining promotion.

A 7-0 loss at Luton was a particular low point, although they were exceptional at home to the weaker sides, winning 11 and drawing one of their 12 fixtures against bottom-half finishers. Derry's interim replacement, Joe Dunne, has since been given the job on a full-time basis.

Longest run without win/loss: 6/5
High/low league position: 7/16
Clean sheets: 18 **Yellows:** 48 **Reds:** 3
Avg attendance: 4,470 **Players used:** 28
Leading scorer: U Ikpeazu 13 (5,11)
Key stat: Cambridge kept 18 clean sheets last season, second only to the 19 of champions Accrington

| | 2017-18 | | Last six seasons at home | | | | | | | |
	H	A	P	W	D	L	OV	UN	BS	CS
Oldham			-	-	-	-	-	-	-	-
Northampton			2	2	0	0	2	0	2	0
MK Dons			-	-	-	-	-	-	-	-
Bury			1	0	0	1	0	1	0	0
Exeter	L	L	4	1	0	3	2	2	2	1
Notts County	W	D	3	3	0	0	2	1	1	2
Lincoln	D	D	3	2	1	0	1	2	1	2
Mansfield	D	L	5	2	2	1	3	2	4	1
Swindon	L	L	1	0	0	1	1	0	1	0
Carlisle	L	D	4	1	2	1	3	1	2	2
Newport County	L	D	5	3	1	1	4	1	2	3
Cambridge Utd										
Colchester	W	D	2	1	1	0	0	2	1	1
Crawley Town	W	W	3	2	0	1	2	1	1	1
Crewe	W	W	2	2	0	0	2	0	2	0
Stevenage	W	W	4	2	2	0	0	4	1	3
Cheltenham	W	D	3	2	0	1	3	0	3	0
Grimsby	W	D	4	1	1	2	2	2	2	1
Yeovil	W	L	3	3	0	0	2	1	1	2
Port Vale	W	L	1	1	0	0	1	0	0	1
Forest Green	W	L	3	2	1	0	2	1	1	2
Morecambe	D	D	4	1	1	2	3	1	2	2
Macclesfield			2	2	0	0	1	0	0	2
Tranmere			1	0	0	1	1	0	1	0

Season	Division	Pos	P	W	D	L	F	A	GD	Pts
2017-18	League Two	12	46	17	13	16	56	60	-4	64
2016-17	League Two	11	46	19	9	18	58	50	+8	66
2015-16	League Two	9	46	18	14	14	66	55	+11	68

Over/Under 48%/52% 12th   **Both score** 48%/52% 23rd

CARLISLE

Nickname: Cumbrians/The Blues
Colours: Blue
Ground: Brunton Park (18,202)
Tel: 01228-526-237   carlisleunited.co.uk

Another solid season for Carlisle, who were unable to match their 2016-17 playoff run as they finished tenth and announced that long-serving boss Keith Curle, who had been at the helm since 2014, will no longer be in charge.

A poor finish cost the Cumbrians with only two wins and seven draws in their last ten matches and they will need to do better against the top sides this season after gaining just one clean sheet against top-half opponents.

Longest run without win/loss: 5/8
High/low league position: 9/18
Clean sheets: 15 **Yellows:** 66 **Reds:** 4
Avg attendance: 4,646 **Players used:** 26
Leading scorer: J Devitt 10 (5,10)
Key stat: Tenth-placed Carlisle won only one match against a team who finished above them

	2017-18 H	2017-18 A	P	W	D	L	OV	UN	BS	CS
Oldham			2	1	0	1	1	1	1	0
Northampton			2	1	0	1	2	0	2	0
MK Dons			2	1	1	0	1	1	1	1
Bury			2	1	0	1	2	0	1	0
Exeter	L	D	4	2	0	2	2	2	2	1
Notts County	D	L	5	2	1	2	4	1	3	1
Lincoln	L	L	1	0	0	1	0	1	0	0
Mansfield	D	L	4	2	1	1	3	1	4	0
Swindon	L	D	3	1	1	1	2	1	2	1
Carlisle										
Newport County	D	D	4	1	1	2	2	2	3	0
Cambridge Utd	D	W	4	0	2	2	2	2	2	0
Colchester	D	W	4	1	1	2	1	3	2	1
Crawley Town	D	W	5	2	2	1	3	2	4	0
Crewe	W	W	4	2	1	1	1	3	1	2
Stevenage	L	D	6	3	2	1	2	4	2	3
Cheltenham	W	W	3	2	1	0	1	2	1	2
Grimsby	W	W	2	1	0	1	1	1	1	1
Yeovil	W	W	4	3	1	0	4	0	3	1
Port Vale	L	W	2	0	0	2	1	1	1	0
Forest Green	W	W	1	1	0	0	0	1	0	1
Morecambe	D	D	4	0	3	1	1	3	4	0
Macclesfield			-	-	-	-	-	-	-	-
Tranmere			3	2	0	1	2	1	1	1

Season	Division	Pos	P	W	D	L	F	A	GD	Pts
2017-18	League Two	10	46	17	16	13	62	54	+8	67
2016-17	League Two	6	46	18	17	11	69	68	+1	71
2015-16	League Two	10	46	17	16	13	67	62	+5	67

Over/Under 41%/59% 25th   **Both score** 52%/48% 16th

CHELTENHAM

Nickname: The Robins
Colours: Red and white
Ground: Whaddon Road (7,066)
Tel: 01242-573-558   ctfc.com

Mohamed Eisa, a speedy striker from Sudan signed from lowly Greenwich Borough, was one of the biggest success stories of the League Two campaign after scoring an impressive 23 goals which was only two off the Golden Boot pace.

However, despite Eisa's best efforts Cheltenham were never able to launch a promotion push and a poor finish of six defeats in seven saw the Robins slip down to 17th. They were better than the final standings would suggest.

Longest run without win/loss: 5/5
High/low league position: 12/21
Clean sheets: 10 **Yellows:** 66 **Reds:** 3
Avg attendance: 3,764 **Players used:** 30
Leading scorer: M Eisa 23 (6,17)
Key stat: Cheltenham's matches produced 140 goals last season, an average of over three per game

	2017-18 H	2017-18 A	P	W	D	L	OV	UN	BS	CS
Oldham			-	-	-	-	-	-	-	-
Northampton			3	2	1	0	1	2	2	1
MK Dons			-	-	-	-	-	-	-	-
Bury			2	1	0	1	2	0	2	0
Exeter	L	L	5	2	0	3	4	1	3	2
Notts County	D	L	2	0	1	1	1	1	2	0
Lincoln	W	L	2	2	0	0	1	1	1	1
Mansfield	W	L	4	1	2	1	2	2	2	2
Swindon	W	W	1	1	0	0	1	0	1	0
Carlisle	L	L	3	1	1	1	0	3	0	2
Newport County	D	L	4	0	3	1	0	4	2	1
Cambridge Utd	D	L	3	1	1	1	1	2	1	1
Colchester	W	W	2	1	0	1	2	0	1	0
Crawley Town	W	W	2	2	0	0	1	1	1	1
Crewe	W	W	2	2	0	0	2	0	2	0
Stevenage	L	L	3	0	1	2	0	3	0	1
Cheltenham										
Grimsby	L	D	3	2	0	1	3	0	3	0
Yeovil	L	D	2	1	0	1	0	2	0	1
Port Vale	W	L	2	1	1	0	1	1	2	0
Forest Green	L	D	2	0	1	1	0	2	1	0
Morecambe	W	L	5	4	1	0	3	2	2	3
Macclesfield			1	1	0	0	0	1	0	1
Tranmere			2	1	0	1	0	2	0	1

Season	Division	Pos	P	W	D	L	F	A	GD	Pts
2017-18	League Two	17	46	13	12	21	67	73	-6	51
2016-17	League Two	21	46	12	14	20	49	69	-20	50
2015-16	Conference	1	46	30	11	5	87	30	+57	101

Over/Under 52%/48% 7th   **Both score** 59%/41% 3rd

COLCHESTER

Nickname: The U's
Colours: Blue and white
Ground: Colchester Community Stadium (10,083)
Tel: 01206-755100   cu-fc.com

Hopes were high in Essex before a ball was kicked that a mainly young side could push towards the top seven, but two wins in the opening ten matches derailed Colchester early on.

Injuries did not help and United improved in the middle of the season before three wins in their last 13 games ended any hopes of a late playoff move. Twelve-goal Sammie Szmodics is a player with potential who reportedly caught the eye of Premier League clubs in January.

Longest run without win/loss: 6/6
High/low league position: 8/20
Clean sheets: 13 **Yellows:** 68 **Reds:** 3
Avg attendance: 4,003 **Players used:** 34
Leading scorer: S Szmodics 12 (4,11)
Key stat: Colchester were the only team who finished in the bottom half to end with a positive goal difference

	2017-18 H	2017-18 A	P	W	D	L	OV	UN	BS	CS
Oldham			4	0	2	2	1	3	1	1
Northampton			-	-	-	-	-	-	-	-
MK Dons			3	1	0	2	1	2	1	0
Bury			2	1	0	1	0	2	0	1
Exeter	W	L	2	1	0	1	2	0	2	0
Notts County	L	L	5	1	0	4	3	2	2	0
Lincoln	W	L	1	1	0	0	0	1	0	1
Mansfield	W	D	2	2	0	0	0	2	0	2
Swindon	D	W	5	0	2	3	2	3	3	1
Carlisle	L	D	4	2	1	1	1	3	2	1
Newport County	W	W	2	1	1	0	0	2	0	2
Cambridge Utd	D	L	2	1	1	0	0	2	0	2
Colchester										
Crawley Town	W	W	5	1	2	2	3	2	5	0
Crewe	W	L	6	2	0	4	6	0	5	1
Stevenage	D	W	4	3	1	0	2	2	1	3
Cheltenham	L	L	2	1	0	1	1	1	1	1
Grimsby	D	D	2	1	1	0	1	1	2	0
Yeovil	L	W	4	3	0	1	0	4	0	3
Port Vale	D	D	4	2	1	1	2	2	3	1
Forest Green	W	W	1	1	0	0	1	0	1	0
Morecambe	D	D	2	0	2	0	1	1	1	1
Macclesfield			-	-	-	-	-	-	-	-
Tranmere			2	0	0	2	2	0	2	0

Season	Division	Pos	P	W	D	L	F	A	GD	Pts
2017-18	League Two	13	46	16	14	16	53	52	+1	62
2016-17	League Two	8	46	19	12	15	67	57	+10	69
2015-16	League One	23	46	9	13	24	57	99	-42	40

Over/Under 43%/57% 19th   **Both score** 54%/46% 12th

CRAWLEY

Nickname: The Red Devils
Colours: Red and white
Ground: Broadfield Stadium (5,996)
Tel: 01293-410000   crawleytownfc.com

Few gave Harry Kewell the benefit of the doubt when he was appointed after some negative vibes from his time as Watford's academy manager but the Australian can be satisfied with a 14th-place finish.

Kewell likes his side to play out from the back and that commitment to playing football in tight spots can backfire, with the Red Devils failing to keep a clean sheet in their last 14 matches. However, Crawley were the only team to beat champions Accrington home and away.

Longest run without win/loss: 7/4
High/low league position: 9/21
Clean sheets: 10 **Yellows:** 92 **Reds:** 5
Avg attendance: 3,267 **Players used:** 26
Leading scorer: E Boldewijn 10 (4,7) J Smith 10 (5,9)
Key stat: Both teams scored in Crawley's last 12 matches of the campaign

	2017-18 H	2017-18 A	P	W	D	L	OV	UN	BS	CS
Oldham			3	2	1	0	0	3	1	2
Northampton			1	0	0	1	1	0	1	0
MK Dons			3	1	1	2	1	2	1	1
Bury			1	1	0	0	1	0	1	0
Exeter	W	D	3	1	0	2	2	1	2	0
Notts County	L	W	6	2	1	3	1	5	1	3
Lincoln	W	D	1	1	0	0	1	0	1	0
Mansfield	W	D	3	1	1	1	1	2	1	1
Swindon	D	D	4	1	3	0	0	4	2	2
Carlisle	L	D	5	0	3	2	1	4	2	1
Newport County	L	L	3	2	0	1	2	1	2	1
Cambridge Utd	L	L	3	1	0	2	1	2	1	1
Colchester	L	L	5	2	2	1	1	4	1	3
Crawley Town										
Crewe	L	L	5	1	1	3	3	2	3	1
Stevenage	W	D	5	2	2	1	2	3	4	1
Cheltenham	L	L	2	0	1	1	1	1	1	1
Grimsby	W	D	2	2	0	0	2	0	1	1
Yeovil	W	W	5	3	0	2	0	5	0	3
Port Vale	L	W	3	0	0	3	3	0	2	0
Forest Green	D	L	1	0	1	0	0	1	1	0
Morecambe	D	W	3	0	2	1	1	2	3	0
Macclesfield			-	-	-	-	-	-	-	-
Tranmere			2	1	0	1	1	1	1	1

Season	Division	Pos	P	W	D	L	F	A	GD	Pts
2017-18	League Two	14	46	16	11	19	58	66	-8	59
2016-17	League Two	19	46	13	12	21	53	71	-18	51
2015-16	League One	20	46	13	8	25	45	78	-33	47

Over/Under 54%/46% 6th   **Both score** 59%/41% 3rd

CREWE

Nickname: The Railwaymen
Colours: Red and white
Ground: Gresty Road (10,118)
Tel: 01270-213-014   crewealex.net

Disturbing off-field events overshadowed Crewe's season and at one stage they seemed certain to be dragged into a relegation battle after losing 19 of 26 matches.

However, David Artell's men turned the tide with a staggering 4-1 win at Lincoln in February and rarely looked back after that with six wins in the final nine games.

No bottom-half side won at Gresty Road but Crewe were beaten home and away by all of the top four by an aggregate 19-7.

Longest run without win/loss: 6/4
High/low league position: 15/22
Clean sheets: 11 **Yellows:** 69 **Reds:** 3
Avg attendance: 4,264 **Players used:** 28
Leading scorer: J Bowery 12 (4,10)
Key stat: Crewe had just one away draw in League Two last season

	2017-18		Last six seasons at home							
---	H	A	P	W	D	L	OV	UN	BS	CS
Oldham			4	1	1	2	0	4	1	1
Northampton			-	-	-	-	-	-	-	-
MK Dons			3	2	0	1	2	1	1	1
Bury			2	1	1	0	1	1	1	1
Exeter	L	L	2	1	0	1	1	1	1	1
Notts County	W	L	5	1	1	3	4	1	3	1
Lincoln	L	W	1	0	0	1	1	0	1	0
Mansfield	D	W	2	0	2	0	1	1	2	0
Swindon	L	L	5	1	2	2	3	2	3	1
Carlisle	L	L	4	2	1	1	2	2	2	1
Newport County	D	W	2	0	1	1	1	1	2	0
Cambridge Utd	L	L	2	0	0	2	1	1	1	0
Colchester	W	L	6	3	2	1	2	4	2	3
Crawley Town	W	W	5	3	1	1	1	4	0	4
Crewe										
Stevenage	W	D	4	1	0	3	3	1	2	1
Cheltenham	W	L	2	1	1	0	1	1	1	1
Grimsby	W	L	2	2	0	0	1	1	0	2
Yeovil	D	L	4	1	1	2	0	4	0	2
Port Vale	D	W	4	1	2	1	3	1	3	1
Forest Green	W	L	1	1	0	0	1	0	1	0
Morecambe	W	W	2	2	0	0	1	1	1	1
Macclesfield			-	-	-	-	-	-	-	-
Tranmere		-	2	1	1	0	1	1	1	1

Season	Division	Pos	P	W	D	L	F	A	GD	Pts
2017-18	League Two	15	46	17	5	24	62	75	-13	56
2016-17	League Two	17	46	14	13	19	58	67	-9	55
2015-16	League One	24	46	7	13	26	46	83	-37	34

Over/Under 59%/41% 3rd   **Both score** 52%/48% 16th

EXETER

Nickname: The Grecians
Colours: Black and white
Ground: St James' Park (9,036)
Tel: 01392-411243   exetercityfc.co.uk

Losing one playoff final is hard going, but to suffer two such defeats in successive years could well be difficult for Exeter to recover from after their Wembley beating at the hands of Coventry.

In truth, the Grecians were fortunate to finish as high as fourth in the regular season with an overall shot ratio (share of total match shots) of just 0.45, which was one of the worst in the league – only Crewe, Forest and Green and Yeovil ended the campaign with poorer figures.

Longest run without win/loss: 4/8
High/low league position: 1/8
Clean sheets: 14 **Yellows:** 60 **Reds:** 2
Avg attendance: 4,379 **Players used:** 28
Leading scorer: J Stockley 19 (6,17)
Key stat: Exeter conceded 306 shots at home, the highest in League Two

	2017-18		Last six seasons at home							
---	H	A	P	W	D	L	OV	UN	BS	CS
Oldham			-	-	-	-	-	-	-	-
Northampton			4	1	1	2	1	3	0	2
MK Dons			-	-	-	-	-	-	-	-
Bury			2	1	1	0	2	0	2	0
Exeter										
Notts County	L	W	3	0	1	2	1	2	1	0
Lincoln	W	L	1	1	0	0	0	1	0	1
Mansfield	L	D	5	1	0	4	2	3	2	1
Swindon	W	D	1	1	0	0	1	0	1	0
Carlisle	D	W	4	1	2	1	2	2	3	1
Newport County	W	L	5	2	1	2	0	5	1	2
Cambridge Utd	W	W	4	2	1	1	2	2	2	2
Colchester	W	L	2	2	0	0	1	1	0	2
Crawley Town	D	L	3	0	2	1	2	1	2	0
Crewe	W	W	2	2	0	0	2	0	0	2
Stevenage	W	L	4	1	3	0	2	2	3	1
Cheltenham	W	W	5	3	1	1	2	3	2	2
Grimsby	W	W	2	1	1	0	0	2	0	2
Yeovil	D	L	3	1	2	0	2	1	2	1
Port Vale	L	W	2	0	0	2	0	2	0	0
Forest Green	W	W	1	1	0	0	0	1	0	1
Morecambe	W	L	6	2	3	1	3	3	5	0
Macclesfield			-	-	-	-	-	-	-	-
Tranmere			1	0	0	1	1	0	1	0

Season	Division	Pos	P	W	D	L	F	A	GD	Pts
2017-18	League Two	4	46	24	8	14	64	54	+10	80
2016-17	League Two	5	46	21	8	17	75	56	+19	71
2015-16	League Two	14	46	17	13	16	63	65	-2	64

Over/Under 50%/50% 9th   **Both score** 57%/43% 8th

FOREST GREEN

Nickname: Rovers
Colours: Green and black
Ground: The New Lawn (5,147)
Tel: 01453 834 860   forestgreenroversfc.com

The Football League newcomers seemed like rabbits in the headlights early in the season as their dream promotion from the National League appeared ready to turn into a nightmare.

Rovers were clearly out of their depth, earning six points after 13 matches including some woeful, heavy defeats. But, backed by a wealthy owner, Forest Green invested heavily in January and ended up 21st with the potential to improve for a second season at this level.

Longest run without win/loss: 10/5
High/low league position: 18/24
Clean sheets: 7 **Yellows:** 76 **Reds:** 3
Avg attendance: 3,635 **Players used:** 35
Leading scorer: C Doidge 20 (4,15)
Key stat: Forest Green committed more fouls (631) than any other side in League Two last season

	2017-18 H	A	P	W	D	L	OV	UN	BS	CS
Oldham			-	-	-	-	-	-	-	-
Northampton			-	-	-	-	-	-	-	-
MK Dons			-	-	-	-	-	-	-	-
Bury			-	-	-	-	-	-	-	-
Exeter	L	L	1	0	0	1	1	0	1	0
Notts County	L	D	1	0	0	1	1	0	1	0
Lincoln	L	L	6	3	1	2	5	1	4	1
Mansfield	W	L	2	1	0	1	1	1	1	1
Swindon	L	L	1	0	0	1	0	1	0	0
Carlisle	L	L	1	0	0	1	0	1	0	0
Newport County	L	D	2	0	0	2	2	0	1	0
Cambridge Utd	W	L	3	2	1	0	2	1	3	0
Colchester	L	L	1	0	0	1	1	0	1	0
Crawley Town	W	D	1	1	0	0	0	1	0	1
Crewe	W	L	1	1	0	0	1	0	1	0
Stevenage	W	W	1	1	0	0	1	0	1	0
Cheltenham	D	W	2	0	2	0	1	1	2	0
Grimsby	L	L	5	2	0	3	3	2	2	0
Yeovil	W	D	1	1	0	0	1	0	1	0
Port Vale	W	D	1	1	0	0	0	1	0	1
Forest Green										
Morecambe	W	D	1	1	0	0	0	1	0	1
Macclesfield			5	3	1	1	4	1	4	1
Tranmere			2	0	1	1	1	1	1	0

Season	Division	Pos	P	W	D	L	F	A	GD	Pts
2017-18	League Two	21	46	13	8	25	54	77	-23	47
2016-17	Conference	3	46	25	11	10	88	56	+32	86
2015-16	Conference	2	46	26	11	9	69	42	+27	89

Over/Under 50%/50% 9th   **Both score** 54%/46% 12th

GRIMSBY

Nickname: The Mariners
Colours: Black and white
Ground: Blundell Park (9,052)
Tel: 01472-605-050

Jolley by name and jolly by nature. The appointment of Michael Jolley seemed to save Grimsby from dropping out of the Football League as they won four and drew one of their last five matches having gone on a run of 20 fixtures without triumphing in League Two.

The supporters felt Russell Slade was given far too long in the post but the club acted in the nick of time. Jolley was brought in from Swedish football boasting references from Sean Dyche.

Longest run without win/loss: 20/7
High/low league position: 11/22
Clean sheets: 12 **Yellows:** 69 **Reds:** 7
Avg attendance: 4,934 **Players used:** 32
Leading scorer: M Rose 8 (5,8)
Key stat: Grimsby failed to score on 20 occasions last season

	2017-18 H	A	P	W	D	L	OV	UN	BS	CS
Oldham			-	-	-	-	-	-	-	-
Northampton			-	-	-	-	-	-	-	-
MK Dons			-	-	-	-	-	-	-	-
Bury			-	-	-	-	-	-	-	-
Exeter	L	L	2	0	0	2	1	1	0	0
Notts County	W	D	2	2	0	0	1	1	1	1
Lincoln	D	L	5	1	3	1	1	4	3	2
Mansfield	D	L	3	2	1	0	2	1	2	1
Swindon	W	W	1	1	0	0	1	0	1	0
Carlisle	L	L	2	0	1	1	1	1	1	0
Newport County	L	L	3	2	0	1	2	1	1	2
Cambridge Utd	D	L	4	1	1	2	1	3	1	1
Colchester	D	D	2	1	1	0	1	1	1	1
Crawley Town	D	L	2	0	2	0	0	2	1	1
Crewe	W	D	2	1	0	1	0	2	0	1
Stevenage	D	L	2	1	1	0	1	1	1	1
Cheltenham	D	W	3	0	1	2	0	3	1	0
Grimsby										
Yeovil	W	L	2	2	0	0	2	0	2	0
Port Vale	D	W	1	0	1	0	0	1	1	0
Forest Green	W	W	5	4	1	0	2	3	3	2
Morecambe	L	D	2	1	0	1	0	2	0	1
Macclesfield			4	0	0	4	2	2	2	0
Tranmere			1	0	1	0	0	1	1	0

Season	Division	Pos	P	W	D	L	F	A	GD	Pts
2017-18	League Two	18	46	13	12	21	42	66	-24	51
2016-17	League Two	14	46	17	11	18	59	63	-4	62
2015-16	Conference	4	46	22	14	10	82	45	+37	80

Over/Under 46%/54% 15th   **Both score** 43%/57% 25th

LINCOLN

Nickname: The Imps
Colours: Red
Ground: Sincil Bank (10,127)
Tel: 0870-899-2005

It was not to be successive promotions for Lincoln as the National League champions lost to Exeter in the playoff semi-finals, but it was still a season of triumph for the Imps, who continue to improve under the management of the Cowley brothers.

There was even a first ever trip to Wembley as Lincoln lifted the Football League Trophy and maybe the fixture congestion played a part in a tired finale to the campaign. They are a direct outfit and few teams enjoy a trip to Sincil Bank.

Longest run without win/loss: 3/6
High/low league position: 3/12
Clean sheets: 15 **Yellows:** 84 **Reds:** 5
Avg attendance: 7,031 **Players used:** 27
Leading scorer: M Green 13 (5,13)
Key stat: Lincoln lost only three times at home in all competitions last term

	2017-18 H	2017-18 A	P	W	D	L	OV	UN	BS	CS
Oldham			-	-	-	-	-	-	-	-
Northampton			-	-	-	-	-	-	-	-
MK Dons			-	-	-	-	-	-	-	-
Bury										
Exeter	W	L	1	1	0	0	1	0	1	0
Notts County	D	L	1	0	1	0	1	0	1	0
Lincoln										
Mansfield	L	D	2	0	0	2	0	2	0	0
Swindon	D	W	1	0	1	0	1	0	1	0
Carlisle	W	W	1	1	0	0	1	0	1	0
Newport County	W	D	2	1	0	1	2	0	2	0
Cambridge Utd	D	D	3	1	2	0	0	3	0	3
Colchester	W	L	1	1	0	0	1	0	1	0
Crawley Town	D	L	1	0	1	0	0	1	0	1
Crewe	L	W	1	0	0	1	1	0	1	0
Stevenage	W	W	1	1	0	0	1	0	0	1
Cheltenham	W	L	2	1	1	0	0	2	1	1
Grimsby	W	D	5	2	1	2	3	2	4	0
Yeovil	D	W	1	0	1	0	0	1	1	0
Port Vale	W	L	1	1	0	0	1	0	1	0
Forest Green	W	W	6	3	0	3	5	1	5	0
Morecambe	D	D	1	0	1	0	0	1	1	0
Macclesfield			5	4	0	1	3	2	3	2
Tranmere			2	2	0	0	1	1	1	1

Season	Division	Pos	P	W	D	L	F	A	GD	Pts
2017-18	League Two	7	46	20	15	11	64	48	+16	75
2016-17	Conference	1	46	30	9	7	83	40	+43	99
2015-16	Conference	13	46	16	13	17	69	68	+1	61

Over/Under 48%/52% 12th **Both score** 54%/46% 12th

MACCLESFIELD

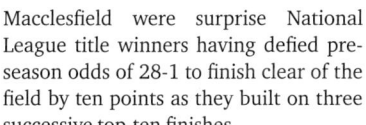

Nickname: The Silkmen
Colours: Blue
Ground: Moss Rose (6,355)
Tel: 01625-264-686

Macclesfield were surprise National League title winners having defied pre-season odds of 28-1 to finish clear of the field by ten points as they built on three successive top-ten finishes.

Scott Wilson top-scored with 14 goals but there was a holistic approach to the attack with many players chipping in.

Club legend John Askey is in charge and they showed nerves of steel, losing just once in their final 16 games and going unbeaten at home since November.

Longest run without win/loss: 4/11
High/low league position: 1/14
Clean sheets: 19 **Yellows:** 39 **Reds:** 2
Avg attendance: 1,755 **Players used:** 23
Leading scorer: S Wilson 14 (8,10)
Key stat: Macclesfield are unbeaten in their last 14 home matches

	2017-18 H	2017-18 A	P	W	D	L	OV	UN	BS	CS
Oldham			-	-	-	-	-	-	-	-
Northampton			-	-	-	-	-	-	-	-
MK Dons			-	-	-	-	-	-	-	-
Bury			-	-	-	-	-	-	-	-
Exeter			-	-	-	-	-	-	-	-
Notts County			-	-	-	-	-	-	-	-
Lincoln			5	3	1	1	4	1	4	1
Mansfield			1	0	0	1	1	0	0	0
Swindon			-	-	-	-	-	-	-	-
Carlisle			-	-	-	-	-	-	-	-
Newport County			1	0	1	0	0	1	1	0
Cambridge Utd			2	1	0	1	1	1	1	0
Colchester			-	-	-	-	-	-	-	-
Crawley Town			-	-	-	-	-	-	-	-
Crewe			-	-	-	-	-	-	-	-
Stevenage			-	-	-	-	-	-	-	-
Cheltenham			1	0	0	1	0	1	0	0
Grimsby			4	1	1	2	2	2	3	0
Yeovil			-	-	-	-	-	-	-	-
Port Vale			-	-	-	-	-	-	-	-
Forest Green			5	1	1	3	4	1	4	0
Morecambe			-	-	-	-	-	-	-	-
Macclesfield										
Tranmere	D	W	3	1	1	1	3	0	3	0

Season	Division	Pos	P	W	D	L	F	A	GD	Pts
2017-18	Conference	1	46	27	11	8	67	46	+21	92
2016-17	Conference	9	46	20	8	18	64	57	+7	68
2015-16	Conference	10	46	19	9	18	60	48	+12	66

Over/Under 43%/57% 22nd **Both score** 50%/50% 16th

MANSFIELD

Nickname: The Stags
Colours: Yellow and blue
Ground: Field Mill (9,186)
Tel: 01623-482 482   mansfieldtown.net

The shock departure of Steve Evans, who claimed he quit to pursue a job outside of the UK and then ended up at Peterborough a few days later, derailed Mansfield's promotion push in February.

With Evans at the helm they were only two points off the automatic promotion places in fifth but missed out on the playoffs after David Flitcroft's appointment from Swindon as the Stags won just two of their last 13 games. Post-Evans Mansfield beat only Chesterfield and Yeovil.

Longest run without win/loss: 9/9
High/low league position: 3/14
Clean sheets: 11 **Yellows:** 10 **Reds:** 4
Avg attendance: 4,405 **Players used:** 27
Leading scorer: K Hemmings 15 (8,14)
Key stat: Mansfield (108) were the only League Two side last season to hit the century mark of players booked

	2017-18		Last six seasons at home							
	H	A	P	W	D	L	OV	UN	BS	CS
Oldham	-	-	-	-	-	-	-	-	-	-
Northampton			3	1	2	0	2	1	2	1
MK Dons			-	-	-	-	-	-	-	-
Bury			2	0	0	2	1	1	1	0
Exeter	D	W	5	0	2	3	2	3	3	1
Notts County	W	D	3	3	0	0	3	0	2	1
Lincoln	D	W	2	0	2	0	0	2	1	1
Mansfield										
Swindon	L	L	1	0	0	1	1	0	1	0
Carlisle	W	D	4	3	1	0	2	2	3	1
Newport County	W	D	6	5	0	1	5	1	3	3
Cambridge Utd	W	D	5	2	3	0	2	3	2	3
Colchester	D	L	2	0	2	0	0	2	1	1
Crawley Town	D	L	3	2	1	0	2	1	2	1
Crewe	L	D	2	1	0	1	2	0	1	1
Stevenage	W	D	4	3	0	1	2	2	2	2
Cheltenham	W	L	4	1	2	1	1	3	3	0
Grimsby	W	D	3	2	0	1	1	2	1	1
Yeovil	D	W	3	1	1	1	0	3	0	2
Port Vale	D	W	1	0	1	0	0	1	1	0
Forest Green	W	L	2	2	0	0	0	2	0	2
Morecambe	W	W	5	3	0	2	3	2	3	1
Macclesfield			1	1	0	0	1	0	1	0
Tranmere			1	1	0	0	0	1	0	1

Season	Division	Pos	P	W	D	L	F	A	GD	Pts
2017-18	League Two	8	46	18	18	10	67	52	+15	72
2016-17	League Two	12	46	17	15	14	54	50	+4	66
2015-16	League Two	12	46	17	13	16	61	53	+8	64

Over/Under 43%/57% 19th   **Both score** 63%/37% 1st

MK DONS

Nickname: The Dons
Colours: White
Ground: stadium:mk (30,500)
Tel: 01908-622-922   mkdons.co.uk

Owner Pete Winkelman was devastated by relegation, saying: "I thought going down from the Championship was bad. To be in this position is just unthinkable. None of us planned or expected to be here. It is probably the worst ever thing that has happened."

Winkelman said he made two bad managerial appointments, first Robbie Neilson then novice Dan Micciche, as the Dons finished in 23rd place, only winning successive matches on two occasions.

Longest run without win/loss: 10/4
High/low league position: 10/23
Clean sheets: 11 **Yellows:** 96 **Reds:** 5
Avg attendance: 8,564 **Players used:** 30
Leading scorer: C Aneke 9 (7,8)
Key stat: No player reached double figures in league goals scored last season

	2017-18		Last six seasons at home							
	H	A	P	W	D	L	OV	UN	BS	CS
Oldham	D	L	5	4	1	0	3	2	2	3
Northampton	D	L	2	1	1	0	1	1	1	1
MK Dons										
Bury	W	W	3	1	1	1	2	1	3	0
Exeter			-	-	-	-	-	-	-	-
Notts County			3	2	1	0	2	1	3	0
Lincoln			-	-	-	-	-	-	-	-
Mansfield			-	-	-	-	-	-	-	-
Swindon			4	3	1	0	2	2	3	1
Carlisle			2	1	0	1	0	2	0	1
Newport County			-	-	-	-	-	-	-	-
Cambridge Utd			-	-	-	-	-	-	-	-
Colchester			3	2	1	0	2	1	1	2
Crawley Town			3	1	1	1	0	3	0	2
Crewe			3	3	0	0	1	2	1	2
Stevenage			2	1	0	1	1	1	1	0
Cheltenham			-	-	-	-	-	-	-	-
Grimsby			-	-	-	-	-	-	-	-
Yeovil			2	2	0	0	1	1	1	1
Port Vale			3	2	0	1	1	2	0	2
Forest Green			-	-	-	-	-	-	-	-
Morecambe			-	-	-	-	-	-	-	-
Macclesfield			-	-	-	-	-	-	-	-
Tranmere			2	1	0	1	1	1	0	1

Season	Division	Pos	P	W	D	L	F	A	GD	Pts
2017-18	League One	23	46	11	12	23	43	69	-26	45
2016-17	League One	12	46	16	13	17	60	58	+2	61
2015-16	Championship	23	46	9	12	25	39	69	-30	39

Over/Under 41%/59% 19th   **Both score** 50%/50% 15th

LEAGUE TWO

MORECAMBE

Nickname: The Shrimps
Colours: Red and white
Ground: Globe Arena (6,476)
Tel: 01524-411-797

Morecambe can look forward to a 12th season in the Football League but it was close for Jim Bentley's boys, who needed a point at Coventry on the final day to survive at the expense of Barnet.

It was not without controversy – the goalless draw was mutually beneficial – and nearly as important was a late-season takeover by a London-based investment firm. Morecambe won only two matches in 2018 and failed to score in each of the last four despite staying up on goal difference.

Longest run without win/loss: 10/5
High/low league position: 16/23
Clean sheets: 12 **Yellows:** 66 **Reds:** 2
Avg attendance: 2,958 **Players used:** 24
Leading scorer: C Lang 10 (3,9)
Key stat: Morecambe notched the fewest League Two goals last season with only 41 scored

	2017-18 H	2017-18 A	P	W	D	L	OV	UN	BS	CS
Oldham			-	-	-	-	-	-	-	-
Northampton			4	0	2	2	1	3	3	0
MK Dons			-	-	-	-	-	-	-	-
Bury			2	1	1	0	0	2	0	2
Exeter	W	L	6	2	1	3	3	3	2	1
Notts County	L	L	3	2	0	1	3	0	3	0
Lincoln	D	D	1	0	1	0	0	1	0	1
Mansfield	L	L	5	1	0	4	4	1	4	0
Swindon	L	D	1	0	0	1	0	1	0	0
Carlisle	D	D	4	0	1	3	2	2	2	0
Newport County	W	D	5	3	0	2	4	1	4	0
Cambridge Utd	D	D	4	1	1	2	1	3	1	2
Colchester	D	D	2	0	2	0	0	2	1	1
Crawley Town	L	D	3	1	0	2	2	1	2	0
Crewe	L	L	2	0	1	1	0	2	0	1
Stevenage	D	L	4	0	2	2	1	3	2	1
Cheltenham	W	L	5	1	2	2	2	3	2	2
Grimsby	D	W	2	1	1	0	0	2	0	2
Yeovil	W	D	3	2	0	1	3	0	3	0
Port Vale	L	D	2	0	0	2	2	0	1	0
Forest Green	D	L	1	0	1	0	0	1	1	0
Morecambe										
Macclesfield			-	-	-	-	-	-	-	-
Tranmere			1	0	1	0	0	1	0	1

Season	Division	Pos	P	W	D	L	F	A	GD	Pts
2017-18	League Two	22	46	9	19	18	41	56	-15	46
2016-17	League Two	18	46	14	10	22	53	73	-20	52
2015-16	League Two	21	46	12	10	24	69	91	-22	46

Over/Under 37%/63% 26th   **Both score** 50%/50% 19th

NEWPORT COUNTY

Nickname: The Exiles
Colours: Yellow and black
Ground: Rodney Parade (7,850)
Tel: 01633-481896

FA Cup runs can often be a distraction for lower-league outfits and so it proved for Newport, who made headlines as they beat Leeds in the third round of the FA Cup and so nearly repeated the trick against Tottenham in round four.

Harry Kane's late equaliser earned Newport a money-spinning Wembley replay but County won only one league game between January 23 and April 7. They finished a respectable 11th and no top-ten team won at Rodney Parade.

Longest run without win/loss: 7/5
High/low league position: 6/14
Clean sheets: 11 **Yellows:** 73 **Reds:** 3
Avg attendance: 3,767 **Players used:** 28
Leading scorer: P Amond 13 (9,12)
Key stat: Newport drew ten of their home matches last season

	2017-18 H	2017-18 A	P	W	D	L	OV	UN	BS	CS
Oldham			-	-	-	-	-	-	-	-
Northampton			3	1	1	1	3	0	3	0
MK Dons			-	-	-	-	-	-	-	-
Bury			2	0	1	1	0	2	0	1
Exeter	W	L	5	1	3	1	3	2	5	0
Notts County	D	L	3	1	1	1	2	1	1	1
Lincoln	D	L	2	1	1	0	1	1	1	1
Mansfield	D	L	6	2	2	2	1	5	3	2
Swindon	W	W	1	1	0	0	1	0	1	0
Carlisle	D	D	4	3	1	0	2	2	2	2
Newport County										
Cambridge Utd	W	W	5	2	1	2	3	2	4	0
Colchester	L	L	2	0	1	1	1	1	2	0
Crawley Town	W	W	3	2	0	1	2	1	1	1
Crewe	L	D	2	0	1	1	1	1	2	0
Stevenage	L	D	4	1	1	2	1	3	1	1
Cheltenham	W	D	4	1	2	1	1	3	2	1
Grimsby	W	W	3	1	2	0	0	3	0	3
Yeovil	W	D	3	2	1	0	3	0	3	0
Port Vale	D	D	1	0	1	0	0	1	1	0
Forest Green	D	W	2	0	1	1	2	0	1	0
Morecambe	D	L	5	0	2	3	2	3	4	0
Macclesfield			1	1	0	0	1	0	1	0
Tranmere			1	0	1	0	0	1	1	0

Season	Division	Pos	P	W	D	L	F	A	GD	Pts
2017-18	League Two	11	46	16	16	14	56	58	-2	64
2016-17	League Two	22	46	12	12	22	51	73	-22	48
2015-16	League Two	22	46	10	13	23	43	64	-21	43

Over/Under 46%/54% 15th   **Both score** 59%/41% 3rd

NORTHAMPTON

Nickname: The Cobblers
Colours: Claret and white
Ground: Sixfields Stadium (7,798)
Tel: 01604-683-700

A season which started with a stack of new players and hope of a bright future finished in relegation for Northampton, who were the subject of a summer Chinese takeover only for the Far East business 5USport to sell back their 60 per cent stake in March following "investment restrictions".

Justin Edinburgh was sacked and so too was replacement Jimmy Floyd Hasselbaink, leaving Dean Austin to take the Cobblers down to League Two despite a late-season rally.

Longest run without win/loss: 10/4
High/low league position: 17/23
Clean sheets: 6 **Yellows:** 88 **Reds:** 7
Avg attendance: 7,081 **Players used:** 39
Leading scorer: C Long 9 (3,7)
Key stat: Northampton had the fewest shots (421) in League One last season

	2017-18 H	2017-18 A	P	W	D	L	OV	UN	BS	CS
Oldham	D	L	2	0	1	1	2	0	2	0
Northampton										
MK Dons	W	D	2	2	0	0	2	0	2	0
Bury	D	W	4	1	1	2	3	1	2	1
Exeter			4	3	0	1	3	1	1	3
Notts County			1	0	1	0	1	0	1	0
Lincoln			-	-	-	-	-	-	-	-
Mansfield			3	2	1	0	0	3	1	2
Swindon			1	1	0	0	1	0	1	0
Carlisle			2	1	0	1	1	1	1	0
Newport County			3	3	0	0	2	1	1	2
Cambridge Utd			2	0	1	1	0	2	1	0
Colchester			-	-	-	-	-	-	-	-
Crawley Town			1	1	0	0	1	0	1	0
Crewe			-	-	-	-	-	-	-	-
Stevenage			2	2	0	0	1	1	1	1
Cheltenham			3	1	1	1	1	2	2	1
Grimsby			-	-	-	-	-	-	-	-
Yeovil			1	1	0	0	0	1	0	1
Port Vale			2	2	0	0	1	1	1	1
Forest Green			-	-	-	-	-	-	-	-
Morecambe			4	3	1	0	3	1	2	2
Macclesfield			-	-	-	-	-	-	-	-
Tranmere			1	1	0	0	0	1	0	1

Season	Division	Pos	P	W	D	L	F	A	GD	Pts
2017-18	League One	22	46	12	11	23	43	77	-34	47
2016-17	League One	16	46	14	11	21	60	73	-13	53
2015-16	League Two	1	46	29	12	5	82	46	+36	99

Over/Under 52%/48% 4th   **Both score** 48%/52% 16th

NOTTS COUNTY

Nickname: The Magpies
Colours: Black and white
Ground: Meadow Lane (19,588)
Tel: 0115-952-9000   nottscountyfc.co.uk

A fifth-placed finish was a strong effort from Notts County in Kevin Nolan's first full season as a manager but the Magpies will be left rueing missed opportunities.

They won eight of their opening ten matches and crucial refereeing decisions went against them in the playoff loss to Coventry. However, the influential Asian betting market was against Notts most weeks, believing they were punching well above their weight, which does not bode particularly well for the 2018-19 season.

Longest run without win/loss: 4/10
High/low league position: 1/5
Clean sheets: 13 **Yellows:** 76 **Reds:** 3
Avg attendance: 5,857 **Players used:** 29
Leading scorer: J Grant 15 (6,10)
Key stat: Notts County scored the most goals (71) of any side not promoted last season

	2017-18 H	2017-18 A	P	W	D	L	OV	UN	BS	CS
Oldham			3	2	1	0	1	2	1	2
Northampton			1	0	0	1	1	0	1	0
MK Dons			3	0	0	3	2	1	2	0
Bury			1	1	0	0	1	0	1	0
Exeter	L	W	3	0	1	2	3	0	3	0
Notts County										
Lincoln	W	D	1	1	0	0	1	0	1	0
Mansfield	D	L	3	0	2	1	0	3	1	1
Swindon	W	L	4	3	0	1	1	3	0	3
Carlisle	W	D	5	3	0	2	4	1	3	1
Newport County	W	D	3	2	0	1	3	0	1	1
Cambridge Utd	D	L	3	0	1	2	2	1	2	0
Colchester	W	W	5	5	0	0	4	1	4	1
Crawley Town	L	W	6	4	1	1	4	2	5	1
Crewe	W	L	5	3	2	0	3	2	4	1
Stevenage	W	D	5	2	1	2	1	4	2	2
Cheltenham	D	W	2	2	0	0	2	0	2	0
Grimsby	D	L	2	0	2	0	1	1	1	1
Yeovil	W	D	5	2	1	2	3	2	3	2
Port Vale	W	W	3	2	0	1	1	2	1	1
Forest Green	D	W	1	0	1	0	0	1	1	0
Morecambe	W	W	3	1	1	1	2	1	2	1
Macclesfield			-	-	-	-	-	-	-	-
Tranmere			2	1	0	1	0	2	0	1

Season	Division	Pos	P	W	D	L	F	A	GD	Pts
2017-18	League Two	5	46	21	14	11	71	48	+23	77
2016-17	League Two	16	46	16	8	22	54	76	-22	56
2015-16	League Two	17	46	14	9	23	54	83	-29	51

Over/Under 50%/50% 9th   **Both score** 59%/41% 3rd

OLDHAM

Nickname: The Latics
Colours: Blue
Ground: Boundary Park (13,500)
Tel: 08712-262-235   oldhamathletic.co.uk

Oldham lost only three matches from February onwards but were still relegated from League One, dropping on the final day after failing to beat a Northampton team who had already been demoted.

That 2-2 draw was the real problem for Richie Wellens, who had replaced John Sheridan as manager, as Athletic shared the spoils in seven of their last eight games and failed to turn decent performances into victories. It's fair to say they were not one of the worst four teams in League One.

Longest run without win/loss: 9/6
High/low league position: 15/24
Clean sheets: 8 **Yellows:** 10 **Reds:** 6
Avg attendance: 6,222 **Players used:** 37
Leading scorer: E Doyle 14 (3,11)
Key stat: Oldham were relegated despite losing just three matches against bottom-half teams last season

| | 2017-18 | | Last six seasons at home | | | | | | | |
	H	A	P	W	D	L	OV	UN	BS	CS
Oldham										
Northampton	W	D	2	1	1	0	1	1	1	1
MK Dons	W	D	5	2	0	3	3	2	3	1
Bury	W	D	4	1	1	2	2	2	2	1
Exeter			-	-	-	-	-	-	-	-
Notts County			3	1	2	0	2	1	2	1
Lincoln			-	-	-	-	-	-	-	-
Mansfield			-	-	-	-	-	-	-	-
Swindon			5	3	0	2	2	3	2	1
Carlisle			2	1	0	1	1	1	1	1
Newport County			-	-	-	-	-	-	-	-
Cambridge Utd			-	-	-	-	-	-	-	-
Colchester			4	0	2	2	0	4	2	0
Crawley Town			3	2	1	0	1	2	2	1
Crewe			4	1	1	2	2	2	3	1
Stevenage			2	1	0	1	0	2	0	1
Cheltenham			-	-	-	-	-	-	-	-
Grimsby			-	-	-	-	-	-	-	-
Yeovil			2	1	0	1	1	1	0	1
Port Vale			4	1	3	0	1	3	3	1
Forest Green			-	-	-	-	-	-	-	-
Morecambe			-	-	-	-	-	-	-	-
Macclesfield			-	-	-	-	-	-	-	-
Tranmere			2	0	0	2	0	2	0	0

Season	Division	Pos	P	W	D	L	F	A	GD	Pts
2017-18	League One	21	46	11	17	18	58	75	-17	50
2016-17	League One	17	46	12	17	17	31	44	-13	53
2015-16	League One	17	46	12	18	16	44	58	-14	54

Over/Under 57%/43% 1st   **Both score** 63%/37% 2nd

PORT VALE

Nickname: The Valiants
Colours: White and black
Ground: Vale Park (19,052)
Tel: 01782-655-800   port-vale.co.uk

Another side who flirted with relegation and those concerns grew as influential target man Tom Pope suffered with injury towards the end of the campaign.

Michael Brown was given the boot as Vale started the season in horrendous fashion – they lost nine of the opening 12 – and replacement Neil Aspin got tough with the players. Gloves were ruled a no-go zone during the winter months but two victories in the last 21 hardly inspires confidence for this season.

Longest run without win/loss: 14/5
High/low league position: 16/24
Clean sheets: 10 **Yellows:** 73 **Reds:** 4
Avg attendance: 4,392 **Players used:** 38
Leading scorer: T Pope 17 (8,14)
Key stat: Tom Pope scored 17 of Port Vale's 49 goals last season

| | 2017-18 | | Last six seasons at home | | | | | | | |
	H	A	P	W	D	L	OV	UN	BS	CS
Oldham			4	1	2	1	1	3	2	1
Northampton			2	0	1	1	2	0	2	0
MK Dons			3	1	2	0	0	3	0	3
Bury			2	1	1	0	1	1	1	1
Exeter	L	W	2	0	0	2	0	2	0	0
Notts County	L	L	3	1	0	2	1	2	1	0
Lincoln	W	L	1	1	0	0	1	0	1	0
Mansfield	L	D	1	0	0	1	1	0	0	0
Swindon	L	L	5	2	0	3	3	2	2	1
Carlisle	L	W	2	1	0	1	2	0	2	0
Newport County	D	D	1	0	1	0	0	1	0	1
Cambridge Utd	W	L	1	1	0	0	0	1	0	1
Colchester	D	D	4	2	1	1	2	2	2	2
Crawley Town	L	W	3	1	0	2	3	0	3	0
Crewe	L	D	4	1	0	3	2	2	1	1
Stevenage	D	L	2	0	2	0	2	0	2	0
Cheltenham	W	L	2	2	0	0	2	0	2	0
Grimsby	L	D	1	0	0	1	1	0	1	0
Yeovil	D	D	2	1	1	0	1	2	0	1
Port Vale										
Forest Green	D	L	1	0	1	0	0	1	1	0
Morecambe	D	W	2	0	1	1	0	2	0	1
Macclesfield			-	-	-	-	-	-	-	-
Tranmere			1	1	0	0	1	0	1	0

Season	Division	Pos	P	W	D	L	F	A	GD	Pts
2017-18	League Two	20	46	11	14	21	49	67	-18	47
2016-17	League One	21	46	12	13	21	45	70	-25	49
2015-16	League One	12	46	18	11	17	56	58	-2	45

Over/Under 46%/54% 15th   **Both score** 52%/48% 16th

STEVENAGE

Nickname: The Boro
Colours: White and red
Ground: Broadhall Way (6,722)
Tel: 01438-223223   stevenagefc.com

Stevenage dropped 12 points in the 2016-17 season and that was enough for a managerial change in March, with Darren Sarll losing his job as head coach only to return to the club ten days later to oversee their youth system.

Sarll's replacement was Dino Maamria from Northwich but there was not much improvement, at least in terms of results. Boro were beaten on the road by each of the top nine teams, including 7-1 at Luton when Sarll was calling the shots.

Longest run without win/loss: 8/5
High/low league position: 6/17
Clean sheets: 9 **Yellows:** 74 **Reds:** 5
Avg attendance: 3,555 **Players used:** 35
Leading scorer: D Newton 14 (8,13)
Key stat: Both teams scored in a joint-high 17 of Stevenage's 23 home league games last season, but only nine times away, a joint-low

	2017-18 H	A	Last six seasons at home P	W	D	L	OV	UN	BS	CS
Oldham			2	0	0	2	2	0	2	0
Northampton			2	1	0	1	2	0	2	0
MK Dons			2	0	0	2	1	1	1	0
Bury			2	0	2	0	1	1	1	1
Exeter	W	L	4	2	0	2	1	3	1	1
Notts County	D	L	5	2	1	2	1	4	1	2
Lincoln	L	L	1	0	0	1	1	0	1	0
Mansfield	D	L	4	1	1	2	1	3	1	1
Swindon	L	L	3	1	0	2	1	2	0	1
Carlisle	D	W	6	1	2	3	2	4	3	2
Newport County	D	W	4	3	1	0	4	0	4	0
Cambridge Utd	L	L	4	2	0	2	2	2	2	1
Colchester	L	D	4	0	0	4	2	2	2	0
Crawley Town	D	L	5	2	1	2	2	3	3	1
Crewe	D	L	4	1	2	1	3	1	3	1
Stevenage										
Cheltenham	W	W	3	3	0	0	3	0	3	0
Grimsby	W	D	2	2	0	0	1	1	1	1
Yeovil	W	L	4	1	2	1	2	2	2	1
Port Vale	W	D	2	1	1	0	0	2	1	1
Forest Green	L	L	1	0	0	1	1	0	1	0
Morecambe	W	D	4	2	1	1	2	2	3	0
Macclesfield			-	-	-	-	-	-	-	-
Tranmere			3	1	2	0	2	1	3	0

Season	Division	Pos	P	W	D	L	F	A	GD	Pts
2017-18	League Two	16	46	14	13	19	60	65	-5	55
2016-17	League Two	10	46	20	7	19	67	63	+4	67
2015-16	League Two	18	46	11	15	20	52	67	-15	48

Over/Under 46%/54% 15th   **Both score** 57%/43% 8th

SWINDON

Nickname: The Robins
Colours: Red and white
Ground: County Ground (15,728)
Tel: 0871-876-1879   swindontownfc.co.uk

If Mansfield were disrupted by Steve Evans leaving for Peterborough it also caused problems for Swindon, who saw their manager David Flitcroft tempted to Field Mill at a crucial stage of the season.

The Robins won only two of their last 12 matches to miss out on the playoffs and whether it was the appointment of Phil Brown to replace Flitcroft or injuries to the defence, the fact remains Swindon were well placed to make the playoffs but finished seven points off the pace.

Longest run without win/loss: 8/4
High/low league position: 5/12
Clean sheets: 14 **Yellows:** 70 **Reds:** 7
Avg attendance: 5,449 **Players used:** 32
Leading scorer: L Norris 13 (7,12)
Key stat: Swindon won only two of their last 12 matches

	2017-18 H	A	Last six seasons at home P	W	D	L	OV	UN	BS	CS
Oldham			5	0	3	2	2	3	3	1
Northampton			1	0	0	1	1	0	1	0
MK Dons			4	1	1	2	2	2	2	1
Bury			3	0	0	3	1	2	1	0
Exeter	D	L	1	0	1	0	0	1	1	0
Notts County	W	L	4	3	1	0	1	3	0	4
Lincoln	L	D	1	0	0	1	0	1	0	0
Mansfield	W	W	1	1	0	0	0	1	0	1
Swindon										
Carlisle	D	W	3	2	1	0	2	1	1	2
Newport County	L	L	1	0	0	1	0	1	0	0
Cambridge Utd	W	W	1	1	0	0	0	1	0	1
Colchester	L	D	5	0	2	3	3	2	3	1
Crawley Town	L	D	4	1	1	2	3	1	2	1
Crewe	W	W	5	5	0	0	4	1	3	2
Stevenage	W	W	3	3	0	0	2	1	1	2
Cheltenham	L	L	1	0	0	1	1	0	0	0
Grimsby	L	L	1	0	0	1	0	1	0	0
Yeovil	D	W	3	1	1	1	2	1	2	0
Port Vale	W	W	5	4	1	0	3	2	3	2
Forest Green	W	W	1	1	0	0	0	1	0	1
Morecambe	D	W	1	0	1	0	0	1	1	0
Macclesfield			-	-	-	-	-	-	-	-
Tranmere			2	2	0	0	1	1	0	2

Season	Division	Pos	P	W	D	L	F	A	GD	Pts
2017-18	League Two	9	46	20	8	18	67	65	+2	68
2016-17	League One	22	46	11	11	24	44	66	-22	44
2015-16	League One	16	46	16	11	19	64	71	-7	59

Over/Under 63%/37% 1st   **Both score** 54%/46% 12th

LEAGUE TWO

TRANMERE

Nickname: The Rovers
Colours: White
Ground: Prenton Park (16,789)
Tel: 0871 221 2001 tranmererovers.co.uk

Tranmere started the National League season as strong 3-1 favourites and while promotion was ultimately achieved via the playoffs, there were nervous moments.

Three wins in their opening 12 fixtures made a return to the Football League look unlikely, but Tranmere lost only five games in 2018 to easily claim second place.

Rovers saw off Ebbsfleet in extra-time in the semis and then beat Boreham Wood 2-1 in the final despite Liam Ridehalgh's first-minute red card.

Longest run without win/loss: 4/7
High/low league position: 2/18
Clean sheets: 19 **Yellows:** 68 **Reds:** 4
Avg attendance: 3,109 **Players used:** 38
Leading scorer: A Cook 26 (7,20)
Key stat: Tranmere had the best goal difference in last season's National League with +32

| | 2017-18 | | Last six seasons at home | | | | | | | |
	H	A	P	W	D	L	OV	UN	BS	CS
Oldham			2	1	1	0	1	1	1	1
Northampton			1	1	0	0	1	0	1	0
MK Dons			2	1	0	1	1	1	1	0
Bury			2	1	0	1	1	1	0	1
Exeter			1	0	0	1	1	0	1	0
Notts County			2	1	1	0	1	1	2	0
Lincoln			2	1	0	1	1	1	1	0
Mansfield			1	0	1	0	0	0	1	0
Swindon			2	0	0	2	2	0	2	0
Carlisle			3	0	1	2	0	3	0	1
Newport County			1	0	1	0	0	1	0	1
Cambridge Utd			1	0	1	0	0	1	1	0
Colchester			2	2	0	0	2	0	1	1
Crawley Town			2	1	1	0	1	1	1	1
Crewe			2	2	0	0	1	1	1	1
Stevenage			3	1	2	0	2	1	2	1
Cheltenham			2	0	0	2	1	1	1	0
Grimsby			1	1	0	0	0	1	0	1
Yeovil			1	1	0	0	1	0	1	0
Port Vale			1	0	0	1	0	1	0	0
Forest Green			2	0	1	1	0	2	1	0
Morecambe			1	1	0	0	1	0	1	0
Macclesfield	L	D	3	1	0	2	1	2	1	1
Tranmere										

Season	Division	Pos	P	W	D	L	F	A	GD	Pts
2017-18	Conference	2	46	24	10	12	78	46	+32	82
2016-17	Conference	2	46	29	8	9	79	39	+40	95
2015-16	Conference	6	46	22	12	12	61	44	+17	78

Over/Under 50%/50% 11th **Both score** 46%/54% 27th

YEOVIL

Nickname: The Glovers
Colours: Green and white
Ground: Huish Park (9,665)
Tel: 01935-423-662 ytfc.net

Most teams start every new season with optimism, but the feelgood factor didn't even last 90 minutes for Yeovil and their supporters with the Glovers gubbed 8-2 on the opening day by Luton at Kenilworth Road.

Yeovil recovered well enough to end the season in 19th, but there were not too many bright spots as they also won only two of their last 14 matches, although their FA Cup tie with Manchester United briefly raised morale in January.

Longest run without win/loss: 8/4
High/low league position: 17/21
Clean sheets: 13 **Yellows:** 70 **Reds:** 10
Avg attendance: 3,849 **Players used:** 30
Leading scorer: F Zoko 13 (2,12)
Key stat: Yeovil conceded the most corners (275) in League Two last season

| | 2017-18 | | Last six seasons at home | | | | | | | |
	H	A	P	W	D	L	OV	UN	BS	CS
Oldham			2	2	0	0	2	0	2	0
Northampton			1	0	1	0	0	1	1	0
MK Dons			2	1	0	1	1	1	1	0
Bury			1	1	0	0	1	0	1	0
Exeter	W	D	3	1	1	1	1	2	1	1
Notts County	D	L	5	2	3	0	0	5	2	3
Lincoln	L	D	1	0	0	1	1	0	0	0
Mansfield	L	D	3	0	1	2	1	2	1	1
Swindon	L	D	3	0	1	2	1	2	2	0
Carlisle	L	L	4	0	1	3	1	3	1	1
Newport County	L	L	3	2	0	1	0	3	0	2
Cambridge Utd	W	L	3	1	1	1	1	2	2	1
Colchester	L	W	4	2	0	2	2	2	2	0
Crawley Town	L	L	5	3	1	1	5	0	4	1
Crewe	L	D	4	3	1	0	1	3	1	3
Stevenage	W	L	4	1	2	1	3	1	3	1
Cheltenham	D	W	2	1	1	0	1	1	1	1
Grimsby	W	L	2	1	1	0	1	1	0	2
Yeovil										
Port Vale	D	D	2	0	1	1	1	1	2	0
Forest Green	D	L	1	0	1	0	0	1	0	1
Morecambe	D	L	3	0	1	2	2	1	2	0
Macclesfield	-	-	-	-	-	-	-	-	-	-
Tranmere			1	1	0	0	0	1	0	1

Season	Division	Pos	P	W	D	L	F	A	GD	Pts
2017-18	League Two	19	46	12	12	22	59	75	-16	48
2016-17	League Two	20	46	11	17	18	49	64	-15	50
2015-16	League Two	19	46	11	15	20	43	59	-16	48

Over/Under 48%/52% 12th **Both score** 50%/50% 19th

League Two stats 2017-18
Key Points in all tables (except the league table) do not include any deductions imposed by the league.
POS H A Overall league position, rank from home games only, rank from away games only **Sup** Average match supremacy **GFA** Goals For Average **GAA** Goals Against Average **PGA** Points Gained Average

Pos	H	A	League Two 2017-18	P	W	D	L	F	A	W	D	L	F	A	GD	Pts
					Home					Away						
1	1	2	Accrington(P)	46	17	3	3	42	19	12	3	8	34	27	30	93
2	2	5	Luton(P)	46	17	2	4	62	24	8	11	4	32	22	48	88
3	8	1	Wycombe(P)	46	12	5	6	43	35	12	7	4	36	25	19	84
4	4	9	Exeter	46	15	4	4	34	19	9	4	10	30	35	10	80
5	3	11	Notts County	46	14	7	2	43	19	7	7	9	28	29	23	77
6	7	6	Coventry(P)	46	13	4	6	36	24	9	5	9	28	23	17	75
7	6	8	Lincoln	46	12	8	3	38	23	8	7	8	26	25	16	75
8	9	7	Mansfield	46	10	10	3	42	26	8	8	7	25	26	15	72
9	15	3	Swindon	46	9	5	9	29	36	11	3	9	38	29	2	68
10	16	4	Carlisle	46	7	10	6	31	23	10	6	7	31	31	8	67
11	10	13	Newport County	46	9	10	4	32	24	7	6	10	24	34	-2	64
12	5	18	Cambridge Utd	46	13	5	5	38	23	4	8	11	18	37	-4	64
13	12	12	Colchester	46	9	7	7	30	23	7	7	9	23	29	1	62
14	20	10	Crawley	46	8	4	11	30	30	8	7	8	28	36	-8	59
15	13	15	Crewe	46	10	4	9	32	32	7	1	15	30	43	-13	56
16	11	21	Stevenage	46	9	9	5	42	27	5	4	14	18	38	-5	55
17	17	16	Cheltenham	46	8	6	9	31	31	5	6	12	36	42	-6	51
18	24	14	Grimsby	46	6	9	8	20	26	7	3	13	22	40	-24	51
19	19	20	Yeovil	46	8	5	10	29	26	4	7	12	30	49	-16	48
20	21	17	Port Vale	46	7	6	10	26	29	4	8	11	23	38	-18	47
21	14	23	Forest Green	46	10	2	11	35	36	3	6	14	19	41	-23	47
22	22	19	Morecambe	46	6	9	8	22	27	3	10	10	19	29	-15	46
23	18	22	Barnet(R)	46	8	6	9	24	25	4	4	15	22	40	-19	46
24	23	24	Chesterfield(R)	46	8	3	12	27	33	2	5	16	20	50	-36	38

Best attack

		GF	GFA
1	Luton	94	2.04
2	Wycombe	79	1.72
3	Accrington	76	1.65
4	Notts County	71	1.54
5	Mansfield	67	1.46
6	Swindon	67	1.46
7	Cheltenham	67	1.46
8	Exeter	64	1.39
9	Lincoln	64	1.39
10	Coventry	64	1.39
11	Carlisle	62	1.35
12	Crewe	62	1.35
13	Stevenage	60	1.3
14	Yeovil	59	1.28
15	Crawley	58	1.26
16	Newport Co	56	1.22
17	Cambridge U	56	1.22
18	Forest Green	54	1.17
19	Colchester	53	1.15
20	Port Vale	49	1.07
21	Chesterfield	47	1.02
22	Barnet	46	1
23	Grimsby	42	0.91
24	Morecambe	41	0.89

Best defence

		GA	GAA
1	Accrington	46	1
2	Luton	46	1
3	Coventry	47	1.02
4	Notts County	48	1.04
5	Lincoln	48	1.04
6	Mansfield	52	1.13
7	Colchester	52	1.13
8	Exeter	54	1.17
9	Carlisle	54	1.17
10	Morecambe	56	1.22
11	Newport Co	58	1.26
12	Wycombe	60	1.3
13	Cambridge U	60	1.3
14	Swindon	65	1.41
15	Stevenage	65	1.41
16	Barnet	65	1.41
17	Crawley	66	1.43
18	Grimsby	66	1.43
19	Port Vale	67	1.46
20	Cheltenham	73	1.59
21	Crewe	75	1.63
22	Yeovil	75	1.63
23	Forest Green	77	1.67
24	Chesterfield	83	1.8

Top scorers

	Team	Goals scored
B Kee	Accrington	25 ▉▉▉▉▉▉▉▉▉▉▉▉▉▉
M Eisa	Cheltenham	23 ▉▉▉▉▉▉▉▉▉▉▉▉▉
M McNulty	Coventry	23 ▉▉▉▉▉▉▉▉▉▉▉▉▉
D Hylton	Luton	21 ▉▉▉▉▉▉▉▉▉▉▉▉
C Doidge	Forest Green	20 ▉▉▉▉▉▉▉▉▉▉▉
J Collins	Luton	19 ▉▉▉▉▉▉▉▉▉▉
K Dennis	Chesterfield	19 ▉▉▉▉▉▉▉▉▉▉
J Stockley	Exeter	19 ▉▉▉▉▉▉▉▉▉▉

Over 2.5 goals

	H	A	%
Swindon	12	17	63%
Wycombe	16	12	61%
Crewe	13	14	59%
Chesterfield	12	14	57%
Luton	16	10	57%

Under 2.5 goals

	H	A	%
Mansfield	17	12	63%
Wycombe	15	13	61%
Cheltenham	11	16	59%
Newport Co	16	11	59%
Crawley, Notts County			59%

Both to score

	H	A	%
Morecambe	13	16	63%
Carlisle	16	11	59%
Colchester	14	12	57%
Mansfield	11	15	57%
Barnet, Coventry			57%

Both not to score

	H	A	%
Grimsby	13	13	57%
Coventry	14	11	54%
Cambridge U	10	14	52%
Accrington, Luton, Morecambe, Yeovil			50%

League Two results 2017-18

Columns (left to right): Acc = Accrington, Bar = Barnet, Cam = Cambridge Utd, Car = Carlisle, Che = Cheltenham, Chf = Chesterfield, Col = Colchester, Cov = Coventry, Cra = Crawley Town, Cre = Crewe, Exe = Exeter, FGn = Forest Green, Gri = Grimsby, Lin = Lincoln, Lut = Luton, Man = Mansfield, Mor = Morecambe, New = Newport County, Not = Notts County, PtV = Port Vale, Ste = Stevenage, Swi = Swindon, Wyc = Wycombe, Yeo = Yeovil

	Acc	Bar	Cam	Car	Che	Chf	Col	Cov	Cra	Cre	Exe	FGn	Gri	Lin	Lut	Man	Mor	New	Not	PtV	Ste	Swi	Wyc	Yeo
Accrington		4-1	1-0	3-0	1-1	4-0	3-1	1-0	2-3	1-0	1-1	3-1	1-2	1-0	0-2	2-1	1-0	1-1	1-0	3-2	3-2	2-1	1-0	2-0
Barnet	1-1		3-1	1-3	0-2	3-0	0-1	0-0	1-2	2-1	1-2	1-0	0-2	1-1	1-0	1-1	2-1	2-0	1-0	1-1	0-1	1-2	0-2	1-1
Cambridge Utd	0-0	1-0		1-2	4-3	2-1	1-0	2-1	3-1	3-1	2-3	3-0	3-1	0-0	1-1	0-0	0-0	1-2	1-0	5-0	1-0	1-3	1-3	2-1
Carlisle	3-1	1-1	1-1		3-0	2-1	1-1	0-1	2-2	1-0	0-1	1-0	2-0	0-1	1-1	1-1	1-1	1-1	1-1	1-2	0-2	1-2	3-3	4-0
Cheltenham	0-2	1-1	0-0	0-1		1-1	3-1	1-6	1-0	1-0	3-4	0-1	2-3	1-0	2-3	3-0	1-1	1-1	5-1	0-1	2-1	0-2	0-2	0-2
Chesterfield	1-2	2-1	2-3	2-2	0-2		0-0	0-0	1-2	0-2	1-0	3-2	1-3	1-3	2-0	0-1	0-2	1-0	3-1	2-0	0-1	2-1	1-2	2-3
Colchester	0-1	0-1	0-0	0-1	1-4	1-1		2-1	3-1	3-1	3-1	5-1	1-1	1-0	2-1	2-0	0-0	2-0	1-3	1-1	1-1	0-0	1-2	0-1
Coventry	0-2	1-0	3-1	2-0	2-1	1-0	0-0		1-1	1-0	2-0	0-1	4-0	2-4	2-2	0-1	0-0	0-1	3-0	1-0	3-1	3-1	3-2	2-6
Crawley Town	2-1	2-0	0-1	0-1	3-5	0-2	0-2	1-2		1-2	3-1	1-1	3-0	3-1	0-0	2-0	1-1	1-2	0-1	1-3	1-0	1-1	2-3	2-0
Crewe	0-2	1-0	0-1	0-5	2-1	5-1	1-0	1-2	3-0		1-2	3-1	2-0	1-4	1-2	2-2	1-0	1-1	2-0	2-2	1-0	0-3	2-3	0-0
Exeter	2-0	2-1	1-0	1-1	2-1	2-1	1-0	1-0	2-2	3-0		2-0	2-0	1-0	1-4	0-1	4-1	1-0	0-3	0-1	2-1	3-1	1-1	0-0
Forest Green	0-1	2-2	5-2	0-1	1-1	4-1	1-2	2-1	2-0	3-2	1-3		0-3	0-1	0-2	2-0	2-0	0-4	1-2	1-0	3-1	0-2	1-2	4-3
Grimsby	0-3	2-2	0-0	0-1	1-1	1-0	2-2	0-2	0-0	0-1	1-0	0-0		0-0	1-1	0-2	1-2	2-1	1-1	0-0	3-2	2-3	2-1	1-1
Lincoln	2-0	2-1	0-0	4-1	1-0	2-1	2-1	1-2	0-0	1-4	3-2	2-1	3-1		0-0	0-1	1-1	3-1	2-2	3-1	3-0	2-2	0-0	1-1
Luton	1-2	2-0	7-0	3-0	2-2	1-0	3-0	0-3	4-1	3-1	1-0	3-1	2-0	4-2		2-1	1-0	3-1	1-1	2-0	7-1	0-3	2-3	8-2
Mansfield	0-1	3-1	2-1	3-1	3-2	2-2	1-1	1-1	1-1	3-4	1-1	2-0	4-1	1-1	2-2		2-1	5-0	3-1	1-1	1-0	1-3	0-0	0-0
Morecambe	1-2	0-1	0-0	1-1	2-1	2-2	0-0	2-0	0-1	0-1	2-1	1-1	0-0	0-0	0-0	1-2		2-1	1-4	0-3	1-1	0-1	2-1	4-3
Newport County	2-1	1-2	2-1	3-3	1-0	4-1	1-2	1-1	2-1	1-2	2-1	3-3	1-0	0-0	1-1	1-1	1-1		0-0	1-1	0-1	2-1	0-0	2-0
Notts County	2-2	2-1	3-3	2-1	3-1	2-0	2-1	2-1	1-2	4-1	1-2	1-1	0-0	4-1	0-0	1-1	2-0	3-0		1-0	2-0	1-0	0-0	4-1
Port Vale	1-2	1-0	2-0	1-2	3-1	2-1	2-2	1-0	1-2	0-1	0-1	1-1	1-2	1-0	4-0	0-4	0-0	0-0	0-1		2-2	0-3	2-3	1-1
Stevenage	3-2	4-1	0-2	0-0	4-1	5-1	0-1	1-1	1-1	2-2	3-1	1-2	1-1	1-0	2-1	3-3	1-1	2-0	0-1	0-0		0-1	0-0	4-1
Swindon	3-0	1-4	2-0	0-0	0-3	2-2	2-3	1-2	0-3	4-3	1-1	1-0	0-1	0-5	1-0	1-1	0-1	1-0	3-2	3-2	1-0		1-0	2-2
Wycombe	0-4	3-1	1-1	4-3	3-3	1-0	3-1	0-1	4-0	3-2	0-0	3-1	2-1	2-2	1-2	1-2	2-4	2-0	2-4	0-0	1-0	3-2		2-1
Yeovil	3-2	2-0	2-0	0-1	0-0	1-2	0-1	2-0	1-2	2-0	3-1	0-0	3-0	0-2	0-3	2-3	2-2	0-2	1-1	1-1	3-0	1-2	0-1	

Record when first to score

		P	W	D	L	F	A	Sup	PGA	Pts
1	Accrington	28	26	0	2	58	17	1.46	2.8	78
2	Coventry	22	20	2	0	47	12	1.59	2.8	62
3	Luton	24	20	4	0	61	15	1.92	2.7	64
4	Wycombe	23	20	1	2	55	26	1.26	2.7	61
5	Notts County	24	19	5	0	52	18	1.42	2.6	62
6	Lincoln	21	16	2	3	44	24	0.95	2.4	50
7	Cambridge Utd	18	14	1	3	37	18	1.06	2.4	43
8	Grimsby	17	12	4	1	30	15	0.88	2.4	40
9	Exeter	25	18	4	3	41	23	0.72	2.3	58
10	Swindon	24	18	2	4	49	27	0.92	2.3	56
11	Carlisle	24	15	9	0	38	14	1.00	2.3	54
12	Colchester	20	14	4	2	34	19	0.75	2.3	46
13	Crawley	18	12	5	1	26	12	0.78	2.3	41
14	Newport County	23	14	8	1	40	22	0.78	2.2	50
15	Mansfield	22	13	8	1	40	15	1.14	2.1	47
16	Forest Green	14	8	6	0	21	8	0.93	2.1	30
17	Crewe	25	16	2	7	46	34	0.48	2	50
18	Barnet	20	11	6	3	30	17	0.65	2	39
19	Stevenage	23	12	7	4	45	27	0.78	1.9	43
20	Cheltenham	21	12	3	6	48	34	0.67	1.9	39
21	Morecambe	12	6	5	1	21	13	0.67	1.9	23
22	Yeovil	20	11	3	6	45	32	0.65	1.8	36
23	Port Vale	20	11	3	6	31	24	0.35	1.8	36
24	Chesterfield	19	9	4	6	30	25	0.26	1.6	31

Record when keeping a clean sheet

		P	W	D	F	Sup	PGA	Pts
1	Accrington	19	18	1	32	1.68	2.9	55
2	Crewe	11	10	1	15	1.36	2.8	31
3	Barnet	8	7	1	10	1.25	2.8	22
4	Carlisle	15	13	2	24	1.60	2.7	41
5	Exeter	14	12	2	17	1.21	2.7	38
6	Swindon	14	12	2	22	1.57	2.7	38
7	Forest Green	7	6	1	9	1.29	2.7	19
8	Luton	18	14	4	35	1.94	2.6	46
9	Cheltenham	10	8	2	16	1.60	2.6	26
10	Coventry	16	12	4	22	1.38	2.5	40
11	Mansfield	11	8	3	16	1.45	2.5	27
12	Notts County	13	9	4	16	1.23	2.4	31
13	Crawley	10	7	3	14	1.40	2.4	24
14	Port Vale	10	7	3	13	1.30	2.4	24
15	Chesterfield	7	5	2	8	1.14	2.4	17
16	Newport County	11	7	4	12	1.09	2.3	25
17	Stevenage	9	6	3	8	0.89	2.3	21
18	Yeovil	13	8	5	17	1.31	2.2	29
19	Colchester	13	7	6	10	0.77	2.1	27
20	Cambridge Utd	18	9	9	16	0.89	2	36
21	Wycombe	14	7	7	13	0.93	2	28
22	Grimsby	12	6	6	9	0.75	2	24
23	Lincoln	15	7	8	11	0.73	1.9	29
24	Morecambe	12	3	9	6	0.50	1.5	18

Salford's swift rise set to stall but Orient ready for Football League return

National League new boys Salford City are the market leaders to make it four promotions in five years, but the influence of their part-owners may be clouding the bookies' judgement, writes Andrew Wilsher. Manchester United legends Gary Neville, Paul Scholes, Ryan Giggs, Phil Neville and Nicky Butt each hold a 10 per cent stake and their guidance has been a driving force behind Salford's rise.

However, shortly after the Ammies won the National League North with 91 points, joint-managers Bernard Morley and Anthony Johnson left by mutual consent after three years with the club and have since been replaced by former Fleetwood and Scunthorpe manager Graham Alexander.

While there is no doubt that the support of the Class of '92 should enable Salford to establish themselves within their new division, there is no value in backing them to win a league that has frequently proven to be one of the toughest to get out of. The likes of Cambridge and Tranmere have highlighted how difficult it is to win the division and, with a questionmark hanging over the new manager, they are best avoided.

One club who do look to have an excellent chance at promotion is Leyton Orient.

The O's only managed to finish 13th last season, but faced a relegation threat around Christmas after a disastrous winter run saw them go 15 matches without a win.

That period can largely be attributed to an unfortunate catalogue of injuries in defence, and Justin Edinburgh's side soon stabilised to finish the season playing the type of football that was expected of them.

Having kept hold of most of their players while gaining the services of former Chester and Tranmere striker James Alabi, Orient are ready to mount a convincing challenge.

Chesterfield drop into the National League after suffering two consecutive relegations and have made plenty of signings to in an attempt to bounce straight back up.

Among the players to join the Spireites are former Macclesfield goalkeeper Shwan Jalal and ex-Barnet duo Curtis Weston and Michael Nelson.

The Derbyshire club have the potential for a promotion push, but the players will need to gel quickly in order to mount a challenge this year.

AFC Fylde were last season's top scorers and reached the playoffs before losing 2-1 to Boreham Wood in the opening round. They have kept hold of striker Danny Rowe and brought in former Wigan defender Luke Burke, but the loss of captain Sam Finley to Accrington is a serious blow.

Barnet enter the National League for the third time since the start of the millennium, but new boss John Still could provide the yo-yo side with a quick escape.

The former Dagenham & Redbridge manager is a veteran of the division and has the credentials to guide the Bees to promotion, having already raided his old side of a number of key players.

Daggers are in freefall after losing their financial backing midway through last season and releasing the majority of their squad as a result. Peter Taylor was appointed

Stakeholder Ryan Giggs takes a dousing during Salford's promotion celebrations

as manager over the summer but with such uncertainty in their future they look the bet to face the drop.

Hampton & Richmond lost to Braintree on penalties in the playoff final last term but can make amends by winning the National League South this season.

The Beavers have made plenty of signings over the summer – nine of which have come from Hendon – while retaining their top talent. At 14-1, they look a decent bet in a competitive field. Chelmsford and St Albans also appeal.

Brackley won the FA Trophy last year, beating Bromley 5-4 on penalties after a last-minute equaliser took the game to extra-time, and also reached the playoff final.

They have lost the services of key defender Alex Gudger to Solihull Moors, but new signing Connor Hall is more than capable of filling the gap.

The Saints should go close again this year, but Stockport and York could also mount a title challenge.

Recommendations
Leyton Orient to be promoted from the National League, 7-1
Dagenham & Redbridge to be relegated from the National League, 15-8
Hampton & Richmond to win the National League South, 16-1
Brackley Town to win the National League North, 16-1

National League 2017-18

Pos	H	A		P	W	D	L	F	A	W	D	L	F	A	GD	Pts
					Home					**Away**						
1	2	1	Macclesfield (P)	46	13	7	3	31	19	14	4	5	36	27	21	92
2	1	3	Tranmere (P)	46	15	2	6	48	23	9	8	6	30	23	32	82
3	5	2	Sutton Utd	46	12	6	5	36	28	11	4	8	31	25	14	79
4	7	5	Boreham Wood	46	12	5	6	33	25	8	10	5	31	22	17	75
5	9	4	Aldershot	46	11	7	5	35	23	9	8	6	29	29	12	75
6	10	6	Ebbsfleet	46	11	7	5	35	23	8	10	5	29	27	14	74
7	3	9	AFC Fylde	46	11	9	3	51	27	9	4	10	31	29	26	73
8	6	7	Dover	46	12	5	6	32	17	8	8	7	30	27	18	73
9	12	8	Bromley	46	10	8	5	38	23	9	5	9	37	35	17	70
10	8	10	Wrexham	46	10	10	3	31	17	7	9	7	18	22	10	70
11	4	16	Dag & Red	46	13	3	7	40	32	6	8	9	29	30	7	68
12	11	17	Maidenhead	46	11	6	6	36	26	6	7	10	29	40	-1	64
13	17	11	Leyton Orient	46	8	6	9	33	26	8	6	9	25	30	2	60
14	18	13	Eastleigh	46	6	11	6	33	34	7	6	10	32	38	-7	56
15	19	12	Hartlepool	46	7	6	10	24	26	7	8	8	29	37	-10	56
16	13	20	Halifax	46	9	6	8	31	30	4	10	9	17	28	-10	55
17	14	19	Gateshead	46	8	8	7	34	27	4	10	9	28	31	4	54
18	16	18	Solihull Moors	46	8	7	8	28	30	6	5	12	21	30	-11	54
19	20	15	Maidstone	46	6	9	8	25	31	7	6	10	27	33	-12	54
20	21	14	Barrow	46	4	10	9	23	29	7	6	10	28	34	-12	49
21	15	23	Woking (R)	46	9	5	9	32	32	4	4	15	23	44	-21	48
22	22	21	Torquay (R)	46	5	6	12	26	36	5	6	12	19	37	-28	42
23	23	22	Chester (R)	46	5	5	13	20	37	3	8	12	22	42	-37	37
24	24	24	Guiseley (R)	46	3	9	11	21	33	4	3	16	23	56	-45	33

National League results

	Aldershot	Barrow	Boreham W	Bromley	Chester	Dag & Red	Dover	Eastleigh	Ebbsfleet	Fylde	Gateshead	Guiseley	Halifax	Hartlepool	Leyton Orient	Macclesfield	Maidenhead	Maidstone	Solihull Moors	Sutton Utd	Torquay	Tranmere	Woking	Wrexham
Aldershot		1-1	2-0	1-1	1-2	0-2	0-2	0-0	2-1	1-0	6-0	0-1	2-1	2-2	1-2	1-0	1-1	1-0	2-2	3-2	2-1	3-1	2-0	
Barrow	3-1		2-1	0-3	1-2	0-1	0-0	3-2	0-1	1-3	1-1	0-0	0-0	1-2	2-2	0-2	1-1	0-1	1-2	1-1	1-1	3-0	1-1	
Boreham Wood	2-1	0-0		2-2	4-2	1-2	2-3	1-0	0-1	1-0	2-1	3-1	1-1	0-0	2-0	0-2	1-1	1-0	4-1	0-4	2-0	2-1	2-1	0-1
Bromley	0-2	0-0	3-2		1-1	3-1	2-2	0-0	4-2	0-1	0-0	2-1	3-0	2-0	6-1	1-1	2-3	2-2	1-0	0-1	3-1	0-1	2-0	1-1
Chester	0-0	3-2	1-2	3-2		0-4	0-2	3-1	1-1	1-1	1-3	0-2	0-0	1-1	0-1	0-2	2-0	1-3	1-0	2-3	0-2	0-2	0-2	0-1
Dag & Red	0-2	2-1	2-3	5-1	3-2		1-0	1-2	3-3	2-0	3-1	3-2	3-1	4-2	0-0	1-0	1-0	2-1	1-3	1-2	1-0	0-4	1-1	0-1
Dover	1-2	1-1	0-1	1-2	4-0	1-0		2-0	1-1	0-2	3-1	0-0	4-0	1-0	2-0	1-1	2-2	1-0	0-1	1-0	0-1	3-1	1-0	
Eastleigh	0-0	0-2	0-2	4-4	2-2	2-2	2-1		0-1	2-2	3-2	4-2	0-0	4-3	0-0	0-2	2-2	0-1	1-2	1-1	1-1	2-0	2-2	1-1
Ebbsfleet	0-2	3-2	0-3	2-1	0-1	1-1	2-1	2-2		3-3	0-0	4-0	2-0	3-0	2-1	2-2	1-1	2-0	1-0	0-1	0-0	2-1	3-0	
Fylde	7-1	1-0	2-2	2-2	1-1	2-2	3-1	2-2	1-1		0-0	2-1	2-0	3-3	0-1	6-0	1-4	3-0	1-1	2-1	2-0	5-2	1-2	2-0
Gateshead	0-1	1-2	1-1	1-2	3-2	0-0	0-0	2-0	2-5	1-2		1-0	0-0	2-2	1-3	3-0	7-1	2-1	2-2	0-2	3-0	1-0	1-1	0-0
Guiseley	1-1	0-1	0-0	0-1	1-1	3-5	1-1	0-0	2-2	1-0	0-1		1-1	0-1	1-3	1-2	1-3	0-0	4-2	0-2	3-2	0-0	1-2	0-2
Halifax	0-2	0-1	2-1	2-1	4-0	2-1	1-2	3-3	1-2	2-1	2-2	2-0		2-0	1-2	1-4	3-2	0-2	0-0	2-1	1-1	0-2	0-0	0-0
Hartlepool	0-2	1-0	0-0	2-1	1-1	1-0	0-1	1-2	0-1	0-2	2-2	0-1	4-0		1-0	1-2	1-2	3-1	0-1	1-1	1-1	1-1	3-2	0-2
Leyton Orient	2-3	4-1	0-0	1-0	1-1	2-2	2-0	1-1	1-1	1-2	0-2	4-1	0-3	1-2		0-1	0-1	2-0	3-1	4-1	0-1	1-0	3-1	4-1
Macclesfield	2-0	3-1	0-0	0-0	1-0	2-0	1-0	1-2	1-0	2-1	0-2	1-1	2-1	2-1	1-1		1-0	1-4	0-0	1-0	1-1	2-2	1-3	4-1
Maidenhead	3-3	0-1	2-1	5-2	3-0	1-1	3-2	3-1	1-1	1-2	0-3	3-0	0-0	2-1	0-1	1-1		0-0	1-0	2-1	1-2	1-0	2-1	1-2
Maidstone	1-1	0-1	0-4	0-2	1-0	0-0	2-2	2-3	1-2	1-0	2-2	1-1	0-0	1-2	0-2	2-2	1-1		1-1	1-0	1-0	2-3	3-1	2-1
Solihull Moors	0-0	3-3	0-0	2-0	2-0	2-2	3-2	1-4	1-3	0-4	1-1	3-1	0-1	1-2	1-0	0-1	3-1	1-0		0-2	1-1	0-2	3-0	0-0
Sutton Utd	2-1	3-2	1-1	0-3	3-2	2-1	2-2	2-0	0-0	2-1	1-1	4-0	3-2	1-1	2-0	2-1	0-2	1-3	1-0		0-1	1-3	2-0	1-1
Torquay	0-0	3-1	2-4	0-4	1-1	0-3	0-2	1-2	1-1	1-3	1-1	3-4	1-0	0-2	3-0	0-1	4-0	0-1	1-2	2-3		0-0	2-1	0-0
Tranmere	2-0	1-0	2-2	1-0	0-0	2-0	0-1	3-1	3-0	4-1	4-2	4-2	1-2	2-1	1-4	3-2	4-0	1-2	0-1	3-0	3-1		3-1	0-1
Woking	1-2	1-2	0-0	0-2	1-0	1-0	1-2	2-1	1-0	2-1	2-3	1-3	1-1	0-2	2-3	1-1	4-4	2-1	2-0	4-1	0-1		2-2	
Wrexham	2-2	3-3	0-1	2-0	2-0	1-2	0-0	2-1	2-0	0-0	1-0	1-1	1-1	0-0	2-1	0-2	1-0	1-0	1-1	4-0	2-2	1-0		

The Macclesfield players celebrate their return to the Football League

National League North 2017-18

	H	A		P	Home					Away					GD	Pts
					W	D	L	F	A	W	D	L	F	A		
1	2	1	Salford City (P)	42	15	2	4	44	24	13	5	3	36	21	35	91
2	1	3	Harrogate (P)	42	15	4	2	60	18	11	3	7	40	31	51	85
3	4	2	Brackley	42	13	5	3	39	16	10	6	5	33	21	35	80
4	3	7	Kidderminster	42	13	5	3	50	25	7	7	7	26	25	26	72
5	5	8	Stockport	42	12	5	4	41	19	8	4	9	34	38	18	69
6	6	6	Chorley	42	10	8	3	28	14	8	6	7	24	25	13	68
7	15	4	Bradford PA	42	9	4	8	38	30	9	5	7	28	26	10	63
8	13	5	Spennymoor	42	9	6	6	31	29	9	3	9	40	39	3	63
9	7	15	Boston Utd	42	11	5	5	40	30	6	4	11	27	36	1	60
10	9	11	Blyth Spartans	42	11	1	9	39	24	8	1	12	37	45	7	59
11	11	12	York	42	9	7	5	31	27	7	3	11	34	35	3	58
12	14	14	Darlington	42	9	5	7	37	26	5	8	8	21	32	0	55
13	16	13	Nuneaton	42	8	7	6	28	23	6	6	9	22	34	-7	55
14	20	9	Telford	42	8	3	10	32	41	8	2	11	23	28	-14	53
15	17	16	Southport	42	8	4	9	34	32	6	4	11	26	40	-12	50
16	8	21	FC United	42	12	2	7	35	26	2	6	13	23	46	-14	50
17	21	10	Alfreton	42	7	3	11	31	33	7	4	10	36	38	-4	49
18	10	18	Curzon Ashton	42	9	7	5	29	23	3	6	12	23	43	-14	49
19	18	17	Leamington	42	8	4	9	30	30	5	6	10	21	35	-14	49
20	12	22	Gainsborough (R)	42	11	1	9	33	30	3	3	15	14	43	-26	46
21	19	19	Tamworth (R)	42	7	6	8	35	34	4	3	14	21	43	-21	42
22	22	20	North Ferriby (R)	42	1	5	15	11	49	3	4	14	14	52	-76	21

National League North results

	Alfreton	Blyth Spartans	Boston Utd	Brackley	Bradford PA	Chorley	Curzon Ashton	Darlington	FC United	Gainsborough	Harrogate	Kidderminster	Leamington	North Ferriby	Nuneaton	Salford City	Southport	Spennymoor	Stockport	Tamworth	Telford	York
Alfreton		2-0	2-3	1-1	1-3	0-2	4-0	1-1	1-0	4-1	1-2	0-2	4-1	1-0	1-1	2-3	0-1	1-4	1-3	2-1	0-1	2-3
Blyth Spartans	0-1		5-2	3-0	3-0	2-0	2-1	3-1	1-1	4-0	0-2	1-2	1-0	0-1	6-3	0-1	2-0	2-3	0-1	4-2	0-1	0-2
Boston Utd	3-1	2-1		2-3	1-2	2-0	3-3	1-1	4-4	2-0	3-0	3-2	0-1	2-1	1-1	0-1	3-2	0-3	2-2	3-1	1-0	2-1
Brackley	1-3	3-1	4-1		0-1	1-2	2-2	3-0	2-1	2-0	0-0	2-0	1-1	3-0	1-0	2-1	4-0	2-0	3-2	0-0	1-1	1-0
Bradford PA	3-3	4-1	2-1	2-0		0-0	3-1	0-1	3-0	5-0	3-1	1-1	1-0	0-1	1-1	1-2	1-2	1-2	2-3	3-4	2-1	0-5
Chorley	1-0	2-0	0-1	0-0	2-0		1-1	4-1	1-0	1-0	0-1	0-0	2-0	2-2	2-2	2-0	0-1	0-0	3-1	1-1	1-1	3-2
Curzon Ashton	2-2	0-3	2-1	0-2	1-1	0-2		1-0	1-0	2-0	1-2	1-2	1-1	4-0	2-2	1-1	2-2	1-0	1-1	1-0	1-0	4-1
Darlington	4-1	3-0	1-2	0-3	2-1	2-2	1-0		3-0	4-3	3-1	2-1	0-0	6-0	0-0	1-2	2-4	1-1	1-1	0-1	0-1	1-2
FC United	3-2	1-3	2-1	1-1	4-0	0-0	2-0	1-2		1-0	3-2	1-2	1-2	0-2	2-1	3-2	1-0	2-3	0-1	3-1	3-1	1-0
Gainsborough	2-1	2-4	1-1	1-2	0-3	1-0	1-0	3-1	1-0		4-5	1-0	1-2	2-0	0-1	0-1	0-3	4-1	2-3	3-0	3-2	1-0
Harrogate	4-3	5-1	3-1	1-1	1-1	4-1	5-0	3-0	6-0	2-0		2-2	2-2	3-0	4-0	1-2	2-0	1-2	4-1	3-0	2-1	2-0
Kidderminster	2-1	5-1	1-1	2-1	1-2	0-1	2-2	3-3	4-0	3-0	0-2		2-0	4-0	4-3	0-2	2-3	2-1	2-2	2-0	2-0	2-1
Leamington	2-3	1-0	0-2	2-2	2-1	2-0	0-0	2-3	1-0	3-0	1-3	1-1		3-0	1-0	0-4	0-1	4-0	2-3	1-2	0-3	2-2
North Ferriby	0-3	1-0	1-5	0-5	0-1	0-2	0-1	1-1	3-3	0-1	0-2	1-3	1-1		0-2	1-1	0-3	0-6	1-3	0-0	0-2	1-4
Nuneaton	2-2	2-2	1-1	0-2	0-0	1-1	1-1	2-1	1-0	0-1	2-1	1-0	4-0	2-2		0-2	3-0	0-1	1-3	4-1	0-2	1-0
Salford City	1-0	4-1	1-2	2-0	2-2	0-3	2-1	0-2	2-2	1-0	2-1	3-0	2-3	4-0	3-0		2-1	3-2	2-1	2-1	3-0	3-2
Southport	1-3	0-3	4-0	0-1	0-4	3-0	3-1	2-0	3-3	2-2	1-4	0-3	2-0	2-2	0-1	0-1		1-2	3-1	3-0	3-0	1-1
Spennymoor	2-1	3-1	0-0	0-3	3-0	1-0	2-4	1-2	4-4	1-1	3-1	1-1	1-0	1-1	0-1	1-1	2-1		1-0	1-1	1-2	2-4
Stockport	1-0	1-3	1-0	0-1	0-0	1-1	3-0	1-1	4-1	1-0	2-2	1-2	4-0	4-1	0-1	2-2	6-0	3-2		3-2	1-0	2-0
Tamworth	2-3	0-3	2-1	1-1	0-1	3-4	4-1	0-0	0-2	1-2	1-1	2-1	0-3	4-1	2-0	1-2	3-3	3-1	3-1		2-2	1-1
Telford	1-2	2-3	2-1	1-3	1-4	1-2	0-3	0-0	1-0	3-2	1-5	0-0	3-2	3-0	1-2	0-2	1-1	3-2	3-2	2-0		3-5
York	1-1	2-3	1-0	2-1	2-1	1-1	2-1	0-0	0-2	1-1	0-2	1-1	2-2	2-0	4-3	1-0	3-2	2-2	2-0	2-3	0-1	

National League South 2017-18

Pos	H	A		P	Home					Away					GD	Pts
					W	D	L	F	A	W	D	L	F	A		
1	3	1	Havant & W (P)	42	11	7	3	40	20	14	4	3	30	10	40	86
2	1	3	Dartford	42	15	3	3	51	20	11	5	5	30	24	37	86
3	8	2	Chelmsford	42	10	6	5	37	24	11	5	5	31	22	22	74
4	5	5	Hampton & R	42	9	11	1	30	16	9	7	5	28	21	21	72
5	2	9	Hemel	42	12	5	4	39	20	7	8	6	34	31	22	70
6	4	8	Braintree (P)	42	11	6	4	40	23	8	7	6	33	32	18	69*
7	11	4	Truro City	42	10	4	7	39	29	10	5	6	32	26	16	69
8	7	11	St Albans	42	11	4	6	40	28	8	4	9	31	31	12	65
9	13	7	Bath City	42	8	7	6	31	20	9	5	7	33	28	16	63
10	14	6	Welling	42	8	4	9	36	31	9	6	6	33	28	10	61
11	9	15	Wealdstone	42	11	3	7	36	29	5	8	8	28	33	2	59
12	10	18	Weston-s-Mare	42	11	2	8	38	30	5	5	11	28	43	-7	55
13	6	19	Chippenham	42	10	7	4	38	25	5	2	14	26	45	-6	54
14	16	14	Gloucester	42	8	3	10	27	31	7	5	9	29	39	-14	53
15	18	10	East Thurrock	42	5	6	10	32	32	8	5	8	36	52	-16	50
16	15	16	Oxford City	42	7	6	8	34	30	6	4	11	26	39	-9	49
17	12	21	Concord Rangers	42	9	5	7	26	26	3	5	13	20	36	-16	46
18	19	12	Eastbourne	42	5	4	12	29	40	8	3	10	28	40	-23	46
19	17	17	Hungerford Town	42	6	4	11	26	29	6	3	12	19	39	-23	43
20	22	13	Poole Town (R)	42	4	4	13	21	42	7	5	9	26	32	-27	42
21	20	20	Whitehawk (R)	42	4	7	10	24	40	4	3	14	27	49	-38	34
22	21	22	Bognor Regis (R)	42	4	4	13	25	39	1	8	12	16	39	-37	27

*Braintree deducted 1pt

National League South results

	Bath City	Bognor Regis	Braintree	Chelmsford	Chippenham	Concord R	Dartford	East Thurrock	Eastbourne	Gloucester	Hampton & W	Havant & W	Hemel	Hungerford	Oxford City	Poole Town	St Albans	Truro City	Wealdstone	Welling	Weston-s-Mare	Whitehawk
Bath City		0-0	1-1	1-2	2-5	2-0	1-2	4-0	0-1	5-1	2-0	1-2	0-0	5-0	2-1	1-0	2-1	0-0	0-0	1-1	0-2	1-1
Bognor Regis	3-2		2-1	0-1	1-3	1-2	1-2	0-2	0-1	2-2	1-2	0-3	2-3	1-2	0-0	1-1	2-1	0-2	0-3	1-3	1-1	6-2
Braintree	0-2	3-0		2-2	2-0	2-1	2-2	4-0	3-2	3-0	2-1	1-3	1-2	5-0	0-0	1-0	1-0	1-1	2-2	1-1	0-1	4-3
Chelmsford	1-1	0-0	2-2		2-0	1-0	1-0	1-2	5-2	2-0	1-2	0-2	3-3	1-1	1-2	2-1	0-2	2-0	3-0	4-1	1-1	4-2
Chippenham	0-3	1-0	1-1	3-2		1-2	2-2	2-2	4-0	2-0	3-3	0-0	5-1	1-2	3-2	0-1	3-3	2-0	0-0	1-0	2-0	2-1
Concord Rangers	0-1	2-1	0-1	0-2	4-2		1-1	1-4	2-1	1-1	1-0	1-1	0-1	0-1	1-2	2-2	3-1	0-2	2-2	1-0		
Dartford	2-0	3-1	1-1	1-2	3-0	2-0		0-1	4-2	4-1	1-0	1-0	3-2	0-0	7-1	0-1	2-1	4-1	3-3	4-1	3-1	3-1
East Thurrock	1-1	2-0	5-3	2-4	0-2	2-3	0-1		0-0	3-0	1-1	0-1	0-1	0-1	4-1	2-2	1-1	1-2	1-1	0-1	3-4	4-2
Eastbourne	2-3	3-0	2-3	0-3	4-2	3-1	0-1	2-2		0-1	1-2	1-4	0-2	4-1	2-0	0-4	1-1	1-3	1-1	0-0	1-2	1-4
Gloucester	2-1	3-2	1-3	0-2	1-0	1-0	0-1	3-1	1-2		1-1	0-1	1-0	4-0	0-1	2-2	1-4	0-3	2-2	0-1	1-3	3-1
Hampton & R	3-1	1-0	1-1	1-1	1-0	1-1	2-2	5-1	1-1	1-1		0-1	0-0	3-1	1-0	1-0	1-0	1-1	1-1	1-1	3-1	1-1
Havant & W	1-2	0-0	0-0	1-1	4-0	3-2	0-0	6-1	3-2	2-1	0-0		1-1	2-0	3-2	2-2	2-1	1-2	1-0	2-3	2-0	4-0
Hemel	1-1	3-1	4-3	4-1	3-1	1-1	0-3	2-0	3-0	3-1	1-0	0-0		1-2	2-0	0-1	3-0	1-0	2-2	2-1	1-3	3-0
Hungerford	1-2	1-1	0-1	1-1	2-2	0-1	2-1	0-2	0-1	0-2	0-1	0-2	1-2		4-0	3-1	0-1	1-3	1-4	2-0	0-1	0-1
Oxford City	1-1	4-0	1-2	2-0	0-1	1-0	0-2	3-3	2-1	0-3	0-0	0-1	4-1	2-0		2-3	2-3	3-1	3-2	1-1	3-3	0-1
Poole Town	0-4	2-2	0-3	0-0	2-0	1-1	0-1	2-3	0-4	0-3	0-1	1-3	2-4	1-2	2-0		0-1	0-3	2-1	2-4	3-1	1-1
St Albans	2-0	1-2	2-1	2-1	2-0	2-1	4-0	7-2	2-2	2-3	1-3	2-1	2-2	0-0	1-1	2-1		0-1	2-1	1-2	3-1	0-3
Truro City	1-2	1-1	1-2	2-0	1-0	2-0	3-1	1-2	0-1	1-1	1-1	1-0	3-3	2-1	2-3	3-1	1-2		1-3	3-2	2-1	7-2
Wealdstone	2-1	3-0	3-1	0-2	4-4	2-1	1-2	3-0	2-3	1-2	0-3	0-1	1-1	1-0	1-1	4-1	1-3	2-1		1-0	2-1	2-1
Welling	0-2	3-3	3-0	0-1	4-0	3-3	2-3	0-3	3-0	2-3	0-1	0-1	0-0	3-2	1-3	2-0	3-1	2-2	1-2		3-1	1-0
Weston-s-Mare	4-2	1-0	1-2	0-1	2-2	1-0	3-0	2-2	5-1	2-1	1-2	1-4	2-1	2-1	4-2	1-2	0-2	0-2	5-1	0-2		1-0
Whitehawk	1-1	2-2	2-1	0-2	1-3	2-0	0-4	2-3	0-1	1-1	1-3	0-0	0-5	0-3	0-3	2-2	1-1	3-2	0-1	2-1	5-1	

Celtic should reign again but the competition looks fierce behind the champs

The arrival of Steven Gerrard at Ibrox as the new manager of Rangers has added some welcome glamour to the 2018-19 Scottish Premiership campaign, but it doesn't alter the fact that the former England captain – and the rest – are playing for second place once again, writes Steve Davies. An eighth-straight Celtic title success is pretty much a given, only the margin of victory meriting a debate.

Last season, Brendan Rodgers' treble winners finished nine points clear of the rest, a marked fall from the 30-point advantage they imposed on the chasers a season earlier.

They actually won only two more matches than second-placed Aberdeen – runners-up for the fourth-straight year – so maybe the gap is closing. And while Celtic look likely to drop more points than they did in their incredible 2016-17 season, they will benefit from the fact that the Dons, Rangers and Hibs will also be taking points off each other.

It means the race for second promises to be every bit as absorbing as last season's, where six points separated second, third and fourth.

It's fair to say Rangers are too short in betting without their Old Firm rivals. Gerrard has attracted players of the calibre of Connor Goldson and Scott Arfield to Ibrox and is overseeing a sizeable squad restructure, but no-one does false dawns quite like the Gers.

This is Gerrard's first management job and it's one that has broken far more experienced coaches than the former Liverpool midfielder.

Derek McInnes played the loan market supremely well last season and will have to do so again if Aberdeen are going to be next best. He's bullish about newcomers like Chris Forrester and Stephen Gleeson and the mood at Pittodrie is definitely upbeat.

The same, though, is the case at Easter Road where the players are relieved that maanger Neil Lennon didn't carry through

his threat to quit after the loss against Hearts in May – their only league defeat in four months as they recovered from a patchy start.

They've clearly got plenty going for them and only Celtic lost fewer games than the Hibbees. They drew too many against bottom-four sides but with more of a cutting edge they could run Celtic closest.

At the other end, Livingston sprang a surprise with the appointment of Kenny Miller. This was a League One club two years ago with not much better than a League One budget and Miller's men face relegation.

In the Championship, Dundee United have to shoulder favouritism again and look worth opposing once more.

The Tangerines have got some serious opposition and you can make a case for many of them, including a progressive outfit like Dunfermline, who finished well last season and can sustain a title charge.

Raith should have gone up from League One last season and can get it right this term, while Peterhead's show of faith in Jim McInally can be rewarded with promotion from the basement.

Recommended bets
Hibernian w/o Celtic, 6-1
Livingston to finish bottom, 9-4
Dunfermline to win the Championship, 10-1
Raith to win League One, 9-4
Peterhead to win League Two, 15-8

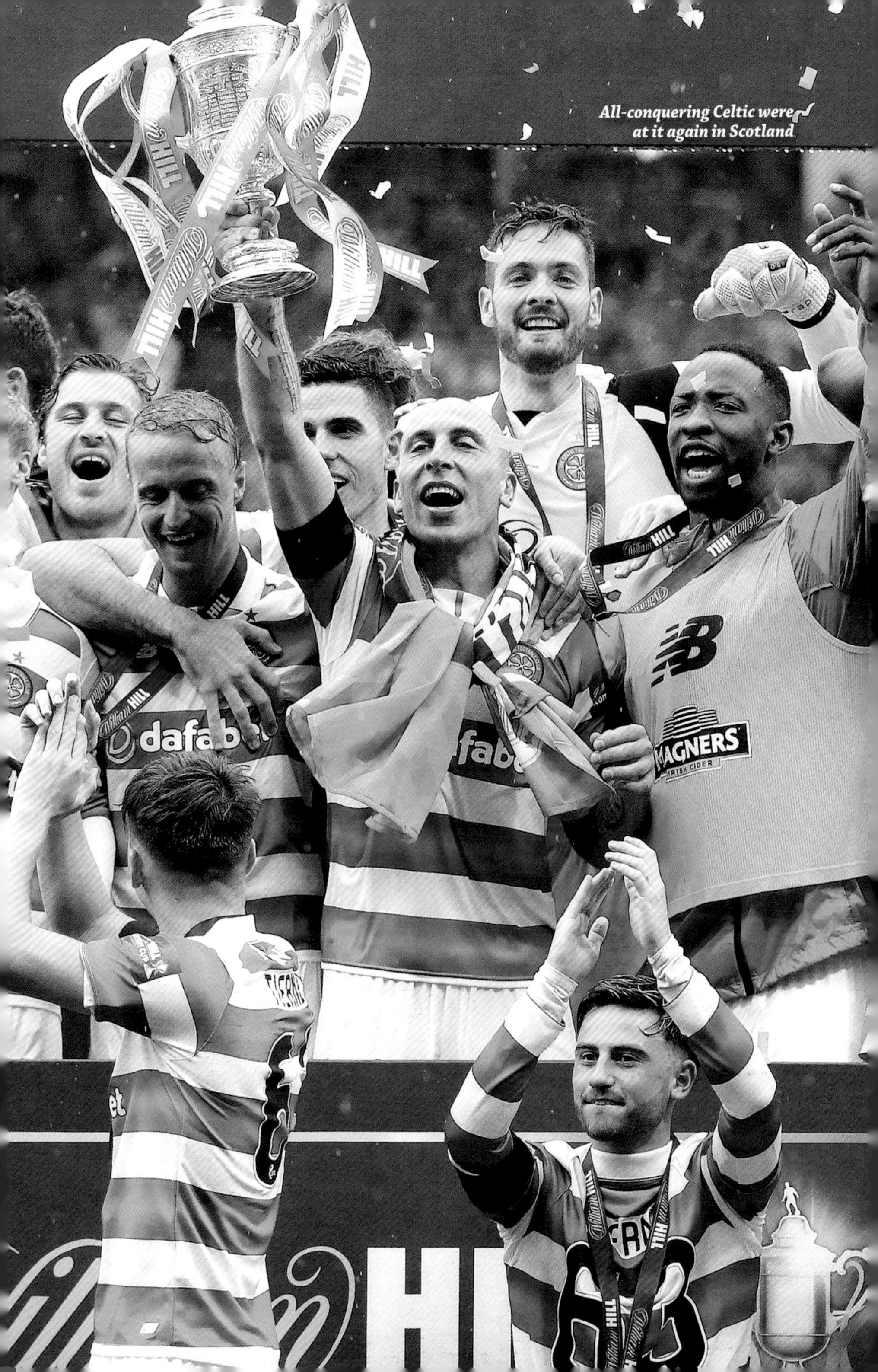

All-conquering Celtic were at it again in Scotland

ABERDEEN

Nickname: The Dons
Colours: Red
Ground: Pittodrie (22,474)
Tel: 01224 650-400   afc.co.uk

The Dons shrugged off Europa League failure at the hands of Apollon Limassol in the third qualifying round by going nine unbeaten at the start of the season.

They were then locked in a titanic battle with Rangers for second spot, not helping themselves by losing all six games against the Old Firm before the split. Eventually they prevailed for those who'd backed them at 6-4 without Celtic as they finished behind Brendan Rodgers' side for the fourth season in a row.

Longest run without win/loss: 3/9
High/low league position: 2/3
Clean sheets: 17 **Yellows:** 69 **Reds:** 3
Avg attendance: 15,425 **Players used:** 27
Leading scorer: A Rooney 9 (3,6)
Key stat: Eleven of Aberdeen's last 12 league matches produced two goals or fewer, six of which produced 2-0 scorelines.

	2017-18 H	A	Last six seasons at home P	W	D	L	OV	UN	BS	CS
Celtic	L L	L W	11	3	0	8	6	5	5	0
Aberdeen										
Rangers	L D	L L	4	1	1	2	3	1	3	0
Hibernian	W D	W L	5	3	2	0	2	3	2	3
Kilmarnock	D W	W W	10	8	1	1	5	5	6	3
Hearts	D W	D L	10	4	4	2	1	9	2	7
Motherwell	L	W W	11	5	3	3	4	7	5	3
St Johnstone	W W	W	12	5	4	3	3	9	4	6
Dundee	W W	W	8	7	1	0	3	5	2	6
Hamilton	W W	D	6	6	0	0	4	2	1	5
St Mirren			5	2	3	0	2	3	1	4
Livingston	-	-	-	-	-	-	-	-	-	-

Season	Division	Pos	P	W	D	L	F	A	GD	Pts
2017-18	Premiership	2	38	22	7	9	56	37	+19	73
2016-17	Premiership	2	38	24	4	10	74	35	+39	76
2015-16	Premiership	2	38	22	5	11	62	48	+14	71

Over/Under 45%/55% 8th   **Both score** 34%/66% 12th

Top league scorers	P	G		Y	R
A Rooney	17 (19)	9		-	-
K McLean	37	8		8	-
G Mackay-Steven	22 (9)	5		2	-
S May	25 (4)	5		3	-
R Christie	28 (4)	4		5	1
A Considine	30 (2)	4		6	-
K Arnason	16 (5)	3		3	-
G Stewart	17 (13)	3		-	-

S Logan, N McGinn, S McKenna, A O'Connor and G Shinnie all scored two goals. Four players scored one goal.

CELTIC

Nickname: The Bhoys
Colours: Green and white
Ground: Celtic Park (60,832)
Tel: 0871-226-1888   celticfc.net

Celtic marched to a seventh-straight league title, winning by nine points. Brendan Rodgers' men added both domestic cup competitions to make it back-to-back trebles, and they are a short price to complete the treble-treble.

They didn't lose a game in the league until a 4-0 humbling by Hearts in mid-December by which time their Champions League dreams had been wrecked. Their subsequent Europa League adventure was ended by Zenit at the last-16 stage.

Longest run without win/loss: 2/17
High/low league position: 1/1
Clean sheets: 20 **Yellows:** 45 **Reds:** 2
Avg attendance: 35,207 **Players used:** 31
Leading scorer: S Sinclair 10 (2,8)
Key stat: Celtic were the clean sheet kings, keeping 20 in their 38 top-flight fixtures, including 15 wins to nil.

	2017-18 H	A	Last six seasons at home P	W	D	L	OV	UN	BS	CS
Celtic										
Aberdeen	W L	W W	12	11	0	1	9	3	7	4
Rangers	D W	W W	4	2	2	0	2	2	2	2
Hibernian	D W	D L	5	3	2	0	3	2	2	3
Kilmarnock	D D	W L	10	6	3	1	5	5	5	4
Hearts	W W	L W	9	8	1	0	5	4	4	5
Motherwell	W	D D	10	8	1	1	5	5	3	7
St Johnstone	D D	W	11	7	3	1	6	5	6	4
Dundee	W D	W	9	7	2	0	5	4	2	7
Hamilton	W	W W	6	5	0	1	3	3	2	3
St Mirren			4	4	0	0	2	2	1	3
Livingston	-	-	-	-	-	-	-	-	-	-

Season	Division	Pos	P	W	D	L	F	A	GD	Pts
2017-18	Premiership	1	38	24	10	4	73	25	+48	82
2016-17	Premiership	1	38	34	4	0	106	25	+81	106
2015-16	Premiership	1	38	26	8	4	93	31	+62	86

Over/Under 50%/50% 4th   **Both score** 39%/61% 11th

Top league scorers	P	G		Y	R
S Sinclair	23 (12)	10		-	-
M Dembele	17 (8)	9		2	-
O Edouard	12 (10)	9		1	-
L Griffiths	11 (14)	9		3	-
J Forrest	31 (4)	8		1	-
C McGregor	29 (7)	7		2	-
Olivier Ntcham	24 (5)	5		4	-
T Rogic	18 (5)	5		1	-
S Armstrong	15 (12)	3		-	-

K Tierney, D Boyata scored two goals. Two players scored one.

DUNDEE

Nickname: The Dark Blues
Colours: Blue and white
Ground: Dens Park (13,565)
Tel: 01382-889966   dundeefc.co.uk

Neil McCann was appointed at the end of 2016-17 tasked with keeping Dundee up and he did it. His reward was to get embroiled in another relegation scrap.

Nine points from their first 14 matches left Dundee bottom of the table and by the time of the split they were still in serious bother. Three wins in those final five matches were nothing if not timely.

There were problems at both ends as the Dark Blues scored just 36 goals in 38 games and kept only seven clean sheets.

Longest run without win/loss: 6/3
High/low league position: 8/12
Clean sheets: 7 **Yellows:** 74 **Reds:** 2
Avg attendance: 9,385 **Players used:** 34
Leading scorer: S Moussa 7 (2,5)
Key stat: Dundee's rotten start was courtesy of not keeping a clean sheet in their opening 13 league matches.

	2017-18 H	2017-18 A	P	W	D	L	OV	UN	BS	CS
Celtic	L	L D	7	0	2	5	2	5	3	1
Aberdeen	L	L L	9	0	3	6	4	5	6	0
Rangers	W	L L	3	2	0	1	3	0	3	0
Hibernian	D L	L	3	1	1	1	1	2	2	0
Kilmarnock	D	D L	9	1	6	2	2	7	6	3
Hearts	W D	L	7	4	1	2	3	4	4	2
Motherwell	L L	D L	8	3	1	4	5	3	4	1
St Johnstone	W L W	W	10	5	2	3	7	3	6	2
Dundee										
Hamilton	L W	L W	10	4	3	3	2	8	3	5
St Mirren			3	1	0	2	2	1	2	0
Livingston			2	1	0	1	1	1	0	1

Season	Division	Pos	P	W	D	L	F	A	GD	Pts
2017-18	Premiership	9	38	11	6	21	36	57	-21	39
2016-17	Premiership	10	38	10	7	21	38	62	-24	37
2015-16	Premiership	8	38	11	15	12	53	57	-4	48

Over/Under 50%/50% 4th   **Both score** 50%/50% 6th

Top league scorers	P	G		Y	R
S Moussa	21 (5)	7		9	-
A Leitch-Smith	14 (14)	6		1	-
M O'Hara	26 (6)	4		4	-
F El-Bakhtaoui	16 (12)	3		1	-
S Murray	13 (1)	3		3	-
K Waddell	10 (6)	3		5	-
M Haber	9 (2)	2		2	-
K Holt	22 (2)	2		5	-

S Caulker, R Deacon, J Hendry, M Henvey, G Kusunga and P McGowan all scored one goal

HAMILTON

Nickname: The Accies
Colours: Red and white
Ground: New Douglas Park (5,396)
Tel: 01698-368-652   acciesfc.co.uk

After a bright enough start the rot quickly set in with six straight defeats and by the time they'd lost 5-3 at home to Rangers in February, the Accies were in 11th place.

Those who'd backed the pre-season 6-4 favourites to finish bottom would have enjoyed Hamilton limping towards the line but they did just enough to avoid a relegation playoff on goal difference.

The worst defence in the top flight – 68 goals conceded – is clearly in need of a tweak.

Longest run without win/loss: 8/6
High/low league position: 7/11
Clean sheets: 5 **Yellows:** 90 **Reds:** 8
Avg attendance: 8,121 **Players used:** 32
Leading scorer: D Templeton 8 (2,8) D Imrie 8 (3,8)
Key stat: Hamilton have kept just one clean sheet in their last 22 away matches in all competitions.

	2017-18 H	2017-18 A	P	W	D	L	OV	UN	BS	CS
Celtic	L L	L	6	0	1	5	4	2	4	0
Aberdeen	D	L L	6	3	2	1	3	3	2	3
Rangers	L L	W	3	0	0	3	3	0	3	0
Hibernian	D	W L	1	0	1	0	0	1	1	0
Kilmarnock	L	D L	8	0	3	5	3	5	3	2
Hearts	L L	D	5	1	2	2	4	1	3	1
Motherwell	L W	W L	8	4	1	3	2	6	2	4
St Johnstone	L L	L L	7	2	2	3	2	5	4	2
Dundee	W L	W L	9	4	2	3	6	3	5	2
Hamilton										
St Mirren			2	2	0	0	1	1	0	2
Livingston			4	2	1	1	1	3	2	2

Season	Division	Pos	P	W	D	L	F	A	GD	Pts
2017-18	Premiership	10	38	9	6	23	47	68	-21	33
2016-17	Premiership	11	38	7	14	17	37	56	-19	35
2015-16	Premiership	10	38	11	10	17	42	63	-21	43

Over/Under 68%/32% 1st   **Both score** 63%/37% 2nd

Top league scorers	P	G		Y	R
D Imrie	33 (2)	8		8	1
D Templeton	20 (7)	8		2	1
R Bingham	18 (14)	5		-	-
G Docherty	21	3		2	-
M Ogboe	12 (4)	3		1	-
A Rojano	14 (12)	3		6	-
G Skondras	20 (1)	3		3	1
D Lyon	21 (6)	2		4	1
D Redmond	11 (14)	2		7	-

S Boyd, A Crawford, A Gogic, L Longridge, D MacKinnon, G Sarris and X Tomas all scored one goal

HEARTS

Nickname: Jambos
Colours: Claret and white
Ground: Tynecastle (17,420)
Tel: 0871-663-1874   heartsfc.co.uk

With Tynecastle being redeveloped, the Jambos played their first 13 matches either away or at Murrayfield and simply couldn't get going.

Under new management – Craig Levein replaced Ian Cathro in July – Hearts were in the bottom half when they finally returned home in November.

They did improve, chalking up an 11-game unbeaten run from mid-November, but finished sixth and were branded "irrelevant" by Hibs' chief Neil Lennon.

Longest run without win/loss: 6/11
High/low league position: 5/8
Clean sheets: 15 **Yellows:** 90 **Reds:** 5
Avg attendance: 17,292 **Players used:** 39
Leading scorer: K Lafferty 12 (8,12)
Key stat: Hearts' only defeat in their last 14 home league games was a 3-1 reverse against champions Celtic.

	2017-18		Last six seasons at home							
	H	A	P	W	D	L	OV	UN	BS	CS
Celtic	W L	L L	9	1	1	7	8	1	5	1
Aberdeen	D W	D L	9	4	2	3	4	5	5	3
Rangers	L	D L L	5	3	1	1	3	2	3	2
Hibernian	D W	L L	8	4	3	1	3	5	4	4
Kilmarnock	L D	W L	9	3	2	4	6	3	4	3
Hearts										
Motherwell	W D	L	8	5	1	2	3	5	2	5
St Johnstone	W W	D	9	5	2	2	4	5	3	4
Dundee	W	L D	6	4	1	1	0	6	1	4
Hamilton	D	W W	4	3	1	0	2	2	2	2
St Mirren			4	3	0	1	2	2	1	2
Livingston			2	2	0	0	1	1	0	2

Season	Division	Pos	P	W	D	L	F	A	GD	Pts
2017-18	Premiership	6	38	12	13	13	39	39	0	49
2016-17	Premiership	5	38	12	10	16	55	52	+3	46
2015-16	Premiership	3	38	18	11	9	59	40	+19	65

Over/Under 37%/63% 12th   **Both score** 47%/53% 8th

Top league scorers	P	G		Y	R
K Lafferty	30 (5)	12		12	[1]
Esmael	16 (4)	6		3	[1]
M Milinkovic	15 (9)	6		3	-
R Callachan	18 (5)	4		4	-
S Naismith	12 (2)	4		3	-
C Berra	37	2		6	-
J Walker	14 (2)	2		5	-
H Cochrane	14 (8)	1		4	[1]
J Souttar	31	1		10	-
D Zanatta	0 (1)	1		-	-

HIBERNIAN

Nickname: The Hibees
Colours: Green and white
Ground: Easter Road (17,458)
Tel: 0131-661-2159   hibernianfc.co.uk

Hibs' return to the top flight after a three-year absence went as well as should have been expected. They found themselves in fourth after a 2-1 home defeat against St Johnstone in November and never shifted from that spot.

Neil Lennon's men finished like a train, losing just one of their last 14 with fourth spot guaranteeing a return to European football. Hibs finished 18 points clear of rivals Hearts and only Celtic lost fewer league games.

Longest run without win/loss: 4/12
High/low league position: 3/7
Clean sheets: 11 **Yellows:** 65 **Reds:** 1
Avg attendance: 17,855 **Players used:** 26
Leading scorer: F Kamberi 9 (3,7)
Key stat: Hibs took 16 points off the top three sides – five off Celtic – which was better than any other team managed.

	2017-18		Last six seasons at home							
	H	A	P	W	D	L	OV	UN	BS	CS
Celtic	D W	D L	5	2	2	1	3	2	3	1
Aberdeen	L W	L D	6	1	1	4	0	6	0	2
Rangers	L D	W W	6	3	1	2	5	1	4	1
Hibernian										
Kilmarnock	D W	W D	6	3	2	1	4	2	4	1
Hearts	W W	D L	8	4	3	1	2	6	4	4
Motherwell	D W	W	5	1	2	2	4	1	4	0
St Johnstone	L	D D	4	1	1	2	2	2	2	2
Dundee	W	D W	4	3	1	0	2	2	2	2
Hamilton	L W	D	2	1	0	1	2	0	2	0
St Mirren			8	4	3	1	4	4	6	2
Livingston			4	4	0	0	4	0	4	0

Season	Division	Pos	P	W	D	L	F	A	GD	Pts
2017-18	Premiership	4	38	18	13	7	62	46	+16	67
2016-17	Championship	1	36	19	14	3	59	25	+34	71
2015-16	Championship	3	36	21	7	8	59	34	+25	70

Over/Under 53%/47% 3rd   **Both score** 66%/34% 1st

Top league scorers	P	G		Y	R
F Kamberi	14	9		3	-
J Maclaren	11 (4)	8		1	-
A Stokes	15 (3)	7		4	-
S Murray	17 (5)	6		1	-
M Boyle	34	5		1	-
J McGinn	35	5		15	-
O Shaw	5 (11)	4		-	-
S Allan	12	3		3	-

E Ambrose, B Barker, P Hanlon, V Slivka and S Whittaker all scored two goals. R Porteous, L Stevenson scored one.

KILMARNOCK

Nickname: Killie
Colours: Blue and white
Ground: (18,128)
Tel: 01563 545-300   kilmarnockfc.co.uk

Bottom after failing to win any of their first eight matches, Kilmarnock were still in the bottom two after a 3-0 home thrashing by Hibs at the end of October.

Steve Clarke had by this time replaced Lee McCulloch and presided over a remarkable turnaround which earned him a trio of manager-of-the-month awards and saw Killie soar to fifth spot.

Between the end of November and end of April they lost once, and landed the Premiership handicap honours.

Longest run without win/loss: 8/11
High/low league position: 5/12
Clean sheets: 11 **Yellows:** 72 **Reds:** 3
Avg attendance: 10,654 **Players used:** 28
Leading scorer: K Boyd 18 (7,15)
Key stat: In their four games against runaway champions Celtic, Killie collected five points and had a goal difference of just minus one.

LIVINGSTON

Nickname: Livi Lions
Colours: Black and yellow
Ground: Almondvale Stadium (6,100)
Tel: 01506-417000   livingstonfc.co.uk

Runners-up behind St Mirren, Livingston landed a second-successive promotion courtesy of a home-and-away playoff final triumph against Partick.

They found the net in each of their first 11 matches and it was an 11-game unbeaten run from the turn of the year which gave them a solid grip on second spot. However, celebrations at a return to the top flight for the first time since 2006 were cut short when boss David Hopkin walked out of Almondvale.

Longest run without win/loss: 3/11
High/low league position: 0/0
Clean sheets: 14 **Yellows:** 72 **Reds:** 3
Avg attendance: 2,081 **Players used:** 27
Leading scorer: R Hardie 8 (0,7)
Key stat: With 26 goals, Livi were the lowest home scorers in the top half of the second tier; they won just eight home games.

	2017-18 H A	P	W	D	L	OV	UN	BS	CS
Celtic	L W D D	9	1	1	7	4	5	3	1
Aberdeen	L L D L	10	0	1	9	6	4	5	0
Rangers	W D W L	3	1	2	0	1	2	2	1
Hibernian	L D D L	6	0	3	3	4	2	5	0
Kilmarnock									
Hearts	L W W D	9	5	2	2	2	7	2	5
Motherwell	W L W	9	3	0	6	4	5	4	3
St Johnstone	L W W	9	3	1	5	5	4	4	3
Dundee	D W D	9	2	3	4	4	5	4	3
Hamilton	D W W	7	2	2	3	3	4	3	3
St Mirren		7	5	1	1	4	3	5	2
Livingston		-	-	-	-	-	-	-	-

Season Division	Pos	P	W	D	L	F	A	GD	Pts
2017-18 Premiership	5	38	16	11	11	49	47	+2	59
2016-17 Premiership	8	38	9	14	15	36	56	-20	41
2015-16 Premiership	11	38	9	9	20	41	64	-23	36

Over/Under 39%/61% 10th   **Both score** 53%/47% 5th

Top league scorers	P	G		Y	R
K Boyd	30 (4)	18		2	-
E Brophy	15 (13)	7		3	-
L Erwin	14 (20)	5		3	-
J Jones	28 (4)	4		8	1
S Findlay	29 (3)	3		1	-
A Frizzell	10 (5)	2		3	-
S O Donnell	35 (1)	2		4	-

S Boyd, K Broadfoot, C Burke, G Greer, Y Mulumbu and I Wilson all scored one goal

	2017-18 H A	P	W	D	L	OV	UN	BS	CS
Celtic		-	-	-	-	-	-	-	-
Aberdeen		-	-	-	-	-	-	-	-
Rangers		4	1	2	1	0	4	2	1
Hibernian		4	0	1	3	2	2	1	1
Kilmarnock		-	-	-	-	-	-	-	-
Hearts		2	0	0	2	1	1	1	0
Motherwell		-	-	-	-	-	-	-	-
St Johnstone		-	-	-	-	-	-	-	-
Dundee		2	1	0	1	1	1	1	0
Hamilton		4	0	3	1	1	3	1	2
St Mirren	L W L D	4	1	0	3	3	1	3	0
Livingston									

Season Division	Pos	P	W	D	L	F	A	GD	Pts
2017-18 Championship	2	36	17	11	8	56	37	+19	62
2016-17 League One	1	36	26	3	7	80	32	+48	81
2015-16 Championship	9	36	8	7	21	37	51	-14	31

Over/Under 50%/50% 5th   **Both score** 47%/53% 6th

Top league scorers	P	G		Y	R
R Hardie	15 (1)	8		1	-
C Halkett	34 (1)	7		6	-
A Lithgow	33	6		5	-
S Robinson	9 (8)	5		2	-
D Mackin	7 (7)	4		1	-
D Mullen	11	4		7	-
S Pittman	35	4		3	-
R De Vita	21 (9)	3		5	-
J Longridge	23 (8)	3		6	-
J Mullin	20 (8)	3		2	-

L Miller, N Todorov scored two goals. Five players scored one.

MOTHERWELL

Nickname: The Well/The Steelmen
Colours: Amber and claret
Ground: Fir Park (13,742)
Tel: 01698-333-333   motherwellfc.co.uk

After a dismal 2016-17, the Well kicked off the new campaign in style with six wins in a spell of eight fixtures hoisting them up to third.

A win at Aberdeen and a draw with Celtic suggested they could carry on the good work only for the wins to dry up. By the time of the split they were eight points off the top six.

They twice beat Aberdeen en route to both domestic cup finals where they lost to Celtic each time.

Longest run without win/loss: 8/4
High/low league position: 4/8
Clean sheets: 13 **Yellows:** 70 **Reds:** 5
Avg attendance: 9,238 **Players used:** 30
Leading scorer: L Moult 8 (1,6)
Key stat: Motherwell's last nine away league matches produced just 12 goals of which the Steelmen scored only four.

| | 2017-18 | | Last six seasons at home | | | | | | | |
	H	A	P	W	D	L	OV	UN	BS	CS
Celtic	D D	L	11	2	3	6	6	5	6	1
Aberdeen	L L	W	9	2	1	6	6	3	6	0
Rangers	L D	L	3	0	1	2	2	1	2	0
Hibernian	L	D L	4	2	0	2	2	2	1	1
Kilmarnock	W L	L	11	5	3	3	5	6	6	3
Hearts	W	L D	8	4	2	2	6	2	5	2
Motherwell										
St Johnstone	W L	L D	12	5	2	5	7	5	8	3
Dundee	D W	W W	9	2	3	4	5	4	7	1
Hamilton	L W	W L	7	3	2	2	6	1	3	3
St Mirren			5	3	2	0	3	2	2	3
Livingston			-	-	-	-	-	-	-	-

Season	Division	Pos	P	W	D	L	F	A	GD	Pts
2017-18	Premiership	7	38	13	9	16	43	49	-6	48
2016-17	Premiership	9	38	10	8	20	46	69	-23	38
2015-16	Premiership	5	38	15	5	18	47	63	-16	50

Over/Under 39%/61% 10th   **Both score** 45%/55% 9th

Top league scorers	P	G		Y	R
L Moult	13 (2)	8		3	-
R Bowman	23 (9)	7		3	-
C Tanner	16 (10)	6		2	-
C Main	16	5		2	-
N Ciftci	8 (3)	3		2	-
A Campbell	25 (4)	2		6	-
P Hartley	14	2		3	1
A Rose	22 (6)	2		3	-

T Aldred, G Bigirimana, E Frear, B Heneghan, C Kipre and R Tait all scored one goal

RANGERS

Nickname: The Gers
Colours: Blue
Ground: Ibrox Stadium (51,082)
Tel: 0871-702-1972   rangers.co.uk

Installed 10-11 favourites in the without Celtic market, Rangers gave it a fair crack, finishing three points behind Aberdeen.

The season began atrociously with defeat to Luxembourg part-timers Progres Niedercorn in the Europa League before Pedro Caixinha was fired in October.

Graeme Murty couldn't quite see out the campaign – given his cards after a 5-0 thrashing at Celtic – which paved the way for ex-England captain Steven Gerrard's arrival at Ibrox.

Longest run without win/loss: 3/5
High/low league position: 2/5
Clean sheets: 11 **Yellows:** 78 **Reds:** 5
Avg attendance: 32,274 **Players used:** 33
Leading scorer: A Morelos 14 (6,12)
Key stat: Rangers signed off with a 5-5 draw at Hibs, their eighth league game to produce five goals or more.

| | 2017-18 | | Last six seasons at home | | | | | | | |
	H	A	P	W	D	L	OV	UN	BS	CS
Celtic	L L	D L	4	0	0	4	3	1	3	0
Aberdeen	W W	W D	4	3	0	1	3	1	2	2
Rangers										
Hibernian	L L	W D	6	2	0	4	4	2	4	1
Kilmarnock	D L W	L	4	2	1	1	1	3	1	2
Hearts	D W W	W	7	5	1	1	4	3	4	3
Motherwell	W	W D	3	2	1	0	1	2	2	1
St Johnstone	L	W W	3	1	1	1	2	1	3	0
Dundee	W W	L	3	3	0	0	2	1	1	2
Hamilton	L	W W	3	1	1	1	1	2	1	1
St Mirren			2	2	0	0	1	1	1	1
Livingston			4	3	1	0	2	2	2	0

Season	Division	Pos	P	W	D	L	F	A	GD	Pts
2017-18	Premiership	3	38	21	7	10	76	50	+26	70
2016-17	Premiership	3	38	19	10	9	56	44	+12	67
2015-16	Championship	1	36	25	6	5	88	34	+54	81

Over/Under 68%/32% 1st   **Both score** 61%/39% 3rd

Top league scorers	P	G		Y	R
A Morelos	29 (6)	14		9	-
J Windass	31 (2)	13		6	-
J Tavernier	37 (1)	8		4	-
D Candeias	34 (3)	6		4	-
G Dorrans	16	5		6	-
J Murphy	16	4		-	-
C Pena	6 (6)	4		1	-
D John	25 (1)	3		2	-
K Miller	15 (3)	3		-	-
D Wilson	12 (2)	3		3	-

Cummings, Goss, Holt, McCrorie scored two. Five scored one.

ST JOHNSTONE

Nickname: The Saints
Colours: Blue and white
Ground: McDiarmid Park (10,673)
Tel: 01738-459090   perthstjohnstonefc.co.uk

St Johnstone began the season as well as they'd finished the previous one, winning their first three games to go top. A 1-1 draw at Celtic in their fourth outing was every bit as impressive. The only downer was exiting the Europa League early.

No consistency thereafter as they sunk into the bottom half, chiefly due to a lack of goals. Top scorer Steve MacLean managed just nine all term. An eighth-place finish ended a sequence of six-successive seasons in the top half.

Longest run without win/loss: 7/5
High/low league position: 2/9
Clean sheets: 9 **Yellows:** 83 **Reds:** 4
Avg attendance: 9,273 **Players used:** 31
Leading scorer: S MacLean 9 (3,7)
Key stat: Saints won only two of their last 15 home league matches, scoring just nine goals.

	2017-18 H	A	Last six seasons at home P	W	D	L	OV	UN	BS	CS
Celtic	L	D D	12	2	3	7	9	3	7	1
Aberdeen	L	L L	10	3	2	5	6	4	5	3
Rangers	L L	W	4	0	1	3	3	1	3	0
Hibernian	D D	W	5	1	2	2	1	4	3	1
Kilmarnock	L	W L	9	4	1	4	5	4	5	2
Hearts	D	L L	8	4	4	0	2	6	2	6
Motherwell	W D	L W	10	7	2	1	6	4	6	4
St Johnstone										
Dundee	L	L W L	7	4	1	2	1	6	2	3
Hamilton	W W	W W	6	4	1	1	3	3	2	3
St Mirren			5	4	0	1	2	3	2	3
Livingston			-	-	-	-	-	-	-	-

Season	Division	Pos	P	W	D	L	F	A	GD	Pts
2017-18	Premiership	8	38	12	10	16	42	53	-11	46
2016-17	Premiership	4	38	17	7	14	50	46	+4	58
2015-16	Premiership	4	38	16	8	14	58	55	+3	56

Over/Under 47%/53% 7th   **Both score** 50%/50% 6th

Top league scorers	P	G		Y	R
S MacLean	26 (4)	9	▮▮▮▮	6	-
M Davidson	29	5	▮▮	14	-
M O'Halloran	12 (4)	5	▮▮	3	-
L Craig	17 (10)	3	▮	8	-
C Kane	10 (2)	3	▮	2	-
D Wotherspoon	25 (10)	3	▮	8	1
B Alston	17 (7)	2	▮	2	-
D Johnstone	8 (12)	2	▮	2	-
D McMillan	2 (2)	2	▮	-	-

S Anderson, G Cummins, J Kerr, S Scougall, J Shaughnessy and M Willock all scored one goal

ST MIRREN

Nickname: The Saints
Colours: Black and white
Ground: St Mirren Park (8,023)
Tel: 0141-889-2558   saintmirren.net

The Buddies are back after romping the Championship by a 12-point margin.

Jack Ross's men hit the top at Christmas and never looked back. They were all but home and hosed by early April and were still streets ahead despite winning just one of their last five matches. St Mirren were also the division's top scorers.

Ross, inevitably, was coveted and joined Sunderland, with former Hibs' chief Alan Stubbs – out of work for almost two years – replacing him.

Longest run without win/loss: 3/9
High/low league position: 0/0
Clean sheets: 14 **Yellows:** 42 **Reds:** 5
Avg attendance: 4,103 **Players used:** 31
Leading scorer: L Morgan 14 (5,10)
Key stat: St Mirren have scored at least two goals in 15 of their last 22 home matches.

	2017-18 H	A	Last six seasons at home P	W	D	L	OV	UN	BS	CS
Celtic			5	0	1	4	3	2	2	0
Aberdeen			5	0	2	3	1	4	2	1
Rangers			2	0	1	1	1	1	1	0
Hibernian			8	2	2	4	3	5	3	3
Kilmarnock			5	2	2	1	2	3	4	1
Hearts			4	2	2	0	0	4	2	2
Motherwell			5	3	0	2	3	2	3	0
St Johnstone			4	1	1	2	1	3	2	0
Dundee			4	1	0	3	3	1	3	0
Hamilton			2	1	0	1	0	2	0	1
St Mirren										
Livingston	W D	W L	4	1	2	1	2	2	3	1

Season	Division	Pos	P	W	D	L	F	A	GD	Pts
2017-18	Championship	1	36	23	5	8	63	36	+27	74
2016-17	Championship	7	36	9	12	15	52	56	-4	39
2015-16	Championship	6	36	11	9	16	44	53	-9	42

Over/Under 56%/44% 3rd   **Both score** 50%/50% 3rd

Top league scorers	P	G		Y	R
L Morgan	34 (1)	14	▮▮▮▮▮	2	-
G Reilly	27 (8)	11	▮▮▮▮	1	-
C Smith	33 (1)	10	▮▮▮▮	4	-
I McShane	26 (5)	5	▮▮	3	-
H Davis	20	3	▮	1	-
D Mullen	11 (8)	3	▮	2	-
K Magennis	25 (2)	2	▮	2	-
L Smith	32	2	▮	1	-

J Baird, G Buchanan, S Demetriou, A Eckersley, R Flynn, D Hilson, M Hippolyte, G MacKenzie, S McGinn, J Sutton all scored one.

Scottish Premiership stats 2017-18
Key Points in all tables (except the league table) do not include any deductions imposed by the league.
POS H A Overall league position, rank from home games only, rank from away games only **Sup** Average match supremacy **GFA** Goals For Average **GAA** Goals Against Average **PGA** Points Gained Average

Scottish Premiership 2017-18			Home					Away						
Pos	H	A		P	W	D	L	F	A	W	D	L	F	A	GD	Pts
1	1	1	Celtic (CL)	38	11	7	1	38	9	13	3	3	35	16	48	82
2	2	3	Aberdeen (EL)	38	11	4	4	30	16	11	3	5	26	21	19	73
3	4	2	Rangers (EL)	38	10	2	7	32	20	11	5	3	44	30	26	70
4	3	4	Hibernian (EL)	38	11	4	4	39	27	7	9	3	23	19	16	67
5	6	5	Kilmarnock	38	9	3	7	27	26	7	8	4	22	21	2	59
6	5	8	Hearts	38	8	7	3	23	13	4	6	10	16	26	0	49
7	7	7	Motherwell	38	8	5	7	26	22	5	4	9	17	27	-6	48
8	9	6	St Johnstone	38	5	7	7	17	27	7	3	9	25	26	-11	46
9	10	9	Dundee	38	6	3	10	18	27	5	3	11	18	30	-21	39
10	11	10	Hamilton	38	5	3	11	26	35	4	3	12	21	33	-21	33
11	8	12	Partick (R)	38	6	4	9	20	24	2	5	12	11	37	-30	33
12	12	11	Ross County (R)	38	3	7	9	23	29	3	4	12	17	33	-22	29

Best attack

		GF	GFA
1	Rangers	76	2
2	Celtic	73	1.92
3	Hibernian	62	1.63
4	Aberdeen	56	1.47
5	Kilmarnock	49	1.29
6	Hamilton	47	1.24
7	Motherwell	43	1.13
8	St Johnstone	42	1.11
9	Ross County	40	1.05
10	Hearts	39	1.03
11	Dundee	36	0.95
12	Partick	31	0.82

Best defence

		GA	GAA
1	Celtic	25	0.66
2	Aberdeen	37	0.97
3	Hearts	39	1.03
4	Hibernian	46	1.21
5	Kilmarnock	47	1.24
6	Motherwell	49	1.29
7	Rangers	50	1.32
8	St Johnstone	53	1.39
9	Dundee	57	1.5
10	Partick	61	1.61
11	Ross County	62	1.63
12	Hamilton	68	1.79

Top scorers

	Team	Goals scored
K Boyd	Kilmarnock	18
A Morelos	Rangers	14
J Windass	Rangers	13
K Lafferty	Hearts	12
A Schalk	Ross County	11
S Sinclair	Celtic	10
M Dembele	Celtic	9
O Edouard	Celtic	9
L Griffiths	Celtic	9
F Kamberi	Hibernian	9
S MacLean	St Johnstone	9
S Murray	Dundee	9
A Rooney	Aberdeen	9

Record when first to score

		P	W	D	L	F	A	Sup	PGA	Pts
1	Celtic	24	21	3	0	63	12	2.13	2.8	66
2	Aberdeen	21	19	2	0	46	11	1.67	2.8	59
3	Kilmarnock	19	15	3	1	32	13	1.00	2.5	48
4	Motherwell	13	10	2	1	20	5	1.15	2.5	32
5	Hibernian	20	14	5	1	38	20	0.90	2.4	47
6	St Johnstone	14	10	4	0	23	9	1.00	2.4	34
7	Rangers	22	16	2	4	50	21	1.32	2.3	50
8	Dundee	14	9	3	2	25	17	0.57	2.1	30
9	Hearts	20	12	5	3	32	16	0.80	2	41
10	Partick	14	6	4	4	19	17	0.14	1.6	22
11	Ross County	13	5	4	4	25	20	0.38	1.5	19
12	Hamilton	16	7	1	8	31	29	0.13	1.4	22

Record when keeping a clean sheet

		P	W	D	F	Sup	PGA	Pts
1	Rangers	11	9	2	22	2.00	2.6	29
2	Hibernian	11	9	2	14	1.27	2.6	29
3	Kilmarnock	11	9	2	12	1.09	2.6	29
4	Hamilton	5	4	1	9	1.80	2.6	13
5	Celtic	20	15	5	36	1.80	2.5	50
6	Aberdeen	17	13	4	23	1.35	2.5	43
7	Motherwell	13	10	3	19	1.46	2.5	33
8	Dundee	7	5	2	9	1.29	2.4	17
9	Partick	6	4	2	5	0.83	2.3	14
10	Hearts	15	9	6	18	1.20	2.2	33
11	St Johnstone	9	5	4	9	1.00	2.1	19
12	Ross County	5	2	3	6	1.20	1.8	9

Over 2.5 goals

	H	A	%
Rangers	10	16	68%
Hamilton	14	12	68%
Hibernian	13	7	53%
Celtic	9	10	50%
Dundee, Ross County			50%

Under 2.5 goals

	H	A	%
Hearts	13	11	63%
Kilmarnock	10	13	61%
Motherwell	11	12	61%
Partick	12	10	58%
Aberdeen	10	11	55%

Both to score

	H	A	%
Hibernian	14	11	66%
Hamilton	13	11	63%
Rangers	8	15	61%
Ross County	13	9	58%
Kilmarnock	9	11	53%

Both not to score

	H	A	%
Aberdeen	11	14	66%
Celtic	12	11	61%
Motherwell	10	11	55%
Partick	10	11	55%
Hearts	11	9	53%

Scottish Premiership results 2017-18

	Aberdeen	Celtic	Dundee	Hamilton	Hearts	Hibernian	Kilmarnock	Motherwell	Partick	Rangers	Ross County	St Johnstone
Aberdeen		0-3/0-2	2-1/1-0	2-0/3-0	0-0/2-0	4-1/0-0	1-1/3-1	0-2	1-0	1-2/1-1	2-1	3-0/4-1
Celtic	3-0/0-1		1-0/0-0	3-1	4-1/3-1	2-2/1-0	1-1/0-0	5-1	2-0	0-0/5-0	4-0/3-0	1-1/0-0
Dundee	0-1	0-2		1-3/1-0	2-1/1-1	1-1/0-1	0-0	0-1/0-1	3-0/0-1	2-1	1-2/1-4	3-2/0-4/2-1
Hamilton	2-2	1-4/1-2	3-0/1-2		1-2/0-3	1-1	1-2	1-2/2-0	0-0/2-1	1-4/3-5	3-2/2-0	0-1/1-2
Hearts	0-0/2-0	4-0/1-3	2-0	1-1		0-0/2-1	1-2/1-1	1-0/1-1	1-1/3-0	1-3	0-0	1-0/1-0
Hibernian	0-1/2-0	2-2/2-1	2-1	1-3/3-1	1-0/2-0		1-1/5-3	2-2/2-1	3-1/2-0	1-2/5-5	2-1	1-2
Kilmarnock	1-3/0-2	0-2/1-0	1-1/3-2	2-2/2-0	0-1/1-0	0-3/2-2		1-0	5-1	2-1	0-2/3-2	1-2/2-0
Motherwell	0-1/0-2	1-1/0-0	1-1/2-1	1-3/3-0	2-1	0-1	2-0/0-1		3-0/1-1	1-2/2-2	2-0/2-0	2-0/1-5
Partick	3-4/0-0	0-1/1-2	2-1/1-2	1-0/2-1	1-1	0-1	0-2/0-1	3-2/0-1		2-2/0-2	2-0/1-1	1-0
Rangers	3-0/2-0	0-2/2-3	4-1/4-0	0-2	0-0/2-0/2-1	2-3/1-2	1-1/0-1/1-0	2-0	3-0		2-1	1-3
Ross County	1-2/2-4	0-1	0-2/0-1	2-1/2-2	1-2/1-1	0-1/1-1	2-2	3-2/0-0	1-1/4-0	1-3/1-2		1-1
St Johnstone	0-3	0-4	0-2	2-1/1-0	0-0	1-1/1-1	1-2	4-1/0-0	1-0/1-3/1-1	0-3/1-4-0/0-2-0/1-1		

Motherwell reached two cup finals but lost both

ALLOA

Nickname: The Wasps — Recreation Park
www.alloaathletic.co.uk

Two wins in the first nine left Alloa eighth in League One. Six months later they were celebrating promotion in dramatic style.

Jim Goodwin's men were 90 seconds from staying in the section before turning their playoff against Dumbarton around.

	2017-18 H	A	Last six seasons at home P	W	D	L	OV	UN	BS	CS
Partick	-	-	-	-	-	-	-	-	-	-
Ross County	-	-	-	-	-	-	-	-	-	-
Dundee United	-	-	-	-	-	-	-	-	-	-
Dunfermline	-	-	-	-	-	-	-	-	-	-
Inverness CT	-	-	-	-	-	-	-	-	-	-
Queen of Sth	8	1	3	4	5	3	5	1		
Morton	4	2	1	1	1	3	1	2		
Falkirk	6	1	2	3	3	3	3	2		
Ayr	L W D W		4	2	1	1	3	1	3	1
Alloa										

Season	Division	Pos	P	W	D	L	F	A	GD	Pts
2017-18	League One	3	36	17	9	10	56	43	+13	60
2016-17	League One	2	36	17	11	8	69	44	+25	62
2015-16	Championship	10	36	4	9	23	22	67	-45	21

Over/Under 53%/47% 12th **Both score** 56%/44% 7th

AYR

Nickname: The Honest Men — Somerset Park
www.ayrunitedfc.co.uk

Promoted straight back as League One champions after a season in the third tier in which they only once failed to find the net.

Ian McCall's Honest Men scored 92 goals and won the title on the final day. Each of their 36 games produced at least two goals.

	2017-18 H	A	Last six seasons at home P	W	D	L	OV	UN	BS	CS
Partick	-	-	-	-	-	-	-	-	-	-
Ross County	-	-	-	-	-	-	-	-	-	-
Dundee United	2	0	1	1	0	2	0	1		
Dunfermline	8	0	2	6	2	6	3	1		
Inverness CT	-	-	-	-	-	-	-	-	-	-
Queen of Sth	4	1	0	3	2	2	2	1		
Morton	4	2	1	1	2	2	3	1		
Falkirk	2	0	0	2	1	1	1	0		
Ayr										
Alloa	D L W L		4	0	2	2	2	2	2	1

Season	Division	Pos	P	W	D	L	F	A	GD	Pts
2017-18	League One	1	36	24	4	8	92	42	+50	76
2016-17	Championship	10	36	7	12	17	33	62	-29	33
2015-16	League One	2	36	19	4	13	65	47	+18	61

Over/Under 81%/19% 1st **Both score** 64%/36% 3rd

DUNDEE UNITED

Nickname: The Terrors — Tannadice Park
www.dundeeunitedfc.co.uk

The pre-season favourites were top of the table in December, but a run of just one win in ten sent them tumbling into the chasing pack.

Csaba Laszlo, appointed in October, got them into the playoffs where they saw off Dunfermline but couldn't topple Livingston.

	2017-18 H	A	Last six seasons at home P	W	D	L	OV	UN	BS	CS
Partick			5	2	1	2	2	3	2	1
Ross County			6	3	2	1	2	4	3	3
Dundee United										
Dunfermline	W D W D		4	3	1	0	1	3	2	2
Inverness CT			8	1	4	3	2	6	5	0
Queen of Sth	W L W L		4	1	2	1	3	1	4	0
Morton	W L W D		4	2	1	1	3	1	3	0
Falkirk	W W D L		4	3	1	0	1	3	1	3
Ayr			2	2	0	0	2	0	1	1
Alloa										

Season	Division	Pos	P	W	D	L	F	A	GD	Pts
2017-18	Championship	3	36	18	7	11	52	42	+10	61
2016-17	Championship	3	36	15	12	9	50	42	+8	57
2015-16	Premiership	12	38	7	9	22	45	70	-25	28

Over/Under 47%/53% 7th **Both score** 44%/56% 8th

DUNFERMLINE

Nickname: The Pars — East End Park
www.dafc.co.uk

In sixth spot after going six without a win in mid-March, Dunfermline finished with a ten-match unbeaten run to nick fourth spot.

They failed against Dundee United in the playoffs but that didn't stop boss Allan Johnstone extending his contract.

	2017-18 H	A	Last six seasons at home P	W	D	L	OV	UN	BS	CS
Partick			2	0	0	2	1	1	0	0
Ross County	-	-	-	-	-	-	-	-	-	-
Dundee United	L D L D		4	0	2	2	2	2	3	1
Dunfermline										
Inverness CT	W W L D		2	2	0	0	1	1	1	1
Queen of Sth	L W D D		4	1	1	2	2	2	3	0
Morton	D D L L		8	2	3	3	6	2	6	1
Falkirk	W W D W		6	2	1	3	2	4	3	1
Ayr			8	5	1	2	5	3	5	1
Alloa										

Season	Division	Pos	P	W	D	L	F	A	GD	Pts
2017-18	Championship	4	36	16	11	9	60	35	+25	59
2016-17	Championship	5	36	12	12	12	46	43	+3	48
2015-16	League One	1	36	24	7	5	83	30	+53	79

Over/Under 56%/44% 3rd **Both score** 50%/50% 3rd

FALKIRK

Nickname: The Bairns   Falkirk Stadium
www.falkirkfc.co.uk

The promotion pick for many punters, Falkirk's eighth-successive season in the second tier was going horribly wrong.

One win in 16 before Christmas saw them drop to ninth before new boss Paul Hartley oversaw a rally in the new year.

	2017-18 H	A	Last six seasons at home P	W	D	L	OV	UN	BS	CS
Partick			2 0	1	1	0	2	0	1	
Ross County			-	-	-	-	-	-	-	
Dundee United	D W	L L	4 3	1	0	3	1	2	2	
Dunfermline	D L	L L	6 3	2	1	3	3	4	2	
Inverness CT	D W	L L	2 1	1	0	1	1	1	1	
Queen of Sth	L W	L D	10 4	5	1	6	4	8	2	
Morton	L W	W W	10 5	2	3	4	6	5	2	
Falkirk										
Ayr			2 1	1	0	0	2	1	1	
Alloa			6 5	1	0	3	3	2	4	

Season	Division	Pos	P	W	D	L	F	A	GD	Pts
2017-18	Championship	8	36	12	11	13	45	49	-4	47
2016-17	Championship	2	36	16	12	8	58	40	+18	60
2015-16	Championship	2	36	19	13	4	61	34	+27	70

Over/Under 50%/50% 5th   **Both score** 50%/50% 3rd

INVERNESS CT

Nickname: Caley   Caledonian Stadium
www.ictfc.com

It was a tough start to Caley's Championship return – Inverness were in the bottom two after nine games having won just one match.

They finished the season unbeaten in 11, with eight wins, but even with their parachute money couldn't fund a playoff push.

	2017-18 H	A	Last six seasons at home P	W	D	L	OV	UN	BS	CS
Partick			6 1	3	2	2	4	1	4	
Ross County			8 3	3	2	4	4	7	1	
Dundee United	L W	W D	12 5	4	3	6	6	6	5	
Dunfermline	W D	L L	2 1	1	0	1	1	1	1	
Inverness CT										
Queen of Sth	D W	D W	2 1	1	0	1	1	1	1	
Morton	D L	L W	2 0	1	1	0	2	1	0	
Falkirk	W W	D L	2 2	0	0	1	1	1	1	
Ayr			-	-	-	-	-	-	-	
Alloa			-	-	-	-	-	-	-	

Season	Division	Pos	P	W	D	L	F	A	GD	Pts
2017-18	Championship	5	36	16	9	11	53	37	+16	57
2016-17	Premiership	12	38	7	13	18	44	71	-27	34
2015-16	Premiership	7	38	14	10	14	54	48	+6	52

Over/Under 42%/58% 8th   **Both score** 39%/61% 9th

MORTON

Nickname: The Ton   Cappielow Park
www.gmfc.net

Ex-Dundee manager Ray McKinnon begins the new campaign in charge of Morton.

The Ton were in the thick of the playoff hunt after taking 19 points from a possible 21 from late January to go third, before losing four of their last five to finish seventh.

	2017-18 H	A	Last six seasons at home P	W	D	L	OV	UN	BS	CS
Partick			2 1	1	0	2	0	2	0	
Ross County			-	-	-	-	-	-	-	
Dundee United	L D	L W	4 0	3	1	0	4	2	1	
Dunfermline	W W	D D	8 6	0	2	5	3	5	1	
Inverness CT	W L	D W	2 1	0	1	1	0	1		
Queen of Sth	L L	W D	8 4	1	3	2	6	3	3	
Morton										
Falkirk	L L	W L	10 1	4	5	2	8	5	1	
Ayr			4 2	1	1	2	2	3	0	
Alloa			4 2	0	2	1	3	1	1	

Season	Division	Pos	P	W	D	L	F	A	GD	Pts
2017-18	Championship	7	36	13	11	12	47	40	+7	50
2016-17	Championship	4	36	13	13	10	44	41	+3	52
2015-16	Championship	5	36	11	10	15	39	42	-3	43

Over/Under 42%/58% 8th   **Both score** 56%/44% 2nd

PARTICK

Nickname: The Jags   Firhill Stadium
www.ptfc.co.uk

In the bottom three all season, the Jags' five-year stay in the top flight came to an end.

Not scoring in 17 matches hurt the league's lowest scorers and despite hoisting themselves up to 11th after the split they lost home-and-away to Livingston in the playoffs.

	2017-18 H	A	Last six seasons at home P	W	D	L	OV	UN	BS	CS
Partick										
Ross County	W D	D L	9 4	3	2	5	4	6	3	
Dundee United			5 2	3	0	2	3	2	3	
Dunfermline			2 1	1	0	2	0	2	0	
Inverness CT			7 4	2	1	3	4	4	3	
Queen of Sth			-	-	-	-	-	-	-	
Morton			2 1	0	1	1	1	1	1	
Falkirk			2 2	0	0	2	0	2	0	
Ayr			-	-	-	-	-	-	-	
Alloa			-	-	-	-	-	-	-	

Season	Division	Pos	P	W	D	L	F	A	GD	Pts
2017-18	Premiership	11	38	8	9	21	31	61	-30	33
2016-17	Premiership	6	38	10	12	16	38	54	-16	42
2015-16	Premiership	9	38	12	10	16	41	50	-9	46

Over/Under 42%/58% 9th   **Both score** 45%/55% 9th

QUEEN OF THE SOUTH

Nickname: The Doonhamers — Palmerston Park
www.qosfc.com

Queens go into their centenary on the back of a solid season which started well – they were third after a 5-2 win at Dunfermline – and finished well, winning 5-1 at Brechin.

Those wins saw Stephen Dobbie bag hat-tricks, two of four for the season.

	2017-18 H	A	Last six seasons at home P	W	D	L	OV	UN	BS	CS
Partick			-	-	-	-	-	-	-	-
Ross County										
Dundee United	L W	L W	4	2	0	2	4	0	3	1
Dunfermline	D D	W L	4	0	3	1	1	3	1	2
Inverness CT	D L	D L	2	0	1	1	0	2	0	1
Queen of Sth										
Morton	L D	W W	8	4	2	2	5	3	3	4
Falkirk	W D	W L	10	5	3	2	6	4	5	4
Ayr			4	3	1	0	1	3	1	3
Alloa			8	6	2	0	2	6	2	6

Season	Division	Pos	P	W	D	L	F	A	GD	Pts
2017-18	Championship	6	36	14	10	12	59	53	+6	52
2016-17	Championship	6	36	11	10	15	46	52	-6	43
2015-16	Championship	7	36	12	6	18	46	56	-10	42

Over/Under 64%/36% 1st   **Both score** 61%/39% 1st

ROSS COUNTY

Nickname: County — Global Energy Stadium
www.rosscountyfootballclub.co.uk

Bottom of the Premiership and relegated after a six-year adventure in the top division.

Joint-managers Steven Ferguson and Stuart Kettlewell replaced Owen Coyle in March, but despite losing just two of their last seven games they couldn't save County.

	2017-18 H	A	Last six seasons at home P	W	D	L	OV	UN	BS	CS
Partick	D W	L D	9	4	2	3	4	5	5	4
Ross County										
Dundee United			7	3	0	4	6	1	4	2
Dunfermline			-	-	-	-	-	-	-	-
Inverness CT			9	3	1	5	7	2	4	3
Queen of Sth			-	-	-	-	-	-	-	-
Morton			-	-	-	-	-	-	-	-
Falkirk			-	-	-	-	-	-	-	-
Ayr			-	-	-	-	-	-	-	-
Alloa			-	-	-	-	-	-	-	-

Season	Division	Pos	P	W	D	L	F	A	GD	Pts
2017-18	Premiership	12	38	6	11	21	40	62	-22	29
2016-17	Premiership	7	38	11	13	14	48	58	-10	46
2015-16	Premiership	6	38	14	6	18	55	61	-6	48

Over/Under 50%/50% 4th   **Both score** 58%/42% 4th

St Mirren finally earned their return to the top tier

Scottish Championship results 2017-18

	Brechin	Dumbarton	Dundee Utd	Dunfermline	Falkirk	Inverness CT	Livingston	Morton	Queen of Sth	St Mirren
Brechin		0-1/1-3	1-1/0-5	0-3/0-3	1-1/0-1	0-4/2-3	2-2/0-2	0-1/1-1	0-1/1-5	1-2/0-1
Dumbarton	2-1/1-0		0-2/3-2	0-4/0-1	0-0/2-5	2-1/0-1	1-4/0-3	0-0/0-1	2-2/0-1	0-2/0-2
Dundee Utd	1-0/4-1	1-1/2-0		2-1/1-1	3-0/1-0	0-2/1-1	3-0/2-0	2-1/0-3	2-1/2-3	2-1/1-0
Dunfermline	2-1/4-0	2-2/4-0	1-3/0-0		3-1/2-0	5-1/1-0	3-1/1-0	1-1/0-0	2-5/3-1	3-0/1-2
Falkirk	3-1/3-0	1-1/0-0	0-0/6-1	1-1/1-2		0-0/3-1	0-2/1-3	0-3/3-1	1-4/3-2	0-0/1-0
Inverness CT	4-0/4-0	1-0/5-1	0-1/1-0	1-0/2-2	4-1/1-0		1-3/1-1	1-1/0-2	0-0/3-1	0-2/2-2
Livingston	3-2/3-0	2-1/2-0	2-0/2-1	1-1/0-0	0-0/0-0	0-0/0-1		1-1/3-2	2-2/0-1	1-3/4-1
Morton	4-1/2-0	1-1/3-2	0-2/1-1	3-2/2-1	0-1/0-1	1-0/0-3	0-1/0-1		1-2/0-1	4-1/1-1
Queen of Sth	4-1/3-1	1-0/0-0	1-3/3-0	0-0/0-0	4-2/2-2	0-0/0-2	0-3/3-3	1-2/1-1		2-3/1-3
St Mirren	2-1/1-0	0-1/5-0	3-0/2-0	1-0/2-0	3-1/1-2	4-2/1-0	3-1/0-0	2-2/2-1	3-1/2-0	

Scottish Championship 2017-18

Pos	H	A		P	Home W	Home D	Home L	Home F	Home A	Away W	Away D	Away L	Away F	Away A	GD	Pts
1	1	3	St Mirren (P)	36	14	2	2	37	12	9	3	6	26	24	27	74
2	5	1	Livingston (P)	36	8	7	3	26	16	9	4	5	30	21	19	62
3	2	7	Dundee Utd	36	12	3	3	30	16	6	4	8	22	26	10	61
4	3	6	Dunfermline	36	11	4	3	38	18	5	7	6	22	17	25	59
5	4	5	Inverness CT	36	9	5	4	31	17	7	4	7	22	20	16	57
6	8	2	Queen of Sth	36	5	7	6	26	26	9	3	6	33	27	6	52
7	7	4	Morton	36	7	3	8	23	22	6	8	4	24	18	7	50
8	6	8	Falkirk	36	7	6	5	27	22	5	5	8	18	27	-4	47
9	9	9	Dumbarton (R)	36	4	3	11	13	32	3	6	9	14	31	-36	30
10	10	10	Brechin (R)	36	0	4	14	10	40	0	0	18	10	50	-70	4

Best attack

		GF	GFA
1	St Mirren	63	1.75
2	Dunfermline	60	1.67
3	Queen of Sth	59	1.64
4	Livingston	56	1.56
5	Inverness CT	53	1.47
6	Dundee Utd	52	1.44
7	Morton	47	1.31
8	Falkirk	45	1.25
9	Dumbarton	27	0.75
10	Brechin	20	0.56

Best defence

		GA	GAA
1	Dunfermline	35	0.97
2	St Mirren	36	1
3	Livingston	37	1.03
4	Inverness CT	37	1.03
5	Morton	40	1.11
6	Dundee Utd	42	1.17
7	Falkirk	49	1.36
8	Queen of Sth	53	1.47
9	Dumbarton	63	1.75
10	Brechin	90	2.5

Top scorers

	Team	Goals scored
S Dobbie	Queen of Sth	18 ▮▮▮▮▮▮▮▮▮▮▮▮▮▮▮▮▮▮
S McDonald	Dundee Utd	15 ▮▮▮▮▮▮▮▮▮▮▮▮▮▮▮
N Clark	Dunfermline	14 ▮▮▮▮▮▮▮▮▮▮▮▮▮▮
L Morgan	St Mirren	14 ▮▮▮▮▮▮▮▮▮▮▮▮▮▮
G Reilly	St Mirren	11 ▮▮▮▮▮▮▮▮▮▮▮
K Higginbotham	Dunfermline	10 ▮▮▮▮▮▮▮▮▮▮
C Smith	St Mirren	10 ▮▮▮▮▮▮▮▮▮▮

Key Points in all tables (except the league table) do not include any deductions imposed by the league.
POS H A Position, home/away rank **Sup** Average supremacy **GFA/GAA** Goals For/Against Average **PGA** Pts Gained Average

Record when first to score

		P	W	D	L	F	A	Sup	PGA	Pts
1	Dundee Utd	20	17	2	1	41	14	1.35	2.6	53
2	St Mirren	25	20	3	2	48	19	1.16	2.5	63
3	Inverness CT	19	15	3	1	36	7	1.53	2.5	48
4	Livingston	18	14	3	1	39	17	1.22	2.5	45
5	Falkirk	13	10	2	1	28	13	1.15	2.5	32
6	Dunfermline	22	16	4	2	52	16	1.64	2.4	52
7	Queen of Sth	17	13	2	2	45	22	1.35	2.4	41
8	Morton	13	10	1	2	27	9	1.38	2.4	31
9	Dumbarton	13	5	5	3	17	20	-0.23	1.5	20
10	Brechin	2	0	1	1	4	8	-2.00	0.5	1

Record when keeping a clean sheet

		P	W	D	F	Sup	PGA	Pts
1	St Mirren	14	12	2	24	1.71	2.7	38
2	Dundee Utd	13	11	2	23	1.77	2.7	35
3	Morton	9	7	2	13	1.44	2.6	23
4	Inverness CT	16	12	4	25	1.56	2.5	40
5	Dunfermline	15	10	5	26	1.73	2.3	35
6	Livingston	14	9	5	19	1.36	2.3	32
7	Queen of Sth	11	6	5	8	0.73	2.1	23
8	Dumbarton	7	3	4	3	0.43	1.9	13
9	Falkirk	12	5	7	7	0.58	1.8	22

Brechin didn't keep a clean sheet in 2017-18

Over 2.5 goals

	H	A	%
Brechin	9	14	64%
Queen of Sth	11	12	64%
Dunfermline, St Mirren			56%

Under 2.5 goals

	H	A	%
Dumbarton	10	11	58%
Inverness CT	10	11	58%
Morton		11	10 58%

Both to score

	H	A	%
Queen of Sth	10	12	61%
Morton		9	11 56%
Dunf'line, Falkirk, St Mirren			50%

Both not to score

	H	A	%
Dumbarton	12	10	61%
Inverness CT	10	12	61%
Dundee Utd	9	11	56%

AIRDRIEONIANS

Nickname: The Diamonds Excelsior Stadium
www.airdriefc.com

An average season on the field – the Diamonds, beaten by Cove Rangers in the Cup, stayed in seventh spot from February – was in contrast to a tumultuous one off it.

The club was taken over in January with the decision taken to go part-time.

	2017-18 H A	Last six seasons at home P	W	D	L	OV	UN	BS	CS
Dumbarton		2	1	0	1	2	0	2	0
Brechin		8	6	1	1	4	4	4	3
Raith	D L L L	4	0	2	2	3	1	3	1
Arbroath	D D L L	4	2	2	0	1	3	2	2
Stranraer	W W L L	10	4	4	2	4	6	7	2
East Fife	L D L L	6	1	3	2	3	3	4	1
Airdrieonians									
Forfar	W L L W	8	3	1	4	5	3	6	0
Montrose		-	-	-	-	-	-	-	-
Stenhousemuir		8	3	2	3	2	6	3	2

Season	Division	Pos	P	W	D	L	F	A	GD	Pts
2017-18	League One	7	36	10	11	15	46	60	-14	41
2016-17	League One	3	36	16	4	16	61	66	-5	52
2015-16	League One	5	36	14	7	15	48	50	-2	49

Over/Under 61%/39% 4th **Both score** 64%/36% 3rd

ARBROATH

Nickname: The Red Lichties Gayfield Park
www.arbroathfc.co.uk

The League Two champions enjoyed a rock-solid return to League One, spending virtually the entire season in the top four.

They scored plenty of goals – 70 in total – but cometh the hour Dick Campbell's side fell short against Dumbarton in the playoffs.

	2017-18 H A	Last six seasons at home P	W	D	L	OV	UN	BS	CS
Dumbarton		-	-	-	-	-	-	-	-
Brechin		4	2	0	2	2	2	2	0
Raith	L D L D	2	0	1	1	1	1	2	0
Arbroath									
Stranraer	L L W W	6	3	0	3	5	1	5	1
East Fife	L D L W	10	3	4	3	3	7	6	2
Airdrieonians	W W D D	4	3	0	1	2	2	2	1
Forfar	W W W W	8	5	1	2	4	4	4	3
Montrose		6	2	3	1	3	3	3	2
Stenhousemuir		4	1	2	1	3	1	3	1

Season	Division	Pos	P	W	D	L	F	A	GD	Pts
2017-18	League One	4	36	17	8	11	70	51	+19	59
2016-17	League Two	1	36	18	12	6	63	36	+27	66
2015-16	League Two	9	36	11	6	19	42	51	-9	39

Over/Under 61%/39% 4th **Both score** 67%/33% 2nd

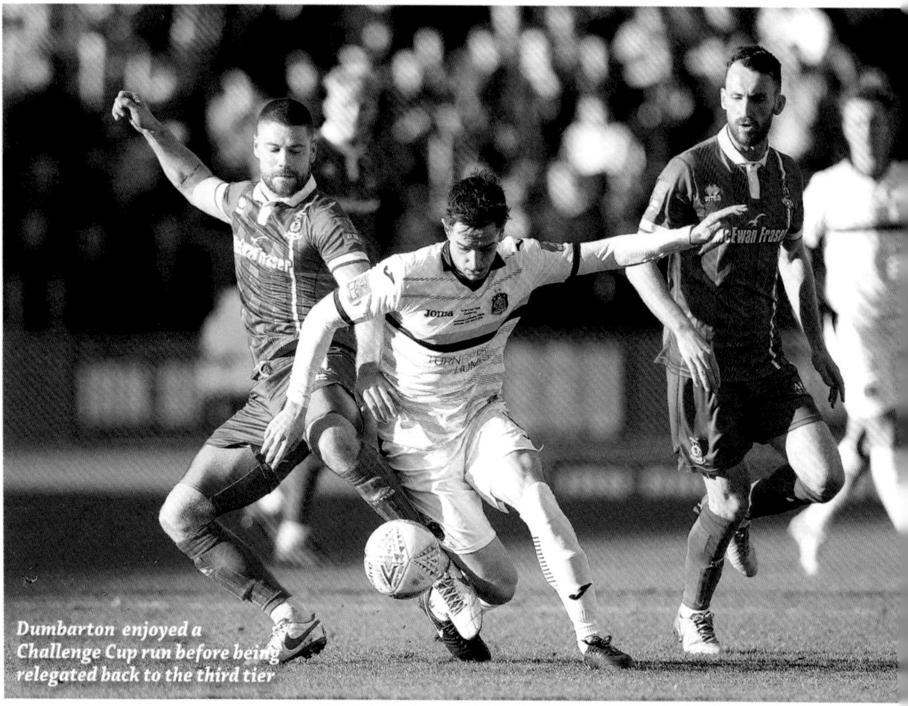

Dumbarton enjoyed a Challenge Cup run before being relegated back to the third tier

BRECHIN

Nickname: The City   Glebe Park
www.brechincity.com

Brechin's promotion to the Championship proved a disaster, returning just four points.

The part-timers, who failed to keep a clean sheet, were the first team in 126 years to go through a league campaign without a win, but stuck behind manager Darren Dods.

	2017-18 H	A	Last six seasons at home P	W	D	L	OV	UN	BS	CS
Dumbarton	L L	L L	2	0	0	2	1	1	1	0
Brechin										
Raith			-	-	-	-	-	-	-	-
Arbroath			4	3	0	1	3	1	3	1
Stranraer			10	4	3	3	5	5	5	5
East Fife			6	5	0	1	4	2	2	3
Airdrieonians			8	3	4	1	5	3	6	2
Forfar			8	3	1	4	7	1	6	1
Montrose			-	-	-	-	-	-	-	-
Stenhousemuir			10	5	1	4	7	3	7	2

Season	Division	Pos	P	W	D	L	F	A	GD	Pts
2017-18	Championship	10	36	0	4	32	20	90	-70	4
2016-17	League One	4	36	15	5	16	43	49	-6	50
2015-16	League One	7	36	12	6	18	47	59	-12	42

Over/Under 64%/36% 1st   **Both score** 47%/53% 6th

DUMBARTON

Nickname: The Sons   C&G Systems Stadium
www.dumbartonfootballclub.com

Part-timers Dumbarton lost out to a 93rd-minute Inverness goal in the Challenge Cup final and also suffered injury-time heartahce against Alloa in the playoffs.

That defeat saw the Sons relegated back to the third tier after six years.

	2017-18 H	A	Last six seasons at home P	W	D	L	OV	UN	BS	CS
Dumbarton										
Brechin	W W	W W	2	2	0	0	1	1	1	1
Raith			10	3	4	3	9	1	8	2
Arbroath			-	-	-	-	-	-	-	-
Stranraer			-	-	-	-	-	-	-	-
East Fife			-	-	-	-	-	-	-	-
Airdrieonians			2	1	0	1	2	0	2	0
Forfar			-	-	-	-	-	-	-	-
Montrose			-	-	-	-	-	-	-	-
Stenhousemuir			-	-	-	-	-	-	-	-

Season	Division	Pos	P	W	D	L	F	A	GD	Pts
2017-18	Championship	9	36	7	9	20	27	63	-36	30
2016-17	Championship	8	36	9	12	15	46	56	-10	39
2015-16	Championship	8	36	10	7	19	35	66	-31	37

Over/Under 42%/58% 8th   **Both score** 39%/61% 9th

EAST FIFE

Nickname: The Fifers   New Bayview Stadium
www.eastfifefc.info

As high as third after a 3-1 defeat of Arbroath in October, the rest of the season was a tale of inconsistency for East Fife.

They conceded at least two goals 19 times, losing six of their last seven. Darren Young's Fifers drew only three games all season.

	2017-18 H	A	Last six seasons at home P	W	D	L	OV	UN	BS	CS
Dumbarton			-	-	-	-	-	-	-	-
Brechin			6	1	1	4	6	0	5	0
Raith	L L	L L	2	0	0	2	2	0	1	0
Arbroath	W L	W D	10	6	0	4	6	4	5	2
Stranraer	D L	L W	8	1	4	3	2	6	5	2
East Fife										
Airdrieonians	W W	W D	6	3	1	2	3	3	2	2
Forfar	W L	L L	6	3	0	3	6	0	4	2
Montrose			4	3	1	0	3	1	1	3
Stenhousemuir			6	3	0	3	3	3	3	2

Season	Division	Pos	P	W	D	L	F	A	GD	Pts
2017-18	League One	6	36	13	3	20	49	67	-18	42
2016-17	League One	5	36	12	10	14	41	44	-3	46
2015-16	League Two	1	36	18	8	10	62	41	+21	62

Over/Under 58%/42% 9th   **Both score** 50%/50% 11th

FORFAR

Nickname: The Loons   Station Park
www.forfarathletic.co.uk

Promoted Forfar endured a torrid campaign, going through three different managers, but they survived in the end.

The division's lowest scorers were still bottom in early February before Jim Weir oversaw a run of four defeats in 11 games.

	2017-18 H	A	Last six seasons at home P	W	D	L	OV	UN	BS	CS
Dumbarton			-	-	-	-	-	-	-	-
Brechin			8	3	1	4	3	5	4	2
Raith	D W	L L	2	1	1	0	1	1	2	0
Arbroath	L L	L L	8	0	3	5	2	6	4	0
Stranraer	D W	L L	10	5	3	2	5	5	7	3
East Fife	W W	L W	6	5	0	1	3	3	3	3
Airdrieonians	W L	L W	8	2	3	3	3	5	5	1
Forfar										
Montrose			2	0	1	1	1	1	1	1
Stenhousemuir			8	5	1	2	6	2	4	3

Season	Division	Pos	P	W	D	L	F	A	GD	Pts
2017-18	League One	8	36	11	5	20	40	65	-25	38
2016-17	League Two	2	36	18	10	8	69	49	+20	64
2015-16	League One	10	36	8	10	18	48	60	-12	34

Over/Under 56%/44% 11th   **Both score** 50%/50% 11th

MONTROSE

Nickname: The Gable Endies   Links Park Stadium
www.montrosefc.co.uk

Pre-season money for Montrose proved shrewd as they bolted up for just the second league title in their history.

They and Peterhead were locked in a titanic fight for top spot before Stewart Petrie's men nicked the spoils.

	2017-18 H	A	P	W	D	L	OV	UN	BS	CS
Dumbarton			-	-	-	-	-	-	-	-
Brechin			-	-	-	-	-	-	-	-
Raith			-	-	-	-	-	-	-	-
Arbroath			6	2	1	3	4	2	3	2
Stranraer			-	-	-	-	-	-	-	-
East Fife			4	0	1	3	4	0	2	0
Airdrieonians			-	-	-	-	-	-	-	-
Forfar			2	1	1	0	0	2	1	1
Montrose										
Stenhousemuir	D W	W W	2	1	1	0	0	2	1	1

Season	Division	Pos	P	W	D	L	F	A	GD	Pts
2017-18	League Two	1	36	23	8	5	60	35	+25	77
2016-17	League Two	4	36	14	10	12	44	53	-9	52
2015-16	League Two	8	36	11	10	15	50	70	-20	43

Over/Under 50%/50% 8th   **Both score** 44%/56% 9th

RAITH

Nickname: The Rovers   Stark's Park
www.raithrovers.net

Raith were 11-8 to bounce straight back up following relegation from the Championship and looked to have it in the bag.

Top going into their final game, they drew 0-0 with Alloa, were pipped by Ayr, and then lost again to Alloa in the promotion playoffs.

	2017-18 H	A	P	W	D	L	OV	UN	BS	CS
Dumbarton			10	6	2	2	8	2	8	2
Brechin			-	-	-	-	-	-	-	-
Raith			-	-	-	-	-	-	-	-
Arbroath	W D	W D	2	1	1	0	1	1	1	1
Stranraer	W W	L W	2	2	0	0	2	0	0	2
East Fife	W W	W W	2	2	0	0	0	2	0	2
Airdrieonians	W W	D W	4	4	0	0	1	3	1	3
Forfar	W W	D L	2	2	0	0	2	0	2	0
Montrose			-	-	-	-	-	-	-	-
Stenhousemuir			-	-	-	-	-	-	-	-

Season	Division	Pos	P	W	D	L	F	A	GD	Pts
2017-18	League One	2	36	22	9	5	68	32	+36	75
2016-17	Championship	9	36	10	9	17	35	52	-17	39
2015-16	Championship	4	36	18	8	10	52	46	+6	62

Over/Under 61%/39% 4th   **Both score** 53%/47% 10th

STENHOUSEMUIR

Nickname: The Warriors   Ochilview Park
www.stenhousemuirfc.com

Relegated last May, Stenhousemuir bounced straight back under Brown Ferguson.

Stenny limped into the playoffs failing to win any of their last four league games and then edged past Queen's Park before riding their luck to see off Peterhead.

	2017-18 H	A	P	W	D	L	OV	UN	BS	CS
Dumbarton			-	-	-	-	-	-	-	-
Brechin			10	3	5	2	7	3	8	1
Raith			-	-	-	-	-	-	-	-
Arbroath			4	2	2	0	3	1	3	1
Stranraer			10	4	3	3	4	6	4	5
East Fife			6	3	2	1	3	3	4	1
Airdrieonians			8	4	2	2	5	3	6	1
Forfar			8	3	2	3	5	3	5	1
Montrose	L L	D L	2	0	0	2	0	2	0	0
Stenhousemuir			-	-	-	-	-	-	-	-

Season	Division	Pos	P	W	D	L	F	A	GD	Pts
2017-18	League Two	4	36	15	9	12	56	47	+9	54
2016-17	League One	10	36	11	6	19	45	64	-19	39
2015-16	League One	8	36	11	7	16	46	80	-34	40

Over/Under 53%/47% 7th   **Both score** 61%/39% 1st

STRANRAER

Nickname: The Blues   Stair Park
www.stranraerfc.org

Stranraer failed to find the net just twice in 2018, a stat slightly offset by conceding at least three goals seven times at home.

It made them entertaining and frustrating but they'll be upbeat for the new term after signing off with five wins in their last six.

	2017-18 H	A	P	W	D	L	OV	UN	BS	CS
Dumbarton			-	-	-	-	-	-	-	-
Brechin			10	5	1	4	4	6	3	4
Raith	W L	L L	2	1	0	1	1	1	0	1
Arbroath	L L	W W	6	2	2	2	3	3	5	1
Stranraer			-	-	-	-	-	-	-	-
East Fife	W L	D W	8	5	1	2	3	5	4	3
Airdrieonians	W W	L L	10	7	1	2	7	3	7	3
Forfar	W W	D L	10	6	2	2	6	4	4	4
Montrose			-	-	-	-	-	-	-	-
Stenhousemuir			10	5	3	2	5	5	7	2

Season	Division	Pos	P	W	D	L	F	A	GD	Pts
2017-18	League One	5	36	16	5	15	58	66	-8	53
2016-17	League One	7	36	12	8	16	46	50	-4	44
2015-16	League One	4	36	15	6	15	43	49	-6	51

Over/Under 67%/33% 3rd   **Both score** 56%/44% 7th

Scottish League One results 2017-18

	Airdrieonians	Albion	Alloa	Arbroath	Ayr	East Fife	Forfar	Queen's Park	Raith	Stranraer
Airdrieonians		2-2/2-0	2-0/2-2	1-1/0-0	2-0/1-2	0-1/0-0	2-1/1-2	4-2/2-1	2-2/1-2	2-0/2-1
Albion	1-2/2-2		0-2/1-3	1-2/1-2	1-5/2-3	3-2/1-0	3-4/0-1	0-1/1-1	2-1/2-2	0-4/1-3
Alloa	1-0/2-2	2-5/3-1		5-3/3-2	1-2/2-1	4-1/1-2	2-1/1-0	1-0/2-2	1-1/0-0	1-0/0-1
Arbroath	7-1/2-0	1-4/1-0	1-1/0-0		1-4/1-1	2-3/1-1	2-1/2-0	2-0/2-1	1-2/1-1	1-2/2-3
Ayr	2-2/3-0	3-2/2-0	3-3/1-2	1-2/1-2		3-0/3-0	3-0/2-3	3-2/4-0	3-0/3-0	2-0/1-2
East Fife	6-1/2-1	5-4/2-0	1-0/2-1	3-1/0-5	1-4/2-3		3-0/1-2	0-1/0-2	0-5/2-3	1-1/2-3
Forfar	2-1/0-1	0-2/4-2	0-2/0-1	0-5/0-1	0-5/0-2	2-0/2-0		0-3/1-1	1-1/2-1	1-1/5-1
Queen's Park	1-1/0-0	2-5/2-2	0-4/1-2	0-2/3-0	0-2/1-4	2-1/2-3	1-1/2-2		0-5/1-3	2-2/2-2
Raith	2-0/2-1	3-1/2-0	2-1/0-0	2-0/2-2	2-1/1-1	1-0/2-0	3-1/2-1	2-0/2-0		3-0/3-0
Stranraer	3-1/3-2	2-2/2-3	2-0/1-0	2-6/1-4	3-4/1-5	1-0/0-2	3-0/2-0	3-0/2-3	1-0/0-3	

Scottish League One 2017-18

Pos	H	A		Home P	W	D	L	F	A	Away W	D	L	F	A	GD	Pts
1	2	1	Ayr (P)	36	11	2	5	43	20	13	2	3	49	22	50	76
2	1	3	Raith	36	15	3	0	36	9	7	6	5	32	23	36	75
3	3	4	Alloa (P)	36	10	4	4	32	24	7	5	6	24	19	13	60
4	6	2	Arbroath	36	7	5	6	30	25	10	3	5	40	26	19	59
5	5	5	Stranraer	36	9	1	8	32	35	7	4	7	26	31	-8	53
6	7	8	East Fife	36	8	1	9	33	37	5	2	11	16	30	-18	42
7	4	10	Airdrieonians	36	8	6	4	28	19	2	5	11	18	41	-14	41
8	8	9	Forfar	36	6	3	9	20	30	5	2	11	20	35	-25	38
9	9	7	Queen's Park (R)	36	2	7	9	22	41	5	3	10	20	31	-30	31
10	10	6	Albion (R)	36	3	3	12	22	40	5	3	10	35	40	-23	30

Best attack

	Team	GF	GFA
1	Ayr	92	2.56
2	Arbroath	70	1.94
3	Raith	68	1.89
4	Stranraer	58	1.61
5	Albion	57	1.58
6	Alloa	56	1.56
7	East Fife	49	1.36
8	Airdrieonians	46	1.28
9	Queen's Park	42	1.17
10	Forfar	40	1.11

Best defence

	Team	GA	GAA
1	Raith	32	0.89
2	Ayr	42	1.17
3	Alloa	43	1.19
4	Arbroath	51	1.42
5	Airdrieonians	60	1.67
6	Forfar	65	1.81
7	Stranraer	66	1.83
8	East Fife	67	1.86
9	Queen's Park	72	2
10	Albion	80	2.22

Top scorers

	Team	Goals scored	
L Shankland	Ayr	26	▮▮▮▮▮▮▮▮▮▮▮▮▮▮▮▮▮▮▮▮▮▮▮▮▮▮
A Trouten	Albion	20	▮▮▮▮▮▮▮▮▮▮▮▮▮▮▮▮▮▮▮▮
C Moore	Ayr	19	▮▮▮▮▮▮▮▮▮▮▮▮▮▮▮▮▮▮▮
R Wallace	Arbroath	16	▮▮▮▮▮▮▮▮▮▮▮▮▮▮▮▮
L Vaughan	Raith	15	▮▮▮▮▮▮▮▮▮▮▮▮▮▮▮
C Duggan	East Fife	14	▮▮▮▮▮▮▮▮▮▮▮▮▮▮

Key POS H A Overall league position, rank from home games, rank from away games **Sup** Avg match supremacy **GFA** Goals For Avg **GAA** Goals Against Avg **PGA** Points Gained Avg

Record when first to score

		P	W	D	L	F	A	Sup	PGA	Pts
1	Raith	23	19	4	0	55	14	1.78	2.7	61
2	Alloa	15	11	4	0	28	10	1.20	2.5	37
3	Ayr	28	21	2	5	77	28	1.75	2.3	65
4	Stranraer	19	13	2	4	40	22	0.95	2.2	41
5	East Fife	16	11	1	4	29	23	0.38	2.1	34
6	Arbroath	16	9	3	4	38	20	1.13	1.9	30
7	Queen's Park	10	6	1	3	19	13	0.60	1.9	19
8	Forfar	17	9	4	4	31	21	0.59	1.8	31
9	Airdrieonians	17	8	4	5	30	31	-0.06	1.6	28
10	Albion	13	5	4	4	27	22	0.38	1.5	19

Record when keeping a clean sheet

		P	W	D	F	Sup	PGA	Pts
1	Ayr	12	12	0	35	2.92	3	36
2	Stranraer	9	9	0	18	2.00	3	27
3	Forfar	3	3	0	5	1.67	3	9
4	Albion	2	2	0	3	1.50	3	6
5	Raith	14	12	2	32	2.29	2.7	38
6	East Fife	6	5	1	9	1.50	2.7	16
7	Queen's Park	6	5	1	10	1.67	2.7	16
8	Arbroath	10	8	2	20	2.00	2.6	26
9	Alloa	11	8	3	13	1.18	2.5	27
10	Airdrieonians	8	5	3	9	1.13	2.3	18

Over 2.5 goals

	H	A	%
Ayr	16	13	81%
Albion	13	12	69%
Stranraer	12	12	67%

Under 2.5 goals

	H	A	%
Alloa	7	10	47%
Forfar	11	5	44%
East Fife	5	10	42%

Both to score

	H	A	%
Albion	13	12	69%
Arbroath	13	11	67%
Airdrieonians, Ayr		64%	

Both not to score

	H	A	%
East Fife	7	11	50%
Forfar	11	7	50%
Raith	10	7	47%

ALBION

Nickname: The Wee Rovers   Cliftonhill Stadium
www.albionroversfc.com

Eight defeats in their last nine matches condemned Albion to relegation.

They scored 57 goals – one more than promoted Alloa – but one clean sheet from the end of August tells its own story. John Brogan has replaced Brian Kerr as manager.

	2017-18 H A	Last six seasons at home P W D L OV UN BS CS
Queens Park	**L** D **W** D	8 5 2 1 2 6 4 3
Albion		
Peterhead		6 1 3 2 1 5 2 3
Stirling		2 1 0 1 1 1 1 0
Clyde		4 2 1 1 2 2 1 2
Elgin		4 2 1 1 3 1 1 2
Annan		4 3 0 1 1 3 1 2
Berwick		4 2 0 2 2 2 1 1
Edinburgh City		- - - - - - - -
Cowdenbeath		2 1 1 0 1 1 1 1

Season	Division	Pos	P	W	D	L	F	A	GD	Pts
2017-18	League One	10	36	8	6	22	57	80	-23	30
2016-17	League One	8	36	11	9	16	41	48	-7	42
2015-16	League One	6	36	13	10	13	40	44	-4	49

Over/Under 69%/31% 2nd   **Both score** 69%/31% 1st

ANNAN

Nickname: Galabankies   Galabank
www.annanathleticfc.com

Player-manager Peter Murphy's first season in charge started well enough with Annan in the top four in mid-January.

Playoff dreams were dashed, however, by a run of one win in 11. Just six home wins – they drew eight at Galabank – proved costly.

	2017-18 H A	Last six seasons at home P W D L OV UN BS CS
Queens Park		8 5 1 2 3 5 4 3
Albion		4 2 1 1 2 2 3 1
Peterhead	**L** D **L** **L**	6 3 2 1 4 2 4 2
Stirling	D **W** **L** **L**	10 4 4 2 7 3 9 0
Clyde	D D **L** D	12 3 3 6 6 6 7 2
Elgin	**W** **W** **W** **L**	12 8 3 1 6 6 7 5
Annan		
Berwick	D D **W** **W**	12 9 3 0 7 5 6 6
Edinburgh City	**W** **L** **W** **L**	4 2 1 1 2 2 3 1
Cowdenbeath	**W** D D **W**	4 3 1 0 0 4 1 3

Season	Division	Pos	P	W	D	L	F	A	GD	Pts
2017-18	League Two	7	36	12	11	13	49	41	+8	47
2016-17	League Two	3	36	18	4	14	61	58	+3	58
2015-16	League Two	5	36	16	8	12	69	57	+12	56

Over/Under 42%/58% 10th   **Both score** 56%/44% 4th

BERWICK

Nickname: The Borderers   Shielfield Park
www.berwickrangersfc.co.uk

New boss Robbie Horn had a mixed season. A lack of consistency hinted at promise – they won five of their first ten games but none back-to-back – but a 3-0 loss at Montrose in early December ushered in a run of one win in 19 which saw them freefall to ninth.

	2017-18 H A	Last six seasons at home P W D L OV UN BS CS
Queens Park		8 5 3 0 2 6 3 5
Albion		4 2 1 1 2 2 3 0
Peterhead	**L** **L** **W** D	6 0 1 5 4 2 5 0
Stirling	**W** **L** **L** **L**	10 6 1 3 4 6 4 4
Clyde	**W** **L** D **W**	12 6 3 3 8 4 5 4
Elgin	**W** D **L** **L**	12 3 3 6 7 5 8 2
Annan	**L** **L** D D	12 6 1 5 7 5 7 2
Berwick		
Edinburgh City	D D **L** **L**	4 1 2 1 2 2 4 0
Cowdenbeath	**W** **W** **W** **W**	4 2 1 1 1 3 2 2

Season	Division	Pos	P	W	D	L	F	A	GD	Pts
2017-18	League Two	8	36	9	10	17	31	59	-28	37
2016-17	League Two	8	36	10	10	16	48	49	-1	40
2015-16	League Two	6	36	14	7	15	45	50	-5	49

Over/Under 47%/53% 9th   **Both score** 39%/61% 11th

CLYDE

Nickname: The Bully Wee   Broadwood Stadium
www.clydefc.co.uk

A run of four straight goalless draws around Christmas summed up the mood, but then Danny Lennon's lads turned on the style.

Led by 25-goal David Goodwillie, Clyde won 12 of their last 18, including home-and-away successes over champions Montrose.

	2017-18 H A	Last six seasons at home P W D L OV UN BS CS
Queens Park		8 2 0 6 4 4 2 2
Albion		4 1 1 2 3 1 2 1
Peterhead	**L** **W** **L** **L**	6 2 0 4 2 4 2 2
Stirling	D **W** **W** **L**	10 5 2 3 6 4 8 1
Clyde		
Elgin	**L** **W** **L** **L**	12 8 2 2 8 4 8 3
Annan	**W** D D D	12 7 2 3 9 3 9 2
Berwick	D **L** **L** **W**	12 5 5 2 8 4 9 2
Edinburgh City	**L** **W** **W** **W**	4 2 1 1 3 1 3 1
Cowdenbeath	D **W** **W** **L**	4 2 1 1 1 3 2 1

Season	Division	Pos	P	W	D	L	F	A	GD	Pts
2017-18	League Two	5	36	14	9	13	52	50	+2	51
2016-17	League Two	9	36	10	8	18	49	64	-15	38
2015-16	League Two	3	36	17	6	13	56	45	+11	57

Over/Under 61%/39% 3rd   **Both score** 61%/39% 1st

COWDENBEATH

Nickname: The Blue Brazil   Central Park
www.cowdenbeathfc.com

One win in their first 26 games left the Blue Brazil stranded and, despite a March flurry, they never recovered.

They failed to score in 18 matches. A fifth straight bottom-two finish saw them edge a relegation playoff 3-2 against Cove Rangers.

	2017-18 H	A	Last six seasons at home P	W	D	L	OV	UN	BS	CS
Queens Park	-	-	-	-	-	-	-	-	-	-
Albion	2	1	0	1	1	1	1	1		
Peterhead	L L	L L	4	0	1	3	3	1	2	0
Stirling	L L	L D	4	0	0	4	2	2	1	0
Clyde	L W	D L	4	3	0	1	1	3	0	3
Elgin	L W	D L	4	1	1	2	2	3	0	
Annan	D L	L D	4	0	2	2	1	3	2	0
Berwick	L L	L L	4	0	0	4	1	3	1	0
Edinburgh City	W L	D D	4	2	0	2	1	3	1	2
Cowdenbeath										

Season	Division	Pos	P	W	D	L	F	A	GD	Pts
2017-18	League Two	10	36	4	10	22	23	56	-33	22
2016-17	League Two	10	36	9	8	19	40	55	-15	35
2015-16	League One	9	36	11	6	19	46	72	-26	39

Over/Under 33%/67% 11th   **Both score** 44%/56% 9th

EDINBURGH CITY

Nickname: City   Meadowbank Stadium
www.edinburghcityfc.com

Five wins in nine after the turn of the year was the bright spot in a season which ended badly as City failed to win any of their last ten.

As a sign of intent they've snaffled Annan's top scorer Blair Henderson, but a record of just six clean sheets hints at other problems.

	2017-18 H	A	Last six seasons at home P	W	D	L	OV	UN	BS	CS
Queens Park	-	-	-	-	-	-	-	-	-	-
Albion	-	-	-	-	-	-	-	-	-	-
Peterhead	L D	L L	2	0	1	1	1	1	0	1
Stirling	L D	L D	4	2	1	1	2	2	2	2
Clyde	L L	W L	4	0	1	3	2	2	1	1
Elgin	L W	D D	4	2	0	2	4	0	1	2
Annan	L W	L W	4	3	0	1	1	3	1	2
Berwick	W W	D D	4	2	1	1	3	1	2	2
Edinburgh City										
Cowdenbeath	D D	L W	4	0	4	0	0	4	3	1

Season	Division	Pos	P	W	D	L	F	A	GD	Pts
2017-18	League Two	9	36	7	9	20	37	62	-25	30
2016-17	League Two	7	36	11	10	15	38	45	-7	43
2015-16	Lowland League 1	28	24	1	3	74	28+46	73		

Over/Under 58%/42% 6th   **Both score** 50%/50% 5th

ELGIN

Nickname: The Black And Whites   Borough Briggs
www.elgincity.com

In the playoff places with four matches left, Gavin Price's men dropped out as they collected just two points from a possible 12.

It was a solid enough start for Price, however, and he's already enticed ex-Celtic man Craig Beattie to Borough Briggs.

	2017-18 H	A	Last six seasons at home P	W	D	L	OV	UN	BS	CS
Queens Park			8	1	3	4	5	3	6	1
Albion			4	1	1	2	2	2	2	1
Peterhead	L L	L L	6	1	0	5	3	3	2	1
Stirling	L W	D L	10	5	1	4	8	2	6	3
Clyde	W W	W L	12	10	1	1	6	6	7	4
Elgin										
Annan	L W	L L	12	4	3	5	9	3	9	1
Berwick	W W	L D	12	8	2	2	10	2	8	4
Edinburgh City	D D	W L	4	2	2	0	2	3	2	2
Cowdenbeath	D W	W L	4	2	2	0	1	3	2	2

Season	Division	Pos	P	W	D	L	F	A	GD	Pts
2017-18	League Two	6	36	14	7	15	54	61	-7	49
2016-17	League Two	5	36	14	9	13	67	47+20	51		
2015-16	League Two	2	36	17	8	11	59	46+13	59		

Over/Under 61%/39% 3rd   **Both score** 50%/50% 5th

PETERHEAD

Nickname: The Blue Toon   Balmoor Stadium
www.peterheadfc.com

The 2-1 favourites won their last six matches only to be touched off by Montrose.

They had only failed to score in three games but the division's top scorers drew a blank against Stenhousemuir in the playoffs, match 49 of a marathon 50-game campaign.

	2017-18 H	A	Last six seasons at home P	W	D	L	OV	UN	BS	CS
Queens Park			6	5	0	1	2	4	4	1
Albion			6	2	4	0	2	4	5	1
Peterhead										
Stirling	L W	W W	8	3	3	2	6	2	6	1
Clyde	W W	W L	6	5	1	0	3	3	2	4
Elgin	W W	W W	6	3	2	1	4	2	3	2
Annan	W W	W D	6	5	1	0	2	4	2	4
Berwick	W W	W W	6	2	3	1	1	5	3	2
Edinburgh City	W W	W D	2	2	0	0	2	1	1	1
Cowdenbeath	W W	W W	4	3	0	1	2	2	1	2

Season	Division	Pos	P	W	D	L	F	A	GD	Pts
2017-18	League Two	2	36	24	4	8	79	39+40	76		
2016-17	League Two	9	36	10	10	16	44	59	-15	40
2015-16	League One	3	36	16	11	9	72	47+25	59		

Over/Under 61%/39% 3rd   **Both score** 50%/50% 5th

QUEEN'S PARK

Nickname: The Spiders Hampden Park
www.queensparkfc.co.uk

A season that began with 150th birthday celebrations ended with a return to the basement after two years courtesy of defeat to Stenhousemuir in the playoffs.

Gus MacPherson's Spiders chalked up the fewest victories in the third tier – just seven.

	2017-18 H A	Last six seasons at home P W D L OV UN BS CS
Queens Park		
Albion	L D W D	8 3 2 3 4 4 4 2
Peterhead		6 1 2 3 2 4 0 3
Stirling		6 2 2 2 4 3 1
Clyde		8 3 3 2 4 4 7 1
Elgin		8 3 4 1 3 5 5 2
Annan		8 1 3 4 4 4 4 2
Berwick		8 3 2 3 4 4 4 2
Edinburgh City		- - - - - - - -
Cowdenbeath		- - - - - - - -

Season	Division	Pos	P	W	D	L	F	A	GD	Pts
2017-18	League One	9	36	7	10	19	42	72	-30	31
2016-17	League One	6	36	12	10	14	37	51	-14	46
2015-16	League Two	4	36	15	11	10	46	32	+14	56

Over/Under 61%/39% 4th **Both score** 56%/44% 7th

STIRLING

Nickname: The Binos Forthbank Stadium
www.stirlingalbionfc.co.uk

Dave Mackay impressed as manager, guiding Stirling to the top of the league after losing just one of their first nine matches.

They couldn't sustain it, however, failing to win any of their last seven and squeezing into the playoffs where Peterhead beat them.

	2017-18 H A	Last six seasons at home P W D L OV UN BS CS
Queens Park		6 1 2 3 5 1 4 2
Albion		2 2 0 0 1 1 1 1
Peterhead	L L W L	8 3 0 5 3 5 3 2
Stirling		
Clyde	L W D L	10 4 2 4 5 5 6 2
Elgin	D W W L	10 3 5 2 6 4 7 2
Annan	W W D L	10 8 1 1 6 4 6 3
Berwick	W W L W	10 7 2 1 7 3 6 4
Edinburgh City	W D W D	4 2 2 0 1 3 2 2
Cowdenbeath	W D W W	4 1 1 2 3 1 2 1

Season	Division	Pos	P	W	D	L	F	A	GD	Pts
2017-18	League Two	3	36	16	7	13	61	52	+9	55
2016-17	League Two	6	36	12	11	13	50	59	-9	47
2015-16	League Two	7	36	13	9	14	47	46	+1	48

Over/Under 67%/33% 2nd **Both score** 61%/39% 1st

SCOTTISH LEAGUE TWO

Edinburgh City enjoyed a comfortable enough second season in the SPFL

Scottish League Two results 2017-18

	Annan	Berwick	Clyde	Cowdenbeath	Edinburgh City	Elgin	Montrose	Peterhead	Stenhousemuir	Stirling
Annan		0-0/0-0	0-0/1-1	1-0/1-1	2-1/2-3	2-0/4-1	0-1/0-1	1-2/3-3	1-1/2-0	1-1/3-1
Berwick	1-5/0-2		3-1/0-1	1-0/1-0	1-1/1-1	3-2/2-2	0-1/2-2	2-3/1-3	0-0/2-2	1-0/0-1
Clyde	2-1/0-0	0-0/1-2		1-1/2-0	2-3/3-2	2-4/1-0	0-0/3-0	1-4/1-0	1-1/0-3	1-1/2-1
Cowdenbeath	1-1/0-2	0-1/1-3	0-3/1-0		1-0/0-2	1-3/3-1	1-3/0-3	0-4/0-2	1-1/1-1	0-3/1-2
Edinburgh City	0-1/3-2	1-0/3-0	0-3/1-3	0-0/1-1		0-3/4-0	1-3/0-2	0-3/0-0	1-2/1-4	1-2/2-2
Elgin	0-1/2-1	5-1/3-0	3-2/2-1	1-1/1-0	1-1/1-1		3-0/2-2	0-2/0-1	2-0/2-0	0-2/3-0
Montrose	1-1/2-1	3-0/1-0	3-2/1-3	1-0/1-1	1-0/3-0	3-0/1-1		2-6/3-2	1-1/1-0	1-3/2-1
Peterhead	1-0/1-0	0-2/1-1	2-1/3-0	3-2/1-0	3-0/2-1	3-0/7-0	1-1/0-1		2-3/1-2	2-4/4-3
Stenhousemuir	1-3/3-2	3-0/4-0	1-1/2-3	1-0/1-2	3-0/1-0	4-1/0-2	0-1/0-2	3-1/1-4		2-3/2-1
Stirling	3-2/3-0	4-0/2-0	2-3/2-1	1-0/2-2	2-0/2-2	2-2/3-1	0-1/0-5	0-1/0-1	1-2/1-1	

Scottish League Two 2017-18

Pos	H	A		P	Home W	Home D	Home L	Home F	Home A	Away W	Away D	Away L	Away F	Away A	GD	Pts
1	1	2	Montrose (P)	36	11	4	3	31	22	12	4	2	29	13	25	77
2	2	1	Peterhead	36	11	2	5	37	21	13	2	3	42	18	40	76
3	5	3	Stirling	36	8	4	6	30	24	8	3	7	31	28	9	55
4	4	4	Stenhousemuir (P)	36	9	1	8	32	26	6	8	4	24	21	9	54
5	6	5	Clyde	36	7	6	5	23	23	7	3	8	29	27	2	51
6	3	8	Elgin City	36	10	4	4	31	16	4	3	11	23	45	-7	49
7	7	6	Annan	36	6	8	4	24	17	6	3	9	25	24	8	47
8	8	7	Berwick	36	5	6	7	21	27	4	4	10	10	32	-28	37
9	9	9	Edinburgh City	36	4	4	10	19	31	3	5	10	18	31	-25	30
10	10	10	Cowdenbeath*	36	3	3	12	12	35	1	7	10	11	21	-33	22

*Cowdenbeath avoided relegation by winning League Two playoff

Best attack
		GF	GFA
1	Peterhead	79	2.19
2	Stirling	61	1.69
3	Montrose	60	1.67
4	Stenhousemuir	56	1.56
5	Elgin City	54	1.5
6	Clyde	52	1.44
7	Annan	49	1.36
8	Edinburgh City	37	1.03
9	Berwick	31	0.86
10	Cowdenbeath	23	0.64

Best defence
		GA	GAA
1	Montrose	35	0.97
2	Peterhead	39	1.08
3	Annan	41	1.14
4	Stenhousemuir	47	1.31
5	Clyde	50	1.39
6	Stirling	52	1.44
7	Cowdenbeath	56	1.56
8	Berwick	59	1.64
9	Elgin City	61	1.69
10	Edinburgh City	62	1.72

Top scorers
	Team	Goals scored	
D Goodwillie	Clyde	25	IIIIIIIIIIIIIIIIIIIIIIIII
D Smith	Stirling	22	IIIIIIIIIIIIIIIIIIIIII
R McAllister	Peterhead	20	IIIIIIIIIIIIIIIIIIII
M McGuigan	Stenhousemuir	20	IIIIIIIIIIIIIIIIIIII
B Henderson	Annan	16	IIIIIIIIIIIIIIII
R McLean	Peterhead	15	IIIIIIIIIIIIIII

Key POS H A Overall league position, rank from home games, rank from away games **Sup** Avg match supremacy **GFA** Goals For Avg **GAA** Goals Against Avg **PGA** Points Gained Avg

Record when first to score
		P	W	D	L	F	A	Sup	PGA	Pts
1	Montrose	23	20	3	0	41	5	1.57	2.7	63
2	Peterhead	24	20	2	2	59	20	1.63	2.6	62
3	Elgin City	16	11	4	1	37	12	1.56	2.3	37
4	Berwick	11	7	3	1	18	13	0.45	2.2	24
5	Stenhousemuir	23	14	6	3	47	25	0.96	2.1	48
6	Stirling	19	12	4	3	37	18	1.00	2.1	40
7	Clyde	21	13	2	6	42	30	0.57	2	41
8	Annan	14	9	1	4	24	13	0.79	2	28
9	Edinburgh City	12	6	5	1	25	15	0.83	1.9	23
10	Cowdenbeath	8	4	3	1	12	9	0.38	1.9	15

Record when keeping a clean sheet
		P	W	D	F	Sup	PGA	Pts
1	Stirling	8	8	0	18	2.25	3	24
2	Elgin City	8	8	0	19	2.38	3	24
3	Montrose	18	17	1	31	1.72	2.9	52
4	Peterhead	15	14	1	33	2.20	2.9	43
5	Stenhousemuir	7	6	1	15	2.14	2.7	19
6	Clyde	11	7	4	14	1.27	2.3	25
7	Annan	11	7	4	11	1.00	2.3	25
8	Edinburgh City	6	4	2	10	1.67	2.3	14
9	Cowdenbeath	3	2	1	2	0.67	2.3	7
10	Berwick	9	5	4	6	0.67	2.1	19

Over 2.5 goals
	H	A	%
Stirling	11	13	67%
Peterhead	11	11	61%
Clyde, Elgin			61%

Under 2.5 goals
	H	A	%
Cowdenbeath	9	15	67%
Annan	12	9	58%
Berwick	10	9	53%

Both to score
	H	A	%
Clyde	10	12	61%
Stenhousemuir	10	12	61%
Stirling	9	13	61%

Both not to score
	H	A	%
Berwick	8	14	61%
Cowdenbeath	10	10	56%
Montrose	7	13	56%

Key to successful betting is to focus on raw facts over noise, hype and distraction

T wo decades in football is, as we've learnt with the passing of the Arsene Wenger era at Arsenal, a time frame in which football has changed beyond recognition. It was a period in the sport marked by some of the most profound changes in the way the game is organised, financed and played. What makes it at least as significant as any previous period is the amount of money sloshing around in the football business.

But the landscape has changed beyond that and in particular the association of the game with the online betting industry that has developed in symbiosis with televised matches.

From shirt sponsorship of domestically irrelevant Far East betting companies to the wall-to-wall betting adverts in every available space of a televised game, we have moved a very long way from how things stood 20 years ago.

At the turn of this century, the Racing & Football Outlook became the very first publication in the world to publish a set of meaningful football ratings derived from the now-standard Elo Ratings. The same type of ratings that at the start of this last World Cup, Fifa belatedly adopted as its own quantification method of ranking international teams. This came after decades of Fifa labouring under one of the most basic and frankly useless rating systems devised.

The contention back then for us at the RFO was that a rating system that had been accepted and used by the world's greatest chess players for many years could serve as the basis for creating, then at least, the most objective measure of a team's worth that had ever been published.

More significant was the fact that the Elo rating system – and with it the RFO's

adaptation of these ratings, the Outlook Index – is by nature a system that is probabilistic, meaning that it could be used in conjunction with other statistical tools to create accurate odds forecasts.

Since then, as the number of betting opportunities and events has increased, so too have the levels of sophistication needed to successfully bet on football.

Where once a traditional reading of football form might well have provided an illusion of being on top of things, in a world of in-play betting across thousands of markets – and against bookmakers well versed in the art of 21st century risk management and odds compilation – that assumption is long dead.

Instead, bar the very rare exception, the bettor who wishes to stay ahead over the long term has to take a more objective view of what they are looking at.

Rather than simply falling back on the clichéd, lazy, football-punter perspective that presents a good narrative to fill airtime on TV or radio – or column inches in tabloids – serious bettors need to look beyond what is at best entertainment and at worst irrelevant and misleading.

We witnessed during last summer's World Cup how taking an objective view of proceedings can pay dividends. While it undoubtedly remains the case that the

Germany crashed out of the World Cup to supposed minnows South Korea

likes of Germany, Spain and Brazil are historically the stronger nations in world football, the truth of the matter – and one shown by analysis of many ratings systems – is that there has also been a significant levelling of strength between nations.

So while many stuck to the historic view of form to reach a relatively superficial comparison between nations, those who didn't and instead went down a more objective route were rewarded time after time as each of those big nations fell flat.

Similar patterns and opportunities are no less prevalent in the Premier League.

While we can easily determine the two or three clubs who have a chance of winning the title, the opportunity for punters is in separating the rest of the pack. And we achieve this not by looking at form lines, historic comparisons or reputations but by using systems such as the Outlook Index to get the most objective and mathematically accurate comparison possible.

You can follow my slow-burning, season-long advice on Twitter at @rfoindex

Manchester City finished a massive 30 Index points clear of closest rivals Tottenham

About the Outlook Index
Our unique ratings provide an objective view of every club. Each team has a rating, roughly on a scale of 0 to 1,000, which goes up or down with league results and takes into account the relative strength of the opposition. The tables show each team's overall rating, plus ratings for home and away form (a separate ratings system) and a Trend rating (-20 to +20). The red and blue bars show the Trend value, based on the last 60 matches but weighted towards more recent games, to help identify the teams in form. Red is hot, blue is not. The tables show final ratings for 2017-18.

Premier League

	Current	H	A		Trend
Man City	996	988	981	‖‖	3
Tottenham	966	980	940	‖	-1
Man Utd	956	976	932	‖‖	-2
Liverpool	955	974	933	‖‖‖	-4
Chelsea	942	967	944	‖‖‖	-4
Arsenal	926	970	886	‖‖‖	-5
Crystal Palace	900	887	894	‖‖‖‖‖	7
Everton	899	936	868		0
Bournemouth	894	889	881	‖	1
West Ham	893	898	874	‖‖‖‖‖	6
Newcastle	893	893	869	‖‖‖‖‖	6
Burnley	887	894	878	‖‖‖	-5
Brighton	885	895	853	‖‖	3
Leicester	884	915	880	‖‖‖‖‖	-7
Southampton	878	887	883	‖	2
Watford	878	898	849		0
West Brom	876	873	856	‖‖‖‖‖	7
Stoke	872	876	869	‖	1
Swansea	868	883	851	‖‖‖‖‖	-9
Huddersfield	864	858	829	‖	-1

Championship

	Current	H	A		Trend
Fulham	886	863	866	‖‖‖	4
Wolves	873	860	858	‖	-1
Cardiff	860	870	840		0
Millwall	854	848	805	‖‖‖‖‖	6
Aston Villa	853	874	825	‖‖	-3
Middlesbro	847	868	826	‖‖	3
Preston	845	834	842	‖‖	4
Brentford	843	836	830		0
Derby	836	850	824	‖‖	-3
Sheff Wed	833	834	828	‖‖‖‖‖‖	9
Sheff Utd	832	832	813	‖	-1
Hull	820	841	801		0
Bristol City	819	832	804	‖‖‖‖‖‖‖	-11
Norwich	819	852	810	‖‖	-3
Ipswich	818	819	808	‖	-1
QPR	814	844	778	‖‖	-2
Leeds	811	838	800	‖‖‖	-5
Nottm Forest	809	818	782		0
Burton	805	782	801	‖‖‖‖	5
Birmingham	804	808	788	‖‖‖‖	6
Sunderland	801	804	820	‖	2
Reading	800	819	794	‖‖‖‖	-6
Barnsley	798	815	779	‖‖‖	-4
Bolton	796	815	766	‖‖‖	-4

SOCCERBASE.COM

League One

	Current	H	A		Trend
Blackburn	831	822	812		9
Blackburn	830	827	808		-1
Wigan	821	806	812		1
Rotherham	790	806	760		3
Shrewsbury	780	780	766		-9
Scunthorpe	778	780	784		0
Plymouth	775	778	745		-4
Bristol Rovers	771	786	720		3
Southend	769	790	745		5
Charlton	768	782	763		3
Blackpool	766	760	739		7
Rochdale	762	760	740		5
Gillingham	761	750	752		-3
Portsmouth	759	763	748		-2
Bradford	759	772	758		-1
Wimbledon	758	750	747		4
Fleetwood	756	755	765		1
Peterborough	755	768	738		-6
Oxford Utd	754	754	745		3
Doncaster	753	750	749		-5
Oldham	746	746	747		0
Northampton	742	746	728		-2
Walsall	741	756	736		-5
MK Dons	737	734	744		-2
Bury	726	730	705		0

League Two

	Current	H	A		Trend
Accrington	760	766	734		4
Luton	744	761	731		-2
Wycombe	740	731	745		2
Lincoln	735	746	702		3
Exeter	734	740	720		3
Coventry	728	745	719		0
Notts Co	727	747	707		2
Cambridge	723	733	696		2
Carlisle	720	706	727		1
Newport Co	714	721	698		0
Mansfield	714	729	727		-8
Crewe	712	710	690		13
Swindon	711	723	720		-4
Crawley	706	703	707		-4
Colchester	699	721	707		-9
Morecambe	699	692	693		0
Barnet	698	709	680		13
Grimsby	697	696	687		6
Stevenage	692	721	684		-2
Port Vale	691	721	695		-5
Yeovil	685	687	690		-2
Forest Green	685	702	670		-4
Cheltenham	683	696	683		-9
Chesterfield	672	703	668		-7

Scottish Premiership

	Current	H	A		Trend
Celtic	918	964	901		-8
Aberdeen	872	866	868		4
Rangers	864	874	846		2
Hibernian	859	848	811		9
Kilmarnock	846	824	826		5
Hearts	824	857	783		-1
Motherwell	814	812	798		5
St Johnstone	809	804	823		-1
Dundee	794	791	787		0
Partick	792	799	778		-1
Ross County	788	791	785		-3
Hamilton	773	794	766		-12

National League

	Current	H	A		Trend
Macclesfield	710	690	699		7
Tranmere	696	705	694		-1
Ebbsfleet	685	675	656		5
Sutton United	676	685	653		-3
Fylde	674	685	656		-2
Aldershot	669	687	663		-6
Solihull M	669	659	658		11
Bromley	669	677	656		-2
Maidenhead	666	674	646		8
Dag & Red	665	682	658		2
Dover	664	695	658		0
Boreham W	664	662	662		-9
Leyton Orient	662	656	676		6
Wrexham	661	676	660		-10
Hartlepool	655	665	659		7
Eastleigh	652	656	652		-2
Halifax	649	653	638		0
Barrow	646	645	660		-2
Maidstone	642	644	642		1
Torquay	641	639	644		3
Gateshead	639	656	647		-9
Chester	625	618	635		4
Woking	621	652	614		-9
Guiseley	611	626	612		-5

Scottish Championship

	Current	H	A		Trend
Inverness CT	785	799	769		12
Dunfermline	778	763	748		12
St Mirren	776	778	760		-7
Livingston	769	750	755		-3
Falkirk	763	772	752		5
Dundee Utd	762	812	738		0
Queen Of Sth	757	736	746		6
Morton	742	741	741		-9
Dumbarton	708	709	704		-10
Brechin	642	665	636		-5

Scottish League One

	Current	H	A		Trend
Ayr	720	702	720		-2
Raith	718	777	692		-3
Alloa	705	711	692		5
Arbroath	689	660	692		3
Stranraer	680	682	676		6
Airdrieonians	657	684	644		-7
Queen's Park	655	647	655		4
Forfar	652	656	652		6
East Fife	648	664	637		-8
Albion	626	640	651		-7

Scottish League Two

	Current	H	A		Trend
Peterhead	676	674	684		5
Montrose	676	652	667		6
Clyde	633	644	613		3
Stirling	625	636	630		-8
Stenhsemuir	624	639	641		-11
Annan	624	658	611		1
Elgin	614	659	592		-5
Berwick	609	621	603		9
Edinburgh C	593	606	604		-4
Cowdenbeath	581	599	610		0

Spanish La Liga

	Current	H	A		Trend
Barcelona	1032	1068	1015	‖‖‖	-5
Real Madrid	1005	1034	1010	‖‖	-3
Atl Madrid	1001	1023	996	‖‖‖‖	-7
Villarreal	969	978	952	‖‖‖	6
Valencia	968	978	952		0
Seville	956	1014	921	‖‖	4
Real Betis	946	946	930	‖	2
Espanyol	944	953	932	‖‖	5
Getafe	943	926	910	‖‖	5
Real Sociedad	943	962	927	‖	3
Celta Vigo	942	958	906	‖	2
Levante	941	944	894	‖‖‖‖‖	15
Alaves	940	938	930	‖	3
Eibar	936	931	935		0
Girona	931	927	937	‖‖	-5
Ath Bilbao	926	966	921	‖‖‖	-9
Leganes	916	939	894	‖	-3
Deportivo	906	912	894	‖	2
Malaga	882	913	875	‖‖‖	-8
Las Palmas	870	906	854	‖‖‖‖	-10

German Bundesliga

	Current	H	A		Trend
B Munich	1006	1024	997	‖‖	-4
Schalke	942	956	914	‖‖‖	7
Hoffenheim	935	966	904	‖‖‖	6
Dortmund	932	982	923	‖‖‖	-7
Stuttgart	928	925	897	‖‖‖‖‖‖	20
Leverkusen	928	921	924	‖	-3
Werder Bremen	924	921	906	‖‖‖‖	10
RB Leipzig	924	931	918	‖	-3
Frankfurt	914	926	881	‖‖	-5
B M'gladbach	913	947	890	‖	-1
H Berlin	903	912	889	‖‖	-5
Augsburg	898	894	896	‖‖	-7
Mainz	895	901	881	‖‖	5
Hamburg	893	898	858	‖‖	6
Freiburg	893	924	867	‖‖‖	-7
Wolfsburg	887	898	895	‖‖‖	-6
Hannover	887	893	872	‖	-2
Cologne	872	894	865	‖‖‖	-6

Italian Serie A

	Current	H	A		Trend
Juventus	984	1044	983	‖‖	-3
Napoli	976	999	983	‖‖	-4
Roma	952	964	973	‖	3
Inter	924	948	934	‖	-2
Lazio	923	930	948	‖	-1
Milan	922	939	926	‖‖	6
Atalanta	918	935	917	‖	-2
Fiorentina	906	940	912	‖	-1
Torino	900	916	898	‖	3
Sassuolo	885	898	902	‖‖	6
Sampdoria	876	922	865	‖‖‖	-8
Cagliari	870	887	864	‖	4
Chievo	868	895	864	‖‖	5
Genoa	864	892	860	‖‖‖	-7
SPAL	859	853	808	‖‖‖‖	13
Crotone	856	880	808	‖‖	6
Udinese	854	883	876	‖‖‖	-8
Bologna	843	877	868	‖‖‖‖	-11
Verona	821	862	839	‖‖‖‖	-10
Benevento	817	834	786	‖‖‖	8

Portuguese Primeira Liga

	Current	H	A		Trend
Porto	958	985	928	‖	2
Benfica	946	977	950	‖‖‖	-6
Sporting Lisbon	940	951	919	‖‖	-4
Braga	920	935	880	‖	3
Rio Ave	868	896	841	‖	-1
Chaves	864	860	856		0
Maritimo	863	906	826	‖	-1
Boavista	862	878	830	‖	4
V Guimaraes	861	882	846	‖	-1
Tondela	854	834	850	‖	1
Belenenses	852	851	842	‖	1
Vitoria Setubal	849	854	801	‖	2
Aves	846	842	846	‖	2
Moreirense	844	852	824	‖	-1
Feirense	841	844	826	‖	2
Portimonense	838	849	824	‖	-3
Estoril	837	840	832		0
Pacos Ferreira	836	869	810	‖	-3

French Ligue 1

	Current	H	A		Trend
Paris St-G	966	1002	954	‖‖‖	-9
Monaco	946	972	928	‖	-3
Lyon	932	937	919	‖	2
Marseille	928	936	906	‖	1
Rennes	898	887	892	‖‖‖	8
Bordeaux	896	898	888	‖‖‖	9
St Etienne	894	909	884	‖‖‖	10
Nice	886	920	878	‖‖	-4
Nantes	881	879	875	‖	-1
Dijon	871	896	812	‖	1
Montpellier	870	878	878	‖	-1
Angers	868	871	843	‖	-2
Lille	866	875	860		0
Guingamp	866	903	837	‖‖	-3
Amiens	865	862	822	‖‖‖	8
Strasbourg	853	868	834	‖	-2
Caen	846	865	838	‖‖	-5
Toulouse	844	870	840	‖‖	-4
Metz	838	836	826	‖‖	-6
Troyes	832	852	803	‖	-2

Dutch Eredivisie

	Current	H	A		Trend
PSV Eindhoven	939	970	912	‖‖	-3
Ajax	932	949	913	‖	2
Feyenoord	906	927	883	‖‖‖	7
AZ Alkmaar	893	885	894	‖‖	4
FC Utrecht	873	900	855	‖‖	-6
Den Haag	848	856	832	‖	3
Groningen	845	872	817	‖‖	6
Vitesse	845	864	843	‖‖	-6
Heracles	844	860	815	‖	2
Heerenveen	839	848	833	‖	2
Willem II	834	835	810	‖‖	8
Excelsior	832	809	836	‖	-2
PEC Zwolle	826	853	811	‖‖‖‖	-15
Roda JC	822	817	804	‖‖	5
NAC Breda	819	821	808	‖	2
VVV Venlo	812	804	800	‖‖‖	-11
FC Twente	811	846	799	‖	-1
Sparta Rotterdam	806	825	784	‖	2

 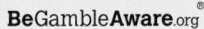

Pools draws chart 2017-18 ⠀⠀⠀⠀⠀⠀⠀⠀⠀⠀**X score-draw, 0 goalless draw**

```
PoolsAug    Sep       Oct      Nov      Dec     Jan      Feb    Mar      Apr      May
No.   5 12 19 26 2 9 16 23 30 7 14 21 28 4 11 18 25 2 9 16 23 30 6 13 20 27 3 10 17 24 3 10 17 24 31 7 14 21 28 5 12   X  0
1    X - - - X - 0 - - - X - - - X - - - X - - - - - - - - - 0 - - - - - - - X - - - - - 0 - -             5  3
2    X - - - - - X 0 0 - X - - - - - - - - X X - - - - - - - - - - X - - - - - X - - - - -               7  2
3    - - - 0 - - X - - X - - X - - X - - X - - - 0 X 0 - - - - - - - - - - - - - X - - - -               6  3
4    - - - - - - - - - - - - X - - - X - X - - 0 X X X X X - X X X - X - - X - - 0 - - 13  2
5    - - - - - - - - - X - - X - - - - - X - - - - - X - - - - X - - - 0 - - - 0 - X - X -             6  2
6    X - - - - - 0 - X - - - - - - - - - - - - 0 0 X - - X - 0 - - - - 0 - - - 0 - - - 4  6
7    - 0 - X - X - - - - - - - - X - - - - X - X 0 0 - X - X X - - 0 - - X X - X X - - 0 - 12  5
8    - - - 0 0 - 0 - 0 - X X - - - - - - - 0 - - - - - - - 0 - - - - - - - - - X - - - - -             3  5
9    - - - X - 0 - - - 0 X - 0 - - - X X - - X - - X X - - - X - - X - - - - - - - - - -             8  3
10   - - - - - - - - - - - - - X - 0 0 - X - - - X - - - - - X - - - - X - X X - - 0 - -             8  2
11   - - 0 - - X X X - - - X 0 - - X - - 0 - - - - X X - - X - - - - X - - - X - X - - - 10  3
12   - - - 0 - - X 0 X - X X - - X - - - - - - - - - - X - 0 - 0 X - X - X - X - - - - 9  4
13   - - - X - - - - - - - X - - - 0 - - - - - - - - - - - - - X - - - - - 0 - - - X - 4  2
14   - - - - - X X 0 - - - - - - - - - - - - - X 0 - 0 - - X - - X - X X X - - - - - - 8  3
15   0 0 - - - - X 0 X - X - - - X 0 X - - - X X - - - - X X X - 0 X - - - - - - 0 - - 11  6
16   - - - - - - - 0 - - - - - - X - - - - - - - - - X - 0 - - - - - - - - - - - - - - 3  2
17   - X - 0 - - X - X - - X - 0 - - - - - X - X - - 0 X - - - - - - - - 0 0 X - - - - 8  5
18   - - - - 0 - - - X - - - - - X - - - - X - - - - - - X X - 0 - - X - - - - X 7  2
19   - X - - - - - - - - - - - - X - - 0 - - - 0 - - - - - - - - - - - - - - - - - - - 2  2
20   - X - - X - - - - - - - - - 0 - X - - X 0 0 - - - X - - X - - - - - X - - - 7  3
21   X - - - - - - 0 - - - - - - - - - - - X - - - - X - X X 0 - - X - 0 - X - 7  3
22   - - - - - - - X - 0 X - X X - - - - X - - - - - X - 0 - - 0 - X - - X - - 9  3
23   - - X - 0 X - - - - - - - X - 0 - 0 - - - 0 X X X X X - X X 0 - - - - - - X 11  5
24   - - - - - 0 - - - - - - - 0 X - - - X 0 - - - X - X 0 - - - - - - - - X - X 6  4
25   - - X - - - - - - - - - - 0 - X - - - 0 - - - - - X - - X - 0 - X X - - - 6  3
26   - - - - - - X - X - 0 - - - - X X - X - X - X - - - X - - - - - 0 - X - - 9  2
27   - - - X X - - X - X - - - - - - - 0 - - 0 X - - - - - - X X - - - - 0 8  3
28   - - - - - X - - - - - - X - - - - X - - - - - - - - - - 0 X 0 0 - 0 X 5  4
29   X X - 0 0 - - - 0 X - - - X - - - - - - - - - - - X - - - - - X - 7  3
30   - - - - 0 X - - - 0 X 0 - - - - - - 0 - X - - - - - X 0 - - - - 5  5
31   X - X X - - X X - - - - 0 - 0 X 0 - - - - 0 - - - - - - - - X - - 7  4
32   - - - X - - X - - - X - - - - - - X X - - - - X 0 - - - - - X - 7  1
33   - - - - 0 - - - - - X - - - - - - 0 - - X - - - - - X 0 - X X - 5  3
34   X - - 0 - X - - - - - - X - - - - - X - - - 0 - X - X - - 0 - 6  3
35   X - - - - - - - 0 X 0 - X - - - - - X - X - - X X - X X - - 10  2
36   - X - - - - 0 - 0 - - - - - X X - - X - X - - - - - - 5  2
37   - - - - - - 0 - X - - 0 - - - - - X - X - X 0 X X 6  3
38   - X - - - X 0 X 0 - X - X - X - X - - X 0 - - X 0 10  4
39   - - - X - - - - - - - X - X X X 0 - X - - X 7  1
40   - X - - 0 - - X - - X - 0 X 0 - - X - - X 7  3
41   0 - - X - X - X 0 0 X - X 0 - 0 - X X - X 8  5
42   - - - - X - X - X 0 - X 0 X X 0 X X - X X 10  3
43   X X - - 0 X - - - - X 0 X 0 - X 6  3
44   - - - 0 X X X - X - X X - 0 0 X X 0 0 8  6
45   - - X - X X 0 X 0 0 0 X 0 0 X 7  6
46   - - - X - X 0 X 0 3  2
47   0 0 X X X X 0 0 X 0 6  5
48   - X 0 X X X 0 0 X X X X 10  3
49   X 0 X X X 0 0 X 0 5  4
```

```
X    9 8 3 9 5 7 11 9 5 9 10 8 9 4 11 8 11 6 7 3 12 9 3 9 8 10 9 14 9 9 9 12 14 10 8 11 10 11 4 10 4  347
0    2 2 2 7 5 5 4 4 4 3 3 6 2 3 4 6 3 4 6 3 7 9 8 3 0 1 2 3 5 4 5 4 6 3 4 2 2 6 5 2  163
```

Football Pools' British weekend coupons only. Some used European or international fixtures. Summer Australian coupons omitted.

BRITISH CUP RESULTS 2017-18

Sixth-tier Dartford hosted Swindon in the first round

FA CUP

First round

Friday November 3, 2017

Hyde............(0) 0-4 (2)...... MK Dons
Notts Co ....(2) 4-2 (2).......Bristol R
Port Vale ......(1) 2-0 (0)..........Oxford

Saturday November 4, 2017

AFC Fylde .....(1) 4-2 (0)Kidderminster
Wimbledon...(1) 1-0 (0)......... Lincoln
Blackburn .....(0) 3-1 (1).......... Barnet
Boreham W ..(0) 2-1 (0)..... Blackpool
Bradford ....(2) 2-0 (0)..Chesterfield
Carlisle ....(2) 3-2 (0)........ Oldham
Cheltenham ..(0) 2-4 (3)....Maidstone
Colchester....(0) 0-1 (0)... Oxford City
Crewe...........(0) 2-1 (1)... Rotherham
Ebbsfleet ......(2) 2-6 (2).....Doncaster
Forest Green .(1) 1-0 (0). Macclesfield
Gainsborough(0)0-6 (1)..........Slough
Gateshead ....(2) 2-0 (0)...Chelmsford
Gillingham....(1) 2-1 (0)Leyton Orient
Hereford FC ..(0) 1-0 (0)..........Telford
Luton............(1) 1-0 (0)...Portsmouth
Morecambe ..(1) 3-0 (0).... Hartlepool
Newport Co ..(1) 2-1 (0)......... Walsall
Northampton(0) 0-0 (0)...Scunthorpe
Peterborough(0) 1-1 (0)...... Tranmere
Plymouth ......(1) 1-0 (0)........Grimsby
Rochdale ......(2) 4-0 (0)........Bromley
Shaw Lane....(1) 1-3 (1).....Mansfield
Shrewsbury ..(2) 5-0 (0)..... Aldershot
Stevenage.....(1) 5-0 (0)..... Nantwich
Wigan...........(1) 2-1 (1)........Crawley
Yeovil...........(1) 1-0 (0)......Southend

Sunday November 5, 2017

Cambridge U (1) 1-0 (0)....Sutton Utd
Charlton ....(1) 3-1 (0)......Truro City

Coventry.......(2) 2-0 (0).Maidenhead
Dartford........(0) 1-5 (3).......Swindon
Exeter ....(0) 3-1 (0).... Heybridge
Guiseley........(0) 0-0 (0)....Accrington
Leatherhead..(1) 1-1 (0)...... Billericay
Solihull M .....(0) 0-2 (2).....Wycombe
Woking.........(1) 1-1 (1)............. Bury

Monday November 6, 2017

Chorley.........(0) 1-2 (0)....Fleetwood

First-round replays

Tuesday November 14, 2017

Accrington ....(0) 1-1 (0)....... Guiseley
AET – 1-1 after 90, Guiseley 4-3 on pens
Bury..............(0) 0-3 (1)........ Woking
Scunthorpe ...(1) 1-0 (0)Northampton

Wednesday November 15, 2017

Tranmere ......(0) 0-5 (2)Peterborough

Thursday November 16, 2017

Billericay.......(0) 1-3 (0). Leatherhead

Second round

Friday December 1, 2017

AFC Fylde .....(0) 1-1 (1).......... Wigan

Saturday December 2, 2017

Bradford ....(1) 3-1 (0)......Plymouth
Fleetwood ....(1) 1-1 (1)..Hereford FC
Forest Green .(1) 3-3 (0)...........Exeter
Gillingham....(1) 1-1 (1).........Carlisle
MK Dons........(0) 4-1 (1)....Maidstone
Notts Co ....(1) 3-2 (0)... Oxford City
Port Vale ....(0) 1-1 (0).......... Yeovil
Shrewsbury ..(2) 2-0 (0)..Morecambe
Stevenage.....(3) 5-2 (2).......Swindon

Isthmian League side Leatherhead reached the FA Cup second round

Sunday December 3, 2017
Wimbledon...(1) 3-1 (1)....... Charlton
Blackburn .....(3) 3-3 (1)......... Crewe
Coventry.......(2) 3-0 (0)..Boreham W
Doncaster .....(1) 3-0 (0)...Scunthorpe
Gateshead ....(0) 0-5 (1)........... Luton
Mansfield .....(1) 3-0 (0)....... Guiseley
Newport Co..(1) 2-0 (0) Cambridge U
Woking.........(0) 1-1 (1)Peterborough
Wycombe .....(1) 3-1 (1). Leatherhead
Monday December 4, 2017
Slough..........(0) 0-4 (1)...... Rochdale

Second-round replays
Tuesday December 12, 2017
Exeter...........(0) 2-1 (1).Forest Green
    AET – 1-1 after 90 mins
Peterborough(2) 5-2 (1)........ Woking
Wigan...........(1) 3-2 (1).....AFC Fylde
Yeovil...........(1) 3-2 (0).......Port Vale
    AET – 1-1 after 90 mins
Wednesday December 13, 2017
Crewe...........(0) 0-1 (1).....Blackburn
Thursday December 14, 2017
Hereford FC ..(0) 0-2 (1)....Fleetwood
Tuesday December 19, 2017
Carlisle ....(2) 3-1 (0)... Gillingham

Third round
Friday January 5, 2018
Liverpool ......(1) 2-1 (0)........ Everton
Man Utd ....(0) 2-0 (0).......... Derby
Saturday January 6, 2018
Aston Villa ....(1) 1-3 (0)Peterborough
Birmingham..(0) 1-0 (0).......... Burton
Blackburn .....(0) 0-1 (0)............. Hull
Bolton...........(0) 1-2 (0).Huddersfield
Bournemouth(0) 2-2 (2)......... Wigan
Brentford ......(0) 0-1 (0).......Notts Co
Cardiff ....(0) 0-0 (0)....... Mansfield
Carlisle ....(0) 0-0 (0).... Sheff Wed
Coventry.......(1) 2-1 (0)............Stoke

Doncaster .....(0) 0-1 (1)...... Rochdale
Exeter ....(0) 0-2 (2)... West Brom
Fleetwood ....(0) 0-0 (0).......Leicester
Fulham ....(0) 0-1 (1)Southampton
Ipswich.........(0) 0-1 (1)..... Sheff Utd
Man City.......(0) 4-1 (1)........Burnley
Middlesbro ...(2) 2-0 (0)...Sunderland
Millwall ....(1) 4-1 (1)....... Barnsley
Newcastle.....(3) 3-1 (0)........ Luton
Norwich........(0) 0-0 (0)........ Chelsea
QPR ....(0) 0-1 (0)... MK Dons
Stevenage.....(0) 0-0 (0).......Reading
Watford ....(1) 3-0 (0)...Bristol City
Wolves ....(0) 0-0 (0)....... Swansea
Wycombe .....(1) 1-5 (2)........Preston
Yeovil............(0) 2-0 (0)....... Bradford

Sunday January 7, 2018
Newport Co..(0) 2-1 (1)........... Leeds
Nottm Forest.(2) 4-2 (1)........Arsenal
Shrewsbury ..(0) 0-0 (0).... West Ham
Tottenham ....(0) 3-0 (0).. Wimbledon
Monday January 8, 2018
Brighton ....(1) 2-1 (0)....... C Palace

Third-round replays
Tuesday January 16, 2018
Leicester ....(1) 2-0 (0)....Fleetwood
Mansfield .....(1) 1-4 (1).........Cardiff
Reading ....(2) 3-0 (0).... Stevenage
Sheff Wed.....(1) 2-0 (0).........Carlisle
West Ham.....(0) 1-0 (0).. Shrewsbury
    AET – 0-0 after 90 mins
Wednesday January 17, 2018
Chelsea.........(0) 1-1 (0)....... Norwich
    AET – 1-1 after 90, Chelsea 5-3 on pens
Swansea.......(1) 2-1 (0)......... Wolves
Wigan...........(1) 3-0 (0)Bournemouth

Fourth round
Friday January 26, 2018
Sheff Wed.....(1) 3-1 (0)........Reading
Yeovil............(0) 0-4 (1).......Man Utd

Saturday January 27, 2018
Huddersfield.(1) 1-1 (0). Birmingham
Hull ....(2) 2-1 (0) Nottm Forest
Liverpool ......(1) 2-3 (3)... West Brom
MK Dons.......(0) 0-1 (0)...... Coventry
Middlesbro ...(0) 0-1 (0)....... Brighton
Millwall ....(1) 2-2 (1)...... Rochdale
Newport Co..(1) 1-1 (1)....Tottenham
Notts County (0) 1-1 (1)....... Swansea
Peterborough(0) 1-5 (3).......Leicester
Sheff Utd ......(0) 1-0 (0).........Preston
Southampton(1) 1-0 (0)........Watford
Wigan...........(1) 2-0 (0).... West Ham
Sunday January 28, 2018
Cardiff ....(0) 0-2 (2)...... Man City
Chelsea.........(2) 3-0 (0).... Newcastle

Fourth-round replays
Tuesday February 6, 2018
Birmingham..(0) 1-4 (0).Huddersfield
    AET – 1-1 after 90 mins
Rochdale ......(0) 1-0 (0)........Millwall
Swansea.......(4) 8-1 (1) Notts County
Wednesday February 7, 2018
Tottenham ....(2) 2-0 (0)..Newport Co

Fifth round
Friday February 16, 2018
Chelsea.........(4) 4-0 (0).............. Hull
Leicester ....(0) 1-0 (0)...... Sheff Utd
Saturday February 17, 2018
Brighton ....(2) 3-1 (0)...... Coventry
Huddersfield.(0) 0-2 (1)......Man Utd
Sheff Wed.....(0) 0-0 (0)...... Swansea
West Brom....(0) 1-2 (1)Southampton
Sunday February 18, 2018
Rochdale ......(1) 2-2 (0)....Tottenham
Monday February 19, 2018
Wigan...........(0) 1-0 (0)...... Man City
Fifth-round replay
Tuesday February 27, 2018
Swansea.......(0) 2-0 (0).... Sheff Wed
Wednesday February 28, 2018
Tottenham ....(1) 6-1 (1)...... Rochdale

Quarter-finals
Saturday March 17, 2018
Man Utd ....(1) 2-0 (0)....... Brighton
Swansea.......(0) 0-3 (2)....Tottenham
Sunday March 18, 2018
Leicester ....(0) 1-2 (1)........ Chelsea
    AET – 1-1 after 90 mins
Wigan...........(0) 0-2 (0)Southampton

Semi-finals
Saturday April 21, 2018
Man Utd ....(1) 2-1 (1)....Tottenham
Sunday April 22, 2018
Chelsea.........(0) 2-0 (0)Southampton

Final
Saturday May 19, 2018
Chelsea.........(1) 1-0 (0).......Man Utd

Wigan stunned Manchester City

Chelsea celebrate their FA Cup final victory over Manchester United

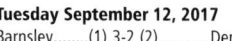

LEAGUE CUP

First round

Tuesday August 8, 2017

AFC W'bledon(1)1-3 (0)......Brentford
AET – 1-1 after 90 mins
Accrington ....(1) 3-2 (0).........Preston
Barnsley........(2) 4-3 (1)..Morecambe
Birmingham..(3) 5-1 (0)........Crawley
Bradford ....(1) 2-3 (1).....Doncaster
Bristol City ....(4) 5-0 (0)......Plymouth
Bristol Rovers (2) 4-1 (0) Cambridge U
Cardiff ....(0) 2-1 (1)....Portsmouth
AET – 1-1 after 90 mins
Coventry.......(1) 1-3 (2).....Blackburn
Exeter ....(0) 1-2 (0)......Charlton
Fleetwood ....(0) 1-2 (1).........Carlisle
AET – 1-1 after 90 mins
Forest Green .(0) 0-1 (0)....... MK Dons
AET – 0-0 after 90 mins
Luton ....(0) 0-2 (1)........ Ipswich
Mansfield .....(0) 0-1 (1)......Rochdale
Millwall ....(0) 2-0 (0).....Stevenage
Norwich.........(3) 3-2 (1)......Swindon
Nottm Forest.(1) 2-1 (0)..Shrewsbury
Oxford ....(3) 3-4 (1)..Cheltenham
AET – 3-3 after 90 mins
Peterborough(1) 1-3 (2)..........Barnet
QPR ....(1) 1-0 (0)Northampton
Reading ....(0) 2-0 (0).... Gillingham
Rotherham....(1) 2-1 (0).........Lincoln
Scunthorpe ...(0) 3-3 (1) Notts County
AET – 2-2 after 90, Scunthorpe won 6-5 pens
Sheff Wed.....(2) 4-1 (1)..Chesterfield
Southend......(0) 0-2 (0)....Newport Co
Wigan...........(2) 2-1 (0)..... Blackpool
Wolves ....(0) 1-0 (0)...........Yeovil
Wycombe .....(0) 0-2 (0).........Fulham

Wednesday August 9, 2017

Colchester.....(1) 1-2 (2)....Aston Villa

Crewe...........(1) 1-2 (0).......... Bolton
Leeds.............(1) 4-1 (1)......Port Vale
Oldham ....(0) 2-3 (0).........Burton
Sheff Utd ......(0) 3-2 (1).........Walsall

Thursday August 10, 2017

Bury..............(0) 0-1 (0)....Sunderland

Tuesday August 22, 2017

Grimsby........(0) 0-1 (0)...........Derby

Second round

Tuesday August 22, 2017

Accrington ....(0) 1-3 (2)... West Brom
Aston Villa ....(3) 4-1 (1).......... Wigan
Birmingham..(1) 1-2 (0)Bournemouth
Bolton...........(1) 3-2 (0)... Sheff Wed
Brighton ....(0) 1-0 (0).......... Barnet
C Palace........(0) 2-1 (0)....... Ipswich
Cardiff ....(0) 1-2 (1)..........Burton
Carlisle ....(0) 1-2 (1)....Sunderland
Doncaster .....(0) 2-0 (0)............. Hull
Fulham..........(0) 0-1 (1)Bristol Rovers
Leeds.............(1) 5-1 (1)..Newport Co
MK Dons.......(1) 1-4 (1)..... Swansea
Middlesbro ...(2) 3-0 (0)....Scunthorpe
Norwich.........(1) 4-1 (1)...... Charlton
QPR ....(1) 1-4 (3)......Brentford
Reading ....(1) 3-1 (1).......Millwall
AET 1-1 after 90 mins
Sheff Utd ......(0) 1-4 (0).......Leicester
Watford ....(0) 2-3 (0)....Bristol City

Wednesday August 23, 2017

Blackburn ......(0) 0-2 (2)........Burnley
Cheltenham ..(0) 0-2 (2).... West Ham
Huddersfield .(0) 2-1 (1)... Rotherham
Newcastle.....(2) 2-3 (2) Nottm Forest
AET – 2-2 after 90 mins
Southampton(0) 0-2 (0).........Wolves
Stoke ....(3) 4-0 (0)...... Rochdale

Tuesday September 12, 2017

Barnsley........(1) 3-2 (2)........... Derby

Third round

Tuesday September 19, 2017

Aston Villa ....(0) 0-2 (0)...Middlesbro
Bournemouth(0) 1-0 (0).......Brighton
AET – 0-0 after 90 mins
Brentford ......(0) 1-3 (1)....... Norwich
Bristol City ....(0) 2-0 (0)............Stoke
Burnley ....(0) 2-2 (0)........... Leeds
AET – 2-2 after 90, Leeds won 5-3 on pens
C Palace........(1) 1-0 (0).Huddersfield
Leicester ....(0) 2-0 (0)...... Liverpool
Reading ....(0) 0-2 (0)...... Swansea
Tottenham ....(0) 1-0 (0)........Barnsley
West Ham.....(2) 3-0 (0).......... Bolton
Wolves ....(0) 1-0 (0)Bristol Rovers
AET – 0-0 after 90 mins

Wednesday September 20, 2017

Arsenal ....(1) 1-0 (0).....Doncaster
Chelsea.........(3) 5-1 (0) Nottm Forest
Everton ....(1) 3-0 (0)....Sunderland
Man Utd ....(3) 4-1 (0).......... Burton
West Brom....(0) 1-2 (1)...... Man City

Fourth round

Tuesday October 24, 2017

Arsenal ....(0) 2-1 (1)...... Norwich
AET – 1-1 after 90 mins
Bournemouth(0) 3-1 (0)...Middlesbro
Bristol City ....(2) 4-1 (1)....... C Palace
Leicester ....(1) 3-1 (1)........... Leeds
Man City.......(0) 0-0 (0)........ Wolves
AET – 0-0 after 90, Man City 4-1 on pens
Swansea.......(0) 0-2 (1).......Man Utd

Wednesday October 25, 2017

Chelsea.........(1) 2-1 (0)........ Everton
Tottenham ....(2) 2-3 (0).... West Ham

Quarter-finals

Tuesday December 19, 2017

Arsenal ....(1) 1-0 (0).... West Ham
Leicester ....(0) 1-1 (1)...... Man City
AET – 1-1 after 90, Man City 4-3 on pens

Wednesday December 20, 2017

Bristol City ....(0) 2-1 (0).......Man Utd
AET – 2-1 after 90 mins
Chelsea.........(1) 2-1 (0)Bournemouth

Semi-finals

Tuesday January 9, 2018

Man City.......(0) 2-1 (1)....Bristol City

Wednesday January 10, 2018

Chelsea.........(0) 0-0 (0).........Arsenal

Second legs

Tuesday January 23, 2018

Bristol City ....(0) 2-3 (1)...... Man City

Wednesday January 24, 2018

Arsenal ....(1) 2-1 (1)........ Chelsea

Final

Sunday February 25, 2018

Arsenal ....(0) 0-3 (1)...... Man City

*City routed Arsenal in
the League Cup final*

EFL TROPHY

Northern Group A – first round

	P	W	D	L	F	A	GD	Pts
Fleetwood	3	3	0	0	7	2	+5	9
Leicester U21	3	1	0	2	3	5	-2	4
Carlisle	3	1	0	2	3	3	+0	3
Morecambe	3	1	0	2	3	6	-3	2

Northern Group B – first round

	P	W	D	L	F	A	GD	Pts
Blackpool	3	2	0	1	7	3	+4	7
Accrington	3	2	0	1	8	4	+4	6
Wigan	3	2	0	1	5	6	-1	5
Middlesbro U21	3	0	0	3	4	11	-7	0

Northern Group C – first round

	P	W	D	L	F	A	GD	Pts
Rochdale	3	2	0	1	5	1	4	6
Bury	3	2	0	1	4	5	-1	6
Blackburn	3	1	0	2	2	2	0	4
Stoke U21	3	1	0	2	1	4	-3	2

Northern Group D – first round

	P	W	D	L	F	A	GD	Pts
Port Vale	3	3	0	0	5	2	3	8
Oldham	3	2	0	1	5	1	4	7
Newcastle U21	3	1	0	2	3	6	-3	3
Crewe	3	0	0	3	3	7	-4	0

Northern Group E – first round

	P	W	D	L	F	A	GD	Pts
Walsall	3	2	0	1	6	3	3	7
Shrewsbury	3	2	0	1	6	3	3	6
Coventry	3	2	0	1	6	6	0	5
West Brom U21	3	0	0	3	2	8	-6	0

Northern Group F – first round

	P	W	D	L	F	A	GD	Pts
Bradford	3	2	0	1	6	6	0	6
Chesterfield	3	2	0	1	6	7	-1	5
Rotherham	3	1	0	2	5	3	2	4
Man City U21	3	1	0	2	4	5	-1	3

Northern Group G – first round

	P	W	D	L	F	A	GD	Pts
Lincoln	3	3	0	0	7	3	4	9
Mansfield	3	2	0	1	4	4	0	6
Notts County	3	1	0	2	4	5	-1	3
Everton U21	3	0	0	3	2	5	-3	0

Northern Group H – first round

	P	W	D	L	F	A	GD	Pts
Scunthorpe	3	3	0	0	6	3	3	7
Doncaster	3	3	0	0	3	2	1	7
Grimsby	3	0	0	3	3	4	-1	2
Sunderland U21	3	1	0	2	2	5	-3	2

Southern Group A – first round

	P	W	D	L	F	A	GD	Pts
Portsmouth	3	2	0	1	7	4	3	7
Charlton	3	2	0	1	5	3	2	6
Fulham U21	3	2	0	1	8	7	1	5
Crawley	3	0	0	3	2	8	-6	0

Southern Group B – first round

	P	W	D	L	F	A	GD	Pts
Gillingham	3	3	0	0	10	6	4	9
Southend	3	2	0	1	4	2	2	6
Colchester	3	1	0	2	2	5	-3	2
Reading U21	3	0	0	3	7	10	-3	1

Southern Group C – first round

	P	W	D	L	F	A	GD	Pts
Swindon	3	2	0	1	7	5	2	6
West Ham U21	3	2	0	1	6	5	1	6
Bristol Rovers	3	1	0	2	8	8	0	3
Wycombe	3	1	0	2	3	6	-3	3

Southern Group D – first round

	P	W	D	L	F	A	GD	Pts
Yeovil	3	3	0	0	6	3	3	8
Chelsea U21	3	1	0	2	6	4	2	5
Plymouth	3	2	0	1	5	6	-1	4
Exeter	3	0	0	3	4	8	-4	1

Southern Group E – first round

	P	W	D	L	F	A	GD	Pts
Swansea U21	3	3	0	0	6	2	4	9
Forest Green	3	2	0	1	4	3	1	6
Cheltenham	3	1	0	2	4	5	-1	3
Newport	3	0	0	3	2	6	-4	0

Southern Group F – first round

	P	W	D	L	F	A	GD	Pts
Luton	3	3	0	0	5	4	1	7
Wimbledon	3	2	0	1	9	8	1	6
Barnet	3	1	0	2	6	6	0	4
Tottenham U21	3	0	0	3	6	8	-2	1

Southern Group G – first round

	P	W	D	L	F	A	GD	Pts
MK Dons	3	3	0	0	6	3	3	8
Oxford U	3	1	0	2	11	8	3	4
Stevenage	3	1	0	2	5	7	-2	4
Brighton U21	3	1	0	2	3	7	-4	2

Southern Group H – first round

	P	W	D	L	F	A	GD	Pts
Peterborough	3	2	0	1	5	4	1	7
Northampton	3	3	0	0	5	5	0	6
So'ton U21	3	1	0	2	4	5	-1	4
Cambridge	3	0	0	3	1	4	-3	1

Second round
Northern section

Tuesday November 28, 2017
Rochdale ......(1) 1-1 (0).....Doncaster
Rochdale 5-4 on pens

Saturday December 2, 2017
Walsall ....(1) 1-2 (1)............ Bury

Tuesday December 5, 2017
Bradford ....(0) 0-1 (1)........ Oldham
Fleetwood ....(1) 2-0 (0)..Chesterfield
Lincoln..........(2) 3-2 (2)....Accrington
Port Vale ....(1) 1-2 (0).. Shrewsbury
Scunthorpe ...(1) 1-2 (2).Leicester U21

Wednesday December 6, 2017
Blackpool ......(1) 1-1 (0).....Mansfield
Blackpool 5-4 on pens

Second round
Southern section

Saturday December 2, 2017
Portsmouth ...(1) 2-0 (0).Northampton

Tuesday December 5, 2017
Gillingham ....(1) 1-2 (1)...... Oxford U
Luton ....(1) 4-0 (0)..West Ham U21
Swansea U21..(2) 2-3 (1)....... Charlton

Lincoln claimed the EFL Trophy

Swindon ....(0) 0-0 (1).Forest Green
Yeovil...........(0) 2-0 (0).. Wimbledon

Wednesday December 6, 2017
MK Dons.......(0) 0-4 (3)..Chelsea U21
Peterborough(1) 2-0 (0)......Southend

Third round
Northern section

Tuesday January 9, 2018
Bury..............(1) 2-3 (2)....Fleetwood
Rochdale ......(0) 0-0 (1)......... Lincoln

Wednesday January 10, 2018
Shrewsbury ..(0) 0-0 (0)..... Blackpool
Shrewsbury 4-2 on pens

Wednesday January 17, 2018
Oldham ....(0) 4-2 (1)..Leicester U21

Third round
Southern section

Tuesday January 9, 2018
Yeovil...........(2) 2-0 (0).Forest Green
Portsmouth...(0) 1-2 (0).Chelsea U21
Charlton ....(1) 1-1 (0)...... Oxford U
Oxford U 3-0 on pens
Luton ....(0) 0-0 (0)..Peterborough
Peterborough 7-6 on pens

Quarter-finals

Tuesday January 23, 2018
Lincoln..........(1) 4-2 (1)Peterborough
Shrewsbury ..(1) 2-1 (0)........Oldham
Chelsea U21 .(2) 3-0 (0)...... Oxford U

Tuesday February 6, 2018
Yeovil...........(1) 3-2 (1)....Fleetwood

Semi-finals

Tuesday February 6, 2018
Lincoln..........(0) 1-1 (0).Chelsea U21
Lincoln 4-2 on pens

Tuesday February 6, 2018
Shrewsbury ..(0) 1-0 (0).......... Yeovil

Final

Sunday April 2, 2018
Lincoln..........(1) 1-0 (0)..Shrewsbury

SCOTTISH CUP
First round
Friday September 22, 2017
Spartans ....(0) 3-0 (0)Vale of Leithen
Saturday September 23, 2017
Banks o'Dee..(0) 4-0 (0)......... Huntly
Brora Rangers .(0) 5-0 (0).........Girvan
Civil Serv Strol(0)2-1 (0). Strathspey T
Clachnacuddin (0) 8-0 (0)..Fort William
Colville Park..(0) 2-1 (0)Cumbernauld
Deveronvale .(0) 3-1 (0)Hawick Royal
Edinburgh Uni(0)2-1 (0).Lossiemouth
Edusport Acad(0)1-1 (0)..........Rothes
Formartine Utd(0) 2-1 (0)........ Turriff U
Fraserburgh ..(0) 2-1 (0). Forres Mech
Gala Fairydean(0) 0-2 (0)............ Keith
Glenafton Ath(0)4-0 (0)Threave Rovers
Lothian Thistle(0)3-2 (0)Inverurie Locos
Nairn County (0) 1-0 (0)..Whitehill W
Selkirk..........(0) 4-0 (0).Gretna 2008
Wick Academy (0) 2-2 (0). Stirling Univ
Sunday September 24, 2017
BSC Glasgow (0) 1-0 (0).... Dalbeattie
First-round replays
Saturday September 30, 2017
Rothes ....(0) 1-3 (0)Edusport Acad
Stirling Univ..(0) 1-0 (0) Wick Academy

Second round
Friday October 13, 2017
Edinburgh C..(0) 0-1 (0) Stenh'semuir
Saturday October 14, 2017
Banks o'Dee..(0) 2-0 (0).......... Selkirk
Berwick ....(0) 1-0 (0).......... Annan
Buckie Thistle(4) 6-2 (0)BSC Glasgow
Civil Serv Strol(0) 0-5 (1).Brora Rangers
Cowdenbeath(0) 0-1 (0). East Kilbride
Deveronvale .(0) 0-2 (0).....Glenafton
Edinburgh Uni(0) 0-2 (2)..Fraserburgh
Elgin City ......(1) 3-1 (0)Edusport Acad
Formartine Utd(2) 4-0 (0)..East Stirling
Keith.............(0) 0-3 (0)............Clyde
Montrose......(2) 4-1 (1). Stirling Univ
Nairn County (0) 1-2 (1)Cove Rangers
Peterhead ....(5) 9-0 (0). Colville Park
Spartans ....(3) 5-0 (0) Clachnacuddin
Stirling..........(1) 3-5 (2)Lothian Thistle

Third round
Saturday November 18, 2017
Airdrieonians(1) 2-3 (1)Cove Rangers
Arbroath ....(2) 3-0 (0)........ Berwick
Banks o'Dee..(2) 2-6 (4)............... Ayr
Buckie Thistle(2) 2-3 (1).......Brechin
Clyde ....(0) 0-2 (1)....... East Fife
Dumbarton ...(1) 1-0 (0)......Elgin City
East Kilbride..(1) 3-4 (1).......... Albion
Formartine Utd(1) 1-0 (0)..........Forfar
Livingston.....(1) 2-0 (0)Glenafton Ath
Lothian Thistle(0) 1-7 (7)...... St Mirren

Montrose......(0) 0-0 (0) Queen of Sth
Peterhead .....(0) 3-0 (0)............ Raith
Queen's Park.(0) 1-4 (0). Dunfermline
Spartans ....(1) 1-2 (0)..Fraserburgh
Stenh'semuir.(1) 1-2 (0)............ Alloa
Stranraer.......(0) 0-1 (0).Brora Rangers
Third-round replays
Tuesday November 21, 2017
Queen of Sth.(1) 2-1 (1)..... Montrose

Fourth round
Saturday January 20, 2018
Aberdeen......(3) 4-1 (1)...... St Mirren
Alloa.............(0) 0-2 (1)..Dundee Utd
Ayr ....(1) 4-1 (0)......Arbroath
Celtic ....(2) 5-0 (0)........Brechin
Dundee.........(0) 2-2 (1).Inverness CT
Dunfermline..(0) 1-2 (1).........Morton
East Fife........(0) 0-1 (1).Brora Rangers
Kilmarnock....(0) 1-0 (0). Ross County
Motherwell...(2) 2-0 (0)...... Hamilton
Queen of Sth.(0) 1-2 (1)......... Partick
Sunday January 21, 2018
Hearts...........(0) 1-0 (0)..... Hibernian
Tuesday January 23, 2018
Livingston.....(0) 0-1 (0).......... Falkirk
Peterhead ....(1) 2-3 (1)...Dumbarton
Monday January 29, 2018
Albion...........(0) 0-4 (1).St Johnstone
Tuesday January 30, 2018
Formartine Utd(0) 0-2 (1)Cove Rangers
Wednesday January 31, 2018
Fraserburgh ..(0) 0-3 (1)........Rangers
Fourth-round replay
Tuesday January 30, 2018
Inverness CT .(0) 0-1 (0)........ Dundee

Fifth round
Saturday February 10, 2018
Celtic ....(2) 3-2 (1)......... Partick
Cove Rangers(1) 1-3 (1)......... Falkirk
Dundee.........(0) 0-2 (1).. Motherwell
Hearts...........(1) 3-0 (0).St Johnstone
Kilmarnock...(1) 4-0 (0).Brora Rangers
Morton ....(1) 3-0 (0)...Dumbarton
Sunday February 11, 2018
Aberdeen......(3) 4-2 (1)..Dundee Utd
Ayr ....(1) 1-6 (1).......Rangers

Quarter-finals
Friday March 2, 2018
Aberdeen......(1) 1-1 (0)... Kilmarnock
Saturday March 3, 2018
Celtic ....(0) 3-0 (0).........Morton
Sunday March 4, 2018
Motherwell...(1) 2-1 (0)........ Hearts
Rangers ....(3) 4-1 (1).......... Falkirk
Quarter-final replay
Tuesday March 13, 2018
Kilmarnock....(0) 1-1 (0)..... Aberdeen
AET – 0-0 after 90, Aberdeen 3-2 on pens

Celtic breezed their way past Motherwell in both cup finals

Semi-finals
Saturday April 14, 2018
Motherwell...(2) 3-0 (0)..... Aberdeen
Sunday April 15, 2018
Celtic ....(2) 4-0 (0)........Rangers
Final
Saturday May 19, 2018
Celtic ....(2) 2-0 (0).. Motherwell

SCOTTISH LEAGUE CUP
Group stage
Friday July 14, 2017
Ayr ....(1) 1-0 (0)... Kilmarnock
Saturday July 15, 2017
Berwick ....(0) 0-1 (1)........Morton
Clyde ....(0) 2-1 (0).......... Annan
Cowdenbeath(2) 4-2 (1)Buckie Thistle
Dundee Utd ..(0) 2-0 (0)........... Raith
Dunfermline..(4) 6-0 (0)......Elgin City
East Kilbride..(0) 1-3 (1)...... Hamilton
Falkirk...........(3) 4-1 (0)......... Stirling
Hibernian......(2) 4-0 (0)..... Montrose
Inverness CT .(2) 3-0 (0).......Brechin
Livingston.....(0) 1-1 (1)......... Partick
Livingston won 3-1 on pens
Peterhead .....(1) 1-0 (0)....... East Fife
Queen's Park.(1) 1-5 (1).. Motherwell
Ross County..(1) 2-0 (0).......... Alloa
Stenh'semuir.(1) 1-3 (0) Queen of Sth
Stranraer.......(1) 1-4 (3)...... St Mirren
Tuesday July 18, 2017
Airdrieonians(1) 1-1 (0)...... Stranraer
Albion...........(0) 1-1 (1) Stenh'semuir
Stenhousemuir won 3-2 on pens
Alloa.............(0) 1-1 (1)......Arbroath
Arbroath won 6-5 on pens

Brechin ....(0) 1-1 (0) .... Forfar
    Brechin won 4-3 on pens
Dumbarton ...(1) 1-3 (1) .... Ayr
East Fife ....(0) 0-0 (0) . Dunfermline
    Dunfermline won 9-8 on pens
Edinburgh C..(2) 2-2 (1) .... Berwick
    Edinburgh City won 4-2 on pens
Elgin City ......(0) 0-1 (0) .... Hearts
Kilmarnock....(1) 4-2 (2) ....Clyde
Montrose ......(0) 0-6 (4). Ross County
Morton ....(0) 2-2 (0) Queen's Park
    Morton won 4-2 on pens
Queen of Sth.(0) 0-0 (0). East Kilbride
    East Kilbride won 4-1 on pens
Raith.............(0) 1-2 (0) .... Dundee
St Mirren ......(0) 0-1 (1).... Livingston
Stirling..........(0) 0-0 (0).Inverness CT
    Inverness CT won 2-0 on pens

Wednesday July 19, 2017
Buckie Thistle(0) 0-3 (3)..Dundee Utd

Friday July 21, 2017
Ross County..(0) 0-0 (0)..... Hibernian
    Ross County won 4-3 on pens

Saturday July 22, 2017
Annan...........(0) 0-2 (1)... Kilmarnock
Arbroath ....(1) 4-0 (0) ..... Montrose
Clyde ....(0) 2-1 (1)...Dumbarton
Dundee........(1) 2-0 (0)Buckie Thistle
Dunfermline..(3) 5-1 (0).....Peterhead
East Kilbride..(0) 2-5 (2).......... Albion
Forfar ....(0) 1-3 (2) .... Stirling
Hamilton.......(0) 1-1 (0) Queen of Sth
    Hamilton won 6-5 on pens
Hearts...........(1) 3-0 (0)...... East Fife
Inverness CT..(0) 0-2 (2).......... Falkirk
Livingston.....(1) 2-0 (0) Airdrieonians
Motherwell...(2) 4-0 (0).........Morton
Partick ....(4) 5-0 (0)..... St Mirren
Queen's Park.(1) 3-0 (0). Edinburgh C

Sunday July 23, 2017
Dundee Utd ..(1) 4-1 (0)Cowdenbeath

Tuesday July 25, 2017
Airdrieonians (0) 1-2 (2).......... Partick
Albion...........(1) 4-4 (2) ..... Hamilton
    Albion won 4-2 on pens
Ayr ....(2) 5-1 (1) ....Clyde
Berwick ....(1) 2-3 (3) Queen's Park
Buckie Thistle(1) 1-6 (3)........... Raith
Dumbarton ...(0) 0-0 (0).......... Annan
    Annan won 4-3 on pens
East Fife........(0) 3-2 (0)......Elgin City
Edinburgh C..(0) 1-2 (0).. Motherwell
Falkirk ....(3) 4-0 (0)........... Forfar
Hibernian......(2) 6-1 (1).......Arbroath
Montrose......(1) 2-1 (0)............ Alloa
Peterhead .....(1) 2-1 (1).......... Hearts
Stenh'semuir.(0) 1-2 (0). East Kilbride
Stirling..........(1) 2-0 (0).........Brechin
Stranraer.......(2) 2-4 (2).... Livingston

Wednesday July 26, 2017
Cowdenbeath(0) 0-3 (3)........ Dundee

Saturday July 29, 2017
Alloa.............(0) 0-3 (1)..... Hibernian
Annan...........(0) 1-6 (4)............. Ayr
Arbroath ....(0) 0-0 (0). Ross County
    Ross County won 5-4 on pens
Brechin ....(0) 0-3 (1).......... Falkirk
Elgin City ......(0) 0-3 (2).....Peterhead
Forfar ....(0) 1-2 (0).Inverness CT
Hamilton.......(1) 3-0 (0) Stenh'semuir
Hearts...........(1) 2-2 (1). Dunfermline
    Dunfermline won 3-1 on pens
Kilmarnock....(0) 3-0 (0)...Dumbarton
Morton ....(1) 5-0 (0). Edinburgh C
Motherwell...(0) 1-0 (0)........ Berwick
Partick ....(0) 1-0 (0)..... Stranraer
Queen of Sth.(0) 2-2 (1).......... Albion
    Queen of Sth won 4-2 on pens
Raith.............(2) 2-0 (0)Cowdenbeath
St Mirren ......(2) 5-0 (0) Airdrieonians

Sunday July 30, 2017
Dundee.........(0) 1-1 (1)..Dundee Utd
    Dundee Utd won 4-3 on pens

Group A

Group A	P	W	D	L	F	A	GD	Pts
Falkirk	4	4	0	0	13	1	12	12
Inverness	4	3	0	1	5	3	2	10
Stirling	4	2	0	2	6	5	1	7
Brechin	4	1	0	3	9	-8	2
Forfar	4	0	0	4	3	10	-7	1

Group B

Group B	P	W	D	L	F	A	GD	Pts
Dunfermline	4	4	0	0	13	3	10	10
Peterhead	4	3	0	1	7	6	1	9
Hearts	4	2	0	2	7	4	3	7
East Fife	4	1	0	3	3	6	-3	4
Elgin City	4	0	0	4	2	13	-11	0

Group C

Group C	P	W	D	L	F	A	GD	Pts
Dundee Utd	4	4	0	0	10	2	8	11
Dundee	4	3	0	1	8	2	6	10
Raith	4	2	0	2	9	5	4	6
Cowdenbeath	4	1	0	3	5	11	-6	3
Buckie Thistle	4	0	0	4	3	15	-12	0

Group D

Group D	P	W	D	L	F	A	GD	Pts
Hibernian	4	3	0	1	13	1	12	10
Ross County	4	4	0	0	8	0	8	10
Arbroath	4	2	0	2	6	7	-1	6
Montrose	4	1	0	3	2	15-13	3
Alloa	4	0	0	4	2	8	-6	1

Group E

Group E	P	W	D	L	F	A	GD	Pts
Ayr Utd	4	4	0	0	15	3	12	12
Kilmarnock	4	3	0	1	9	3	6	9
Clyde	4	2	0	2	7	11	-4	6
Annan	4	1	0	3	2	10	-8	2
Dumbarton	4	0	0	4	2	8	-6	1

Group F

Group F	P	W	D	L	F	A	GD	Pts
Motherwell	4	4	0	0	12	2	10	12
Morton	4	3	0	1	8	6	2	8
Queen's Park	4	2	0	2	9	9	0	7
Edinburgh	4	1	0	3	3	12	-9	2
Berwick	4	0	0	4	4	7	-3	1

Group G

Group G	P	W	D	L	F	A	GD	Pts
Hamilton	4	3	0	1	11	6	5	9
Albion	4	2	0	2	12	9	3	7
Queen of Sth	4	2	0	2	6	4	2	7
East Kilbride	4	2	0	2	5	9	-4	5
Stenh'semuir	4	1	0	3	3	9	-6	2

Group H

Group H	P	W	D	L	F	A	GD	Pts
Livingston	4	4	0	0	8	3	5	11
Partick	4	3	0	1	9	2	7	10
St Mirren	4	2	0	2	9	7	2	6
Airdrieonians	4	1	0	3	4	10	-6	3
Stranraer	4	0	0	4	4	12	-8	0

Second round

Tuesday August 8, 2017
Celtic ....(3) 5-0 (0)... Kilmarnock
Falkirk...........(1) 1-2 (1).... Livingston
    AET – 1-1 after 90 mins
Hibernian......(2) 5-0 (0).............. Ayr
St Johnstone .(0) 0-3 (0).......... Partick

Wednesday August 9, 2017
Dundee.........(1) 2-1 (1)..Dundee Utd
Hamilton.......(0) 0-1 (1)..... Aberdeen
Rangers ....(4) 6-0 (0). Dunfermline
Ross County..(0) 2-3 (0).. Motherwell
    AET – 1-1 after 90 mins

Quarter-finals

Tuesday September 19, 2017
Hibernian......(2) 3-2 (2).... Livingston
Partick ....(0) 1-3 (0)........Rangers
    AET 1-1 after 90 mins

Wednesday September 20, 2017
Dundee.........(0) 0-4 (2)...........Celtic

Thursday September 21, 2017
Motherwell...(2) 3-0 (0)..... Aberdeen

Semi-finals

Saturday October 21, 2017
Hibernian......(0) 2-4 (2)...........Celtic

Sunday October 22, 2017
Rangers ....(0) 0-2 (0).. Motherwell

Final

Sunday November 26, 2017
Motherwell...(0) 0-2 (0)...........Celtic

Magical Messi should lead Catalans to another title triumph over rivals Real

The 2017-18 season went largely as planned across Europe, writes Joe Champion. Juventus were pushed hard by a brilliant Napoli side but eventually won a seventh consecutive Scudetto, Paris Saint-Germain splashed the cash to return to the summit of Ligue 1, Bayern Munich dominated Germany again while Barcelona wrestled back La Liga supremacy from Real Madrid.

Barcelona's victory was a surprise due to the manner in which they did it in their first season under Ernesto Valverde, but also because of a complete lack of a challenge from Real.

The Catalans became hard to beat while still retaining some of the irresistible football of previous regimes – indeed only a dramatic 5-4 defeat against Levante on the penultimate day of the season prevented La Blaugrana from going unbeaten in La Liga.

They finished 14 points clear of Atletico Madrid and a further three clear of Real. Los Blancos never landed a blow but re-grouped to seal a third straight Champions League crown before Zinedine Zidane quit the Bernabeu to be replaced by former Spanish national team manager Julen Lopetegui.

Once again bookmakers are struggling to split the Spanish giants – with Barcelona the slim favourites. They look the team to back this time around.

While Andres Iniesta paid an emotional departure at the end of the season, they still have Lionel Messi to lead the team while Philippe Coutinho and Ousmane Dembele will have parts to play this season.

With Cristiano Ronaldo departing Real, Lopetegui faces a serious rebuilding job in the Spanish capital.

Diego Simeone remains in charge at Atletico while Antoine Griezmann has announced his intention to remain at the club for another season. Los Rojiblancos, however, may have to be content with third place.

Real Valladolid and Rayo Vallecano both return to La Liga while vulnerable minnows Huesca make their top-flight debut in tiny 5,500 capacity Estadio El Alcoraz.

Juventus top the Serie A betting but Napoli, Roma and Inter will all fancy their chances of upsetting the odds.

Massimiliano Allegri remains in Turin, which is a big bonus for the Old Lady, though he loses the dressing room experience of Gianluigi Buffon and Stephan Lichtsteiner in defence and, like Lopetegui, he needs to bring in a few new faces. Of course, landing Ronaldo is not a bad place to start.

Napoli came close to winning the Scudetto last season and will be itching to narrow the gap under new manager Carlo Ancelotti, who takes over from Maurizio Sarri at the San Paolo.

The veteran Italian coach has not managed in Serie A since 2009 but is a class act and knows the division well. There could be value in backing Napoli to upset the odds if they can hold on to their key players.

Roma will look to build on a strong finish to the 2017-18 campaign which saw them finish third and reach the Champions League semi-finals, but big-spending Inter could be better placed in their second season under Luciano Spalletti.

Milan are facing severe spending restrictions while Lazio tailed off after a strong start in 2017-18.

The new season will see the return of Parma, declared bankrupt in 2015 before being re-founded in Serie D and achieving three consecutive promotions. Expect a season of consolidation from Robeto D'Aversa's team.

Serie B champions Empoli and playoff winners Frosinone join Parma back in Italy's top tier and will be among the favourites to make a swift return.

In the Bundesliga, Niko Kovac takes over as manager of Bayern Munich following the retirement of Jupp Heynckes.

Kovac led Eintracht Frankfurt to a thrilling 3-1 victory over his new club in the German Cup final and has done a fine job in establishing the Eagles as a top-half Bundesliga club.

The German-born Croat favours a direct, pressing style of football and will want to put his own stamp on a team who will once again be sent off at short odds to retain their title.

Schalke got closest to Bayern last time, though a 21-point margin tells its own story and the Miners have lost key man Leon Goretzka to the Bavarian giants.

Dortmund's season was chaotic under Peter Bosz and then Peter Stoger but new boss Lucien Favre did a fine job at Monchengladbach, where he helped to mould Marco Reus into one of the finest attacking players in world football, before guiding Nice to third place in France.

Favre can harness a talented group of players and Dortmund look worthy favourites in the without Bayern market ahead of Schalke and Leipzig, who could do better without the demands of Champions League football.

Last season saw Hamburg relegated from the Bundesliga for the first time, replaced by Nuremberg and Fortuna Dusseldorf. Much like the Premier League, there are a number of relegation candidates in 2018-19.

Monaco bucked the trend in France in 2016-17 but Paris Saint-Germain returned to the summit following the additions of Neymar and Kylian Mbappe.

It looks likely that at least one of them will leave the Parc des Princes this summer but that may not stop the Parisian giants from retaining their title following the appointment of Thomas Tuchel, even if the German coach may need some time to find his feet in unfamiliar surroundings.

Monaco responded superbly to losing several key players following their title-winning season. Leonardo Jardim continues to impress as manager and they will probably fight it out with Lyon and Marseille again for the two remaining Champions League places.

Favre's departure from Nice could harm their chances of a European challenge but Patrick Vieira takes over at Allianz Riviera in a fascinating appointment.

Reims bolted up in Ligue 2 and survival looks entirely possible on their return to Ligue 1 but the same cannot be said for Nimes.

The Crocodiles return to the top flight for the first time since 1993 and will surely be vulnerable after sealing promotion on a shoestring budget.

Recommendations
Barcelona to win La Liga, 5-6
Huesca to be relegated from La Liga, 11-13
Napoli to win Serie A, 13-2
Dortmund w/o Bayern (Bundesliga), 3-4
Monaco w/o Paris St-Germain (Ligue 1), 2-1

Barcelona can count on Lionel Messi to star for them once again

ATALANTA

Atleti Azzurri d'Italia — atalanta.it

	2017-18 H	A	P	W	D	L	OV	UN	BS	CS
			Last six seasons at home							
Juventus	D	L	6	0	2	4	4	2	3	0
Napoli	L	L	6	3	1	2	2	4	2	3
Roma	L	W	6	1	2	3	4	2	5	0
Inter	D	L	6	2	3	1	3	3	5	1
Lazio	D	D	6	2	2	2	4	2	5	0
Milan	D	W	6	2	2	2	3	3	5	0
Atalanta										
Fiorentina	D	D	6	0	2	4	1	5	2	1
Torino	W	D	6	3	0	3	4	2	4	1
Sampdoria	L	L	6	3	1	2	4	2	3	3
Sassuolo	W	W	5	2	2	1	2	3	4	0
Genoa	W	W	6	2	1	3	3	3	3	1
Chievo	W	D	6	4	2	0	2	4	3	3
Udinese	W	L	6	2	3	1	1	5	3	3
Bologna	W	W	5	4	1	0	2	3	3	2
Cagliari	L	L	5	3	1	1	2	3	3	2
SPAL	D	D	1	0	1	0	0	1	1	0
Empoli			3	1	2	0	1	2	1	1
Parma			3	2	0	1	2	1	1	1
Frosinone			1	1	0	0	0	1	0	1

Season	Division	Pos	P	W	D	L	F	A	GD	Pts
2017-18	Serie A	7	38	16	12	10	57	39	+18	60
2016-17	Serie A	4	38	21	9	8	62	41	+21	72
2015-16	Serie A	13	38	11	12	15	41	47	-6	45

Over/Under 45%/55% 16th Both score 58%/42% 2nd

BOLOGNA

Renato Dall'Ara — bolognafc.it

	2017-18 H	A	P	W	D	L	OV	UN	BS	CS
			Last six seasons at home							
Juventus	L	L	5	0	1	4	2	3	1	1
Napoli	L	L	5	1	1	3	5	0	3	0
Roma	D	L	5	0	3	2	3	2	3	0
Inter	D	L	5	0	2	3	1	4	3	0
Lazio	L	D	5	0	3	2	2	3	2	2
Milan	L	L	5	0	1	4	3	2	3	0
Atalanta	L	L	5	2	0	3	2	3	1	1
Fiorentina	L	L	5	1	1	3	3	2	3	0
Torino	D	L	5	1	2	2	2	3	3	1
Sampdoria	W	L	5	3	2	0	3	2	3	2
Sassuolo	W	W	4	1	2	1	1	3	2	1
Genoa	W	W	5	3	1	1	0	5	0	4
Chievo	L	W	5	2	1	2	3	2	2	2
Udinese	L	L	5	1	1	3	3	2	3	1
Bologna										
Cagliari	D	D	4	3	1	0	2	2	2	2
SPAL	W	L	1	1	0	0	1	0	1	0
Empoli			2	0	1	1	1	1	1	1
Parma			2	0	1	1	1	1	2	0
Frosinone			2	1	1	0	1	1	1	1

Season	Division	Pos	P	W	D	L	F	A	GD	Pts
2017-18	Serie A	15	38	11	6	21	40	52	-12	39
2016-17	Serie A	15	38	11	8	19	40	58	-18	41
2015-16	Serie A	14	38	11	9	18	33	45	-12	42

Over/Under 53%/47% 10th Both score 53%/47% 6th

CAGLIARI

Sardegna Arena — cagliaricalcio.net

	2017-18 H	A	P	W	D	L	OV	UN	BS	CS
			Last six seasons at home							
Juventus	L	L	5	0	0	5	3	2	3	0
Napoli	L	L	5	0	1	4	3	2	1	0
Roma	L	L	5	0	1	4	4	1	3	0
Inter	L	L	5	1	1	3	3	2	4	1
Lazio	D	L	5	1	2	2	2	3	2	2
Milan	L	L	5	1	2	2	3	2	5	0
Atalanta	W	W	5	3	1	1	3	2	3	2
Fiorentina	L	W	5	2	0	3	3	2	2	1
Torino	L	L	5	2	0	3	5	0	4	0
Sampdoria	D	L	5	2	3	0	5	0	5	0
Sassuolo	L	D	4	2	1	1	3	1	3	0
Genoa	L	L	5	3	1	1	4	1	5	0
Chievo	L	L	5	1	0	4	1	4	0	1
Udinese	W	W	5	4	0	1	4	1	3	1
Bologna	D	D	4	1	2	1	1	3	1	2
Cagliari										
SPAL	W	W	1	1	0	0	0	1	0	1
Empoli			2	1	1	0	1	1	2	0
Parma			3	2	0	1	1	2	0	2
Frosinone			-	-	-	-	-	-	-	-

Season	Division	Pos	P	W	D	L	F	A	GD	Pts
2017-18	Serie A	16	38	11	6	21	33	61	-28	39
2016-17	Serie A	11	38	14	5	19	55	76	-21	47
2015-16	Serie B	1	42	25	8	9	78	41	+37	83

Over/Under 55%/45% 7th Both score 45%/55% 13th

CHIEVO

Marc'Antonio Bentegodi — chievoverona.tv

	2017-18 H	A	P	W	D	L	OV	UN	BS	CS
			Last six seasons at home							
Juventus	L	L	6	0	0	6	4	2	3	0
Napoli	D	L	6	1	1	4	3	3	3	2
Roma	D	L	6	1	3	2	2	4	2	3
Inter	L	L	6	2	0	4	2	4	2	1
Lazio	L	L	6	1	2	3	3	3	3	2
Milan	L	D	6	0	3	3	2	4	2	3
Atalanta	D	L	6	2	2	2	1	5	3	2
Fiorentina	W	L	6	1	2	3	4	2	4	1
Torino	D	D	6	1	3	2	1	5	2	3
Sampdoria	W	L	6	4	1	1	4	2	5	0
Sassuolo	D	D	5	1	3	1	1	4	3	1
Genoa	L	D	6	2	1	3	2	4	2	2
Chievo										
Udinese	D	W	6	1	4	1	3	3	5	1
Bologna	L	W	5	2	1	2	3	2	3	3
Cagliari	W	W	5	3	2	0	1	4	1	4
SPAL	W	D	1	1	0	0	1	0	1	0
Empoli			3	1	2	0	1	2	2	1
Parma			3	0	1	2	1	3	1	0
Frosinone			1	1	0	0	1	0	1	0

Season	Division	Pos	P	W	D	L	F	A	GD	Pts
2017-18	Serie A	13	38	10	10	18	36	59	-23	40
2016-17	Serie A	14	38	12	7	19	43	61	-18	43
2015-16	Serie A	9	38	13	11	14	43	45	-2	50

Over/Under 50%/50% 12th Both score 58%/42% 2nd

ITALIAN SERIE A

EMPOLI

Stadio Carlo Castellani empolicalcio.it

	2017-18 H	A	Last six seasons at home P	W	D	L	OV	UN	BS	CS
Juventus			3	0	0	3	2	1	1	0
Napoli			3	1	1	1	3	0	3	0
Roma			3	0	1	2	1	2	1	1
Inter			3	0	1	2	0	3	0	1
Lazio			3	2	0	1	2	1	2	1
Milan			3	0	2	1	3	0	3	0
Atalanta			3	0	1	2	0	3	0	1
Fiorentina			3	1	0	2	2	1	1	1
Torino			3	1	2	0	1	2	2	1
Sampdoria			3	0	2	1	0	3	2	0
Sassuolo			4	2	0	2	3	1	2	1
Genoa			3	1	1	1	0	3	1	1
Chievo			3	1	1	2	1	1	1	2
Udinese			3	1	1	1	1	2	2	1
Bologna			2	1	1	0	1	1	1	1
Cagliari			2	1	0	1	1	1	0	1
SPAL			-	-	-	-	-	-	-	-
Empoli										
Parma	W	W	2	1	1	0	2	0	1	1
Frosinone	D	W	2	0	1	1	2	0	2	0

Season	Division	Pos	P	W	D	L	F	A	GD	Pts
2017-18	Serie B	1	42	24	13	5	88	49	+39	85
2016-17	Serie A	18	38	8	8	22	29	61	-32	32
2015-16	Serie A	10	38	12	10	16	40	49	-9	46

Over/Under 60%/40% 3rd **Both score** 71%/29% 2nd

FIORENTINA

Artemio Franchi violachannel.tv

	2017-18 H	A	Last six seasons at home P	W	D	L	OV	UN	BS	CS
Juventus	L	L	6	2	2	2	3	3	3	2
Napoli	W	D	6	1	3	2	3	3	4	1
Roma	L	W	6	1	1	4	2	4	3	1
Inter	D	L	6	4	1	1	5	1	5	1
Lazio	L	D	6	2	0	4	3	3	3	1
Milan	D	L	6	2	3	1	2	4	3	2
Atalanta	D	D	6	4	2	0	3	3	3	3
Fiorentina										
Torino	W	W	6	3	3	0	4	2	4	2
Sampdoria	L	L	6	2	3	1	3	3	5	1
Sassuolo	W	L	5	3	1	1	4	1	3	2
Genoa	D	W	6	2	4	0	3	3	3	3
Chievo	W	L	6	6	0	0	3	3	2	4
Udinese	W	W	6	6	0	0	6	0	3	3
Bologna	W	W	5	5	0	0	2	3	1	4
Cagliari	L	W	5	2	1	2	2	3	3	1
SPAL	D	D	1	0	1	0	0	1	0	1
Empoli										
Parma			3	0	2	1	2	1	3	0
Frosinone			1	1	0	0	1	0	1	0

Season	Division	Pos	P	W	D	L	F	A	GD	Pts
2017-18	Serie A	8	38	16	9	13	54	46	+8	57
2016-17	Serie A	8	38	16	12	10	63	57	+6	60
2015-16	Serie A	5	38	18	10	10	60	42	+18	64

Over/Under 50%/50% 12th **Both score** 50%/50% 10th

FROSINONE

Stadio Benito Stirpe frosinonecalcio.com

	2017-18 H	A	Last six seasons at home P	W	D	L	OV	UN	BS	CS
Juventus			1	0	0	1	0	1	0	0
Napoli			1	0	0	1	1	0	1	0
Roma			1	0	0	1	0	1	0	0
Inter			1	0	0	1	0	1	0	0
Lazio			1	0	1	0	0	1	0	1
Milan			1	0	0	1	1	0	1	0
Atalanta			1	0	1	0	0	1	0	1
Fiorentina			1	0	1	0	0	1	0	1
Torino			1	0	0	1	1	0	1	0
Sampdoria			1	1	0	0	0	1	0	1
Sassuolo			1	0	0	1	0	1	0	0
Genoa			1	0	1	0	1	0	1	0
Chievo			1	0	0	1	0	1	0	0
Udinese			1	1	0	0	0	1	0	1
Bologna			2	2	0	0	1	1	1	1
Cagliari			-	-	-	-	-	-	-	-
SPAL			1	1	0	0	1	0	1	0
Empoli	L	D	2	1	0	1	1	1	1	1
Parma	W	L	1	1	0	0	1	0	1	0
Frosinone										

Season	Division	Pos	P	W	D	L	F	A	GD	Pts
2017-18	Serie B	3	42	19	15	8	65	47	+18	72
2016-17	Serie B	3	42	21	11	10	57	42	+15	74
2015-16	Serie A	19	38	8	7	23	35	76	-41	31

Over/Under 45%/55% 17th **Both score** 55%/45% 12th

GENOA

Luigi Ferraris genoafc.it

	2017-18 H	A	Last six seasons at home P	W	D	L	OV	UN	BS	CS
Juventus	L	L	6	2	0	4	3	3	3	1
Napoli	L	L	6	0	2	4	3	3	3	2
Roma	D	L	6	1	1	4	2	4	3	1
Inter	W	L	6	5	1	0	1	5	1	5
Lazio	L	W	6	3	2	1	3	3	3	3
Milan	L	D	6	3	0	3	2	4	1	3
Atalanta	L	L	6	0	3	3	4	2	5	0
Fiorentina	L	D	6	1	2	3	4	3	2	0
Torino	L	D	6	3	2	1	4	2	6	0
Sampdoria	L	D	6	0	1	5	1	5	2	0
Sassuolo	W	W	5	3	1	1	2	3	2	2
Genoa										
Chievo	D	W	6	2	1	3	4	2	5	0
Udinese	L	L	6	2	3	1	2	4	4	1
Bologna	L	L	5	1	2	2	0	5	1	2
Cagliari	W	W	5	4	0	1	3	2	3	2
SPAL	D	L	1	0	1	0	0	1	1	0
Empoli			3	1	2	0	0	3	1	2
Parma			3	2	1	0	0	3	1	2
Frosinone			1	1	0	0	1	0	0	1

Season	Division	Pos	P	W	D	L	F	A	GD	Pts
2017-18	Serie A	12	38	11	8	19	33	43	-10	41
2016-17	Serie A	16	38	9	9	20	38	64	-26	36
2015-16	Serie A	11	38	13	7	18	45	48	-3	46

Over/Under 32%/68% 20th **Both score** 39%/61% 17th

INTER

San Siro — inter.it

	2017-18		Last six seasons at home							
	H	A	P	W	D	L	OV	UN	BS	CS
Juventus	L	D	6	1	2	3	4	2	5	1
Napoli	D	D	6	2	3	1	2	4	2	3
Roma	D	W	6	2	1	3	4	2	4	1
Inter										
Lazio	D	W	6	2	2	2	5	1	4	2
Milan	W	D	6	3	3	0	2	4	3	3
Atalanta	W	D	6	4	0	2	3	3	3	3
Fiorentina	W	D	6	4	0	2	5	1	4	1
Torino	D	L	6	2	2	2	3	3	4	1
Sampdoria	W	W	6	4	1	1	4	2	5	1
Sassuolo	L	L	5	2	0	3	3	2	2	2
Genoa	W	L	6	5	1	0	1	5	2	4
Chievo	W	W	6	4	2	0	3	3	3	3
Udinese	L	W	6	2	1	3	5	1	5	1
Bologna	W	D	5	2	2	1	3	2	4	0
Cagliari	W	W	5	1	2	2	4	1	4	1
SPAL	W	D	1	1	0	0	0	1	0	1
Empoli			3	3	0	0	2	1	2	1
Parma			3	1	2	0	1	2	2	1
Frosinone			1	1	0	0	1	0	0	1

Season	Division	Pos	P	W	D	L	F	A	GD	Pts
2017-18	Serie A	4	38	20	12	6	66	30	+36	72
2016-17	Serie A	7	38	19	5	14	72	49	+23	62
2015-16	Serie A	4	38	20	7	11	50	38	+12	60

Over/Under 47%/53% 14th **Both score** 47%/53% 12th

JUVENTUS

Juventus Stadium — juventus.com

	2017-18		Last six seasons at home							
	H	A	P	W	D	L	OV	UN	BS	CS
Juventus										
Napoli	L	W	6	5	0	1	3	3	2	3
Roma	W	D	6	6	0	0	3	3	2	4
Inter	D	W	6	3	2	1	2	4	3	3
Lazio	L	W	6	4	1	1	3	3	2	4
Milan	W	W	6	6	0	0	4	2	4	2
Atalanta	W	D	6	6	0	0	3	3	2	4
Fiorentina	W	W	6	6	0	0	3	3	3	3
Torino	W	W	6	5	1	0	4	2	3	3
Sampdoria	W	L	6	4	1	1	5	1	4	2
Sassuolo	W	W	5	5	0	0	3	2	1	4
Genoa	W	W	6	5	1	0	1	5	1	5
Chievo	W	W	6	5	1	0	2	4	2	4
Udinese	W	W	6	5	0	1	2	4	1	4
Bologna	W	W	5	5	0	0	4	1	3	2
Cagliari	W	W	5	3	2	0	3	2	2	3
SPAL	W	D	1	1	0	0	1	0	1	0
Empoli			3	3	0	0	0	3	0	3
Parma			3	3	0	0	2	1	1	2
Frosinone			1	0	1	0	0	1	1	0

Season	Division	Pos	P	W	D	L	F	A	GD	Pts
2017-18	Serie A	1	38	30	5	3	86	24	+62	95
2016-17	Serie A	1	38	29	4	5	77	27	+50	91
2015-16	Serie A	1	38	29	4	5	75	20	+55	91

Over/Under 55%/45% 7th **Both score** 39%/61% 17th

LAZIO

Stadio Olimpico — sslazio.it

	2017-18		Last six seasons at home							
	H	A	P	W	D	L	OV	UN	BS	CS
Juventus	L	W	6	0	1	5	1	5	1	0
Napoli	L	L	6	0	1	5	3	3	3	0
Roma	D	L	6	1	2	3	3	3	3	2
Inter	L	D	6	3	0	3	3	3	3	3
Lazio										
Milan	W	L	6	3	2	1	4	2	6	0
Atalanta	D	D	6	4	1	1	2	4	2	3
Fiorentina	D	W	6	2	2	2	3	3	3	2
Torino	L	W	6	3	2	1	5	1	5	1
Sampdoria	W	W	6	5	1	0	3	3	2	4
Sassuolo	W	W	5	4	0	1	4	1	4	0
Genoa	L	W	6	2	0	4	2	4	2	1
Chievo	W	W	6	3	1	2	3	3	3	1
Udinese	W	W	6	5	0	1	3	3	1	4
Bologna	D	W	5	3	2	0	2	3	3	2
Cagliari	W	D	5	5	0	0	4	1	3	2
SPAL	D	W	1	0	1	0	0	1	0	1
Empoli			3	3	0	0	1	2	0	3
Parma			3	3	0	0	3	0	2	1
Frosinone			1	1	0	0	1	0	1	0

Season	Division	Pos	P	W	D	L	F	A	GD	Pts
2017-18	Serie A	5	38	21	9	8	89	49	+40	72
2016-17	Serie A	5	38	21	7	10	74	51	+23	70
2015-16	Serie A	8	38	15	9	14	52	52	0	54

Over/Under 76%/24% 1st **Both score** 68%/32% 1st

MILAN

San Siro — acmilan.com

	2017-18		Last six seasons at home							
	H	A	P	W	D	L	OV	UN	BS	CS
Juventus	L	L	6	2	0	4	1	5	1	2
Napoli	D	L	6	1	2	3	3	3	3	2
Roma	L	W	6	1	2	3	4	2	4	1
Inter	D	L	6	2	3	1	2	4	2	3
Lazio	W	L	6	4	2	0	3	3	4	2
Milan										
Atalanta	L	D	6	1	2	3	1	5	0	3
Fiorentina	W	D	6	3	1	2	3	3	4	1
Torino	D	D	6	4	2	0	2	4	2	4
Sampdoria	W	L	6	3	1	2	1	5	2	2
Sassuolo	D	W	5	3	1	1	4	1	5	0
Genoa	D	W	6	3	2	1	2	4	3	3
Chievo	W	W	6	6	0	0	4	2	3	3
Udinese	W	D	6	4	1	1	2	4	3	2
Bologna	W	W	5	4	0	1	3	2	2	2
Cagliari	W	W	5	5	0	0	3	2	3	2
SPAL	W	W	1	1	0	0	0	1	0	1
Empoli			3	1	1	1	2	1	3	0
Parma			3	2	0	1	3	0	3	0
Frosinone			1	0	1	0	1	0	1	0

Season	Division	Pos	P	W	D	L	F	A	GD	Pts
2017-18	Serie A	6	38	18	10	10	56	42	+14	64
2016-17	Serie A	6	38	18	9	11	57	45	+12	63
2015-16	Serie A	7	38	15	12	11	49	43	+6	57

Over/Under 47%/53% 14th **Both score** 53%/47% 6th

ITALIAN SERIE A

NAPOLI

San Paolo — ssnapoli.it

	2017-18 H	2017-18 A	P	W	D	L	OV	UN	BS	CS
Juventus	L	W	6	2	2	2	2	4	4	1
Napoli										
Roma	L	W	6	3	1	2	3	3	3	3
Inter	D	D	6	4	2	0	5	1	4	2
Lazio	W	W	6	4	1	1	5	1	4	2
Milan	W	D	6	4	2	0	5	1	5	1
Atalanta	W	W	6	4	1	1	3	3	4	1
Fiorentina	D	L	6	4	1	1	4	2	3	2
Torino	D	W	6	4	2	0	4	2	5	1
Sampdoria	W	W	6	4	2	0	4	2	4	2
Sassuolo	W	D	5	3	2	0	2	3	4	1
Genoa	W	W	6	5	1	0	2	4	3	3
Chievo	W	D	6	4	1	1	2	4	3	2
Udinese	W	W	6	5	1	0	5	1	4	2
Bologna	W	W	5	4	0	1	5	0	3	2
Cagliari	W	W	5	4	1	0	5	0	3	2
SPAL	W	W	1	1	0	0	0	1	0	1
Empoli			3	2	1	0	2	1	2	1
Parma			3	2	0	1	1	2	1	1
Frosinone			1	1	0	0	1	0	0	1

Season	Division	Pos	P	W	D	L	F	A	GD	Pts
2017-18	Serie A	2	38	28	7	3	77	29	+48	91
2016-17	Serie A	3	38	26	8	4	94	39	+55	86
2015-16	Serie A	2	38	25	7	6	80	32	+48	82

Over/Under 55%/45% 7th **Both score** 45%/55% 13th

PARMA

Ennio Tardini — fcparma.com

	2017-18 H	2017-18 A	P	W	D	L	OV	UN	BS	CS
Juventus			3	1	1	1	0	3	1	1
Napoli			3	1	1	1	2	1	2	1
Roma			3	1	0	2	3	0	3	0
Inter			3	2	0	1	0	3	0	2
Lazio			3	0	2	1	1	2	2	1
Milan			3	1	1	1	2	1	3	0
Atalanta			3	2	1	0	1	2	1	2
Fiorentina			3	1	2	0	1	2	2	1
Torino			3	2	0	1	2	1	2	0
Sampdoria			3	2	0	1	1	2	1	1
Sassuolo			2	1	0	1	2	0	2	0
Genoa			3	0	2	1	1	2	2	1
Chievo			3	1	1	1	0	3	0	2
Udinese			3	2	0	1	1	2	0	2
Bologna			2	0	1	1	0	2	1	0
Cagliari			3	1	2	0	1	2	1	2
SPAL			-	-	-	-	-	-	-	-
Empoli	L	L	2	0	0	2	1	1	1	0
Parma										
Frosinone	W	L	1	1	0	0	0	1	0	1

Season	Division	Pos	P	W	D	L	F	A	GD	Pts
2017-18	Serie B	2	42	21	9	12	57	37	+20	72
2016-17	Serie C (Grp B)	2	38	20	10	8	55	36	+19	70
2015-16	Serie D	1	38	28	10	0	82	17	+65	94

Over/Under 45%/55% 17th **Both score** 40%/60% 34th

ROMA
Stadio Olimpico — asroma.it

	2017-18 H	2017-18 A	P	W	D	L	OV	UN	BS	CS
Juventus	D	L	6	3	2	1	2	4	3	2
Napoli	L	W	6	4	0	2	2	4	2	3
Roma										
Inter	L	D	6	2	3	1	3	3	5	1
Lazio	W	D	6	3	2	1	3	3	4	2
Milan	L	W	6	3	2	1	1	5	2	3
Atalanta	L	W	6	2	2	2	2	4	4	1
Fiorentina	L	W	6	5	0	1	4	2	3	2
Torino	W	W	6	6	0	0	5	1	3	3
Sampdoria	L	D	6	3	1	2	3	3	3	1
Sassuolo	D	W	5	1	4	0	3	2	5	0
Genoa	W	W	6	6	0	0	4	2	3	3
Chievo	W	D	6	5	0	1	4	2	2	3
Udinese	W	W	6	5	0	1	6	0	5	1
Bologna	W	D	5	3	1	1	3	2	2	3
Cagliari	W	W	5	3	1	1	4	1	4	4
SPAL	W	W	1	1	0	0	1	0	1	0
Empoli			3	2	1	0	1	2	2	1
Parma			3	2	1	0	1	2	1	2
Frosinone			1	1	0	0	1	0	0	1

Season	Division	Pos	P	W	D	L	F	A	GD	Pts
2017-18	Serie A	3	38	23	8	7	61	28	+33	77
2016-17	Serie A	2	38	28	3	7	90	38	+52	87
2015-16	Serie A	3	38	23	11	4	83	41	+42	80

Over/Under 37%/63% 19th **Both score** 39%/61% 17th

SAMPDORIA

Stadio Luigi Ferraris — sampdoria.it

	2017-18 H	2017-18 A	P	W	D	L	OV	UN	BS	CS
Juventus	W	L	6	2	0	4	3	3	3	0
Napoli	L	L	6	0	1	5	3	3	4	0
Roma	D	W	6	3	2	1	3	3	4	1
Inter	L	L	6	2	1	3	2	4	1	2
Lazio	L	L	6	1	1	4	3	3	4	0
Milan	W	L	6	1	2	3	1	5	1	2
Atalanta	W	W	6	4	1	1	3	3	3	3
Fiorentina	W	W	6	2	2	2	4	2	3	1
Torino	D	D	6	2	4	0	2	4	2	2
Sampdoria										
Sassuolo	L	L	5	1	1	3	3	2	4	0
Genoa	D	W	6	2	2	2	4	2	3	1
Chievo	W	L	6	4	1	1	3	3	4	1
Udinese	W	L	6	3	2	1	3	3	2	3
Bologna	W	L	5	4	1	0	1	4	2	3
Cagliari	W	D	5	3	1	1	1	4	2	2
SPAL	W	L	1	1	0	0	0	1	0	1
Empoli			3	1	2	0	0	3	1	2
Parma			3	1	2	0	1	2	2	1
Frosinone			1	1	0	0	0	1	0	1

Season	Division	Pos	P	W	D	L	F	A	GD	Pts
2017-18	Serie A	10	38	16	6	16	56	60	-4	54
2016-17	Serie A	10	38	12	12	14	49	55	-6	48
2015-16	Serie A	15	38	10	10	18	48	61	-13	40

Over/Under 63%/37% 2nd **Both score** 53%/47% 6th

SASSUOLO

Citta del Tricolore — sassuolocalcio.it

	2017-18 H	A	Last six seasons at home P	W	D	L	OV	UN	BS	CS
Juventus	L	L	5	1	1	3	2	3	3	1
Napoli	D	L	5	1	2	2	2	3	3	0
Roma	L	D	5	0	0	5	2	3	1	0
Inter	W	W	5	3	0	2	3	2	2	1
Lazio	L	L	5	1	1	3	5	0	3	0
Milan	L	D	5	3	0	2	2	3	2	1
Atalanta	L	L	5	1	2	2	3	2	1	2
Fiorentina	W	L	5	1	2	2	2	3	3	1
Torino	D	L	5	0	4	1	0	5	3	1
Sampdoria	W	W	5	2	2	1	2	3	2	3
Sassuolo										
Genoa	D	L	5	3	1	1	2	3	2	2
Chievo	D	D	5	1	2	2	1	4	2	2
Udinese	L	W	5	1	2	2	1	4	3	1
Bologna	L	L	4	1	0	3	1	3	1	0
Cagliari	D	W	4	1	3	0	1	3	3	1
SPAL	D	W	1	0	1	0	0	1	1	0
Empoli			4	3	1	0	3	1	3	1
Parma			2	1	0	1	1	1	1	0
Frosinone			1	0	1	0	1	0	1	0

Season	Division	Pos	P	W	D	L	F	A	GD	Pts
2017-18	Serie A	11	38	11	10	17	29	59	-30	43
2016-17	Serie A	12	38	13	7	18	58	63	-5	46
2015-16	Serie A	6	38	16	13	9	49	40	+9	61

Over/Under 42%/58% 17th   Both score 45%/55% 13th

SPAL

Stadio Paolo Mazza — spalferrara.it

	2017-18 H	A	Last six seasons at home P	W	D	L	OV	UN	BS	CS
Juventus	D	L	1	0	1	0	0	1	0	1
Napoli	L	L	1	0	0	1	1	0	1	0
Roma	L	L	1	0	0	1	0	1	0	0
Inter	D	L	1	0	1	0	0	1	1	0
Lazio	L	D	1	0	0	1	1	0	1	0
Milan	L	L	1	0	0	1	0	1	0	0
Atalanta	D	D	1	0	1	0	0	1	1	0
Fiorentina	D	D	1	0	1	0	0	1	1	0
Torino	D	L	1	0	1	0	1	0	1	0
Sampdoria	W	L	1	1	0	0	1	0	1	0
Sassuolo	L	D	1	0	0	1	0	1	0	0
Genoa	W	D	1	1	0	0	0	1	0	1
Chievo	D	L	1	0	1	0	0	1	0	1
Udinese	W	D	1	1	0	0	1	0	1	0
Bologna	W	L	1	1	0	0	0	1	0	1
Cagliari	L	L	1	0	0	1	0	1	0	0
SPAL										
Empoli			-	-	-	-	-	-	-	-
Parma			-	-	-	-	-	-	-	-
Frosinone			1	0	0	1	0	1	0	0

Season	Division	Pos	P	W	D	L	F	A	GD	Pts
2017-18	Serie A	17	38	8	14	16	39	59	-20	38
2016-17	Serie B	1	42	22	12	8	66	39	+27	78
2015-16	Serie C (Grp B)	1	34	21	8	5	59	25	+34	71

Over/Under 42%/58% 17th   Both score 58%/42% 2nd

TORINO

Stadio Olimpico Grande Torino — torino.it

	2017-18 H	A	Last six seasons at home P	W	D	L	OV	UN	BS	CS
Juventus	L	L	6	1	0	5	3	3	3	0
Napoli	L	D	6	1	0	5	4	2	3	1
Roma	L	L	6	1	3	2	2	4	5	0
Inter	W	D	6	1	3	2	2	4	2	2
Lazio	L	W	6	2	2	2	1	5	2	2
Milan	D	D	6	0	5	1	3	3	6	0
Atalanta	D	L	6	3	3	0	2	4	4	2
Fiorentina	L	L	6	2	3	1	4	2	5	1
Torino										
Sampdoria	D	D	6	2	3	1	2	4	3	2
Sassuolo	W	D	5	3	0	2	3	2	2	2
Genoa	D	W	6	3	3	0	3	3	3	3
Chievo	D	D	6	4	1	1	3	3	4	2
Udinese	W	W	6	3	2	1	1	5	1	4
Bologna	W	D	5	4	0	1	3	2	2	3
Cagliari	W	W	5	3	1	1	3	2	4	0
SPAL	W	D	1	1	0	0	1	0	1	0
Empoli			3	0	1	2	0	3	0	1
Parma			3	1	1	1	1	2	2	1
Frosinone			1	0	1	0	1	0	1	0

Season	Division	Pos	P	W	D	L	F	A	GD	Pts
2017-18	Serie A	9	38	13	15	10	54	46	+8	54
2016-17	Serie A	9	38	13	14	11	71	66	+5	53
2015-16	Serie A	12	38	12	9	17	52	55	-3	45

Over/Under 58%/42% 5th   Both score 58%/42% 2nd

UDINESE

Stadio Friuli — udinese.it

	2017-18 H	A	Last six seasons at home P	W	D	L	OV	UN	BS	CS
Juventus	L	L	6	0	2	4	3	3	3	1
Napoli	L	L	6	2	2	2	2	4	3	2
Roma	L	L	6	0	1	5	1	5	2	0
Inter	L	W	6	1	0	5	6	0	2	1
Lazio	L	L	6	1	1	4	3	3	2	2
Milan	D	L	6	4	1	1	4	2	5	1
Atalanta	W	L	6	4	2	0	3	3	5	1
Fiorentina	L	L	6	3	2	1	4	2	4	1
Torino	L	L	6	2	1	3	4	2	4	1
Sampdoria	W	L	6	3	2	1	4	2	4	2
Sassuolo	L	W	5	1	1	3	2	3	2	2
Genoa	W	W	6	3	2	1	2	4	2	4
Chievo	L	D	6	2	2	2	4	2	4	2
Udinese										
Bologna	W	W	5	2	2	1	0	5	1	3
Cagliari	L	L	5	3	1	1	3	2	3	1
SPAL	D	L	1	0	1	0	0	1	1	0
Empoli			3	2	0	1	1	2	1	2
Parma			3	2	1	0	3	0	3	0
Frosinone			1	1	0	0	1	0	1	0

Season	Division	Pos	P	W	D	L	F	A	GD	Pts
2017-18	Serie A	14	38	12	4	22	48	63	-15	40
2016-17	Serie A	13	38	12	9	17	47	56	-9	45
2015-16	Serie A	17	38	10	9	19	35	60	-25	39

Over/Under 58%/42% 5th   Both score 53%/47% 6th

Serie A 2017-18

Pos	H	A	Team	P	Home					Away					GD	Pts
					W	D	L	F	A	W	D	L	F	A		
1	1	1	Juventus (CL)	38	16	1	2	45	8	14	4	1	41	16	62	95
2	2	2	Napoli (CL)	38	14	3	2	43	18	14	4	1	34	11	48	91
3	5	3	Roma (CL)	38	11	2	6	31	19	12	6	1	30	9	33	77
4	4	5	Inter (CL)	38	11	5	3	37	16	9	7	3	29	14	36	72
5	8	4	Lazio (EL)	38	9	5	5	45	21	12	4	3	44	28	40	72
6	6	6	Milan (EL)	38	10	5	4	25	16	8	5	6	31	26	14	64
7	7	8	Atalanta (EL)	38	9	6	4	30	18	7	6	6	27	21	18	60
8	10	7	Fiorentina	38	8	5	6	27	22	8	4	7	27	24	8	57
9	9	9	Torino	38	8	6	5	29	18	5	9	5	25	28	8	54
10	3	16	Sampdoria	38	12	3	4	36	20	4	3	12	20	40	-4	54
11	18	10	Sassuolo	38	4	7	8	11	22	7	3	9	18	37	-30	43
12	15	11	Genoa	38	6	3	10	23	27	5	5	9	10	16	-10	41
13	11	17	Chievo	38	7	6	6	22	24	3	4	12	14	35	-23	40
14	17	12	Udinese	38	6	2	11	24	30	6	2	11	24	33	-15	40
15	14	14	Bologna	38	6	4	9	25	26	5	2	12	15	26	-12	39
16	16	13	Cagliari	38	6	3	10	18	30	5	3	11	15	31	-28	39
17	13	15	SPAL	38	5	8	6	22	29	3	6	10	17	30	-20	38
18	12	18	Crotone (R)	38	6	6	7	23	25	3	2	14	17	41	-26	35
19	20	19	Hellas Verona (R)	38	5	1	13	14	35	2	3	14	16	43	-48	25
20	19	20	Benevento (R)	38	5	2	12	23	40	1	1	17	10	44	-51	21

Serie A results 2017-18

	Atalanta	Benevento	Bologna	Cagliari	Chievo	Crotone	Fiorentina	Genoa	Hellas Verona	Inter	Juventus	Lazio	Milan	Napoli	Roma	Sampdoria	Sassuolo	SPAL	Torino	Udinese
Atalanta		1-0	1-0	1-2	1-0	5-1	1-1	3-1	3-0	0-0	2-2	3-3	1-1	0-1	0-1	1-2	2-1	1-1	2-1	2-0
Benevento	0-3		0-1	1-2	1-0	3-2	0-3	1-0	3-0	1-2	2-4	1-5	2-2	0-2	0-4	3-2	1-2	1-2	0-1	3-3
Bologna	0-1	3-0		1-1	1-2	2-3	1-2	2-0	2-0	1-1	0-3	1-2	1-2	0-3	1-1	3-0	2-1	2-1	1-1	1-2
Cagliari	1-0	2-1	0-0		0-2	1-0	0-1	2-3	2-1	1-3	0-1	2-2	1-2	0-5	0-1	2-2	0-1	2-0	0-4	2-1
Chievo	1-1	1-0	2-3	2-1		2-1	2-1	0-1	3-2	1-2	0-2	1-2	1-4	0-0	0-0	2-1	1-1	2-1	0-0	1-1
Crotone	1-1	2-0	1-0	1-1	1-0		2-1	0-1	0-0	0-2	1-1	2-2	0-3	0-1	0-2	4-1	4-1	2-3	2-2	0-3
Fiorentina	1-1	1-0	2-1	0-1	1-0	2-0		0-0	1-4	1-1	0-2	3-4	1-1	3-0	2-4	1-2	3-0	0-0	3-0	2-1
Genoa	1-2	1-0	0-1	2-1	1-1	1-0	2-3		3-1	2-0	2-4	2-3	0-1	2-3	0-1	0-2	1-0	1-1	1-2	0-1
Hellas Verona	0-5	1-0	2-3	1-0	1-0	0-3	0-5	0-1		1-2	1-3	0-3	3-0	1-3	0-1	0-0	0-1	1-3	2-1	0-1
Inter	2-0	2-0	2-1	4-0	5-0	1-1	3-0	1-0	3-0		2-3	0-0	3-2	0-0	1-1	3-2	1-2	2-0	1-1	1-3
Juventus	2-0	2-1	3-1	3-0	3-0	3-0	1-0	1-0	2-1	0-0		1-2	3-1	0-1	1-0	3-0	7-0	4-1	4-0	2-0
Lazio	1-1	6-2	1-1	3-0	5-1	4-0	1-1	1-2	2-0	2-3	0-1		4-1	1-4	0-0	4-0	6-1	0-0	1-3	3-0
Milan	0-2	0-1	2-1	2-1	3-2	1-0	5-1	0-0	4-1	0-0	0-2	2-1		0-0	0-2	1-0	1-1	2-0	0-0	2-1
Napoli	3-1	6-0	3-1	3-0	2-1	2-1	0-0	1-0	2-0	0-0	0-1	4-1	2-1		2-4	3-2	3-1	1-0	2-2	4-2
Roma	1-2	5-2	1-0	1-0	4-1	1-0	0-2	2-1	3-0	1-0	0-1	0-2	0-1	0-1		0-1	1-1	3-1	3-0	3-1
Sampdoria	3-1	2-1	1-0	4-1	4-1	5-0	3-1	2-0	0-5	3-2	1-2	2-0	0-2	0-2	1-1		0-1	2-0	1-1	2-1
Sassuolo	0-3	2-2	0-1	0-0	0-0	2-1	1-0	0-0	0-2	1-0	1-3	0-3	0-2	1-1	0-1	1-0		1-1	1-1	0-1
SPAL	1-1	2-0	1-0	0-2	0-0	1-1	1-1	1-0	2-2	1-1	0-0	2-5	0-4	2-3	0-3	3-1	0-1		2-2	3-2
Torino	1-1	3-0	3-0	2-1	1-1	4-1	1-2	0-0	2-2	1-0	0-1	0-1	1-1	1-3	0-1	2-2	3-0	2-1		2-0
Udinese	2-1	2-0	1-0	0-1	1-2	1-2	0-2	1-0	4-0	0-4	2-6	1-2	1-1	0-1	0-2	4-0	1-2	1-1	2-3	

Top scorers

	Team	Goals scored
M Icardi	Inter	29 ▊▊▊▊▊▊▊▊▊▊▊▊▊▊▊▊▊▊▊▊▊▊▊
C Immobile	Lazio	29 ▊▊▊▊▊▊▊▊▊▊▊▊▊▊▊▊▊▊▊▊▊▊▊
P Dybala	Juventus	22 ▊▊▊▊▊▊▊▊▊▊▊▊▊▊▊▊▊
F Quagliarella	Sampdoria	19 ▊▊▊▊▊▊▊▊▊▊▊▊▊▊
D Mertens	Napoli	18 ▊▊▊▊▊▊▊▊▊▊▊▊▊
E Dzeko (Roma), G Higuain (Juve)		16 ▊▊▊▊▊▊▊▊▊▊▊

Over 2.5 goals

	H	A	%
Lazio	12	17	76%
Hellas Verona	11	13	63%
Sampdoria	10	14	63%
Benevento	14	9	61%
Torino	10	12	58%
Udinese	10	12	58%

Both teams to score

	H	A	%
Lazio	11	15	68%
Atalanta	11	11	58%
Chievo	13	9	58%
SPAL	10	12	58%
Torino	10	12	58%
Bol, Mil, Samp, Udin			53%

AUGSBURG

Augsburg Arena — fcaugsburg.de

	2017-18 H	A	Last six seasons at home P	W	D	L	OV	UN	BS	CS
Bayern Munich	L	L	6	1	0	5	4	2	3	1
Schalke	L	L	6	1	3	2	3	3	4	2
Hoffenheim	L	D	6	3	0	3	3	3	3	1
Dortmund	L	L	6	0	1	5	5	1	5	0
Leverkusen	D	D	6	0	3	3	5	1	6	0
RB Leipzig	W	L	2	1	1	0	1	1	1	1
Stuttgart	L	D	5	4	0	1	3	2	2	2
E Frankfurt	W	W	6	3	3	0	3	3	3	3
M'gladbach	D	L	6	2	4	0	4	2	5	1
Hertha Berlin	D	D	5	1	3	1	0	5	1	3
Werder Bremen	L	W	6	4	0	2	6	0	6	0
Augsburg										
Hannover	L	W	5	1	1	3	2	3	3	1
Mainz	W	W	6	2	2	2	3	3	4	1
Freiburg	D	L	5	2	3	0	2	3	4	1
Wolfsburg	W	D	6	2	2	2	2	4	2	3
Fortuna Dusseldorf			1	0	0	1	0	1	0	0
Nurnberg			2	0	0	2	1	1	1	0

Season	Division	Pos	P	W	D	L	F	A	GD	Pts
2017-18	Bundesliga	12	34	10	11	13	43	46	-3	41
2016-17	Bundesliga	13	34	9	11	14	35	51	-16	38
2015-16	Bundesliga	12	34	9	11	14	42	52	-10	38

Over/Under 53%/47% 8th **Both score** 53%/47% 11th

BAYERN MUNICH

Allianz Arena — fcbayern.de

	2017-18 H	A	Last six seasons at home P	W	D	L	OV	UN	BS	CS
Bayern Munich										
Schalke	W	W	6	4	2	0	4	2	4	2
Hoffenheim	W	L	6	4	2	0	3	3	3	3
Dortmund	W	W	6	4	1	1	5	1	4	1
Leverkusen	W	W	6	5	0	1	5	1	4	2
RB Leipzig	W	L	2	2	0	0	1	1	0	2
Stuttgart	L	W	5	4	0	1	3	2	2	3
E Frankfurt	W	W	6	6	0	0	4	2	1	5
M'gladbach	W	L	6	3	2	1	2	4	4	1
Hertha Berlin	D	D	5	4	1	0	2	3	1	4
Werder Bremen	W	W	6	6	0	0	6	0	3	3
Augsburg	W	W	6	5	0	1	5	1	1	4
Hannover	W	W	5	5	0	0	4	1	2	3
Mainz	W	W	6	4	1	1	5	1	4	2
Freiburg	W	W	5	5	0	0	3	2	1	4
Wolfsburg	D	W	6	5	1	0	5	1	3	3
Fortuna Dusseldorf			1	1	0	0	1	0	1	0
Nurnberg			2	2	0	0	1	1	0	2

Season	Division	Pos	P	W	D	L	F	A	GD	Pts
2017-18	Bundesliga	1	34	27	3	4	92	28	+64	84
2016-17	Bundesliga	1	34	25	7	2	89	22	+67	82
2015-16	Bundesliga	1	34	28	4	2	80	17	+63	88

Over/Under 74%/26% 1st **Both score** 50%/50% 14th

DORTMUND

Westfalenstadion — bvb.de

	2017-18 H	A	Last six seasons at home P	W	D	L	OV	UN	BS	CS
Bayern Munich	L	L	6	1	2	3	2	4	2	2
Schalke	D	L	6	2	3	1	4	2	3	3
Hoffenheim	W	L	6	5	0	1	5	1	5	1
Dortmund										
Leverkusen	W	D	6	4	0	2	4	2	1	3
RB Leipzig	L	D	2	1	0	1	1	1	1	1
Stuttgart	W	L	5	3	2	0	4	1	3	2
E Frankfurt	W	D	6	6	0	0	5	1	3	3
M'gladbach	W	W	6	5	0	1	5	1	3	3
Hertha Berlin	W	D	5	3	1	1	2	3	3	2
Werder Bremen	L	D	6	5	0	1	5	1	5	1
Augsburg	D	W	6	2	3	1	3	3	5	0
Hannover	W	L	5	4	0	1	1	4	1	3
Mainz	L	W	6	5	0	1	4	2	4	2
Freiburg	D	D	5	4	1	0	5	0	4	1
Wolfsburg	D	W	6	3	2	1	5	1	4	2
Fortuna Dusseldorf			1	0	1	0	0	1	1	0
Nurnberg			2	2	0	0	2	0	0	2

Season	Division	Pos	P	W	D	L	F	A	GD	Pts
2017-18	Bundesliga	4	34	15	10	9	64	47	+17	55
2016-17	Bundesliga	3	34	18	10	6	72	40	+32	64
2015-16	Bundesliga	2	34	24	6	4	82	34	+48	78

Over/Under 62%/38% 2nd **Both score** 59%/41% 4th

GERMAN BUNDESLIGA

EINTRACHT FRANKFURT

Commerzbank-Arena eintracht.de

	2017-18		Last six seasons at home							
	H	A	P	W	D	L	OV	UN	BS	CS
Bayern Munich	L	L	6	0	2	4	2	4	1	1
Schalke	D	L	6	3	3	0	2	4	2	4
Hoffenheim	D	D	6	2	2	2	3	3	4	1
Dortmund	D	L	6	3	2	1	4	2	4	2
Leverkusen	L	L	6	3	0	3	4	2	4	0
RB Leipzig	W	L	2	1	1	0	2	0	2	0
Stuttgart	W	L	5	2	0	3	5	0	5	0
E Frankfurt										
M'gladbach	W	W	6	2	2	2	1	5	1	4
Hertha Berlin	L	W	5	1	3	1	3	2	3	1
Werder Bremen	W	L	6	4	2	0	5	1	5	1
Augsburg	L	L	6	2	2	2	3	3	5	0
Hannover	W	W	5	3	1	1	3	2	3	2
Mainz	W	D	6	4	1	1	5	1	3	3
Freiburg	D	D	5	2	1	2	3	2	4	1
Wolfsburg	L	W	6	1	2	3	3	3	4	0
Fortuna Dusseldorf			1	1	0	0	1	0	1	0
Nurnberg			2	0	2	0	0	2	1	1

Season	Division	Pos	P	W	D	L	F	A	GD	Pts
2017-18	Bundesliga	8	34	14	7	13	45	45	0	49
2016-17	Bundesliga	11	34	11	9	14	36	43	-7	42
2015-16	Bundesliga	16	34	9	9	16	34	52	-18	36

Over/Under 59%/41% 5th **Both score** 59%/41% 4th

FORTUNA DUSSELDORF

Esprit Arena fortuna-duesseldorf.de

	2017-18		Last six seasons at home							
	H	A	P	W	D	L	OV	UN	BS	CS
Bayern Munich			1	0	0	1	1	0	0	0
Schalke			1	0	1	0	1	0	1	0
Hoffenheim			1	0	1	0	0	1	1	0
Dortmund			1	0	0	1	1	0	1	0
Leverkusen			1	0	0	1	1	0	1	0
RB Leipzig			2	0	1	1	2	0	2	0
Stuttgart			2	2	0	0	1	1	1	1
E Frankfurt			1	1	0	0	1	0	0	1
M'gladbach			1	0	1	0	0	1	0	1
Hertha Berlin			-	-	-	-	-	-	-	-
Werder Bremen			1	0	1	0	1	0	1	0
Augsburg			1	0	0	1	1	0	1	0
Hannover			2	1	1	0	2	0	2	0
Mainz			1	0	1	0	0	1	1	0
Freiburg			2	0	1	1	1	1	1	1
Wolfsburg			1	0	0	1	1	0	1	0
Fortuna Dusseldorf										
Nurnberg	L	W	5	0	1	4	2	3	3	0

Season	Division	Pos	P	W	D	L	F	A	GD	Pts
2017-18	2.Bundesliga	1	34	19	6	9	57	44	+13	63
2016-17	2.Bundesliga	11	34	10	12	12	37	39	-2	42

Over/Under 62%/38% 3rd **Both score** 65%/35% 3rd

Another season, another title for 28-time German champions Bayern

FREIBURG

Schwarzwald-Stadion scfreiburg.com

	2017-18		Last six seasons at home							
	H	A	P	W	D	L	OV	UN	BS	CS
Bayern Munich	L	L	5	1	1	3	3	2	3	0
Schalke	L	L	5	2	0	3	1	4	1	2
Hoffenheim	W	D	5	2	3	0	2	3	5	0
Dortmund	D	D	5	0	1	4	2	3	0	1
Leverkusen	D	L	5	2	3	0	2	3	2	3
RB Leipzig	W	L	3	2	0	1	3	0	3	0
Stuttgart	L	L	4	1	0	3	4	0	3	1
E Frankfurt	D	D	5	2	3	0	1	4	2	3
M'gladbach	W	L	5	4	1	0	2	3	2	3
Hertha Berlin	D	D	4	1	3	0	2	2	4	0
Werder Bremen	W	D	5	2	0	3	3	2	3	1
Augsburg	W	D	5	4	0	1	2	3	2	3
Hannover	D	L	4	2	2	0	3	1	4	0
Mainz	W	D	5	2	1	2	3	2	4	1
Freiburg										
Wolfsburg	L	L	5	0	0	5	4	1	2	0
Fortuna Dusseldorf			2	1	0	1	1	1	1	1
Nurnberg			3	3	0	0	3	0	2	1

Season	Division	Pos	P	W	D	L	F	A	GD	Pts
2017-18	Bundesliga	15	34	8	12	14	32	56	-24	36
2016-17	Bundesliga	7	34	14	6	14	42	60	-18	48
2015-16	2.Bundesliga	1	34	22	6	6	75	39	+36	72

Over/Under 47%/53% 11th **Both score** 47%/53% 16th

HANNOVER

Niedersachsenstadion hannover96.de

	2017-18		Last six seasons at home							
	H	A	P	W	D	L	OV	UN	BS	CS
Bayern Munich	L	L	5	0	0	5	4	1	2	0
Schalke	W	D	5	3	1	1	4	1	4	1
Hoffenheim	W	L	5	3	0	2	2	3	2	3
Dortmund	W	L	5	1	1	3	4	1	4	0
Leverkusen	D	L	5	1	2	2	3	2	4	0
RB Leipzig	L	L	1	0	0	1	1	0	1	0
Stuttgart	D	D	6	1	4	1	1	5	3	3
E Frankfurt	L	L	5	2	1	2	2	3	2	3
M'gladbach	L	L	5	2	0	3	3	2	2	1
Hertha Berlin	W	L	4	1	2	1	2	2	4	0
Werder Bremen	W	L	5	3	1	1	3	2	4	1
Augsburg	L	W	5	3	0	2	2	3	2	2
Hannover										
Mainz	W	W	5	2	2	1	3	2	4	0
Freiburg	W	D	4	3	0	1	4	0	4	0
Wolfsburg	L	D	5	2	0	3	3	2	2	1
Fortuna Dusseldorf			2	2	0	0	1	1	0	2
Nurnberg			3	2	1	0	2	1	2	1

Season	Division	Pos	P	W	D	L	F	A	GD	Pts
2017-18	Bundesliga	13	34	10	9	15	44	54	-10	39
2016-17	2.Bundesliga	2	34	19	10	5	51	32	+19	67
2015-16	Bundesliga	18	34	7	4	23	31	62	-31	25

Over/Under 53%/47% 8th   **Both score** 68%/32% 1st

HERTHA BERLIN

Olympiastadion herthabsc.de

	2017-18		Last six seasons at home							
	H	A	P	W	D	L	OV	UN	BS	CS
Bayern Munich	D	D	5	0	2	3	2	3	3	0
Schalke	L	L	5	2	1	2	1	4	1	2
Hoffenheim	D	D	5	1	2	2	2	3	3	1
Dortmund	D	L	5	2	2	1	2	3	2	2
Leverkusen	W	W	5	2	0	3	3	2	3	0
RB Leipzig	L	W	2	0	0	2	2	0	2	0
Stuttgart	W	L	4	3	0	1	2	2	2	1
E Frankfurt	L	W	5	3	1	1	2	3	2	3
M'gladbach	L	L	5	2	0	3	4	1	3	2
Hertha Berlin										
Werder Bremen	D	D	5	1	3	1	2	3	4	0
Augsburg	D	D	5	2	3	0	1	4	1	4
Hannover	D	L	4	1	1	2	3	1	2	0
Mainz	L	L	5	3	0	2	3	2	3	1
Freiburg	D	D	4	1	2	1	1	3	1	2
Wolfsburg	D	D	5	2	2	1	1	4	2	3
Fortuna Dusseldorf			-	-	-	-	-	-	-	-
Nurnberg			1	0	0	1	1	0	1	0

Season	Division	Pos	P	W	D	L	F	A	GD	Pts
2017-18	Bundesliga	10	34	10	13	11	43	46	-3	43
2016-17	Bundesliga	6	34	15	4	15	43	47	-4	49
2015-16	Bundesliga	7	34	14	8	12	42	42	0	50

Over/Under 44%/56% 14th   **Both score** 59%/41% 4th

HOFFENHEIM

Rhein-Neckar Arena achtzehn99.de

	2017-18		Last six seasons at home							
	H	A	P	W	D	L	OV	UN	BS	CS
Bayern Munich	W	L	6	2	0	4	2	4	2	2
Schalke	W	L	6	4	1	1	5	1	5	1
Hoffenheim										
Dortmund	W	L	6	1	4	1	4	2	6	0
Leverkusen	L	D	6	1	1	4	3	3	4	1
RB Leipzig	W	W	2	1	1	0	2	0	1	1
Stuttgart	W	L	5	3	1	1	3	2	3	1
E Frankfurt	D	D	6	2	3	1	2	4	2	3
M'gladbach	L	D	6	2	2	2	5	1	5	1
Hertha Berlin	D	D	5	3	1	1	3	2	4	1
Werder Bremen	W	D	6	1	2	3	4	2	5	1
Augsburg	D	W	6	3	3	0	2	4	2	4
Hannover	W	L	5	5	0	0	4	1	4	1
Mainz	W	W	6	4	1	1	4	2	3	3
Freiburg	D	L	5	2	3	0	4	1	5	0
Wolfsburg	W	D	6	3	2	1	3	3	3	3
Fortuna Dusseldorf			1	1	0	0	1	0	0	1
Nurnberg			2	1	1	0	2	0	2	0

Season	Division	Pos	P	W	D	L	F	A	GD	Pts
2017-18	Bundesliga	3	34	15	10	9	66	48	+18	55
2016-17	Bundesliga	4	34	16	14	4	64	37	+27	62
2015-16	Bundesliga	15	34	9	10	15	39	54	-15	37

Over/Under 56%/44% 6th   **Both score** 62%/38% 3rd

LEVERKUSEN

BayArena bayer04.de

	2017-18		Last six seasons at home							
	H	A	P	W	D	L	OV	UN	BS	CS
Bayern Munich	L	L	6	1	3	2	2	4	3	3
Schalke	L	D	6	2	1	3	2	4	3	2
Hoffenheim	D	W	6	3	1	2	5	1	3	2
Dortmund	D	L	6	1	3	2	2	4	3	2
Leverkusen										
RB Leipzig	D	W	2	0	1	1	2	0	2	0
Stuttgart	L	W	5	4	0	1	4	1	3	1
E Frankfurt	W	W	6	4	1	1	4	2	3	2
M'gladbach	W	W	6	3	2	1	3	3	4	2
Hertha Berlin	L	L	5	4	0	1	4	1	4	0
Werder Bremen	W	D	6	3	2	1	3	3	4	2
Augsburg	D	D	6	3	3	0	2	4	3	3
Hannover	W	D	5	5	0	0	4	1	2	3
Mainz	W	L	6	2	2	1	5	1	3	3
Freiburg	W	D	5	4	1	0	2	3	2	3
Wolfsburg	D	W	6	2	3	1	5	1	5	1
Fortuna Dusseldorf			1	1	0	0	1	0	1	0
Nurnberg			2	2	0	0	1	1	0	2

Season	Division	Pos	P	W	D	L	F	A	GD	Pts
2017-18	Bundesliga	5	34	15	10	9	58	44	+14	55
2016-17	Bundesliga	12	34	11	8	15	53	55	-2	41
2015-16	Bundesliga	3	34	18	6	10	56	40	+16	60

Over/Under 56%/44% 6th   **Both score** 56%/44% 9th

GERMAN BUNDESLIGA

MAINZ

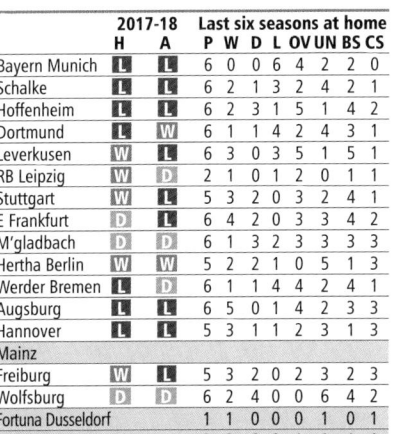

1. FSV Mainz 05 Arena mainz05.de

	2017-18		Last six seasons at home							
	H	A	P	W	D	L	OV	UN	BS	CS
Bayern Munich	L	L	6	0	0	6	4	2	2	0
Schalke	L	L	6	2	1	3	2	4	2	1
Hoffenheim	L	L	6	2	3	1	5	1	4	2
Dortmund	L	W	6	1	1	4	2	4	3	1
Leverkusen	W	L	6	3	0	3	5	1	5	1
RB Leipzig	W	D	2	1	0	1	2	0	1	1
Stuttgart	W	L	5	3	2	0	3	2	4	1
E Frankfurt	D	L	6	4	2	0	3	3	4	2
M'gladbach	D	D	6	1	3	2	3	3	3	3
Hertha Berlin	W	W	5	2	2	1	0	5	1	3
Werder Bremen	L	D	6	1	1	4	4	2	4	1
Augsburg	L	L	6	5	0	1	4	2	3	3
Hannover	L	L	5	3	1	1	2	3	1	3
Mainz										
Freiburg	W	L	5	3	2	0	2	3	2	3
Wolfsburg	D	D	6	2	4	0	0	6	4	2
Fortuna Dusseldorf			1	1	0	0	0	1	0	1
Nurnberg			2	2	0	0	1	1	1	1

Season	Division	Pos	P	W	D	L	F	A	GD	Pts
2017-18	Bundesliga	14	34	9	9	16	38	52	-14	36
2016-17	Bundesliga	15	34	10	7	17	44	55	-11	37
2015-16	Bundesliga	6	34	14	8	12	46	42	+4	50

Over/Under 44%/56% 14th **Both score** 50%/50% 14th

MONCHENGLADBACH

Borussia-Park borussia.de

	2017-18		Last six seasons at home							
	H	A	P	W	D	L	OV	UN	BS	CS
Bayern Munich	W	L	6	2	1	3	3	3	3	1
Schalke	D	D	6	4	1	1	4	2	5	0
Hoffenheim	D	W	6	3	3	0	5	1	6	0
Dortmund	L	L	6	2	1	3	3	3	4	1
Leverkusen	L	L	6	3	1	2	5	1	4	1
RB Leipzig	L	D	2	0	0	2	1	1	1	0
Stuttgart	W	L	5	2	2	1	2	3	3	2
E Frankfurt	L	L	6	3	1	2	3	3	2	3
M'gladbach										
Hertha Berlin	W	W	5	5	0	0	4	1	2	3
Werder Bremen	D	W	6	4	2	0	5	1	6	0
Augsburg	W	D	6	3	1	2	3	3	4	2
Hannover	W	W	5	5	0	0	3	2	2	3
Mainz	D	D	6	3	2	1	2	4	4	2
Freiburg	W	W	5	4	1	0	2	3	2	3
Wolfsburg	W	L	6	4	1	1	3	3	2	4
Fortuna Dusseldorf			1	1	0	0	1	0	1	0
Nurnberg			2	1	0	1	2	0	2	0

Season	Division	Pos	P	W	D	L	F	A	GD	Pts
2017-18	Bundesliga	9	34	13	8	13	47	52	-5	47
2016-17	Bundesliga	9	34	12	9	13	45	49	-4	45
2015-16	Bundesliga	4	34	17	4	13	67	50	+17	55

Over/Under 53%/47% 8th **Both score** 56%/44% 9th

NURNBERG

Stadion Nurnberg fcn.de

	2017-18		Last six seasons at home							
	H	A	P	W	D	L	OV	UN	BS	CS
Bayern Munich			2	0	1	1	0	2	1	0
Schalke			2	1	1	0	1	1	0	2
Hoffenheim			2	2	0	0	2	0	1	1
Dortmund			2	0	2	0	0	2	2	0
Leverkusen			2	0	0	2	1	1	1	0
RB Leipzig			2	2	0	0	1	1	1	1
Stuttgart			3	1	0	2	1	2	1	1
E Frankfurt			2	0	0	2	2	0	2	0
M'gladbach			2	1	0	1	1	1	1	0
Hertha Berlin			1	0	1	0	1	0	1	0
Werder Bremen			2	1	0	1	1	1	1	0
Augsburg			2	0	1	1	0	2	0	1
Hannover			3	1	1	1	1	2	1	1
Mainz			2	1	1	0	1	1	1	0
Freiburg			3	1	1	1	2	1	2	0
Wolfsburg			2	1	1	0	0	2	1	1
Fortuna Dusseldorf	L	W	5	2	0	3	2	3	2	2
Nurnberg										

Season	Division	Pos	P	W	D	L	F	A	GD	Pts
2017-18	2.Bundesliga	2	34	17	9	8	61	39	+22	60
2016-17	2.Bundesliga	12	34	12	6	16	46	52	-6	42
2015-16	2.Bundesliga	3	34	19	8	7	68	41	+27	65

Over/Under 53%/47% 9th **Both score** 62%/38% 7th

RB LEIPZIG

Red Bull Arena dierotenbullen.com

	2017-18		Last six seasons at home							
	H	A	P	W	D	L	OV	UN	BS	CS
Bayern Munich	W	L	2	1	0	1	2	0	2	0
Schalke	W	L	2	2	0	0	2	0	2	0
Hoffenheim	L	L	2	1	0	1	2	0	2	0
Dortmund	D	W	2	1	1	0	0	2	1	1
Leverkusen	L	D	2	1	0	1	1	1	1	1
RB Leipzig										
Stuttgart	W	D	1	1	0	0	0	1	0	1
E Frankfurt	W	L	2	2	0	0	2	0	1	1
M'gladbach	D	W	2	0	2	0	1	1	2	0
Hertha Berlin	L	L	2	1	0	1	1	1	1	1
Werder Bremen	W	D	2	2	0	0	1	1	1	1
Augsburg	W	L	2	2	0	0	1	1	1	1
Hannover	W	W	1	1	0	0	1	0	1	0
Mainz	D	L	2	1	1	0	2	0	2	0
Freiburg	W	L	3	2	1	0	2	1	2	1
Wolfsburg	W	D	2	1	0	1	1	1	1	0
Fortuna Dusseldorf			2	2	0	0	2	0	2	0
Nurnberg			2	2	0	0	2	0	2	0

Season	Division	Pos	P	W	D	L	F	A	GD	Pts
2017-18	Bundesliga	6	34	15	8	11	57	53	+4	53
2016-17	Bundesliga	2	34	20	7	7	66	39	+27	67
2015-16	2.Bundesliga	2	34	20	7	7	54	32	+22	67

Over/Under 62%/38% 2nd **Both score** 68%/32% 1st

SCHALKE

Veltins-Arena schalke04.de

	2017-18		Last six seasons at home							
	H	A	P	W	D	L	OV	UN	BS	CS
Bayern Munich	L	L	6	0	1	5	3	3	2	0
Schalke										
Hoffenheim	W	L	6	5	1	0	4	2	3	3
Dortmund	W	D	6	3	2	1	4	2	5	1
Leverkusen	D	W	6	1	2	3	2	4	3	1
RB Leipzig	W	L	2	1	1	0	0	2	1	1
Stuttgart	W	W	5	3	1	1	4	1	4	1
E Frankfurt	W	D	6	3	2	1	1	5	2	3
M'gladbach	D	D	6	3	2	1	2	4	3	2
Hertha Berlin	W	W	5	5	0	0	1	4	1	4
Werder Bremen	L	W	6	3	1	2	5	1	6	0
Augsburg	W	W	6	5	1	0	4	2	4	2
Hannover	D	L	5	4	1	0	2	3	3	2
Mainz	W	W	6	5	1	0	4	2	2	4
Freiburg	W	W	5	2	2	1	1	4	2	3
Wolfsburg	D	W	6	5	1	0	5	1	4	2
Fortuna Dusseldorf			1	1	0	0	1	0	1	0
Nurnberg			2	2	0	0	1	1	1	1

Season	Division	Pos	P	W	D	L	F	A	GD	Pts
2017-18	Bundesliga	2	34	18	9	7	53	37	+16	63
2016-17	Bundesliga	10	34	11	10	13	45	40	+5	43
2015-16	Bundesliga	5	34	15	7	12	51	49	+2	52

Over/Under 41%/59% 17th **Both score** 53%/47% 11th

STUTTGART

Mercedes-Benz Arena vfb.de

	2017-18		Last six seasons at home							
	H	A	P	W	D	L	OV	UN	BS	CS
Bayern Munich	L	W	5	0	0	5	2	3	2	0
Schalke	L	L	5	2	0	3	3	2	2	0
Hoffenheim	W	L	5	3	0	2	3	2	2	1
Dortmund	W	L	5	1	0	4	5	0	4	0
Leverkusen	L	W	5	0	2	3	2	3	2	0
RB Leipzig	D	L	1	0	1	0	0	1	0	1
Stuttgart										
E Frankfurt	W	L	5	3	1	1	3	2	4	1
M'gladbach	W	L	5	2	0	3	1	4	1	2
Hertha Berlin	W	L	4	2	1	1	1	3	1	3
Werder Bremen	W	L	5	2	2	1	2	3	4	1
Augsburg	D	W	5	1	1	3	2	2	2	1
Hannover	D	D	6	2	1	3	4	2	5	1
Mainz	W	L	5	2	1	2	3	2	3	2
Freiburg	W	W	4	3	1	0	3	1	2	2
Wolfsburg	W	D	5	2	0	3	3	2	2	1
Fortuna Dusseldorf			2	1	1	0	0	2	0	2
Nurnberg			3	1	2	0	1	2	3	0

Season	Division	Pos	P	W	D	L	F	A	GD	Pts
2017-18	Bundesliga	7	34	15	6	13	36	36	0	51
2016-17	2.Bundesliga	1	34	21	6	7	63	37	+26	69
2015-16	Bundesliga	17	34	9	6	19	50	75	-25	33

Over/Under 32%/68% 18th **Both score** 38%/62% 18th

WERDER BREMEN

Weserstadion werder.de

	2017-18		Last six seasons at home							
	H	A	P	W	D	L	OV	UN	BS	CS
Bayern Munich	L	L	6	0	0	6	3	3	1	0
Schalke	L	W	6	1	1	4	4	2	2	1
Hoffenheim	D	L	6	1	4	1	3	3	6	0
Dortmund	D	W	6	1	1	4	5	1	5	0
Leverkusen	D	L	6	3	1	2	4	2	3	2
RB Leipzig	D	L	2	1	1	0	1	1	1	1
Stuttgart	W	L	5	3	2	0	2	3	3	2
E Frankfurt	W	L	6	3	1	2	3	3	3	2
M'gladbach	L	D	6	2	1	3	2	4	2	1
Hertha Berlin	D	D	5	3	2	0	1	4	1	4
Werder Bremen										
Augsburg	L	W	6	2	0	4	4	2	3	1
Hannover	W	L	5	4	1	0	4	1	3	2
Mainz	D	W	6	1	3	2	4	2	5	1
Freiburg	D	L	5	0	3	2	2	3	3	2
Wolfsburg	W	D	6	3	0	3	6	0	5	0
Fortuna Dusseldorf			1	1	0	0	1	0	1	0
Nurnberg			2	0	2	0	1	1	2	0

Season	Division	Pos	P	W	D	L	F	A	GD	Pts
2017-18	Bundesliga	11	34	10	12	12	37	40	-3	42
2016-17	Bundesliga	8	34	13	6	15	61	64	-3	45
2015-16	Bundesliga	13	34	10	8	16	50	65	-15	38

Over/Under 44%/56% 14th **Both score** 53%/47% 11th

WOLFSBURG

Volkswagen Arena vfl-wolfsburg.de

	2017-18		Last six seasons at home							
	H	A	P	W	D	L	OV	UN	BS	CS
Bayern Munich	L	D	6	1	0	5	4	2	3	0
Schalke	D	D	6	2	1	3	3	3	2	2
Hoffenheim	D	L	6	4	2	0	5	1	5	1
Dortmund	L	D	6	2	1	3	6	0	5	0
Leverkusen	D	D	6	4	0	2	6	0	6	0
RB Leipzig	D	L	2	0	1	1	0	2	1	0
Stuttgart	D	L	5	4	1	0	3	2	4	1
E Frankfurt	L	W	6	3	1	2	4	2	4	1
M'gladbach	W	L	6	5	1	0	4	2	4	2
Hertha Berlin	D	D	5	3	1	1	3	2	3	2
Werder Bremen	D	L	6	3	2	1	4	2	4	2
Augsburg	D	L	6	1	3	2	1	5	3	2
Hannover	W	W	5	0	3	2	3	2	4	0
Mainz	D	D	6	2	3	1	2	4	2	3
Freiburg	W	W	5	2	1	2	3	2	2	1
Wolfsburg										
Fortuna Dusseldorf			1	0	1	0	0	1	1	0
Nurnberg			2	1	1	0	2	0	2	0

Season	Division	Pos	P	W	D	L	F	A	GD	Pts
2017-18	Bundesliga	16	34	6	15	13	36	48	-12	33
2016-17	Bundesliga	16	34	10	7	17	34	52	-18	37
2015-16	Bundesliga	8	34	12	9	13	47	49	-2	45

Over/Under 47%/53% 11th **Both score** 59%/41% 4th

Bundesliga 2017-18

Pos	H	A		P	W	D	L	F	A	W	D	L	F	A	GD	Pts
					Home					Away						
1	1	1	Bayern Munich (CL)	34	14	2	1	56	15	13	1	3	36	13	64	84
2	3	2	Schalke (CL)	34	10	5	2	27	15	8	4	5	26	22	16	63
3	2	9	Hoffenheim (CL)	34	11	4	2	38	16	4	6	7	28	32	18	55
4	5	4	B Dortmund (CL)	34	9	4	4	40	21	6	6	5	24	26	17	55
5	8	3	B Leverkusen (EL)	34	8	5	4	29	19	7	5	5	29	25	14	55
6	6	5	RB Leipzig (EL)	34	9	4	4	34	26	6	4	7	23	27	4	53
7	4	11	Stuttgart	34	10	4	3	18	9	5	2	10	18	27	0	51
8	9	7	E Frankfurt (EL)	34	8	4	5	26	19	6	3	8	19	26	0	49
9	7	13	B M'gladbach	34	9	4	4	28	20	4	4	9	19	32	-5	47
10	16	6	Hertha Berlin	34	5	7	5	23	27	5	6	6	20	19	-3	43
11	12	10	Werder Bremen	34	6	7	4	20	17	4	5	8	17	23	-3	42
12	14	8	Augsburg	34	6	4	7	24	24	4	7	6	19	22	-3	41
13	10	14	Hannover	34	8	3	6	28	25	2	6	9	16	29	-10	39
14	13	15	Mainz	34	7	3	7	22	21	2	6	9	16	31	-14	36
15	11	17	Freiburg	34	7	6	4	17	17	1	6	10	15	39	-24	36
16	17	12	Wolfsburg*	34	3	8	6	23	25	3	7	7	13	23	-12	33
17	15	16	Hamburg (R)	34	6	4	7	17	19	2	3	12	12	34	-24	31
18	18	18	Cologne (R)	34	3	5	9	20	30	2	2	13	15	40	-35	22

*Wolfsburg avoided relegation by winning relegation playoff

Bundesliga results 2017-18

	Augsburg	Bayern Munich	Cologne	Dortmund	Ein Frankfurt	Freiburg	Hamburg	Hannover	Hertha Berlin	Hoffenheim	Leverkusen	Mainz	M'gladbach	RB Leipzig	Schalke	Stuttgart	Werder Bremen	Wolfsburg
Augsburg		1-4	3-0	1-2	3-0	3-3	1-0	1-2	1-1	0-2	1-1	2-0	2-2	1-0	1-2	0-1	1-3	2-1
Bayern Munich	3-0		1-0	6-0	4-1	5-0	6-0	3-1	0-0	5-2	3-1	4-0	5-1	2-0	2-1	1-4	4-2	2-2
Cologne	1-1	1-3		2-3	0-1	3-4	1-3	1-1	0-2	0-3	2-0	1-1	2-1	1-2	2-2	2-3	0-0	1-0
Dortmund	1-1	1-3	5-0		3-2	2-2	2-0	1-0	2-0	2-1	4-0	1-2	6-1	2-3	4-4	3-0	1-2	0-0
Eintacht Frankfurt	1-2	0-1	4-2	2-2		1-1	3-0	1-0	0-3	1-1	0-1	3-0	2-0	2-1	2-2	2-1	2-1	0-1
Freiburg	2-0	0-4	3-2	0-0	0-0		0-0	1-1	1-1	3-2	0-0	2-1	1-0	2-1	0-1	1-2	1-0	0-2
Hamburg	1-0	0-1	0-2	0-3	1-2	1-0		1-1	1-2	3-0	1-2	0-0	2-1	0-2	3-2	3-1	1-0	0-0
Hannover	1-3	0-3	0-0	4-2	1-2	2-1	2-0		3-1	2-0	4-4	3-2	0-1	2-3	1-0	1-1	2-1	0-1
Hertha Berlin	2-2	2-2	2-1	1-1	1-2	0-0	2-1	3-1		1-1	2-1	0-2	2-4	2-6	0-2	2-0	1-1	0-0
Hoffenheim	2-2	2-0	6-0	3-1	1-1	1-1	2-0	3-1	1-1		1-4	4-2	1-3	4-0	2-0	1-0	1-0	3-0
Leverkusen	0-0	1-3	2-1	1-1	4-1	4-0	3-0	3-2	0-2	2-2		2-0	2-0	2-2	0-2	0-1	1-0	2-2
Mainz	1-3	0-2	1-0	0-2	1-1	2-0	3-2	0-1	1-0	2-3	3-1		0-0	3-0	0-1	3-2	1-2	1-1
M'gladbach	2-0	2-1	1-0	0-1	0-1	3-1	3-1	2-1	2-1	3-3	1-5	1-1		0-1	1-1	2-0	2-2	3-0
RB Leipzig	2-0	2-1	1-2	1-1	2-1	4-1	1-1	2-1	2-3	2-5	1-4	2-2	2-2		3-1	1-0	2-0	4-1
Schalke	3-2	0-3	2-2	2-0	1-0	0-0	2-0	1-1	1-0	2-1	1-1	2-0	1-1	2-0		3-1	1-2	1-1
Stuttgart	0-0	0-1	2-1	2-1	1-0	3-0	1-1	1-1	1-0	2-0	0-2	1-0	1-0	0-0	0-2		2-0	1-0
Werder Bremen	0-3	0-2	3-1	1-1	2-1	0-0	1-0	4-0	0-0	1-1	0-0	2-2	0-2	1-1	1-2	1-0		3-1
Wolfsburg	0-0	1-2	4-1	0-3	1-3	3-1	1-3	1-1	3-3	1-1	1-2	1-1	3-0	1-1	0-1	1-1	1-1	

Top scorers

	Team	Goals scored	
R Lewandowski	Bayern	29	▖▖▖▖▖▖▖▖▖▖▖▖▖▖▖
N Petersen	Freiburg	15	▖▖▖▖▖▖▖▖
N Fullkrug	Hannover	14	▖▖▖▖▖▖▖
M Uth	Hoffenheim	14	▖▖▖▖▖▖▖
K Volland	Leverkusen	14	▖▖▖▖▖▖▖

Over 2.5 goals top five

	H	A	%
Bayern Munich	14	11	74%
Cologne	9	12	62%
Dortmund	12	9	62%
RB Leipzig	12	9	62%
E Frankfurt	10	10	59%

Both to score top five

	H	A	%
Hannover	10	13	68%
RB Leipzig	14	9	68%
Hoffenheim	9	12	62%
Cologne, Dortmund, Hertha, Frankfurt, Wolfsburg			59%

VORSPRUNG DURCH TECHNIK SOCCERBASE.COM

ALAVES

Estadio de Mendizorroza · deportivoalaves.com

	2017-18 H	A	Last six seasons at home P	W	D	L	OV	UN	BS	CS
Barcelona	L	L	2	0	0	2	1	1	0	0
Atl Madrid	L	L	2	0	1	1	0	2	0	1
Real Madrid	L	L	2	0	0	2	2	0	2	0
Valencia	L	L	2	1	0	1	2	0	2	0
Villarreal	L	W	2	1	0	1	2	0	1	0
Betis	L	L	3	1	0	2	2	1	2	1
Sevilla	W	L	2	1	1	0	0	2	1	1
Getafe	W	L	1	1	0	0	0	1	0	1
Eibar	L	W	3	0	1	2	1	2	1	1
Girona	L	W	4	1	1	2	2	2	2	1
Espanyol	W	D	2	1	0	1	0	2	0	1
Sociedad	L	L	2	1	0	1	0	2	0	1
Celta	W	L	2	2	0	0	2	0	2	0
Alaves										
Levante	W	W	1	1	0	0	0	1	0	1
Ath Bilbao	W	L	2	2	0	0	1	1	1	1
Leganes	D	L	4	1	3	0	2	2	2	2
Vallecano	-	-	-	-	-	-	-	-	-	-
Huesca			1	1	0	0	0	1	0	1
Valladolid			2	1	0	1	1	1	1	0

Season	Division	Pos	P	W	D	L	F	A	GD	Pts
2017-18	La Liga	14	38	15	2	21	40	50	-10	47
2016-17	La Liga	9	38	14	13	11	41	43	-2	55
2015-16	Liga Segunda	1	42	21	12	9	49	35	+14	75

Over/Under 47%/53% 13th **Both score** 37%/63% 17th

ATHLETIC BILBAO

San Mames · athletic-club.net

	2017-18 H	A	Last six seasons at home P	W	D	L	OV	UN	BS	CS
Barcelona	L	L	6	1	1	4	2	4	2	1
Atl Madrid	L	L	6	1	1	4	5	1	4	1
Real Madrid	D	D	6	1	2	3	3	3	3	2
Valencia	D	L	6	3	3	0	2	4	5	1
Villarreal	D	W	5	3	2	0	1	4	1	4
Betis	W	W	5	4	0	1	4	1	4	1
Sevilla	W	L	6	6	0	0	4	2	4	2
Getafe	D	D	5	3	1	1	3	2	2	3
Eibar	D	W	4	2	2	0	2	2	3	1
Girona	W	L	1	1	0	0	0	1	0	1
Espanyol	L	D	6	3	0	3	4	2	3	1
Sociedad	D	L	6	1	3	2	2	4	4	1
Celta	D	L	6	4	2	0	3	3	5	1
Alaves	W	L	2	1	1	0	0	2	0	2
Ath Bilbao										
Levante	L	W	5	3	0	2	3	2	2	2
Leganes	W	L	2	1	1	0	0	2	1	1
Vallecano			4	3	0	1	2	2	2	2
Huesca	-	-	-	-	-	-	-	-	-	-
Valladolid			2	2	0	0	1	1	1	1

Season	Division	Pos	P	W	D	L	F	A	GD	Pts
2017-18	La Liga	16	38	10	13	15	41	49	-8	43
2016-17	La Liga	7	38	19	6	13	53	43	+10	63
2015-16	La Liga	5	38	18	8	12	58	45	+13	62

Over/Under 34%/66% 17th **Both score** 50%/50% 7th

ATLETICO MADRID

Wanda Metropolitano · clubatleticodemadrid.com

	2017-18 H	A	Last six seasons at home P	W	D	L	OV	UN	BS	CS
Barcelona	D	L	6	0	2	4	3	3	4	1
Atl Madrid										
Real Madrid	D	D	6	1	3	2	4	2	3	2
Valencia	W	D	6	4	2	0	3	3	3	3
Villarreal	D	L	5	1	2	2	0	5	1	2
Betis	D	W	5	4	1	0	2	3	1	4
Sevilla	W	W	6	4	2	0	3	3	2	4
Getafe	W	W	5	5	0	0	1	4	0	5
Eibar	D	W	4	3	1	0	3	1	3	1
Girona	D	D	1	0	1	0	0	1	1	0
Espanyol	L	L	6	4	1	1	0	6	0	5
Sociedad	W	L	6	5	0	1	3	3	1	4
Celta	W	W	6	5	1	0	4	2	3	3
Alaves	W	W	2	1	1	0	0	2	1	1
Levante	W	W	5	5	0	0	3	2	2	3
Ath Bilbao	W	W	6	5	1	0	3	3	2	4
Leganes	W	D	2	2	0	0	1	1	0	2
Vallecano			4	4	0	0	3	1	2	2
Huesca	-	-	-	-	-	-	-	-	-	-
Valladolid			2	2	0	0	2	0	1	1

Season	Division	Pos	P	W	D	L	F	A	GD	Pts
2017-18	La Liga	2	38	23	10	5	58	22	+36	79
2016-17	La Liga	3	38	23	9	6	70	27	+43	78
2015-16	La Liga	3	38	28	4	6	63	18	+45	88

Over/Under 34%/66% 17th **Both score** 29%/71% 20th

BARCELONA

Camp Nou · fcbarcelona.cat

	2017-18 H	A	Last six seasons at home P	W	D	L	OV	UN	BS	CS
Barcelona										
Atl Madrid	W	D	6	4	2	0	3	3	5	1
Real Madrid	D	W	6	2	3	1	5	1	6	0
Valencia	W	D	6	4	0	2	4	2	4	2
Villarreal	W	W	5	5	0	0	5	0	4	1
Betis	W	W	5	5	0	0	4	1	3	2
Sevilla	W	D	6	6	0	0	6	0	5	1
Getafe	D	W	5	3	2	0	4	1	2	3
Eibar	W	W	4	4	0	0	4	0	3	1
Girona	W	W	1	1	0	0	1	0	1	0
Espanyol	W	D	6	6	0	0	5	1	2	4
Sociedad	W	W	6	6	0	0	4	2	3	3
Celta	D	D	6	4	1	1	5	1	3	2
Alaves	W	W	2	1	0	1	2	0	2	0
Levante	W	L	5	5	0	0	4	1	1	4
Ath Bilbao	W	W	6	6	0	0	4	2	2	4
Leganes	W	W	2	2	0	0	2	0	2	0
Vallecano			4	4	0	0	4	0	3	1
Huesca	-	-	-	-	-	-	-	-	-	-
Valladolid			2	2	0	0	2	0	2	0

Season	Division	Pos	P	W	D	L	F	A	GD	Pts
2017-18	La Liga	1	38	28	9	1	99	29	+70	93
2016-17	La Liga	2	38	28	6	4	116	37	+79	90
2015-16	La Liga	1	38	29	4	5	112	29	+83	91

Over/Under 61%/39% 4th **Both score** 50%/50% 7th

BETIS

Benito Villamarin — realbetisbalompie.es

	2017-18 H	A	Last six seasons at home P	W	D	L	OV	UN	BS	CS
Barcelona	L	L	5	0	1	4	3	2	3	0
Atl Madrid	L	D	5	0	1	4	1	4	2	0
Real Madrid	L	W	5	1	1	3	3	2	3	1
Valencia	L	L	5	3	1	1	2	3	2	3
Villarreal	W	L	4	2	1	1	1	3	2	1
Betis										
Sevilla	D	W	5	0	3	2	3	2	3	1
Getafe	D	W	4	2	2	0	2	2	2	2
Eibar	W	L	3	2	0	1	1	2	0	2
Girona	D	W	2	1	1	0	2	0	2	0
Espanyol	W	L	5	3	0	2	2	3	1	3
Sociedad	D	D	5	2	1	2	1	4	1	3
Celta	W	L	5	2	2	1	3	2	4	1
Alaves	W	W	3	1	0	2	2	1	2	1
Levante	W	W	4	3	1	0	1	3	0	4
Ath Bilbao	L	L	5	1	1	3	1	4	2	1
Leganes	W	L	5	2	0	1	2	1	2	1
Vallecano			3	0	2	1	3	0	3	0
Huesca			-	-	-	-	-	-	-	-
Valladolid			3	2	1	0	2	1	1	2

Season	Division	Pos	P	W	D	L	F	A	GD	Pts
2017-18	La Liga	6	38	18	6	14	60	61	-1	60
2016-17	La Liga	15	38	10	9	19	41	64	-23	39
2015-16	La Liga	10	38	11	12	15	34	52	-18	45

Over/Under 53%/47% 9th   **Both score** 42%/58% 12th

CELTA VIGO

Estadio Municipal de Balaidos — celtavigo.net

	2017-18 H	A	Last six seasons at home P	W	D	L	OV	UN	BS	CS
Barcelona	D	D	6	2	2	2	5	1	4	0
Atl Madrid	L	L	6	1	0	5	2	4	1	1
Real Madrid	D	L	6	1	1	4	5	1	5	1
Valencia	D	L	6	2	2	2	3	5	5	0
Villarreal	L	L	5	0	2	3	1	4	1	2
Betis	W	L	5	2	1	2	2	3	3	0
Sevilla	W	L	6	3	2	1	2	4	2	3
Getafe	D	L	5	2	3	0	2	3	4	1
Eibar	W	W	4	2	0	2	1	3	1	1
Girona	D	L	1	0	1	0	1	0	1	0
Espanyol	D	L	6	3	3	0	4	2	4	2
Sociedad	L	W	6	1	4	1	4	2	5	1
Celta										
Alaves	W	L	2	2	0	0	0	2	0	2
Levante	W	W	5	3	1	1	3	2	3	1
Ath Bilbao	W	D	6	1	2	3	3	3	3	1
Leganes	W	L	2	1	0	1	0	2	0	1
Vallecano			4	2	0	2	2	2	1	1
Huesca			-	-	-	-	-	-	-	-
Valladolid			2	2	0	0	2	0	2	0

Season	Division	Pos	P	W	D	L	F	A	GD	Pts
2017-18	La Liga	13	38	13	10	15	59	60	-1	49
2016-17	La Liga	13	38	13	6	19	53	69	-16	45
2015-16	La Liga	6	38	17	9	12	51	59	-8	60

Over/Under 66%/34% 3rd   **Both score** 63%/37% 1st

EIBAR

Estadio Municipal de Ipurua — sdeibar.com

	2017-18 H	A	Last six seasons at home P	W	D	L	OV	UN	BS	CS
Barcelona	L	L	4	0	0	4	2	2	0	0
Atl Madrid	L	D	4	0	0	4	1	3	1	0
Real Madrid	L	L	4	0	0	4	3	1	2	0
Valencia	W	D	4	2	1	1	3	2	1	
Villarreal	W	L	4	2	1	1	2	2	3	1
Betis	W	L	3	2	1	0	2	1	2	1
Sevilla	W	L	4	1	2	1	2	2	4	0
Getafe	L	D	3	2	0	1	2	1	2	0
Eibar										
Girona	W	W	2	1	0	1	2	0	1	0
Espanyol	W	W	4	2	1	1	2	2	3	0
Sociedad	D	L	4	3	1	0	1	3	1	3
Celta	L	L	4	1	1	2	1	3	1	1
Alaves	L	W	3	1	1	1	0	3	0	2
Levante	D	L	3	1	2	0	2	1	2	1
Ath Bilbao	L	D	4	1	0	3	0	4	0	1
Leganes	W		2	2	0	0	0	2	0	2
Vallecano			2	1	0	1	1	1	1	1
Huesca			-	-	-	-	-	-	-	-
Valladolid			-	-	-	-	-	-	-	-

Season	Division	Pos	P	W	D	L	F	A	GD	Pts
2017-18	La Liga	9	38	14	9	15	44	50	-6	51
2016-17	La Liga	10	38	15	9	14	56	51	+5	54
2015-16	La Liga	14	38	11	10	17	49	61	-12	43

Over/Under 47%/53% 13th   **Both score** 42%/58% 12th

ESPANYOL

Estadi Cornella-El Prat — rcdespanyol.com

	2017-18 H	A	Last six seasons at home P	W	D	L	OV	UN	BS	CS
Barcelona	D	L	6	0	2	4	1	5	1	1
Atl Madrid	W	W	6	2	1	3	1	5	1	3
Real Madrid	W	L	6	1	1	4	2	4	2	1
Valencia	L	L	6	2	1	3	3	3	3	1
Villarreal	D	D	5	0	4	1	2	3	4	1
Betis	W	L	5	3	1	1	2	3	1	3
Sevilla	D	D	6	2	1	3	5	1	4	1
Getafe	W	L	5	3	0	2	0	5	0	3
Eibar	L	L	4	1	1	2	3	1	3	0
Girona	L	W	1	0	0	1	0	0	1	0
Espanyol										
Sociedad	W	D	6	2	1	3	5	1	4	1
Celta	W	D	6	4	1	1	1	5	2	3
Alaves	D	L	2	1	1	0	0	2	0	2
Levante	D	D	5	2	3	0	2	3	3	2
Ath Bilbao	D	W	6	3	3	0	3	3	4	2
Leganes	L	L	2	1	0	1	1	1	0	1
Vallecano			4	2	2	0	3	1	4	0
Huesca			-	-	-	-	-	-	-	-
Valladolid			2	1	1	0	1	1	1	1

Season	Division	Pos	P	W	D	L	F	A	GD	Pts
2017-18	La Liga	11	38	12	13	13	36	42	-6	49
2016-17	La Liga	8	38	15	11	12	49	50	-1	56
2015-16	La Liga	13	38	12	7	19	49	74	-34	43

Over/Under 29%/71% 20th   **Both score** 39%/61% 14th

GETAFE

Coliseum Alfonso Perez — getafecf.com

	2017-18 H	A	Last six seasons at home P	W	D	L	OV	UN	BS	CS
Barcelona	L	D	5	0	1	4	3	2	3	1
Atl Madrid	L	L	5	0	1	4	0	5	0	1
Real Madrid	L	L	5	1	0	4	5	0	3	0
Valencia	W	W	5	1	1	3	2	3	1	1
Villarreal	W	L	4	2	1	1	1	3	1	2
Betis	L	D	4	2	0	2	2	2	2	1
Sevilla	L	D	5	2	2	1	1	4	3	1
Getafe										
Eibar	D	W	3	0	3	0	0	3	2	1
Girona	D	L	2	0	1	1	0	2	1	0
Espanyol	W	L	5	3	1	1	2	3	2	2
Sociedad	W	W	5	2	2	1	3	2	4	0
Celta	W	D	5	4	0	1	3	2	2	2
Alaves	W	W	1	1	0	0	1	0	1	0
Levante	L	D	6	3	0	3	1	5	0	3
Ath Bilbao	D	D	5	1	1	3	2	3	2	1
Leganes	D	W	1	0	1	0	0	1	0	1
Vallecano			5	1	1	3	2	3	3	1
Huesca			1	0	1	0	0	1	1	0
Valladolid			3	2	1	0	2	1	2	1

Season	Division	Pos	P	W	D	L	F	A	GD	Pts
2017-18	La Liga	8	38	15	10	13	42	33	+9	55
2016-17	Liga Segunda	3	42	18	14	10	55	43	+12	68
2015-16	La Liga	19	38	9	9	20	37	67	-30	36

Over/Under 37%/63% 16th **Both score** 39%/61% 14th

GIRONA

Estadi Montilivi — gironafc.cat

	2017-18 H	A	Last six seasons at home P	W	D	L	OV	UN	BS	CS
Barcelona	L	L	1	0	0	1	1	0	0	0
Atl Madrid	D	D	1	0	1	0	1	0	1	0
Real Madrid	W	L	1	1	0	0	1	0	1	0
Valencia	L	L	1	0	0	1	0	1	0	0
Villarreal	L	W	2	1	0	1	1	1	1	1
Betis	L	D	2	0	0	2	1	1	1	0
Sevilla	L	L	1	0	0	1	0	1	0	0
Getafe	W	D	2	2	0	0	1	1	1	1
Eibar	L	L	2	0	1	1	1	1	2	0
Girona										
Espanyol	L	W	1	0	0	1	0	1	0	0
Sociedad	D	L	1	0	1	0	0	1	1	0
Celta	W	D	1	1	0	0	0	1	0	1
Alaves	L	W	4	2	1	1	2	2	2	2
Levante	D	W	2	1	1	0	1	1	2	0
Ath Bilbao	W	L	1	1	0	0	0	1	0	1
Leganes	W	D	3	2	1	0	2	1	2	1
Vallecano			1	0	0	1	0	1	0	1
Huesca			3	2	1	0	2	1	2	1
Valladolid			3	3	0	0	2	1	2	1

Season	Division	Pos	P	W	D	L	F	A	GD	Pts
2017-18	La Liga	10	38	14	9	15	50	59	-9	51
2016-17	Liga Segunda	2	42	20	10	12	65	45	+20	70
2015-16	Liga Segunda	4	42	17	15	10	46	28	+18	66

Over/Under 50%/50% 11th **Both score** 50%/50% 7th

HUESCA

Estadio El Alcoraz — sdhuesca.es

	2017-18 H	A	Last six seasons at home P	W	D	L	OV	UN	BS	CS
Barcelona	-	-	-	-	-	-	-	-	-	-
Atl Madrid	-	-	-	-	-	-	-	-	-	-
Real Madrid	-	-	-	-	-	-	-	-	-	-
Valencia	-	-	-	-	-	-	-	-	-	-
Villarreal			1	0	0	1	0	1	0	0
Betis	-	-	-	-	-	-	-	-	-	-
Sevilla	-	-	-	-	-	-	-	-	-	-
Getafe			1	0	1	0	0	1	0	1
Eibar	-	-	-	-	-	-	-	-	-	-
Girona			3	0	1	2	1	2	1	1
Espanyol	-	-	-	-	-	-	-	-	-	-
Sociedad	-	-	-	-	-	-	-	-	-	-
Celta	-	-	-	-	-	-	-	-	-	-
Alaves			1	0	0	1	1	0	1	0
Levante			1	0	0	1	0	1	0	0
Ath Bilbao	-	-	-	-	-	-	-	-	-	-
Leganes			1	0	1	0	0	1	1	0
Vallecano	W	L	2	2	0	0	1	1	1	1
Huesca										
Valladolid	W	L	3	2	1	0	0	3	1	2

Season	Division	Pos	P	W	D	L	F	A	GD	Pts
2017-18	Liga Segunda	2	42	21	12	9	61	40	+21	75
2016-17	Liga Segunda	6	42	16	15	11	53	43	+10	63
2015-16	Liga Segunda	12	42	14	13	15	48	49	-1	55

Over/Under 43%/57% 17th **Both score** 50%/50% 16th

LEGANES

Estadio de Butarque — deportivoleganes.com

	2017-18 H	A	Last six seasons at home P	W	D	L	OV	UN	BS	CS
Barcelona	L	L	2	0	0	2	2	0	1	0
Atl Madrid	D	L	2	0	2	0	0	2	0	2
Real Madrid	L	L	2	0	0	2	0	2	2	0
Valencia	L	L	2	0	0	2	1	1	1	0
Villarreal	W	L	2	1	1	0	1	1	1	1
Betis	W	L	3	3	0	0	2	1	1	2
Sevilla	W	L	2	1	0	2	0	2	2	0
Getafe	L	D	1	0	0	1	1	0	1	0
Eibar	L	L	2	0	1	1	0	2	1	0
Girona	D	L	3	0	2	1	2	1	2	1
Espanyol	W	W	2	1	0	1	1	1	1	0
Sociedad	W	L	2	1	0	1	0	2	0	1
Celta	W	L	2	1	0	1	0	2	0	1
Alaves	W	D	4	2	2	0	0	4	2	2
Levante	W	D	1	0	0	1	1	0	0	0
Ath Bilbao	W	L	2	1	1	0	0	2	0	2
Leganes										
Vallecano	-	-	-	-	-	-	-	-	-	-
Huesca			1	0	0	1	1	0	1	0
Valladolid			2	2	0	0	1	1	0	2

Season	Division	Pos	P	W	D	L	F	A	GD	Pts
2017-18	La Liga	17	38	12	7	19	34	51	-17	43
2016-17	La Liga	17	38	8	11	19	36	55	-19	35
2015-16	Liga Segunda	2	42	20	14	8	59	34	+25	74

Over/Under 47%/53% 13th **Both score** 34%/66% 18th

LEVANTE

Ciutat de Valencia — levanteud.com

	2017-18 H	A	Last six seasons at home P	W	D	L	OV	UN	BS	CS
Barcelona	W	L	5	1	1	3	3	2	2	0
Atl Madrid	L	L	5	2	2	1	3	2	3	1
Real Madrid	D	D	5	0	1	4	5	0	4	0
Valencia	D	L	5	4	1	0	1	4	2	3
Villarreal	W	L	4	2	0	2	1	3	0	2
Betis	L	L	4	0	1	3	1	3	2	0
Sevilla	W	D	5	2	2	1	2	3	3	2
Getafe	D	W	6	1	5	0	1	5	3	3
Eibar	W	D	3	2	1	0	3	0	3	0
Girona	L	D	2	1	0	1	2	0	2	0
Espanyol	D	D	5	3	2	0	4	1	4	1
Sociedad	W	L	5	2	2	1	3	2	2	2
Celta	L	L	5	0	0	5	1	4	1	0
Alaves	L	L	1	0	0	1	0	1	0	0
Levante										
Ath Bilbao	L	W	5	1	1	3	4	1	4	0
Leganes	D	W	1	0	1	0	0	1	0	1
Vallecano			5	2	1	2	2	3	2	2
Huesca			1	0	0	1	1	0	1	0
Valladolid			3	2	1	0	2	1	3	0

Season	Division	Pos	P	W	D	L	F	A	GD	Pts
2017-18	La Liga	15	38	11	13	14	44	58	-14	46
2016-17	Liga Segunda	1	42	25	9	8	57	32	+25	84
2015-16	La Liga	20	38	8	8	22	37	70	-33	32

Over/Under 55%/45% 6th   **Both score** 50%/50% 7th

REAL MADRID

Santiago Bernabeu — realmadrid.com

	2017-18 H	A	Last six seasons at home P	W	D	L	OV	UN	BS	CS
Barcelona	L	D	6	2	0	4	6	0	4	0
Atl Madrid	D	D	6	1	2	3	1	5	3	1
Real Madrid										
Valencia	D	W	6	2	4	0	5	1	6	0
Villarreal	L	D	5	2	2	1	2	3	3	1
Betis	L	W	5	4	0	1	4	1	3	1
Sevilla	W	L	6	6	0	0	6	0	4	2
Getafe	W	W	5	5	0	0	5	0	4	1
Eibar	W	W	4	3	1	0	3	1	1	3
Girona	W	L	1	1	0	0	1	0	1	0
Espanyol	W	L	6	5	1	0	4	2	2	4
Sociedad	W	W	6	6	0	0	6	0	5	1
Celta	W	D	6	6	0	0	5	1	2	4
Alaves	W	W	2	2	0	0	2	0	0	2
Levante	D	D	5	4	1	0	3	2	2	3
Ath Bilbao	D	D	6	5	1	0	5	1	5	1
Leganes	W	W	2	2	0	0	2	0	1	1
Vallecano			4	4	0	0	3	1	2	2
Huesca			-	-	-	-	-	-	-	-
Valladolid			2	2	0	0	2	0	1	1

Season	Division	Pos	P	W	D	L	F	A	GD	Pts
2017-18	La Liga	3	38	22	10	6	94	44	+50	76
2016-17	La Liga	1	38	29	6	3	106	41	+65	93
2015-16	La Liga	2	38	28	6	4	110	34	+76	90

Over/Under 76%/24% 1st   **Both score** 63%/37% 1st

SEVILLA

Ramon Sanchez Pizjuan — sevillafc.es

	2017-18 H	A	Last six seasons at home P	W	D	L	OV	UN	BS	CS
Barcelona	D	L	6	1	2	3	6	0	6	0
Atl Madrid	L	L	6	1	1	4	3	3	2	2
Real Madrid	W	L	6	5	0	1	5	1	5	1
Valencia	L	L	6	3	2	1	2	4	3	2
Villarreal	D	W	5	2	3	0	3	2	3	2
Betis	L	D	5	4	0	1	3	2	2	3
Sevilla										
Getafe	D	W	5	4	1	0	3	2	2	3
Eibar	W	L	4	3	1	0	1	3	0	4
Girona	W	W	1	1	0	0	0	1	0	1
Espanyol	D	W	6	5	1	0	4	2	4	2
Sociedad	W	L	6	3	1	2	2	4	3	3
Celta	W	L	6	4	0	2	4	2	4	1
Alaves	W	L	2	2	0	0	1	1	1	1
Levante	D	L	5	1	3	1	2	3	3	2
Ath Bilbao	W	L	6	5	1	0	1	5	2	4
Leganes	W	L	2	1	1	0	1	1	2	0
Vallecano			4	4	0	0	3	1	3	1
Huesca			-	-	-	-	-	-	-	-
Valladolid			2	1	0	1	2	0	2	0

Season	Division	Pos	P	W	D	L	F	A	GD	Pts
2017-18	La Liga	7	38	17	7	14	49	58	-9	58
2016-17	La Liga	4	38	21	9	8	69	49	+20	72
2015-16	La Liga	7	38	14	10	14	51	50	+1	52

Over/Under 53%/47% 9th   **Both score** 45%/55% 11th

REAL SOCIEDAD

Anoeta — realsociedad.com

	2017-18 H	A	Last six seasons at home P	W	D	L	OV	UN	BS	CS
Barcelona	L	L	6	4	1	1	3	3	4	2
Atl Madrid	W	L	6	3	0	3	3	3	2	2
Real Madrid	L	L	6	1	1	4	5	1	3	0
Valencia	L	L	6	4	1	1	3	3	4	2
Villarreal	W	L	5	1	1	3	2	3	1	2
Betis	D	D	5	3	2	0	4	1	4	1
Sevilla	W	L	6	4	1	1	4	2	4	1
Getafe	L	L	5	1	1	3	3	2	4	1
Eibar	W	D	4	3	1	0	3	1	3	1
Girona	W	D	1	1	0	0	1	0	0	1
Espanyol	D	L	6	2	2	2	4	2	4	1
Sociedad										
Celta	L	W	6	3	1	2	4	2	5	1
Alaves	W	W	2	2	0	0	2	0	1	1
Levante	W	L	5	2	3	0	2	3	2	3
Ath Bilbao	W	D	6	3	2	1	1	5	2	3
Leganes	W	L	2	1	1	0	1	1	2	0
Vallecano			4	2	0	2	3	1	2	1
Huesca			-	-	-	-	-	-	-	-
Valladolid			2	2	0	0	1	1	1	1

Season	Division	Pos	P	W	D	L	F	A	GD	Pts
2017-18	La Liga	12	38	14	7	17	66	59	+7	49
2016-17	La Liga	6	38	19	7	12	59	53	+6	64
2015-16	La Liga	9	38	13	9	16	45	48	-3	48

Over/Under 68%/32% 2nd   **Both score** 58%/42% 3rd

VALENCIA

Mestalla — valenciafc.com

	2017-18 H	A	Last six seasons at home P	W	D	L	OV	UN	BS	CS
Barcelona	D	L	6	0	3	3	2	4	5	0
Atl Madrid	D	L	6	2	1	3	2	4	2	2
Real Madrid	L	D	6	2	1	3	6	0	5	0
Valencia										
Villarreal	L	L	5	1	1	3	2	3	2	1
Betis	W	W	5	3	1	1	3	2	1	4
Sevilla	W	W	6	5	1	0	4	2	3	3
Getafe	L	L	5	2	1	2	4	1	4	1
Eibar	D	L	4	2	1	1	3	1	1	2
Girona	W	W	1	1	0	0	1	0	1	0
Espanyol	W	W	6	5	1	0	5	1	5	1
Sociedad	W	W	6	2	0	4	2	4	4	1
Celta	W	D	6	4	1	1	4	2	5	0
Alaves	W	W	2	2	0	0	2	0	2	0
Levante	W	D	5	4	1	0	4	1	2	3
Ath Bilbao	W	D	6	3	2	1	3	3	3	2
Leganes	W	W	2	2	0	0	1	1	0	2
Vallecano			4	2	1	1	2	2	1	2
Huesca			-	-	-	-	-	-	-	-
Valladolid			2	1	1	0	2	0	2	0

Season	Division	Pos	P	W	D	L	F	A	GD	Pts
2017-18	La Liga	4	38	22	7	9	65	38	+27	73
2016-17	La Liga	12	38	13	7	18	56	65	-9	46
2015-16	La Liga	12	38	11	11	16	46	48	-2	44

Over/Under 55%/45% 6th **Both score** 58%/42% 3rd

VALLADOLID

Nuevo Jose Zorrilla — realvalladolid.es

	2017-18 H	A	Last six seasons at home P	W	D	L	OV	UN	BS	CS
Barcelona			2	1	0	1	1	1	1	1
Atl Madrid			2	0	0	2	1	1	0	0
Real Madrid			2	0	1	1	1	1	2	0
Valencia			2	0	2	0	0	2	1	1
Villarreal			1	1	0	0	0	1	0	1
Betis			3	0	2	1	0	3	0	2
Sevilla			2	0	2	0	1	1	2	0
Getafe			3	3	0	0	1	2	1	2
Eibar			-	-	-	-	-	-	-	-
Girona			3	2	1	0	2	1	2	1
Espanyol			2	1	1	0	0	2	1	1
Sociedad			2	0	2	0	2	0	2	0
Celta			2	1	0	1	1	1	0	1
Alaves			2	1	0	1	1	1	1	1
Levante			3	1	1	1	1	2	1	1
Ath Bilbao			2	0	1	1	2	0	2	0
Leganes			2	1	1	0	0	2	1	1
Vallecano	D	L	4	2	2	0	2	2	4	0
Huesca	W	L	3	1	0	2	2	1	2	0
Valladolid										

Season	Division	Pos	P	W	D	L	F	A	GD	Pts
2017-18	Liga Segunda	5	42	19	10	13	69	55	+14	67
2016-17	Liga Segunda	7	42	18	9	15	52	47	+5	63
2015-16	Liga Segunda	16	42	12	15	15	47	52	-5	51

Over/Under 57%/43% 2nd **Both score** 60%/40% 1st

VALLECANO

Campo de Vallecas — rayovallecano.es

	2017-18 H	A	Last six seasons at home P	W	D	L	OV	UN	BS	CS
Barcelona			4	0	0	4	3	1	1	0
Atl Madrid			4	1	1	2	2	2	2	1
Real Madrid			4	0	0	4	2	2	2	0
Valencia			4	1	2	1	1	3	1	2
Villarreal			3	2	0	1	2	1	2	1
Betis			3	2	0	1	2	1	1	1
Sevilla			4	0	2	2	1	3	1	1
Getafe			5	4	0	1	2	3	2	3
Eibar			2	0	1	1	1	1	2	0
Girona			1	1	0	0	1	0	1	0
Espanyol			4	2	0	2	3	1	2	2
Sociedad			4	1	1	2	2	2	2	1
Celta			4	4	0	0	3	1	1	3
Alaves			-	-	-	-	-	-	-	-
Levante			5	4	0	1	5	0	4	1
Ath Bilbao			4	1	1	2	4	0	2	0
Leganes			-	-	-	-	-	-	-	-
Vallecano										
Huesca	W	L	2	1	1	0	2	0	1	1
Valladolid	W	D	4	1	1	2	3	1	2	1

Season	Division	Pos	P	W	D	L	F	A	GD	Pts
2017-18	Liga Segunda	1	42	21	13	8	67	48	+19	76
2016-17	Liga Segunda	12	42	14	11	17	44	44	+0	53
2015-16	La Liga	18	38	9	11	18	52	73	-21	38

Over/Under 52%/48% 4th **Both score** 57%/43% 3rd

VILLARREAL

Estadio de la Ceramica — villarrealcf.es

	2017-18 H	A	Last six seasons at home P	W	D	L	OV	UN	BS	CS
Barcelona	L	L	5	0	2	3	2	3	3	0
Atl Madrid	W	D	5	3	1	1	2	3	2	2
Real Madrid	D	W	5	1	2	2	3	2	3	1
Valencia	W	W	5	3	0	2	2	3	2	2
Villarreal										
Betis	W	L	4	2	2	0	1	3	2	2
Sevilla	L	D	5	1	1	3	3	2	3	1
Getafe	W	L	4	3	0	1	1	3	1	2
Eibar	W	L	4	2	1	1	2	2	2	2
Girona	L	W	2	1	0	1	1	1	1	0
Espanyol	D	D	5	3	1	1	3	2	2	2
Sociedad	W	L	5	4	1	0	4	1	3	2
Celta	W	W	5	3	0	2	4	1	3	1
Alaves	L	W	2	0	0	2	1	1	1	0
Levante	W	L	4	4	0	0	2	2	1	3
Ath Bilbao	L	D	5	3	1	1	3	2	4	1
Leganes	W	L	2	2	0	0	2	0	2	0
Vallecano			3	3	0	0	3	0	2	1
Huesca			1	0	1	0	0	1	0	0
Valladolid			1	1	0	0	1	0	1	0

Season	Division	Pos	P	W	D	L	F	A	GD	Pts
2017-18	La Liga	5	38	18	7	13	57	50	+7	61
2016-17	La Liga	5	38	19	10	9	56	33	+23	67
2015-16	La Liga	4	38	18	10	10	44	35	+9	64

Over/Under 55%/45% 6th **Both score** 53%/47% 6th

La Liga 2017-18

Pos	H	A		P	Home					Away					GD	Pts
					W	D	L	F	A	W	D	L	F	A		
1	1	1	Barcelona (CL)	38	16	3	0	53	11	12	6	1	46	18	70	93
2	2	2	Atl Madrid (CL)	38	12	6	1	30	8	11	4	4	28	14	36	79
3	4	3	Real Madrid (CL)	38	12	4	3	54	20	10	6	3	40	24	50	76
4	3	4	Valencia (CL)	38	13	3	3	36	16	9	4	6	29	22	27	73
5	6	6	Villarreal (EL)	38	11	3	5	35	22	7	4	8	22	28	7	61
6	7	5	Real Betis (EL)	38	10	4	5	35	31	8	2	9	25	30	-1	60
7	5	10	Sevilla (EL)	38	11	5	3	31	22	6	2	11	18	36	-9	58
8	10	7	Getafe	38	9	4	6	26	13	6	6	7	16	20	9	55
9	13	9	Eibar	38	8	4	7	26	19	6	5	8	18	31	-6	51
10	15	8	Girona	38	8	3	8	26	22	6	6	7	24	37	-9	51
11	12	12	Espanyol	38	8	6	5	20	16	4	7	8	16	26	-6	49
12	8	16	Real Sociedad	38	10	3	6	47	29	4	4	11	19	30	7	49
13	9	15	Celta Vigo	38	8	8	3	34	23	5	2	12	25	37	-1	49
14	14	11	Alaves	38	9	1	9	21	23	6	1	12	19	27	-10	47
15	16	13	Levante	38	7	6	6	25	28	4	7	8	19	30	-14	46
16	17	14	Athletic Bilbao	38	6	8	5	19	16	4	5	10	22	33	-8	43
17	11	17	Leganes	38	9	4	6	19	19	3	3	13	15	32	-17	43
18	18	18	Deportivo (R)	38	4	6	9	22	33	2	5	12	16	43	-38	29
19	20	19	Las Palmas (R)	38	4	2	13	15	38	1	5	13	9	36	-50	22
20	19	20	Malaga (R)	38	4	3	12	14	27	1	2	16	10	34	-37	20

La Liga results 2017-18

	Alaves	Ath Bilbao	Atl Madrid	Barcelona	Betis	Celta	Deportivo	Eibar	Espanyol	Getafe	Girona	Las Palmas	Leganes	Levante	Malaga	Real Madrid	Sevilla	Sociedad	Valencia	Villarreal
Alaves		3-1	0-1	0-2	1-3	2-1	1-0	1-2	1-0	2-0	1-2	2-0	2-2	1-0	1-0	1-2	1-0	0-2	1-2	0-3
Ath Bilbao	2-0		1-2	0-2	2-0	1-1	2-3	1-1	0-1	0-0	2-0	0-0	2-0	1-3	2-1	0-0	1-0	0-0	1-1	1-1
Atl Madrid	1-0	2-0		1-1	0-0	3-0	1-0	2-2	0-2	2-0	1-1	3-0	4-0	3-0	1-0	0-0	2-0	2-1	1-0	1-1
Barcelona	2-1	2-0	1-0		2-0	2-2	4-0	6-1	5-0	0-0	6-1	3-0	3-1	3-0	2-0	2-2	2-1	1-0	2-1	5-1
Betis	2-0	0-2	0-1	0-5		2-1	2-1	2-0	3-0	2-2	2-2	1-1	3-2	4-0	2-1	3-5	2-2	0-0	3-6	2-1
Celta	1-0	3-1	0-1	2-2	3-2		1-1	2-0	2-2	1-1	3-3	2-1	1-0	4-2	0-0	2-2	4-0	2-3	1-1	0-1
Dep La Coruna	1-0	2-2	0-1	2-4	0-1	1-3		1-1	0-0	2-1	1-2	1-1	1-0	2-2	3-2	0-3	0-0	2-4	1-2	2-4
Eibar	0-1	0-1	0-1	0-2	5-0	0-4	0-0		3-1	0-1	4-1	1-0	1-0	2-2	1-1	1-2	5-1	0-0	2-1	1-0
Espanyol	0-0	1-1	1-0	1-1	1-0	2-1	4-1	0-1		1-0	0-1	1-1	0-1	0-0	4-1	1-0	0-3	2-1	0-2	1-1
Getafe	4-1	2-2	0-1	1-2	0-1	3-0	3-0	0-0	1-0		1-1	2-0	0-0	0-1	1-0	1-2	0-1	2-1	1-0	4-0
Girona	2-3	2-0	2-2	0-3	0-1	1-0	2-0	1-4	0-2	1-0		6-0	3-0	1-1	2-1	0-1	1-1	0-1	0-1	1-2
Las Palmas	0-4	1-0	1-5	1-1	1-0	2-5	1-3	1-2	2-2	0-1	1-2		0-2	0-2	1-0	0-3	1-2	0-1	2-1	0-2
Leganes	1-0	1-0	0-0	0-3	3-2	1-0	0-0	3-2	1-2	0-0	0-0			0-3	2-0	1-3	2-1	1-0	0-1	3-1
Levante	0-2	1-2	0-5	5-4	0-2	0-1	2-2	2-1	1-1	1-1	1-2	2-1	0-0		1-0	2-2	2-1	3-0	1-1	1-0
Malaga	0-3	3-3	0-1	0-2	0-2	2-1	3-2	0-1	0-1	0-1	0-0	1-3	0-2	0-0		1-2	0-1	2-0	1-2	1-0
Real Madrid	4-0	1-1	1-1	0-3	0-1	6-0	7-1	3-0	2-0	3-1	6-3	3-0	2-1	1-1	3-2		5-0	5-2	2-2	0-1
Sevilla	1-0	2-0	2-5	2-2	3-5	2-1	2-0	3-0	1-1	1-1	1-0	1-0	2-1	0-0	2-0	3-2		1-0	0-2	2-2
Sociedad	2-1	3-1	3-0	2-4	4-4	1-2	5-0	3-1	1-1	1-2	5-0	2-2	3-2	3-0	0-2	1-3	3-1		2-3	3-0
Valencia	3-1	3-2	0-0	1-1	2-0	2-1	2-1	0-0	1-0	1-2	2-1	1-0	3-0	3-1	5-0	1-4	4-0	2-1		0-1
Villarreal	1-2	1-3	2-1	0-2	3-1	4-1	1-1	3-0	0-0	1-0	0-2	4-0	2-1	2-1	2-0	2-2	2-3	4-2	1-0	

Top scorers

	Team	Goals scored
L Messi	Barcelona	34
C Ronaldo	Real Madrid	26
L Suarez	Barcelona	25
I Aspas	Celta Vigo	22
C Stuani	Girona	21
A Griezmann	Atl Madrid	19

Over 2.5 goals

	H	A	%
Real Madrid	13	16	76%
Sociedad	17	9	68%
Celta Vigo	10	15	66%
Barcelona	13	10	61%
Deportivo	11	11	58%
Levante, Valencia, Villarreal			55%

Both teams to score

	H	A	%
Celta Vigo	12	12	63%
Real Madrid	10	14	63%
Deportivo	12	10	58%
Sociedad	13	9	58%
Valencia	10	12	58%
Villarreal	11	9	53%

AMIENS

Stade de la Licorne — amiensfootball.com

	2017-18 H	A	Last six seasons at home P	W	D	L	OV	UN	BS	CS
Paris SG	D	L	1	0	1	0	1	0	1	0
Monaco	D	D	1	0	1	0	0	1	1	0
Lyon	L	L	1	0	0	1	1	0	1	0
Marseille	L	L	1	0	0	1	0	1	0	0
Rennes	L	L	1	0	0	1	0	1	0	0
Bordeaux	W	L	1	1	0	0	0	1	0	1
St Etienne	L	L	1	0	0	1	0	1	0	0
Nice	W	L	1	1	0	0	1	0	0	1
Nantes	L	W	1	0	0	1	0	1	0	0
Montpellier	D	D	1	0	1	0	0	1	1	0
Dijon	W	D	1	1	0	0	1	0	1	0
Guingamp	W	D	1	1	0	0	1	0	1	0
Amiens										
Angers	L	L	1	0	0	1	0	1	0	0
Strasbourg	W	W	2	2	0	0	2	0	2	0
Caen	W	L	1	1	0	0	1	0	0	1
Lille	W	W	1	1	0	0	1	0	0	1
Toulouse	D	L	1	0	1	0	0	1	0	1
Reims			1	0	1	0	0	1	1	0
Nimes			1	0	0	1	1	0	1	0

Season	Division	Pos	P	W	D	L	F	A	GD	Pts
2017-18	Ligue 1	13	38	12	9	17	37	42	-5	45
2016-17	Ligue 2	2	38	19	9	10	56	38	+18	66
2015-16	Championnat	3	34	14	13	7	44	35	+9	55

Over/Under 32%/68% 19th **Both score** 34%/66% 20th

ANGERS

Stade Raymond Kopa — angers-sco.fr

	2017-18 H	A	Last six seasons at home P	W	D	L	OV	UN	BS	CS
Paris SG	L	L	3	0	1	2	1	2	0	1
Monaco	L	L	4	1	0	3	3	1	1	1
Lyon	D	D	3	0	1	2	3	0	2	0
Marseille	D	D	3	0	2	1	0	3	2	0
Rennes	L	L	3	0	1	2	1	2	1	1
Bordeaux	D	D	3	0	3	0	1	2	3	0
St Etienne	L	D	3	0	1	2	1	2	1	1
Nice	D	D	3	0	2	1	0	3	2	0
Nantes	L	L	4	1	1	2	0	4	0	2
Montpellier	D	L	3	1	1	1	1	2	2	1
Dijon	W	L	5	3	2	0	3	2	3	2
Guingamp	W	D	4	2	1	1	3	1	1	3
Amiens	W	W	1	1	0	0	0	1	0	1
Angers										
Strasbourg	D	D	1	0	1	0	0	1	1	0
Caen	W	W	5	3	1	1	3	2	3	2
Lille	D	W	3	2	1	0	0	3	1	2
Toulouse	L	L	3	0	1	2	1	2	1	1
Reims			1	0	1	0	0	1	0	1
Nimes			3	1	1	1	2	1	1	2

Season	Division	Pos	P	W	D	L	F	A	GD	Pts
2017-18	Ligue 1	14	38	9	14	15	42	52	-10	41
2016-17	Ligue 1	12	38	13	7	18	40	49	-9	46
2015-16	Ligue 1	9	38	13	11	14	40	38	+2	50

Over/Under 45%/55% 14th **Both score** 55%/45% 7th

BORDEAUX

Nouveau Stade de Bordeaux — girondins.com

	2017-18 H	A	Last six seasons at home P	W	D	L	OV	UN	BS	CS
Paris SG	L	L	6	1	1	4	2	4	2	0
Monaco	L	L	5	2	0	3	3	2	2	0
Lyon	W	D	6	2	1	3	5	1	4	0
Marseille	D	L	6	2	4	0	0	6	4	2
Rennes	L	L	6	3	2	1	3	3	3	2
Bordeaux										
St Etienne	W	W	6	4	1	1	3	3	2	4
Nice	D	L	6	0	5	1	1	5	3	3
Nantes	D	W	5	3	1	1	2	3	2	2
Montpellier	L	W	6	4	1	1	3	3	3	2
Dijon	W	L	2	2	0	0	2	0	2	0
Guingamp	W	L	5	4	1	0	3	2	3	2
Amiens	W	L	1	1	0	0	1	0	1	0
Angers	D	D	3	0	1	2	1	2	1	1
Strasbourg	L	W	1	1	0	0	1	0	0	0
Caen	L	L	4	0	2	2	1	3	2	1
Lille	W	D	6	4	1	1	1	5	2	3
Toulouse	W	W	6	4	1	1	2	4	3	2
Reims			4	0	3	1	1	3	2	2
Nimes			-	-	-	-	-	-	-	-

Season	Division	Pos	P	W	D	L	F	A	GD	Pts
2017-18	Ligue 1	6	38	16	7	15	53	48	+5	55
2016-17	Ligue 1	6	38	15	14	9	53	43	+10	59
2015-16	Ligue 1	11	38	12	14	12	50	57	-7	50

Over/Under 47%/53% 12th **Both score** 45%/55% 15th

CAEN

Stade Michel D'Ornano — smcaen.fr

	2017-18 H	A	Last six seasons at home P	W	D	L	OV	UN	BS	CS
Paris SG	D	L	4	0	1	3	2	2	0	1
Monaco	L	L	5	1	1	3	5	0	2	1
Lyon	L	L	4	2	0	2	4	0	2	1
Marseille	L	L	4	0	0	4	3	1	3	0
Rennes	D	W	4	1	1	2	1	3	1	1
Bordeaux	W	W	4	2	0	2	2	2	1	2
St Etienne	L	L	4	2	0	2	0	4	0	2
Nice	D	L	4	2	1	1	1	3	2	2
Nantes	W	L	5	1	0	4	2	3	2	0
Montpellier	L	L	4	1	1	2	2	2	3	0
Dijon	W	L	4	2	2	0	4	0	4	0
Guingamp	D	D	5	1	2	2	3	3	3	1
Amiens	W	L	1	1	0	0	0	1	0	1
Angers	L	L	5	1	2	2	1	4	2	2
Strasbourg	W	D	1	1	0	0	0	1	0	1
Caen										
Lille	L	W	4	0	0	4	1	3	1	0
Toulouse	D		4	3	1	0	0	4	0	4
Reims			2	1	0	1	1	1	0	2
Nimes			2	1	1	0	0	2	1	1

Season	Division	Pos	P	W	D	L	F	A	GD	Pts
2017-18	Ligue 1	16	38	10	8	20	27	52	-25	38
2016-17	Ligue 1	17	38	10	7	21	36	65	-29	37
2015-16	Ligue 1	7	38	16	6	16	39	52	-13	54

Over/Under 34%/66% 18th **Both score** 32%/68% 21st

FRENCH LIGUE 1

DIJON

Stade Gaston Gérard — dfco.fr

	2017-18 H	2017-18 A	Last six seasons at home P	W	D	L	OV	UN	BS	CS
Paris SG	L	L	2	0	0	2	2	0	2	0
Monaco	L	L	3	0	1	2	1	2	2	0
Lyon	L	D	2	1	0	1	2	0	2	0
Marseille	L	L	2	0	0	2	2	0	2	0
Rennes	W	D	2	2	0	0	2	0	1	1
Bordeaux	W	L	2	1	1	0	1	1	1	1
St Etienne	L	D	2	0	0	2	0	2	0	0
Nice	W	L	2	1	0	1	1	1	1	0
Nantes	W	D	3	2	0	1	1	2	1	1
Montpellier	W	D	2	1	1	0	2	0	2	0
Dijon										
Guingamp	W	L	3	2	1	0	2	1	2	1
Amiens	D	L	1	0	1	0	0	1	1	0
Angers	W	L	5	2	2	1	3	2	4	1
Strasbourg	D	L	1	0	1	0	0	1	1	0
Caen	W	L	4	3	1	0	1	3	1	3
Lille	W	L	2	1	1	0	1	1	0	2
Toulouse	W	W	2	2	0	0	1	1	1	1
Reims			-	-	-	-	-	-	-	-
Nimes			4	2	0	2	3	1	3	0

Season	Division	Pos	P	W	D	L	F	A	GD	Pts
2017-18	Ligue 1	11	38	13	9	16	55	73	-18	48
2016-17	Ligue 1	16	38	8	13	17	46	58	-12	37
2015-16	Ligue 2	2	38	20	10	8	62	36	+26	70

Over/Under 74%/26% 1st **Both score** 71%/29% 1st

GUINGAMP

Stade Municipal du Roudourou — eaguingamp.com

	2017-18 H	2017-18 A	Last six seasons at home P	W	D	L	OV	UN	BS	CS
Paris SG	L	D	5	2	1	2	2	3	2	1
Monaco	W	L	6	2	1	3	4	2	4	1
Lyon	L	L	5	1	0	4	2	3	2	0
Marseille	D	L	5	2	1	2	3	2	3	1
Rennes	W	W	5	2	1	2	0	5	1	2
Bordeaux	W	L	5	2	1	2	3	2	4	0
St Etienne	W	L	5	2	1	2	1	4	1	2
Nice	L	L	5	1	0	4	3	2	3	1
Nantes	L	L	6	3	1	2	3	3	2	2
Montpellier	D	D	5	0	3	2	2	3	3	1
Dijon	W	L	3	3	0	0	2	1	0	3
Guingamp										
Amiens	D	L	1	0	1	0	0	1	1	0
Angers	D	L	4	2	2	0	2	2	3	1
Strasbourg	W	W	1	1	0	0	0	1	0	1
Caen	D	D	5	2	2	1	1	4	2	2
Lille	W	W	5	2	2	1	0	5	1	3
Toulouse	D	L	5	4	1	0	2	3	3	2
Reims			3	1	0	2	2	1	2	1
Nimes			1	1	0	0	1	0	0	1

Season	Division	Pos	P	W	D	L	F	A	GD	Pts
2017-18	Ligue 1	12	38	12	11	15	48	59	-11	47
2016-17	Ligue 1	10	38	14	8	16	46	53	-7	50
2015-16	Ligue 1	16	38	11	11	16	47	56	-9	44

Over/Under 55%/45% 8th **Both score** 50%/50% 10th

LILLE

Stade Pierre-Mauroy — losc.fr

	2017-18 H	2017-18 A	Last six seasons at home P	W	D	L	OV	UN	BS	CS
Paris SG	L	L	6	0	1	5	3	3	3	0
Monaco	L	L	5	2	0	3	3	2	2	1
Lyon	D	W	6	2	3	1	2	4	3	2
Marseille	L	L	6	1	2	3	2	4	1	3
Rennes	L	L	6	2	3	1	2	4	4	2
Bordeaux	D	L	6	3	2	1	3	3	3	3
St Etienne	W	L	6	3	3	0	1	5	4	2
Nice	D	L	6	0	3	3	1	5	3	1
Nantes	W	D	5	3	1	1	2	3	0	4
Montpellier	D	L	6	4	2	0	2	4	3	3
Dijon	W	L	2	2	0	0	1	1	1	1
Guingamp	D	L	5	2	1	2	3	2	2	3
Amiens	L	L	1	0	0	1	0	1	0	0
Angers	L	D	3	0	1	2	2	1	2	1
Strasbourg	W	L	1	1	0	0	1	0	1	0
Caen	L	W	4	3	0	1	1	3	1	2
Lille										
Toulouse	W	W	6	5	0	1	2	4	1	5
Reims			4	3	0	1	3	1	2	2
Nimes			-	-	-	-	-	-	-	-

Season	Division	Pos	P	W	D	L	F	A	GD	Pts
2017-18	Ligue 1	17	38	10	8	20	41	67	-26	38
2016-17	Ligue 1	11	38	13	7	18	40	47	-7	46
2015-16	Ligue 1	5	38	15	15	8	39	27	+12	60

Over/Under 68%/32% 4th **Both score** 53%/47% 9th

LYON

Stade de Lyon — olweb.fr

	2017-18 H	2017-18 A	Last six seasons at home P	W	D	L	OV	UN	BS	CS
Paris SG	W	L	6	3	1	2	3	3	4	1
Monaco	W	L	5	3	0	2	5	0	5	0
Lyon										
Marseille	W	W	6	3	3	0	2	4	3	3
Rennes	L	W	6	3	1	2	1	5	1	4
Bordeaux	D	L	6	1	3	2	3	3	4	1
St Etienne	D	W	6	2	3	1	3	3	4	2
Nice	W	W	6	3	2	1	5	1	4	2
Nantes	W	D	5	5	0	0	2	3	2	3
Montpellier	D	D	6	3	2	1	3	3	3	3
Dijon	D	W	2	1	1	0	2	0	2	0
Guingamp	W	W	5	4	0	1	4	1	4	1
Amiens	W	W	1	1	0	0	1	0	0	1
Angers	D	D	3	1	1	1	0	3	1	1
Strasbourg	W	L	1	1	0	0	1	0	0	1
Caen	W	W	4	4	0	0	2	2	1	3
Lille	L	D	6	1	2	3	4	2	3	3
Toulouse	W	W	6	5	1	0	4	2	2	4
Reims			4	3	0	1	2	2	1	2
Nimes			-	-	-	-	-	-	-	-

Season	Division	Pos	P	W	D	L	F	A	GD	Pts
2017-18	Ligue 1	3	38	23	9	6	87	43	+44	78
2016-17	Ligue 1	4	38	21	4	13	77	48	+29	67
2015-16	Ligue 1	2	38	19	8	11	67	43	+24	65

Over/Under 66%/34% 5th **Both score** 55%/45% 7th

MARSEILLE

Stade Velodrome — om.net

	2017-18 H	A	Last six seasons at home P	W	D	L	OV	UN	BS	CS
Paris SG	D	L	6	0	2	4	6	0	6	0
Monaco	D	L	5	1	2	2	5	0	5	0
Lyon	L	L	6	1	3	2	3	3	4	2
Marseille										
Rennes	L	W	6	3	0	3	4	2	3	2
Bordeaux	W	D	6	3	3	0	2	4	2	4
St Etienne	W	D	6	5	1	0	4	2	3	3
Nice	W	W	6	3	1	2	4	2	3	1
Nantes	D	W	5	2	2	1	1	4	3	1
Montpellier	D	W	6	3	2	1	3	3	3	2
Dijon	W	W	2	1	1	0	1	1	1	1
Guingamp	W	D	5	4	1	0	1	4	1	4
Amiens	W	W	1	1	0	0	1	0	1	0
Angers	D	D	3	1	1	1	2	1	2	1
Strasbourg	W	D	1	1	0	0	0	1	0	1
Caen	W	W	4	2	0	2	2	2	1	2
Lille	W	W	6	4	2	0	2	4	3	3
Toulouse	W	W	6	3	3	0	2	4	3	3
Reims			4	1	2	1	2	2	2	2
Nimes	-	-	-	-	-	-	-	-	-	-

Season	Division	Pos	P	W	D	L	F	A	GD	Pts
2017-18	Ligue 1	4	38	22	11	5	80	47	+33	77
2016-17	Ligue 1	5	38	17	11	10	57	41	+16	62
2015-16	Ligue 1	13	38	10	18	10	48	42	+6	48

Over/Under 61%/39% 7th **Both score** 58%/42% 3rd

MONACO

Stade Louis II — asm-fc.com

	2017-18 H	A	Last six seasons at home P	W	D	L	OV	UN	BS	CS
Paris SG	L	L	5	1	2	2	3	2	3	1
Monaco										
Lyon	W	L	5	2	2	1	3	2	4	1
Marseille	W	D	5	5	0	0	3	2	2	3
Rennes	W	D	5	3	2	0	2	3	3	2
Bordeaux	W	W	5	2	2	1	3	2	4	1
St Etienne	W	W	5	4	1	0	1	4	2	3
Nice	D	L	5	3	1	1	2	3	1	3
Nantes	W	L	5	5	0	1	3	3	2	3
Montpellier	D	D	5	3	2	0	2	3	3	2
Dijon	W	W	3	2	1	0	2	1	2	1
Guingamp	W	L	6	3	3	0	4	2	4	2
Amiens	D	D	1	0	1	0	0	1	0	1
Angers	W	W	4	3	1	0	2	2	2	2
Strasbourg	W	W	1	1	0	0	1	0	0	1
Caen	W	W	5	2	2	1	2	3	3	1
Lille	W	W	5	2	3	0	2	3	3	2
Toulouse	W	D	5	4	1	0	4	1	3	2
Reims			3	1	2	0	2	1	3	0
Nimes			1	0	1	0	0	1	1	0

Season	Division	Pos	P	W	D	L	F	A	GD	Pts
2017-18	Ligue 1	2	38	24	8	6	85	45	+40	80
2016-17	Ligue 1	3	38	30	5	3	107	31	+76	95
2015-16	Ligue 1	3	38	17	14	7	57	50	+7	65

Over/Under 71%/29% 2nd **Both score** 58%/42% 3rd

MONTPELLIER

Stade de la Mosson — mhscfoot.com

	2017-18 H	A	Last six seasons at home P	W	D	L	OV	UN	BS	CS
Paris SG	D	L	6	1	3	2	2	4	3	2
Monaco	D	L	5	0	2	3	2	3	3	1
Lyon	D	D	6	1	1	4	4	2	5	0
Marseille	D	D	6	2	1	3	3	3	4	0
Rennes	L	D	6	2	3	1	0	6	1	4
Bordeaux	L	W	6	2	1	3	2	4	2	2
St Etienne	L	W	6	1	1	4	2	4	3	0
Nice	W	L	6	4	1	1	3	3	4	1
Nantes	L	W	5	2	1	2	3	2	3	1
Montpellier										
Dijon	D	L	2	0	2	0	1	1	2	0
Guingamp	D	D	5	2	3	0	2	3	5	0
Amiens	D	D	1	0	1	0	0	1	1	0
Angers	W	D	3	2	0	1	1	2	1	1
Strasbourg	D	D	1	0	1	0	0	1	1	0
Caen	W	W	4	3	0	1	2	2	2	2
Lille	W	D	6	2	1	3	4	2	1	3
Toulouse	W	L	6	4	1	1	2	4	3	2
Reims			4	3	1	0	3	1	3	1
Nimes	-	-	-	-	-	-	-	-	-	-

Season	Division	Pos	P	W	D	L	F	A	GD	Pts
2017-18	Ligue 1	10	38	11	18	9	36	33	+3	51
2016-17	Ligue 1	15	38	10	9	19	48	66	-18	39
2015-16	Ligue 1	12	38	14	7	17	49	47	+2	49

Over/Under 24%/76% 21st **Both score** 47%/53% 14th

NANTES

Beaujoire-Louis Fonteneau — fcnantes.com

	2017-18 H	A	Last six seasons at home P	W	D	L	OV	UN	BS	CS
Paris SG	L	L	5	0	0	5	2	3	2	0
Monaco	W	L	6	1	2	3	0	6	1	2
Lyon	D	L	5	0	3	2	3	2	2	2
Marseille	L	D	5	2	1	2	1	4	2	1
Rennes	D	L	5	0	2	3	2	3	3	0
Bordeaux	L	D	5	1	2	2	2	3	2	1
St Etienne	L	D	5	1	2	2	3	2	2	2
Nice	L	D	5	3	1	1	2	3	3	2
Nantes										
Montpellier	L	W	5	3	0	2	1	4	1	2
Dijon	D	L	3	2	1	0	1	2	2	1
Guingamp	W	W	6	5	1	0	2	4	4	3
Amiens	L	W	1	0	0	1	0	1	0	0
Angers	W	W	4	4	0	0	1	3	1	3
Strasbourg	W	W	1	1	0	0	0	1	0	1
Caen	W	L	5	3	0	2	3	2	3	2
Lille	D	L	5	0	3	2	2	3	2	1
Toulouse	W	D	5	1	2	2	3	2	5	0
Reims			3	1	2	0	0	3	1	0
Nimes			1	0	0	1	1	0	1	0

Season	Division	Pos	P	W	D	L	F	A	GD	Pts
2017-18	Ligue 1	9	38	14	10	14	36	41	-5	52
2016-17	Ligue 1	7	38	14	9	15	40	54	-14	51
2015-16	Ligue 1	14	38	12	12	14	33	44	-11	48

Over/Under 32%/68% 19th **Both score** 45%/55% 15th

NICE

Stade de Nice · ogcnice.com

	2017-18		Last six seasons at home								
	H	A	P	W	D	L	OV	UN	BS	CS	
Paris SG	L	L	6	2	0	4	5	1	4	0	
Monaco	W	D	5	2	0	3	4	1	1	2	
Lyon	L	L	6	2	1	3	3	3	2	2	
Marseille	L	L	6	3	1	2	3	3	4	1	
Rennes	D	W	6	4	1	1	3	3	3	3	
Bordeaux	W	D	6	3	0	3	4	2	4	1	
St Etienne	W	L	6	3	2	1	0	6	1	4	
Nice											
Nantes	D	W	5	1	3	1	2	3	3	2	
Montpellier	W	L	6	4	2	0	2	4	3	3	
Dijon	W	L	2	2	0	0	1	1	1	1	
Guingamp	W	W	5	3	0	2	2	3	2	2	
Amiens	W	L	1	1	0	0	0	1	0	1	
Angers	D	D	3	1	1	1	2	1	2	0	
Strasbourg	L	D	1	0	0	1	1	0	1	0	
Caen	W	D	4	2	2	0	3	1	4	0	
Lille	W	D	6	3	3	0	2	4	3	3	
Toulouse	L	W	6	4	0	2	2	4	1	3	
Reims			4	3	1	0	0	4	0	4	
Nimes			-	-	-	-	-	-	-	-	

Season	Division	Pos	P	W	D	L	F	A	GD	Pts
2017-18	Ligue 1	8	38	15	9	14	53	52	+1	54
2016-17	Ligue 1	3	38	22	12	4	63	36	+27	78
2015-16	Ligue 1	4	38	18	9	11	58	41	+17	63

Over/Under 53%/47% 10th **Both score** 58%/42% 3rd

NIMES

Stade des Costieres · nimes-olympique.com

	2017-18		Last six seasons at home								
	H	A	P	W	D	L	OV	UN	BS	CS	
Paris SG			-	-	-	-	-	-	-	-	
Monaco			1	0	0	1	0	1	0	0	
Lyon			-	-	-	-	-	-	-	-	
Marseille			-	-	-	-	-	-	-	-	
Rennes			-	-	-	-	-	-	-	-	
Bordeaux			-	-	-	-	-	-	-	-	
St Etienne			-	-	-	-	-	-	-	-	
Nice			-	-	-	-	-	-	-	-	
Nantes			1	0	1	0	0	1	0	1	
Montpellier			-	-	-	-	-	-	-	-	
Dijon			4	0	4	0	1	3	4	0	
Guingamp			1	1	0	0	1	0	1	0	
Amiens			1	0	0	1	0	1	0	0	
Angers			3	2	0	1	2	1	1	1	
Strasbourg			1	0	1	0	1	0	1	0	
Caen			2	1	0	1	1	1	1	0	
Lille			-	-	-	-	-	-	-	-	
Toulouse			-	-	-	-	-	-	-	-	
Reims	L	D	2	1	0	1	1	1	0	1	
Nimes											

Season	Division	Pos	P	W	D	L	F	A	GD	Pts
2017-18	Ligue 2	2	38	22	7	9	75	37	+38	73
2016-17	Ligue 2	6	38	17	13	8	58	40	+18	64
2015-16	Ligue 2	14	38	13	12	13	50	52	-2	43

Over/Under 63%/37% 2nd **Both score** 53%/47% 14th

PARIS SAINT-GERMAIN

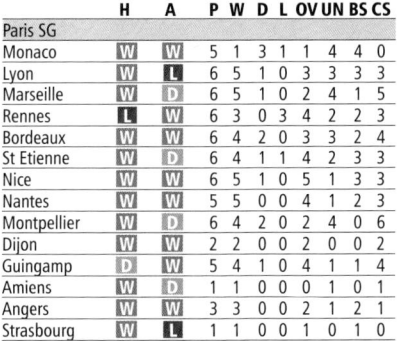

Parc des Princes · psg.fr

	2017-18		Last six seasons at home								
	H	A	P	W	D	L	OV	UN	BS	CS	
Paris SG											
Monaco	W	W	5	1	3	1	4	4	4	0	
Lyon	W	L	6	5	1	0	3	3	3	3	
Marseille	W	D	6	5	1	0	2	4	1	5	
Rennes	L	W	6	3	0	3	4	2	2	3	
Bordeaux	W	W	6	4	2	0	3	3	2	4	
St Etienne	W	D	6	4	1	1	4	2	3	3	
Nice	W	W	6	5	1	0	5	1	3	3	
Nantes	W	W	5	5	0	0	4	1	2	3	
Montpellier	W	D	6	4	2	0	2	4	0	6	
Dijon	W	W	2	2	0	0	2	0	2	0	
Guingamp	D	W	5	4	1	0	4	1	1	4	
Amiens	W	D	1	1	0	0	0	1	0	1	
Angers	W	W	3	3	0	0	2	1	2	1	
Strasbourg	W	L	1	1	0	0	1	0	1	0	
Caen	W	D	4	2	2	0	3	1	3	1	
Lille	W	W	6	4	2	0	4	2	4	2	
Toulouse	W	W	6	5	1	0	3	3	2	4	
Reims			4	4	0	0	3	1	2	2	
Nimes			-	-	-	-	-	-	-	-	

Season	Division	Pos	P	W	D	L	F	A	GD	Pts
2017-18	Ligue 1	1	38	29	6	3	108	29	+79	93
2016-17	Ligue 1	2	38	27	6	5	83	27	+56	87
2015-16	Ligue 1	1	38	30	6	2	102	19	+83	96

Over/Under 71%/29% 2nd **Both score** 50%/50% 10th

REIMS

Stade Auguste-Delaune II · stade-de-reims.com

	2017-18		Last six seasons at home								
	H	A	P	W	D	L	OV	UN	BS	CS	
Paris SG			4	1	2	1	2	2	2	1	
Monaco			3	0	1	2	1	2	2	0	
Lyon			4	2	0	2	2	2	1	1	
Marseille			4	1	1	2	1	3	1	1	
Rennes			4	2	1	1	2	2	2	2	
Bordeaux			4	3	1	0	1	3	1	3	
St Etienne			4	0	3	1	2	2	4	0	
Nice			4	2	1	1	3	2	1	
Nantes			3	2	1	0	2	1	2	1	
Montpellier			4	2	0	2	3	1	3	1	
Dijon			-	-	-	-	-	-	-	-	
Guingamp			3	0	1	2	1	2	2	0	
Amiens			1	0	0	1	1	0	1	0	
Angers			1	1	0	0	1	0	1	0	
Strasbourg			1	0	1	0	0	1	1	0	
Caen			2	0	0	2	0	2	0	0	
Lille			4	3	1	0	1	3	2	2	
Toulouse			4	1	1	2	2	2	3	1	
Reims											
Nimes	D	W	2	0	2	0	1	1	2	0	

Season	Division	Pos	P	W	D	L	F	A	GD	Pts
2017-18	Ligue 2	1	38	28	4	6	74	24	+50	88
2016-17	Ligue 2	7	38	14	13	11	42	39	+3	55
2015-16	Ligue 1	18	38	10	9	19	44	57	-13	39

Over/Under 53%/47% 8th **Both score** 39%/61% 29th

RENNES

Roazhon Park   staderennais.com

	2017-18 H	A	P	W	D	L	OV	UN	BS	CS
Paris SG	L	W	6	0	1	5	2	4	3	0
Monaco	D	L	5	1	2	2	1	4	3	1
Lyon	L	W	6	1	2	3	2	4	3	1
Marseille	L	W	6	1	3	2	3	3	4	0
Rennes										
Bordeaux	W	W	6	1	4	1	1	5	4	1
St Etienne	D	D	6	2	3	1	2	4	3	2
Nice	L	D	6	1	2	3	4	2	3	1
Nantes	W	D	5	2	2	1	3	2	4	1
Montpellier	D	W	6	3	2	1	3	3	3	2
Dijon	D	L	2	0	2	0	1	1	2	0
Guingamp	L	L	5	2	0	3	1	4	0	2
Amiens	W	W	1	1	0	0	0	1	0	1
Angers	W	W	3	2	1	0	0	3	1	2
Strasbourg	W	L	1	1	0	0	1	0	1	0
Caen	L	D	4	1	1	2	1	3	2	1
Lille	W	W	6	4	2	0	0	6	1	5
Toulouse	W	L	6	4	0	2	4	2	3	2
Reims			4	3	0	1	3	1	3	1
Nimes			-	-	-	-	-	-	-	-

Season	Division	Pos	P	W	D	L	F	A	GD	Pts
2017-18	Ligue 1	5	38	16	10	12	50	44	+6	58
2016-17	Ligue 1	9	38	12	14	12	36	42	-6	50
2015-16	Ligue 1	8	38	13	13	12	52	54	-2	52

Over/Under 45%/55% 14th **Both score** 61%/39% 2nd

ST ETIENNE

Stade Geoffroy-Guichard   asse.fr

	2017-18 H	A	P	W	D	L	OV	UN	BS	CS
Paris SG	D	L	6	0	3	3	3	3	3	0
Monaco	L	L	5	1	3	1	1	4	3	1
Lyon	L	D	6	3	0	3	3	3	1	3
Marseille	D	L	6	1	4	1	2	4	3	2
Rennes	D	D	6	1	5	0	1	5	3	3
Bordeaux	L	L	6	1	4	1	3	3	5	1
St Etienne										
Nice	W	L	6	3	1	2	3	3	2	3
Nantes	D	W	5	3	2	0	0	5	2	3
Montpellier	L	W	6	5	0	1	3	3	2	3
Dijon	D	W	2	0	2	0	1	1	2	0
Guingamp	W	L	5	5	0	0	2	3	1	4
Amiens	W	W	1	1	0	0	1	0	0	1
Angers	D	W	3	2	1	0	1	2	2	1
Strasbourg	D	W	1	0	1	0	1	0	1	0
Caen	W	W	4	2	0	2	2	2	2	1
Lille	W	L	6	4	0	2	3	3	2	3
Toulouse	W	D	6	1	3	2	2	4	2	3
Reims			4	3	1	0	3	1	1	3
Nimes			-	-	-	-	-	-	-	-

Season	Division	Pos	P	W	D	L	F	A	GD	Pts
2017-18	Ligue 1	7	38	15	10	13	47	50	-3	55
2016-17	Ligue 1	8	38	12	14	12	41	42	-1	50
2015-16	Ligue 1	6	38	17	7	14	42	37	+5	58

Over/Under 53%/47% 10th **Both score** 42%/58% 17th

STRASBOURG

Stade de la Meinau   rcstrasbourgalsace.fr

	2017-18 H	A	P	W	D	L	OV	UN	BS	CS
Paris SG	W	L	1	1	0	0	1	0	1	0
Monaco	L	L	1	0	0	1	1	0	1	0
Lyon	W	L	1	1	0	0	1	0	1	0
Marseille	D	L	1	0	1	0	1	0	1	0
Rennes	W	L	1	1	0	0	1	0	1	0
Bordeaux	L	W	1	0	0	1	0	1	0	0
St Etienne	L	D	1	0	0	1	0	0	0	0
Nice	D	W	1	0	1	0	0	1	1	0
Nantes	L	L	1	0	0	1	1	0	1	0
Montpellier	D	D	1	0	1	0	0	1	0	1
Dijon	W	D	1	1	0	0	1	0	1	0
Guingamp	L	L	1	0	0	1	0	1	0	0
Amiens	L	L	2	1	0	1	0	2	0	1
Angers	D	D	1	0	1	0	1	0	1	0
Strasbourg										
Caen	D	L	1	0	1	0	0	1	0	1
Lille	W	L	1	1	0	0	1	0	0	1
Toulouse	W	D	1	1	0	0	1	0	1	0
Reims			1	0	0	1	1	0	1	0
Nimes			1	0	1	0	0	1	1	0

Season	Division	Pos	P	W	D	L	F	A	GD	Pts
2017-18	Ligue 1	15	38	9	11	18	44	67	-23	38
2016-17	Ligue 1	1	38	19	10	9	63	47	+16	67
2015-16	Championnat	1	34	15	13	6	35	19	+16	58

Over/Under 63%/37% 6th **Both score** 58%/42% 3rd

TOULOUSE

Stadium Municipal   tfc.info

	2017-18 H	A	P	W	D	L	OV	UN	BS	CS
Paris SG	L	L	6	1	1	4	2	4	2	1
Monaco	D	L	5	1	2	2	3	3	3	0
Lyon	L	L	6	2	1	3	5	1	4	2
Marseille	L	L	6	0	3	3	2	4	4	1
Rennes	W	L	6	2	2	2	5	1	4	1
Bordeaux	L	L	6	3	2	1	3	3	3	2
St Etienne	D	L	6	2	3	1	3	3	3	2
Nice	L	W	6	2	1	3	3	3	4	2
Nantes	D	L	5	0	4	1	0	5	3	1
Montpellier	W	L	6	4	2	0	0	6	2	4
Dijon	L	L	2	0	1	1	0	2	0	1
Guingamp	W	D	5	2	2	1	3	2	4	1
Amiens	W	D	1	1	0	0	0	1	0	1
Angers	W	W	3	2	0	1	2	1	1	2
Strasbourg	D	L	1	0	1	0	1	0	1	0
Caen	W	D	4	2	1	1	3	1	2	1
Lille	L	L	6	2	2	2	4	2	6	0
Toulouse										
Reims			4	2	2	0	2	2	3	1
Nimes			-	-	-	-	-	-	-	-

Season	Division	Pos	P	W	D	L	F	A	GD	Pts
2017-18	Ligue 1	18	38	9	10	19	38	54	-16	37
2016-17	Ligue 1	13	38	10	14	14	37	41	-4	44
2015-16	Ligue 1	17	38	9	13	16	45	55	-10	40

Over/Under 42%/58% 16th **Both score** 50%/50% 10th

Ligue 1 2017-18

Pos	H	A	Team	P	Home W	D	L	F	A	Away W	D	L	F	A	GD	Pts
1	1	1	Paris St-G (CL)	38	17	1	1	70	15	12	5	2	38	14	79	
2	2	4	Monaco (CL)	38	15	3	1	47	17	9	5	5	38	28	40	
3	4	2	Lyon (CL)	38	12	5	2	38	18	11	4	4	49	25	44	
4	3	3	Marseille (EL)	38	12	5	2	44	19	10	6	3	36	28	33	7.
5	11	5	Rennes (EL)	38	8	4	7	21	22	8	6	5	29	22	6	58
6	9	7	Bordeaux (EL)	38	9	4	6	27	23	7	3	9	26	25	5	55
7	8	9	St-Etienne	38	8	7	4	32	27	7	3	9	15	23	-3	55
8	6	10	Nice	38	10	3	6	29	23	5	6	8	24	29	1	54
9	12	8	Nantes	38	8	4	7	15	17	6	6	7	21	24	-5	52
10	16	6	Montpellier	38	5	9	5	20	19	6	9	4	16	14	3	51
11	5	17	Dijon	38	11	3	5	35	28	2	6	11	20	45	-18	48
12	7	13	Guingamp	38	8	7	4	30	24	4	4	11	18	35	-11	47
13	10	12	Amiens	38	8	5	6	26	19	4	4	11	11	23	-5	45
14	19	11	Angers	38	5	7	7	23	28	4	7	8	19	24	-10	41
15	13	19	Strasbourg	38	7	6	6	27	27	2	5	12	17	40	-23	38
16	15	16	Caen	38	7	5	7	17	19	3	3	13	10	33	-25	38
17	17	14	Lille	38	6	6	7	24	27	4	2	13	17	40	-26	38
18	14	18	Toulouse*	38	7	5	7	23	21	2	5	12	15	33	-16	37
19	18	20	Troyes (R)	38	7	3	9	17	22	2	3	14	15	37	-27	33
20	20	15	Metz (R)	38	3	4	12	16	37	3	4	12	18	39	-42	26

*Toulouse avoided relegation by winning relegation playoff

Ligue 1 results 2017-18

	Amiens	Angers	Bordeaux	Caen	Dijon	Guingamp	Lille	Lyon	Marseille	Metz	Monaco	Montpellier	Nantes	Nice	Paris St-G	Rennes	St Etienne	Strasbourg	Toulouse	Troyes
Amiens		0-2	1-0	3-0	2-1	3-1	3-0	1-2	0-2	2-0	1-1	1-1	0-1	3-0	2-2	0-2	0-2	3-1	0-0	1-1
Angers	1-0		2-2	3-0	2-1	3-0	1-1	3-3	1-1	0-1	0-4	1-1	0-2	1-1	0-5	1-2	0-1	1-1	0-1	3-1
Bordeaux	3-2	0-0		0-2	3-1	3-1	2-1	3-1	1-1	2-0	0-2	0-2	1-1	0-0	0-1	0-2	3-0	0-3	4-2	2-1
Caen	1-0	0-2	1-0		2-1	0-0	0-1	1-2	0-2	1-0	1-2	1-3	3-2	1-1	0-0	2-2	0-1	2-0	0-0	1-0
Dijon	1-1	2-1	3-2	2-0		3-1	3-0	2-5	1-3	1-1	1-4	2-1	1-0	3-2	1-2	2-1	0-1	1-1	3-1	3-1
Guingamp	1-1	1-1	2-1	0-0	4-0		1-0	0-2	3-3	2-2	3-1	0-0	0-3	2-5	0-3	2-0	2-1	2-0	1-1	4-0
Lille	0-1	1-2	0-0	0-2	2-1	2-2		2-2	0-1	3-1	0-4	1-1	3-0	1-1	0-3	1-2	3-1	2-1	1-0	2-2
Lyon	3-0	1-1	3-3	1-0	3-3	2-1	1-2		2-0	2-0	3-2	0-0	2-0	3-2	2-1	0-2	1-1	4-0	2-0	3-0
Marseille	2-1	1-1	1-0	5-0	3-0	1-0	5-1	2-3		6-3	2-2	0-0	1-1	2-1	2-2	1-3	3-0	2-0	2-0	3-1
Metz	0-2	1-2	0-4	1-1	1-2	1-3	0-3	0-5	0-3		0-1	0-1	1-1	2-1	1-5	1-1	3-0	3-0	1-1	0-1
Monaco	0-0	1-0	2-1	2-0	4-0	6-0	2-1	3-2	6-1	3-1		1-1	2-1	2-2	1-2	2-0	1-0	3-0	3-2	3-2
Montpellier	1-1	2-1	3-1	1-0	2-2	1-1	3-0	1-1	1-1	1-3	0-0		0-1	2-0	0-0	0-1	0-1	1-1	2-1	1-1
Nantes	0-1	1-0	0-1	1-0	1-1	2-1	2-2	0-0	0-1	1-0	1-0	0-2		1-2	0-1	1-1	0-3	1-0	2-1	1-0
Nice	1-0	2-2	1-0	4-1	1-0	2-0	2-1	0-5	2-4	3-1	4-0	1-0	1-1		1-2	1-1	1-0	1-2	0-1	1-2
Paris St-Germain	2-0	2-1	6-2	3-1	8-0	2-2	3-1	2-0	3-0	5-0	7-1	4-0	4-1	3-0		0-2	3-0	5-2	6-2	2-0
Rennes	2-0	1-0	1-0	0-1	2-2	0-1	1-0	1-2	0-3	1-2	1-1	1-1	2-1	0-1	1-4		1-1	2-1	2-1	2-0
St Etienne	3-0	1-1	1-3	2-1	2-2	2-0	5-0	0-5	2-2	3-1	0-4	0-1	1-1	1-0	1-1	2-2		2-2	2-0	2-1
Strasbourg	0-1	2-2	0-2	0-0	3-2	0-2	3-0	3-2	3-3	2-2	1-3	0-0	1-2	1-1	2-1	2-1	0-1		2-1	2-1
Toulouse	1-0	2-0	0-1	2-0	0-1	2-1	2-3	1-2	1-2	0-0	3-3	1-1	1-2	0-1	3-2	0-0	2-2	2-2		1-0
Troyes	1-0	3-0	0-1	3-1	0-0	0-1	1-0	0-5	2-3	1-0	0-3	0-1	0-1	0-2	0-2	1-1	2-1	3-0	0-0	

Top scorers

	Team	Goals scored
E Cavani	Paris St-G	28
F Thauvin	Marseille	22
Neymar	Paris St-G	19
M Depay	Lyon	19
M Balotelli (Nice), M Diaz (Lyon), N Fekir (Lyon), R Falcao (Monaco)		18

Over 2.5 goals

	H	A	%
Dijon	13	15	74%
Monaco	14	13	71%
Paris St-G	15	12	71%
Lille	12	14	68%
Lyon	10	15	66%
Strasbourg	12	12	63%

Both teams to score

	H	A	%
Dijon	15	12	71%
Rennes	10	13	61%
Marseille	11	11	58%
Monaco	12	10	58%
Nice	10	12	58%
Strasbourg	12	10	58%

Uefa Association Coefficients

Pos	Change	Country	13-14	14-15	15-16	16-17	17-18	Pts	Change
1	–	Spain	23	20.214	23.928	20.142	19.428	106.712	1.714
2	1	England	16.785	13.571	14.25	14.928	20.071	79.605	3.643
3	1	Italy	14.166	19	11.5	14.25	17.333	76.249	2.917
4	-2	Germany	14.714	15.857	16.428	14.571	9.857	71.427	-8.071
5	–	France	8.5	10.916	11.083	14.416	11.5	56.415	-0.25
6	–	Russia	10.416	9.666	11.5	9.2	12.6	53.382	2.85
7	–	Portugal	9.916	9.083	10.5	8.083	9.666	47.248	-2.084
8	–	Ukraine	7.833	10	9.8	5.5	8	41.133	-1.5
9	–	Belgium	6.4	9.6	7.4	12.5	2.6	38.5	-3.9
10	–	Turkey	6.7	6	6.6	9.7	6.8	35.8	-3.4
11	4	Austria	7.8	4.125	3.8	7.375	9.75	32.85	7.5
12	–	Switzerland	7.2	6.9	5.3	4.3	6.5	30.2	-1.875
13	-2	Czech Republic	8	3.875	7.3	5.5	5.5	30.175	-3
14	-1	Netherlands	5.916	6.083	5.75	9.1	2.9	29.749	-1.314
15	-1	Greece	6.1	6.2	5.4	5.8	5.1	28.6	0.7
16	–	Croatia	4.375	6.875	4.5	5.125	5.125	26	0.75
17	1	Denmark	3.8	2.9	5.5	8.5	5.25	25.95	1.95
18	4	Israel	5.75	1.375	2.25	6.75	5.625	21.75	2.375
19	5	Cyprus	2.75	3.3	3	5.5	7	21.55	3
20	-3	Romania	6.875	5.125	2.25	3.3	2.9	20.45	-3.9
21	-1	Poland	3.125	4.75	5.5	3.875	2.875	20.125	0.375
22	-1	Sweden	3.2	3.9	4.75	2.75	5.375	19.975	0.25
23	3	Azerbaijan	2.5	3.625	4.375	4.25	4.375	19.125	1.375
24	3	Bulgaria	5.625	4.25	1	4.25	4	19.125	3.25
25	3	Serbia	2.5	2.75	4.25	2.875	6.375	18.75	3.375
26	-3	Scotland	3.25	4	3	4.375	4	18.625	-0.3
27	-8	Belarus	1.75	5.5	5.125	3	3.25	18.625	-1.25
28	1	Kazakhstan	3.125	3.375	4.625	2.75	4.25	18.125	2.875
29	-4	Norway	2.6	2.2	7.25	1.375	4	17.425	-0.9
30	–	Slovenia	2.625	4	1	2.25	4.625	14.5	1.375
31	1	Liechtenstein	1	2.5	5	2.5	2	13	2
32	-1	Slovakia	1.625	2.75	3.75	2.125	1.875	12.125	0.375
33	1	Moldova	3.375	1.75	1.25	0.875	2.75	10	0.5
34	3	Albania	2	0.875	2.125	0.875	2.625	8.5	1.875
35	–	Iceland	2.5	2.5	1.125	1	1.125	8.25	-0.125
36	-3	Hungary	0.875	2.125	1.625	1.875	1.625	8.125	-1.375
37	5	Macedonia	0.5	1.125	1.5	1.25	3.125	7.5	1.875
38	-2	Finland	0.5	2.4	1	1.75	1.25	6.9	-0.75
39	-1	Ireland	0.25	2	0.7	2.625	1.125	6.7	0.125
40	-1	Bosnia-Hz	1.5	1.75	1.5	0.5	1.375	6.625	0.125
41	–	Latvia	1.625	0.25	1.625	1.375	0.75	5.625	-0.5
42	1	Estonia	1	1.5	1	1.375	0.625	5.5	0.25
43	5	Lithuania	1.25	0.5	0.75	0.5	2.375	5.375	1.25
44	–	Montenegro	1.25	0.75	1	0.875	1.125	5	-0.25
45	-5	Georgia	1.875	1.25	0.625	1.125	0.125	5	-1.375
46	-1	Armenia	1.125	0.375	1.625	1.125	0.625	4.875	-0.25
47	2	Malta	0.875	0.125	0.875	1.25	1.375	4.5	0.5
48	-2	Luxembourg	1.5	0.5	0.75	0.75	0.875	4.375	-0.5
49	-2	Northern Ireland	0.875	1.375	0.75	0.5	0.75	4.25	-0.25
50	–	Wales	0.75	0.125	1.5	1	0.5	3.875	0
51	–	Faroe Islands	0.875	1.375	0.375	0.375	0.75	3.75	0.25
52	–	Gibraltar	No entry	0.25	0.75	1.5	0.5	3	0.5
53	–	Andorra	0.333	0.5	0.166	0.166	0.166	1.331	0.166
54	–	San Marino	0.333	0	0	0	0.166	0.499	0.166
55	–	Kosovo	Not a UEFA member			No entry	0	0	0

Uefa's country coefficients are calculated from performances of each FA's clubs in the last five Europa League and Champions League seasons. They are used to allocate places in Uefa's club competitions and determine seedings with the top 12 receiving at least one place in the Champions League group stage.

Two points are awarded for a win and one for a draw, and half that in qualifying matches. An extra point is awarded for every round from the last 16 of the Champions League and the quarter-finals of the Europa League. Four extra points are given for reaching the group stage of the Champions League and four more for the knockout rounds.

The country coefficient is the sum of the average points for each nation in each of the last five seasons. England's clubs have averaged 16.785, 13.571, 14.25, 14.928 and 20.071 over the last five campaigns – add them together and you get 79.605, England's country coefficient.

Russia

		P	W	D	L	F	A	GD	Pts
1	Lokomotiv Mos.	30	18	6	6	41	21	20	60
2	CSKA Moscow	30	17	7	6	49	23	26	58
3	Spartak Moscow	30	16	8	6	51	32	19	56
4	Krasnodar	30	16	6	8	46	30	16	54
5	Zenit	30	14	11	5	46	21	25	53
6	Ufa	30	11	10	9	34	30	4	43
7	Arsenal Tula	30	12	6	12	35	41	-6	42
8	Dinamo Moscow	30	10	10	10	29	30	-1	40
9	Akhmat Grozny	30	10	9	11	30	34	-4	39
10	Rubin Kazan	30	9	11	10	32	25	7	38
11	Rostov	30	9	10	11	27	28	-1	37
12	Ural	30	8	13	9	31	32	-1	37
13	Amkar Perm	30	9	8	13	20	30	-10	35
14	Anzhi	30	6	6	18	31	55	-24	24
15	Tosno	30	6	6	18	23	54	-31	24
16	Khabarovsk	30	2	7	21	16	55	-39	13

Portugal

		P	W	D	L	F	A	GD	Pts
1	Porto	34	28	4	2	82	18	64	88
2	Benfica	34	25	6	3	80	22	58	81
3	Sporting CP	34	24	6	4	63	24	39	78
4	Braga	34	24	3	7	74	29	45	75
5	Rio Ave	34	15	6	13	40	42	-2	51
6	Chaves	34	13	8	13	47	55	-8	47
7	Maritimo	34	13	8	13	36	49	-13	47
8	Boavista	34	13	6	15	35	44	-9	45
9	V Guimaraes	34	13	4	17	45	56	-11	43
10	Portimonense	34	10	8	16	52	60	-8	38
11	Tondela	34	10	8	16	41	50	-9	38
12	Belenenses	34	9	10	15	33	46	-13	37
13	Aves	34	9	7	18	36	51	-15	34
14	Vitoria Setubal	34	7	11	16	39	62	-23	32
15	Moreirense	34	8	8	18	29	50	-21	32
16	Feirense	34	9	4	21	32	48	-16	31
17	Pacos Ferreira	34	7	9	18	33	59	-26	30
18	Estoril	34	8	6	20	29	61	-32	30

Ukraine

		P	W	D	L	F	A	GD	Pts
1	Shakhtar Don.	22	16	3	3	51	18	33	51
2	Dynamo Kyiv	22	13	6	3	42	20	22	45
3	Vorskla	22	11	4	7	28	22	6	37
4	Zorya	22	8	9	5	38	28	10	33
5	Veres	22	7	11	4	26	17	9	32
6	Mariupol	22	9	5	8	30	27	3	32
7	Olimpik Donetsk	22	7	7	8	24	26	-2	28
8	Oleksandria	22	4	11	7	19	23	-4	23
9	Zirka	22	4	7	11	13	31	-18	19
10	Karpaty	22	3	10	9	13	35	-22	19
11	Chornomorets	22	3	9	10	16	36	-20	18
12	Stal Kamianske	22	3	6	13	15	32	-17	15

Belgium (Championship playoff)

		P	W	D	L	F	A	GD	Pts
1	Club Brugge	10	3	3	4	17	12	5	46
2	Standard Liege	10	6	3	1	20	9	11	43
3	Anderlecht	10	4	0	6	12	15	-3	40
4	Gent	10	4	2	4	8	8	0	39
5	Genk	10	4	2	4	13	13	0	38
6	Charleroi	10	2	2	6	9	22	-13	34

Points from regular season are halved, rounded up and carried over into round-robin championship playoff

Turkey

		P	W	D	L	F	A	GD	Pts
1	Galatasaray	34	24	3	7	75	33	42	75
2	Fenerbahce	34	21	9	4	78	36	42	72
3	Basaksehir	34	22	6	6	62	34	28	72
4	Besiktas	34	21	8	5	69	30	39	71
5	Trabzonspor	34	15	10	9	63	51	12	55
6	Goztepe	34	13	10	11	49	50	-1	49
7	Sivasspor	34	14	7	13	45	53	-8	49
8	Kasimpasa	34	13	7	14	57	58	-1	46
9	Kayserispor	34	12	8	14	44	55	-11	44
10	Malatyaspor	34	11	10	13	38	45	-7	43
11	Akhisarspor	34	11	9	14	44	53	-9	42
12	Alanyaspor	34	11	7	16	55	59	-4	40
13	Bursaspor	34	11	6	17	43	48	-5	39
14	Antalyaspor	34	10	8	16	40	59	-19	38
15	Konyaspor	34	9	9	16	38	42	-4	36
16	Osmanlispor	34	8	9	17	49	60	-11	33
17	Genclerbirligi	34	8	9	17	37	54	-17	33
18	Karabukspor	34	3	3	28	20	86	-66	12

Austria

		P	W	D	L	F	A	GD	Pts
1	Salzburg	36	25	8	3	81	29	52	83
2	Sturm Graz	36	22	4	10	68	45	23	70
3	Rapid Vienna	36	17	11	8	68	43	25	62
4	LASK	36	17	6	13	49	41	8	57
5	Admira	36	15	6	15	59	66	-7	51
6	Mattersburg	36	12	10	14	50	56	-6	46
7	Austria Vienna	36	12	7	17	51	55	-4	43
8	Rheindorf Altach	36	10	8	18	35	51	-16	38
9	Wolfsberger	36	8	9	19	31	57	-26	33
10	St Polten	36	5	5	26	28	77	-49	20

Switzerland

		P	W	D	L	F	A	GD	Pts
1	Young Boys	36	26	6	4	84	41	43	84
2	Basel	36	20	9	7	72	36	36	69
3	Luzern	36	15	9	12	51	51	0	54
4	Zurich	36	12	13	11	50	44	6	49
5	St Gallen	36	14	3	19	52	72	-20	45
6	Sion	36	11	9	16	53	56	-3	42
7	Thun	36	12	6	18	53	68	-15	42
8	Lugano	36	12	6	18	38	55	-17	42
9	Grasshopper	36	10	9	17	43	52	-9	39
10	Lausanne	36	9	8	19	46	67	-21	35

Holland

		P	W	D	L	F	A	GD	Pts
1	PSV Eindhoven	34	26	5	3	87	39	48	83
2	Ajax	34	25	4	5	89	33	56	79
3	AZ Alkmaar	34	22	5	7	72	38	34	71
4	Feyenoord	34	20	6	8	76	39	37	66
5	FC Utrecht	34	14	12	8	58	53	5	54
6	Vitesse	34	13	10	11	63	47	16	49
7	Den Haag	34	13	8	13	45	53	-8	47
8	Heerenveen	34	12	10	12	48	53	-5	46
9	PEC Zwolle	34	12	8	14	42	54	-12	44
10	Heracles	34	11	9	14	50	64	-14	42
11	Excelsior	34	11	7	16	41	56	-15	40
12	Groningen	34	8	14	12	50	50	0	38
13	Willem II	34	10	7	17	50	63	-13	37
14	NAC Breda	34	9	7	18	41	57	-16	34
15	VVV Venlo	34	7	13	14	35	54	-19	34
16	Roda JC	34	8	6	20	42	69	-27	30
17	Sparta Rotterdam	34	7	6	21	34	75	-41	27
18	Twente	34	5	9	20	37	63	-26	24

EUROPA LEAGUE

First qualifying round
Thursday June 29, 2017

AEK Larnaca.... (1) 5-0 (0) ......Lincoln R I
Bala Town....... (0) 1-2 (2) .... Vaduz
Beitar J'salem.. (1) 4-3 (2) ....Vasas
Chikhura Sach. (0) 0-1 (1) ....Altach
Connah's Q..... (1) 1-0 (0) ....HJK Helsinki
Crusaders .... (2) 3-1 (0) ... Dag Liepaja
Dinamo Batumi(0) 0-1 (0) .... Jagiellonia
Dinamo Minsk (1) 2-1 (0) ....NSI Runavik
Domzale .... (0) 2-0 (0) .... Flora Tallinn
Dukla Trencin.. (2) 5-1 (1)Torpedo Kutaisi
Ferencvaros .... (1) 2-0 (0) .... Jelgava
Fola Esch .... (1) 2-1 (0) . Milsami Orhei
Haugesund .... (3) 7-0 (0) .... Coleraine
Irtysh .... (1) 1-0 (0) .... Dunav Ruse
KR Reykjavik ... (0) 0-0 (0) ....SJK
Kairat Almaty.. (4) 6-0 (0) ....Atlantas
Ki Klaksvik ..... (0) 0-0 (0) ......AIK Solna
Lech Poznan.. (3) 4-0 (0) ..Pelister Bitola
Levadia Tallinn (0) 0-2 (1) ......Cork City
Levski Sofia..... (3) 3-1 (0) ....Sutjeska
Lyngby........... (1) 1-0 (0) ...Bangor City
M. Tel Aviv..... (1) 2-0 (0) ...... SK Tirana
Midtjylland .... (3) 6-1 (0) ... Derry City
Mladost Lucani(0) 0-3 (2) ....Inter Baku
Mladost Pod. .. (0) 1-0 (0) .... Gandzasar
NK Siroki Brijeg(2) 2-0 (0) ....Ordabasy
Nomme Kalju... (1) 2-1 (0) ..B36 Torshavn
Norrkoping ..... (5) 5-0 (0) .... Prishtina
Odd Grenland . (1) 3-0 (0) .....Ballymena
Partizan Tirana (1) 1-3 (1) ..Botev Plovdiv
Pyunik Yerevan(1) 1-4 (1) ...S. Bratislava
Rangers .... (0) 1-0 (0) ...P Niedercorn
Red Star.......... (1) 3-0 (0) .... Floriana FC
Shakhtyor .... (0) 0-0 (0) ......FK Suduva
Shirak Gumri... (0) 0-2 (1) .ND HIT Gorica
Shkendija......... (2) 3-0 (0) .... Dacia
Skenderbeu ..... (0) 0-0 (0) ...UE Sant Julia
St Johnstone ... (1) 1-2 (2) ....FK Trakai
St Josephs....... (0) 0-4 (1) ...AEL Limassol
Stjarnan .... (0) 0-1 (1) .....Shamrock R
Tre Penne........ (0) 0-1 (0) ......Rabotnicki
UE Santa.......... (0) 0-2 (0) .... Osijek
VPS Vaasa....... (1) 1-0 (0) ... O. Ljubljana
Valletta .... (1) 2-0 (0) Folgore Falciano
Ventspils........ (0) 0-0 (0) ....Valur
Videoton......... (0) 2-0 (0) .... Balzan
Vojvodina NS.. (2) 2-1 (0) ... Ruzomberok
Zaria Balti ...... (2) 2-1 (0) .... Sarajevo
Zeljeznicar ...... (0) 1-0 (0) ....Zeta
Zira................. (1) 2-0 (0) .....Differdange

Second legs
Tuesday July 4, 2017

Balzan .... (1) 3-3 (2) ....Videoton
Videoton 5-3 on agg
P Niedercorn... (0) 2-0 (0) .... Rangers
Progres Niederkorn 2-1 on agg

Thursday July 6, 2017
AEL Limassol... (3) 6-0 (0) ....St Josephs
AEL 10-0 on agg
AIK Solna........ (5) 5-0 (0) ...... Ki Klaksvik
AIK 5-0 on agg
Altach .... (1) 1-1 (0) Chikhura Sach.
Altach 2-1 on agg
Atlantas........... (1) 1-2 (2) ..Kairat Almaty
Kairat 8-1 on agg
B36 Torshavn.. (0) 1-2 (1)..Nomme Kalju
Nomme Kalju 4-2 on agg
Ballymena........ (0) 0-2 (0) . Odd Grenland
Odd 5-0 on agg
Bangor City..... (0) 0-3 (3) ....Lyngby
Lyngby 8-0 on agg
Botev Plovdiv.. (1) 1-0 (0) Partizan Tirana
Botev Plovdiv 4-1 on agg
Coleraine .... (0) 0-0 (0) ..... Haugesund
Haugesund 7-0 on agg
Cork City........ (1) 4-2 (2) Levadia Tallinn
Cork City 6-2 on agg
Dacia .... (0) 0-4 (2) ....Shkendija
Shkendija 7-0 on agg
Derry City .... (1) 1-4 (2) ... Midtjylland
Midtjylland 10-2 on agg
Differdange..... (1) 1-2 (0) ....Zira
Zira 4-1 on agg
Dunav Ruse .... (0) 0-1 (0) ....Irtysh
Irtysh 3-0 on agg
FK Suduva....... (1) 2-1 (1) ...... Shakhtyor
FK Suduva 2-1 on agg
FK Trakai........ (0) 1-0 (0) ... St Johnstone
FK Trakai 3-1 on agg
Flora Tallinn ... (2) 2-3 (1) .... Domzale
Domzale 5-2 on agg
Floriana FC..... (1) 3-3 (1) ....Red Star
Red Star 6-3 on agg
Folgore Falciano(0)0-1 (0) ....Valletta
Valletta 3-0 on agg
Gandzasar ...... (0) 0-3 (0) .. Mladost Pod.
Mladost Pod. 4-0 on agg
HJK Helsinki .... (2) 3-0 (0) ....Connah's Q
HJK 3-1 on agg
Inter Baku....... (1) 2-0 (0)Mladost Lucani
Inter Baku 5-0 on agg
Jagiellonia ..... (0) 4-0 (0)Dinamo Batumi
Jagiellonia 5-0 on agg
Jelgava .... (0) 0-1 (1) ... Ferencvaros
Ferencvaros 3-0 on agg
Liepaja............ (1) 2-0 (0) ...... Crusaders
3-3 on agg, Liepaja won on away goals
Lincoln R I ...... (1) 1-1 (0) ....AEK Larnaca
AEK Larnaca 6-1 on agg
Milsami Orhei . (1) 1-1 (0) .... Fola Esch
Fola Esch 3-2 on agg
ND HIT Gorica. (1) 2-2 (1) ...Shirak Gumri
ND HIT Gorica 4-2 on agg
NSI Runavik.... (0) 0-2 (1) Dinamo Minsk
Dinamo Minsk 4-1 on agg
O. Ljubljana .... (1) 0-1 (0) .....VPS Vaasa
VPS 2-0 on agg
Ordabasy........ (0) 0-0 (0)NK Siroki Brijeg
NK Siroki Brijeg 2-0 on agg
Osijek.............. (2) 4-0 (0) ....UE Santa
Osijek 6-0 on agg
Pelister Bitola.. (0) 0-3 (1) ....Lech Poznan
Lech Poznan 7-0 on agg

Prishtina .... (0) 0-1 (0) ..... Norrkoping
Norrkoping 6-0 on agg
Rabotnicki....... (2) 6-0 (0) ....Tre Penne
Rabotnicki 7-0 on agg
Ruzomberok ... (0) 2-0 (0) .. Vojvodina NS
Ruzomberok 3-2 on agg
S. Bratislava.... (2) 5-0 (0)Pyunik Yerevan
Slovan Bratislava 9-1 on agg
SJK................... (0) 0-2 (0) ... KR Reykjavik
KR 2-0 on agg
SK Tirana .... (0) 0-3 (0) ......M. Tel Aviv
Maccabi Tel Aviv 5-0 on agg
Sarajevo .... (2) 2-1 (0) ...... Zaria Balti
AET – 2-1 after 90, 3-3 agg. Zaria 6-5 pens
Shamrock R...... (1) 1-0 (0) ....Stjarnan
Shamrock Rovers 2-0 on agg
Sutjeska.......... (0) 0-0 (0) .....Levski Sofia
Levski Sofia 3-1 on agg
Torpedo Kutaisi(0) 0-3 (1) ..Dukla Trencin
Dukla Trencin 8-1 on agg
UE Sant Julia.... (0) 0-5 (2) ... Skenderbeu
Skenderbeu 6-0 on agg
Vaduz .... (3) 3-0 (0) ......Bala Town
Vaduz 5-1 on agg
Valur................ (0) 0-1 (0) .... Ventspils
Valur 1-0 on agg
Vasas............... (0) 0-3 (1) ..Beitar J'salem
Beitar Jerusalem 7-3 on agg
Zeta................. (1) 2-2 (1) ...... Zeljeznicar
Zeljeznicar 3-2 on agg

Second qualifying round
Wednesday July 12, 2017
Inter Baku....... (0) 1-0 (0) .... Fola Esch

Thursday July 13, 2017
Aberdeen........ (1) 1-1 (0)NK Siroki Brijeg
Altach.............. (0) 0-0 (0)..Dinamo Brest
Ap Limassol ... (3) 3-0 (0) .... Zaria Balti
Astra Giurgiu .. (1) 3-1 (1) ....Zira
Beitar J'salem.. (1) 1-1 (0) ..Botev Plovdiv
Brondby.......... (2) 2-0 (0) ....VPS Vaasa
Cork City........ (0) 0-1 (0) ...AEK Larnaca
Dag Liepaja .... (0) 0-2 (1) .....FK Suduva
Dukla Trencin.. (1) 1-1 (1) ...Bnei Yehuda
Ferencvaros .... (2) 2-4 (1) ... Midtjylland
Hajduk Split ... (1) 1-0 (0) .....Levski Sofia
Haugesund .... (1) 3-2 (0) ....Lech Poznan
Irtysh .... (0) 1-1 (0) ....Red Star
Kairat Almaty.. (1) 1-1 (0) ... Skenderbeu
M. Tel Aviv..... (0) 3-1 (0) ... KR Reykjavik
Nomme Kalju.. (0) 0-3 (1) ....Videoton
Norrkoping ..... (1) 2-1 (0) ......FK Trakai
Osijek.............. (2) 2-0 (0) ....Lucerne
Ostersunds..... (0) 2-0 (0) ..Galatasaray
P Niedercorn... (0) 0-1 (0) ...AEL Limassol
Panionios........ (1) 2-0 (0).ND HIT Gorica
Qabala............. (0) 1-1 (1) ..... Jagiellonia
Rabotnicki....... (1) 1-1 (0) Dinamo Minsk
Ruzomberok ... (0) 0-1 (0) ....Brann
S. Bratislava.... (0) 0-1 (0) ....Lyngby
Shamrock R...... (0) 2-3 (1)Mlada Boleslav
Shkendija........ (1) 3-1 (1) ... HJK Helsinki

Clockwise from above: Everton's season got off to an early start against Slovakians Ruzomberok; St Johnstone and Rangers fell at the first hurdle, Derek McInnes' Aberdeen reached the third qualifying round before bowing out

Sturm Graz...... (0) 0-1 (1) .. Mladost Pod.
Vaduz .... (0) 0-1 (1) . Odd Grenland
Valletta .... (0) 0-0 (0) .... FC Utrecht
Valur............... (1) 1-2 (1) .... Domzale
Zeljeznicar ...... (0) 0-0 (0) .... AIK Solna

Second legs
Thursday July 20, 2017
AEK Larnaca.... (1) 1-0 (0) .... Cork City
  AEK Larnaca 2-0 on agg
AEL Limassol... (0) 2-1 (0) .. P Niedercorn
  AEL 3-1 on agg
AIK Solna........ (0) 2-0 (0) ...... Zeljeznicar
  AIK 2-0 on agg
Bnei Yehuda.... (0) 2-0 (0) .. Dukla Trencin
  Bnei Yehuda 3-1 on agg
Botev Plovdiv.. (2) 4-0 (0) .. Beitar J'salem
  Botev Plovdiv 5-1 on agg
Brann............. (0) 0-2 (0) ... Ruzomberok
  Ruzomberok 2-1 on agg
Dinamo Brest.. (0) 0-3 (2) .... Altach
  Altach 4-1 on agg
Dinamo Minsk (1) 3-0 (0) .... Rabotnicki
  Dinamo Minsk 4-1 on agg
Domzale .... (1) 3-2 (2) .... Valur
  Domzale 5-3 on agg
FC Utrecht....... (0) 3-1 (0) .... Valletta
  FC Utrecht 3-1 on agg
FK Suduva....... (0) 0-1 (0) .... Dag Liepaja
  FK Suduva 2-1 on agg

FK Trakai......... (2) 2-1 (0) ..... Norrkoping
  AET. 2-1 after 90, 3-3 on agg. Trakai 5-3 pens
Fola Esch .... (2) 4-1 (0) .... Inter Baku
  Fola Esch 4-2 on agg
Galatasaray .... (0) 1-1 (0) ..... Ostersunds
  Ostersunds 3-1 on agg
HJK Helsinki..... (1) 1-1 (0) .... Shkendija
  Shkendija 4-2 on agg
Jagiellonia ...... (0) 0-2 (1) .... Qabala
  Qabala 3-1 on agg
KR Reykjavik... (0) 0-2 (0) ...... M. Tel Aviv
  Maccabi Tel Aviv 5-1 on agg
Lech Poznan.... (1) 2-0 (0) ..... Haugesund
  Lech Poznan 4-3 on agg
Levski Sofia..... (0) 1-2 (0) .... Hajduk Split
  Hajduk Split 3-1 on agg
Lucerne........... (1) 2-1 (0) .... Osijek
  Osijek 3-2 on agg
Lyngby........... (2) 2-1 (0) .... S. Bratislava
  Lyngby 3-1 on agg
Midtjylland ..... (1) 3-1 (0) .... Ferencvaros
  Midtjylland 7-3 on agg
Mlada Boleslav (2) 2-0 (0) .... Shamrock R
  Mlada Boleslav 5-2 on agg
Mladost Pod... (0) 0-3 (2) ...... Sturm Graz
  Sturm Graz 3-1 on agg
ND HIT Gorica.. (1) 2-3 (3) .... Panionios
  Panionios 5-2 on agg
NK Siroki Brijeg(0) 0-2 (0) .... Aberdeen
  Aberdeen 3-1 on agg

Odd Grenland. (0) 1-0 (0) .... Vaduz
  Odd 2-0 on agg
Red Star........... (1) 2-0 (0) .... Irtysh
  Red Star 3-1 on agg
Skenderbeu .... (0) 2-0 (0) .. Kairat Almaty
  Skenderbeu 3-1 on agg
VPS Vaasa....... (2) 2-1 (1) .... Brondby
  Brondby 3-2 on agg
Videoton.......... (1) 1-1 (0) .. Nomme Kalju
  Videoton 4-1 on agg
Zaria Balti .... (0) 1-2 (1) .... Ap Limassol
  Apollon Limassol 5-1 on agg
Zira................ (0) 0-0 (0) .. Astra Giurgiu
  Astra 3-1 on agg

Third qualifying round
Thursday July 27, 2017
AEK Larnaca.... (1) 2-0 (0) Dinamo Minsk
AIK Solna........ (1) 1-1 (1) .... Braga
Aberdeen........ (1) 2-1 (0) .... Ap Limassol
Arka Gdynia.... (2) 3-2 (2) ..... Midtjylland
Astra Giurgiu .. (0) 0-0 (0) .... Oleksandria
Aus. Vienna .... (0) 0-0 (0) ... AEL Limassol
Bnei Yehuda.... (0) 0-2 (0) .... Zenit
Bordeaux........ (2) 2-1 (1) .... Videoton
Botev Plovdiv.. (0) 0-0 (0) .... Maritimo
Brondby.......... (0) 0-0 (0) .... Hajduk Split
Din Zagreb...... (2) 2-1 (1) . Odd Grenland
Din. Bucharest (0) 1-1 (1) ..... Ath Bilbao

Arsenal's season finished with a whimper in Madrid

Everton .... (0) 1-0 (0) ... Ruzomberok
FC Utrecht .... (0) 0-0 (0) ....Lech Poznan
FK Suduva .... (2) 3-0 (0) .... FC Sion
FK Trakai .... (1) 2-1 (1) .... Shkendija
Freiburg .... (1) 1-0 (0) .... Domzale
Gent .... (0) 1-1 (1) .... Altach
Krasnodar .... (0) 2-1 (0) .... Lyngby
M. Tel Aviv ..... (0) 1-0 (0) .... Panionios
Marseille .... (2) 4-2 (1) .... Oostende
Mlada Boleslav (1) 2-1 (0) .... Skenderbeu
Olimpik Donetsk(0)1-1 (0) PAOK Salonika
Ostersunds ..... (0) 1-0 (0) ...... Fola Esch
PSV Eindhoven (0) 0-1 (0) .... Osijek
Panathinaikos . (1) 1-0 (0) .... Qabala
Red Star .... (1) 2-0 (0) . Sparta Prague
Sturm Graz ...... (1) 1-2 (2) ..... Fenerbahce
Uni Craiova ..... (0) 0-1 (1) .... Milan

Second legs

Wednesday August 2, 2017

AEL Limassol ... (0) 1-2 (1) .... Aus. Vienna
Austria Vienna 2-1 on agg
FC Sion .... (0) 1-1 (0) .... FK Suduva
FK Suduva 4-1 on agg

Thursday August 3, 2017

Altach .... (1) 3-1 (1) .... Gent
Altach 4-2 on agg
Ap Limassol ..... (1) 2-0 (0) ...... Aberdeen
Apollon Limassol won 3-2 on agg
Ath Bilbao ...... (2) 3-0 (0) Din. Bucharest
Athletic Bilbao 4-1 on agg
Braga .... (0) 2-0 (0) .... AIK Solna
Braga 3-2 on agg
Dinamo Minsk (0) 1-1 (0) ....AEK Larnaca
AEK Larnaca 3-1 on agg

Domzale .... (0) 2-0 (0) .... Freiburg
Domzale 2-1 on agg
Fenerbahce ..... (1) 1-1 (0) ...... Sturm Graz
Fenerbahce 3-2 on agg
Fola Esch .... (0) 1-2 (0) .... Ostersunds
Ostersunds 3-1 on agg
Hajduk Split .... (0) 2-0 (0) .... Brondby
Hajduk Split 2-0 on agg
Lech Poznan .... (1) 2-2 (1) .... FC Utrecht
2-2 on agg. FC Utrecht won on away goals
Lyngby .... (1) 1-3 (2) ...... Krasnodar
Krasnodar 5-2 on agg
Maritimo .... (1) 2-0 (0) ..Botev Plovdiv
Maritimo 2-0 on agg
Midtjylland ..... (0) 2-0 (0) ....Arka Gdynia
4-4 on agg. Midtjylland won on away goals
Milan .... (1) 2-0 (0) .... Uni Craiova
Milan 3-0 on agg
Odd Grenland . (0) 0-0 (0) ...... Din Zagreb
Dinamo Zagreb 2-1 on agg
Oleksandria ..... (1) 1-0 (0) .. Astra Giurgiu
Oleksandria 1-0 on agg
Oostende .... (0) 0-0 (0) .... Marseille
Marseille 4-2 on agg
Osijek .... (1) 1-0 (0) PSV Eindhoven
Osijek 2-0 on agg
PAOK Salonika (2) 2-0 (0)Olimpik Donetsk
PAOK 3-1 on agg
Panionios .... (0) 0-1 (0) ..... M. Tel Aviv
Maccabi Tel Aviv 2-0 on agg
Qabala .... (0) 1-2 (0) . Panathinaikos
Panathinaikos 3-1 on agg
Ruzomberok ... (0) 0-1 (0) .... Everton
Everton 2-0 on agg
Shkendija .... (2) 3-0 (0) .... FK Trakai
Shkendija 4-2 on agg

Skenderbeu .... (0) 2-1 (1)Mlada Boleslav
AET. 2-1 after 90, 3-3 agg. Skenderbeu 4-2 pens
Sparta Prague . (0) 0-1 (1) .... Red Star
Red Star 3-0 on agg
Videoton .... (1) 1-0 (0) .... Bordeaux
2-2 on agg. Videoton won on away goals
Zenit .... (0) 0-1 (0) ....Bnei Yehuda
Zenit 2-1 on agg

Playoff round

Wednesday August 16, 2017

FC Utrecht .... (0) 1-0 (0) .... Zenit

Thursday August 17, 2017

Ajax .... (0) 0-1 (0) ...... Rosenborg
Altach .... (0) 0-1 (0) ..... M. Tel Aviv
Ap Limassol .... (1) 3-2 (1) ..... Midtjylland
BATE Borisov .. (1) 1-1 (1) ..... Oleksandria
Club Brugge.... (0) 0-0 (0) ....AEK Athens
Din Zagreb ..... (0) 1-1 (1) .... Skenderbeu
Domzale .... (1) 1-1 (0) .... Marseille
Everton .... (2) 2-0 (0) ... Hajduk Split
Hafnarfjordur.. (1) 1-2 (0) .... Braga
Krasnodar .... (1) 3-2 (0) .... Red Star
Legia Warsaw . (0) 1-1 (0) ...... FC Sheriff
Ludogorets .... (0) 2-0 (0) .....FK Suduva
Maritimo .... (0) 0-0 (0) .. Dynamo Kiev
Milan .... (3) 6-0 (0) .... Shkendija
Osijek .... (1) 1-2 (1) ..... Aus. Vienna
PAOK Salonika (1) 3-1 (1) ..... Ostersunds
Panathinaikos . (1) 2-3 (0) ...... Ath Bilbao
Partizan .... (0) 0-0 (0) .... Videoton
Vardar Skopje . (1) 2-0 (0) .....Fenerbahce
Viitorul C .... (1) 1-3 (3) .... RB Salzburg
Viktoria Plzen.. (2) 3-1 (1) ....AEK Larnaca

Second legs
Thursday August 25, 2017
AEK Athens..... (2) 3-0 (0) ....Club Brugge
AEK Athens 3-0 on agg
AEK Larnaca.... (0) 0-0 (0)..Viktoria Plzen
Viktoria Plzen 3-1 on agg
Ath Bilbao ...... (1) 1-0 (0) . Panathinaikos
Athletic Bilbao 4-2 on agg
Aus. Vienna .... (0) 0-1 (0) .... Osijek
2-2 on agg. Aus. Vienna won on away goals
Braga.............. (1) 3-2 (1)..Hafnarfjordur
Braga 5-3 on agg
Dynamo Kiev .. (2) 3-1 (0) ....Maritimo
Dynamo Kiev 3-1 on agg
FC Sheriff........ (0) 0-0 (0). Legia Warsaw
1-1 on agg. FC Sheriff won on away goals
FK Suduva....... (0) 0-0 (0) ..... Ludogorets
Ludogorets 2-0 on agg
Fenerbahce ..... (0) 1-2 (0) . Vardar Skopje
Vardar 4-1 on agg
Hajduk Split .... (1) 1-1 (0)............Everton
Everton 3-1 on agg
M. Tel Aviv...... (1) 2-2 (1)..............Altach
Maccabi Tel Aviv 3-2 on agg
Marseille......... (1) 3-0 (0) ....Domzale
Marseille 4-1 on agg
Midtjylland ..... (1) 1-1 (0) .... Ap Limassol
Apollon Limassol 4-3 on agg
Oleksandria ..... (1) 1-2 (0) . BATE Borisov
BATE 3-2 on agg
Ostersunds ..... (0) 2-0 (0) PAOK Salonika
3-3 on agg. Ostersunds won on away goals
RB Salzburg .... (2) 4-0 (0) .... Viitorul C
RB Salzburg 7-1 on agg
Red Star.......... (1) 2-1 (0) ...... Krasnodar
4-4 on agg. Red Star won on away goals
Rosenborg ...... (1) 3-2 (0) ....Ajax
Rosenborg 4-2 on agg
Shkendija........ (0) 0-1 (1) ....Milan
Milan 7-0 on agg
Skenderbeu .... (0) 0-0 (0) ......Din Zagreb
1-1 on agg. Skenderbeu won on away goals
Videoton......... (0) 0-4 (3) ....Partizan
Partizan 4-0 on agg
Zenit.............. (1) 2-0 (0) ....FC Utrecht
AET – 1-0 after 90. Zenit won 2-1 on agg

Group A
	P	W	D	L	F	A	GD	Pts
Villarreal	6	3	2	1	10	6	4	11
Astana	6	3	1	2	10	7	3	10
Slavia Prague	6	2	2	2	6	6	0	8
M. Tel Aviv	6	1	1	4	1	8	-7	4

Thursday September 14, 2017
Slavia Prague.. (1) 1-0 (0) .....M. Tel Aviv
Villarreal .... (1) 3-1 (0) ....Astana

Thursday September 28, 2017
Astana .... (1) 1-1 (1)..Slavia Prague
M. Tel Aviv..... (0) 0-0 (0) ....Villarreal

Thursday October 19, 2017
Astana .... (2) 4-0 (0)....M. Tel Aviv
Villarreal .... (2) 2-2 (0)..Slavia Prague

Thursday November 2, 2017
M. Tel Aviv..... (0) 0-1 (0) ....Astana
Slavia Prague.. (0) 0-2 (1) ....Villarreal

Thursday November 23, 2017
Astana .... (1) 2-3 (1) ....Villarreal
M. Tel Aviv...... (0) 0-2 (1)..Slavia Prague

Thursday December 7, 2017
Slavia Prague.. (0) 0-1 (1) ....Astana
Villarreal .... (0) 0-1 (1) ......M. Tel Aviv

Group B
	P	W	D	L	F	A	GD	Pts
Dynamo Kiev	6	4	1	1	15	9	6	13
Partizan	6	2	2	2	8	9	-1	8
Young Boys	6	1	3	2	7	8	-1	6
Skenderbeu	6	1	2	3	6	10	-4	5

Thursday September 14, 2017
Dynamo Kiev .. (0) 3-1 (1) ... Skenderbeu
Young Boys..... (1) 1-1 (1) .... Partizan

Thursday September 28, 2017
Partizan .... (2) 2-3 (0).. Dynamo Kiev
Skenderbeu .... (0) 1-1 (0) ....Young Boys

Thursday October 19, 2017
Dynamo Kiev .. (1) 2-2 (2)....Young Boys
Skenderbeu .... (0) 0-0 (0) .... Partizan

Thursday November 2, 2017
Partizan .... (1) 2-0 (0) ... Skenderbeu
Young Boys..... (0) 0-1 (0).. Dynamo Kiev

Thursday November 23, 2017
Skenderbeu .... (1) 3-2 (1).. Dynamo Kiev
Partizan .... (2) 2-1 (1) ....Young Boys

Thursday December 7, 2017
Dynamo Kiev .. (3) 4-1 (1) .... Partizan
Young Boys..... (0) 2-1 (0) ... Skenderbeu

Group C
	P	W	D	L	F	A	GD	Pts
Braga	6	3	1	2	9	8	1	10
Ludogorets	6	2	3	1	7	5	2	9
Basaksehir	6	2	2	2	7	8	-1	8
Hoffenheim	6	1	2	3	8	10	-2	5

Thursday September 14, 2017
Hoffenheim ..... (1) 1-2 (1) ....Braga
Basaksehir ...... (0) 0-0 (0) .... Ludogorets

Thursday September 28, 2017
Braga.............. (1) 2-1 (1) ... Basaksehir
Ludogorets ..... (0) 2-1 (1) ....Hoffenheim

Thursday October 19, 2017
Braga.............. (0) 0-2 (1) .... Ludogorets
Hoffenheim..... (0) 3-1 (0) ... Basaksehir

Thursday November 2, 2017
Basaksehir ...... (0) 1-1 (0) ....Hoffenheim
Ludogorets ..... (0) 1-1 (0) ....Braga

Thursday November 23, 2017
Braga.............. (1) 3-1 (0) ....Hoffenheim
Ludogorets ..... (0) 1-2 (2) .... Basaksehir

Thursday December 7, 2017
Hoffenheim ..... (1) 1-1 (0) .... Ludogorets
Basaksehir ...... (1) 2-1 (0) ....Braga

Group D
	P	W	D	L	F	A	GD	Pts
Milan	6	3	2	1	13	6	7	11
AEK Athens	6	1	5	0	6	5	1	8
Rijeka	6	2	1	3	11	12	-1	7
Austria Vienna	6	1	2	3	9	16	-7	5

Thursday September 14, 2017
Aus. Vienna ..... (0) 1-5 (3) ....Milan
Rijeka .... (1) 1-2 (1) ....AEK Athens

Thursday September 28, 2017
AEK Athens..... (1) 2-2 (1) .... Aus. Vienna
Milan.............. (1) 3-2 (0) ....Rijeka

Thursday October 19, 2017
Aus. Vienna .... (0) 1-3 (2) .... Rijeka
Milan .... (0) 0-0 (0).....AEK Athens

Thursday November 2, 2017
AEK Athens..... (0) 0-0 (0) ....Milan
Rijeka .... (0) 1-4 (1) ... Aus. Vienna

Thursday November 23, 2017
AEK Athens..... (1) 2-2 (2) .... Rijeka
Milan .... (3) 5-1 (1) .... Aus. Vienna

Thursday December 7, 2017
Aus. Vienna .... (0) 0-0 (0)......AEK Athens
Rijeka .... (1) 2-0 (0) ....Milan

Group E
	P	W	D	L	F	A	GD	Pts
Atalanta	6	4	2	0	14	4	10	14
Lyon	6	3	2	1	11	4	7	11
Everton	6	1	1	4	7	15	-8	4
Ap Limassol	6	0	3	3	5	14	-9	3

Thursday September 14, 2017
Ap Limassol .... (0) 1-1 (0) .... Lyon
Atalanta .... (3) 3-0 (0)...........Everton

Thursday September 28, 2017
Everton .... (1) 2-2 (1) .... Ap Limassol
Lyon .... (1) 1-1 (0) .... Atalanta

Thursday October 19, 2017
Atalanta .... (1) 3-1 (0) .... Ap Limassol
Everton .... (0) 1-2 (1) .... Lyon

Thursday November 2, 2017
Ap Limassol .... (0) 1-1 (1) .... Atalanta
Lyon .... (0) 3-0 (0) ....Everton

Thursday November 23, 2017
Everton .... (0) 1-5 (1) .... Atalanta
Lyon .... (2) 4-0 (0) .... Ap Limassol

Thursday December 7, 2017
Ap Limassol .... (0) 0-3 (2) ....Everton
Atalanta .... (1) 1-0 (0) .... Lyon

Group F
	P	W	D	L	F	A	GD	Pts
Lok. Moscow	6	3	2	1	9	4	5	11
Copenhagen	6	2	3	1	7	3	4	9
FC Sheriff	6	2	3	1	4	0	4	9
Zlin	6	0	2	4	1	10	-9	2

Thursday September 14, 2017
FC Copenhagen(0) 0-0 (0) .. Lok. Moscow
Zlin .... (0) 0-0 (0) .... FC Sheriff

Thursday September 28, 2017
FC Sheriff........ (0) 0-0 (0)FC Copenhagen
Lok. Moscow .. (3) 3-0 (0) ....Zlin

Thursday October 19, 2017
FC Sheriff........ (1) 1-1 (1) .. Lok. Moscow
Zlin .... (1) 1-1 (1)FC Copenhagen

Thursday November 2, 2017
FC Copenhagen(3) 3-0 (0) ....Zlin
Lok. Moscow .. (1) 1-2 (1) ...... FC Sheriff

Thursday November 23, 2017
FC Sheriff........ (1) 1-0 (0) ....Zlin
Lok. Moscow .. (1) 2-1 (1)FC Copenhagen

Thursday December 7, 2017
FC Copenhagen(2) 0-0 (0) ....FC Sheriff
Zlin .... (0) 0-2 (0) .. Lok. Moscow

Group G

	P	W	D	L	F	A	GD	Pts
Viktoria Plzen	6	4	0	2	13	8	5	12
Steaua	6	3	1	2	9	7	2	10
Lugano	6	3	0	3	9	11	-2	9
H Be'er Sheva	6	1	1	4	5	10	-5	4

Thursday Septe mber 14, 2017
H Be'er Sheva . (1) 2-1 (0) .... Lugano
Steaua .... (2) 3-0 (0) .. Viktoria Plzen
Thursday September 28, 2017
Lugano .... (1) 1-2 (0) .... Steaua
Viktoria Plzen.. (1) 3-1 (0). H Be'er Sheva
Thursday October 19, 2017
H Be'er Sheva . (0) 1-2 (0) .... Steaua
Lugano .... (0) 3-2 (0) .. Viktoria Plzen
Thursday November 2, 2017
Steaua .... (1) 1-1 (1). H Be'er Sheva
Viktoria Plzen.. (3) 4-1 (1) .... Lugano
Thursday November 23, 2017
Lugano .... (0) 1-0 (0). H Be'er Sheva
Viktoria Plzen.. (0) 2-0 (0) .... Steaua
Thursday December 7, 2017
H Be'er Sheva . (0) 0-2 (1) .. Viktoria Plzen
Steaua .... (0) 1-2 (2) .... Lugano

Group H

	P	W	D	L	F	A	GD	Pts
Arsenal	6	4	1	1	14	4	10	13
Red Star	6	2	3	1	3	2	1	9
Cologne	6	2	0	4	7	8	-1	6
BATE Borisov	6	1	2	3	6	16	-10	5

Thursday September 14, 2017
Arsenal .... (0) 3-1 (1) .... Cologne
Red Star.......... (0) 1-1 (0).. BATE Borisov
Thursday September 28, 2017
BATE Borisov .. (1) 2-4 (3) .... Arsenal
Cologne.......... (0) 0-1 (1) .... Red Star
Thursday October 19, 2017
BATE Borisov .. (0) 1-0 (0) .... Cologne
Red Star.......... (0) 0-1 (0) .... Arsenal
Thursday November 2, 2017
Arsenal .... (0) 0-0 (0) .... Red Star
Cologne.......... (1) 5-2 (2) .. BATE Borisov
Thursday November 23, 2017
BATE Borisov .. (0) 0-0 (0) .... Red Star
Cologne.......... (0) 1-0 (0) .... Arsenal
Thursday December 7, 2017
Arsenal .... (3) 6-0 (0) .. BATE Borisov
Red Star.......... (1) 1-0 (0) .... Cologne

Group I

	P	W	D	L	F	A	GD	Pts
RB Salzburg	6	3	3	0	7	1	6	12
Marseille	6	2	2	2	4	4	0	8
Konyaspor	6	1	3	2	4	6	-2	6
V Guimaraes	6	1	2	3	5	9	-4	5

Thursday September 14, 2017
Marseille......... (0) 1-0 (0) ...... Konyaspor
V Guimaraes ... (1) 1-1 (1) ... RB Salzburg
Thursday September 28, 2017
Konyaspor ...... (1) 2-1 (0) .. V Guimaraes
RB Salzburg ... (0) 1-0 (0) .... Marseille

Thursday October 19, 2017
Marseille......... (1) 2-1 (1) ... V Guimaraes
Konyaspor ...... (0) 0-2 (1) .... RB Salzburg
Thursday November 2, 2017
RB Salzburg .... (0) 0-0 (0) ...... Konyaspor
V Guimaraes ... (0) 1-0 (0) .... Marseille
Thursday November 23, 2017
Konyaspor ...... (0) 1-1 (0) .... Marseille
RB Salzburg ... (2) 3-0 (0) .. V Guimaraes
Thursday December 7, 2017
Marseille......... (0) 0-0 (0) ... RB Salzburg
V Guimaraes ... (1) 1-1 (1) ...... Konyaspor

Group J

	P	W	D	L	F	A	GD	Pts
Ath Bilbao	6	3	2	1	8	5	3	11
Ostersunds	6	3	2	1	8	4	4	11
Zorya	6	2	0	4	3	9	-6	6
Hertha Berlin	6	1	2	3	6	7	-1	5

Thursday September 14, 2017
Hertha Berlin... (0) 0-0 (0) ...... Ath Bilbao
Zorya .... (0) 0-2 (0) ..... Ostersunds
Thursday September 28, 2017
Ath Bilbao ...... (0) 0-1 (1) .... Zorya
Ostersunds ..... (1) 1-0 (0) ...Hertha Berlin
Thursday October 19, 2017
Ostersunds ..... (0) 2-2 (1) ...... Ath Bilbao
Zorya .... (1) 2-1 (0) ...Hertha Berlin
Thursday November 2, 2017
Ath Bilbao ...... (0) 1-0 (0) .... Ostersunds
Hertha Berlin... (1) 2-0 (0) .... Zorya
Thursday November 23, 2017
Ath Bilbao ...... (1) 3-2 (2) ...Hertha Berlin
Ostersunds ..... (1) 2-0 (0) .... Zorya
Thursday December 7, 2017
Hertha Berlin... (0) 1-1 (0) ..... Ostersunds
Zorya .... (0) 0-2 (1) ...... Ath Bilbao

Group K

	P	W	D	L	F	A	GD	Pts
Lazio	6	4	1	1	12	7	5	13
Nice	6	3	0	3	12	7	5	9
Waregem	6	2	1	3	8	13	-5	7
Vitesse	6	1	2	3	5	10	-5	5

Thursday September 14, 2017
Vitesse............ (1) 2-3 (0) .... Lazio
Waregem........ (0) 1-5 (3) .... Nice
Thursday September 28, 2017
Lazio .... (1) 2-0 (0) .... Waregem
Nice .... (2) 3-0 (0) .... Vitesse
Thursday October 19, 2017
Nice .... (1) 1-3 (0) .... Lazio
Waregem........ (1) 1-1 (1) .... Vitesse
Thursday November 2, 2017
Lazio .... (0) 1-0 (0) .... Nice
Vitesse............ (0) 0-2 (1) .... Waregem
Thursday November 23, 2017
Lazio .... (1) 1-1 (1) .... Vitesse
Nice .... (2) 3-1 (0) .... Waregem
Thursday December 7, 2017
Vitesse............ (0) 1-0 (0) .... Nice
Waregem........ (1) 3-2 (0) .... Lazio

Group L

	P	W	D	L	F	A	GD	Pts
Zenit	6	5	1	0	17	5	12	16
Sociedad	6	4	0	2	16	6	10	12
Rosenborg	6	1	2	3	6	11	-5	5
Vardar Skopje	6	0	1	5	3	20	-17	1

Thursday September 14, 2017
Sociedad......... (3) 4-0 (0) ...... Rosenborg
Vardar Skopje .. (0) 0-5 (3) .... Zenit
Thursday September 28, 2017
Rosenborg ...... (1) 3-1 (0). Vardar Skopje
Zenit................ (2) 3-1 (1) .... Sociedad
Thursday October 19, 2017
Vardar Skopje . (0) 0-6 (3) .... Sociedad
Zenit................ (1) 3-1 (0) ...... Rosenborg
Thursday November 2, 2017
Rosenborg ...... (0) 1-1 (0) .... Zenit
Sociedad......... (1) 3-0 (0). Vardar Skopje
Thursday November 23, 2017
Rosenborg ...... (0) 0-1 (0) .... Sociedad
Zenit................ (2) 2-1 (0). Vardar Skopje
Thursday December 7, 2017
Sociedad......... (0) 1-3 (1) .... Zenit
Vardar Skopje . (1) 1-1 (1) ...... Rosenborg

Round of 32

Tuesday February 13, 2018
Red Star.......... (0) 0-0 (0) CSKA Moscow
Thursday February 15, 2018
AEK Athens..... (0) 1-1 (1).. Dynamo Kiev
Astana .... (1) 1-3 (0).......... Sporting
B Dortmund .... (1) 3-2 (0) .... Atalanta
Celtic .... (0) 1-0 (0) .... Zenit
FC Copenhagen (1) 1-4 (2) ...... Atl Madrid
Ludogorets ..... (0) 0-3 (1).............. Milan
Lyon .... (0) 3-1 (0) .... Villarreal
Marseille.......... (1) 3-0 (0) .... Braga
Napoli .... (0) 1-3 (0) .... RB Leipzig
Nice................. (2) 2-3 (1).. Lok. Moscow
Ostersunds ..... (0) 0-3 (2) .... Arsenal
Partizan .... (0) 1-1 (0) .. Viktoria Plzen
Sociedad......... (0) 2-2 (1) ... RB Salzburg
Spartak Moscow (0) 1-3 (3) ..... Ath Bilbao
Steaua .... (1) 1-0 (0) .... Lazio

Second legs

Wednesday February 21, 2018
CSKA Moscow (1) 1-0 (0) ....Red Star
CSKA Moscow 1-0 on agg
Thursday February 22, 2018
Arsenal .... (0) 1-2 (2) ..... Ostersunds
Arsenal 4-2 on agg
Atalanta .... (1) 1-1 (0) ... B Dortmund
Dortmund 4-3 on agg
Ath Bilbao ...... (0) 1-2 (1)Spartak Moscow
Athletic Bilbao 4-3 on agg
Atl Madrid ...... (1) 1-0 (0)FC Copenhagen
Atletico Madrid 5-1 on agg
Braga.............. (1) 1-0 (0) ....Marseille
Marseille 3-1 on agg
Dynamo Kiev .. (1) 1-0 (0) .....AEK Athens
1-1 on agg. Kiev won on away goals
Lazio................ (3) 5-1 (0) .... Steaua
Lazio 5-2 on agg

Thursday October 19, 2017
Marseille......... (1) 2-1 (1)...V Guimaraes
Konyaspor ...... (0) 0-2 (1).... RB Salzburg
Thursday November 2, 2017
RB Salzburg .... (0) 0-0 (0) ...... Konyaspor
V Guimaraes ... (0) 1-0 (0) ....Marseille
Thursday November 23, 2017
Konyaspor ...... (0) 1-1 (0) ....Marseille
RB Salzburg ... (2) 3-0 (0) .. V Guimaraes
Thursday December 7, 2017
Marseille......... (0) 0-0 (0) ... RB Salzburg
V Guimaraes ... (0) 1-1 (1) ...... Konyaspor

A dominant Atletico outfit claimed Europa League glory

Lok. Moscow .. (1) 1-0 (0) .... Nice
Lokomotiv Moscow 4-2 on agg
Milan .... (1) 1-0 (0) ..... Ludogorets
Milan 4-0 on agg
RB Leipzig .... (0) 0-2 (1) .... Napoli
3-3 on agg. RB Leipzig won on away goals
RB Salzburg .... (1) 2-1 (1) .... Sociedad
RB Salzburg 4-3 on agg
Sporting .... (1) 3-3 (1) .... Astana
Sporting 6-4 on agg
Viktoria Plzen.. (0) 2-0 (0) .... Partizan
Viktoria Plzen 3-1 on agg
Villarreal .... (0) 0-1 (0) .... Lyon
Lyon 4-1 on agg
Zenit .... (2) 3-0 (0) .... Celtic
Zenit 3-1 on agg

Round of 16
Thursday March 8, 2018
Atl Madrid ...... (1) 3-0 (0) .. Lok. Moscow
B Dortmund .... (0) 1-2 (0) .... RB Salzburg
CSKA Moscow .. (0) 0-1 (0) .... Lyon
Lazio .... (0) 2-2 (0) .. Dynamo Kiev
Marseille .... (2) 3-1 (1) ...... Ath Bilbao
Milan .... (0) 0-2 (2) .... Arsenal
RB Leipzig .... (0) 2-1 (0) .... Zenit
Sporting .... (1) 2-0 (0) .. Viktoria Plzen

Second legs
Thursday March 15, 2018
Arsenal .... (1) 3-1 (1) .... Milan
Arsenal 5-1 on agg
Ath Bilbao ...... (0) 1-2 (1) .... Marseille
Marseille 5-2 on agg
Dynamo Kiev .. (0) 0-2 (1) .... Lazio
Lazio 4-2 on agg
Lok. Moscow .. (1) 1-5 (1) ...... Atl Madrid
Atletico Madrid 8-1 on agg
Lyon .... (0) 2-3 (1) CSKA Moscow
3-3 on agg – CSKA won on away goals
RB Salzburg .... (0) 0-0 (0) .... B Dortmund
RB Salzburg 2-1 on agg
Viktoria Plzen.. (1) 2-1 (0) .... Sporting
AET – 2-0 after 90. Sporting won 3-2 on agg
Zenit .... (1) 1-1 (1) .... RB Leipzig
RB Leipzig 3-2 on agg

Quarter-finals
Thursday April 5, 2018
Arsenal .... (4) 4-1 (1) CSKA Moscow
Atl Madrid ...... (2) 2-0 (0) .... Sporting
Lazio .... (1) 4-2 (1) .... RB Salzburg
RB Leipzig .... (1) 1-0 (0) .... Marseille

Second legs
Thursday April 12, 2018
CSKA Moscow (1) 2-2 (0) .... Arsenal
Arsenal 6-3 on agg
Marseille .... (3) 5-2 (1) ...... RB Leipzig
Marseille 5-3 on agg
RB Salzburg .... (0) 4-1 (0) .... Lazio
RB Salzburg 6-5 on agg
Sporting .... (1) 1-0 (0) ...... Atl Madrid
Atletico Madrid 2-1 on agg

Semi-finals
Thursday April 26, 2018
Arsenal .... (0) 1-1 (0) ...... Atl Madrid
Marseille .... (1) 2-0 (0) .... RB Salzburg

Second legs
Thursday May 3, 2018
Atl Madrid ...... (1) 1-0 (0) .... Arsenal
Atletico Madrid 2-1 on agg
RB Salzburg .... (0) 2-1 (0) .... Marseille
AET – 2-0 after 90. Marseille 3-2 on agg

Europa League final
Wednesday May 16, 2018
Marseille .... (0) 0-3 (1) ...... Atl Madrid
POS 57/43 SH ON 2/4 SH OFF 8/4 CRN 1/6
SCORERS **Atl Madrid:** Griezmann (21, 49)
Fernandez (89)

CHAMPIONS LEAGUE

First qualifying round

Tuesday June 27, 2017

Alashkert ....(1) 1-0 (0)FC Santa Coloma
Hibernians ......(0) 2-0 (0)Tallinna Infonet
The New Saints(1) 1-2 (1) .... Europa FC
Vikingur..........(1) 2-1 (1) .... Trepca '89

Wednesday June 28, 2017

Linfield ....(0) 1-0 (0) .... La Fiorita

Second legs

Tuesday July 4, 2017

Europa FC........(0) 1-3 (2)The New Saints
   AET – 1-2 after 90. TNS won 4-3 on agg
FC Santa Coloma(0) 1-1 (1) .... Alashkert
   Alashkert 2-1 on agg
La Fiorita ....(0) 0-0 (0) .... Linfield
   Linfield 1-0 on agg
Tallinna Infonet(0) 0-1 (0) ...... Hibernians
   Hibernians 3-0 on agg
Trepca '89.......(0) 1-4 (2) .... Vikingur
   Vikingur 6-2 on agg

Second qualifying round

Tuesday July 11, 2017

Hibernians ......(0) 0-3 (2) .... RB Salzburg
Partizan ....(0) 2-0 (0) .... Buducnost P.
Qarabag ....(3) 5-0 (0) .... Samtredia
Rijeka ....(1) 2-0 (0)The New Saints

Wednesday July 12, 2017

APOEL ....(0) 1-0 (0)F91 Dudelange
BATE Borisov ..(1) 1-1 (0) .... Alashkert
Dundalk..........(1) 1-1 (1) ..... Rosenborg
FC Sheriff........(0) 1-0 (0) ....Kukesi
H Beer Sheva ..(1) 2-1 (0) ....Honved
Hafnarfjordur..(0) 1-1 (0) ....Vikingur
Malmo............(0) 1-1 (0) . Vardar Skopje
Mariehamn .....(0) 0-3 (3) .Legia Warsaw
Spart. Jurmala.(0) 0-1 (0) ....Astana
Zalgiris Vilnius (0) 2-1 (1) .... Ludogorets
Zilina ....(1) 1-3 (0)FC Copenhagen
Zrinjski Mostar (0) 1-2 (1) .... Maribor

Friday July 14, 2017

Linfield ....(0) 0-2 (2) .... Celtic

Second legs

Tuesday July 18, 2017

Alashkert ....(1) 1-3 (2) .. BATE Borisov
   BATE Borisov 4-2 on agg
Astana ....(0) 1-1 (0) .Spart. Jurmala
   Astana 2-1 on agg
Buducnost P. ...(0) 0-0 (0) .... Partizan
   Partizan 2-0 on agg
Samtredia ....(0) 1-5 (1) .... Qarabag
   Qarabag 6-0 on agg
The New Saints(0) 1-5 (1) .... Rijeka
   Rijeka 7-1 on agg
Vardar Skopje .(0) 3-1 (1) ....Malmo
   Vardar 4-2 on agg
Vikingur..........(0) 0-2 (0) .Hafnarfjordur
   Hafnarfjordur 3-1 on agg

Wednesday July 19, 2017

Celtic ....(1) 4-0 (0) .... Linfield
   Celtic 6-0 on agg
F91 Dudelange(0) 0-1 (1) .... APOEL
   APOEL 2-0 on agg
FC Copenhagen(0) 1-2 (1) .... Zilina
   FC Copenhagen 4-3 on agg
Honved...........(1) 2-3 (2) .. H Beer Sheva
   Hapoel Be'er Sheva 5-3 on agg
Kukesi.............(2) 2-1 (0) .... FC Sheriff
   2-2 on agg, FC Sheriff won on away goals
Legia Warsaw.(3) 6-0 (0) .....Mariehamn
   Legia Warsaw 9-0 on agg
Ludogorets .....(1) 4-1 (1) Zalgiris Vilnius
   Ludogorets 5-3 on agg
Maribor ....(1) 1-1 (1) Zrinjski Mostar
   Maribor 3-2 on agg
RB Salzburg ....(2) 3-0 (0) ...... Hibernians
   RB Salzburg 6-0 on agg
Rosenborg ......(1) 2-1 (1) ....Dundalk
   AET – 1-1 after 90. Rosenborg 3-2 on agg

Third qualifying round

Tuesday July 25, 2017

AEK Athens.....(0) 0-2 (1) CSKA Moscow
Partizan ....(1) 1-3 (1) .....Olympiakos
Qarabag ....(0) 0-0 (0) .... FC Sheriff
Slavia Prague ..(1) 1-0 (0) .. BATE Borisov
Steaua ....(1) 2-2 (1) ..Viktoria Plzen
Vardar Skopje .(0) 1-0 (0)FC Copenhagen

Clockwise from top left: Celtic's Scott Sinclair was joint-top scorer in Champions League qualifying; Trent Alexander-Arnold took the first step for Liverpool in their long road to the final; Linfield found Celtic too hot to handle; Ajax's dismal European campaign saw them dumped out of both competitions before the group stage

Wednesday July 26, 2017

Astana .... (2) 3-1 (0) . Legia Warsaw
Celtic .... (0) 0-0 (0) ...... Rosenborg
Club Brugge.... (2) 3-3 (0)Istanbul Buyuk.
Dynamo Kiev .. (2) 3-1 (0) ..... Young Boys
H Beer Sheva .. (1) 2-0 (0) ..... Ludogorets
Maribor .... (0) 1-0 (0) .. Hafnarfjordur
Nice .... (1) 1-1 (0) .... Ajax
RB Salzburg .... (0) 1-1 (1) .... Rijeka
Viitorul C .... (0) 1-0 (0) .... APOEL

Second legs

Tuesday August 1, 2017
FC Sheriff........ (0) 1-2 (1) .... Qarabag
Qarabag 2-1 on agg

Wednesday August 2, 2017
Ajax .... (1) 2-2 (1) .... Nice
3-3 on agg, Nice won on away goals
APOEL .... (0) 4-0 (0) .... Viitorul C
APOEL 4-1 on agg
BATE Borisov .. (1) 2-1 (1) .. Slavia Prague
2-2 on agg, Slavia Prague won on away goals

CSKA Moscow (0) 1-0 (0) .....AEK Athens
CSKA Moscow 3-0 on agg
FC Copenhagen(2) 4-1 (1) . Vardar Skopje
FC Copenhagen 4-2 on agg
Hafnarfjordur.. (0) 0-1 (0) .... Maribor
Maribor 2-0 on agg
Istanbul Buyuk.(2) 2-0 (0) ....Club Brugge
Istanbul 5-3 on agg
Legia Warsaw. (0) 1-0 (0) ....Astana
Astana 3-2 on agg
Ludogorets ..... (2) 3-1 (0) .. H Beer Sheva
3-3 on agg, H Be'er Sheva won on away goals
Olympiakos..... (1) 2-2 (1) .... Partizan
Olympiakos 5-3 on agg
Rijeka .... (0) 0-0 (0) ..... RB Salzburg
1-1 on agg, Rijeka won on away goals
Rosenborg ...... (0) 0-1 (0) .... Celtic
Celtic 1-0 on agg
Viktoria Plzen.. (0) 1-4 (1) .... Steaua
Steaua Bucharest 6-3 on agg
Young Boys..... (1) 2-0 (0) .. Dynamo Kiev
3-3 on agg, Young Boys won on away goals

Tuesday August 15, 2017
APOEL .... (2) 2-0 (0) ..Slavia Prague
Hoffenheim..... (0) 1-2 (1) .... Liverpool
Qarabag .... (1) 1-0 (0)FC Copenhagen
Sporting.......... (0) 0-0 (0) .... Steaua
Young Boys..... (0) 0-1 (0) CSKA Moscow

Wednesday August 16, 2017
Celtic .... (2) 5-0 (0) ....Astana
H Be'er Sheva . (2) 2-1 (1) .... Maribor
Istanbul Buyuk.(0) 1-2 (1) ....Sevilla
Napoli .... (1) 2-0 (0) ....Nice
Olympiakos..... (0) 2-1 (1) .... Rijeka

Second legs

Tuesday August 22, 2017
Astana .... (1) 4-3 (1) .... Celtic
Celtic 8-4 on agg
Maribor .... (1) 1-0 (0) . H Be'er Sheva
2-2 on agg, Maribor won on away goals
Nice .... (0) 0-2 (0) .... Napoli
Napoli 4-0 on agg
Rijeka .... (0) 0-1 (1) ....Olympiakos
Olympiakos 3-1 on agg
Sevilla............. (0) 2-2 (1)Istanbul Buyuk.
Sevilla 4-3 on agg

Wednesday August 23, 2017
CSKA Moscow (1) 2-0 (0) .....Young Boys
CSKA Moscow 3-0 on agg

FC Copenhagen(1) 2-1 (0) .... Qarabag
2-2 on agg, Qarabag won away goals
Liverpool ....(3) 4-2 (1) .....Hoffenheim
Liverpool 6-3 on agg
Slavia Prague.. (0) 0-0 (0) .... APOEL
APOEL 2-0 on agg
Steaua ....(1) 1-5 (1) ....Sporting
Sporting 5-1 on agg

Group A

	P	W	D	L	F	A	GD	Pts
Man United	6	5	0	1	12	3	9	15
Basel	6	4	0	2	11	5	6	12
CSKA Moscow	6	3	0	3	8	10	-2	9
Benfica	6	0	0	6	1	14	-13	0

Tuesday September 12, 2017
Benfica ....(0) 1-2 (0) CSKA Moscow
Man Utd ....(1) 3-0 (0) .... Basel
Wednesday September 27, 2017
Basel ....(2) 5-0 (0) .... Benfica
CSKA Moscow (0) 1-4 (3) .... Man Utd
Wednesday October 18, 2017
Benfica ....(0) 0-1 (0) .... Man Utd
CSKA Moscow (0) 0-2 (1) .... Basel
Tuesday October 31, 2017
Basel ....(1) 1-2 (0) CSKA Moscow
Man Utd ....(1) 2-0 (0) .... Benfica
Wednesday November 22, 2017
Basel ....(0) 1-0 (0) .... Man Utd
CSKA Moscow (1) 2-0 (0) .... Benfica
Tuesday December 5, 2017
Benfica ....(0) 0-2 (1) .... Basel
Man Utd ....(0) 2-1 (1) CSKA Moscow

Group B

	P	W	D	L	F	A	GD	Pts
Paris St-G	6	5	0	1	25	4	21	15
Bayern Munich	6	5	0	1	13	6	7	15
Celtic	6	1	0	5	5	18	-13	3
Anderlecht	6	1	0	5	2	17	-15	3

Tuesday September 12, 2017
Bayern Munich(1) 3-0 (0) .....Anderlecht
Celtic ....(0) 0-5 (3) ....Paris St-G
Wednesday September 27, 2017
Anderlecht.......(0) 0-3 (1) .... Celtic
Paris St-G........(2) 3-0 (0)Bayern Munich
Wednesday October 18, 2017
Anderlecht.......(0) 0-4 (2) ....Paris St-G
Bayern Munich (2) 3-0 (0) .... Celtic
Tuesday October 31, 2017
Celtic ....(0) 1-2 (1)Bayern Munich
Paris St-G........(2) 5-0 (0) .....Anderlecht
Wednesday November 22, 2017
Anderlecht.......(0) 1-2 (0)Bayern Munich
Paris St-G........(4) 7-1 (1) .... Celtic
Tuesday December 5, 2017
Bayern Munich (2) 3-1 (0) ....Paris St-G
Celtic ....(0) 0-1 (0) .....Anderlecht

Group C

	P	W	D	L	F	A	GD	Pts
Roma	6	3	2	1	9	6	3	11
Chelsea	6	3	2	1	16	8	8	11
Atl Madrid	6	1	4	1	5	4	1	7
Qarabag	6	0	2	4	2	14	-12	2

Tuesday September 12, 2017
Chelsea...........(2) 6-0 (0) .... Qarabag
Roma..............(0) 0-0 (0) ...... Atl Madrid
Wednesday September 27, 2017
Atl Madrid ......(1) 1-2 (0) ....Chelsea
Qarabag ....(1) 1-2 (2) ....Roma
Wednesday October 18, 2017
Chelsea...........(2) 3-3 (1) ....Roma
Qarabag ....(0) 0-0 (0) ...... Atl Madrid
Tuesday October 31, 2017
Atl Madrid ......(0) 1-1 (1) .... Qarabag
Roma..............(2) 3-0 (0) ....Chelsea
Wednesday November 22, 2017
Atl Madrid ......(0) 2-0 (0) ....Roma
Qarabag ....(0) 0-4 (2) ....Chelsea
Tuesday December 5, 2017
Chelsea...........(0) 1-1 (0) ...... Atl Madrid
Roma..............(0) 1-0 (0) .... Qarabag

Group D

	P	W	D	L	F	A	GD	Pts
Barcelona	6	4	2	0	9	1	8	14
Juventus	6	3	2	1	7	5	2	11
Sporting	6	2	1	3	8	9	-1	7
Olympiakos	6	0	1	5	4	13	-9	1

Tuesday September 12, 2017
Barcelona ....(1) 3-0 (0) ....Juventus
Olympiakos.....(0) 2-3 (3) ....Sporting

Wednesday September 27, 2017
Juventus ....(0) 2-0 (0) .....Olympiakos
Sporting..........(0) 0-1 (0) .... Barcelona
Wednesday October 18, 2017
Barcelona ....(1) 3-1 (0) .....Olympiakos
Juventus ....(1) 2-1 (1) ....Sporting
Tuesday October 31, 2017
Olympiakos.....(0) 0-0 (0) .... Barcelona
Sporting..........(1) 1-1 (0) ....Juventus
Wednesday November 22, 2017
Juventus ....(0) 0-0 (0) .... Barcelona
Sporting..........(2) 3-1 (0) .....Olympiakos
Tuesday December 5, 2017
Barcelona ....(0) 2-0 (0) ....Sporting
Olympiakos.....(0) 0-2 (1) ....Juventus

Group E

	P	W	D	L	F	A	GD	Pts
Liverpool	6	3	3	0	23	6	17	12
Sevilla	6	2	3	1	12	12	0	9
Sp. Moscow	6	1	3	2	9	13	-4	6
Maribor	6	0	3	3	3	16	-13	3

Wednesday September 13, 2017
Liverpool ....(2) 2-2 (1) ....Sevilla
Maribor ....(0) 1-1 (0)Spartak Moscow
Tuesday September 26, 2017
Sevilla.............(2) 3-0 (0) .... Maribor
Spartak Moscow(1) 1-1 (1) .... Liverpool

Clockwise from main: Liverpool blitzed Man City in the quarter-finals; Juventus were too savvy for spirited Spurs; Lionel Messi outclassed Chelsea: United limped out in tame fashion against Sevilla

Tuesday October 17, 2017
Maribor .... (0) 0-7 (4) .... Liverpool
Spartak Moscow(1) 5-1 (1) .... Sevilla
Wednesday November 1, 2017
Liverpool .... (0) 3-0 (0) .... Maribor
Sevilla .... (1) 2-1 (0)Spartak Moscow
Tuesday November 21, 2017
Sevilla .... (0) 3-3 (3) .... Liverpool
Spartak Moscow(0) 1-1 (0) .... Maribor
Wednesday December 6, 2017
Liverpool .... (3) 7-0 (0)Spartak Moscow
Maribor .... (1) 1-1 (0) .... Sevilla

Group F

	P	W	D	L	F	A	GD	Pts
Man City	6	5	0	1	14	5	9	15
Shakhtar	6	4	0	2	9	9	0	12
Napoli	6	2	0	4	11	11	0	6
Feyenoord	6	1	0	5	5	14	-9	3

Wednesday September 13, 2017
Feyenoord ...... (0) 0-4 (3) .... Man City
Shakhtar .... (1) 2-1 (0) .... Napoli
Tuesday September 26, 2017
Man City .... (0) 2-0 (0) .... Shakhtar
Napoli .... (1) 3-1 (0) ..... Feyenoord
Tuesday October 17, 2017
Feyenoord ...... (1) 1-2 (1) .... Shakhtar
Man City .... (2) 2-1 (0) .... Napoli

Wednesday November 1, 2017
Napoli .... (1) 2-4 (1) .... Man City
Shakhtar .... (2) 3-1 (1) ...... Feyenoord
Tuesday November 21, 2017
Man City .... (0) 1-0 (0) ..... Feyenoord
Napoli .... (0) 3-0 (0) .... Shakhtar
Wednesday December 6, 2017
Feyenoord ...... (1) 2-1 (1) .... Napoli
Shakhtar .... (2) 2-1 (0) .... Man City

Group G

	P	W	D	L	F	A	GD	Pts
Besiktas	6	4	2	0	11	5	6	14
Porto	6	3	1	2	15	10	5	10
RB Leipzig	6	2	1	3	10	11	-1	7
Monaco	6	0	2	4	6	16	-10	2

Wednesday September 13, 2017
Porto .... (1) 1-3 (2) .... Besiktas
RB Leipzig .... (1) 1-1 (1) .... Monaco
Tuesday September 26, 2017
Besiktas .... (2) 2-0 (0) .... RB Leipzig
Monaco .... (0) 0-3 (1) .... Porto
Tuesday October 17, 2017
Monaco .... (1) 1-2 (1) .... Besiktas
RB Leipzig .... (3) 3-2 (2) .... Porto
Wednesday November 1, 2017
Besiktas .... (0) 1-1 (1) .... Monaco
Porto .... (1) 3-1 (0) ....RB Leipzig

Tuesday November 21, 2017
Besiktas .... (1) 1-1 (1) .... Porto
Monaco .... (1) 1-4 (4) ......RB Leipzig
Wednesday December 6, 2017
Porto .... (3) 5-2 (0) .... Monaco
RB Leipzig .... (0) 1-2 (1) .... Besiktas

Group H

	P	W	D	L	F	A	GD	Pts
Tottenham	6	5	1	0	15	4	11	16
Real Madrid	6	4	1	1	17	7	10	13
Dortmund	6	0	2	4	7	13	-6	2
APOEL	6	0	2	4	2	17	-15	2

Wednesday September 13, 2017
Real Madrid ... (1) 3-0 (0) .... APOEL
Tottenham ...... (2) 3-1 (1) .... B Dortmund
Tuesday September 26, 2017
APOEL .... (0) 0-3 (1) ...... Tottenham
B Dortmund .... (0) 1-3 (1) .... Real Madrid
Tuesday October 17, 2017
APOEL .... (0) 1-1 (0) .... B Dortmund
Real Madrid ... (1) 1-1 (1) ...... Tottenham
Wednesday November 1, 2017
B Dortmund .... (1) 1-1 (0) .... APOEL
Tottenham ...... (1) 3-1 (0) .... Real Madrid

Gareth Bale's sensational strike helped Real Madrid to a third-consecutive Champions League title

Tuesday November 21, 2017
APOEL .... (0) 0-6 (4) .... Real Madrid
B Dortmund .... (1) 1-2 (0) ...... Tottenham

Wednesday December 6, 2017
Real Madrid .... (2) 3-2 (1) .... B Dortmund
Tottenham ...... (2) 3-0 (0) .... APOEL

Round of 16

First legs

Tuesday February 13, 2018
Basel .... (0) 0-4 (3) .... Man City
Juventus .... (2) 2-2 (1) ...... Tottenham

Wednesday February 14, 2018
Porto.............. (0) 0-5 (2) .... Liverpool
Real Madrid .... (1) 3-1 (1) .... Paris St-G

Tuesday February 20, 2018
Bayern Munich (1) 5-0 (0) .... Besiktas
Chelsea........... (0) 1-1 (0) ...... Barcelona

Wednesday February 21, 2018
Sevilla............. (0) 0-0 (0) .... Man Utd
Shakhtar .... (0) 2-1 (1) .... Roma

Second legs

Tuesday March 6, 2018
Liverpool .... (0) 0-0 (0) .... Porto
Liverpool 5-0 on agg
Paris St-G .... (0) 1-2 (0) .... Real Madrid
Real Madrid 5-2 on agg

Wednesday March 7, 2018
Man City .... (1) 1-2 (1) .... Basel
Man City 5-2 on agg
Tottenham ...... (1) 1-2 (0) .... Juventus
Juventus 4-3 on agg

Tuesday March 13, 2018
Man Utd .... (0) 1-2 (0) .... Sevilla
Sevilla 2-1 on agg
Roma.............. (0) 1-0 (0) .... Shakhtar
2-2 on agg, Roma won on away goals

Wednesday March 14, 2018
Barcelona .... (2) 3-0 (0) .... Chelsea
Barcelona 4-1 on agg
Besiktas .... (0) 1-3 (1) Bayern Munich
Bayern Munich 8-1 on agg

Quarter-finals

Tuesday April 3, 2018
Juventus .... (0) 0-3 (1) .... Real Madrid
Sevilla............. (1) 1-2 (1) Bayern Munich

Wednesday April 4, 2018
Barcelona .... (1) 4-1 (0) .... Roma
Liverpool .... (3) 3-0 (0) .... Man City

Second legs

Tuesday April 10, 2018
Man City .... (1) 1-2 (0) ...... Liverpool
Liverpool 5-1 on agg
Roma.............. (1) 3-0 (0) .... Barcelona
4-4 on agg, Roma won on away goals

Wednesday April 11, 2018
Bayern Munich (0) 0-0 (0) .... Sevilla
Bayern Munich 2-1 on agg
Real Madrid .... (0) 1-3 (2) .... Juventus
Real Madrid 4-3 on agg

Semi-finals

Tuesday April 24, 2018
Liverpool .... (2) 5-2 (0) .... Roma

Wednesday April 25, 2018
Bayern Munich (1) 1-2 (1) .... Real Madrid

Second legs

Tuesday May 1, 2018
Real Madrid .... (1) 2-2 (1) .... B Munich
Real Madrid 4-3 on agg

Wednesday May 2, 2018
Roma.............. (1) 4-2 (2) .... Liverpool
Liverpool 7-6 on agg

Champions League final

Saturday May 26, 2018
Real Madrid .... (0) 3-1 (0) .... Liverpool
POS 65/35 SH ON 5/2 SH OFF 6/3 CRN 9/5
SCORERS **Real Madrid:** Benzema (51)
Bale (64, 83) **Liverpool:** Mane (55)

Ladbrokes

9/2
LIVERPOOL TO WIN
THE PREMIER LEAGUE 18/19

PREMIER LEAGUE OUTRIGHT

MAN CITY	4/6	NEWCASTLE	500/1
LIVERPOOL	9/2	SOUTHAMPTON	500/1
MAN UTD	6/1	WEST HAM	500/1
CHELSEA	9/1	BOURNEMOUTH	750/1
TOTTENHAM	11/1	BURNLEY	750/1
ARSENAL	25/1	BRIGHTON	1000/1
WOLVES	100/1	CARDIFF	1000/1
EVERTON	200/1	FULHAM	1000/1
LEICESTER	200/1	HUDDERSFIELD	1000/1
CRYSTAL PALACE	500/1	WATFORD	1000/1

Each-way 1/3 the odds a place 1-2

Uefa – 13 qualifiers

Comprised of nine round-robin home-and-away six-team groups. Group winners qualify for World Cup finals while eight best-ranked runners-up playoff for final four Uefa slots.

EUROPE

Sunday September 4, 2016
Czech Rep ...... (0) 0-0 (0) .... N Ireland
Denmark .... (1) 1-0 (0) ....Armenia
Kazakhstan .... (0) 2-2 (2) ....Poland
Lithuania........ (2) 2-2 (0) ....Slovenia
Malta .... (1) 1-5 (1)........ Scotland
Norway .... (0) 0-3 (2) ....Germany
Romania......... (0) 1-1 (0) ... Montenegro
San Marino .... (0) 0-1 (1).......Azerbaijan
Slovakia .... (0) 0-1 (0) ....England

Monday September 5, 2016
Albania .... (1) 2-1 (0) ... Macedonia
Croatia........... (1) 1-1 (1)............Turkey
Finland .... (1) 1-1 (0) ....Kosovo
Georgia........... (0) 1-2 (2) ....Austria
Israel .... (1) 1-3 (2) ....Italy
Serbia............. (0) 2-2 (1)..........Ireland
Spain .... (1) 8-0 (0) .. Liechtenstein
Ukraine .... (1) 1-1 (0)..........Iceland
Wales.............. (2) 4-0 (0) ....Moldova

Tuesday September 6, 2016
Andorra........... (0) 0-1 (0) ....Latvia
Belarus........... (0) 0-0 (0) ....France
Bosnia-Hz...... (2) 5-0 (0) .... Estonia
Bulgaria .... (1) 4-3 (0) .. Luxembourg
Cyprus............ (0) 0-3 (1) ....Belgium
Faroe Islands.. (0) 0-0 (1).......Hungary
Gibraltar......... (1) 1-4 (4) ....Greece
Sweden........... (1) 1-1 (0)........Holland
Switzerland.... (2) 2-0 (0) .... Portugal

Thursday October 6, 2016
Austria .... (1) 2-2 (2) .... Wales
Iceland............ (1) 3-2 (2) .... Finland
Ireland .... (0) 1-0 (0) .... Georgia
Italy................. (0) 1-1 (0) .... Spain
Kosovo .... (0) 0-6 (3) ....Croatia
Liechtenstein .. (0) 0-2 (1)..........Albania
Macedonia...... (0) 1-2 (2) .... Israel
Moldova......... (0) 0-3 (2) ....Serbia
Turkey .... (1) 2-2 (2) ....Ukraine

Friday October 7, 2016
Belgium........... (2) 4-0 (0) ..... Bosnia-Hz
Estonia............ (2) 4-0 (0) ....Gibraltar
France .... (3) 4-1 (1).......Bulgaria
Greece............. (2) 2-0 (0) ....Cyprus
Holland .... (2) 4-1 (0) ....Belarus
Hungary .... (0) 2-3 (0) ... Switzerland
Latvia.............. (0) 0-2 (1)... Faroe Islands
Luxembourg.... (0) 1-0 (0)........Sweden
Portugal.......... (3) 6-0 (0) ....Andorra

Saturday October 8, 2016
Armenia........... (0) 0-5 (4) .... Romania
Azerbaijan....... (1) 1-0 (0) ....Norway
England........... (2) 2-0 (0) ....Malta
Germany.......... (1) 3-0 (0) ....Czech Rep
Montenegro..... (1) 5-0 (0) ....Kazakhstan
N Ireland......... (1) 4-0 (0) .... San Marino
Poland............. (2) 3-2 (0) ....Denmark
Scotland.......... (0) 1-1 (0) ....Lithuania
Slovenia .... (0) 1-0 (0) ....Slovakia

Sunday October 9, 2016
Albania .... (0) 0-2 (0) .... Spain
Finland .... (0) 0-1 (1)............Croatia
Iceland............ (2) 2-0 (0) ....Turkey
Israel .... (2) 2-1 (0) .. Liechtenstein
Macedonia...... (0) 2-3 (1)............Italy
Moldova......... (1) 1-3 (1)..........Ireland
Serbia............. (2) 3-2 (1)..........Austria
Ukraine .... (1) 3-0 (0) ....Kosovo
Wales.............. (1) 1-1 (0) ....Georgia

Monday October 10, 2016
Andorra........... (0) 1-2 (1).... Switzerland
Belarus........... (0) 1-1 (0) ... Luxembourg
Bosnia-Hz...... (0) 2-0 (0) ....Cyprus
Estonia............ (0) 0-2 (1)...........Greece
Faroe Islands.. (0) 0-6 (3) .... Portugal
Gibraltar......... (0) 0-6 (3) ....Belgium
Holland .... (0) 1-1 (0)............France
Latvia.............. (0) 0-2 (1)...........Hungary
Sweden........... (2) 3-0 (0) ....Bulgaria

Tuesday October 11, 2016
Kazakhstan ..... (0) 0-0 (0) .... Romania
Czech Rep ...... (0) 0-0 (0) ......Azerbaijan
Germany .... (2) 2-0 (0) .... N Ireland
Norway .... (1) 4-1 (0) .... San Marino
Denmark .... (0) 0-1 (1)... Montenegro
Poland............. (0) 2-1 (0) ....Armenia;
Lithuania......... (0) 2-0 (0) ....Malta
Slovakia .... (1) 3-0 (0) ....Scotland
Slovenia .... (0) 0-0 (0) ....England

Friday November 11, 2016
Armenia........... (0) 3-2 (2) ... Montenegro
France .... (0) 2-1 (0) ....Sweden
Czech Rep ...... (1) 2-1 (0) ....Norway
N Ireland......... (2) 4-0 (0) ....Azerbaijan
San Marino ..... (0) 0-8 (3) ....Germany
Denmark .... (2) 4-1 (1)....Kazakhstan
Romania.......... (0) 0-3 (1) ....Poland
England........... (1) 3-0 (0) ....Scotland
Malta .... (0) 0-1 (0) ....Slovenia
Slovakia .... (3) 4-0 (0) ....Lithuania

Saturday November 12, 2016
Austria .... (0) 0-1 (0) ....Ireland
Georgia........... (1) 1-1 (0) ....Moldova
Croatia........... (1) 2-0 (0) ....Iceland
Wales.............. (1) 1-1 (0) ....Serbia
Albania .... (3) 3-0 (1)............Israel
Liechtenstein .. (0) 0-4 (4) ....Italy
Spain .... (1) 4-0 (0) .... Macedonia
Ukraine .... (1) 1-0 (0) ....Finland
Turkey .... (0) 2-0 (0) ....Kosovo

Group A	P	W	D	L	F	A	GD	Pts
France (Q)	10	7	2	1	18	6	12	23
Sweden (Q)	10	6	1	3	26	9	17	19
Holland	10	6	1	3	21	12	9	19
Bulgaria	10	4	1	5	14	19	-5	13
Luxembourg	10	1	3	6	8	26	-18	6
Belarus	10	1	2	7	6	21	-15	5

Group B	P	W	D	L	F	A	GD	Pts
Portugal (Q)	10	9	0	1	32	4	28	27
Switzerland (Q)	10	9	0	1	23	7	16	27
Hungary	10	4	1	5	14	14	0	13
Faroe Islands	10	2	3	5	4	16	-12	9
Latvia	10	2	1	7	7	18	-11	7
Andorra	10	1	1	8	2	23	-21	4

Group C	P	W	D	L	F	A	GD	Pts
Germany (Q)	10	10	0	0	43	4	39	30
N Ireland	10	6	1	3	17	6	11	19
Czech Rep	10	4	3	3	17	10	7	15
Norway	10	4	1	5	17	16	1	13
Azerbaijan	10	3	1	6	10	19	-9	10
San Marino	10	0	0	10	2	51	-49	0

Group D	P	W	D	L	F	A	GD	Pts
Serbia (Q)	10	6	3	1	20	10	10	21
Ireland	10	5	4	1	12	6	6	19
Wales	10	4	5	1	13	6	7	17
Austria	10	4	3	3	14	12	2	15
Georgia	10	0	5	5	8	14	-6	5
Moldova	10	0	2	8	4	23	-19	2

Group E	P	W	D	L	F	A	GD	Pts
Poland (Q)	10	8	1	1	28	14	14	25
Denmark (Q)	10	6	2	2	20	8	12	20
Montenegro	10	5	1	4	20	12	8	16
Romania	10	3	4	3	12	10	2	13
Armenia	10	2	1	7	10	26	-16	7
Kazakhstan	10	0	3	7	6	26	-20	3

Group F	P	W	D	L	F	A	GD	Pts
England (Q)	10	8	2	0	18	3	15	26
Slovakia	10	6	0	4	17	7	10	18
Scotland	10	5	3	2	17	12	5	18
Slovenia	10	4	3	3	12	7	5	15
Lithuania	10	1	3	6	7	20	-13	6
Malta	10	0	1	9	3	25	-22	1

Group G	P	W	D	L	F	A	GD	Pts
Spain (Q)	10	9	1	0	36	3	33	28
Italy	10	7	2	1	21	8	13	23
Albania	10	4	1	5	10	13	-3	13
Israel	10	4	0	6	10	15	-5	12
Macedonia	10	3	2	5	15	15	0	11
Liechtenstein	10	0	0	10	1	39	-38	0

Group H	P	W	D	L	F	A	GD	Pts
Belgium (Q)	10	9	1	0	43	6	37	28
Greece	10	5	4	1	17	6	11	19
Bosnia-Hz	10	5	2	3	24	13	11	17
Estonia	10	3	5	13	19	19	-6	11
Cyprus	10	3	1	6	9	18	-9	10
Gibraltar	10	0	0	10	3	47	-44	0

Group I	P	W	D	L	F	A	GD	Pts
Iceland (Q)	10	7	1	2	16	7	9	22
Croatia (Q)	10	6	2	2	15	4	11	20
Ukraine	10	5	2	3	13	9	4	17
Turkey	10	4	3	3	14	13	1	15
Finland	10	2	3	5	9	13	-4	9
Kosovo	10	0	1	9	3	24	-21	1

Sunday November 13, 2016
Bulgaria........ (1) 1-0 (0)......... Belarus
Luxembourg... (1) 1-3 (1)...........Holland
Hungary........ (2) 4-0 (0)......... Andorra
Portugal........ (1) 4-1 (0)............ Latvia
Switzerland.... (1) 2-0 (0).. Faroe Islands
Belgium........ (3) 8-1 (1)......... Estonia
Greece........... (0) 1-1 (1)....... Bosnia-Hz
Cyprus............ (1) 3-1 (0)........ Gibraltar
Friday March 24, 2017
Austria........... (0) 2-0 (0)........ Moldova
Croatia........... (1) 1-0 (0).........Ukraine
Georgia........... (1) 1-3 (1)............ Serbia
Ireland .... (0) 0-0 (0)............ Wales
Italy............... (1) 2-0 (0)..........Albania
Kosovo........... (0) 1-2 (2)...........Iceland
Liechtenstein . (0) 0-3 (1)..... Macedonia
Spain............. (2) 4-1 (0)............. Israel
Turkey............ (2) 2-0 (0)............ Finland
Saturday March 25, 2017
Andorra......... (0) 0-0 (0).. Faroe Islands
Belgium......... (0) 1-1 (0)...........Greece
Bosnia-Hz...... (2) 5-0 (0)........Gibraltar
Bulgaria .... (2) 2-0 (0)...........Holland
Cyprus............ (0) 0-0 (0)........... Estonia
Luxembourg... (1) 1-3 (2)............France
Portugal........ (2) 3-0 (0)..........Hungary
Sweden.......... (1) 4-0 (0)......... Belarus
Switzerland.... (1) 1-0 (0)............ Latvia
Sunday March 26, 2017
Armenia......... (0) 2-0 (0)...Kazakhstan
Azerbaijan...... (1) 1-4 (3).......Germany
England.......... (1) 2-0 (0)....... Lithuania
Malta .... (1) 1-3 (2)..... Slovakia
Montenegro.... (1) 2-1 (0).......... Poland
N Ireland........ (2) 2-0 (0)..........Norway
Romania......... (0) 0-0 (0).......Denmark
San Marino ..... (0) 0-6 (5).....Czech Rep
Scotland........ (1) 1-0 (0)........Slovenia
Friday June 9, 2017
Andorra......... (1) 1-0 (0).........Hungary
Belarus.......... (1) 2-1 (0)..........Bulgaria
Bosnia-Hz...... (0) 0-0 (0)........... Greece
Estonia.......... (0) 0-2 (1).......... Belgium
Faroe Islands.. (0) 0-2 (1)..... Switzerland
Gibraltar........ (1) 1-2 (1)............ Cyprus
Holland .... (2) 5-0 (0).. Luxembourg
Latvia............ (0) 0-3 (1)........... Portugal
Sweden.......... (1) 2-1 (1).............France
Saturday June 10, 2017
Azerbaijan...... (0) 0-1 (0).... N Ireland
Germany .... (4) 7-0 (0).....San Marino
Kazakhstan .... (0) 1-3 (1).......Denmark
Lithuania .... (0) 1-2 (1)..... Slovakia
Montenegro.... (2) 4-1 (0).......Armenia
Norway .... (0) 1-1 (1)....Czech Rep
Poland............ (1) 3-1 (0)......... Romania
Scotland........ (0) 2-2 (0)........ England
Slovenia........ (1) 2-0 (0)............Malta
Sunday June 11, 2017
Finland........... (0) 1-2 (0)........Ukraine
Iceland .... (0) 1-0 (0)..........Croatia
Ireland .... (0) 1-1 (1)...........Austria
Israel............. (0) 0-3 (2).........Albania
Italy............... (1) 5-0 (0)...Liechtenstein
Kosovo........... (1) 1-4 (2)..........Turkey
Macedonia..... (0) 1-2 (2)........... Spain
Moldova......... (2) 2-2 (0)....... Georgia
Serbia............ (0) 1-1 (1)............. Wales
Thursday August 31, 2017
Belgium.......... (6) 9-0 (0)........Gibraltar
Bulgaria .... (2) 3-2 (2)..........Sweden
Cyprus............ (0) 3-2 (2)...... Bosnia-Hz

France........... (1) 4-0 (0)..........Holland
Greece............ (0) 0-0 (0).......... Estonia
Hungary........ (2) 3-1 (1).............. Latvia
Luxembourg... (0) 1-0 (0)......... Belarus
Portugal........ (2) 5-1 (1)....Faroe Islands
Switzerland.... (1) 3-0 (0)..........Andorra
Friday September 1, 2017
Czech Rep...... (0) 1-2 (1)..........Germany
Denmark........ (2) 4-0 (0)............Poland
Kazakhstan .... (0) 0-3 (1)... Montenegro
Lithuania .... (0) 0-3 (2)......... Scotland
Malta .... (0) 0-4 (0)........... England
Norway .... (1) 2-0 (0).......Azerbaijan
Romania......... (0) 1-0 (0).........Armenia
San Marino ..... (0) 0-3 (0)..... N Ireland
Slovakia......... (0) 1-0 (0).........Slovenia
Saturday September 2, 2017
Albania........... (0) 2-0 (0)... Liechtenstein
Finland........... (1) 1-0 (0)............Iceland
Georgia........... (1) 1-1 (1)...........Ireland
Israel............. (0) 0-1 (0)..... Macedonia
Serbia............ (2) 3-0 (0).......... Moldova
Spain............. (2) 3-0 (0)............. Italy
Ukraine.......... (2) 2-0 (0)..........Turkey
Wales............. (0) 1-0 (0)...........Austria
Sunday September 3, 2017
Belarus.......... (0) 0-4 (3)..........Sweden
Croatia........... (0) 1-0 (0)...........Kosovo
Estonia.......... (0) 1-0 (0)........... Cyprus
Faroe Islands.. (1) 1-0 (0)..........Andorra
France........... (0) 0-0 (0)... Luxembourg
Gibraltar........ (0) 0-4 (1)........ Bosnia-Hz
Greece............ (0) 1-2 (0)..........Belgium
Holland .... (1) 3-1 (0)...........Bulgaria
Hungary........ (0) 0-1 (0)......... Portugal
Latvia............ (0) 0-3 (1)....... Switzerland
Monday September 4, 2017
Armenia......... (1) 1-4 (2)..........Denmark
Azerbaijan...... (2) 5-1 (0).....San Marino
England.......... (1) 2-1 (1)......... Slovakia
Germany .... (4) 6-0 (0).........Norway
Montenegro... (1) 1-0 (0)......... Romania
N Ireland........ (2) 2-0 (0)Czech Republic
Poland............ (1) 3-0 (0)....Kazakhstan
Scotland........ (1) 2-0 (0)............Malta
Slovenia........ (1) 4-0 (0)....... Lithuania
Tuesday September 5, 2017
Austria........... (1) 1-1 (1)........... Georgia
Iceland .... (0) 2-0 (0).........Ukraine
Ireland .... (0) 1-0 (0)............ Serbia
Italy............... (1) 1-0 (0)............ Israel
Kosovo........... (0) 0-1 (0)............ Finland
Liechtenstein . (0) 0-8 (4)............ Spain
Macedonia..... (0) 1-1 (0)..........Albania
Moldova......... (0) 0-2 (0)............ Wales
Turkey............ (0) 1-0 (0)...........Croatia
Thursday October 5, 2017
Armenia......... (1) 1-6 (3)........... Poland
Azerbaijan...... (0) 1-2 (1)....Czech Rep
England.......... (0) 1-0 (0)........ Slovenia
Malta .... (1) 1-1 (0)..... Lithuania
Montenegro... (0) 0-1 (1).......Denmark
N Ireland........ (1) 1-3 (2)........Germany
Romania......... (2) 3-1 (0)....Kazakhstan
San Marino ..... (0) 0-8 (4)..........Norway
Scotland........ (0) 1-0 (0)......... Slovakia
Friday October 6, 2017
Austria........... (1) 3-2 (1)............ Serbia
Croatia........... (0) 1-1 (0)............ Finland

Georgia........... (0) 0-1 (0)............. Wales
Ireland .... (2) 2-0 (0)........ Moldova
Italy............... (1) 1-1 (0)..... Macedonia
Kosovo........... (0) 0-2 (0)...........Ukraine
Liechtenstein . (0) 0-1 (1).............. Israel
Spain............. (3) 3-0 (0)...........Albania
Turkey............ (0) 0-3 (2)............Iceland
Saturday October 7, 2017
Andorra......... (0) 0-2 (0)........ Portugal
Belarus.......... (0) 1-3 (1)...........Holland
Bosnia-Hz...... (2) 3-4 (1)......... Belgium
Bulgaria .... (0) 0-1 (1)............France
Cyprus............ (1) 1-2 (2)...........Greece
Faroe Islands.. (0) 0-0 (0)............ Latvia
Gibraltar........ (0) 0-6 (3).......... Estonia
Sweden.......... (3) 8-0 (0).. Luxembourg
Switzerland.... (3) 5-2 (0)..........Hungary
Sunday October 8, 2017
Czech Rep...... (3) 5-0 (0).....San Marino
Denmark........ (0) 1-1 (0)......... Romania
Germany .... (1) 5-1 (1)....... Azerbaijan
Kazakhstan .... (0) 1-1 (1)..........Armenia
Lithuania .... (0) 0-1 (1)........... England
Norway .... (1) 1-0 (0)..... N Ireland
Poland............ (2) 4-2 (0)... Montenegro
Slovakia......... (1) 3-0 (0)............Malta
Slovenia........ (0) 2-2 (1)......... Scotland
Monday October 9, 2017
Albania........... (0) 0-1 (0)............. Italy
Finland........... (0) 2-2 (0)..........Romania
Iceland .... (1) 2-0 (0)...........Kosovo
Israel............. (0) 0-1 (0)............. Spain
Macedonia..... (2) 4-0 (0).. Liechtenstein
Moldova......... (0) 0-0 (0)...........Austria
Serbia............ (0) 1-0 (0)......... Georgia
Ukraine.......... (0) 0-2 (0)...........Croatia
Wales............. (0) 0-1 (0)............Ireland
Tuesday October 10, 2017
Belgium.......... (1) 4-0 (0)......... Cyprus
Estonia.......... (0) 1-2 (0)..... Bosnia-Hz
France........... (2) 2-1 (1)......... Belarus
Greece............ (1) 4-0 (0).........Gibraltar
Holland .... (2) 2-0 (0)...........Sweden
Hungary........ (0) 1-0 (0).. Faroe Islands
Latvia............ (2) 4-0 (0)..........Andorra
Luxembourg... (1) 1-1 (0)..........Bulgaria
Portugal........ (1) 2-0 (0).... Switzerland

Uefa playoff round
Thursday November 9, 2017
Croatia........... (3) 4-1 (1)...........Greece
N Ireland........ (0) 0-1 (0).... Switzerland
Friday November 10, 2017
Sweden.......... (0) 1-0 (0).............. Italy
Saturday November 11, 2017
Denmark........ (0) 0-0 (0)............Ireland
Second legs
Sunday November 12, 2017
Greece............ (0) 0-0 (0)...........Croatia
Croatia won 4-1 on aggregate
Switzerland.... (0) 0-0 (0)..... N Ireland
Switzerland won 1-0 on aggregate
Monday November 13, 2017
Italy............... (0) 0-0 (0)...........Sweden
Sweden won 1-0 on aggregate
Tuesday November 14, 2017
Ireland .... (1) 1-5 (2).........Denmark
Denmark won 5-1 on aggregate

GROUP STAGE

Group A

	P	W	D	L	F	A	GD	Pts
Uruguay	3	3	0	0	5	0	5	9
Russia	3	2	0	1	8	4	4	6
Saudi Arabia	3	1	0	2	2	7	-5	3
Egypt	3	0	0	3	2	6	-4	0

Thursday June 14
Russia .... (2) 5-0 (0) ...Saudi Arabia
Russia: Gazinskiy (12) Cheryshev (43, 90) Dzyuba (71) Golovin (90)
Friday June 15
Egypt.............. (0) 0-1 (0) ....Uruguay
Uruguay: Gimenez (89)
Tuesday June 19
Russia .... (0) 3-1 (0) ....Egypt
Russia: Fathy (47 og) Cheryshev (59) Dzyuba (62)
Egypt: Salah (pen 73)
Wednesday June 20
Uruguay .... (1) 1-0 (0) ...Saudi Arabia
Uruguay: Suarez (23)
Monday June 25
Russia .... (0) 0-3 (2) ....Uruguay
Uruguay: Suarez (10) Cheryshev (23 og) Cavani (90)
Saudi Arabia .. (1) 2-1 (1).............Egypt
Saudi Arabia: Al Faraj (pen 45) Al Dawsari (90)
Egypt: Salah (22)

Group B

	P	W	D	L	F	A	GD	Pts
Spain	3	1	2	0	6	5	1	5
Portugal	3	1	2	0	5	4	1	5
Iran	3	1	1	1	2	2	0	4
Morocco	3	0	1	2	2	4	-2	1

Friday June 15
Morocco......... (0) 0-1 (0) ....Iran
Iran: Bouhaddouz (90 og)
Portugal.......... (2) 3-3 (1).............. Spain
Portugal: Ronaldo (pen 4, 44, 88)
Spain: Costa (24, 55) Nacho Fernandez (58)
Wednesday June 20
Iran .... (0) 0-1 (0) .... Spain
Spain: Costa (54)
Portugal......... (1) 1-0 (0) .... Morocco
Portugal: Ronaldo (4)
Monday June 25
Iran .... (0) 1-1 (1)......... Portugal
Iran: Ansarifard (pen 90)
Portugal: Quaresma (45)
Spain............... (1) 2-2 (1)......... Morocco
Spain: Isco (19) Aspas (90)
Morocco: Boutaib (14) En-Nesyri (81)

Group C

	P	W	D	L	F	A	GD	Pts
France	3	2	1	0	3	1	2	7
Denmark	3	1	2	0	2	1	1	5
Peru	3	1	0	2	2	2	0	3
Australia	3	0	1	2	2	5	-3	1

Saturday June 16
France .... (0) 2-1 (0) ....Australia
France: Griezmann (pen 58) Behich (80 og)
Australia: Jedinak (pen 62)
Peru .... (0) 0-1 (0) ....Denmark
Denmark: Poulsen (59)

Thursday June 21
Denmark .... (1) 1-1 (1).........Australia
Denmark: Eriksen (7)
Australia: Jedinak (pen 38)
France .... (1) 1-0 (0) .... Peru
France: Mbappe (34)
Tuesday June 26
Australia .... (0) 0-2 (1)................. Peru
Peru: Carrillo (18) Guerrero (50)
Denmark .... (0) 0-0 (0) ....France

Group D

	P	W	D	L	F	A	GD	Pts
Croatia	3	3	0	0	7	1	6	9
Argentina	3	1	1	1	3	5	-2	4
Nigeria	3	1	0	2	3	4	-1	3
Iceland	3	0	1	2	2	5	-3	1

Saturday June 16
Argentina .... (1) 1-1 (1)............Iceland
Argentina: Aguero (19)
Iceland: Finnbogason (23)
Croatia .... (1) 2-0 (0) ....Nigeria
Croatia: Oghenekaro (32 og) Modric (pen 71)
Thursday June 21
Argentina ...... (0) 0-3 (0) ....Croatia
Croatia: Rebic (53) Modric (80) Rakitic (90)
Friday June 22
Nigeria .... (0) 2-0 (0) ....Iceland
Nigeria: Musa (49, 75)
Tuesday June 26
Iceland .... (0) 1-2 (0) ....Croatia
Iceland: Sigurdsson (pen 76)
Croatia: Badelj (53) Perisic (90)
Nigeria .... (0) 1-2 (1)........ Argentina
Nigeria: Moses (pen 51)
Argentina: Messi (14) Rojo (86)

Group E

	P	W	D	L	F	A	GD	Pts
Brazil	3	2	1	0	5	1	4	7
Switzerland	3	1	2	0	5	4	1	5
Serbia	3	1	0	2	4	4	-2	3
Costa Rica	3	0	1	2	2	5	-3	1

Sunday June 17
Brazil.............. (1) 1-1 (1) .... Switzerland
Brazil: Coutinho (20) **Switzerland:** Zuber (50)
Costa Rica...... (0) 0-1 (0) .... Serbia
Serbia: Kolarov (56)
Friday June 22
Brazil.............. (0) 2-0 (0) ...... Costa Rica
Brazil: Neymar (90) Coutinho (90)
Serbia .... (1) 1-2 (0) .... Switzerland
Serbia: Mitrovic (5)
Switzerland: Xhaka (52) Shaqiri (90)
Wednesday June 27
Serbia.............. (0) 0-2 (1).............. Brazil
Brazil: Paulinho (36) Silva (68)
Switzerland..... (0) 2-2 (1) ...... Costa Rica
Switzerland: Dzemaili (31) Drmic (88)
Costa Rica: Waston (56) Sommer (90 og)

Group F

	P	W	D	L	F	A	GD	Pts
Sweden	3	2	0	1	5	2	3	6
Mexico	3	2	0	1	3	4	-1	6
South Korea	3	1	0	2	3	3	0	3
Germany	3	1	0	2	2	4	-2	3

Sunday June 17
Germany .... (0) 0-1 (1)............Mexico
Mexico: Lozano (35)

Monday June 18
Sweden .... (0) 1-0 (0) ....South Korea
Sweden: Granqvist (pen 65)
Saturday June 23
Germany .... (0) 2-1 (1)............Sweden
Germany: Reus (48) Kroos (90)
Sweden: Toivonen (32)
South Korea ... (0) 1-2 (1)............Mexico
South Korea: Heung-Min Son (90)
Mexico: Vela (pen 26) Hernandez (66)
Wednesday June 27
Mexico .... (0) 0-3 (0) ....Sweden
Sweden: Augustinsson (50) Granqvist (pen 62) Alvarez (74 og)
South Korea ... (0) 2-0 (0) ....Germany
South Korea: Heung-Min (90) Young-Gwon (90)

Group G

	P	W	D	L	F	A	GD	Pts
Belgium	3	3	0	0	9	2	7	9
England	3	2	0	1	8	3	5	6
Tunisia	3	1	0	2	5	8	-3	3
Panama	3	0	0	3	2	11	-9	0

Monday June 18
Belgium .... (1) 3-0 (0) .... Panama
Belgium: Mertens (47) Lukaku (69, 75)
Tunisia............ (1) 1-2 (1).......... England
Tunisia: Sassi (pen 35) **England:** Kane (11, 90)
Saturday June 23
Belgium.......... (3) 5-2 (1)............ Tunisia
Belgium: Hazard (pen 6, 51) Lukaku (16, 45) Batshuayi (90) **Tunisia:** Bronn (18) Khazri (90)
Sunday June 24
England.......... (5) 6-1 (0) .... Panama
England: Stones (8, 40) Kane (pen 22, pen 45, 62) Lingard (36) **Panama:** Baloy (78)
Thursday June 28
England.......... (0) 0-1 (1) .... Belgium
Belgium: Januzaj (51)
Panama........... (1) 1-2 (1) .... Tunisia
Panama: Meriah (33 og)
Tunisia: Ben Youssef (51) Khazri (66)

Group H

	P	W	D	L	F	A	GD	Pts
Colombia	3	2	0	1	5	2	3	6
Japan	3	1	1	1	4	4	0	4
Senegal	3	1	1	1	4	4	0	4
Poland	3	1	0	2	2	5	-3	3

Tuesday June 19
Colombia .... (1) 1-2 (1)..............Japan
Colombia: Quintero (38)
Japan: Kagawa (pen 6) Osako (73)
Poland............ (0) 1-2 (1) .... Senegal
Poland: Krychowiak (86)
Senegal: Cionek (37 og) Niang (60)
Sunday June 24
Japan .... (1) 2-2 (1).......... Senegal
Japan: Inui (34) Honda (78)
Senegal: Mane (11) Wague (71)
Poland............. (0) 0-3 (1)........Colombia
Colombia: Mina (40) Falcao (70) Cuadrado (75)
Thursday June 28
Japan .... (0) 0-1 (0) .... Poland
Poland: Bednarek (59)
Senegal........... (0) 0-1 (0) .... Colombia
Colombia: Mina (74)

Saturday June 30

France .... (1) 4-3 (1)........ Argentina
France: Griezmann (pen 13) Pavard (57)
Mbappe (64, 68) **Argentina:** Di Maria (41)
Mercado (48) Aguero (90)

Uruguay .... (1) 2-1 (0) .... Portugal
Uruguay: Cavani (7, 62) **Portugal:** Pepe (55)

Sunday July 1

Croatia .... (1) 1-1 (1)..........Denmark
AET – 1-1 after 90, Croatia won 3-2 pens
Croatia: Mandzukic (4) **Denmark:** Jorgensen (1)

Spain.............. (1) 1-1 (1)..............Russia
AET – 1-1 after 90, Russia won 4-3 pens
Spain: Ignashevich (11 og)
Russia: Dzyuba (pen 41)

Monday July 2

Belgium.......... (0) 3-2 (0) ....Japan
Belgium: Vertonghen (69) Fellaini (74) Chadli (90)
Japan: Haraguchi (48) Inui (52)

Brazil.............. (0) 2-0 (0) ....Mexico
Brazil: Neymar (51) Firmino (88)

Tuesday July 3

Colombia .... (0) 1-1 (0) .... England
AET – 1-1 after 90, England won 4-3 pens
Colombia: Mina (90) **England:** Kane (pen 57)

Sweden .... (0) 1-0 (0) .... Switzerland
Sweden: Forsberg (66)

Friday July 6

Brazil.............. (0) 1-2 (2) .... Belgium
Brazil: Augusto (76)
Belgium: Fernandinho (13 og) De Bruyne (31)

Uruguay .... (0) 0-2 (1).............France
France: Varane (40) Griezmann (61)

Saturday July 7

Russia .... (1) 2-2 (1).............Croatia
AET – 1-1 after 90, Croatia won 4-3 pens
Russia: Cheryshev (31) Mario Fernandes (115)
Croatia: Kramaric (39) Vida (100)

Sweden .... (0) 0-2 (1)...........England
England: Maguire (30) Alli (58)

Tuesday July 10

France .... (0) 1-0 (0) .... Belgium
France: Umtiti (51)

Wednesday July 11

Croatia .... (0) 2-1 (1).......... England
AET – 1-1 after 90 mins
Croatia: Perisic (68) Mandzukic (109)
England: Trippier (5)

Saturday July 14

Belgium.......... (1) 2-0 (0) .... England
Belgium: Meunier (4) Hazard (82)

Sunday July 15

France .... (2) 4-2 (1).............Croatia
France: Mandzukic (18 og) Griezmann (pen 38)
Pogba (59) Mbappe (65)
Croatia: Perisic (28) Mandzukic (69)

To the right of each fixture are results for the corresponding league match in each of the last six seasons. The most recent result – 2017-18 – is on the right. The results cover matches in the Premier League, Championship, League One, League Two, National League, Scottish Premiership, Scottish Championship, Scottish League One and Scottish League Two.
Where Scottish clubs have met more than once at the same venue in the same season, results are separated by an oblique stroke with the most recent to the right. The Scottish Premiership will split into top- and bottom-six sections later in the season. These fixtures cover the period until the split.
Please note that TV coverage and postponements will cause alterations to the fixture list.

	2012-13	2013-14	2014-15	2015-16	2016-17	2017-18
Friday August 3, 2018						
Championship						
Reading v Derby	-	0-0	0-3	0-1	1-1	3-3
Saturday August 4, 2018						
Championship						
Birmingham v Norwich	-	-	0-0	-	3-0	0-2
Friday August 3, 2018						
Championship						
Reading v Derby	-	0-0	0-3	0-1	1-1	3-3
Saturday August 4, 2018						
Championship						
Birmingham v Norwich	-	-	0-0	-	3-0	0-2
Brentford v Rotherham	-	0-1	1-0	2-1	4-2	-
Bristol City v Nottm Forest	2-0	-	-	2-0	2-1	2-1
Ipswich v Blackburn	1-1	3-1	1-1	2-0	3-2	-
Millwall v Middlesbrough	3-1	0-2	1-5	-	-	2-1
Preston v QPR	-	-	-	1-1	2-1	1-0
Sheffield United v Swansea	-	-	-	-	-	-
West Brom v Bolton	-	-	-	-	-	-
Wigan v Sheffield Weds	-	1-0	0-1	-	0-1	-
League One						
Accrington v Gillingham	1-1	-	-	-	-	-
Barnsley v Oxford	-	-	-	-	-	-
Burton v Rochdale	3-2	1-0	-	1-0	-	-
Coventry v Scunthorpe	1-2	-	1-1	1-2	0-1	-
Fleetwood Town v AFC Wimbledon	1-1	0-0	-	-	0-0	2-0
Peterborough v Bristol Rovers	-	-	-	-	4-2	1-1
Portsmouth v Luton	-	-	2-0	0-0	1-0	-
Shrewsbury v Bradford	-	2-1	-	1-1	1-0	0-1
Southend v Doncaster	-	-	-	0-3	-	0-0
Sunderland v Charlton	-	-	-	-	-	-
Walsall v Plymouth	-	-	-	-	-	2-1
Wycombe v Blackpool	-	-	-	-	0-0	-
League Two						
Bury v Yeovil	3-2	-	-	-	-	-
Cheltenham v Crawley Town	-	-	-	-	2-1	1-0
Crewe v Morecambe	-	-	-	-	2-1	1-0
Exeter v Carlisle	-	-	2-0	2-2	2-3	1-1
Grimsby v Forest Green	1-0	3-1	2-1	1-1	-	1-0
Mansfield v Newport County	3-4	2-1	1-0	3-0	2-1	5-0
Northampton v Lincoln	-	-	-	-	-	-
Notts County v Colchester	3-1	2-0	2-1	-	3-1	2-1
Oldham v MK Dons	3-1	1-2	1-3	-	0-2	1-0
Port Vale v Cambridge U	-	-	-	-	-	2-0
Stevenage v Tranmere	1-1	3-1	2-2	-	-	-
Swindon v Macclesfield	-	-	-	-	-	-

Results cover matches from Premier League to National League and Scottish Premiership to Scottish League Two

	2012-13	2013-14	2014-15	2015-16	2016-17	2017-18
National League						
Aldershot v Barnet	1-0	3-3	1-3	-	-	-
Barrow v Havant & W	-	-	-	-	-	-
Boreham Wood v Dag & Red	-	-	-	-	1-3	1-2
Braintree v Halifax	-	1-0	0-0	2-0	-	-
Dover v Wrexham	-	-	2-0	2-1	1-1	1-0
Eastleigh v Solihull Moors	-	-	-	-	2-0	1-2
Ebbsfleet v Chesterfield	-	-	-	-	-	-
Fylde v Bromley	-	-	-	-	-	2-2
Harrogate T v Sutton Utd	-	-	-	-	-	-
Maidenhead v Gateshead	-	-	-	-	-	0-3
Maidstone v Hartlepool	-	-	-	-	-	1-2
Salford City v Leyton Orient	-	-	-	-	-	-
Ladbrokes Premiership						
Celtic v Livingston	-	-	-	-	-	-
Hamilton v Hearts	-	-	-	3-2/0-0	3-3	1-2/0-3
Hibernian v Motherwell	2-3	0-1/3-3	-	-	-	2-2/2-1
Kilmarnock v St Johnstone	1-2	0-0/1-2	0-1	2-1/3-0	0-1	1-2/2-0
St Mirren v Dundee	3-1/1-2	-	0-1/1-2	-	-	-
Ladbrokes Championship						
Ayr v Partick	-	-	-	-	-	-
Dundee United v Dunfermline	-	-	-	-	1-0/1-0	2-1/1-1
Falkirk v Inverness CT	-	-	-	-	-	0-0/3-1
Morton v Queen of Sth	-	0-2/1-1	-	2-0/3-2	1-0/1-0	1-2/0-1
Ross County v Alloa	-	-	-	-	-	-
Ladbrokes League One						
East Fife v Dumbarton	-	-	-	-	-	-
Forfar v Airdrieonians	-	3-3/1-1	1-1/2-0	2-3/0-2	-	2-1/0-1
Montrose v Arbroath	-	-	1-5/3-0	3-0/0-2	1-1/1-3	-
Stenhousemuir v Brechin	3-1/3-3	3-2/4-2	0-2/2-2	2-2/0-0	1-3/1-1	-
Stranraer v Raith	-	-	-	-	-	1-0/0-3
Ladbrokes League Two						
Annan v Elgin	2-0/2-2	2-1/2-0	3-3/2-3	1-1/4-2	1-0/1-0	2-0/4-1
Berwick v Stirling	4-1/1-0	1-1/4-0	-	1-2/1-0	3-2/0-1	1-0/0-1
Clyde v Cowdenbeath	-	-	-	-	5-3/0-2	1-1/2-0
Edinburgh City v Albion	-	-	-	-	-	-
Peterhead v Queens Park	1-0/0-2	2-1/1-0	-	-	2-0/4-0	-

Sunday August 5, 2018

	2012-13	2013-14	2014-15	2015-16	2016-17	2017-18
Championship						
Leeds v Stoke	-	-	-	-	-	-
Ladbrokes Premiership						
Aberdeen v Rangers	-	-	-	-	2-1/0-3	1-2/1-1

Monday August 6, 2018

	2012-13	2013-14	2014-15	2015-16	2016-17	2017-18
Championship						
Hull v Aston Villa	-	0-0	2-0	-	-	0-0

Tuesday August 7, 2018

	2012-13	2013-14	2014-15	2015-16	2016-17	2017-18
Championship						
Middlesbrough v Sheffield United	-	-	-	-	-	1-0
Nottm Forest v West Brom	-	-	-	-	-	-
National League						
Barnet v Braintree	-	1-1	3-0	-	-	-
Bromley v Dover	-	0-4	-	1-1	0-2	2-2
Chesterfield v Aldershot	0-0	-	-	-	-	-
Dag & Red v Maidstone	-	-	-	-	0-2	2-1
Gateshead v Salford City	-	-	-	-	-	-

Results cover matches from Premier League to National League and Scottish Premiership to Scottish League Two

	2012-13	2013-14	2014-15	2015-16	2016-17	2017-18
Halifax v Barrow	-	-	-	3-1	-	0-1
Hartlepool v Harrogate T	-	-	-	-	-	-
Havant & W v Boreham Wood	-	1-1	2-1	-	-	-
Leyton Orient v Ebbsfleet	-	-	-	-	-	1-1
Solihull Moors v Maidenhead	-	-	-	-	-	3-1
Sutton Utd v Eastleigh	-	1-1	-	-	1-1	2-0
Wrexham v Fylde	-	-	-	-	-	0-0

Saturday August 11, 2018

Premier League

	2012-13	2013-14	2014-15	2015-16	2016-17	2017-18
Arsenal v Man City	0-2	1-1	2-2	2-1	2-2	0-3
Bournemouth v Cardiff	-	-	5-3	-	-	-
Fulham v Crystal Palace	-	2-2	-	-	-	-
Huddersfield v Chelsea	-	-	-	-	-	1-3
Liverpool v West Ham	0-0	4-1	2-0	0-3	2-2	4-1
Man United v Leicester	-	-	3-1	1-1	4-1	2-0
Newcastle v Tottenham	2-1	0-4	1-3	5-1	-	0-2
Southampton v Burnley	-	-	2-0	-	3-1	0-1
Watford v Brighton	0-1	2-0	1-1	-	-	0-0
Wolves v Everton	-	-	-	-	-	-

Championship

	2012-13	2013-14	2014-15	2015-16	2016-17	2017-18
Aston Villa v Wigan	0-3	-	-	-	1-0	-
Blackburn v Millwall	0-2	3-2	2-0	-	-	-
Bolton v Bristol City	3-2	-	-	0-0	-	1-0
Derby v Leeds	3-1	3-1	2-0	1-2	1-0	2-2
Middlesbrough v Birmingham	0-1	3-1	2-0	0-0	-	2-0
Norwich v West Brom	4-0	0-1	-	0-1	-	-
Nottm Forest v Reading	-	2-3	4-0	3-1	3-2	1-1
QPR v Sheffield United	-	-	-	-	-	1-0
Rotherham v Ipswich	-	-	2-0	2-5	1-0	-
Sheffield Weds v Hull	0-1	-	-	1-1	-	2-2
Stoke v Brentford	-	-	-	-	-	-
Swansea v Preston	-	-	-	-	-	-

League One

	2012-13	2013-14	2014-15	2015-16	2016-17	2017-18
AFC Wimbledon v Coventry	-	-	-	-	1-1	-
Blackpool v Portsmouth	-	-	-	-	3-1	2-3
Bradford v Barnsley	-	-	1-0	0-1	-	-
Bristol Rovers v Accrington	0-1	0-1	-	0-1	-	-
Charlton v Shrewsbury	-	-	-	-	3-0	0-2
Doncaster v Wycombe	-	-	-	-	2-2	-
Gillingham v Burton	4-1	-	-	0-3	-	-
Luton v Sunderland	-	-	-	-	-	-
Oxford v Fleetwood Town	1-2	0-2	-	-	1-3	0-1
Plymouth v Southend	1-1	1-1	2-0	-	-	4-0
Rochdale v Peterborough	-	-	0-1	2-0	2-3	2-0
Scunthorpe v Walsall	1-1	-	2-1	0-1	0-0	1-0

League Two

	2012-13	2013-14	2014-15	2015-16	2016-17	2017-18
Cambridge U v Notts County	-	-	-	3-1	4-0	1-0
Carlisle v Northampton	-	-	2-1	1-4	-	-
Colchester v Port Vale	-	1-0	1-2	2-1	-	1-1
Crawley Town v Stevenage	1-1	1-1	-	2-1	1-2	1-0
Forest Green v Oldham	-	-	-	-	-	-
Lincoln v Swindon	-	-	-	-	-	2-2
Macclesfield v Grimsby	1-3	1-1	0-1	2-1	-	-
MK Dons v Bury	1-1	-	-	-	1-3	2-1
Morecambe v Exeter	0-3	2-0	0-2	1-1	0-3	2-1
Newport County v Crewe	-	-	-	-	1-1	1-2
Tranmere v Cheltenham	-	-	2-3	0-1	-	-
Yeovil v Mansfield	-	-	-	0-1	0-0	2-3

Results cover matches from Premier League to National League and Scottish Premiership to Scottish League Two

	2012-13	2013-14	2014-15	2015-16	2016-17	2017-18
National League						
Barnet v Eastleigh	-	-	1-0	-	-	-
Bromley v Harrogate T	-	-	-	-	-	-
Chesterfield v Braintree	-	-	-	-	-	-
Dag & Red v Maidenhead	-	-	-	-	-	1-0
Gateshead v Dover	-	-	1-2	2-3	4-2	0-0
Halifax v Maidstone	-	-	-	-	-	0-2
Hartlepool v Ebbsfleet	-	-	-	-	-	0-1
Havant & W v Fylde	-	-	-	-	-	-
Leyton Orient v Barrow	-	-	-	-	-	4-1
Solihull Moors v Aldershot	-	-	-	-	0-2	0-0
Sutton Utd v Salford City	-	-	-	-	-	-
Wrexham v Boreham Wood	-	-	-	1-0	2-1	0-1
Ladbrokes Premiership						
Dundee v Aberdeen	1-3/1-1	-	2-3/1-1/1-1	0-2	1-3/0-7	0-1
Hearts v Celtic	0-4	1-3/0-2	-	2-2/1-3	1-2/0-5	4-0/1-3
Livingston v Kilmarnock	-	-	-	-	-	-
Motherwell v Hamilton	-	-	0-4/4-0	3-3	4-2/0-0	1-3/3-0
Rangers v St Mirren	-	-	-	3-1/1-0	-	-
St Johnstone v Hibernian	0-1	1-2/2-0	-	-	-	1-1/1-1
Ladbrokes Championship						
Alloa v Morton	-	2-0/2-0	-	0-1/2-2	-	-
Dunfermline v Ross County	-	-	-	-	-	-
Inverness CT v Ayr	-	-	-	-	-	-
Partick v Falkirk	3-1/4-1	-	-	-	-	-
Queen of Sth v Dundee United	-	-	-	-	1-4/4-2	1-3/3-0
Ladbrokes League One						
Airdrieonians v Montrose	-	-	-	-	-	-
Arbroath v Stranraer	2-1/1-0	1-2/4-2	-	-	-	1-2/2-3
Brechin v East Fife	2-1/6-0	2-0/3-0	-	-	0-1/2-1	-
Dumbarton v Forfar	-	-	-	-	-	-
Raith v Stenhousemuir	-	-	-	-	-	-
Ladbrokes League Two						
Albion v Peterhead	-	1-2/0-0	-	1-0/1-1	0-1/0-0	-
Cowdenbeath v Annan	-	-	-	-	2-2/0-1	1-1/0-2
Elgin v Edinburgh City	-	-	-	-	3-0/3-1	1-1/1-1
Queens Park v Berwick	1-1/2-1	0-4/1-3	2-0/2-1	0-1/0-0	-	-
Stirling v Clyde	0-1/2-0	1-1/4-1	-	0-1/1-2	1-1/3-0	2-3/2-1
Tuesday August 14, 2018						
National League						
Aldershot v Dag & Red	1-0	-	-	-	3-1	1-1
Barrow v Chesterfield	-	-	-	-	-	-
Boreham Wood v Gateshead	-	-	-	2-3	0-4	2-1
Braintree v Hartlepool	-	-	-	-	-	-
Dover v Havant & W	-	0-0	-	-	-	-
Eastleigh v Bromley	-	2-1	-	2-0	2-1	4-4
Ebbsfleet v Sutton Utd	-	2-0	3-0	1-0	-	0-1
Fylde v Solihull Moors	-	-	-	-	-	1-1
Harrogate T v Barnet	-	-	-	-	-	-
Maidenhead v Wrexham	-	-	-	-	-	1-2
Maidstone v Leyton Orient	-	-	-	-	-	0-2
Salford City v Halifax	-	-	-	-	2-2	-
Friday August 17, 2018						
Championship						
Birmingham v Swansea	-	-	-	-	-	-
League Two						
Notts County v Yeovil	1-2	-	1-2	2-0	0-0	4-1

Results cover matches from Premier League to National League and Scottish Premiership to Scottish League Two

Saturday August 18, 2018

Premier League

	2012-13	2013-14	2014-15	2015-16	2016-17	2017-18
Brighton v Man United	-	-	-	-	-	1-0
Burnley v Watford	1-1	0-0	-	-	2-0	1-0
Cardiff v Newcastle	-	1-2	-	-	0-2	-
Chelsea v Arsenal	2-1	6-0	2-0	2-0	3-1	0-0
Crystal Palace v Liverpool	-	3-3	3-1	1-2	2-4	1-2
Everton v Southampton	3-1	2-1	1-0	1-1	3-0	1-1
Leicester v Wolves	2-1	-	-	-	-	-
Man City v Huddersfield	-	-	-	-	-	0-0
Tottenham v Fulham	0-1	3-1	-	-	-	-
West Ham v Bournemouth	-	-	-	3-4	1-0	1-1

Championship

	2012-13	2013-14	2014-15	2015-16	2016-17	2017-18
Bristol City v Middlesbrough	2-0	-	-	1-0	-	2-1
Hull v Blackburn	2-0	-	-	1-1	-	-
Ipswich v Aston Villa	-	-	-	-	0-0	0-4
Leeds v Rotherham	-	-	0-0	0-1	3-0	-
Millwall v Derby	2-1	1-5	3-3	-	-	0-0
Preston v Stoke	-	-	-	-	-	-
Reading v Bolton	-	7-1	0-0	2-1	-	1-1
Sheffield United v Norwich	-	-	-	-	-	0-1
West Brom v QPR	3-2	-	1-4	-	-	-
Wigan v Nottm Forest	-	2-1	0-0	-	0-0	-

League One

	2012-13	2013-14	2014-15	2015-16	2016-17	2017-18
Accrington v Charlton	-	-	-	-	-	-
Barnsley v AFC Wimbledon	-	-	-	-	-	-
Burton v Doncaster	-	-	-	3-3	-	-
Coventry v Plymouth	-	-	-	-	-	-
Fleetwood Town v Rochdale	0-3	0-0	1-0	1-1	0-0	2-2
Peterborough v Luton	-	-	-	-	-	-
Portsmouth v Oxford	-	1-4	0-0	0-1	-	3-0
Shrewsbury v Blackpool	-	-	-	2-0	-	1-0
Southend v Bradford	2-2	-	-	0-1	3-0	1-2
Walsall v Gillingham	-	1-1	1-1	3-2	1-2	0-1
Wycombe v Bristol Rovers	2-0	1-2	-	1-0	-	-

League Two

	2012-13	2013-14	2014-15	2015-16	2016-17	2017-18
Bury v Forest Green	-	-	-	-	-	-
Cheltenham v Carlisle	-	-	0-0	-	1-0	0-1
Crewe v MK Dons	2-1	2-0	0-5	-	-	-
Exeter v Newport County	-	0-2	2-0	1-1	0-1	1-0
Grimsby v Lincoln	1-1	1-1	1-3	2-0	-	0-0
Mansfield v Colchester	-	-	-	-	0-0	1-1
Northampton v Cambridge U	-	-	0-1	1-1	-	-
Oldham v Macclesfield	-	-	-	-	-	-
Port Vale v Crawley Town	-	2-1	2-3	-	-	1-2
Stevenage v Morecambe	-	-	1-1	4-3	0-1	2-1
Swindon v Tranmere	5-0	1-0	-	-	-	-

National League

	2012-13	2013-14	2014-15	2015-16	2016-17	2017-18
Aldershot v Harrogate T	-	-	-	-	-	-
Barnet v Ebbsfleet	-	-	-	-	-	-
Braintree v Havant & W	-	-	-	-	-	1-3
Bromley v Gateshead	-	-	-	3-0	3-2	0-0
Eastleigh v Wrexham	-	-	2-2	1-1	1-1	1-1
Fylde v Dover	-	-	-	-	-	3-1
Halifax v Dag & Red	-	-	-	-	-	2-1
Hartlepool v Maidenhead	-	-	-	-	-	1-2
Leyton Orient v Boreham Wood	-	-	-	-	-	0-0
Maidstone v Barrow	-	-	-	-	2-1	0-1
Salford City v Chesterfield	-	-	-	-	-	-
Solihull Moors v Sutton Utd	-	-	-	-	3-0	0-2

Results cover matches from Premier League to National League and Scottish Premiership to Scottish League Two

Ladbrokes League One

	2012-13	2013-14	2014-15	2015-16	2016-17	2017-18
Dumbarton v Arbroath	-	-	-	-	-	-
Forfar v Stranraer	4-0/3-1	1-2/1-0	1-1/1-0	1-2/1-1	-	1-1/5-1
Montrose v Brechin	-	-	-	-	-	-
Raith v East Fife	-	-	-	-	-	1-0/2-0
Stenhousemuir v Airdrieonians	-	1-1/1-2	1-0/0-2	2-1/3-2	2-2/4-2	-

Ladbrokes League Two

	2012-13	2013-14	2014-15	2015-16	2016-17	2017-18
Albion v Elgin	-	0-0/5-2	3-0/0-3	-	-	-
Annan v Queens Park	2-3/2-0	3-2/1-1	0-1/2-0	3-1/1-0	-	-
Cowdenbeath v Berwick	-	-	-	-	0-2/0-1	0-1/1-3
Edinburgh City v Stirling	-	-	-	-	2-0/1-0	1-2/2-2
Peterhead v Clyde	1-0/3-0	1-1/2-0	-	-	-	2-1/3-0

Sunday August 19, 2018

Championship

	2012-13	2013-14	2014-15	2015-16	2016-17	2017-18
Brentford v Sheffield Weds	-	-	0-0	1-2	1-1	2-0

League One

	2012-13	2013-14	2014-15	2015-16	2016-17	2017-18
Sunderland v Scunthorpe	-	-	-	-	-	-

Tuesday August 21, 2018

Championship

	2012-13	2013-14	2014-15	2015-16	2016-17	2017-18
Derby v Ipswich	0-1	4-4	1-1	0-1	0-1	0-1
QPR v Bristol City	-	-	-	1-0	1-0	1-1
Rotherham v Hull	-	-	-	2-0	-	-
Swansea v Leeds	-	-	-	-	-	-

League One

	2012-13	2013-14	2014-15	2015-16	2016-17	2017-18
AFC Wimbledon v Walsall	-	-	-	-	1-0	1-2
Blackpool v Coventry	-	-	-	0-1	-	-
Bradford v Burton	1-0	-	-	2-0	-	-
Bristol Rovers v Portsmouth	-	2-0	-	1-2	-	2-1
Charlton v Peterborough	2-0	-	-	-	0-2	2-2
Doncaster v Shrewsbury	1-0	-	-	0-1	-	1-2
Luton v Southend	-	-	2-0	-	-	-
Oxford v Accrington	5-0	1-2	3-1	1-2	-	-
Plymouth v Wycombe	0-1	0-3	0-1	0-1	3-3	-
Rochdale v Barnsley	-	-	0-1	3-0	-	-

League Two

	2012-13	2013-14	2014-15	2015-16	2016-17	2017-18
Cambridge U v Exeter	-	-	1-2	0-1	1-0	2-3
Carlisle v Port Vale	-	0-1	-	-	-	1-2
Colchester v Crewe	1-2	1-2	2-3	2-3	4-0	3-1
Crawley Town v Swindon	1-1	0-0	1-0	-	-	1-1
Forest Green v Stevenage	-	-	-	-	-	3-1
Lincoln v Bury	-	-	-	-	-	-
Macclesfield v Cheltenham	-	-	-	0-1	-	-
MK Dons v Grimsby	-	-	-	-	-	-
Morecambe v Northampton	1-1	1-1	0-1	2-4	-	-
Newport County v Notts County	-	-	-	0-1	2-1	0-0
Tranmere v Mansfield	-	-	0-0	-	-	-
Yeovil v Oldham	4-1	-	2-1	-	-	-

Wednesday August 22, 2018

Championship

	2012-13	2013-14	2014-15	2015-16	2016-17	2017-18
Aston Villa v Brentford	-	-	-	-	1-1	0-0
Blackburn v Reading	-	0-0	3-1	3-1	2-3	-
Bolton v Birmingham	3-1	2-2	0-1	0-1	-	0-1
Norwich v Preston	-	-	-	-	0-1	1-1
Sheffield Weds v Millwall	3-2	2-2	1-1	-	-	2-1
Stoke v Wigan	2-2	-	-	-	-	-

Results cover matches from Premier League to National League and Scottish Premiership to Scottish League Two

League One

	2012-13	2013-14	2014-15	2015-16	2016-17	2017-18
Gillingham v Sunderland	-	-	-	-	-	-
Scunthorpe v Fleetwood Town	-	0-0	0-2	1-0	0-2	1-1

Friday August 24, 2018

Championship

	2012-13	2013-14	2014-15	2015-16	2016-17	2017-18
Middlesbrough v West Brom	-	-	-	-	1-1	-

Saturday August 25, 2018

Premier League

	2012-13	2013-14	2014-15	2015-16	2016-17	2017-18
Arsenal v West Ham	5-1	3-1	3-0	0-2	3-0	4-1
Bournemouth v Everton	-	-	-	3-3	1-0	2-1
Fulham v Burnley	-	-	-	2-3	-	-
Huddersfield v Cardiff	0-0	-	0-0	2-3	0-3	-
Liverpool v Brighton	-	-	-	-	-	4-0
Man United v Tottenham	2-3	1-2	3-0	1-0	1-0	1-0
Newcastle v Chelsea	3-2	2-0	2-1	2-2	-	3-0
Southampton v Leicester	-	-	2-0	2-2	3-0	1-4
Watford v Crystal Palace	2-2	-	-	0-1	1-1	0-0
Wolves v Man City	-	-	-	-	-	-

Championship

	2012-13	2013-14	2014-15	2015-16	2016-17	2017-18
Aston Villa v Reading	1-0	-	-	-	1-3	3-0
Blackburn v Brentford	-	-	2-3	1-1	3-2	-
Bolton v Sheffield United	-	-	-	-	1-0	0-1
Derby v Preston	-	-	-	0-0	1-1	1-0
Norwich v Leeds	-	-	1-1	-	2-3	2-1
Nottm Forest v Birmingham	2-2	1-0	1-3	1-1	3-1	2-1
QPR v Wigan	1-1	1-0	-	-	2-1	-
Rotherham v Millwall	-	-	2-1	-	-	-
Sheffield Weds v Ipswich	1-1	1-1	1-1	1-1	1-2	1-2
Stoke v Hull	-	1-0	1-0	-	3-1	-
Swansea v Bristol City	-	-	-	-	-	-

League One

	2012-13	2013-14	2014-15	2015-16	2016-17	2017-18
AFC Wimbledon v Sunderland	-	-	-	-	-	-
Blackpool v Accrington	-	-	-	-	0-0	-
Bradford v Wycombe	1-0	-	-	-	-	-
Bristol Rovers v Southend	2-3	0-0	-	-	2-0	3-0
Charlton v Fleetwood Town	-	-	-	-	1-1	0-0
Doncaster v Portsmouth	1-1	-	-	-	3-1	2-1
Gillingham v Coventry	-	4-2	3-1	0-0	2-1	-
Luton v Shrewsbury	-	-	0-0	-	-	-
Oxford v Burton	1-1	1-2	0-1	-	-	-
Plymouth v Peterborough	-	-	-	-	-	2-1
Rochdale v Walsall	-	-	4-0	1-2	4-0	1-1
Scunthorpe v Barnsley	-	-	0-1	2-0	-	-

League Two

	2012-13	2013-14	2014-15	2015-16	2016-17	2017-18
Cambridge U v Cheltenham	-	-	1-2	-	3-1	4-3
Carlisle v Crewe	0-0	2-1	-	-	0-2	1-0
Colchester v Northampton	-	-	-	-	-	-
Crawley Town v Bury	3-2	-	-	-	-	-
Forest Green v Swindon	-	-	-	-	-	0-2
Lincoln v Notts County	-	-	-	-	-	2-2
Macclesfield v Mansfield	0-3	-	-	-	-	-
MK Dons v Exeter	-	-	-	-	-	-
Morecambe v Oldham	-	-	-	-	-	-
Newport County v Grimsby	0-0	-	-	-	0-0	1-0
Tranmere v Port Vale	-	0-1	-	-	-	-
Yeovil v Stevenage	1-3	-	-	2-2	1-1	3-0

Results cover matches from Premier League to National League and Scottish Premiership to Scottish League Two

	2012-13	2013-14	2014-15	2015-16	2016-17	2017-18
National League						
Barrow v Braintree	0-1	-	-	2-0	2-1	-
Boreham Wood v Halifax	-	-	-	3-1	-	1-1
Chesterfield v Barnet	0-1	-	-	-	-	2-1
Dag & Red v Hartlepool	-	0-2	2-0	0-1	-	4-2
Dover v Eastleigh	-	1-2	2-1	1-2	3-0	2-0
Ebbsfleet v Aldershot	-	-	-	-	-	0-2
Gateshead v Leyton Orient	-	-	-	-	-	1-3
Harrogate T v Solihull Moors	-	2-1	0-4	6-0	-	-
Havant & W v Salford City	-	-	-	-	-	-
Maidenhead v Maidstone	-	-	-	0-2	-	0-0
Sutton Utd v Fylde	-	-	-	-	-	2-1
Wrexham v Bromley	-	-	-	2-0	2-1	2-0
Ladbrokes Premiership						
Celtic v Hamilton	-	-	0-1/4-0	8-1	1-0/2-0	3-1
Hibernian v Aberdeen	0-1/0-0	0-2/0-2	-	-	-	0-1/2-0
Kilmarnock v Hearts	1-0/0-1	2-0/4-2	-	2-2	2-0/0-0	0-1/1-0
Motherwell v Rangers	-	-	-	-	0-2	1-2/2-2
St Johnstone v Dundee	1-0	-	0-1/1-0	1-1	2-1/2-0	0-2
St Mirren v Livingston	-	-	-	1-1/1-4	-	3-1/0-0
Ladbrokes Championship						
Ayr v Dunfermline	-	2-4/1-1	0-1/0-2	1-2/0-2	0-0/0-2	-
Dundee United v Partick	-	4-1	1-0/0-2	0-1/3-3	-	-
Falkirk v Queen of Sth	-	2-1/1-0	1-1/1-1	0-0/3-1	2-2/2-2	1-4/3-2
Inverness CT v Alloa	-	-	-	-	-	-
Morton v Ross County	-	-	-	-	-	-
Ladbrokes League One						
Airdrieonians v Raith	0-0/1-2	-	-	-	-	2-2/1-2
Brechin v Dumbarton	-	-	-	-	-	0-1/1-3
East Fife v Arbroath	2-1/0-1	2-1/1-0	1-5/2-0	0-1/2-1	-	3-1/0-5
Forfar v Stenhousemuir	3-2/3-3	1-2/3-0	3-0/1-0	4-1/0-1	-	-
Stranraer v Montrose	-	-	-	-	-	-
Ladbrokes League Two						
Berwick v Annan	3-1/0-2	4-2/1-4	2-0/2-2	0-2/3-2	2-0/4-1	1-5/0-2
Clyde v Edinburgh City	-	-	-	-	0-0/3-1	2-3/3-2
Elgin v Cowdenbeath	-	-	-	-	3-1/0-0	1-1/1-0
Queens Park v Albion	-	1-1/4-0	0-1/0-1	-	2-1/2-0	2-5/2-2
Stirling v Peterhead	1-0/0-1	2-0/1-2	2-3/2-1	-	-	0-1/0-1
Monday August 27, 2018						
National League						
Aldershot v Sutton Utd	-	-	-	-	2-0	2-2
Barnet v Dag & Red	0-0	-	-	3-1	-	-
Braintree v Maidenhead	-	-	-	-	-	-
Bromley v Havant & W	-	2-0	2-0	-	-	-
Eastleigh v Ebbsfleet	-	3-1	-	-	-	0-1
Fylde v Harrogate T	-	-	-	-	-	-
Halifax v Gateshead	-	3-3	2-2	1-1	-	2-2
Hartlepool v Chesterfield	-	1-2	-	-	-	-
Leyton Orient v Dover	-	-	-	-	-	1-1
Maidstone v Boreham Wood	-	-	-	-	1-0	0-4
Salford City v Barrow	-	-	-	-	-	-
Solihull Moors v Wrexham	-	-	-	-	0-1	0-0
Saturday September 1, 2018						
Premier League						
Brighton v Fulham	-	-	1-2	5-0	2-1	-
Burnley v Man United	-	-	0-0	-	0-2	0-1
Cardiff v Arsenal	-	0-3	-	-	-	-
Chelsea v Bournemouth	-	-	-	0-1	3-0	0-3
Crystal Palace v Southampton	-	0-1	1-3	1-0	3-0	0-1

Results cover matches from Premier League to National League and Scottish Premiership to Scottish League Two

	2012-13	2013-14	2014-15	2015-16	2016-17	2017-18
Everton v Huddersfield	-	-	-	-	-	2-0
Leicester v Liverpool	-	-	1-3	2-0	3-1	2-3
Man City v Newcastle	4-0	4-0	5-0	6-1	-	3-1
Watford v Tottenham	-	-	-	1-2	1-4	1-1
West Ham v Wolves	-	-	-	-	-	-
Championship						
Birmingham v QPR	-	0-2	-	2-1	1-4	1-2
Brentford v Nottm Forest	-	-	2-2	2-1	1-0	3-4
Hull v Derby	2-1	-	-	0-2	-	0-0
Leeds v Middlesbrough	2-1	2-1	1-0	0-0	-	2-1
Millwall v Swansea	-	-	-	-	-	-
Preston v Bolton	-	-	-	0-0	-	0-0
Reading v Sheffield Weds	-	0-2	2-0	1-1	2-1	0-0
Sheffield United v Aston Villa	-	-	-	-	-	0-1
West Brom v Stoke	0-1	1-2	1-0	2-1	1-0	1-1
Wigan v Rotherham	-	-	1-2	-	3-2	0-0
League One						
Accrington v Scunthorpe	-	2-3	-	-	-	-
Barnsley v Gillingham	-	-	4-1	2-0	-	-
Burton v AFC Wimbledon	6-2	1-1	0-0	-	-	-
Coventry v Rochdale	-	-	2-2	0-1	2-0	-
Fleetwood Town v Bradford	2-2	-	0-2	1-1	2-1	1-2
Peterborough v Doncaster	-	-	0-0	4-0	-	1-1
Portsmouth v Plymouth	-	3-3	2-1	1-2	1-1	1-0
Shrewsbury v Bristol Rovers	-	-	-	-	2-0	4-0
Southend v Charlton	-	-	-	-	1-1	3-1
Sunderland v Oxford	-	-	-	-	-	-
Walsall v Blackpool	-	-	-	1-1	-	1-1
Wycombe v Luton	-	-	1-1	0-1	1-1	1-2
League Two						
Bury v Morecambe	-	0-2	1-2	-	-	-
Cheltenham v Colchester	-	-	-	-	0-3	3-1
Crewe v Macclesfield	-	-	-	-	-	-
Exeter v Lincoln	-	-	-	-	-	1-0
Grimsby v Yeovil	-	-	-	-	4-2	2-1
Mansfield v Carlisle	-	-	3-2	1-1	2-0	3-1
Northampton v Tranmere	-	-	1-0	-	-	-
Notts County v Forest Green	-	-	-	-	-	1-1
Oldham v Crawley Town	2-1	1-0	1-1	-	-	-
Port Vale v Newport County	-	-	-	-	-	0-0
Stevenage v Cambridge U	-	-	3-2	2-0	1-2	0-2
Swindon v MK Dons	1-0	1-2	0-3	-	1-1	-
National League						
Barrow v Solihull Moors	-	0-2	1-3	-	2-1	1-2
Boreham Wood v Braintree	-	-	-	1-0	0-1	-
Chesterfield v Leyton Orient	-	-	2-3	-	-	-
Dag & Red v Salford City	-	-	-	-	-	-
Dover v Barnet	-	-	0-3	-	-	-
Ebbsfleet v Fylde	-	-	-	-	-	3-3
Gateshead v Maidstone	-	-	-	-	1-2	2-1
Harrogate T v Eastleigh	-	-	-	-	-	-
Havant & W v Hartlepool	-	-	-	-	-	-
Maidenhead v Bromley	-	0-1	4-4	-	-	5-2
Sutton Utd v Halifax	-	-	-	-	-	3-2
Wrexham v Aldershot	-	2-1	3-1	3-0	0-2	2-2
Ladbrokes Premiership						
Aberdeen v Kilmarnock	0-2/1-0	2-1/2-1	1-0	2-0/2-1	5-1	1-1/3-1
Celtic v Rangers	-	-	-	-	5-1/1-1	0-0/5-0
Dundee v Motherwell	1-2/0-3	-	4-1	2-1/2-2	2-0	0-1/0-1

Results cover matches from Premier League to National League and Scottish Premiership to Scottish League Two

	2012-13	2013-14	2014-15	2015-16	2016-17	2017-18
Hamilton v St Johnstone	-	-	1-0/1-1	2-4	1-1/1-0	0-1/1-2
Hearts v St Mirren	1-0/3-0	0-2/2-1	-	-	-	-
Livingston v Hibernian	-	-	0-4/1-3	0-1/0-0	-	-

Ladbrokes Championship

Alloa v Dundee United	-	-	-	-	-	-
Dunfermline v Inverness CT	-	-	-	-	-	5-1/1-0
Partick v Morton	1-2/1-0	-	-	-	-	-
Queen of Sth v Ayr	2-0/2-0	-	-	-	4-1/0-0	-
Ross County v Falkirk	-	-	-	-	-	-

Ladbrokes League One

Airdrieonians v Stranraer	-	3-2/1-1	3-3/1-1	0-1/1-1	1-0/1-2	2-0/2-1
Arbroath v Brechin	3-1/0-1	2-1/0-1	-	-	-	-
Montrose v East Fife	-	-	0-4/0-3	1-4/2-2	-	-
Raith v Forfar	-	-	-	-	-	3-1/2-1
Stenhousemuir v Dumbarton	-	-	-	-	-	-

Ladbrokes League Two

Albion v Berwick	-	0-2/0-3	2-1/2-0	-	-	-
Annan v Clyde	1-3/0-1	1-2/0-1	2-1/0-1	2-3/3-3	3-2/1-0	0-0/1-1
Elgin v Stirling	3-1/1-2	4-0/2-3	-	1-0/2-1	2-3/2-2	0-2/3-0
Peterhead v Edinburgh City	-	-	-	-	-	3-0/2-1
Queens Park v Cowdenbeath	-	-	-	-	-	-

Sunday September 2, 2018

Championship

Bristol City v Blackburn	3-5	-	-	0-2	1-0	-
Ipswich v Norwich	-	-	0-1	-	1-1	0-1

Tuesday September 4, 2018

National League

Boreham Wood v Chesterfield	-	-	-	-	-	-
Bromley v Barnet	-	-	-	-	-	-
Dag & Red v Braintree	-	-	-	-	3-0	-
Dover v Ebbsfleet	-	2-1	-	-	-	1-1
Fylde v Salford City	-	-	-	-	-	-
Gateshead v Harrogate T	-	-	-	-	-	-
Hartlepool v Barrow	-	-	-	-	-	1-0
Havant & W v Aldershot	-	-	-	-	-	-
Leyton Orient v Solihull Moors	-	-	-	-	-	3-1
Maidenhead v Eastleigh	-	1-3	-	-	-	3-1
Maidstone v Sutton Utd	-	-	-	1-2	1-1	1-0
Wrexham v Halifax	-	0-0	0-0	3-1	-	1-1

Saturday September 8, 2018

League One

Accrington v Burton	3-3	0-1	1-0	-	-	-
Barnsley v Walsall	-	-	3-0	0-2	-	-
Blackpool v Bradford	-	-	-	0-1	-	5-0
Bristol Rovers v Plymouth	2-1	2-1	-	1-1	-	2-1
Charlton v Wycombe	-	-	-	-	-	-
Doncaster v Luton	-	-	-	-	1-1	-
Gillingham v AFC Wimbledon	2-2	-	-	-	2-2	2-2
Oxford v Coventry	-	-	-	-	4-1	-
Portsmouth v Shrewsbury	3-1	-	0-2	-	-	0-1
Scunthorpe v Rochdale	-	3-0	2-1	1-1	2-1	1-1
Southend v Peterborough	-	-	-	2-1	1-1	1-1
Sunderland v Fleetwood Town	-	-	-	-	-	-

League Two

Bury v Grimsby	-	-	-	-	-	-
Cambridge U v Carlisle	-	-	5-0	0-0	2-2	1-2
Crewe v Mansfield	-	-	-	-	1-1	2-2
Exeter v Notts County	-	-	-	1-1	0-2	0-3

Results cover matches from Premier League to National League and Scottish Premiership to Scottish League Two

	2012-13	2013-14	2014-15	2015-16	2016-17	2017-18
Forest Green v Port Vale	-	-	-	-	-	1-0
Lincoln v Crawley Town	-	-	-	-	-	0-0
Morecambe v Swindon	-	-	-	-	-	0-1
Northampton v Cheltenham	2-3	1-1	2-0	-	-	-
Oldham v Newport County	-	-	-	-	-	-
Stevenage v Macclesfield	-	-	-	-	-	-
Tranmere v Colchester	4-0	2-1	-	-	-	-
Yeovil v MK Dons	2-1	-	0-2	-	-	-

National League

	2012-13	2013-14	2014-15	2015-16	2016-17	2017-18
Aldershot v Bromley	-	-	-	1-1	4-0	1-1
Barnet v Maidenhead	-	-	-	-	-	-
Barrow v Dag & Red	-	-	-	-	2-1	0-1
Braintree v Wrexham	1-5	3-0	1-0	1-0	1-2	-
Chesterfield v Dover	-	-	-	-	-	-
Eastleigh v Fylde	-	-	-	-	-	2-2
Ebbsfleet v Gateshead	3-1	-	-	-	-	0-0
Halifax v Leyton Orient	-	-	-	-	-	1-2
Harrogate T v Havant & W	-	-	-	-	-	-
Salford City v Maidstone	-	-	-	-	-	-
Solihull Moors v Hartlepool	-	-	-	-	-	1-2
Sutton Utd v Boreham Wood	-	1-0	1-3	-	1-0	1-1

Saturday September 15, 2018

Premier League

	2012-13	2013-14	2014-15	2015-16	2016-17	2017-18
Bournemouth v Leicester	-	0-1	-	1-1	1-0	0-0
Chelsea v Cardiff	-	4-1	-	-	-	-
Everton v West Ham	2-0	1-0	2-1	2-3	2-0	4-0
Huddersfield v Crystal Palace	1-0	-	-	-	-	0-2
Man City v Fulham	2-0	5-0	-	-	-	-
Newcastle v Arsenal	0-1	0-1	1-2	0-1	-	2-1
Southampton v Brighton	-	-	-	-	-	1-1
Tottenham v Liverpool	2-1	0-5	0-3	0-0	1-1	4-1
Watford v Man United	-	-	-	1-2	3-1	2-4
Wolves v Burnley	1-2	-	-	0-0	-	-

Championship

	2012-13	2013-14	2014-15	2015-16	2016-17	2017-18
Birmingham v West Brom	-	-	-	-	-	-
Blackburn v Aston Villa	-	-	-	-	1-0	-
Bolton v QPR	-	0-1	-	1-1	-	1-1
Brentford v Wigan	-	-	3-0	-	0-0	-
Bristol City v Sheffield United	-	0-1	1-3	-	-	2-3
Hull v Ipswich	2-1	-	-	3-0	-	2-2
Millwall v Leeds	1-0	2-0	2-0	-	-	1-0
Norwich v Middlesbrough	-	-	0-1	-	-	1-0
Preston v Reading	-	-	-	1-0	3-0	1-0
Rotherham v Derby	-	-	3-3	3-3	1-1	-
Sheffield Weds v Stoke	-	-	-	-	-	-
Swansea v Nottm Forest	-	-	-	-	-	-

League One

	2012-13	2013-14	2014-15	2015-16	2016-17	2017-18
AFC Wimbledon v Scunthorpe	-	3-2	-	-	1-2	1-1
Bradford v Charlton	-	-	-	-	0-0	0-1
Burton v Sunderland	-	-	-	-	-	0-2
Coventry v Barnsley	-	-	2-2	4-3	-	-
Fleetwood Town v Accrington	1-3	3-1	-	-	-	-
Luton v Bristol Rovers	-	-	-	0-1	-	-
Peterborough v Portsmouth	-	-	-	-	-	2-1
Plymouth v Blackpool	-	-	-	-	0-3	1-3
Rochdale v Gillingham	1-1	-	1-1	1-1	4-1	3-0
Shrewsbury v Southend	-	-	1-1	1-2	1-0	1-0
Walsall v Doncaster	0-3	-	3-0	2-0	-	4-2
Wycombe v Oxford	1-3	0-1	2-3	2-1	-	-

Results cover matches from Premier League to National League and Scottish Premiership to Scottish League Two

	2012-13	2013-14	2014-15	2015-16	2016-17	2017-18
League Two						
Carlisle v Tranmere	0-3	4-1	1-0	-	-	-
Cheltenham v Crewe	-	-	-	-	2-0	1-0
Colchester v Cambridge U	-	-	-	-	2-0	0-0
Crawley Town v Morecambe	-	-	-	1-1	1-3	1-1
Grimsby v Oldham	-	-	-	-	-	-
Macclesfield v Lincoln	2-1	3-1	3-0	1-1	1-2	-
Mansfield v Exeter	-	0-0	2-3	0-2	1-2	1-1
MK Dons v Forest Green	-	-	-	-	-	-
Newport County v Yeovil	-	-	-	0-0	1-0	2-0
Notts County v Stevenage	1-2	0-1	-	1-0	1-1	2-0
Port Vale v Northampton	2-2	-	-	-	2-3	-
Swindon v Bury	0-1	-	-	0-1	1-2	-
National League						
Boreham Wood v Barrow	-	-	-	0-2	1-1	0-0
Bromley v Salford City	-	-	-	-	-	-
Dag & Red v Chesterfield	0-1	0-1	-	-	-	-
Dover v Solihull Moors	-	-	-	-	0-0	1-0
Fylde v Aldershot	-	-	-	-	-	7-1
Gateshead v Braintree	1-2	1-0	3-1	2-3	1-1	-
Hartlepool v Eastleigh	-	-	-	-	-	1-2
Havant & W v Sutton Utd	-	0-5	2-2	0-2	-	-
Leyton Orient v Barnet	-	-	-	2-0	1-3	-
Maidenhead v Halifax	-	-	-	-	-	0-0
Maidstone v Harrogate T	-	-	-	-	-	-
Wrexham v Ebbsfleet	4-1	-	-	-	-	2-0
Ladbrokes Premiership						
Hibernian v Kilmarnock	2-1/2-2	3-0/0-1	-	-	-	1-1/5-3
Livingston v Hamilton	0-3/0-0	0-0/1-1	-	-	-	-
Motherwell v Hearts	0-0	2-1/4-1	-	2-2/1-0	1-3/0-3	2-1
Rangers v Dundee	-	-	-	-	1-0	4-1/4-0
St Johnstone v Aberdeen	1-2/3-1	0-2	1-0/1-1	3-4/3-0	0-0/1-2	0-3
St Mirren v Celtic	0-5/1-1	0-4	1-2/0-2	-	-	-
Ladbrokes Championship						
Ayr v Falkirk	-	-	-	-	0-1/1-4	-
Dundee United v Morton	-	-	-	-	2-1/1-1	2-1/0-3
Dunfermline v Alloa	-	-	-	-	-	-
Inverness CT v Partick	-	1-2/1-0	0-4	0-0/0-0	0-0	-
Queen of Sth v Ross County	-	-	-	-	-	-
Ladbrokes League One						
Arbroath v Forfar	1-1/3-1	3-0/2-3	-	-	2-0/0-1	2-1/2-0
Brechin v Raith	-	-	-	-	-	-
Dumbarton v Montrose	-	-	-	-	-	-
East Fife v Airdrieonians	-	1-0/0-0	-	-	0-1/0-4	6-1/2-1
Stranraer v Stenhousemuir	1-1/1-1	1-0/1-1	0-2/3-2	1-2/3-1	3-1/3-0	-
Ladbrokes League Two						
Berwick v Elgin	0-0/2-1	2-3/2-3	1-1/0-2	2-3/2-0	2-4/0-1	3-2/2-2
Clyde v Albion	-	2-2/4-0	0-1/2-3	-	-	-
Cowdenbeath v Peterhead	-	-	-	2-2/2-3	-	0-4/0-2
Edinburgh City v Annan	-	-	-	-	1-0/2-0	0-1/3-2
Stirling v Queens Park	1-2/2-3	3-0/2-2	-	1-2/0-0	-	-
Tuesday September 18, 2018						
Championship						
Aston Villa v Rotherham	-	-	-	-	3-0	-
Derby v Blackburn	1-1	1-1	2-0	1-0	1-2	-
Ipswich v Brentford	-	-	1-1	1-3	1-1	2-0
Leeds v Preston	-	-	-	1-0	3-0	0-0
Stoke v Swansea	2-0	1-1	2-1	2-2	3-1	2-1
West Brom v Bristol City	-	-	-	-	-	-
Wigan v Hull	-	-	-	-	-	-

Results cover matches from Premier League to National League and Scottish Premiership to Scottish League Two

Wednesday September 19, 2018

Championship

	2012-13	2013-14	2014-15	2015-16	2016-17	2017-18
Middlesbrough v Bolton	2-1	1-0	1-0	3-0	-	2-0
Nottm Forest v Sheffield Weds	1-0	3-3	0-2	0-3	1-2	0-3
QPR v Millwall	-	1-1	-	-	-	2-2
Reading v Norwich	0-0	-	2-1	-	3-1	1-2
Sheffield United v Birmingham	-	-	-	-	-	1-1

Saturday September 22, 2018

Premier League

	2012-13	2013-14	2014-15	2015-16	2016-17	2017-18
Arsenal v Everton	0-0	1-1	2-0	2-1	3-1	5-1
Brighton v Tottenham	-	-	-	-	-	1-1
Burnley v Bournemouth	-	1-1	-	-	3-2	1-2
Cardiff v Man City	-	3-2	-	-	-	-
Crystal Palace v Newcastle	-	0-3	1-1	5-1	-	1-1
Fulham v Watford	-	-	0-5	-	-	-
Leicester v Huddersfield	6-1	2-1	-	-	-	3-0
Liverpool v Southampton	1-0	0-1	2-1	1-1	0-0	3-0
Man United v Wolves	-	-	-	-	-	-
West Ham v Chelsea	3-1	0-3	0-1	2-1	1-2	1-0

Championship

	2012-13	2013-14	2014-15	2015-16	2016-17	2017-18
Aston Villa v Sheffield Weds	-	-	-	-	2-0	1-2
Derby v Brentford	-	-	1-1	2-0	0-0	3-0
Ipswich v Bolton	1-0	1-0	1-0	2-0	-	2-0
Leeds v Birmingham	0-1	4-0	1-1	0-2	1-2	2-0
Middlesbrough v Swansea	-	-	-	-	3-0	-
Nottm Forest v Rotherham	-	-	2-0	2-1	2-0	-
QPR v Norwich	0-0	-	-	-	2-1	4-1
Reading v Hull	-	-	-	1-2	-	1-1
Sheffield United v Preston	0-0	0-1	2-1	-	-	0-1
Stoke v Blackburn	-	-	-	-	-	-
West Brom v Millwall	-	-	-	-	-	-
Wigan v Bristol City	-	-	-	-	0-1	-

League One

	2012-13	2013-14	2014-15	2015-16	2016-17	2017-18
Accrington v AFC Wimbledon	4-0	3-2	1-0	3-4	-	-
Barnsley v Burton	-	-	-	1-0	1-1	1-2
Blackpool v Luton	-	-	-	-	0-2	-
Bristol Rovers v Coventry	-	-	-	-	4-1	-
Charlton v Plymouth	-	-	-	-	-	2-0
Doncaster v Bradford	-	-	0-3	0-1	-	2-0
Gillingham v Peterborough	-	2-2	2-1	2-1	0-1	1-1
Oxford v Walsall	-	-	-	-	0-0	1-2
Portsmouth v Wycombe	-	2-2	1-1	2-1	4-2	-
Scunthorpe v Shrewsbury	0-0	-	-	2-1	0-1	1-2
Southend v Fleetwood Town	1-1	2-0	-	2-2	0-2	1-2
Sunderland v Rochdale	-	-	-	-	-	-

League Two

	2012-13	2013-14	2014-15	2015-16	2016-17	2017-18
Bury v Carlisle	1-1	-	2-1	-	-	-
Cambridge U v Mansfield	4-1	-	3-1	1-1	1-3	0-0
Crewe v Port Vale	-	1-2	2-1	0-0	-	2-2
Exeter v Cheltenham	0-1	1-1	1-0	-	3-0	2-1
Forest Green v Crawley Town	-	-	-	-	-	2-0
Lincoln v MK Dons	-	-	-	-	-	-
Morecambe v Macclesfield	-	-	-	-	-	-
Northampton v Notts County	-	-	-	2-2	-	-
Oldham v Colchester	1-1	0-2	0-1	1-1	-	-
Stevenage v Grimsby	-	-	-	-	2-0	3-1
Tranmere v Newport County	-	-	0-0	-	-	-
Yeovil v Swindon	0-2	-	1-1	-	-	1-2

Results cover matches from Premier League to National League and Scottish Premiership to Scottish League Two

	2012-13	2013-14	2014-15	2015-16	2016-17	2017-18
National League						
Aldershot v Dover	-	-	3-1	1-1	1-0	0-2
Barnet v Fylde	-	-	-	-	-	-
Barrow v Maidenhead	-	-	-	-	-	1-1
Braintree v Maidstone	-	-	-	-	0-0	-
Chesterfield v Gateshead	-	-	-	-	-	-
Eastleigh v Dag & Red	-	-	-	-	0-1	2-2
Ebbsfleet v Havant & W	-	0-0	1-0	2-2	-	-
Halifax v Hartlepool	-	-	-	-	-	2-0
Harrogate T v Leyton Orient	-	-	-	-	-	-
Salford City v Boreham Wood	-	-	-	-	-	-
Solihull Moors v Bromley	-	-	-	-	1-0	2-0
Sutton Utd v Wrexham	-	-	-	-	1-0	1-1
Ladbrokes Premiership						
Aberdeen v Motherwell	3-3/0-0	0-1/0-1	1-0/2-1	1-1/4-1	7-2/1-0	0-2
Dundee v Hibernian	3-1	-	-	-	-	1-1/0-1
Hamilton v St Mirren	-	-	3-0/1-0	-	-	-
Hearts v Livingston	-	-	5-0/1-0	-	-	-
Kilmarnock v Celtic	1-3	2-5/0-3	0-2	2-2/0-1	0-1	0-2/1-0
Rangers v St Johnstone	-	-	-	-	1-1/3-2	1-3
Ladbrokes Championship						
Alloa v Ayr	1-0/2-2	-	-	-	-	1-2/2-1
Falkirk v Dundee United	-	-	-	-	3-1/3-0	0-0/6-1
Morton v Dunfermline	4-2/0-1	-	2-1/2-0	-	2-1/0-1	3-2/2-1
Partick v Queen of Sth	-	-	-	-	-	-
Ross County v Inverness CT	0-0/1-0	0-3/1-2	1-3	1-2/0-3	3-2/4-0	-
Ladbrokes League One						
Airdrieonians v Dumbarton	4-1/1-2	-	-	-	-	-
Forfar v Brechin	1-0/1-4	2-0/1-1	3-1/0-2	0-1/1-2	-	-
Raith v Montrose	-	-	-	-	-	-
Stenhousemuir v Arbroath	2-2/1-0	3-2/2-2	-	-	-	-
Stranraer v East Fife	2-6/3-1	2-0/2-0	-	-	1-1/2-1	1-0/0-2
Ladbrokes League Two						
Clyde v Elgin	2-2/1-1	2-1/4-0	2-1/0-2	4-2/1-0	2-1/3-2	2-4/1-0
Cowdenbeath v Albion	-	-	-	1-0/1-2	-	-
Peterhead v Berwick	1-0/1-1	1-1/3-0	-	-	-	0-2/1-1
Queens Park v Edinburgh City	-	-	-	-	-	-
Stirling v Annan	5-1/2-1	0-2/1-1	-	1-0/2-1	3-1/1-0	3-2/3-0

Tuesday September 25, 2018

	2012-13	2013-14	2014-15	2015-16	2016-17	2017-18
National League						
Aldershot v Maidstone	-	-	-	-	1-0	1-1
Barnet v Havant & W	-	-	-	-	-	-
Barrow v Gateshead	0-2	-	-	0-0	0-0	1-1
Braintree v Leyton Orient	-	-	-	-	-	-
Chesterfield v Maidenhead	-	-	-	-	-	-
Eastleigh v Boreham Wood	-	0-1	-	1-0	2-2	0-2
Ebbsfleet v Bromley	-	1-3	0-1	-	-	2-1
Halifax v Fylde	-	-	-	-	-	2-1
Harrogate T v Wrexham	-	-	-	-	-	-
Salford City v Hartlepool	-	-	-	-	-	-
Solihull Moors v Dag & Red	-	-	-	-	2-5	2-2
Sutton Utd v Dover	-	1-0	-	-	0-6	2-2

Saturday September 29, 2018

	2012-13	2013-14	2014-15	2015-16	2016-17	2017-18
Premier League						
Arsenal v Watford	-	-	-	4-0	1-2	3-0
Bournemouth v Crystal Palace	-	-	-	0-0	0-2	2-2
Cardiff v Burnley	4-0	-	-	2-2	-	-
Chelsea v Liverpool	1-1	2-1	1-1	1-3	1-2	1-0

Results cover matches from Premier League to National League and Scottish Premiership to Scottish League Two

	2012-13	2013-14	2014-15	2015-16	2016-17	2017-18
Everton v Fulham	1-0	4-1	-	-	-	-
Huddersfield v Tottenham	-	-	-	-	-	0-4
Man City v Brighton	-	-	-	-	-	3-1
Newcastle v Leicester	-	-	1-0	0-3	-	2-3
West Ham v Man United	2-2	0-2	1-1	3-2	0-2	0-0
Wolves v Southampton	-	-	-	-	-	-
Championship						
Birmingham v Ipswich	0-1	1-1	2-2	3-0	2-1	1-0
Blackburn v Nottm Forest	3-0	0-1	3-3	0-0	2-1	-
Bolton v Derby	2-0	2-2	0-2	0-0	-	1-2
Brentford v Reading	-	-	3-1	1-3	4-1	1-1
Bristol City v Aston Villa	-	-	-	-	3-1	1-1
Hull v Middlesbrough	1-0			3-0	4-2	1-3
Millwall v Sheffield United	-	-	-	1-0	2-1	3-1
Norwich v Wigan	2-1	-	0-1	-	2-1	-
Preston v West Brom	-	-	-	-	-	-
Rotherham v Stoke	-	-	-	-	-	-
Sheffield Weds v Leeds	1-1	6-0	1-2	2-0	0-2	3-0
Swansea v QPR	4-1	-	2-0	-	-	-
League One						
AFC Wimbledon v Oxford	0-3	0-2	0-0	1-2	2-1	2-1
Bradford v Bristol Rovers	4-1	-	-	-	1-1	3-1
Burton v Scunthorpe	-	2-2	-	2-1	-	-
Coventry v Sunderland	-	-	-	-	-	-
Fleetwood Town v Barnsley	-	-	0-0	0-2	-	-
Luton v Charlton	-	-	-	-	-	-
Peterborough v Blackpool	1-4	-	-	5-1	-	0-1
Plymouth v Doncaster	-	-	-	-	2-0	0-3
Rochdale v Portsmouth	-	3-0	-	-	-	3-3
Shrewsbury v Gillingham	-	2-0	-	2-2	2-3	1-1
Walsall v Accrington	-	-	-	-	-	-
Wycombe v Southend	1-2	2-1	4-1	-	-	-
League Two						
Carlisle v Stevenage	2-1	0-0	3-0	1-0	1-1	0-2
Cheltenham v Lincoln	-	-	-	3-1	-	1-0
Colchester v Bury	2-0	-	-	0-1	-	-
Crawley Town v Yeovil	0-1	-	2-0	0-1	2-0	2-0
Grimsby v Morecambe	-	-	-	-	2-0	0-2
Macclesfield v Forest Green	1-2	1-2	2-2	4-1	0-1	-
Mansfield v Northampton	-	3-0	1-1	2-2	-	-
MK Dons v Tranmere	3-0	0-1	-	-	-	-
Newport County v Cambridge U	6-2	-	1-1	0-1	1-2	2-1
Notts County v Crewe	1-1	4-0	2-1	-	1-1	4-1
Port Vale v Exeter	0-2	-	-	-	-	0-1
Swindon v Oldham	1-1	0-1	2-2	1-2	0-0	-
National League						
Boreham Wood v Harrogate T	-	-	-	-	-	-
Bromley v Halifax	-	-	-	1-0	-	3-0
Dag & Red v Ebbsfleet	-	-	-	-	-	3-3
Dover v Barrow	-	-	-	3-1	3-1	1-1
Fylde v Braintree	-	-	-	-	-	-
Gateshead v Eastleigh	-	-	2-3	2-1	2-2	2-0
Hartlepool v Aldershot	-	-	-	-	-	0-2
Havant & W v Solihull Moors	-	-	-	-	-	-
Leyton Orient v Sutton Utd	-	-	-	-	-	4-1
Maidenhead v Salford City	-	-	-	-	-	-
Maidstone v Chesterfield	-	-	-	-	-	-
Wrexham v Barnet	-	0-1	1-0	-	-	-

Results cover matches from Premier League to National League and Scottish Premiership to Scottish League Two

Ladbrokes Premiership						
Celtic v Aberdeen	1-0/4-3	3-1/5-2	2-1/4-0	3-1/3-2	4-1/1-0	3-0/0-1
Hamilton v Dundee	-	0-3/1-1	2-1	1-1/2-1	0-1/4-0	3-0/1-2
Hearts v St Johnstone	2-0/2-0	0-2	-	4-3/0-3/2-2	2-2	1-0/1-0
Kilmarnock v Motherwell	1-2/2-0	0-2	2-0/1-2	0-1	1-2/1-2	1-0
Livingston v Rangers	-	-	0-1/1-1	1-1/1-0	-	-
St Mirren v Hibernian	1-2/0-1	0-0/2-0	-	1-4/2-2	0-2/2-0	-

Ladbrokes Championship						
Alloa v Falkirk	-	0-0/3-0	2-3/1-3	1-1/0-1	-	-
Dundee United v Ross County	0-0/1-1	1-0	2-1/1-2	1-0	-	-
Dunfermline v Partick	0-1/0-4	-	-	-	-	-
Inverness CT v Queen of Sth	-	-	-	-	-	0-0/3-1
Morton v Ayr	-	-	0-1/2-1	-	2-1/1-1	-

Ladbrokes League One						
Arbroath v Airdrieonians	-	3-2/0-1	-	-	-	7-1/2-0
Brechin v Stranraer	3-0/2-2	1-1/1-3	1-2/1-3	2-0/1-0	2-0/0-0	-
Dumbarton v Raith	4-2/1-2	2-4/3-3	2-1/2-2	3-3/2-3	0-0/4-0	-
East Fife v Stenhousemuir	3-2/1-2	1-0/1-2	-	-	0-1/1-0	-
Montrose v Forfar	-	-	-	-	1-1/1-0	-

Ladbrokes League Two						
Albion v Stirling	-	2-1/0-2	-	-	-	-
Annan v Peterhead	2-1/0-0	2-0/2-1	-	-	-	1-2/3-3
Berwick v Clyde	2-1/3-3	0-1/3-0	4-0/0-0	0-5/3-0	1-1/4-3	3-1/0-1
Edinburgh City v Cowdenbeath	-	-	-	-	1-1/1-1	0-0/1-1
Elgin v Queens Park	0-4/3-5	3-2/1-1	1-4/1-2	0-0/1-1	-	-

Tuesday October 2, 2018

Championship						
Aston Villa v Preston	-	-	-	-	2-2	1-1
Brentford v Birmingham	-	-	1-1	0-2	1-2	5-0
Ipswich v Middlesbrough	4-0	3-1	2-0	0-2	-	2-2
Reading v QPR	0-0	1-1	-	0-1	0-1	1-0
Stoke v Bolton	-	-	-	-	-	-
Wigan v Swansea	2-3	-	-	-	-	-

League One						
Accrington v Doncaster	-	-	-	-	3-2	-
AFC Wimbledon v Bradford	2-1	-	-	-	2-3	2-1
Barnsley v Plymouth	-	-	-	-	-	-
Burton v Southend	2-0	0-1	2-1	1-0	-	-
Coventry v Portsmouth	1-1	-	-	-	-	-
Fleetwood Town v Wycombe	0-1	1-0	-	-	-	-
Gillingham v Blackpool	-	-	-	2-1	-	0-3
Oxford v Luton	-	-	1-1	2-3	-	-
Rochdale v Bristol Rovers	2-1	2-0	-	-	0-0	1-0
Scunthorpe v Charlton	-	-	-	-	0-0	2-0
Sunderland v Peterborough	-	-	-	-	-	-
Walsall v Shrewsbury	3-1	1-0	-	2-1	3-2	1-1

League Two						
Cambridge U v Forest Green	0-0	2-1	-	-	-	3-0
Carlisle v Grimsby	-	-	-	-	1-3	2-0
Cheltenham v Morecambe	2-0	3-0	1-1	-	3-1	3-0
Colchester v Yeovil	2-0	-	2-0	-	2-0	0-1
Crewe v Swindon	2-1	1-1	0-0	1-3	-	0-3
Exeter v Stevenage	-	-	0-0	3-3	1-1	2-1
Mansfield v Oldham	-	-	-	-	-	-
Newport County v Macclesfield	4-1	-	-	-	-	-
Northampton v Bury	-	0-3	2-3	-	3-2	0-0
Notts County v Crawley Town	1-1	1-0	5-3	4-1	2-1	1-2
Port Vale v MK Dons	-	1-0	0-0	-	0-0	-
Tranmere v Lincoln	-	-	-	3-2	0-1	-

Results cover matches from Premier League to National League and Scottish Premiership to Scottish League Two

Wednesday October 3, 2018

Championship

	2012-13	2013-14	2014-15	2015-16	2016-17	2017-18
Blackburn v Sheffield United	-	-	-	-	-	-
Derby v Norwich	-	-	2-2	-	1-0	1-1
Hull v Leeds	2-0	-	-	2-2	-	0-0
Nottm Forest v Millwall	1-4	1-2	0-1	-	-	1-0
Rotherham v Bristol City	-	2-1	-	3-0	2-2	-
Sheffield Weds v West Brom	-	-	-	-	-	-

Saturday October 6, 2018

Premier League

	2012-13	2013-14	2014-15	2015-16	2016-17	2017-18
Brighton v West Ham	-	-	-	-	-	3-1
Burnley v Huddersfield	0-1	3-2	-	2-1	-	0-0
Crystal Palace v Wolves	3-1	-	-	-	-	-
Fulham v Arsenal	0-1	1-3	-	-	-	-
Leicester v Everton	-	-	2-2	3-1	0-2	2-0
Liverpool v Man City	2-2	3-2	2-1	3-0	1-0	4-3
Man United v Newcastle	4-3	0-1	3-1	0-0	-	4-1
Southampton v Chelsea	2-1	0-3	1-1	1-2	0-2	2-3
Tottenham v Cardiff	-	1-0	-	-	-	-
Watford v Bournemouth	-	6-1	1-1	0-0	2-2	2-2

Championship

	2012-13	2013-14	2014-15	2015-16	2016-17	2017-18
Birmingham v Rotherham	-	-	2-1	0-2	4-2	-
Bolton v Blackburn	1-0	4-0	2-1	1-0	-	-
Leeds v Brentford	-	-	0-1	1-1	1-0	1-0
Middlesbrough v Nottm Forest	1-0	1-1	3-0	0-1	-	2-0
Millwall v Aston Villa	-	-	-	-	-	1-0
Norwich v Stoke	1-0	1-1	-	1-1	-	-
Preston v Wigan	-	-	-	-	1-0	-
QPR v Derby	-	2-1	-	2-0	0-1	1-1
Sheffield United v Hull	-	-	-	-	-	4-1
Swansea v Ipswich	-	-	-	-	-	-
West Brom v Reading	1-0	-	-	-	-	-

League One

	2012-13	2013-14	2014-15	2015-16	2016-17	2017-18
Blackpool v Rochdale	-	-	-	0-2	-	0-0
Bradford v Sunderland	-	-	-	-	-	-
Bristol Rovers v Walsall	-	-	-	-	1-1	2-1
Charlton v Coventry	-	-	-	-	3-0	-
Doncaster v Fleetwood Town	-	-	0-0	2-0	-	3-0
Luton v Scunthorpe	-	-	-	-	-	-
Peterborough v Barnsley	2-1	-	2-1	3-2	-	-
Plymouth v AFC Wimbledon	1-2	1-2	1-1	1-2	-	4-2
Portsmouth v Gillingham	-	-	-	-	-	1-3
Shrewsbury v Accrington	-	-	4-0	-	-	-
Southend v Oxford	1-0	3-0	1-1	-	2-1	1-1
Wycombe v Burton	3-0	1-2	1-3	-	-	-

League Two

	2012-13	2013-14	2014-15	2015-16	2016-17	2017-18
Bury v Mansfield	-	0-0	2-0	-	-	-
Crawley Town v Cambridge U	-	-	-	1-0	1-3	0-1
Forest Green v Newport County	1-2	-	-	-	-	0-4
Grimsby v Port Vale	-	-	-	-	-	1-1
Lincoln v Crewe	-	-	-	-	-	1-4
Macclesfield v Notts County	-	-	-	-	-	-
MK Dons v Cheltenham	-	-	-	-	-	-
Morecambe v Tranmere	-	-	0-0	-	-	-
Oldham v Carlisle	1-2	1-0	-	-	-	-
Stevenage v Colchester	0-2	2-3	-	-	2-4	0-1
Swindon v Northampton	-	-	-	-	1-3	-
Yeovil v Exeter	-	-	-	0-2	0-0	3-1

Results cover matches from Premier League to National League and Scottish Premiership to Scottish League Two

	2012-13	2013-14	2014-15	2015-16	2016-17	2017-18
National League						
Aldershot v Halifax	-	2-2	1-1	3-2	-	0-1
Barnet v Solihull Moors	-	-	-	-	-	-
Barrow v Sutton Utd	-	-	-	-	0-0	1-1
Braintree v Eastleigh	-	-	1-5	2-0	1-1	-
Chesterfield v Fylde	-	-	-	-	-	-
Dover v Salford City	-	-	-	-	-	-
Ebbsfleet v Harrogate T	-	-	-	-	-	-
Gateshead v Dag & Red	-	-	-	-	1-0	0-0
Hartlepool v Boreham Wood	-	-	-	-	-	0-0
Maidenhead v Leyton Orient	-	-	-	-	-	0-1
Maidstone v Bromley	-	-	-	-	0-2	0-2
Wrexham v Havant & W	-	-	-	-	-	-
Ladbrokes Premiership						
Aberdeen v St Mirren	0-0/0-0	2-0	2-2/3-0	-	-	-
Dundee v Kilmarnock	0-0/2-3	-	1-1/1-0	1-2/1-1	1-1/1-1	0-0
Hibernian v Hamilton	-	-	-	-	-	1-3/3-1
Motherwell v Livingston	-	-	-	-	-	-
Rangers v Hearts	-	-	1-2/2-1	-	2-0/2-1	0-0/2-0/2-1
St Johnstone v Celtic	2-1/1-1	0-1/3-3	0-3/1-2/0-0	0-3/2-1	2-4/2-5	0-4
Ladbrokes Championship						
Ayr v Dundee United	-	-	-	-	0-1/0-0	-
Falkirk v Dunfermline	2-2/1-0	-	-	-	2-1/2-0	1-1/1-2
Inverness CT v Morton	-	-	-	-	-	1-1/0-2
Partick v Ross County	-	3-3/2-3	4-0/1-3	1-0	1-1/2-1	2-0/1-1
Queen of Sth v Alloa	1-0/0-0	0-0/3-1	2-0/1-0	3-1/1-0	-	-
Ladbrokes League One						
Airdrieonians v Brechin	-	3-1/2-1	4-0/1-1	1-0/0-2	1-0/3-1	-
Forfar v East Fife	3-2/3-2	2-0/1-2	-	-	-	2-0/2-0
Raith v Arbroath	-	-	-	-	-	2-0/2-2
Stenhousemuir v Montrose	-	-	-	-	-	0-1/0-2
Stranraer v Dumbarton	-	-	-	-	-	-
Ladbrokes League Two						
Annan v Albion	-	1-1/2-0	2-1/1-3	-	-	-
Cowdenbeath v Stirling	-	-	-	-	0-2/0-2	0-3/1-2
Edinburgh City v Berwick	-	-	-	-	1-2/2-2	1-0/3-0
Peterhead v Elgin	1-1/0-1	2-2/2-1	-	-	-	3-0/7-0
Queens Park v Clyde	1-0/4-1	1-1/1-3	1-2/1-1	1-1/2-1	-	-
Sunday October 7, 2018						
Championship						
Bristol City v Sheffield Weds	1-1	-	-	4-1	2-2	4-0
Friday October 12, 2018						
League Two						
Tranmere v Macclesfield	-	-	-	0-1	1-0	1-4
Saturday October 13, 2018						
League One						
Accrington v Bradford	1-1	-	-	-	-	-
AFC Wimbledon v Portsmouth	-	4-0	1-0	0-1	-	0-2
Barnsley v Luton	-	-	-	-	-	-
Burton v Bristol Rovers	1-1	1-0	-	-	-	-
Coventry v Wycombe	-	-	-	-	-	3-2
Fleetwood Town v Shrewsbury	-	-	-	0-0	3-0	1-2
Gillingham v Southend	1-0	-	-	1-1	2-1	3-3
Oxford v Plymouth	2-1	2-3	0-0	1-0	-	0-1
Rochdale v Doncaster	-	-	1-3	2-2	-	2-1
Scunthorpe v Peterborough	-	-	2-0	0-4	1-1	2-1
Sunderland v Blackpool	-	-	-	-	-	-
Walsall v Charlton	-	-	-	-	1-2	2-2

Results cover matches from Premier League to National League and Scottish Premiership to Scottish League Two

	2012-13	2013-14	2014-15	2015-16	2016-17	2017-18
League Two						
Cambridge U v MK Dons	-	-	-	-	-	-
Carlisle v Morecambe	-	-	1-1	2-3	1-1	1-1
Cheltenham v Yeovil	-	-	-	-	2-0	0-2
Colchester v Crawley Town	1-1	1-1	2-3	-	2-3	3-1
Crewe v Bury	1-0	-	-	3-3	-	-
Exeter v Swindon	-	-	-	-	-	3-1
Mansfield v Grimsby	2-0	-	-	-	0-1	4-1
Newport County v Stevenage	-	-	2-0	2-2	0-2	0-1
Northampton v Forest Green	-	-	-	-	-	-
Notts County v Oldham	1-0	3-2	0-0	-	-	-
Port Vale v Lincoln	-	-	-	-	-	1-0
National League						
Boreham Wood v Maidenhead	-	2-2	2-1	-	-	1-1
Bromley v Barrow	-	-	-	5-0	4-1	0-0
Dag & Red v Wrexham	-	-	-	-	3-0	0-1
Eastleigh v Aldershot	-	-	1-0	1-1	1-1	0-0
Fylde v Maidstone	-	-	-	-	-	3-0
Halifax v Chesterfield	-	-	-	-	-	-
Harrogate T v Dover	-	-	-	-	-	-
Havant & W v Gateshead	-	-	-	-	-	-
Leyton Orient v Hartlepool	1-0	-	-	0-2	2-1	1-2
Salford City v Braintree	-	-	-	-	-	-
Solihull Moors v Ebbsfleet	-	-	-	-	-	1-3
Sutton Utd v Barnet	-	-	-	-	-	-
Saturday October 20, 2018						
Premier League						
Arsenal v Leicester	-	-	2-1	2-1	1-0	4-3
Bournemouth v Southampton	-	-	-	2-0	1-3	1-1
Cardiff v Fulham	-	3-1	1-0	1-1	2-2	2-4
Chelsea v Man United	2-3	3-1	1-0	1-1	4-0	1-0
Everton v Crystal Palace	-	2-3	2-3	1-1	1-1	3-1
Huddersfield v Liverpool	-	-	-	-	-	0-3
Man City v Burnley	-	-	2-2	-	2-1	3-0
Newcastle v Brighton	-	-	-	-	2-0	0-0
West Ham v Tottenham	2-3	2-0	0-1	1-0	1-0	2-3
Wolves v Watford	1-1	-	2-2	-	-	-
Championship						
Aston Villa v Swansea	2-0	1-1	0-1	1-2	-	-
Blackburn v Leeds	0-0	1-0	2-1	1-2	1-2	-
Brentford v Bristol City	-	3-1	-	1-1	2-0	2-2
Derby v Sheffield United	-	-	-	-	-	1-1
Hull v Preston	-	-	-	2-0	-	1-2
Ipswich v QPR	-	1-3	-	2-1	3-0	0-0
Nottm Forest v Norwich	-	-	2-1	-	1-2	1-0
Reading v Millwall	-	1-1	3-2	-	-	0-2
Rotherham v Bolton	-	-	4-2	4-0	-	-
Sheffield Weds v Middlesbrough	2-0	1-0	2-0	1-3	-	1-2
Stoke v Birmingham	-	-	-	-	-	-
Wigan v West Brom	1-2	-	-	-	-	-
League One						
Blackpool v AFC Wimbledon	-	-	-	-	-	1-0
Bradford v Rochdale	2-4	-	1-2	2-2	4-0	4-3
Bristol Rovers v Oxford	0-2	1-1	-	0-1	2-1	0-1
Charlton v Barnsley	0-1	1-2	-	-	-	-
Doncaster v Gillingham	-	-	1-2	2-2	-	0-0
Luton v Walsall	-	-	-	-	-	-
Peterborough v Accrington	-	-	-	-	-	-
Plymouth v Burton	1-2	0-1	1-1	-	-	-

Results cover matches from Premier League to National League and Scottish Premiership to Scottish League Two

	2012-13	2013-14	2014-15	2015-16	2016-17	2017-18
Portsmouth v Fleetwood Town	-	0-1	-	-	-	4-1
Shrewsbury v Sunderland	-	-	-	-	-	-
Southend v Coventry	-	-	-	3-0	3-1	-
Wycombe v Scunthorpe	-	1-1	-	-	-	-

League Two

	2012-13	2013-14	2014-15	2015-16	2016-17	2017-18
Bury v Notts County	0-2	-	-	-	-	-
Crawley Town v Newport County	-	-	-	2-0	3-1	1-2
Forest Green v Cheltenham	-	-	-	2-2	-	1-1
Grimsby v Exeter	-	-	-	-	0-3	0-1
Lincoln v Cambridge U	0-0	1-0	-	-	-	0-0
Macclesfield v Carlisle	-	-	-	-	-	-
MK Dons v Northampton	-	-	-	-	5-3	0-0
Morecambe v Colchester	-	-	-	-	1-1	0-0
Oldham v Port Vale	-	3-1	1-1	1-1	0-0	-
Stevenage v Crewe	2-2	1-0	-	-	1-2	2-2
Swindon v Mansfield	-	-	-	-	-	1-0
Yeovil v Tranmere	1-0	-	-	-	-	-

Ladbrokes Premiership

	2012-13	2013-14	2014-15	2015-16	2016-17	2017-18
Celtic v Hibernian	2-2/3-0	1-0	-	-	-	2-2/1-0
Hamilton v Rangers	-	-	-	-	1-2	1-4/3-5
Hearts v Aberdeen	2-0	2-1/1-1	-	1-3/2-1	0-1/1-2	0-0/2-0
Livingston v Dundee	-	2-1/0-2	-	-	-	-
Motherwell v St Johnstone	1-1/3-2	4-0/2-1	0-1/1-1	2-0/1-2	1-2/1-2	2-0/1-5
St Mirren v Kilmarnock	1-1	1-1/2-0	1-2/4-1	-	-	-

Ladbrokes Championship

	2012-13	2013-14	2014-15	2015-16	2016-17	2017-18
Alloa v Partick	-	-	-	-	-	-
Dundee United v Inverness CT	4-4	0-1/2-1	1-1	1-1/0-2	-	0-2/1-1
Dunfermline v Queen of Sth	-	-	-	-	0-1/1-1	2-5/3-1
Morton v Falkirk	1-2/2-0	0-2/1-1	-	1-1/0-1	1-1/2-2	0-1/0-1
Ross County v Ayr	-	-	-	-	-	-

Ladbrokes League One

	2012-13	2013-14	2014-15	2015-16	2016-17	2017-18
Arbroath v Dumbarton	-	-	-	-	-	-
East Fife v Brechin	2-2/0-3	1-3/1-2	-	-	1-2/3-2	-
Montrose v Airdrieonians	-	-	-	-	-	-
Raith v Stranraer	-	-	-	-	-	3-0/3-0
Stenhousemuir v Forfar	0-4/2-0	1-1/4-1	0-2/1-3	2-2/2-1	-	-

Tuesday October 23, 2018

Championship

	2012-13	2013-14	2014-15	2015-16	2016-17	2017-18
Birmingham v Reading	-	1-2	6-1	2-1	0-1	0-2
Middlesbrough v Rotherham	-	-	2-0	1-0	-	-
Millwall v Wigan	-	2-1	2-0	0-0	-	-
Norwich v Aston Villa	1-2	0-1	-	2-0	1-0	3-1
QPR v Sheffield Weds	-	2-1	-	0-0	1-2	4-2
Sheffield United v Stoke	-	-	-	-	-	-
Swansea v Blackburn	-	-	-	-	-	-

League One

	2012-13	2013-14	2014-15	2015-16	2016-17	2017-18
Blackpool v Scunthorpe	-	-	-	5-0	-	2-3
Bradford v Coventry	-	3-3	3-2	0-0	3-1	-
Bristol Rovers v AFC Wimbledon	1-0	3-0	-	3-1	2-0	1-3
Charlton v Oxford	-	-	-	-	0-1	2-3
Doncaster v Sunderland	-	-	-	-	-	-
Luton v Accrington	-	-	2-0	0-2	1-0	1-2
Peterborough v Fleetwood Town	-	-	1-0	2-1	1-2	2-0
Plymouth v Gillingham	2-2	-	-	-	-	2-1
Portsmouth v Burton	-	0-0	1-1	-	-	-
Shrewsbury v Barnsley	-	-	-	0-3	-	-
Southend v Walsall	-	-	-	0-2	3-2	0-3
Wycombe v Rochdale	1-2	0-2	-	-	-	-

Results cover matches from Premier League to National League and Scottish Premiership to Scottish League Two

	2012-13	2013-14	2014-15	2015-16	2016-17	2017-18
League Two						
Bury v Newport County	-	0-0	1-3	-	-	-
Crawley Town v Exeter	-	-	-	0-2	1-2	3-1
Forest Green v Tranmere	-	-	-	0-2	2-2	-
Grimsby v Colchester	-	-	-	-	1-0	2-2
Lincoln v Carlisle	-	-	-	-	-	4-1
Macclesfield v Northampton	-	-	-	-	-	-
MK Dons v Notts County	1-1	3-1	4-1	-	-	-
Morecambe v Mansfield	-	0-1	2-1	1-2	1-3	1-2
Oldham v Cheltenham	-	-	-	-	-	-
Stevenage v Port Vale	-	1-1	-	-	-	2-0
Swindon v Cambridge U	-	-	-	-	-	2-0
Yeovil v Crewe	1-0	-	1-1	-	3-0	2-0
Wednesday October 24, 2018						
Championship						
Bolton v Nottm Forest	2-2	1-1	2-2	1-1	-	3-2
Bristol City v Hull	1-2	-	-	1-1	-	5-5
Leeds v Ipswich	2-0	1-1	2-1	0-1	1-0	3-2
Preston v Brentford	1-1	0-3	-	1-3	4-2	2-3
West Brom v Derby	-	-	-	-	-	-
Saturday October 27, 2018						
Premier League						
Brighton v Wolves	2-0	-	1-1	0-1	1-0	-
Burnley v Chelsea	-	-	1-3	-	1-1	1-2
Crystal Palace v Arsenal	-	0-2	1-2	1-2	3-0	2-3
Fulham v Bournemouth	-	-	1-5	-	-	-
Leicester v West Ham	-	-	2-1	2-2	1-0	0-2
Liverpool v Cardiff	-	3-1	-	-	-	-
Man United v Everton	2-0	0-1	2-1	1-0	1-1	4-0
Southampton v Newcastle	2-0	4-0	4-0	3-1	-	2-2
Tottenham v Man City	3-1	1-5	0-1	4-1	2-0	1-3
Watford v Huddersfield	4-0	1-4	4-2	-	-	1-4
Championship						
Birmingham v Sheffield Weds	0-0	4-1	0-2	1-2	2-1	1-0
Bolton v Hull	4-1	-	-	1-0	-	1-0
Bristol City v Stoke	-	-	-	-	-	-
Leeds v Nottm Forest	2-1	0-2	0-0	0-1	2-0	0-0
Middlesbrough v Derby	2-2	1-0	2-0	2-0	-	0-3
Millwall v Ipswich	0-0	1-0	1-3	-	-	3-4
Norwich v Brentford	-	-	1-2	-	5-0	1-2
Preston v Rotherham	-	3-3	-	2-1	1-1	-
QPR v Aston Villa	1-1	-	2-0	-	0-1	1-2
Sheffield United v Wigan	-	-	-	0-2	-	-
Swansea v Reading	2-2	-	-	-	-	-
West Brom v Blackburn	-	-	-	-	-	-
League One						
Accrington v Portsmouth	-	2-2	1-1	1-3	1-0	-
AFC Wimbledon v Luton	-	-	3-2	4-1	-	-
Barnsley v Bristol Rovers	-	-	-	-	-	-
Burton v Peterborough	-	-	-	2-1	-	-
Coventry v Doncaster	1-0	-	1-3	2-2	-	-
Fleetwood Town v Blackpool	-	-	-	0-0	-	0-0
Gillingham v Bradford	3-1	0-1	1-0	3-0	1-1	0-1
Oxford v Shrewsbury	-	-	0-2	-	2-0	1-1
Rochdale v Charlton	-	-	-	-	3-3	1-0
Scunthorpe v Plymouth	-	1-0	-	-	-	2-0
Sunderland v Southend	-	-	-	-	-	-
Walsall v Wycombe	-	-	-	-	-	-

Results cover matches from Premier League to National League and Scottish Premiership to Scottish League Two

FIXTURES 2018-19

	2012-13	2013-14	2014-15	2015-16	2016-17	2017-18
League Two						
Cambridge U v Macclesfield	2-0	3-0	-	-	-	-
Carlisle v Yeovil	3-3	-	-	3-2	2-1	4-0
Cheltenham v Stevenage	-	-	0-1	-	0-0	0-1
Colchester v Lincoln	-	-	-	-	-	1-0
Crewe v Grimsby	-	-	-	-	5-0	2-0
Exeter v Forest Green	-	-	-	-	-	2-0
Mansfield v MK Dons	-	-	-	-	-	-
Newport County v Morecambe	-	2-3	0-1	1-2	1-1	1-1
Northampton v Oldham	-	-	-	-	1-2	2-2
Notts County v Swindon	1-0	2-0	0-3	-	-	1-0
Port Vale v Bury	-	-	-	1-0	2-2	-
Tranmere v Crawley Town	2-0	3-3	-	-	-	-
National League						
Barrow v Barnet	-	-	-	-	-	-
Boreham Wood v Bromley	-	1-1	1-1	2-3	0-0	2-2
Braintree v Dover	-	-	3-0	1-0	1-2	-
Chesterfield v Wrexham	-	-	-	-	-	-
Dag & Red v Harrogate T	-	-	-	-	-	-
Gateshead v Aldershot	-	0-0	1-1	3-2	1-1	0-1
Halifax v Eastleigh	-	-	0-2	0-0	-	3-3
Hartlepool v Sutton Utd	-	-	-	-	-	1-1
Leyton Orient v Havant & W	-	-	-	-	-	-
Maidenhead v Fylde	-	-	-	-	-	1-2
Maidstone v Solihull Moors	-	-	-	-	2-4	1-1
Salford City v Ebbsfleet	-	-	-	-	-	-
Ladbrokes Premiership						
Aberdeen v Livingston	-	-	-	-	-	-
Celtic v Motherwell	1-0	2-0/3-0	1-1/4-0	1-2/7-0	2-0/2-0	5-1
Dundee v Hearts	1-0/1-0	-	-	1-2/0-1	3-2	2-1/1-1
Hibernian v Rangers	-	-	4-0/0-2	2-1/3-2	-	1-2/5-5
Kilmarnock v Hamilton	-	-	1-0/2-3	1-2/0-1	0-0	2-2/2-0
St Johnstone v St Mirren	2-1/1-0	2-0	1-2/2-0	-	-	-
Ladbrokes Championship						
Alloa v Inverness CT	-	-	-	-	-	-
Dunfermline v Dundee United	-	-	-	-	1-3/1-1	1-3/0-0
Partick v Ayr	-	-	-	-	-	-
Queen of Sth v Falkirk	-	2-0/1-2	3-0/1-0	2-2/2-2	2-0/0-2	4-2/2-2
Ross County v Morton	-	-	-	-	-	-
Ladbrokes League One						
Airdrieonians v Stenhousemuir	-	0-1/1-1	2-0/2-1	0-1/1-1	0-5/1-0	-
Brechin v Montrose	-	-	-	-	-	-
Dumbarton v East Fife	-	-	-	-	-	-
Forfar v Raith	-	-	-	-	-	1-1/2-1
Stranraer v Arbroath	1-1/2-0	3-2/1-1	-	-	-	2-6/1-4
Ladbrokes League Two						
Albion v Queens Park	-	2-1/1-0	1-0/2-1	-	2-0/1-1	0-1/1-1
Berwick v Cowdenbeath	-	-	-	-	1-1/1-3	1-0/1-0
Clyde v Peterhead	0-2/2-0	1-3/0-2	-	-	-	1-4/1-0
Elgin v Annan	2-2/3-1	2-3/2-3	0-0/4-5	3-2/2-2	0-2/3-2	0-1/2-1
Stirling v Edinburgh City	-	-	-	-	1-1/1-0	2-0/2-2
Tuesday October 30, 2018						
National League						
Aldershot v Boreham Wood	-	-	-	1-2	2-0	2-0
Barnet v Salford City	-	-	-	-	-	-
Bromley v Braintree	-	-	-	1-2	0-5	-
Dover v Dag & Red	-	-	-	-	1-2	1-0
Eastleigh v Leyton Orient	-	-	-	-	-	0-0
Ebbsfleet v Maidstone	-	-	-	0-1	-	2-0

Results cover matches from Premier League to National League and Scottish Premiership to Scottish League Two

	2012-13	2013-14	2014-15	2015-16	2016-17	2017-18
Fylde v Gateshead	-	-	-	-	-	0-0
Harrogate T v Barrow	-	3-1	2-2	-	-	-
Havant & W v Maidenhead	-	1-3	1-1	3-1	-	-
Solihull Moors v Halifax	-	-	-	-	-	0-1
Sutton Utd v Chesterfield	-	-	-	-	-	-
Wrexham v Hartlepool	-	-	-	-	-	0-0

Ladbrokes Championship

	2012-13	2013-14	2014-15	2015-16	2016-17	2017-18
Ayr v Alloa	0-0/0-2	-	-	-	-	3-3/1-2
Falkirk v Ross County	-	-	-	-	-	-
Inverness CT v Dunfermline	-	-	-	-	-	1-0/2-2
Partick v Dundee United	-	0-0/1-1	2-2	3-0/1-0	-	-
Queen of Sth v Morton	-	2-0/3-0	-	2-2/1-0	0-5/3-0	1-2/1-1

Wednesday October 31, 2018

Ladbrokes Premiership

	2012-13	2013-14	2014-15	2015-16	2016-17	2017-18
Aberdeen v Hamilton	-	-	3-0	1-0/3-0	2-1	2-0/3-0
Dundee v Celtic	0-2	-	1-1/1-2	0-0	0-1/1-2	0-2
Hearts v Hibernian	0-0/1-2	1-0/2-0	2-1/1-1	-	-	0-0/2-1
Livingston v St Johnstone	-	-	-	-	-	-
Rangers v Kilmarnock	-	-	-	-	3-0	1-1/0-1/1-0
St Mirren v Motherwell	2-1	0-1/3-2	0-1/2-1	-	-	-

Saturday November 3, 2018

Premier League

	2012-13	2013-14	2014-15	2015-16	2016-17	2017-18
Arsenal v Liverpool	2-2	2-0	4-1	0-0	3-4	3-3
Bournemouth v Man United	-	-	-	2-1	1-3	0-2
Cardiff v Leicester	1-1	-	-	-	-	-
Chelsea v Crystal Palace	-	2-1	1-0	1-2	1-2	2-1
Everton v Brighton	-	-	-	-	-	2-0
Huddersfield v Fulham	-	-	0-2	1-1	1-4	-
Man City v Southampton	3-2	4-1	2-0	3-1	1-1	2-1
Newcastle v Watford	-	-	-	1-2	-	0-3
West Ham v Burnley	-	-	1-0	-	1-0	0-3
Wolves v Tottenham	-	-	-	-	-	-

Championship

	2012-13	2013-14	2014-15	2015-16	2016-17	2017-18
Aston Villa v Bolton	-	-	-	-	-	1-0
Blackburn v QPR	-	2-0	-	1-1	1-0	-
Brentford v Millwall	-	-	2-2	-	-	1-0
Derby v Birmingham	3-2	1-1	2-2	0-3	1-0	1-1
Hull v West Brom	-	2-0	0-0	-	1-1	-
Ipswich v Preston	-	-	-	1-1	1-0	3-0
Nottm Forest v Sheffield United	-	-	-	-	-	2-1
Reading v Bristol City	-	-	-	1-0	2-1	0-1
Rotherham v Swansea	-	-	-	-	-	-
Sheffield Weds v Norwich	-	-	0-0	-	5-1	5-1
Stoke v Middlesbrough	-	-	-	-	2-0	-
Wigan v Leeds	-	1-0	0-1	-	1-1	-

League One

	2012-13	2013-14	2014-15	2015-16	2016-17	2017-18
AFC Wimbledon v Shrewsbury	-	-	2-2	-	1-1	0-1
Barnsley v Southend	-	-	-	0-2	-	-
Blackpool v Bristol Rovers	-	-	-	-	-	0-0
Bradford v Portsmouth	-	-	-	-	-	3-1
Charlton v Doncaster	-	2-0	-	-	-	1-0
Coventry v Accrington	-	-	-	-	-	0-2
Gillingham v Fleetwood Town	2-2	-	0-1	5-1	2-3	2-1
Plymouth v Sunderland	-	-	-	-	-	-
Rochdale v Luton	-	-	-	-	-	-
Scunthorpe v Oxford	-	1-0	-	-	1-1	1-0
Walsall v Burton	-	-	-	2-0	-	-
Wycombe v Peterborough	-	-	-	-	-	-

Results cover matches from Premier League to National League and Scottish Premiership to Scottish League Two

	2012-13	2013-14	2014-15	2015-16	2016-17	2017-18
League Two						
Cambridge U v Grimsby	0-0	1-2	-	-	0-1	3-1
Carlisle v Newport County	-	-	2-3	0-1	2-1	1-1
Cheltenham v Mansfield	-	1-2	1-1	-	0-0	3-0
Colchester v Swindon	0-1	1-2	1-1	1-4	-	0-0
Crawley Town v MK Dons	2-0	0-2	2-2	-	-	-
Lincoln v Forest Green	1-2	2-1	1-2	0-1	3-1	2-1
Macclesfield v Bury	-	-	-	-	-	-
Morecambe v Yeovil	-	-	-	2-1	1-3	4-3
Northampton v Crewe	-	-	-	-	-	-
Port Vale v Notts County	-	2-1	0-2	-	-	0-1
Stevenage v Oldham	1-2	3-4	-	-	-	-
Tranmere v Exeter	-	-	1-2	-	-	-
National League						
Aldershot v Braintree	-	2-1	1-3	2-1	2-0	-
Barnet v Maidstone	-	-	-	-	-	-
Bromley v Hartlepool	-	-	-	-	-	2-0
Dover v Maidenhead	-	2-0	-	-	-	1-1
Eastleigh v Salford City	-	-	-	-	-	-
Ebbsfleet v Barrow	2-4	-	-	-	-	3-2
Fylde v Leyton Orient	-	-	-	-	-	0-1
Harrogate T v Chesterfield	-	-	-	-	-	-
Havant & W v Halifax	-	-	-	-	-	-
Solihull Moors v Boreham Wood	-	-	-	-	1-1	0-0
Sutton Utd v Dag & Red	-	-	-	-	1-0	2-1
Wrexham v Gateshead	1-1	3-2	0-3	4-0	0-2	1-0
Ladbrokes Premiership						
Celtic v Hearts	1-0/4-1	2-0	-	0-0/3-1	4-0/2-0	4-1/3-1
Hamilton v Livingston	1-2/1-1	2-0/2-0	-	-	-	-
Hibernian v St Johnstone	2-0/1-3	0-0	-	-	-	1-2
Kilmarnock v Aberdeen	1-3/1-1	0-1	0-2/1-2	0-4	0-4/1-2	1-3/0-2
Motherwell v Dundee	1-1	-	1-3/0-1	3-1	0-0/1-5/2-3	1-1/2-1
St Mirren v Rangers	-	-	-	0-1/2-2	-	-
Ladbrokes Championship						
Alloa v Dunfermline	-	-	-	-	-	-
Dundee United v Queen of Sth	-	-	-	-	1-1/3-3	2-1/2-3
Falkirk v Ayr	-	-	-	-	2-0/1-1	-
Inverness CT v Ross County	3-1/2-1	1-2	1-1/1-1	2-0	2-3/1-1	-
Morton v Partick	3-1/2-2	-	-	-	-	-
Ladbrokes League One						
Airdrieonians v Forfar	-	0-2/5-1	1-2/3-1	0-1/1-1	-	2-1/1-2
Arbroath v East Fife	2-0/1-0	2-2/2-1	0-2/1-1	1-1/0-1	-	2-3/1-1
Montrose v Dumbarton	-	-	-	-	-	-
Raith v Brechin	-	-	-	-	-	-
Stenhousemuir v Stranraer	0-0/1-2	1-0/1-1	2-2/1-0	1-0/1-5	0-5/1-0	-
Ladbrokes League Two						
Cowdenbeath v Elgin	-	-	-	-	0-1/1-1	1-3/3-1
Edinburgh City v Clyde	-	-	-	-	0-1/0-0	0-3/1-3
Peterhead v Albion	-	1-1/2-0	-	1-1/5-1	2-2/1-1	-
Queens Park v Annan	2-2/2-2	2-5/0-1	0-0/2-0	0-1/1-3	-	-
Stirling v Berwick	6-3/1-0	3-1/2-1	-	1-3/2-1	0-0/2-2	4-0/2-0

Saturday November 10, 2018

	2012-13	2013-14	2014-15	2015-16	2016-17	2017-18
Premier League						
Arsenal v Wolves	-	-	-	-	-	-
Cardiff v Brighton	0-2	-	0-0	4-1	0-0	-
Chelsea v Everton	2-1	1-0	1-0	3-3	5-0	2-0
Crystal Palace v Tottenham	-	0-1	2-1	1-3	0-1	0-1
Huddersfield v West Ham	-	-	-	-	-	1-4

Results cover matches from Premier League to National League and Scottish Premiership to Scottish League Two

	2012-13	2013-14	2014-15	2015-16	2016-17	2017-18
Leicester v Burnley	2-1	1-1	2-2	-	3-0	1-0
Liverpool v Fulham	4-0	4-0	-	-	-	-
Man City v Man United	2-3	4-1	1-0	0-1	0-0	2-3
Newcastle v Bournemouth	-	-	-	1-3	-	0-1
Southampton v Watford	-	-	-	2-0	1-1	0-2
Championship						
Birmingham v Hull	2-3	-	-	1-0	-	3-0
Blackburn v Rotherham	-	-	2-1	1-0	4-2	2-0
Bolton v Swansea	-	-	-	-	-	-
Bristol City v Preston	-	1-1	0-1	1-2	1-2	1-2
Derby v Aston Villa	-	-	-	-	0-0	2-0
Middlesbrough v Wigan	-	0-0	1-0	-	-	-
Norwich v Millwall	-	-	6-1	-	-	2-1
Nottm Forest v Stoke	-	-	-	-	-	-
QPR v Brentford	-	-	-	3-0	0-2	2-2
Reading v Ipswich	-	2-1	1-0	5-1	2-1	0-4
Sheffield United v Sheffield Weds	-	-	-	-	-	0-0
West Brom v Leeds	-	-	-	-	-	-
Ladbrokes Premiership						
Aberdeen v Hibernian	2-1/0-0	1-0	-	-	-	4-1/0-0
Dundee v St Mirren	0-2/2-1	-	1-3	-	-	-
Hearts v Kilmarnock	1-3/0-3	0-4/5-0	-	1-1/1-0	4-0	1-2/1-1
Livingston v Celtic	-	-	-	-	-	-
Rangers v Motherwell	-	-	-	-	2-1/1-1	2-0
St Johnstone v Hamilton	-	-	0-1	4-1/0-0	3-0	2-1/1-0
Ladbrokes Championship						
Ayr v Queen of Sth	2-4/1-5	-	-	-	1-0/0-2	-
Dunfermline v Falkirk	0-1/0-2	-	-	-	1-1/1-2	3-1/2-0
Morton v Alloa	-	0-2/0-1	-	1-0/4-1	-	-
Partick v Inverness CT	-	0-0	3-1/1-0	2-1/1-4	2-0/1-1	-
Ross County v Dundee United	1-2/1-0	2-4/3-0	2-3	2-1/0-3	-	-
Ladbrokes League One						
Arbroath v Montrose	-	-	3-1/2-2	3-1/0-0	0-0/0-1	-
Brechin v Forfar	4-1/3-4	2-1/1-5	3-3/2-3	0-2/4-0	-	-
Dumbarton v Stenhousemuir	-	-	-	-	-	-
East Fife v Raith	-	-	-	-	-	0-5/2-3
Stranraer v Airdrieonians	-	3-1/1-1	1-0/1-0	1-3/4-0	1-2/2-1	3-1/3-2
Ladbrokes League Two						
Albion v Edinburgh City	-	-	-	-	-	-
Annan v Cowdenbeath	-	-	-	-	2-0/1-0	1-0/1-1
Clyde v Stirling	2-1/1-2	2-1/1-0	-	0-1/3-1	1-1/2-3	1-1/2-1
Elgin v Berwick	3-1/1-2	2-0/1-3	2-1/3-3	4-1/1-0	6-0/2-2	5-1/3-0
Queens Park v Peterhead	0-0/0-3	0-5/0-2	-	-	0-0/2-0	-
Saturday November 17, 2018						
League One						
Accrington v Barnsley	-	-	-	-	-	-
Bristol Rovers v Scunthorpe	-	0-0	-	-	1-1	1-1
Burton v Coventry	-	-	-	1-2	-	-
Doncaster v AFC Wimbledon	-	-	-	-	-	0-0
Fleetwood Town v Walsall	-	-	0-1	0-1	2-1	2-0
Luton v Plymouth	-	-	0-1	1-2	1-1	-
Oxford v Gillingham	0-0	-	-	-	1-0	3-0
Peterborough v Bradford	-	2-1	2-0	0-4	0-1	1-3
Portsmouth v Charlton	-	-	-	-	-	0-1
Shrewsbury v Rochdale	-	-	-	2-0	1-0	3-2
Southend v Blackpool	-	-	-	1-0	-	2-1
Sunderland v Wycombe	-	-	-	-	-	-

Results cover matches from Premier League to National League and Scottish Premiership to Scottish League Two

League Two						
Bury v Stevenage	2-0	-	2-1	-	-	-
Crewe v Tranmere	0-0	2-1	-	-	-	-
Exeter v Northampton	3-0	0-1	0-2	0-0	-	-
Forest Green v Morecambe	-	-	-	-	-	2-0
Grimsby v Crawley Town	-	-	-	-	1-1	0-0
Mansfield v Port Vale	-	-	-	-	-	1-1
MK Dons v Macclesfield	-	-	-	-	-	-
Newport County v Colchester	-	-	-	-	1-1	1-2
Notts County v Cheltenham	-	-	-	-	2-1	3-1
Oldham v Cambridge U	-	-	-	-	-	-
Swindon v Carlisle	4-0	3-1	-	-	-	0-0
Yeovil v Lincoln	-	-	-	-	-	0-2
National League						
Barrow v Eastleigh	-	-	-	1-0	4-0	3-2
Boreham Wood v Ebbsfleet	-	2-1	1-3	-	-	0-1
Braintree v Solihull Moors	-	-	-	-	0-1	-
Chesterfield v Havant & W	-	-	-	-	-	-
Dag & Red v Fylde	-	-	-	-	-	2-0
Gateshead v Sutton Utd	-	-	-	-	1-0	0-2
Halifax v Dover	-	-	3-2	4-2	-	1-2
Hartlepool v Barnet	-	-	-	1-1	0-2	-
Leyton Orient v Bromley	-	-	-	-	-	0-1
Maidenhead v Harrogate T	-	-	-	-	-	-
Maidstone v Wrexham	-	-	-	-	2-2	2-1
Salford City v Aldershot	-	-	-	-	-	-
Ladbrokes Championship						
Ayr v Morton	-	-	1-0/1-1	-	2-1/1-4	-
Dundee United v Alloa	-	-	-	-	-	-
Falkirk v Partick	0-0/0-2	-	-	-	-	-
Queen of Sth v Inverness CT	-	-	-	-	-	0-0/0-2
Ross County v Dunfermline	-	-	-	-	-	-
Ladbrokes League One						
Airdrieonians v East Fife	-	1-3/2-1	-	-	1-1/2-2	0-1/0-0
Brechin v Arbroath	3-2/2-0	3-1/2-4	-	-	-	-
Forfar v Dumbarton	-	-	-	-	-	-
Montrose v Stranraer	-	-	-	-	-	-
Stenhousemuir v Raith	-	-	-	-	-	-
Ladbrokes League Two						
Annan v Stirling	5-2/0-1	4-4/1-2	-	1-1/2-2	3-2/4-1	1-1/3-1
Berwick v Albion	-	2-1/3-1	1-1/0-2	-	-	-
Cowdenbeath v Queens Park	-	-	-	-	-	-
Edinburgh City v Peterhead	-	-	-	-	-	0-3/0-0
Elgin v Clyde	2-1/4-2	1-0/3-1	1-0/2-0	1-1/1-0	0-2/4-1	3-2/2-1

Saturday November 24, 2018

Premier League						
Bournemouth v Arsenal	-	-	-	0-2	3-3	2-1
Brighton v Leicester	1-1	3-1	-	-	-	0-2
Burnley v Newcastle	-	-	1-1	-	-	1-0
Everton v Cardiff	-	2-1	-	-	-	-
Fulham v Southampton	1-1	0-3	-	-	-	-
Man United v Crystal Palace	-	2-0	1-0	2-0	2-0	4-0
Tottenham v Chelsea	2-4	1-1	5-3	0-0	2-0	1-2
Watford v Liverpool	-	-	-	3-0	0-1	3-3
West Ham v Man City	0-0	1-3	2-1	2-2	0-4	1-4
Wolves v Huddersfield	1-3	-	1-3	3-0	0-1	-

Results cover matches from Premier League to National League and Scottish Premiership to Scottish League Two

	2012-13	2013-14	2014-15	2015-16	2016-17	2017-18
Championship						
Brentford v Middlesbrough	-	-	0-1	0-1	-	1-1
Hull v Nottm Forest	1-2	-	-	1-1	-	2-3
Ipswich v West Brom	-	-	-	-	-	-
Leeds v Bristol City	1-0	-	-	1-0	2-1	2-2
Millwall v Bolton	2-1	1-1	0-1	-	0-2	1-1
Preston v Blackburn	-	-	-	1-2	3-2	-
Rotherham v Sheffield United	-	3-1	-	-	-	-
Sheffield Weds v Derby	2-2	0-1	0-0	0-0	2-1	2-0
Stoke v QPR	1-0	-	3-1	-	-	-
Swansea v Norwich	3-4	3-0	-	1-0	-	-
Wigan v Reading	3-2	3-0	2-2	-	0-3	-
League One						
AFC Wimbledon v Southend	0-4	0-1	0-0	-	0-2	2-0
Barnsley v Doncaster	-	0-0	1-1	1-0	-	-
Blackpool v Burton	-	-	-	1-2	-	-
Bradford v Oxford	1-2	-	-	-	1-0	3-2
Charlton v Bristol Rovers	-	-	-	-	4-1	1-0
Coventry v Peterborough	-	4-2	3-2	3-2	1-0	-
Gillingham v Luton	-	-	-	-	-	-
Plymouth v Fleetwood Town	2-1	0-2	-	-	-	1-2
Rochdale v Accrington	0-3	2-1	-	-	-	-
Scunthorpe v Portsmouth	2-1	5-1	-	-	-	2-0
Walsall v Sunderland	-	-	-	-	-	-
Wycombe v Shrewsbury	-	-	1-0	-	-	-
League Two						
Cambridge U v Bury	-	-	0-2	-	-	-
Carlisle v Forest Green	-	-	-	-	-	1-0
Cheltenham v Newport County	-	0-0	0-1	-	1-1	1-1
Colchester v Exeter	-	-	-	-	2-3	3-1
Crawley Town v Crewe	2-0	1-2	1-1	-	0-3	1-2
Lincoln v Mansfield	0-1	-	-	-	-	0-1
Macclesfield v Yeovil	-	-	-	-	-	-
Morecambe v Notts County	-	-	-	4-1	4-1	1-4
Northampton v Grimsby	-	-	-	-	-	-
Port Vale v Swindon	-	2-3	0-1	1-0	3-2	0-3
Stevenage v MK Dons	0-2	2-3	-	-	-	-
Tranmere v Oldham	1-0	2-2	-	-	-	-
National League						
Aldershot v Barrow	-	-	-	0-1	2-2	1-1
Barnet v Gateshead	-	0-1	2-0	-	-	-
Bromley v Dag & Red	-	-	-	-	1-3	3-1
Dover v Hartlepool	-	-	-	-	-	4-0
Eastleigh v Chesterfield	-	-	-	-	-	-
Ebbsfleet v Halifax	-	-	-	-	-	2-0
Fylde v Boreham Wood	-	-	-	-	-	2-2
Harrogate T v Braintree	-	-	-	-	-	-
Havant & W v Maidstone	-	-	-	2-1	-	-
Solihull Moors v Salford City	-	-	-	-	-	-
Sutton Utd v Maidenhead	-	3-2	1-2	2-2	-	0-2
Wrexham v Leyton Orient	-	-	-	-	-	2-2
Ladbrokes Premiership						
Hamilton v Celtic	-	-	0-2	1-2/1-1	0-3	1-4/1-2
Hibernian v Dundee	3-0/1-1/1-0	-	-	-	-	2-1
Motherwell v Aberdeen	4-1	1-3/2-2	0-2	1-2/2-1	1-3	0-1/0-2
Rangers v Livingston	-	-	2-0/1-1	3-0/4-1	-	-
St Johnstone v Kilmarnock	2-1/2-0	3-1	1-2/0-0	2-1	0-1/0-2	1-2
St Mirren v Hearts	2-0/2-0	1-1/1-1	-	-	-	-

Results cover matches from Premier League to National League and Scottish Premiership to Scottish League Two

Sunday November 25, 2018

Championship					
Aston Villa v Birmingham	-	-	-	-	1-0	2-0

Tuesday November 27, 2018

Championship					
Brentford v Sheffield United	2-0	3-1	-	-	-	1-1
Hull v Norwich	-	1-0	-	-	-	4-3
Leeds v Reading	-	2-4	0-0	3-2	2-0	0-1
Preston v Middlesbrough	-	-	-	0-0	-	2-3
Rotherham v QPR	-	-	-	0-3	1-0	-
Sheffield Weds v Bolton	1-2	1-3	1-2	3-2	-	1-1

League One					
Accrington v Wycombe	0-2	1-1	1-1	1-1	2-2	1-0
Bristol Rovers v Gillingham	0-2	-	-	-	2-1	1-1
Burton v Charlton	-	-	-	-	-	-
Doncaster v Blackpool	-	1-3	-	0-1	0-1	3-3
Fleetwood Town v Coventry	-	-	0-2	0-1	2-0	-
Luton v Bradford	-	-	-	-	-	-
Oxford v Rochdale	3-0	1-1	-	-	1-0	2-1
Peterborough v AFC Wimbledon	-	-	-	-	0-1	1-1
Portsmouth v Walsall	1-2	-	-	-	-	1-1
Shrewsbury v Plymouth	-	-	0-2	-	-	1-2
Southend v Scunthorpe	-	0-1	-	2-1	3-1	3-2
Sunderland v Barnsley	-	-	-	-	-	0-1

League Two					
Bury v Cheltenham	-	4-1	0-1	-	-	-
Crewe v Cambridge U	-	-	-	-	1-2	0-1
Exeter v Macclesfield	-	-	-	-	-	-
Forest Green v Colchester	-	-	-	-	-	1-2
Grimsby v Tranmere	-	-	-	1-1	-	-
Mansfield v Crawley Town	-	-	-	4-0	3-1	1-1
MK Dons v Morecambe	-	-	-	-	-	-
Newport County v Northampton	-	1-2	3-2	2-2	-	-
Notts County v Carlisle	1-0	4-1	-	0-5	2-3	2-1
Oldham v Lincoln	-	-	-	-	-	-
Swindon v Stevenage	3-0	1-0	-	-	-	3-2
Yeovil v Port Vale	-	-	1-2	-	-	1-1

National League					
Barrow v Wrexham	0-1	-	-	2-0	1-1	1-1
Boreham Wood v Dover	-	2-2	-	3-0	5-0	2-3
Braintree v Sutton Utd	-	-	-	-	1-0	-
Chesterfield v Bromley	-	-	-	-	-	-
Dag & Red v Havant & W	-	-	-	-	-	-
Gateshead v Solihull Moors	-	-	-	-	0-0	2-2
Halifax v Barnet	-	2-1	1-1	-	-	-
Hartlepool v Fylde	-	-	-	-	-	0-2
Leyton Orient v Aldershot	-	-	-	-	-	2-3
Maidenhead v Ebbsfleet	-	1-0	0-4	0-0	1-2	1-1
Maidstone v Eastleigh	-	-	-	-	2-1	2-3
Salford City v Harrogate T	-	-	-	-	0-0	2-1

Wednesday November 28, 2018

Championship					
Aston Villa v Nottm Forest	-	-	-	-	2-2	2-1
Ipswich v Bristol City	1-1	-	-	2-2	2-1	1-3
Millwall v Birmingham	3-3	2-3	1-3	-	-	2-0
Stoke v Derby	-	-	-	-	-	-
Swansea v West Brom	3-1	1-2	3-0	1-0	2-1	1-0
Wigan v Blackburn	-	2-1	1-1	-	3-0	0-0

Results cover matches from Premier League to National League and Scottish Premiership to Scottish League Two

Saturday December 1, 2018

Premier League

	2012-13	2013-14	2014-15	2015-16	2016-17	2017-18
Arsenal v Tottenham	5-2	1-0	1-1	1-1	1-1	2-0
Cardiff v Wolves	3-1	-	0-1	2-0	2-1	0-1
Chelsea v Fulham	0-0	2-0	-	-	-	-
Crystal Palace v Burnley	4-3	-	0-0	-	0-2	1-0
Huddersfield v Brighton	1-2	1-1	1-1	1-1	3-1	2-0
Leicester v Watford	1-2	2-2	-	2-1	3-0	2-0
Liverpool v Everton	0-0	4-0	1-1	4-0	3-1	1-1
Man City v Bournemouth	-	-	-	5-1	4-0	4-0
Newcastle v West Ham	0-1	0-0	2-0	2-1	-	3-0
Southampton v Man United	2-3	1-1	1-2	2-3	0-0	0-1

Championship

	2012-13	2013-14	2014-15	2015-16	2016-17	2017-18
Birmingham v Preston	-	-	-	2-2	2-2	1-3
Blackburn v Sheffield Weds	1-0	0-0	1-2	2-2	0-1	-
Bolton v Wigan	-	1-1	3-1	-	-	-
Derby v Swansea	-	-	-	-	-	-
Middlesbrough v Aston Villa	-	-	-	-	-	0-1
Norwich v Rotherham	-	-	1-1	-	3-1	-
Nottm Forest v Ipswich	1-0	0-0	2-2	1-1	3-0	2-1
QPR v Hull	-	-	0-1	1-2	-	2-1
Reading v Stoke	1-1	-	-	-	-	-
Sheffield United v Leeds	-	-	-	-	-	2-1
West Brom v Brentford	-	-	-	-	-	-

National League

	2012-13	2013-14	2014-15	2015-16	2016-17	2017-18
Aldershot v Ebbsfleet	-	-	-	-	-	0-0
Barnet v Chesterfield	0-2	-	-	-	-	3-0
Braintree v Barrow	2-3	-	-	1-1	0-2	-
Bromley v Wrexham	-	-	-	3-1	4-3	1-1
Eastleigh v Dover	-	1-0	0-1	2-5	2-4	2-1
Fylde v Sutton Utd	-	-	-	-	-	2-1
Halifax v Boreham Wood	-	-	-	3-2	-	2-1
Hartlepool v Dag & Red	-	2-1	0-2	3-1	-	1-0
Leyton Orient v Gateshead	-	-	-	-	-	0-2
Maidstone v Maidenhead	-	-	-	1-2	-	1-1
Salford City v Havant & W	-	-	-	-	-	-
Solihull Moors v Harrogate T	-	3-0	0-1	1-0	-	-

Ladbrokes Premiership

	2012-13	2013-14	2014-15	2015-16	2016-17	2017-18
Aberdeen v Dundee	2-0/1-0	-	3-3	2-0/1-0	3-0	2-1/1-0
Celtic v St Johnstone	1-1/4-0	2-1/3-0	0-1	3-1/3-1	1-0/4-1	1-1/0-0
Hearts v Rangers	-	-	2-0/2-2	-	2-0/4-1	1-3
Kilmarnock v Hibernian	1-1/1-3	1-2/1-1	-	-	-	0-3/2-2
Livingston v Motherwell	-	-	-	-	-	-
St Mirren v Hamilton	-	-	0-2/1-0	-	-	-

Ladbrokes Championship

	2012-13	2013-14	2014-15	2015-16	2016-17	2017-18
Alloa v Ross County	-	-	-	-	-	-
Dundee United v Ayr	-	-	-	-	3-0/2-1	-
Dunfermline v Morton	2-2/1-4	-	1-2/0-4	-	2-1/3-1	1-1/0-0
Inverness CT v Falkirk	-	-	-	-	-	4-1/1-0
Queen of Sth v Partick	-	-	-	-	-	-

Ladbrokes League One

	2012-13	2013-14	2014-15	2015-16	2016-17	2017-18
Arbroath v Stenhousemuir	2-2/0-0	3-4/2-1	-	-	-	-
Dumbarton v Brechin	-	-	-	-	-	2-1/1-0
East Fife v Montrose	-	-	3-0/3-0	1-1/3-0	-	-
Raith v Airdrieonians	2-0/2-0	-	1-1/4-2	-	-	2-0/2-1
Stranraer v Forfar	4-1/0-3	0-4/3-1	1-1/4-2	0-0/1-0	-	3-0/2-0

Results cover matches from Premier League to National League and Scottish Premiership to Scottish League Two

Ladbrokes League Two						
Albion v Cowdenbeath	-	-	-	2-1/0-0	-	-
Clyde v Berwick	2-1/2-1	1-0/3-3	3-3/0-3	1-1/2-1	3-2/1-1	0-0/1-2
Edinburgh City v Queens Park	-	-	-	-	-	-
Peterhead v Annan	2-0/2-0	2-2/3-1	-	-	-	1-0/1-0
Stirling v Elgin	1-4/1-1	1-1/2-2	-	3-1/0-0	0-4/1-0	2-2/3-1

Sunday December 2, 2018

Championship						
Bristol City v Millwall	1-1	-	-	-	-	0-0

Tuesday December 4, 2018

Premier League						
Bournemouth v Huddersfield	-	2-1	1-1	-	-	4-0
Brighton v Crystal Palace	3-0	-	-	-	-	0-0
Burnley v Liverpool	-	-	0-1	-	2-0	1-2
Fulham v Leicester	-	-	-	-	-	-
Man United v Arsenal	2-1	1-0	1-1	3-2	1-1	2-1
Watford v Man City	-	-	-	1-2	0-5	0-6
West Ham v Cardiff	-	2-0	-	-	-	-
Wolves v Chelsea	-	-	-	-	-	-

Wednesday December 5, 2018

Premier League						
Everton v Newcastle	2-2	3-2	3-0	3-0	-	1-0
Tottenham v Southampton	1-0	3-2	1-0	1-2	2-1	5-2

Ladbrokes Premiership						
Dundee v Hamilton	-	0-0/1-0	2-0/1-1	4-0/0-1	1-1/0-2	1-3/1-0
Hibernian v St Mirren	2-1/3-3	2-0/2-3	-	1-1/3-1	2-0/1-1	-
Kilmarnock v Livingston	-	-	-	-	-	-
Motherwell v Celtic	0-2/2-1/3-1	0-5/3-3	0-1	0-1/1-2	3-4	1-1/0-0
Rangers v Aberdeen	-	-	-	-	2-1/1-2	3-0/2-0
St Johnstone v Hearts	2-2	1-0/3-3	-	0-0	1-0/1-0/1-0	0-0

Saturday December 8, 2018

Premier League						
Arsenal v Huddersfield	-	-	-	-	-	5-0
Bournemouth v Liverpool	-	-	-	1-2	4-3	0-4
Burnley v Brighton	1-3	0-0	-	1-1	-	0-0
Cardiff v Southampton	-	0-3	-	-	-	-
Chelsea v Man City	0-0	2-1	1-1	0-3	2-1	0-1
Everton v Watford	-	-	-	2-2	1-0	3-2
Leicester v Tottenham	-	-	1-2	1-1	1-6	2-1
Man United v Fulham	3-2	2-2	-	-	-	-
Newcastle v Wolves	-	-	-	-	0-2	-
West Ham v Crystal Palace	-	0-1	1-3	2-2	3-0	1-1

Championship						
Birmingham v Bristol City	2-0	-	-	4-2	1-0	2-1
Brentford v Swansea	-	-	-	-	-	-
Leeds v QPR	-	0-1	-	1-1	0-0	2-0
Middlesbrough v Blackburn	1-0	0-0	1-1	1-1	-	-
Millwall v Hull	0-1	-	-	-	-	0-0
Norwich v Bolton	-	-	2-1	-	-	0-0
Nottm Forest v Preston	-	-	-	1-0	1-1	0-3
Reading v Sheffield United	-	-	-	-	-	1-3
Sheffield Weds v Rotherham	-	-	0-0	0-1	1-0	-
Stoke v Ipswich	-	-	-	-	-	-
West Brom v Aston Villa	2-2	2-2	1-0	0-0	-	-
Wigan v Derby	-	1-3	0-2	-	0-1	-

Results cover matches from Premier League to National League and Scottish Premiership to Scottish League Two

	2012-13	2013-14	2014-15	2015-16	2016-17	2017-18
League One						
Accrington v Sunderland	-	-	-	-	-	-
AFC Wimbledon v Rochdale	1-2	0-3	-	-	3-1	0-0
Blackpool v Charlton	0-2	0-3	0-3	-	-	1-0
Bristol Rovers v Doncaster	-	-	-	-	-	0-1
Burton v Shrewsbury	-	-	1-0	1-2	-	-
Luton v Fleetwood Town	-	-	-	-	-	-
Peterborough v Oxford	-	-	-	-	1-2	1-4
Plymouth v Bradford	0-0	-	-	-	-	1-0
Portsmouth v Southend	-	1-2	1-2	-	-	1-0
Scunthorpe v Gillingham	-	-	2-1	0-0	5-0	1-3
Walsall v Coventry	4-0	0-1	0-2	2-1	1-1	-
Wycombe v Barnsley	-	-	-	-	-	-
League Two						
Bury v Exeter	-	2-0	1-1	-	-	-
Cheltenham v Grimsby	-	-	-	3-1	2-1	2-3
Colchester v Macclesfield	-	-	-	-	-	-
Crawley Town v Northampton	-	-	-	1-2	-	-
Crewe v Oldham	0-2	1-1	0-1	1-0	-	-
Mansfield v Notts County	-	-	-	5-0	3-1	3-1
MK Dons v Carlisle	2-0	0-1	-	-	-	-
Morecambe v Port Vale	1-3	-	-	-	-	0-3
Stevenage v Lincoln	-	-	-	-	-	1-2
Swindon v Newport County	-	-	-	-	-	0-1
Tranmere v Cambridge U	-	-	1-1	-	-	-
Yeovil v Forest Green	-	-	-	-	-	0-0
National League						
Barrow v Maidstone	-	-	-	-	3-0	0-1
Boreham Wood v Leyton Orient	-	-	-	-	-	2-0
Chesterfield v Salford City	-	-	-	-	-	-
Dag & Red v Halifax	-	-	-	-	-	3-1
Dover v Fylde	-	-	-	-	-	0-1
Ebbsfleet v Barnet	-	-	-	-	-	-
Gateshead v Bromley	-	-	-	3-1	0-2	1-2
Harrogate T v Aldershot	-	-	-	-	-	-
Havant & W v Braintree	-	-	-	-	-	0-0
Maidenhead v Hartlepool	-	-	-	-	-	2-1
Sutton Utd v Solihull Moors	-	-	-	-	1-3	1-0
Wrexham v Eastleigh	-	-	3-0	2-3	0-0	2-1
Ladbrokes Premiership						
Aberdeen v St Johnstone	2-0	0-0/1-0/1-1	2-0/0-1	1-5/1-1	0-0/0-2	3-0/4-1
Celtic v Kilmarnock	0-2/4-1	4-0	2-0/4-1	0-0	6-1/3-1	1-1/0-0
Dundee v Rangers	-	-	-	-	1-2/2-1	2-1
Hamilton v Hibernian	-	-	-	-	-	1-1
Hearts v Motherwell	1-0/1-2	0-1	-	2-0/6-0	3-0	1-0/1-1
Livingston v St Mirren	-	-	-	0-1/2-3	-	1-3/4-1
Ladbrokes Championship						
Ayr v Inverness CT	-	-	-	-	-	-
Falkirk v Alloa	-	0-0/3-1	2-1/1-0	5-0/2-0	-	-
Morton v Dundee United	-	-	-	-	0-0/1-1	0-2/1-1
Partick v Dunfermline	5-1/3-3	-	-	-	-	-
Ross County v Queen of Sth	-	-	-	-	-	-
Ladbrokes League One						
Brechin v Stenhousemuir	7-2/1-2	0-1/1-3	1-0/2-1	1-2/1-0	2-1/2-2	-
Dumbarton v Airdrieonians	3-4/4-1	-	-	-	-	-
East Fife v Stranraer	0-1/1-1	1-2/1-1	-	-	2-0/0-0	1-1/2-3
Forfar v Arbroath	1-1/2-4	1-1/0-2	-	-	0-1/1-1	0-5/0-1
Montrose v Raith	-	-	-	-	-	-

Results cover matches from Premier League to National League and Scottish Premiership to Scottish League Two

	2012-13	2013-14	2014-15	2015-16	2016-17	2017-18
Ladbrokes League Two						
Annan v Edinburgh City	-	-	-	-	1-1/1-0	2-1/2-3
Berwick v Peterhead	1-1/0-2	1-3/1-2	-	-	-	2-3/1-3
Cowdenbeath v Clyde	-	-	-	-	1-0/1-0	0-3/1-0
Elgin v Albion	-	1-2/1-1	0-4/2-0	-	-	-
Queens Park v Stirling	2-1/2-2	0-2/0-1	-	1-0/1-1	-	-

Saturday December 15, 2018

	2012-13	2013-14	2014-15	2015-16	2016-17	2017-18
Premier League						
Brighton v Chelsea	-	-	-	-	-	0-4
Crystal Palace v Leicester	2-2	-	2-0	0-1	2-2	5-0
Fulham v West Ham	3-1	2-1	-	-	-	-
Huddersfield v Newcastle	-	-	-	-	1-3	1-0
Liverpool v Man United	1-2	1-0	1-2	0-1	0-0	0-0
Man City v Everton	1-1	3-1	1-0	0-0	1-1	1-1
Southampton v Arsenal	1-1	2-2	2-0	4-0	0-2	1-1
Tottenham v Burnley	-	-	2-1	-	2-1	1-1
Watford v Cardiff	0-0	-	0-1	-	-	-
Wolves v Bournemouth	-	-	1-2	-	-	-
Championship						
Aston Villa v Stoke	0-0	1-4	1-2	0-1	-	-
Blackburn v Birmingham	1-1	2-3	1-0	2-0	1-1	-
Bolton v Leeds	2-2	0-1	1-1	1-1	-	2-3
Bristol City v Norwich	-	-	-	-	1-1	0-1
Derby v Nottm Forest	1-1	5-0	1-2	1-0	3-0	2-0
Hull v Brentford	-	-	-	2-0	-	3-2
Ipswich v Wigan	-	1-3	0-0	-	3-0	-
Preston v Millwall	-	-	-	-	-	0-0
QPR v Middlesbrough	-	2-0	-	2-3	-	0-3
Rotherham v Reading	-	-	2-1	1-1	0-1	-
Sheffield United v West Brom	-	-	-	-	-	-
Swansea v Sheffield Weds	-	-	-	-	-	-
League One						
Barnsley v Portsmouth	-	-	-	-	-	-
Bradford v Walsall	-	0-2	1-1	4-0	1-0	1-1
Charlton v AFC Wimbledon	-	-	-	-	1-2	1-0
Coventry v Luton	-	-	-	-	-	2-2
Doncaster v Scunthorpe	4-0	-	5-2	0-1	-	0-1
Fleetwood Town v Burton	0-4	2-3	-	4-0	-	-
Gillingham v Wycombe	0-1	-	-	-	-	-
Oxford v Blackpool	-	-	-	-	-	1-0
Rochdale v Plymouth	1-0	3-0	-	-	-	1-1
Shrewsbury v Peterborough	-	2-4	-	3-4	1-1	3-1
Southend v Accrington	0-1	1-0	1-2	-	-	-
Sunderland v Bristol Rovers	-	-	-	-	-	-
League Two						
Cambridge U v Yeovil	-	-	-	3-0	1-0	2-1
Carlisle v Colchester	0-2	2-4	-	-	2-0	1-1
Exeter v Crewe	-	-	-	-	4-0	3-0
Forest Green v Mansfield	1-2	-	-	-	-	2-0
Grimsby v Swindon	-	-	-	-	-	3-2
Lincoln v Morecambe	-	-	-	-	-	1-1
Macclesfield v Crawley Town	-	-	-	-	-	-
Newport County v MK Dons	-	-	-	-	-	-
Northampton v Stevenage	-	-	1-0	2-1	-	-
Notts County v Tranmere	0-1	2-0	-	-	-	-
Oldham v Bury	1-2	-	-	0-1	0-0	2-1
Port Vale v Cheltenham	3-2	-	-	-	-	3-1

Results cover matches from Premier League to National League and Scottish Premiership to Scottish League Two

	2012-13	2013-14	2014-15	2015-16	2016-17	2017-18
Ladbrokes Premiership						
Hibernian v Celtic	1-0	1-1/0-4	-	-	-	2-2/2-1
Kilmarnock v Dundee	0-0/1-2	-	1-3	0-4/0-0	2-0/0-1	1-1/3-2
Livingston v Hearts	-	-	0-1/2-3	-	-	-
Rangers v Hamilton	-	-	-	-	1-1/4-0	0-2
St Johnstone v Motherwell	1-3/2-0	2-0/3-0	2-1	2-1/2-1	1-1	4-1/0-0
St Mirren v Aberdeen	1-4/0-0	1-1/0-1	0-2	-	-	-
Ladbrokes Championship						
Ayr v Ross County	-	-	-	-	-	-
Falkirk v Morton	0-1/4-1	3-1/1-1	-	1-0/1-0	1-1/0-1	0-3/3-1
Inverness CT v Dundee United	4-0/0-0/1-2	1-1/1-1	1-0/2-1/3-0	2-2/2-3	-	0-1/1-0
Partick v Alloa	-	-	-	-	-	-
Queen of Sth v Dunfermline	-	-	-	-	2-2/0-1	0-0/0-0
Ladbrokes League One						
Airdrieonians v Arbroath	-	2-1/2-0	-	-	-	1-1/0-0
Forfar v Montrose	-	-	-	-	1-3/0-0	-
Raith v Dumbarton	2-2/3-2	2-1/1-3	3-1/2-1	1-0/0-0	3-2/1-3	-
Stenhousemuir v East Fife	3-0/2-1	1-1/1-1	-	-	0-1/3-1	-
Stranraer v Brechin	0-2/3-2	3-0/1-2	2-2/0-2	1-0/2-0	0-1/2-0	-
Ladbrokes League Two						
Berwick v Queens Park	2-0/4-1	4-0/1-0	0-0/1-1	1-0/1-1	-	-
Clyde v Annan	2-1/2-3	2-1/0-3	1-1/1-0	4-2/2-1	2-3/2-1	2-1/0-0
Edinburgh City v Elgin	-	-	-	-	1-2/3-0	0-3/4-0
Peterhead v Cowdenbeath	-	-	-	7-0/0-1	-	3-2/1-0
Stirling v Albion	-	2-1/2-0	-	-	-	-

Saturday December 22, 2018

	2012-13	2013-14	2014-15	2015-16	2016-17	2017-18
Premier League						
Arsenal v Burnley	-	-	3-0	-	2-1	5-0
Bournemouth v Brighton	-	1-1	3-2	-	-	2-1
Cardiff v Man United	-	2-2	-	-	-	-
Chelsea v Leicester	-	-	2-0	1-1	3-0	0-0
Everton v Tottenham	2-1	0-0	0-1	1-1	1-1	0-3
Huddersfield v Southampton	-	-	-	-	-	0-0
Man City v Crystal Palace	-	1-0	3-0	4-0	5-0	5-0
Newcastle v Fulham	1-0	1-0	-	-	1-3	-
West Ham v Watford	-	-	-	3-1	2-4	2-0
Wolves v Liverpool	-	-	-	-	-	-
Championship						
Aston Villa v Leeds	-	-	-	-	1-1	1-0
Blackburn v Norwich	-	-	1-2	-	1-4	-
Brentford v Bolton	-	-	2-2	3-1	-	2-0
Derby v Bristol City	3-0	-	-	4-0	3-3	0-0
Hull v Swansea	-	1-0	0-1	-	2-1	-
Ipswich v Sheffield United	-	-	-	-	-	0-0
Nottm Forest v QPR	-	2-0	-	0-0	1-1	4-0
Reading v Middlesbrough	-	2-0	0-0	2-0	-	0-2
Rotherham v West Brom	-	-	-	-	-	-
Sheffield Weds v Preston	-	-	-	3-1	2-1	4-1
Stoke v Millwall	-	-	-	-	-	-
Wigan v Birmingham	-	0-0	4-0	-	1-1	-
League One						
Blackpool v Barnsley	1-2	1-0	-	1-1	-	-
Bradford v Scunthorpe	-	-	1-1	1-0	0-0	1-2
Bristol Rovers v Fleetwood Town	0-0	1-3	-	-	2-1	3-1
Charlton v Gillingham	-	-	-	-	3-0	1-2
Doncaster v Oxford	-	-	-	-	-	0-1

Results cover matches from Premier League to National League and Scottish Premiership to Scottish League Two

	2012-13	2013-14	2014-15	2015-16	2016-17	2017-18
Luton v Burton	-	-	0-1	-	-	-
Peterborough v Walsall	-	0-0	0-0	1-1	1-1	2-1
Plymouth v Accrington	0-0	0-0	1-0	1-0	0-1	-
Portsmouth v Sunderland	-	-	-	-	-	-
Shrewsbury v Coventry	4-1	1-1	-	2-1	0-0	-
Southend v Rochdale	3-1	1-1	-	2-2	2-1	0-0
Wycombe v AFC Wimbledon	0-1	0-3	2-0	1-2	-	-

League Two

	2012-13	2013-14	2014-15	2015-16	2016-17	2017-18
Bury v Tranmere	0-1	-	2-0	-	-	-
Crawley Town v Carlisle	1-1	0-0	-	0-1	3-3	0-1
Forest Green v Crewe	-	-	-	-	-	3-2
Grimsby v Notts County	-	-	-	-	2-0	2-1
Lincoln v Newport County	2-4	-	-	-	-	3-1
Macclesfield v Port Vale	-	-	-	-	-	-
MK Dons v Colchester	5-1	0-0	6-0	-	-	-
Morecambe v Cambridge U	-	-	0-2	2-4	2-0	0-0
Oldham v Exeter	-	-	-	-	-	-
Stevenage v Mansfield	-	-	3-0	0-2	0-1	1-1
Swindon v Cheltenham	-	-	-	-	-	0-3
Yeovil v Northampton	-	-	-	1-1	-	-

National League

	2012-13	2013-14	2014-15	2015-16	2016-17	2017-18
Aldershot v Wrexham	-	2-0	1-1	0-1	2-0	2-0
Barnet v Dover	-	-	2-2	-	-	-
Braintree v Boreham Wood	-	-	-	0-2	1-2	-
Bromley v Maidenhead	-	6-1	4-2	-	-	2-3
Eastleigh v Harrogate T	-	-	-	-	-	1-1
Fylde v Ebbsfleet	-	-	-	-	-	1-1
Halifax v Sutton Utd	-	-	-	-	-	2-1
Hartlepool v Havant & W	-	-	-	-	-	-
Leyton Orient v Chesterfield	-	-	1-2	-	-	-
Maidstone v Gateshead	-	-	-	-	0-2	2-2
Salford City v Dag & Red	-	-	-	-	-	-
Solihull Moors v Barrow	-	0-2	3-4	-	2-4	3-3

Ladbrokes Premiership

	2012-13	2013-14	2014-15	2015-16	2016-17	2017-18
Aberdeen v Hearts	0-0/2-0/1-1	1-3	-	1-0/0-1	0-0/2-0	0-0/2-0
Celtic v Dundee	2-0/5-0	-	2-1/5-0	6-0/0-0	2-1	1-0/0-0
Hamilton v Kilmarnock	-	-	0-0/0-0	0-1/0-4	1-2/1-1/0-2	1-2
Hibernian v Livingston	-	-	2-1/2-1	2-1/2-1	-	-
Motherwell v St Mirren	1-1/2-2	3-0	1-0/5-0	-	-	-
St Johnstone v Rangers	-	-	-	-	1-1/1-2	0-3/1-4

Ladbrokes Championship

	2012-13	2013-14	2014-15	2015-16	2016-17	2017-18
Alloa v Queen of Sth	1-0/1-2	0-3/0-1	1-1/2-2	1-2/2-2	-	-
Dundee United v Falkirk	-	-	-	-	1-0/1-1	3-0/1-0
Dunfermline v Ayr	-	5-1/3-0	4-2/2-1	0-2/3-2	1-1/0-1	-
Morton v Inverness CT	-	-	-	-	-	1-0/0-3
Ross County v Partick	-	1-3/1-1	1-0/1-2	1-0/1-0	1-3	1-1/4-0

Ladbrokes League One

	2012-13	2013-14	2014-15	2015-16	2016-17	2017-18
Arbroath v Raith	-	-	-	-	-	1-2/1-1
Brechin v Airdrieonians	-	4-3/1-1	1-1/0-0	1-2/3-3	3-2/3-0	-
Dumbarton v Stranraer	-	-	-	-	-	-
East Fife v Forfar	3-0/1-2	1-3/2-1	-	-	-	3-0/1-2
Montrose v Stenhousemuir	-	-	-	-	-	1-1/1-0

Ladbrokes League Two

	2012-13	2013-14	2014-15	2015-16	2016-17	2017-18
Albion v Clyde	-	3-0/1-0	2-2/0-2	-	-	-
Annan v Berwick	3-2/2-2	3-2/4-0	2-0/4-2	1-0/1-0	3-1/2-1	0-0/0-0
Cowdenbeath v Edinburgh City	-	-	-	-	2-0/1-2	1-0/0-2
Peterhead v Stirling	2-2/0-0	3-1/0-4	1-1/2-1	-	-	2-4/4-3
Queens Park v Elgin	1-1/0-1	3-3/2-0	2-1/1-1	3-1/0-0	-	-

Results cover matches from Premier League to National League and Scottish Premiership to Scottish League Two

Wednesday December 26, 2018

Premier League

	2012-13	2013-14	2014-15	2015-16	2016-17	2017-18
Brighton v Arsenal	-	-	-	-	-	2-1
Burnley v Everton	-	-	1-3	-	2-1	2-1
Crystal Palace v Cardiff	3-2	2-0	-	-	-	-
Fulham v Wolves	-	-	0-1	0-3	1-3	2-0
Leicester v Man City	-	-	0-1	0-0	4-2	0-2
Liverpool v Newcastle	1-1	2-1	2-0	2-2	-	2-0
Man United v Huddersfield	-	-	-	-	-	2-0
Southampton v West Ham	1-1	0-0	0-0	1-0	1-3	3-2
Tottenham v Bournemouth	-	-	-	3-0	4-0	1-0
Watford v Chelsea	-	-	-	0-0	1-2	4-1

Championship

	2012-13	2013-14	2014-15	2015-16	2016-17	2017-18
Birmingham v Stoke	-	-	-	-	-	-
Bolton v Rotherham	-	-	3-2	2-1	-	-
Bristol City v Brentford	-	1-2	-	2-4	0-1	0-1
Leeds v Blackburn	3-3	1-2	0-3	0-2	2-1	-
Middlesbrough v Sheffield Weds	3-1	1-1	2-3	1-0	-	0-0
Millwall v Reading	-	0-3	0-0	-	-	2-1
Norwich v Nottm Forest	-	-	3-1	-	5-1	0-0
Preston v Hull	-	-	-	1-0	-	2-1
QPR v Ipswich	-	1-0	-	1-0	2-1	2-1
Sheffield United v Derby	-	-	-	-	-	3-1
Swansea v Aston Villa	2-2	4-1	1-0	1-0	-	-
West Brom v Wigan	2-3	-	-	-	-	-

League One

	2012-13	2013-14	2014-15	2015-16	2016-17	2017-18
Accrington v Shrewsbury	-	-	1-2	-	-	-
AFC Wimbledon v Plymouth	1-1	1-1	0-0	0-2	-	0-1
Barnsley v Peterborough	0-2	-	1-1	1-0	-	-
Burton v Wycombe	2-0	1-0	1-0	-	-	-
Coventry v Charlton	-	-	-	-	1-1	-
Fleetwood Town v Doncaster	-	-	3-1	0-0	-	0-0
Gillingham v Portsmouth	-	-	-	-	-	0-1
Oxford v Southend	2-0	0-2	2-3	-	0-2	2-0
Rochdale v Blackpool	-	-	-	3-0	-	1-2
Scunthorpe v Luton	-	-	-	-	-	-
Sunderland v Bradford	-	-	-	-	-	-
Walsall v Bristol Rovers	-	-	-	-	3-1	0-0

League Two

	2012-13	2013-14	2014-15	2015-16	2016-17	2017-18
Cambridge U v Crawley Town	-	-	-	0-3	2-0	3-1
Carlisle v Oldham	3-1	0-1	-	-	-	-
Cheltenham v MK Dons	-	-	-	-	-	-
Colchester v Stevenage	1-0	4-0	-	-	4-0	1-1
Crewe v Lincoln	-	-	-	-	-	1-4
Exeter v Yeovil	-	-	-	3-2	3-3	0-0
Mansfield v Bury	-	1-4	0-1	-	-	-
Newport County v Forest Green	0-5	-	-	-	-	3-3
Northampton v Swindon	-	-	-	-	2-1	-
Notts County v Macclesfield	-	-	-	-	-	-
Port Vale v Grimsby	-	-	-	-	-	1-2
Tranmere v Morecambe	-	-	2-1	-	-	-

National League

	2012-13	2013-14	2014-15	2015-16	2016-17	2017-18
Barrow v Fylde	-	-	-	-	-	1-3
Boreham Wood v Barnet	-	-	-	-	-	-
Chesterfield v Solihull Moors	-	-	-	-	-	-
Dag & Red v Leyton Orient	-	-	-	1-3	-	0-0
Dover v Maidstone	-	-	-	-	1-1	2-2
Ebbsfleet v Braintree	0-1	-	-	-	-	-
Gateshead v Hartlepool	-	-	-	-	-	2-2
Harrogate T v Halifax	-	-	-	-	0-3	-

Results cover matches from Premier League to National League and Scottish Premiership to Scottish League Two

	2012-13	2013-14	2014-15	2015-16	2016-17	2017-18
Havant & W v Eastleigh	-	1-0	-	-	-	-
Maidenhead v Aldershot	-	-	-	-	-	3-3
Sutton Utd v Bromley	-	1-0	1-2	-	2-0	0-3
Wrexham v Salford City	-	-	-	-	-	-

Ladbrokes Premiership

	2012-13	2013-14	2014-15	2015-16	2016-17	2017-18
Aberdeen v Celtic	0-2	0-2/2-1	1-2/0-1	2-1/2-1	0-1/1-3	0-3/0-2
Dundee v Livingston	-	3-0/0-1	-	-	-	-
Hearts v Hamilton	-	-	-	2-0	3-1/4-0	1-1
Motherwell v Kilmarnock	2-2	2-1/1-2	1-1/3-1	1-0/0-2	0-0/3-1	2-0/0-1
Rangers v Hibernian	-	-	1-3/0-2	1-0/4-2	-	2-3/1-2
St Mirren v St Johnstone	1-1	4-3/0-1	0-1	-	-	-

Saturday December 29, 2018

Premier League

	2012-13	2013-14	2014-15	2015-16	2016-17	2017-18
Brighton v Everton	-	-	-	-	-	1-1
Burnley v West Ham	-	-	1-3	-	1-2	1-1
Crystal Palace v Chelsea	-	1-0	1-2	0-3	0-1	2-1
Fulham v Huddersfield	-	-	3-1	1-1	5-0	-
Leicester v Cardiff	0-1	-	-	-	-	-
Liverpool v Arsenal	0-2	5-1	2-2	3-3	3-1	4-0
Man United v Bournemouth	-	-	-	3-1	1-1	1-0
Southampton v Man City	3-1	1-1	0-3	4-2	0-3	0-1
Tottenham v Wolves	-	-	-	-	-	-
Watford v Newcastle	-	-	-	2-1	-	2-1

Championship

	2012-13	2013-14	2014-15	2015-16	2016-17	2017-18
Birmingham v Brentford	-	-	1-0	2-1	1-3	0-2
Bolton v Stoke	-	-	-	-	-	-
Bristol City v Rotherham	-	1-2	-	1-1	1-0	-
Leeds v Hull	2-3	-	-	2-1	-	1-0
Middlesbrough v Ipswich	2-0	2-0	4-1	0-0	-	2-0
Millwall v Nottm Forest	0-1	2-2	0-0	-	-	2-0
Norwich v Derby	-	-	1-1	-	3-0	1-2
Preston v Aston Villa	-	-	-	-	2-0	0-2
QPR v Reading	1-1	1-3	-	1-1	1-1	2-0
Sheffield United v Blackburn	-	-	-	-	-	-
Swansea v Wigan	2-1	-	-	-	-	-
West Brom v Sheffield Weds	-	-	-	-	-	-

League One

	2012-13	2013-14	2014-15	2015-16	2016-17	2017-18
Accrington v Peterborough	-	-	-	-	-	-
AFC Wimbledon v Blackpool	-	-	-	-	-	2-0
Barnsley v Charlton	0-6	2-2	-	-	-	-
Burton v Plymouth	1-0	1-0	1-1	-	-	-
Coventry v Southend	-	-	-	2-2	0-2	-
Fleetwood Town v Portsmouth	-	3-1	-	-	-	1-2
Gillingham v Doncaster	-	-	1-1	1-0	-	0-0
Oxford v Bristol Rovers	0-2	0-1	-	1-2	0-2	1-2
Rochdale v Bradford	0-0	-	0-2	1-3	1-1	1-1
Scunthorpe v Wycombe	-	0-0	-	-	-	-
Sunderland v Shrewsbury	-	-	-	-	-	-
Walsall v Luton	-	-	-	-	-	-

League Two

	2012-13	2013-14	2014-15	2015-16	2016-17	2017-18
Cambridge U v Lincoln	2-1	1-0	-	-	-	0-0
Carlisle v Macclesfield	-	-	-	-	-	-
Cheltenham v Forest Green	-	-	-	1-1	-	0-1
Colchester v Morecambe	-	-	-	-	2-2	0-0
Crewe v Stevenage	1-2	0-3	-	-	1-2	1-0
Exeter v Grimsby	-	-	-	-	0-0	2-0
Mansfield v Swindon	-	-	-	-	-	1-3
Newport County v Crawley Town	-	-	-	0-3	1-0	2-1
Northampton v MK Dons	-	-	-	-	3-2	2-1
Notts County v Bury	4-1	-	-	-	-	-
Port Vale v Oldham	-	1-0	0-1	1-1	2-2	-
Tranmere v Yeovil	3-2	-	-	-	-	-

Results cover matches from Premier League to National League and Scottish Premiership to Scottish League Two

National League

	2012-13	2013-14	2014-15	2015-16	2016-17	2017-18
Barrow v Salford City	-	-	-	-	-	-
Boreham Wood v Maidstone	-	-	-	-	0-1	1-0
Chesterfield v Hartlepool	-	1-1	-	-	-	-
Dag & Red v Barnet	1-0	-	-	0-2	-	-
Dover v Leyton Orient	-	-	-	-	-	1-0
Ebbsfleet v Eastleigh	-	3-1	-	-	-	2-2
Gateshead v Halifax	-	1-1	2-2	1-4	-	0-0
Harrogate T v Fylde	-	-	-	-	-	-
Havant & W v Bromley	-	1-0	1-3	-	-	-
Maidenhead v Braintree	-	-	-	-	-	-
Sutton Utd v Aldershot	-	-	-	-	2-0	2-1
Wrexham v Solihull Moors	-	-	-	-	1-0	1-0

Ladbrokes Premiership

	2012-13	2013-14	2014-15	2015-16	2016-17	2017-18
Dundee v St Johnstone	1-3/2-2	-	1-1/0-2	2-1/2-0	3-0	3-2/0-4/2-1
Hamilton v Motherwell	-	-	5-0/2-0	1-0/0-1	1-1/0-1	1-2/2-0
Hibernian v Hearts	1-1/0-0	2-1/1-2	1-1/2-0	-	-	1-0/2-0
Kilmarnock v St Mirren	3-1/1-1/1-3	2-1/1-0	2-1/1-0	-	-	-
Livingston v Aberdeen	-	-	-	-	-	-
Rangers v Celtic	-	-	-	-	1-2/1-5	0-2/2-3

Ladbrokes Championship

	2012-13	2013-14	2014-15	2015-16	2016-17	2017-18
Alloa v Dundee United	-	-	-	-	-	-
Falkirk v Dunfermline	2-2/1-0	-	-	-	2-1/2-0	1-1/1-2
Partick v Morton	1-2/1-0	-	-	-	-	-
Queen of Sth v Ayr	2-0/2-0	-	-	-	4-1/0-0	-
Ross County v Inverness CT	0-0/1-0	0-3/1-2	1-3	1-2/0-3	3-2/4-0	-

Ladbrokes League One

	2012-13	2013-14	2014-15	2015-16	2016-17	2017-18
Airdrieonians v Stranraer	-	3-2/1-1	3-3/1-1	0-1/1-1	1-0/1-2	2-0/2-1
Forfar v Brechin	1-0/1-4	2-0/1-1	3-1/0-2	0-1/1-2	-	-
Montrose v Arbroath	-	-	1-5/3-0	3-0/0-2	1-1/1-3	-
Raith v East Fife	-	-	-	-	-	1-0/2-0
Stenhousemuir v Dumbarton	-	-	-	-	-	-

Ladbrokes League Two

	2012-13	2013-14	2014-15	2015-16	2016-17	2017-18
Albion v Annan	-	2-0/0-2	2-1/2-0	-	-	-
Berwick v Edinburgh City	-	-	-	-	1-3/3-2	1-1/1-1
Clyde v Queens Park	0-3/2-3	3-0/1-2	0-2/2-0	0-2/0-1	-	-
Elgin v Peterhead	2-0/0-3	2-4/2-3	-	-	-	0-2/0-1
Stirling v Cowdenbeath	-	-	-	-	1-2/0-3	1-0/2-2

Tuesday January 1, 2019

Premier League

	2012-13	2013-14	2014-15	2015-16	2016-17	2017-18
Arsenal v Fulham	3-3	2-0	-	-	-	-
Bournemouth v Watford	-	1-1	2-0	1-1	2-2	0-2
Cardiff v Tottenham	-	0-1	-	-	-	-
Chelsea v Southampton	2-2	3-1	1-1	1-3	4-2	1-0
Everton v Leicester	-	-	2-2	2-3	4-2	2-1
Huddersfield v Burnley	2-0	2-1	-	1-3	-	0-0
Man City v Liverpool	2-2	2-1	3-1	1-4	1-1	5-0
Newcastle v Man United	0-3	0-4	0-1	3-3	-	1-0
West Ham v Brighton	-	-	-	-	-	0-3
Wolves v Crystal Palace	1-2	-	-	-	-	-

Championship

	2012-13	2013-14	2014-15	2015-16	2016-17	2017-18
Aston Villa v QPR	3-2	-	3-3	-	1-0	1-3
Blackburn v West Brom	-	-	-	-	-	-
Brentford v Norwich	-	-	0-3	-	0-0	0-1
Derby v Middlesbrough	3-1	2-1	0-1	1-1	-	1-2
Hull v Bolton	3-1	-	-	1-0	-	4-0
Ipswich v Millwall	3-0	3-0	2-0	-	-	2-2

Results cover matches from Premier League to National League and Scottish Premiership to Scottish League Two

	2012-13	2013-14	2014-15	2015-16	2016-17	2017-18
Nottm Forest v Leeds	4-2	2-1	1-1	1-1	3-1	0-2
Reading v Swansea	0-0	-	-	-	-	-
Rotherham v Preston	-	0-0	-	0-0	1-3	-
Sheffield Weds v Birmingham	3-2	4-1	0-0	3-0	3-0	1-3
Stoke v Bristol City	-	-	-	-	-	-
Wigan v Sheffield United	-	-	-	3-3	-	-

League One						
Blackpool v Sunderland	-	-	-	-	-	-
Bradford v Accrington	2-1	-	-	-	-	-
Bristol Rovers v Burton	3-0	2-0	-	-	-	-
Charlton v Walsall	-	-	-	-	1-1	3-1
Doncaster v Rochdale	-	-	1-1	0-2	-	2-0
Luton v Barnsley	-	-	-	-	-	-
Peterborough v Scunthorpe	-	-	1-2	0-2	0-2	2-2
Plymouth v Oxford	0-1	0-2	1-2	2-2	-	0-4
Portsmouth v AFC Wimbledon	-	1-0	0-2	0-0	-	2-1
Shrewsbury v Fleetwood Town	-	-	-	1-1	0-1	1-0
Southend v Gillingham	0-1	-	-	1-1	1-3	4-0
Wycombe v Coventry	-	-	-	-	-	0-1

League Two						
Bury v Crewe	2-2	-	-	0-0	-	-
Crawley Town v Colchester	3-0	1-0	0-0	-	1-1	0-2
Forest Green v Northampton	-	-	-	-	-	-
Grimsby v Mansfield	4-1	-	-	-	3-0	1-1
Lincoln v Port Vale	-	-	-	-	-	3-1
Macclesfield v Tranmere	-	-	-	1-2	4-2	2-2
MK Dons v Cambridge U	-	-	-	-	-	-
Morecambe v Carlisle	-	-	0-1	1-2	0-3	1-1
Oldham v Notts County	2-2	1-1	3-0	-	-	-
Stevenage v Newport County	-	-	2-1	2-1	3-1	3-3
Swindon v Exeter	-	-	-	-	-	1-1
Yeovil v Cheltenham	-	-	-	-	4-2	0-0

National League						
Aldershot v Maidenhead	-	-	-	-	-	1-0
Barnet v Boreham Wood	-	-	-	-	-	-
Braintree v Ebbsfleet	3-1	-	-	-	-	-
Bromley v Sutton Utd	-	2-4	2-1	-	1-0	0-1
Eastleigh v Havant & W	-	0-0	-	-	-	-
Fylde v Barrow	-	-	-	-	-	1-0
Halifax v Harrogate T	-	-	-	-	0-1	-
Hartlepool v Gateshead	-	-	-	-	-	2-2
Leyton Orient v Dag & Red	-	-	-	3-2	-	2-0
Maidstone v Dover	-	-	-	-	1-4	2-2
Salford City v Wrexham	-	-	-	-	-	-
Solihull Moors v Chesterfield	-	-	-	-	-	-

Saturday January 5, 2019

League One						
AFC Wimbledon v Fleetwood Town	2-1	2-0	-	-	2-2	0-1
Blackpool v Wycombe	-	-	-	-	0-0	-
Bradford v Shrewsbury	-	2-1	-	1-1	2-0	0-0
Bristol Rovers v Peterborough	-	-	-	-	1-2	1-4
Charlton v Sunderland	-	-	-	-	-	-
Doncaster v Southend	-	-	-	0-0	-	4-1
Gillingham v Accrington	1-0	-	-	-	-	-
Luton v Portsmouth	-	-	1-1	1-2	1-3	-
Oxford v Barnsley	-	-	-	-	-	-
Plymouth v Walsall	-	-	-	-	-	1-0
Rochdale v Burton	0-1	1-1	-	2-1	-	-
Scunthorpe v Coventry	1-2	-	2-1	1-0	3-1	-

Results cover matches from Premier League to National League and Scottish Premiership to Scottish League Two

	2012-13	2013-14	2014-15	2015-16	2016-17	2017-18
League Two						
Cambridge U v Stevenage	-	-	1-1	1-0	0-0	1-0
Carlisle v Mansfield	-	-	2-1	1-2	5-2	1-1
Colchester v Notts County	0-2	0-4	0-1	-	2-1	1-3
Crawley Town v Cheltenham	-	-	-	-	0-0	3-5
Forest Green v Grimsby	0-1	2-1	2-1	0-1	-	0-3
Lincoln v Exeter	-	-	-	-	-	3-2
Macclesfield v Swindon	-	-	-	-	-	-
MK Dons v Oldham	2-0	2-1	7-0	-	1-0	4-4
Morecambe v Crewe	-	-	-	-	0-0	0-1
Newport County v Port Vale	-	-	-	-	-	1-1
Tranmere v Northampton	-	-	2-1	-	-	-
Yeovil v Bury	2-1	-	-	-	-	-
National League						
Barnet v Aldershot	0-1	1-3	1-0	-	-	-
Bromley v Fylde	-	-	-	-	-	0-1
Chesterfield v Ebbsfleet	-	-	-	-	-	-
Dag & Red v Boreham Wood	-	-	-	-	0-2	2-3
Gateshead v Maidenhead	-	-	-	-	-	7-1
Halifax v Braintree	-	0-0	1-0	3-6	-	-
Hartlepool v Maidstone	-	-	-	-	-	3-1
Havant & W v Barrow	-	-	-	-	-	-
Leyton Orient v Salford City	-	-	-	-	-	-
Solihull Moors v Eastleigh	-	-	-	-	2-0	1-4
Sutton Utd v Harrogate T	-	-	-	-	-	-
Wrexham v Dover	-	-	1-1	0-1	0-0	0-0
Ladbrokes Championship						
Ayr v Falkirk	-	-	-	-	0-1/1-4	-
Dundee United v Partick	-	4-1	1-0/0-2	0-1/3-3	-	-
Dunfermline v Alloa	-	-	-	-	-	-
Inverness CT v Queen of Sth	-	-	-	-	-	0-0/3-1
Morton v Ross County	-	-	-	-	-	-
Ladbrokes League One						
Arbroath v Brechin	3-1/0-1	2-1/0-1	-	-	-	-
Dumbarton v Forfar	-	-	-	-	-	-
East Fife v Airdrieonians	-	1-0/0-0	-	-	0-1/0-4	6-1/2-1
Raith v Stenhousemuir	-	-	-	-	-	-
Stranraer v Montrose	-	-	-	-	-	-
Ladbrokes League Two						
Annan v Elgin	2-0/2-2	2-1/2-0	3-3/2-3	1-1/4-2	1-0/1-0	2-0/4-1
Cowdenbeath v Berwick	-	-	-	-	0-2/0-1	0-1/1-3
Edinburgh City v Stirling	-	-	-	-	2-0/1-0	1-2/2-2
Peterhead v Clyde	1-0/3-0	1-1/2-0	-	-	-	2-1/3-0
Queens Park v Albion	-	1-1/4-0	0-1/0-1	-	2-1/2-0	2-5/2-2

Saturday January 12, 2019

	2012-13	2013-14	2014-15	2015-16	2016-17	2017-18
Premier League						
Brighton v Liverpool	-	-	-	-	-	1-5
Burnley v Fulham	-	-	-	3-1	-	-
Cardiff v Huddersfield	1-0	-	3-1	2-0	3-2	-
Chelsea v Newcastle	2-0	3-0	2-0	5-1	-	3-1
Crystal Palace v Watford	2-3	-	-	1-2	1-0	2-1
Everton v Bournemouth	-	-	-	2-1	6-3	2-1
Leicester v Southampton	-	-	2-0	1-0	0-0	0-0
Man City v Wolves	-	-	-	-	-	-
Tottenham v Man United	1-1	2-2	0-0	3-0	2-1	2-0
West Ham v Arsenal	1-3	1-3	1-2	3-3	1-5	0-0

Results cover matches from Premier League to National League and Scottish Premiership to Scottish League Two

	2012-13	2013-14	2014-15	2015-16	2016-17	2017-18
Championship						
Birmingham v Middlesbrough	3-2	2-2	1-1	2-2	-	0-1
Brentford v Stoke	-	-	-	-	-	-
Bristol City v Bolton	1-2	-	-	6-0	-	2-0
Hull v Sheffield Weds	1-3	-	-	0-0	-	0-1
Ipswich v Rotherham	-	-	2-0	0-1	2-2	-
Leeds v Derby	1-2	1-1	2-0	2-2	1-0	1-2
Millwall v Blackburn	1-2	2-2	2-2	-	-	-
Preston v Swansea	-	-	-	-	-	-
Reading v Nottm Forest	-	1-1	0-3	2-1	2-0	3-1
Sheffield United v QPR	-	-	-	-	-	2-1
West Brom v Norwich	2-1	0-2	-	0-1	-	-
Wigan v Aston Villa	2-2	-	-	-	0-2	-
League One						
Accrington v Bristol Rovers	1-0	2-1	-	1-0	-	-
Barnsley v Bradford	-	-	3-1	0-0	-	-
Burton v Gillingham	3-2	-	-	2-1	-	-
Coventry v AFC Wimbledon	-	-	-	-	2-2	-
Fleetwood Town v Oxford	3-0	1-1	-	-	2-0	2-0
Peterborough v Rochdale	-	-	2-1	1-2	3-1	0-1
Portsmouth v Blackpool	-	-	-	-	2-0	0-2
Shrewsbury v Charlton	-	-	-	-	4-3	0-2
Southend v Plymouth	0-2	1-0	0-0	-	-	1-1
Sunderland v Luton	-	-	-	-	-	-
Walsall v Scunthorpe	1-4	-	1-4	0-0	1-4	1-0
Wycombe v Doncaster	-	-	-	-	2-1	-
League Two						
Bury v MK Dons	1-4	-	-	-	0-0	0-2
Cheltenham v Tranmere	-	-	2-0	0-1	-	-
Crewe v Newport County	-	-	-	-	1-2	1-1
Exeter v Morecambe	0-3	1-1	1-1	1-1	3-1	4-1
Grimsby v Macclesfield	0-1	2-3	1-2	0-2	-	-
Mansfield v Yeovil	-	-	-	0-1	1-0	0-0
Northampton v Carlisle	-	-	0-2	3-2	-	-
Notts County v Cambridge U	-	-	-	1-2	0-1	3-3
Oldham v Forest Green	-	-	-	-	-	-
Port Vale v Colchester	-	2-0	1-2	2-0	-	2-2
Stevenage v Crawley Town	1-2	2-0	-	0-1	2-1	1-1
Swindon v Lincoln	-	-	-	-	-	0-1
Ladbrokes Championship						
Alloa v Morton	-	2-0/2-0	-	0-1/2-2	-	-
Dundee United v Dunfermline	-	-	-	-	1-0/1-0	2-1/1-1
Inverness CT v Ayr	-	-	-	-	-	-
Partick v Falkirk	3-1/4-1	-	-	-	-	-
Queen of Sth v Ross County	-	-	-	-	-	-
Ladbrokes League One						
Airdrieonians v Raith	0-0/1-2	-	-	-	-	2-2/1-2
Brechin v Dumbarton	-	-	-	-	-	0-1/1-3
Forfar v Stranraer	4-0/3-1	1-2/1-0	1-1/1-0	1-2/1-1	-	1-1/5-1
Montrose v East Fife	-	-	0-4/0-3	1-4/2-2	-	-
Stenhousemuir v Arbroath	2-2/1-0	3-2/2-2	-	-	-	-
Ladbrokes League Two						
Albion v Peterhead	-	1-2/0-0	-	1-0/1-1	0-1/0-0	-
Berwick v Clyde	2-1/3-3	0-1/3-0	4-0/0-0	0-5/3-0	1-1/4-3	3-1/0-1
Elgin v Cowdenbeath	-	-	-	-	3-1/0-0	1-1/1-0
Queens Park v Edinburgh City	-	-	-	-	-	-
Stirling v Annan	5-1/2-1	0-2/1-1	-	1-0/2-1	3-1/1-0	3-2/3-0

Results cover matches from Premier League to National League and Scottish Premiership to Scottish League Two

Saturday January 19, 2019

Premier League

	2012-13	2013-14	2014-15	2015-16	2016-17	2017-18
Arsenal v Chelsea	1-2	0-0	0-0	0-1	3-0	2-2
Bournemouth v West Ham	-	-	-	1-3	3-2	3-3
Fulham v Tottenham	0-3	1-2	-	-	-	-
Huddersfield v Man City	-	-	-	-	-	1-2
Liverpool v Crystal Palace	-	3-1	1-3	1-2	1-2	1-0
Man United v Brighton	-	-	-	-	-	1-0
Newcastle v Cardiff	-	3-0	-	-	2-1	-
Southampton v Everton	0-0	2-0	3-0	0-3	1-0	4-1
Watford v Burnley	3-3	1-1	-	-	2-1	1-2
Wolves v Leicester	2-1	-	-	-	-	-

Championship

	2012-13	2013-14	2014-15	2015-16	2016-17	2017-18
Aston Villa v Hull	-	3-1	2-1	-	-	1-1
Blackburn v Ipswich	1-0	2-0	3-2	2-0	0-0	-
Bolton v West Brom	-	-	-	-	-	-
Derby v Reading	-	1-3	0-3	1-1	3-2	2-4
Middlesbrough v Millwall	1-2	1-2	3-0	-	-	2-0
Norwich v Birmingham	-	-	2-2	-	2-0	1-0
Nottm Forest v Bristol City	1-0	-	-	1-2	1-0	0-0
QPR v Preston	-	-	-	0-0	0-2	1-2
Rotherham v Brentford	-	3-0	0-2	2-1	1-0	-
Sheffield Weds v Wigan	-	0-3	2-1	-	2-1	-
Stoke v Leeds	-	-	-	-	-	-
Swansea v Sheffield United	-	-	-	-	-	-

League One

	2012-13	2013-14	2014-15	2015-16	2016-17	2017-18
AFC Wimbledon v Barnsley	-	-	-	-	-	-
Blackpool v Shrewsbury	-	-	-	2-3	-	1-1
Bradford v Southend	2-2	-	-	2-0	1-1	0-2
Bristol Rovers v Wycombe	1-0	0-1	-	3-0	-	-
Charlton v Accrington	-	-	-	-	-	-
Doncaster v Burton	-	-	-	0-0	-	-
Gillingham v Walsall	-	2-2	0-0	1-2	1-1	0-0
Luton v Peterborough	-	-	-	-	-	-
Oxford v Portsmouth	-	0-0	0-1	1-1	-	3-0
Plymouth v Coventry	-	-	-	-	-	-
Rochdale v Fleetwood Town	0-0	1-2	0-2	1-0	2-1	0-2
Scunthorpe v Sunderland	-	-	-	-	-	-

League Two

	2012-13	2013-14	2014-15	2015-16	2016-17	2017-18
Cambridge U v Northampton	-	-	2-1	2-1	-	-
Carlisle v Cheltenham	-	-	1-0	-	1-1	3-0
Colchester v Mansfield	-	-	-	-	2-0	2-0
Crawley Town v Port Vale	-	0-3	1-2	-	-	1-3
Forest Green v Bury	-	-	-	-	-	-
Lincoln v Grimsby	1-4	0-2	3-2	1-1	-	3-1
Macclesfield v Oldham	-	-	-	-	-	-
MK Dons v Crewe	1-0	1-0	6-1	-	-	-
Morecambe v Stevenage	-	-	0-0	1-4	0-2	1-1
Newport County v Exeter	-	1-1	2-2	1-1	1-4	2-1
Tranmere v Swindon	1-3	1-2	-	-	-	-
Yeovil v Notts County	0-0	-	1-1	1-0	2-0	1-1

National League

	2012-13	2013-14	2014-15	2015-16	2016-17	2017-18
Aldershot v Chesterfield	0-1	-	-	-	-	-
Barrow v Halifax	-	-	-	4-1	-	0-0
Boreham Wood v Havant & W	-	0-2	1-2	-	-	-
Braintree v Barnet	-	0-3	1-1	-	-	-
Dover v Bromley	-	0-2	-	2-3	1-0	1-2
Eastleigh v Sutton Utd	-	1-0	-	-	2-1	1-0
Ebbsfleet v Leyton Orient	-	-	-	-	-	2-1

Results cover matches from Premier League to National League and Scottish Premiership to Scottish League Two

	2012-13	2013-14	2014-15	2015-16	2016-17	2017-18
Fylde v Wrexham	-	-	-	-	-	2-0
Harrogate T v Hartlepool	-	-	-	-	-	-
Maidenhead v Solihull Moors	-	-	-	-	-	1-0
Maidstone v Dag & Red	-	-	-	-	0-1	0-0
Salford City v Gateshead	-	-	-	-	-	-

Ladbrokes League Two

	2012-13	2013-14	2014-15	2015-16	2016-17	2017-18
Clyde v Elgin	2-2/1-1	2-1/4-0	2-1/0-2	4-2/1-0	2-1/3-2	2-4/1-0
Cowdenbeath v Albion	-	-	-	1-0/1-2	-	-
Edinburgh City v Annan	-	-	-	-	1-0/2-0	0-1/3-2
Peterhead v Berwick	1-0/1-1	1-1/3-0	-	-	-	0-2/1-1
Stirling v Queens Park	1-2/2-3	3-0/2-2	-	1-2/0-0	-	-

Wednesday January 23, 2019

Ladbrokes Premiership

	2012-13	2013-14	2014-15	2015-16	2016-17	2017-18
Celtic v St Mirren	2-0	1-0/3-0	4-1	-	-	-
Hamilton v Aberdeen	-	-	3-0/0-3	1-1	1-0/1-0	2-2
Hearts v Dundee	0-1/1-0	-	-	1-1	2-0/1-0	2-0
Kilmarnock v Rangers	-	-	-	-	1-1/0-0	2-1
Motherwell v Hibernian	0-4/4-1	1-0	-	-	-	0-1
St Johnstone v Livingston	-	-	-	-	-	-

Saturday January 26, 2019

Championship

	2012-13	2013-14	2014-15	2015-16	2016-17	2017-18
Aston Villa v Ipswich	-	-	-	-	0-1	2-0
Blackburn v Hull	1-0	-	-	0-2	-	-
Bolton v Reading	-	1-1	1-1	0-1	-	2-2
Derby v Millwall	1-0	0-1	0-0	-	-	3-0
Middlesbrough v Bristol City	1-3	-	-	0-1	-	2-1
Norwich v Sheffield United	-	-	-	-	-	1-2
Nottm Forest v Wigan	-	1-4	3-0	-	4-3	-
QPR v West Brom	1-2	-	3-2	-	-	-
Rotherham v Leeds	-	-	2-1	2-1	1-2	-
Sheffield Weds v Brentford	-	-	1-0	4-0	1-2	2-1
Stoke v Preston	-	-	-	-	-	-
Swansea v Birmingham	-	-	-	-	-	-

League One

	2012-13	2013-14	2014-15	2015-16	2016-17	2017-18
Accrington v Oxford	0-3	0-0	1-0	1-3	-	-
Barnsley v Rochdale	-	-	5-0	6-1	-	-
Burton v Bradford	1-0	-	-	3-1	-	-
Coventry v Blackpool	-	-	-	0-0	-	-
Fleetwood Town v Scunthorpe	-	0-1	2-2	2-1	2-2	2-3
Peterborough v Charlton	2-2	-	-	-	2-0	4-1
Portsmouth v Bristol Rovers	-	3-2	-	3-1	-	3-0
Shrewsbury v Doncaster	1-2	-	-	1-2	-	2-2
Southend v Luton	-	-	1-0	-	-	-
Sunderland v Gillingham	-	-	-	-	-	-
Walsall v AFC Wimbledon	-	-	-	-	3-1	2-3
Wycombe v Plymouth	1-1	0-1	0-2	1-2	1-1	-

League Two

	2012-13	2013-14	2014-15	2015-16	2016-17	2017-18
Bury v Lincoln	-	-	-	-	-	-
Cheltenham v Macclesfield	-	-	-	2-0	-	-
Crewe v Colchester	3-2	0-0	0-3	1-1	2-0	1-0
Exeter v Cambridge U	-	-	2-2	1-0	1-2	1-0
Grimsby v MK Dons	-	-	-	-	-	-
Mansfield v Tranmere	-	-	1-0	-	-	-
Northampton v Morecambe	3-0	0-0	2-1	3-1	-	-
Notts County v Newport County	-	-	-	4-3	0-3	3-0
Oldham v Yeovil	1-0	-	0-4	-	-	-
Port Vale v Carlisle	-	2-1	-	-	-	1-2
Stevenage v Forest Green	-	-	-	-	-	1-2
Swindon v Crawley Town	3-0	1-1	1-2	-	-	0-3

Results cover matches from Premier League to National League and Scottish Premiership to Scottish League Two

National League						
Barnet v Harrogate T	-	-	-	-	-	-
Bromley v Eastleigh	-	1-2	-	2-2	0-5	0-0
Chesterfield v Barrow	-	-	-	-	-	-
Dag & Red v Aldershot	0-0	-	-	-	1-0	0-2
Gateshead v Boreham Wood	-	-	-	2-1	1-1	1-1
Halifax v Salford City	-	-	-	-	4-2	-
Hartlepool v Braintree	-	-	-	-	-	-
Havant & W v Dover	-	3-4	-	-	-	-
Leyton Orient v Maidstone	-	-	-	-	-	2-0
Solihull Moors v Fylde	-	-	-	-	-	0-4
Sutton Utd v Ebbsfleet	-	3-1	2-1	2-0	-	0-0
Wrexham v Maidenhead	-	-	-	-	-	2-0
Ladbrokes Premiership						
Aberdeen v Kilmarnock	0-2/1-0	2-1/2-1	1-0	2-0/2-1	5-1	1-1/3-1
Celtic v Hamilton	-	-	0-1/4-0	8-1	1-0/2-0	3-1
Dundee v Motherwell	1-2/0-3	-	4-1	2-1/2-2	2-0	0-1/0-1
Hearts v St Johnstone	2-0/2-0	0-2	-	4-3/0-3/2-2	2-2	1-0/1-0
Livingston v Rangers	-	-	0-1/1-1	1-1/1-0	-	-
St Mirren v Hibernian	1-2/0-1	0-0/2-0	-	1-4/2-2	0-2/2-0	-
Ladbrokes Championship						
Ayr v Dundee United	-	-	-	-	0-1/0-0	-
Falkirk v Inverness CT	-	-	-	-	-	0-0/3-1
Morton v Dunfermline	4-2/0-1	-	2-1/2-0	-	2-1/0-1	3-2/2-1
Partick v Queen of Sth	-	-	-	-	-	-
Ross County v Alloa	-	-	-	-	-	-
Ladbrokes League One						
Arbroath v Forfar	1-1/3-1	3-0/2-3	-	-	2-0/0-1	2-1/2-0
Brechin v Raith	-	-	-	-	-	-
Dumbarton v Montrose	-	-	-	-	-	-
Stenhousemuir v Airdrieonians	-	1-1/1-2	1-0/0-2	2-1/3-2	2-2/4-2	-
Stranraer v East Fife	2-6/3-1	2-0/2-0	-	-	1-1/2-1	1-0/0-2
Ladbrokes League Two						
Albion v Stirling	-	2-1/0-2	-	-	-	-
Annan v Peterhead	2-1/0-0	2-0/2-1	-	-	-	1-2/3-3
Clyde v Cowdenbeath	-	-	-	-	5-3/0-2	1-1/2-0
Elgin v Edinburgh City	-	-	-	-	3-0/3-1	1-1/1-1
Queens Park v Berwick	1-1/2-1	0-4/1-3	2-0/2-1	0-1/0-0	-	-

Tuesday January 29, 2019

Premier League						
Arsenal v Cardiff	-	2-0	-	-	-	-
Bournemouth v Chelsea	-	-	-	1-4	1-3	0-1
Fulham v Brighton	-	-	0-2	1-2	1-2	-
Huddersfield v Everton	-	-	-	-	-	0-2
Man United v Burnley	-	-	3-1	-	0-0	2-2
Wolves v West Ham	-	-	-	-	-	-

Wednesday January 30, 2019

Premier League						
Liverpool v Leicester	-	-	2-2	1-0	4-1	2-1
Newcastle v Man City	1-3	0-2	0-2	1-1	-	0-1
Southampton v Crystal Palace	-	2-0	1-0	4-1	3-1	1-2
Tottenham v Watford	-	-	-	1-0	4-0	2-0

Saturday February 2, 2019

Premier League						
Brighton v Watford	1-3	1-1	0-2	-	-	1-0
Burnley v Southampton	-	-	1-0	-	1-0	1-1
Cardiff v Bournemouth	-	-	1-1	-	-	-
Chelsea v Huddersfield	-	-	-	-	-	1-1

Results cover matches from Premier League to National League and Scottish Premiership to Scottish League Two

	2012-13	2013-14	2014-15	2015-16	2016-17	2017-18
Crystal Palace v Fulham	-	1-4	-	-	-	-
Everton v Wolves	-	-	-	-	-	-
Leicester v Man United	-	-	5-3	1-1	0-3	2-2
Man City v Arsenal	1-1	6-3	0-2	2-2	2-1	3-1
Tottenham v Newcastle	2-1	0-1	1-2	1-2	-	1-0
West Ham v Liverpool	2-3	1-2	3-1	2-0	0-4	1-4
Championship						
Birmingham v Nottm Forest	2-1	0-0	2-1	0-1	0-0	1-0
Brentford v Blackburn	-	-	3-1	0-1	1-3	-
Bristol City v Swansea	-	-	-	-	-	-
Hull v Stoke	-	0-0	1-1	-	0-2	-
Ipswich v Sheffield Weds	0-3	2-1	2-1	2-1	0-1	2-2
Leeds v Norwich	-	-	0-2	-	3-3	1-0
Millwall v Rotherham	-	-	0-1	-	-	-
Preston v Derby	-	-	-	1-2	0-1	0-1
Reading v Aston Villa	1-2	-	-	-	1-2	2-1
Sheffield United v Bolton	-	-	-	-	2-0	0-1
West Brom v Middlesbrough	-	-	-	-	0-0	-
Wigan v QPR	2-2	0-0	-	-	0-1	-
League One						
Accrington v Blackpool	-	-	-	-	2-1	-
Barnsley v Scunthorpe	-	-	1-2	0-0	-	-
Burton v Oxford	4-0	0-2	2-0	-	-	-
Coventry v Gillingham	-	2-1	1-0	4-1	2-1	-
Fleetwood Town v Charlton	-	-	-	-	2-2	1-3
Peterborough v Plymouth	-	-	-	-	-	2-1
Portsmouth v Doncaster	0-1	-	-	-	1-2	2-2
Shrewsbury v Luton	-	-	2-0	-	-	-
Southend v Bristol Rovers	0-0	1-1	-	-	1-1	0-0
Sunderland v AFC Wimbledon	-	-	-	-	-	-
Walsall v Rochdale	-	-	3-2	0-3	0-2	0-3
Wycombe v Bradford	0-3	-	-	-	-	-
League Two						
Bury v Crawley Town	0-2	-	-	-	-	-
Cheltenham v Cambridge U	-	-	3-1	-	0-1	0-0
Crewe v Carlisle	1-0	2-1	-	-	1-1	0-5
Exeter v MK Dons	-	-	-	-	-	-
Grimsby v Newport County	3-0	-	-	-	1-0	1-2
Mansfield v Macclesfield	3-1	-	-	-	-	-
Northampton v Colchester	-	-	-	-	-	-
Notts County v Lincoln	-	-	-	-	-	4-1
Oldham v Morecambe	-	-	-	-	-	-
Port Vale v Tranmere	-	3-2	-	-	-	-
Stevenage v Yeovil	0-2	-	-	0-0	2-2	4-1
Swindon v Forest Green	-	-	-	-	-	1-0
National League						
Aldershot v Solihull Moors	-	-	-	-	2-0	1-0
Barrow v Leyton Orient	-	-	-	-	-	2-2
Boreham Wood v Wrexham	-	-	-	0-1	0-1	0-1
Braintree v Chesterfield	-	-	-	-	-	-
Dover v Gateshead	-	-	1-0	4-0	2-0	3-2
Eastleigh v Barnet	-	-	1-2	-	-	-
Ebbsfleet v Hartlepool	-	-	-	-	-	3-0
Fylde v Havant & W	-	-	-	-	-	-
Harrogate T v Bromley	-	-	-	-	-	-
Maidenhead v Dag & Red	-	-	-	-	-	1-1
Maidstone v Halifax	-	-	-	-	-	0-0
Salford City v Sutton Utd	-	-	-	-	-	-

Results cover matches from Premier League to National League and Scottish Premiership to Scottish League Two

Ladbrokes Premiership

	2012-13	2013-14	2014-15	2015-16	2016-17	2017-18
Hamilton v Dundee	-	0-3/1-1	2-1	1-1/2-1	0-1/4-0	3-0/1-2
Hibernian v Aberdeen	0-1/0-0	0-2/0-2	-	-	-	0-1/2-0
Kilmarnock v Hearts	1-0/0-1	2-0/4-2	-	2-2	2-0/0-0	0-1/1-0
Motherwell v Livingston	-	-	-	-	-	-
Rangers v St Mirren	-	-	-	3-1/1-0	-	-
St Johnstone v Celtic	2-1/1-1	0-1/3-3	0-3/1-2/0-0	0-3/2-1	2-4/2-5	0-4

Ladbrokes Championship

	2012-13	2013-14	2014-15	2015-16	2016-17	2017-18
Alloa v Ayr	1-0/2-2	-	-	-	-	1-2/2-1
Dundee United v Morton	-	-	-	-	2-1/1-1	2-1/0-3
Dunfermline v Ross County	-	-	-	-	-	-
Falkirk v Queen of Sth	-	2-1/1-0	1-1/1-1	0-0/3-1	2-2/2-2	1-4/3-2
Inverness CT v Partick	-	1-2/1-0	0-4	0-0/0-0	0-0	-

Ladbrokes League One

	2012-13	2013-14	2014-15	2015-16	2016-17	2017-18
Airdrieonians v Dumbarton	4-1/1-2	-	-	-	-	-
East Fife v Arbroath	2-1/0-1	2-1/1-0	1-5/2-0	0-1/2-1	-	3-1/0-5
Montrose v Brechin	-	-	-	-	-	-
Raith v Forfar	-	-	-	-	-	3-1/2-1
Stranraer v Stenhousemuir	1-1/1-1	1-0/1-1	0-2/3-2	1-2/3-1	3-1/3-0	-

Ladbrokes League Two

	2012-13	2013-14	2014-15	2015-16	2016-17	2017-18
Berwick v Annan	3-1/0-2	4-2/1-4	2-0/2-2	0-2/3-2	2-0/4-1	1-5/0-2
Cowdenbeath v Peterhead	-	-	-	2-2/2-3	-	0-4/0-2
Edinburgh City v Albion	-	-	-	-	-	-
Elgin v Queens Park	0-4/3-5	3-2/1-1	1-4/1-2	0-0/1-1	-	-
Stirling v Clyde	0-1/2-0	1-1/4-1	-	0-1/1-2	1-1/3-0	2-3/2-1

Wednesday February 6, 2019

Ladbrokes Premiership

	2012-13	2013-14	2014-15	2015-16	2016-17	2017-18
Aberdeen v Rangers	-	-	-	-	2-1/0-3	1-2/1-1
Celtic v Hibernian	2-2/3-0	1-0	-	-	-	2-2/1-0
Dundee v Kilmarnock	0-0/2-3	-	1-1/1-0	1-2/1-1	1-1/1-1	0-0
Hamilton v St Johnstone	-	-	1-0/1-1	2-4	1-1/1-0	0-1/1-2
Hearts v Livingston	-	-	5-0/1-0	-	-	-
St Mirren v Motherwell	2-1	0-1/3-2	0-1/2-1	-	-	-

Saturday February 9, 2019

Premier League

	2012-13	2013-14	2014-15	2015-16	2016-17	2017-18
Brighton v Burnley	1-0	2-0	-	2-2	-	0-0
Crystal Palace v West Ham	-	1-0	1-3	1-3	0-1	2-2
Fulham v Man United	0-1	1-3	-	-	-	-
Huddersfield v Arsenal	-	-	-	-	-	0-1
Liverpool v Bournemouth	-	-	-	1-0	2-2	3-0
Man City v Chelsea	2-0	0-1	1-1	3-0	1-3	1-0
Southampton v Cardiff	-	0-1	-	-	-	-
Tottenham v Leicester	-	-	4-3	0-1	1-1	5-4
Watford v Everton	-	-	-	1-1	3-2	1-0
Wolves v Newcastle	-	-	-	-	0-1	-

Championship

	2012-13	2013-14	2014-15	2015-16	2016-17	2017-18
Aston Villa v Sheffield United	-	-	-	-	-	2-2
Blackburn v Bristol City	2-0	-	-	2-2	1-1	-
Bolton v Preston	-	-	-	1-2	-	1-3
Derby v Hull	1-2	-	-	4-0	-	5-0
Middlesbrough v Leeds	1-0	0-0	0-1	3-0	-	3-0
Nottm Forest v Brentford	-	-	1-3	0-3	2-3	0-1
QPR v Birmingham	-	1-0	-	2-0	1-1	3-1
Rotherham v Wigan	-	-	1-2	-	3-2	1-3
Sheffield Weds v Reading	-	5-2	1-0	1-1	0-2	3-0
Stoke v West Brom	0-0	0-0	2-0	0-1	1-1	3-1
Swansea v Millwall	-	-	-	-	-	-

Results cover matches from Premier League to National League and Scottish Premiership to Scottish League Two

	2012-13	2013-14	2014-15	2015-16	2016-17	2017-18
League One						
AFC Wimbledon v Burton	1-1	3-1	3-0	-	-	-
Blackpool v Walsall	-	-	-	0-4	-	2-2
Bradford v Fleetwood Town	1-0	-	2-2	2-1	2-1	0-3
Bristol Rovers v Shrewsbury	-	-	-	-	2-0	1-2
Charlton v Southend	-	-	-	-	2-1	2-1
Doncaster v Peterborough	-	-	0-2	1-2	-	0-0
Gillingham v Barnsley	-	-	0-1	2-1	-	-
Luton v Wycombe	-	-	2-3	0-2	4-1	2-3
Oxford v Sunderland	-	-	-	-	-	-
Plymouth v Portsmouth	-	1-1	3-0	1-2	2-2	0-0
Rochdale v Coventry	-	-	1-0	0-0	2-0	-
Scunthorpe v Accrington	-	0-2	-	-	-	-
League Two						
Cambridge U v Port Vale	-	-	-	-	-	5-0
Carlisle v Exeter	-	-	1-3	1-0	3-2	0-1
Colchester v Cheltenham	-	-	-	-	2-0	1-4
Crawley Town v Oldham	1-1	1-0	2-0	-	-	-
Forest Green v Notts County	-	-	-	-	-	1-2
Lincoln v Northampton	-	-	-	-	-	-
Macclesfield v Crewe	-	-	-	-	-	-
MK Dons v Swindon	2-0	1-1	2-1	-	3-2	-
Morecambe v Bury	-	0-0	1-0	-	-	-
Newport County v Mansfield	2-0	1-1	0-1	1-0	2-3	1-1
Tranmere v Stevenage	3-1	0-0	2-2	-	-	-
Yeovil v Grimsby	-	-	-	-	0-0	3-0
National League						
Aldershot v Eastleigh	-	-	0-2	1-2	0-1	0-2
Barnet v Sutton Utd	-	-	-	-	-	-
Barrow v Bromley	-	-	-	1-1	1-1	0-3
Braintree v Salford City	-	-	-	-	-	-
Chesterfield v Halifax	-	-	-	-	-	-
Dover v Harrogate T	-	-	-	-	-	-
Ebbsfleet v Solihull Moors	-	-	-	-	-	1-0
Gateshead v Havant & W	-	-	-	-	-	-
Hartlepool v Leyton Orient	2-1	-	-	3-1	1-3	1-0
Maidenhead v Boreham Wood	-	0-1	0-1	-	-	2-1
Maidstone v Fylde	-	-	-	-	-	1-0
Wrexham v Dag & Red	-	-	-	-	0-1	1-2
Ladbrokes League One						
Arbroath v Stranraer	2-1/1-0	1-2/4-2	-	-	-	1-2/2-3
Brechin v East Fife	2-1/6-0	2-0/3-0	-	-	0-1/2-1	-
Dumbarton v Raith	4-2/1-2	2-4/3-3	2-1/2-2	3-3/2-3	0-0/4-0	-
Forfar v Airdrieonians	-	3-3/1-1	1-1/2-0	2-3/0-2	-	2-1/0-1
Stenhousemuir v Montrose	-	-	-	-	-	0-1/0-2
Ladbrokes League Two						
Albion v Elgin	-	0-0/5-2	3-0/0-3	-	-	-
Annan v Clyde	1-3/0-1	1-2/0-1	2-1/0-1	2-3/3-3	3-2/1-0	0-0/1-1
Berwick v Stirling	4-1/1-0	1-1/4-0	-	1-2/1-0	3-2/0-1	1-0/0-1
Peterhead v Edinburgh City	-	-	-	-	-	3-0/2-1
Queens Park v Cowdenbeath	-	-	-	-	-	-
Sunday February 10, 2019						
Championship						
Norwich v Ipswich	-	-	2-0	-	1-1	1-1
Tuesday February 12, 2019						
Championship						
Birmingham v Bolton	2-1	1-2	0-1	1-0	-	0-0
Hull v Rotherham	-	-	-	5-1	-	-
Millwall v Sheffield Weds	1-2	1-1	1-3	-	-	2-1
West Brom v Nottm Forest	-	-	-	-	-	-

Results cover matches from Premier League to National League and Scottish Premiership to Scottish League Two

Wednesday February 13, 2019

Championship

	2012-13	2013-14	2014-15	2015-16	2016-17	2017-18
Brentford v Aston Villa	-	-	-	-	3-0	2-1
Bristol City v QPR	-	-	-	1-1	2-1	2-0
Ipswich v Derby	1-2	2-1	0-1	0-1	0-3	1-2
Leeds v Swansea	-	-	-	-	-	-
Preston v Norwich	-	-	-	-	1-3	0-0
Reading v Blackburn	-	0-1	0-0	1-0	3-1	-
Sheffield United v Middlesbrough	-	-	-	-	-	2-1
Wigan v Stoke	2-2	-	-	-	-	-

Saturday February 16, 2019

Championship

	2012-13	2013-14	2014-15	2015-16	2016-17	2017-18
Aston Villa v West Brom	1-1	4-3	2-1	0-1	-	-
Blackburn v Middlesbrough	1-2	1-0	0-0	2-1	-	-
Bolton v Norwich	-	-	1-2	-	-	2-1
Bristol City v Birmingham	0-1	-	-	0-0	0-1	3-1
Derby v Wigan	-	0-1	1-2	-	0-0	-
Hull v Millwall	4-1	-	-	-	-	1-2
Ipswich v Stoke	-	-	-	-	-	-
Preston v Nottm Forest	-	-	-	1-0	1-1	1-1
QPR v Leeds	-	1-1	-	1-0	3-0	1-3
Rotherham v Sheffield Weds	-	-	2-3	1-2	0-2	-
Sheffield United v Reading	-	-	-	-	-	2-1
Swansea v Brentford	-	-	-	-	-	-

League One

	2012-13	2013-14	2014-15	2015-16	2016-17	2017-18
Barnsley v Wycombe	-	-	-	-	-	-
Bradford v Plymouth	1-0	-	-	-	-	0-1
Charlton v Blackpool	2-1	0-0	2-2	-	-	1-1
Coventry v Walsall	5-1	2-1	0-0	1-1	1-0	-
Doncaster v Bristol Rovers	-	-	-	-	-	1-3
Fleetwood Town v Luton	-	-	-	-	-	-
Gillingham v Scunthorpe	-	-	0-3	2-1	3-2	0-0
Oxford v Peterborough	-	-	-	-	2-1	2-1
Rochdale v AFC Wimbledon	0-1	1-2	-	-	1-1	1-1
Shrewsbury v Burton	-	-	1-0	0-1	-	-
Southend v Portsmouth	-	2-1	2-0	-	-	3-1
Sunderland v Accrington	-	-	-	-	-	-

League Two

	2012-13	2013-14	2014-15	2015-16	2016-17	2017-18
Cambridge U v Tranmere	-	-	1-2	-	-	-
Carlisle v MK Dons	1-1	3-0	-	-	-	-
Exeter v Bury	-	2-2	2-1	-	-	-
Forest Green v Yeovil	-	-	-	-	-	4-3
Grimsby v Cheltenham	-	-	-	0-1	0-1	1-1
Lincoln v Stevenage	-	-	-	-	-	3-0
Macclesfield v Colchester	-	-	-	-	-	-
Newport County v Swindon	-	-	-	-	-	2-1
Northampton v Crawley Town	-	-	-	2-1	-	-
Notts County v Mansfield	-	-	-	0-2	0-0	1-1
Oldham v Crewe	1-2	1-1	1-2	1-0	-	-
Port Vale v Morecambe	0-1	-	-	-	-	0-0

National League

	2012-13	2013-14	2014-15	2015-16	2016-17	2017-18
Boreham Wood v Hartlepool	-	-	-	-	-	0-0
Bromley v Maidstone	-	-	-	-	2-0	2-2
Dag & Red v Gateshead	-	-	-	-	0-5	3-1
Eastleigh v Braintree	-	-	1-0	0-2	0-2	-
Fylde v Chesterfield	-	-	-	-	-	-
Halifax v Aldershot	-	4-0	1-0	0-2	-	0-2

Results cover matches from Premier League to National League and Scottish Premiership to Scottish League Two

	2012-13	2013-14	2014-15	2015-16	2016-17	2017-18
Harrogate T v Ebbsfleet	-	-	-	-	-	-
Havant & W v Wrexham	-	-	-	-	-	-
Leyton Orient v Maidenhead	-	-	-	-	-	0-1
Salford City v Dover	-	-	-	-	-	-
Solihull Moors v Barnet	-	-	-	-	-	-
Sutton Utd v Barrow	-	-	-	-	0-0	3-2

Ladbrokes Premiership

	2012-13	2013-14	2014-15	2015-16	2016-17	2017-18
Aberdeen v St Mirren	0-0/0-0	2-0	2-2/3-0	-	-	-
Hibernian v Hamilton	-	-	-	-	-	1-3/3-1
Kilmarnock v Celtic	1-3	2-5/0-3	0-2	2-2/0-1	0-1	0-2/1-0
Livingston v Dundee	-	2-1/0-2	-	-	-	-
Motherwell v Hearts	0-0	2-1/4-1	-	2-2/1-0	1-3/0-3	2-1
Rangers v St Johnstone	-	-	-	-	1-1/3-2	1-3

Ladbrokes Championship

	2012-13	2013-14	2014-15	2015-16	2016-17	2017-18
Alloa v Partick	-	-	-	-	-	-
Dunfermline v Inverness CT	-	-	-	-	-	5-1/1-0
Morton v Ayr	-	-	0-1/2-1	-	2-1/1-1	-
Queen of Sth v Dundee United	-	-	-	-	1-4/4-2	1-3/3-0
Ross County v Falkirk	-	-	-	-	-	-

Ladbrokes League One

	2012-13	2013-14	2014-15	2015-16	2016-17	2017-18
Airdrieonians v Brechin	-	3-1/2-1	4-0/1-1	1-0/0-2	1-0/3-1	-
East Fife v Stenhousemuir	3-2/1-2	1-0/1-2	-	-	0-1/1-0	-
Montrose v Forfar	-	-	-	-	1-1/1-0	-
Raith v Arbroath	-	-	-	-	-	2-0/2-2
Stranraer v Dumbarton	-	-	-	-	-	-

Ladbrokes League Two

	2012-13	2013-14	2014-15	2015-16	2016-17	2017-18
Clyde v Albion	-	2-2/4-0	0-1/2-3	-	-	-
Cowdenbeath v Annan	-	-	-	-	2-2/0-1	1-1/0-2
Edinburgh City v Berwick	-	-	-	-	1-2/2-2	1-0/3-0
Elgin v Stirling	3-1/1-2	4-0/2-3	-	1-0/2-1	2-3/2-2	0-2/3-0
Peterhead v Queens Park	1-0/0-2	2-1/1-0	-	-	2-0/4-0	-

Saturday February 23, 2019

Premier League

	2012-13	2013-14	2014-15	2015-16	2016-17	2017-18
Arsenal v Southampton	6-1	2-0	1-0	0-0	2-1	3-2
Bournemouth v Wolves	-	-	2-1	-	-	-
Burnley v Tottenham	-	-	0-0	-	0-2	0-3
Cardiff v Watford	2-1	-	2-4	-	-	-
Chelsea v Brighton	-	-	-	-	-	2-0
Everton v Man City	2-0	2-3	1-1	0-2	4-0	1-3
Leicester v Crystal Palace	1-2	-	0-1	1-0	3-1	0-3
Man United v Liverpool	2-1	0-3	3-0	3-1	1-1	2-1
Newcastle v Huddersfield	-	-	-	-	1-2	1-0
West Ham v Fulham	3-0	3-0	-	-	-	-

Championship

	2012-13	2013-14	2014-15	2015-16	2016-17	2017-18
Birmingham v Blackburn	1-1	2-4	2-2	0-0	1-0	-
Brentford v Hull	-	-	-	0-2	-	1-1
Leeds v Bolton	1-0	1-5	1-0	2-1	-	2-1
Middlesbrough v QPR	-	1-3	-	1-0	-	3-2
Millwall v Preston	-	-	-	-	-	1-1
Norwich v Bristol City	-	-	-	-	1-0	0-0
Nottm Forest v Derby	0-1	1-0	1-1	1-0	2-2	0-0
Reading v Rotherham	-	-	3-0	1-0	2-1	-
Sheffield Weds v Swansea	-	-	-	-	-	-
Stoke v Aston Villa	1-3	2-1	0-1	2-1	-	-
West Brom v Sheffield United	-	-	-	-	-	-
Wigan v Ipswich	-	2-0	1-2	-	2-3	-

Results cover matches from Premier League to National League and Scottish Premiership to Scottish League Two

	2012-13	2013-14	2014-15	2015-16	2016-17	2017-18
League One						
Accrington v Southend	1-1	1-1	0-1	-	-	-
AFC Wimbledon v Charlton	-	-	-	-	1-1	1-0
Blackpool v Oxford	-	-	-	-	-	3-1
Bristol Rovers v Sunderland	-	-	-	-	-	-
Burton v Fleetwood Town	0-1	2-4	-	2-1	-	-
Luton v Coventry	-	-	-	-	-	0-3
Peterborough v Shrewsbury	-	1-0	-	1-1	2-1	1-0
Plymouth v Rochdale	3-1	1-0	-	-	-	1-1
Portsmouth v Barnsley	-	-	-	-	-	-
Scunthorpe v Doncaster	2-3	-	1-2	2-0	-	1-1
Walsall v Bradford	-	0-2	0-0	2-1	1-1	3-3
Wycombe v Gillingham	0-1	-	-	-	-	-
League Two						
Bury v Oldham	0-1	-	-	1-1	0-1	2-2
Cheltenham v Port Vale	1-1	-	-	-	-	5-1
Colchester v Carlisle	2-0	1-1	-	-	4-1	0-1
Crawley Town v Macclesfield	-	-	-	-	-	-
Crewe v Exeter	-	-	-	-	2-0	1-2
Mansfield v Forest Green	1-0	-	-	-	-	2-0
MK Dons v Newport County	-	-	-	-	-	-
Morecambe v Lincoln	-	-	-	-	-	0-0
Stevenage v Northampton	-	-	2-1	2-3	-	-
Swindon v Grimsby	-	-	-	-	-	0-1
Tranmere v Notts County	1-1	3-2	-	-	-	-
Yeovil v Cambridge U	-	-	-	2-3	1-1	2-0
National League						
Barrow v Ebbsfleet	1-1	-	-	-	-	0-1
Boreham Wood v Solihull Moors	-	-	-	-	0-0	4-1
Braintree v Aldershot	-	1-0	1-1	1-2	2-0	-
Chesterfield v Harrogate T	-	-	-	-	-	-
Dag & Red v Sutton Utd	-	-	-	-	2-2	1-2
Gateshead v Wrexham	0-1	0-3	3-1	2-1	2-2	0-0
Halifax v Havant & W	-	-	-	-	-	-
Hartlepool v Bromley	-	-	-	-	-	2-1
Leyton Orient v Fylde	-	-	-	-	-	1-2
Maidenhead v Dover	-	1-2	-	-	-	3-2
Maidstone v Barnet	-	-	-	-	-	-
Salford City v Eastleigh	-	-	-	-	-	-
Ladbrokes Premiership						
Celtic v Motherwell	1-0	2-0/3-0	1-1/4-0	1-2/7-0	2-0/2-0	5-1
Dundee v Hibernian	3-1	-	-	-	-	1-1/0-1
Hamilton v Rangers	-	-	-	-	1-2	1-4/3-5
Hearts v St Mirren	1-0/3-0	0-2/2-1	-	-	-	-
Livingston v Kilmarnock	-	-	-	-	-	-
St Johnstone v Aberdeen	1-2/3-1	0-2	1-0/1-1	3-4/3-0	0-0/1-2	0-3
Ladbrokes Championship						
Ayr v Dunfermline	-	2-4/1-1	0-1/0-2	1-2/0-2	0-0/0-2	-
Falkirk v Dundee United	-	-	-	-	3-1/3-0	0-0/6-1
Inverness CT v Morton	-	-	-	-	-	1-1/0-2
Partick v Ross County	-	3-3/2-3	4-0/1-3	1-0	1-1/2-1	2-0/1-1
Queen of Sth v Alloa	1-0/0-0	0-0/3-1	2-0/1-0	3-1/1-0	-	-
Ladbrokes League One						
Arbroath v Airdrieonians	-	3-2/0-1	-	-	-	7-1/2-0
Brechin v Stranraer	3-0/2-2	1-1/1-3	1-2/1-3	2-0/1-0	2-0/0-0	-
East Fife v Dumbarton	-	-	-	-	-	-
Forfar v Stenhousemuir	3-2/3-3	1-2/3-0	3-0/1-0	4-1/0-1	-	-
Raith v Montrose	-	-	-	-	-	-

Results cover matches from Premier League to National League and Scottish Premiership to Scottish League Two

	2012-13	2013-14	2014-15	2015-16	2016-17	2017-18
Ladbrokes League Two						
Annan v Albion	-	1-1/2-0	2-1/1-3	-	-	-
Berwick v Elgin	0-0/2-1	2-3/2-3	1-1/0-2	2-3/2-0	2-4/0-1	3-2/2-2
Edinburgh City v Cowdenbeath	-	-	-	-	1-1/1-1	0-0/1-1
Queens Park v Clyde	1-0/4-1	1-1/1-3	1-2/1-1	1-1/2-1	-	-
Stirling v Peterhead	1-0/0-1	2-0/1-2	2-3/2-1	-	-	0-1/0-1
Tuesday February 26, 2019						
Premier League						
Arsenal v Bournemouth	-	-	-	2-0	3-1	3-0
Cardiff v Everton	-	0-0	-	-	-	-
Crystal Palace v Man United	-	0-2	1-2	0-0	1-2	2-3
Huddersfield v Wolves	2-1	-	1-4	1-0	1-0	-
Leicester v Brighton	1-0	1-4	-	-	-	2-0
Ladbrokes Championship						
Alloa v Falkirk	-	0-0/3-0	2-3/1-3	1-1/0-1	-	-
Dundee United v Inverness CT	4-4	0-1/2-1	1-1	1-1/0-2	-	0-2/1-1
Dunfermline v Partick	0-1/0-4	-	-	-	-	-
Morton v Queen of Sth	-	0-2/1-1	-	2-0/3-2	1-0/1-0	1-2/0-1
Ross County v Ayr	-	-	-	-	-	-
Wednesday February 27, 2019						
Premier League						
Chelsea v Tottenham	2-2	4-0	3-0	2-2	2-1	1-3
Liverpool v Watford	-	-	-	2-0	6-1	5-0
Man City v West Ham	2-1	2-0	2-0	1-2	3-1	2-1
Newcastle v Burnley	-	-	3-3	-	-	1-1
Southampton v Fulham	2-2	2-0	-	-	-	-
Ladbrokes Premiership						
Aberdeen v Hamilton	-	-	3-0	1-0/3-0	2-1	2-0/3-0
Hearts v Celtic	0-4	1-3/0-2	-	2-2/1-3	1-2/0-5	4-0/1-3
Kilmarnock v Motherwell	1-2/2-0	0-2	2-0/1-2	0-1	1-2/1-2	1-0
Rangers v Dundee	-	-	-	-	1-0	4-1/4-0
St Johnstone v Hibernian	0-1	1-2/2-0	-	-	-	1-1/1-1
St Mirren v Livingston	-	-	-	1-1/1-4	-	3-1/0-0
Saturday March 2, 2019						
Premier League						
Bournemouth v Man City	-	-	-	0-4	0-2	1-2
Brighton v Huddersfield	4-1	0-0	0-0	2-1	1-0	1-1
Burnley v Crystal Palace	1-0	-	2-3	-	3-2	1-0
Everton v Liverpool	2-2	3-3	0-0	1-1	0-1	0-0
Fulham v Chelsea	0-3	1-3	-	-	-	-
Man United v Southampton	2-1	1-1	0-1	0-1	2-0	0-0
Tottenham v Arsenal	2-1	0-1	2-1	2-2	2-0	1-0
Watford v Leicester	2-1	0-3	-	0-1	2-1	2-1
West Ham v Newcastle	0-0	1-3	1-0	2-0	-	2-3
Wolves v Cardiff	1-2	-	1-0	1-3	3-1	1-2
Championship						
Aston Villa v Derby	-	-	-	-	1-0	1-1
Brentford v QPR	-	-	-	1-0	3-1	2-1
Hull v Birmingham	5-2	-	-	2-0	-	6-1
Ipswich v Reading	-	2-0	0-1	2-1	2-2	2-0
Leeds v West Brom	-	-	-	-	-	-
Millwall v Norwich	-	-	1-4	-	-	4-0
Preston v Bristol City	-	1-0	1-1	1-1	5-0	2-1
Rotherham v Blackburn	-	-	2-0	0-1	1-1	1-1
Sheffield Weds v Sheffield United	-	-	-	-	-	2-4
Stoke v Nottm Forest	-	-	-	-	-	-
Swansea v Bolton	-	-	-	-	-	-
Wigan v Middlesbrough	-	2-2	1-1	-	-	-

Results cover matches from Premier League to National League and Scottish Premiership to Scottish League Two

	2012-13	2013-14	2014-15	2015-16	2016-17	2017-18
League One						
Accrington v Coventry	-	-	-	-	-	1-0
Bristol Rovers v Blackpool	-	-	-	-	-	3-1
Burton v Walsall	-	-	-	0-0	-	-
Doncaster v Charlton	-	3-0	-	-	-	1-1
Fleetwood Town v Gillingham	2-2	-	1-0	2-1	2-1	0-2
Luton v Rochdale	-	-	-	-	-	-
Oxford v Scunthorpe	-	0-2	-	-	2-1	1-1
Peterborough v Wycombe	-	-	-	-	-	-
Portsmouth v Bradford	-	-	-	-	-	0-1
Shrewsbury v AFC Wimbledon	-	-	2-0	-	2-1	1-0
Southend v Barnsley	-	-	-	2-1	-	-
Sunderland v Plymouth	-	-	-	-	-	-
League Two						
Bury v Macclesfield	-	-	-	-	-	-
Crewe v Northampton	-	-	-	-	-	-
Exeter v Tranmere	-	-	1-2	-	-	-
Forest Green v Lincoln	3-0	4-1	3-3	3-1	2-3	0-1
Grimsby v Cambridge U	0-1	0-1	-	-	2-1	0-0
Mansfield v Cheltenham	-	0-2	1-1	-	1-1	3-2
MK Dons v Crawley Town	0-0	0-2	2-0	-	-	-
Newport County v Carlisle	-	-	2-1	1-0	2-0	3-3
Notts County v Port Vale	-	4-2	0-1	-	-	1-0
Oldham v Stevenage	0-1	1-0	-	-	-	-
Swindon v Colchester	0-1	0-0	2-2	1-2	-	2-3
Yeovil v Morecambe	-	-	-	2-4	0-1	2-2
National League						
Aldershot v Gateshead	-	1-2	1-2	1-2	3-0	1-0
Barnet v Barrow	-	-	-	-	-	-
Bromley v Boreham Wood	-	2-1	2-1	1-2	1-0	3-2
Dover v Braintree	-	-	1-0	0-0	6-1	-
Eastleigh v Halifax	-	-	4-1	2-1	-	0-0
Ebbsfleet v Salford City	-	-	-	-	-	-
Fylde v Maidenhead	-	-	-	-	-	1-4
Harrogate T v Dag & Red	-	-	-	-	-	-
Havant & W v Leyton Orient	-	-	-	-	-	-
Solihull Moors v Maidstone	-	-	-	-	2-0	1-0
Sutton Utd v Hartlepool	-	-	-	-	-	1-1
Wrexham v Chesterfield	-	-	-	-	-	-
Ladbrokes Championship						
Ayr v Partick	-	-	-	-	-	-
Dundee United v Ross County	0-0/1-1	1-0	2-1/1-2	1-0	-	-
Dunfermline v Queen of Sth	-	-	-	-	0-1/1-1	2-5/3-1
Inverness CT v Alloa	-	-	-	-	-	-
Morton v Falkirk	1-2/2-0	0-2/1-1	-	1-1/0-1	1-1/2-2	0-1/0-1
Ladbrokes League One						
Airdrieonians v Montrose	-	-	-	-	-	-
Dumbarton v Arbroath	-	-	-	-	-	-
Forfar v East Fife	3-2/3-2	2-0/1-2	-	-	-	2-0/2-0
Stenhousemuir v Brechin	3-1/3-3	3-2/4-2	0-2/2-2	2-2/0-0	1-3/1-1	-
Stranraer v Raith	-	-	-	-	-	1-0/0-3
Ladbrokes League Two						
Albion v Berwick	-	0-2/0-3	2-1/2-0	-	-	-
Annan v Queens Park	2-3/2-0	3-2/1-1	0-1/2-0	3-1/1-0	-	-
Clyde v Edinburgh City	-	-	-	-	0-0/3-1	2-3/3-2
Cowdenbeath v Stirling	-	-	-	-	0-2/0-2	0-3/1-2
Peterhead v Elgin	1-1/0-1	2-2/2-1	-	-	-	3-0/7-0

Results cover matches from Premier League to National League and Scottish Premiership to Scottish League Two

Tuesday March 5, 2019

League Two

	2012-13	2013-14	2014-15	2015-16	2016-17	2017-18
Cheltenham v Bury	-	2-1	1-2	-	-	-

Friday March 8, 2019

League Two

	2012-13	2013-14	2014-15	2015-16	2016-17	2017-18
Lincoln v Yeovil	-	-	-	-	-	1-1
Tranmere v Crewe	2-1	1-0	-	-	-	-

Saturday March 9, 2019

Premier League

	2012-13	2013-14	2014-15	2015-16	2016-17	2017-18
Arsenal v Man United	1-1	0-0	1-2	3-0	2-0	1-3
Cardiff v West Ham	-	0-2	-	-	-	-
Chelsea v Wolves	-	-	-	-	-	-
Crystal Palace v Brighton	3-0	-	-	-	-	3-2
Huddersfield v Bournemouth	-	5-1	0-4	-	-	4-1
Leicester v Fulham	-	-	-	-	-	-
Liverpool v Burnley	-	-	2-0	-	2-1	1-1
Man City v Watford	-	-	-	2-0	2-0	3-1
Newcastle v Everton	1-2	0-3	3-2	0-1	-	0-1
Southampton v Tottenham	1-2	2-3	2-2	0-2	1-4	1-1

Championship

	2012-13	2013-14	2014-15	2015-16	2016-17	2017-18
Blackburn v Preston	-	-	-	1-2	2-2	-
Bolton v Millwall	1-1	3-1	2-0	-	2-0	0-2
Bristol City v Leeds	2-3	-	-	2-2	1-0	0-3
Derby v Sheffield Weds	2-2	3-0	3-2	1-1	2-0	2-0
Middlesbrough v Brentford	-	-	4-0	3-1	-	2-2
Norwich v Swansea	2-2	1-1	-	1-0	-	-
Nottm Forest v Hull	1-2	-	-	0-1	-	0-2
QPR v Stoke	0-2	-	2-2	-	-	-
Reading v Wigan	0-3	1-2	0-1	-	1-0	-
Sheffield United v Rotherham	-	1-0	-	-	-	-
West Brom v Ipswich	-	-	-	-	-	-

League One

	2012-13	2013-14	2014-15	2015-16	2016-17	2017-18
AFC Wimbledon v Doncaster	-	-	-	-	-	2-0
Barnsley v Accrington	-	-	-	-	-	-
Blackpool v Southend	-	-	-	2-0	-	1-1
Bradford v Peterborough	-	1-0	0-1	0-2	1-0	1-3
Charlton v Portsmouth	-	-	-	-	-	0-1
Coventry v Burton	-	-	-	0-2	-	-
Gillingham v Oxford	0-1	-	-	-	0-1	1-1
Plymouth v Luton	-	-	0-1	0-1	0-3	-
Rochdale v Shrewsbury	-	-	-	3-2	2-1	3-1
Scunthorpe v Bristol Rovers	-	1-1	-	-	3-1	1-0
Walsall v Fleetwood Town	-	-	1-0	3-1	0-1	4-2
Wycombe v Sunderland	-	-	-	-	-	-

League Two

	2012-13	2013-14	2014-15	2015-16	2016-17	2017-18
Cambridge U v Oldham	-	-	-	-	-	-
Carlisle v Swindon	2-2	1-0	-	-	-	1-2
Cheltenham v Notts County	-	-	-	-	2-3	1-1
Colchester v Newport County	-	-	-	-	0-0	2-0
Crawley Town v Grimsby	-	-	-	-	3-2	3-0
Macclesfield v MK Dons	-	-	-	-	-	-
Morecambe v Forest Green	-	-	-	-	-	1-1
Northampton v Exeter	3-0	1-2	1-0	3-0	-	-
Port Vale v Mansfield	-	-	-	-	-	0-4
Stevenage v Bury	2-2	-	0-0	-	-	-

National League

	2012-13	2013-14	2014-15	2015-16	2016-17	2017-18
Barrow v Aldershot	-	-	-	1-3	1-0	3-1
Boreham Wood v Fylde	-	-	-	-	-	1-0
Braintree v Harrogate T	-	-	-	-	-	-

Results cover matches from Premier League to National League and Scottish Premiership to Scottish League Two

	2012-13	2013-14	2014-15	2015-16	2016-17	2017-18
Chesterfield v Eastleigh	-	-	-	-	-	-
Dag & Red v Bromley	-	-	-	-	2-1	5-1
Gateshead v Barnet	-	1-2	0-2	-	-	-
Halifax v Ebbsfleet	-	-	-	-	-	1-2
Hartlepool v Dover	-	-	-	-	-	0-1
Leyton Orient v Wrexham	-	-	-	-	-	1-0
Maidenhead v Sutton Utd	-	3-2	2-1	1-1	-	2-1
Maidstone v Havant & W	-	-	-	1-0	-	-
Salford City v Solihull Moors	-	-	-	-	-	-

Ladbrokes Premiership

	2012-13	2013-14	2014-15	2015-16	2016-17	2017-18
Celtic v Aberdeen	1-0/4-3	3-1/5-2	2-1/4-0	3-1/3-2	4-1/1-0	3-0/0-1
Dundee v Hearts	1-0/1-0	-	-	1-2/0-1	3-2	2-1/1-1
Hibernian v Rangers	-	-	4-0/0-2	2-1/3-2	-	1-2/5-5
Livingston v St Johnstone	-	-	-	-	-	-
Motherwell v Hamilton	-	-	0-4/4-0	3-3	4-2/0-0	1-3/3-0
St Mirren v Kilmarnock	1-1	1-1/2-0	1-2/4-1	-	-	-

Ladbrokes Championship

	2012-13	2013-14	2014-15	2015-16	2016-17	2017-18
Alloa v Dunfermline	-	-	-	-	-	-
Falkirk v Ayr	-	-	-	-	2-0/1-1	-
Partick v Dundee United	-	0-0/1-1	2-2	3-0/1-0	-	-
Queen of Sth v Inverness CT	-	-	-	-	-	0-0/0-2
Ross County v Morton	-	-	-	-	-	-

Ladbrokes League One

	2012-13	2013-14	2014-15	2015-16	2016-17	2017-18
Arbroath v Stenhousemuir	2-2/0-0	3-4/2-1	-	-	-	-
Brechin v Forfar	4-1/3-4	2-1/1-5	3-3/2-3	0-2/4-0	-	-
East Fife v Stranraer	0-1/1-1	1-2/1-1	-	-	2-0/0-0	1-1/2-3
Montrose v Dumbarton	-	-	-	-	-	-
Raith v Airdrieonians	2-0/2-0	-	-	-	-	2-0/2-1

Ladbrokes League Two

	2012-13	2013-14	2014-15	2015-16	2016-17	2017-18
Berwick v Cowdenbeath	-	-	-	-	1-1/1-3	1-0/1-0
Edinburgh City v Queens Park	-	-	-	-	-	-
Elgin v Clyde	2-1/4-2	1-0/3-1	1-0/2-0	1-1/1-0	0-2/4-1	3-2/2-1
Peterhead v Annan	2-0/2-0	2-2/3-1	-	-	-	1-0/1-0
Stirling v Albion	-	2-1/2-0	-	-	-	-

Sunday March 10, 2019

Championship

	2012-13	2013-14	2014-15	2015-16	2016-17	2017-18
Birmingham v Aston Villa	-	-	-	-	1-1	0-0

Tuesday March 12, 2019

Championship

	2012-13	2013-14	2014-15	2015-16	2016-17	2017-18
Blackburn v Wigan	-	4-3	3-1	-	1-0	2-2
Bolton v Sheffield Weds	0-1	1-1	0-0	0-0	-	2-1
Bristol City v Ipswich	2-1	-	-	2-1	2-0	1-0
Reading v Leeds	-	1-0	0-2	0-0	1-0	2-2
Sheffield United v Brentford	2-2	0-0	-	-	-	1-0

League One

	2012-13	2013-14	2014-15	2015-16	2016-17	2017-18
AFC Wimbledon v Peterborough	-	-	-	-	0-0	2-2
Barnsley v Sunderland	-	-	-	-	-	3-0
Blackpool v Doncaster	-	1-1	-	0-2	4-2	1-2
Bradford v Luton	-	-	-	-	-	-
Charlton v Burton	-	-	-	-	-	-
Coventry v Fleetwood Town	-	-	1-1	1-2	0-1	-
Gillingham v Bristol Rovers	4-0	-	-	-	3-1	4-1
Plymouth v Shrewsbury	-	-	1-0	-	-	1-1
Rochdale v Oxford	2-0	3-0	-	-	0-4	0-0
Scunthorpe v Southend	-	2-2	-	1-0	4-0	3-1
Walsall v Portsmouth	2-0	-	-	-	-	0-1
Wycombe v Accrington	0-1	0-0	2-2	0-1	1-1	0-4

Results cover matches from Premier League to National League and Scottish Premiership to Scottish League Two

	2012-13	2013-14	2014-15	2015-16	2016-17	2017-18
League Two						
Cambridge U v Crewe	-	-	-	-	2-1	3-1
Carlisle v Notts County	0-4	2-1	-	3-0	1-2	1-1
Colchester v Forest Green	-	-	-	-	-	5-1
Crawley Town v Mansfield	-	-	-	0-1	2-2	2-0
Lincoln v Oldham	-	-	-	-	-	-
Macclesfield v Exeter	-	-	-	-	-	-
Morecambe v MK Dons	-	-	-	-	-	-
Northampton v Newport County	-	3-1	3-0	1-0	-	-
Port Vale v Yeovil	-	-	4-1	-	-	1-1
Stevenage v Swindon	0-4	2-0	-	-	-	0-1
Tranmere v Grimsby	-	-	-	1-0	-	-
National League						
Aldershot v Leyton Orient	-	-	-	-	-	2-2
Barnet v Halifax	-	0-4	3-0	-	-	-
Bromley v Chesterfield	-	-	-	-	-	-
Dover v Boreham Wood	-	0-0	-	2-1	1-4	0-1
Eastleigh v Maidstone	-	-	-	-	3-0	0-1
Ebbsfleet v Maidenhead	-	1-1	1-0	3-1	2-3	1-1
Fylde v Hartlepool	-	-	-	-	-	3-3
Harrogate T v Salford City	-	-	-	-	3-3	1-2
Havant & W v Dag & Red	-	-	-	-	-	-
Solihull Moors v Gateshead	-	-	-	-	0-2	1-1
Sutton Utd v Braintree	-	-	-	-	1-2	-
Wrexham v Barrow	3-0	-	-	4-1	2-2	3-3

Wednesday March 13, 2019

	2012-13	2013-14	2014-15	2015-16	2016-17	2017-18
Championship						
Birmingham v Millwall	1-1	4-0	0-1	-	-	0-1
Derby v Stoke	-	-	-	-	-	-
Middlesbrough v Preston	-	-	-	1-0	-	0-0
Norwich v Hull	-	1-0	-	-	-	1-1
Nottm Forest v Aston Villa	-	-	-	-	2-1	0-1
QPR v Rotherham	-	-	-	4-2	5-1	-
West Brom v Swansea	2-1	0-2	2-0	1-1	3-1	1-1

Saturday March 16, 2019

	2012-13	2013-14	2014-15	2015-16	2016-17	2017-18
Premier League						
Bournemouth v Newcastle	-	-	-	0-1	-	2-2
Brighton v Cardiff	0-0	-	1-1	1-1	1-0	-
Burnley v Leicester	0-1	0-2	0-1	-	1-0	2-1
Everton v Chelsea	1-2	1-0	3-6	3-1	0-3	0-0
Fulham v Liverpool	1-3	2-3	-	-	-	-
Man United v Man City	1-2	0-3	4-2	0-0	1-2	1-2
Tottenham v Crystal Palace	-	2-0	0-0	1-0	1-0	1-0
Watford v Southampton	-	-	-	0-0	3-4	2-2
West Ham v Huddersfield	-	-	-	-	-	2-0
Wolves v Arsenal	-	-	-	-	-	-
Championship						
Aston Villa v Middlesbrough	-	-	-	-	-	0-0
Brentford v West Brom	-	-	-	-	-	-
Hull v QPR	-	-	2-1	1-1	-	4-0
Ipswich v Nottm Forest	3-1	1-1	2-1	1-0	0-2	4-2
Leeds v Sheffield United	-	-	-	-	-	1-2
Millwall v Bristol City	2-1	-	-	-	-	2-0
Preston v Birmingham	-	-	-	1-1	2-1	1-1
Rotherham v Norwich	-	-	1-1	-	2-1	-
Sheffield Weds v Blackburn	3-2	3-3	1-2	2-1	2-1	-
Stoke v Reading	2-1	-	-	-	-	-
Swansea v Derby	-	-	-	-	-	-
Wigan v Bolton	-	3-2	1-1	-	-	-

Results cover matches from Premier League to National League and Scottish Premiership to Scottish League Two

	2012-13	2013-14	2014-15	2015-16	2016-17	2017-18
League One						
Accrington v Rochdale	2-3	1-2	-	-	-	-
Bristol Rovers v Charlton	-	-	-	-	1-5	1-1
Burton v Blackpool	-	-	-	1-0	-	-
Doncaster v Barnsley	-	2-2	1-0	2-1	-	-
Fleetwood Town v Plymouth	3-0	0-4	-	-	-	1-1
Luton v Gillingham	-	-	-	-	-	-
Oxford v Bradford	0-2	-	-	-	1-0	2-2
Peterborough v Coventry	-	1-0	0-1	3-1	1-1	-
Portsmouth v Scunthorpe	2-1	1-2	-	-	-	1-1
Shrewsbury v Wycombe	-	-	0-0	-	-	-
Southend v AFC Wimbledon	1-3	0-1	0-1	-	3-0	1-0
Sunderland v Walsall	-	-	-	-	-	-
League Two						
Bury v Cambridge U	-	-	2-0	-	-	-
Crewe v Crawley Town	2-0	1-0	0-0	-	0-2	3-0
Exeter v Colchester	-	-	-	-	3-0	1-0
Forest Green v Carlisle	-	-	-	-	-	0-1
Grimsby v Northampton	-	-	-	-	-	-
Mansfield v Lincoln	0-0	-	-	-	-	1-1
MK Dons v Stevenage	0-1	4-1	-	-	-	-
Newport County v Cheltenham	-	0-1	1-1	-	2-2	1-0
Notts County v Morecambe	-	-	-	2-2	1-2	2-0
Oldham v Tranmere	0-1	0-1	-	-	-	-
Swindon v Port Vale	-	5-2	1-0	2-2	1-0	3-2
Yeovil v Macclesfield	-	-	-	-	-	-
National League						
Aldershot v Salford City	-	-	-	-	-	-
Barnet v Hartlepool	-	-	-	1-3	3-2	-
Bromley v Leyton Orient	-	-	-	-	-	6-1
Dover v Halifax	-	-	0-1	1-0	-	0-0
Eastleigh v Barrow	-	-	-	3-1	2-0	0-2
Ebbsfleet v Boreham Wood	-	0-0	1-1	-	-	0-3
Fylde v Dag & Red	-	-	-	-	-	2-2
Harrogate T v Maidenhead	-	-	-	-	-	-
Havant & W v Chesterfield	-	-	-	-	-	-
Solihull Moors v Braintree	-	-	-	-	3-3	-
Sutton Utd v Gateshead	-	-	-	-	3-0	1-1
Wrexham v Maidstone	-	-	-	-	1-3	1-0
Ladbrokes Premiership						
Aberdeen v Livingston	-	-	-	-	-	-
Dundee v Celtic	0-2	-	1-1/1-2	0-0	0-1/1-2	0-2
Hamilton v Hearts	-	-	-	3-2/0-0	3-3	1-2/0-3
Hibernian v Motherwell	2-3	0-1/3-3	-	-	-	2-2/2-1
Rangers v Kilmarnock	-	-	-	-	3-0	1-1/0-1/1-0
St Johnstone v St Mirren	2-1/1-0	2-0	1-2/2-0	-	-	-
Ladbrokes Championship						
Ayr v Queen of Sth	2-4/1-5	-	-	-	1-0/0-2	-
Dunfermline v Dundee United	-	-	-	-	1-3/1-1	1-3/0-0
Falkirk v Partick	0-0/0-2	-	-	-	-	-
Inverness CT v Ross County	3-1/2-1	1-2	1-1/1-1	2-0	2-3/1-1	-
Morton v Alloa	-	0-2/0-1	-	1-0/4-1	-	-
Ladbrokes League One						
Arbroath v East Fife	2-0/1-0	2-2/2-1	0-2/1-1	1-1/0-1	-	2-3/1-1
Brechin v Montrose	-	-	-	-	-	-
Dumbarton v Airdrieonians	3-4/4-1	-	-	-	-	-
Forfar v Raith	-	-	-	-	-	1-1/2-1
Stenhousemuir v Stranraer	0-0/1-2	1-0/1-1	2-2/1-0	1-0/1-5	0-5/1-0	-

Results cover matches from Premier League to National League and Scottish Premiership to Scottish League Two

Ladbrokes League Two

	2012-13	2013-14	2014-15	2015-16	2016-17	2017-18
Albion v Cowdenbeath	-	-	-	2-1/0-0	-	-
Annan v Edinburgh City	-	-	-	-	1-1/1-0	2-1/2-3
Berwick v Peterhead	1-1/0-2	1-3/1-2	-	-	-	2-3/1-3
Clyde v Stirling	2-1/1-2	2-1/1-0	-	0-1/3-1	1-1/2-3	1-1/2-1
Queens Park v Elgin	1-1/0-1	3-3/2-0	2-1/1-1	3-1/0-0	-	-

Saturday March 23, 2019

League One

	2012-13	2013-14	2014-15	2015-16	2016-17	2017-18
AFC Wimbledon v Gillingham	0-1	-	-	-	2-0	1-1
Bradford v Blackpool	-	-	-	1-0	-	2-1
Burton v Accrington	1-0	2-1	3-0	-	-	-
Coventry v Oxford	-	-	-	-	2-1	-
Fleetwood Town v Sunderland	-	-	-	-	-	-
Luton v Doncaster	-	-	-	-	3-1	-
Peterborough v Southend	-	-	-	0-0	1-4	0-1
Plymouth v Bristol Rovers	1-1	1-0	-	1-1	-	3-2
Rochdale v Scunthorpe	-	0-4	3-1	2-1	3-2	1-1
Shrewsbury v Portsmouth	3-2	-	2-1	-	-	2-0
Walsall v Barnsley	-	-	3-1	1-3	-	-
Wycombe v Charlton	-	-	-	-	-	-

League Two

	2012-13	2013-14	2014-15	2015-16	2016-17	2017-18
Carlisle v Cambridge U	-	-	0-1	4-4	0-3	1-1
Cheltenham v Northampton	1-0	1-1	3-2	-	-	-
Colchester v Tranmere	1-5	1-2	-	-	-	-
Crawley Town v Lincoln	-	-	-	-	-	3-1
Grimsby v Bury	-	-	-	-	-	-
Macclesfield v Stevenage	-	-	-	-	-	-
Mansfield v Crewe	-	-	-	-	3-0	3-4
MK Dons v Yeovil	1-0	-	5-1	-	-	-
Newport County v Oldham	-	-	-	-	-	-
Notts County v Exeter	-	-	-	1-4	2-2	1-2
Port Vale v Forest Green	-	-	-	-	-	1-1
Swindon v Morecambe	-	-	-	-	-	1-1

National League

	2012-13	2013-14	2014-15	2015-16	2016-17	2017-18
Barrow v Harrogate T	-	1-0	1-1	-	-	-
Boreham Wood v Aldershot	-	-	-	0-1	1-1	2-1
Braintree v Bromley	-	-	-	1-0	2-2	-
Chesterfield v Sutton Utd	-	-	-	-	-	-
Dag & Red v Dover	-	-	-	-	2-0	1-0
Gateshead v Fylde	-	-	-	-	-	1-2
Halifax v Solihull Moors	-	-	-	-	-	0-0
Hartlepool v Wrexham	-	-	-	-	-	0-2
Leyton Orient v Eastleigh	-	-	-	-	-	1-1
Maidenhead v Havant & W	-	1-3	0-2	2-2	-	-
Maidstone v Ebbsfleet	-	-	-	0-2	-	1-2
Salford City v Barnet	-	-	-	-	-	-

Ladbrokes Championship

	2012-13	2013-14	2014-15	2015-16	2016-17	2017-18
Ayr v Morton	-	-	1-0/1-1	-	2-1/1-4	-
Dundee United v Alloa	-	-	-	-	-	-
Partick v Inverness CT	-	0-0	3-1/1-0	2-1/1-4	2-0/1-1	-
Queen of Sth v Falkirk	-	2-0/1-2	3-0/1-0	2-2/2-2	2-0/0-2	4-2/2-2
Ross County v Dunfermline	-	-	-	-	-	-

Ladbrokes League One

	2012-13	2013-14	2014-15	2015-16	2016-17	2017-18
Airdrieonians v Forfar	-	0-2/5-1	1-2/3-1	0-1/1-1	-	2-1/1-2
East Fife v Brechin	2-2/0-3	1-3/1-2	-	-	1-2/3-2	-
Montrose v Stenhousemuir	-	-	-	-	-	1-1/1-0
Raith v Dumbarton	2-2/3-2	2-1/1-3	3-1/2-1	1-0/0-0	3-2/1-3	-
Stranraer v Arbroath	1-1/2-0	3-2/1-1	-	-	-	2-6/1-4

Results cover matches from Premier League to National League and Scottish Premiership to Scottish League Two

	2012-13	2013-14	2014-15	2015-16	2016-17	2017-18
Ladbrokes League Two						
Clyde v Annan	2-1/2-3	2-1/0-3	1-1/1-0	4-2/2-1	2-3/2-1	2-1/0-0
Cowdenbeath v Queens Park	-	-	-	-	-	-
Edinburgh City v Peterhead	-	-	-	-	-	0-3/0-0
Elgin v Albion	-	1-2/1-1	0-4/2-0	-	-	-
Stirling v Berwick	6-3/1-0	3-1/2-1	-	1-3/2-1	0-0/2-2	4-0/2-0
Saturday March 30, 2019						
Premier League						
Arsenal v Newcastle	7-3	3-0	4-1	1-0	-	1-0
Brighton v Southampton	-	-	-	-	-	1-1
Burnley v Wolves	2-0	-	-	1-1	-	-
Cardiff v Chelsea	-	1-2	-	-	-	-
Crystal Palace v Huddersfield	1-1	-	-	-	-	0-3
Fulham v Man City	1-2	2-4	-	-	-	-
Leicester v Bournemouth	-	2-1	-	0-0	1-1	1-1
Liverpool v Tottenham	3-2	4-0	3-2	1-1	2-0	2-2
Man United v Watford	-	-	-	1-0	2-0	1-0
West Ham v Everton	1-2	2-3	1-2	1-1	0-0	3-1
Championship						
Aston Villa v Blackburn	-	-	-	-	2-1	-
Derby v Rotherham	-	-	1-0	3-0	3-0	-
Ipswich v Hull	1-2	-	-	0-1	-	0-3
Leeds v Millwall	1-0	2-1	1-0	-	-	3-4
Middlesbrough v Norwich	-	-	4-0	-	-	0-1
Nottm Forest v Swansea	-	-	-	-	-	-
QPR v Bolton	-	2-1	-	4-3	-	2-0
Reading v Preston	-	-	-	1-2	1-0	1-0
Sheffield United v Bristol City	-	3-0	1-2	-	-	1-2
Stoke v Sheffield Weds	-	-	-	-	-	-
West Brom v Birmingham	-	-	-	-	-	-
Wigan v Brentford	-	-	0-0	-	2-1	-
League One						
Accrington v Fleetwood Town	0-3	2-0	-	-	-	-
Barnsley v Coventry	-	-	1-0	2-0	-	-
Blackpool v Plymouth	-	-	-	-	0-1	2-2
Bristol Rovers v Luton	-	-	-	2-0	-	-
Charlton v Bradford	-	-	-	-	1-1	1-1
Doncaster v Walsall	1-2	-	0-2	1-2	-	0-3
Gillingham v Rochdale	1-2	-	1-0	2-0	3-0	2-1
Oxford v Wycombe	0-1	2-2	1-2	3-0	-	-
Portsmouth v Peterborough	-	-	-	-	-	2-0
Scunthorpe v AFC Wimbledon	-	0-0	-	-	1-2	1-1
Southend v Shrewsbury	-	-	1-0	0-1	1-1	1-2
Sunderland v Burton	-	-	-	-	-	1-2
League Two						
Bury v Swindon	0-1	-	-	2-2	1-0	-
Cambridge U v Colchester	-	-	-	-	1-1	1-0
Crewe v Cheltenham	-	-	-	-	0-0	2-1
Exeter v Mansfield	-	0-1	1-2	2-3	2-0	0-1
Forest Green v MK Dons	-	-	-	-	-	-
Lincoln v Macclesfield	2-3	1-0	2-0	5-3	2-1	-
Morecambe v Crawley Town	-	-	-	3-1	2-3	0-1
Northampton v Port Vale	2-0	-	-	-	2-1	-
Oldham v Grimsby	-	-	-	-	-	-
Stevenage v Notts County	2-0	0-1	-	0-2	3-0	1-1
Tranmere v Carlisle	0-1	0-0	0-2	-	-	-
Yeovil v Newport County	-	-	-	1-0	1-0	0-2

Results cover matches from Premier League to National League and Scottish Premiership to Scottish League Two

|---|---|---|---|---|---|---|
National League						
Aldershot v Fylde	-	-	-	-	-	2-1
Barnet v Leyton Orient	-	-	-	3-0	0-0	-
Barrow v Boreham Wood	-	-	-	0-0	1-1	2-1
Braintree v Gateshead	2-1	0-0	1-0	0-0	1-4	-
Chesterfield v Dag & Red	1-2	1-1	-	-	-	-
Eastleigh v Hartlepool	-	-	-	-	-	4-3
Ebbsfleet v Wrexham	1-1	-	-	-	-	3-0
Halifax v Maidenhead	-	-	-	-	-	3-2
Harrogate T v Maidstone	-	-	-	-	-	-
Salford City v Bromley	-	-	-	-	-	-
Solihull Moors v Dover	-	-	-	-	2-3	3-2
Sutton Utd v Havant & W	-	3-1	1-0	3-0	-	-
Ladbrokes Premiership						
Celtic v Rangers	-	-	-	-	5-1/1-1	0-0/5-0
Hearts v Aberdeen	2-0	2-1/1-1	-	1-3/2-1	0-1/1-2	0-0/2-0
Kilmarnock v Hamilton	-	-	1-0/2-3	1-2/0-1	0-0	2-2/2-0
Livingston v Hibernian	-	-	0-4/1-3	0-1/0-0	-	-
Motherwell v St Johnstone	1-1/3-2	4-0/2-1	0-1/1-1	2-0/1-2	1-2/1-2	2-0/1-5
St Mirren v Dundee	3-1/1-2	-	0-1/1-2	-	-	-
Ladbrokes Championship						
Alloa v Ross County	-	-	-	-	-	-
Dundee United v Queen of Sth	-	-	-	-	1-1/3-3	2-1/2-3
Dunfermline v Ayr	-	5-1/3-0	4-2/2-1	0-2/3-2	1-1/0-1	-
Inverness CT v Falkirk	-	-	-	-	-	4-1/1-0
Morton v Partick	3-1/2-2	-	-	-	-	-
Ladbrokes League One						
Brechin v Airdrieonians	-	4-3/1-1	1-1/0-0	1-2/3-3	3-2/3-0	-
Dumbarton v Stenhousemuir	-	-	-	-	-	-
East Fife v Raith	-	-	-	-	-	0-5/2-3
Forfar v Arbroath	1-1/2-4	1-1/0-2	-	-	0-1/1-1	0-5/0-1
Montrose v Stranraer	-	-	-	-	-	-
Ladbrokes League Two						
Albion v Clyde	-	3-0/1-0	2-2/0-2	-	-	-
Berwick v Edinburgh City	-	-	-	-	1-3/3-2	1-1/1-1
Elgin v Annan	2-2/3-1	2-3/2-3	0-0/4-5	3-2/2-2	0-2/3-2	0-1/2-1
Peterhead v Cowdenbeath	-	-	-	7-0/0-1	-	3-2/1-0
Queens Park v Stirling	2-1/2-2	0-2/0-1	-	1-0/1-1	-	-
Wednesday April 3, 2019						
Ladbrokes Premiership						
Aberdeen v Motherwell	3-3/0-0	0-1/0-1	1-0/2-1	1-1/4-1	7-2/1-0	0-2
Hibernian v Kilmarnock	2-1/2-2	3-0/0-1	-	-	-	1-1/5-3
Livingston v Hamilton	0-3/0-0	0-0/1-1	-	-	-	-
Rangers v Hearts	-	-	1-2/2-1	-	2-0/2-1	0-0/2-0/2-1
St Johnstone v Dundee	1-0	-	0-1/1-0	1-1	2-1/2-0	0-2
St Mirren v Celtic	0-5/1-1	0-4	1-2/0-2	-	-	-
Saturday April 6, 2019						
Premier League						
Bournemouth v Burnley	-	1-1	-	-	2-1	1-2
Chelsea v West Ham	2-0	0-0	2-0	2-2	2-1	1-1
Everton v Arsenal	1-1	3-0	2-2	0-2	2-1	2-5
Huddersfield v Leicester	0-2	0-2	-	-	-	1-1
Man City v Cardiff	-	4-2	-	-	-	-
Newcastle v Crystal Palace	-	1-0	3-3	1-0	-	1-0
Southampton v Liverpool	3-1	0-3	0-2	3-2	0-0	0-2
Tottenham v Brighton	-	-	-	-	-	2-0
Watford v Fulham	-	-	1-0	-	-	-
Wolves v Man United	-	-	-	-	-	-

Results cover matches from Premier League to National League and Scottish Premiership to Scottish League Two

	2012-13	2013-14	2014-15	2015-16	2016-17	2017-18
Championship						
Birmingham v Leeds	1-0	1-3	1-1	1-2	1-3	1-0
Blackburn v Stoke	-	-	-	-	-	-
Bolton v Ipswich	1-2	1-1	0-0	2-2	-	1-1
Brentford v Derby	-	-	2-1	1-3	4-0	1-1
Bristol City v Wigan	-	-	-	-	2-1	-
Hull v Reading	-	-	-	2-1	-	0-0
Millwall v West Brom	-	-	-	-	-	-
Norwich v QPR	1-1	-	-	-	4-0	2-0
Preston v Sheffield United	0-1	0-0	1-1	-	-	1-0
Rotherham v Nottm Forest	-	-	0-0	0-0	2-2	-
Sheffield Weds v Aston Villa	-	-	-	-	1-0	2-4
Swansea v Middlesbrough	-	-	-	-	0-0	-
League One						
AFC Wimbledon v Accrington	1-2	1-1	2-1	0-0	-	-
Bradford v Doncaster	-	-	1-2	2-1	-	2-0
Burton v Barnsley	-	-	-	0-0	0-0	2-4
Coventry v Bristol Rovers	-	-	-	-	1-0	-
Fleetwood Town v Southend	0-0	1-1	-	1-1	1-1	2-4
Luton v Blackpool	-	-	-	-	1-0	-
Peterborough v Gillingham	-	2-0	1-2	1-1	1-1	0-1
Plymouth v Charlton	-	-	-	-	-	2-0
Rochdale v Sunderland	-	-	-	-	-	-
Shrewsbury v Scunthorpe	0-1	-	-	2-2	0-1	2-0
Walsall v Oxford	-	-	-	-	1-1	2-1
Wycombe v Portsmouth	-	0-1	0-0	2-2	1-0	-
League Two						
Carlisle v Bury	2-1	-	0-3	-	-	-
Cheltenham v Exeter	3-0	1-0	1-2	-	1-3	3-4
Colchester v Oldham	0-2	0-1	2-2	0-0	-	-
Crawley Town v Forest Green	-	-	-	-	-	1-1
Grimsby v Stevenage	-	-	-	-	5-2	0-0
Macclesfield v Morecambe	-	-	-	-	-	-
Mansfield v Cambridge U	3-1	-	0-0	0-0	0-0	2-1
MK Dons v Lincoln	-	-	-	-	-	-
Newport County v Tranmere	-	-	1-1	-	-	-
Notts County v Northampton	-	-	-	1-2	-	-
Port Vale v Crewe	-	1-3	0-1	3-0	-	0-1
Swindon v Yeovil	4-1	-	0-1	-	-	2-2
National League						
Boreham Wood v Sutton Utd	-	1-3	2-0	-	1-0	0-4
Bromley v Aldershot	-	-	-	1-3	2-2	0-2
Dag & Red v Barrow	-	-	-	-	1-4	2-1
Dover v Chesterfield	-	-	-	-	-	-
Fylde v Eastleigh	-	-	-	-	-	2-2
Gateshead v Ebbsfleet	2-0	-	-	-	-	2-5
Hartlepool v Solihull Moors	-	-	-	-	-	0-1
Havant & W v Harrogate T	-	-	-	-	-	-
Leyton Orient v Halifax	-	-	-	-	-	0-3
Maidenhead v Barnet	-	-	-	-	-	-
Maidstone v Salford City	-	-	-	-	-	-
Wrexham v Braintree	1-1	2-3	3-0	2-3	0-1	-
Ladbrokes Premiership						
Celtic v Livingston	-	-	-	-	-	-
Dundee v Aberdeen	1-3/1-1	-	2-3/1-1/1-1	0-2	1-3/0-7	0-1
Hamilton v St Mirren	-	-	3-0/1-0	-	-	-
Hearts v Hibernian	0-0/1-2	1-0/2-0	2-1/1-1	-	-	0-0/2-1
Kilmarnock v St Johnstone	1-2	0-0/1-2	0-1	2-1/3-0	0-1	1-2/2-0
Motherwell v Rangers	-	-	-	-	0-2	1-2/2-2

Results cover matches from Premier League to National League and Scottish Premiership to Scottish League Two

	2012-13	2013-14	2014-15	2015-16	2016-17	2017-18
Ladbrokes Championship						
Ayr v Inverness CT	-	-	-	-	-	-
Falkirk v Alloa	-	0-0/3-1	2-1/1-0	5-0/2-0	-	-
Partick v Dunfermline	5-1/3-3	-	-	-	-	-
Queen of Sth v Morton	-	2-0/3-0	-	2-2/1-0	0-5/3-0	1-2/1-1
Ross County v Dundee United	1-2/1-0	2-4/3-0	2-3	2-1/0-3	-	-
Ladbrokes League One						
Airdrieonians v East Fife	-	1-3/2-1	-	-	1-1/2-2	0-1/0-0
Arbroath v Montrose	-	-	3-1/2-2	3-1/0-0	0-0/0-1	-
Dumbarton v Brechin	-	-	-	-	-	2-1/1-0
Stenhousemuir v Raith	-	-	-	-	-	-
Stranraer v Forfar	4-1/0-3	0-4/3-1	1-1/4-2	0-0/1-0	-	3-0/2-0
Ladbrokes League Two						
Albion v Queens Park	-	2-1/1-0	1-0/2-1	-	2-0/1-1	0-1/1-1
Annan v Berwick	3-2/2-2	3-2/4-0	2-0/4-2	1-0/1-0	3-1/2-1	0-0/0-0
Clyde v Peterhead	0-2/2-0	1-3/0-2	-	-	-	1-4/1-0
Cowdenbeath v Edinburgh City	-	-	-	-	2-0/1-2	1-0/0-2
Stirling v Elgin	1-4/1-1	1-1/2-2	-	3-1/0-0	0-4/1-0	2-2/3-1
Tuesday April 9, 2019						
Championship						
Blackburn v Derby	2-0	1-1	2-3	0-0	1-0	-
Bolton v Middlesbrough	2-1	2-2	1-2	1-2	-	0-3
Bristol City v West Brom	-	-	-	-	-	-
Norwich v Reading	2-1	-	1-2	-	7-1	3-2
Preston v Leeds	-	-	-	1-1	1-4	3-1
Sheffield Weds v Nottm Forest	0-1	0-1	0-1	1-0	2-1	3-1
Swansea v Stoke	3-1	3-3	2-0	0-1	2-0	1-2
Wednesday April 10, 2019						
Championship						
Birmingham v Sheffield United	-	-	-	-	-	2-1
Brentford v Ipswich	-	-	2-4	2-2	2-0	1-0
Hull v Wigan	-	-	-	-	-	-
Millwall v QPR	-	2-2	-	-	-	1-0
Rotherham v Aston Villa	-	-	-	-	0-2	-
Saturday April 13, 2019						
Premier League						
Brighton v Bournemouth	-	1-1	0-2	-	-	2-2
Burnley v Cardiff	1-1	-	-	0-0	-	-
Crystal Palace v Man City	-	0-2	2-1	0-1	1-2	0-0
Fulham v Everton	2-2	1-3	-	-	-	-
Leicester v Newcastle	-	-	3-0	1-0	-	1-2
Liverpool v Chelsea	2-2	0-2	1-2	1-1	1-1	1-1
Man United v West Ham	1-0	3-1	2-1	0-0	1-1	4-0
Southampton v Wolves	-	-	-	-	-	-
Tottenham v Huddersfield	-	-	-	-	-	2-0
Watford v Arsenal	-	-	-	0-3	1-3	2-1
Championship						
Aston Villa v Bristol City	-	-	-	-	2-0	5-0
Derby v Bolton	1-1	0-0	4-1	4-1	-	3-0
Ipswich v Birmingham	3-1	1-0	4-2	1-1	1-1	1-0
Leeds v Sheffield Weds	2-1	1-1	1-1	1-1	1-0	1-2
Middlesbrough v Hull	2-0	-	-	1-0	1-0	3-1
Nottm Forest v Blackburn	0-0	4-1	1-3	1-1	0-1	-
QPR v Swansea	0-5	-	1-1	-	-	-
Reading v Brentford	-	-	0-2	1-2	3-2	0-1
Sheffield United v Millwall	-	-	-	1-2	2-0	1-1
Stoke v Rotherham	-	-	-	-	-	-
West Brom v Preston	-	-	-	-	-	-
Wigan v Norwich	1-0	-	0-1	-	2-2	-

Results cover matches from Premier League to National League and Scottish Premiership to Scottish League Two

	2012-13	2013-14	2014-15	2015-16	2016-17	2017-18
League One						
Accrington v Walsall	-	-	-	-	-	-
Barnsley v Fleetwood Town	-	-	1-2	0-1	-	-
Blackpool v Peterborough	0-1	-	-	2-0	-	1-1
Bristol Rovers v Bradford	3-3	-	-	-	1-1	3-1
Charlton v Luton	-	-	-	-	-	-
Doncaster v Plymouth	-	-	-	-	0-1	1-1
Gillingham v Shrewsbury	-	1-1	-	2-3	1-1	1-2
Oxford v AFC Wimbledon	3-2	2-1	0-0	1-0	1-3	3-0
Portsmouth v Rochdale	-	3-0	-	-	-	2-0
Scunthorpe v Burton	-	1-0	-	1-0	-	-
Southend v Wycombe	1-0	1-1	2-2	-	-	-
Sunderland v Coventry	-	-	-	-	-	-
League Two						
Bury v Colchester	1-2	-	-	5-2	-	-
Cambridge U v Newport County	0-0	-	4-0	3-0	3-2	1-2
Crewe v Notts County	1-2	1-3	0-3	-	2-2	2-0
Exeter v Port Vale	0-2	-	-	-	-	0-1
Forest Green v Macclesfield	1-1	2-3	3-1	2-1	3-0	-
Lincoln v Cheltenham	-	-	-	1-1	-	1-0
Morecambe v Grimsby	-	-	-	-	1-0	0-0
Northampton v Mansfield	-	1-1	1-0	1-0	-	-
Oldham v Swindon	0-2	2-1	2-1	2-0	0-2	-
Stevenage v Carlisle	1-1	1-3	1-0	0-1	1-2	0-0
Tranmere v MK Dons	0-1	3-2	-	-	-	-
Yeovil v Crawley Town	2-2	-	2-1	2-1	5-0	1-2
National League						
Aldershot v Hartlepool	-	-	-	-	-	2-1
Barnet v Wrexham	-	1-1	0-1	-	-	-
Barrow v Dover	-	-	-	2-1	2-3	0-0
Braintree v Fylde	-	-	-	-	-	-
Chesterfield v Maidstone	-	-	-	-	-	-
Eastleigh v Gateshead	-	-	2-2	1-2	1-1	3-2
Ebbsfleet v Dag & Red	-	-	-	-	-	1-1
Halifax v Bromley	-	-	-	2-2	-	2-1
Harrogate T v Boreham Wood	-	-	-	-	-	-
Salford City v Maidenhead	-	-	-	-	-	-
Solihull Moors v Havant & W	-	-	-	-	-	-
Sutton Utd v Leyton Orient	-	-	-	-	-	2-0
Ladbrokes Championship						
Alloa v Queen of Sth	1-0/1-2	0-3/0-1	1-1/2-2	1-2/2-2	-	-
Dundee United v Ayr	-	-	-	-	3-0/2-1	-
Dunfermline v Falkirk	0-1/0-2	-	-	-	1-1/1-2	3-1/2-0
Morton v Inverness CT	-	-	-	-	-	1-0/0-3
Ross County v Partick	-	1-3/1-1	1-0/1-2	1-0/1-0	1-3	1-1/4-0
Ladbrokes League One						
Airdrieonians v Stenhousemuir	-	0-1/1-1	2-0/2-1	0-1/1-1	0-5/1-0	-
Brechin v Arbroath	3-2/2-0	3-1/2-4	-	-	-	-
East Fife v Montrose	-	-	3-0/3-0	1-1/3-0	-	-
Forfar v Dumbarton	-	-	-	-	-	-
Raith v Stranraer	-	-	-	-	-	3-0/3-0
Ladbrokes League Two						
Annan v Stirling	5-2/0-1	4-4/1-2	-	1-1/2-2	3-2/4-1	1-1/3-1
Berwick v Queens Park	2-0/4-1	4-0/1-0	0-0/1-1	1-0/1-1	-	-
Cowdenbeath v Elgin	-	-	-	-	0-1/1-1	1-3/3-1
Edinburgh City v Clyde	-	-	-	-	0-1/0-0	0-3/1-3
Peterhead v Albion	-	1-1/2-0	-	1-1/5-1	2-2/1-1	-

Results cover matches from Premier League to National League and Scottish Premiership to Scottish League Two

Friday April 19, 2019

Championship

	2012-13	2013-14	2014-15	2015-16	2016-17	2017-18
Birmingham v Derby	3-1	3-3	0-4	1-1	1-2	0-3
Bolton v Aston Villa	-	-	-	-	-	1-0
Bristol City v Reading	-	-	-	0-2	2-3	2-0
Leeds v Wigan	-	2-0	0-2	-	1-1	-
Middlesbrough v Stoke	-	-	-	-	1-1	-
Millwall v Brentford	-	-	2-3	-	-	1-0
Norwich v Sheffield Weds	-	-	2-0	-	0-0	3-1
Preston v Ipswich	-	-	-	1-2	1-1	0-1
QPR v Blackburn	-	0-0	-	2-2	1-1	-
Sheffield United v Nottm Forest	-	-	-	-	-	0-0
Swansea v Rotherham	-	-	-	-	-	-
West Brom v Hull	-	1-1	1-0	-	3-1	-

League One

	2012-13	2013-14	2014-15	2015-16	2016-17	2017-18
Accrington v Luton	-	-	2-2	1-1	1-4	0-2
AFC Wimbledon v Bristol Rovers	3-1	0-0	-	0-0	0-1	1-0
Barnsley v Shrewsbury	-	-	-	1-2	-	-
Burton v Portsmouth	-	1-2	2-0	-	-	-
Coventry v Bradford	-	0-0	1-1	1-0	0-2	-
Fleetwood Town v Peterborough	-	-	1-1	2-0	2-0	2-3
Gillingham v Plymouth	2-1	-	-	-	-	5-2
Oxford v Charlton	-	-	-	-	1-1	1-1
Rochdale v Wycombe	4-1	3-2	-	-	-	-
Scunthorpe v Blackpool	-	-	-	0-1	-	0-0
Sunderland v Doncaster	-	-	-	-	-	-
Walsall v Southend	-	-	-	1-0	0-0	0-1

League Two

	2012-13	2013-14	2014-15	2015-16	2016-17	2017-18
Cambridge U v Swindon	-	-	-	-	-	1-3
Carlisle v Lincoln	-	-	-	-	-	0-1
Cheltenham v Oldham	-	-	-	-	-	-
Colchester v Grimsby	-	-	-	-	3-2	1-1
Crewe v Yeovil	0-1	-	1-0	-	0-1	0-0
Exeter v Crawley Town	-	-	-	2-2	0-1	2-2
Mansfield v Morecambe	-	1-2	1-0	2-1	0-1	2-1
Newport County v Bury	-	0-0	0-2	-	-	-
Northampton v Macclesfield	-	-	-	-	-	-
Notts County v MK Dons	1-2	1-3	0-1	-	-	-
Port Vale v Stevenage	-	2-2	-	-	-	2-2
Tranmere v Forest Green	-	-	-	1-1	0-1	-

National League

	2012-13	2013-14	2014-15	2015-16	2016-17	2017-18
Boreham Wood v Salford City	-	-	-	-	-	-
Bromley v Solihull Moors	-	-	-	-	0-1	1-0
Dag & Red v Eastleigh	-	-	-	-	4-0	1-2
Dover v Aldershot	-	-	3-0	5-2	1-2	1-2
Fylde v Barnet	-	-	-	-	-	-
Gateshead v Chesterfield	-	-	-	-	-	-
Hartlepool v Halifax	-	-	-	-	-	4-0
Havant & W v Ebbsfleet	-	1-0	2-0	1-4	-	-
Leyton Orient v Harrogate T	-	-	-	-	-	-
Maidenhead v Barrow	-	-	-	-	-	0-1
Maidstone v Braintree	-	-	-	-	2-1	-
Wrexham v Sutton Utd	-	-	-	-	1-0	1-1

Saturday April 20, 2019

Premier League

	2012-13	2013-14	2014-15	2015-16	2016-17	2017-18
Arsenal v Crystal Palace	-	2-0	2-1	1-1	2-0	4-1
Bournemouth v Fulham	-	-	2-0	-	-	-
Cardiff v Liverpool	-	3-6	-	-	-	-
Chelsea v Burnley	-	-	1-1	-	3-0	2-3
Everton v Man United	1-0	2-0	3-0	0-3	1-1	0-2
Huddersfield v Watford	2-3	1-2	3-1	-	-	1-0
Man City v Tottenham	2-1	6-0	4-1	1-2	2-2	4-1

Results cover matches from Premier League to National League and Scottish Premiership to Scottish League Two

	2012-13	2013-14	2014-15	2015-16	2016-17	2017-18
Newcastle v Southampton	4-2	1-1	1-2	2-2	-	3-0
West Ham v Leicester	-	-	2-0	1-2	2-3	1-1
Wolves v Brighton	3-3	-	1-1	0-0	0-2	-

Ladbrokes Championship

	2012-13	2013-14	2014-15	2015-16	2016-17	2017-18
Ayr v Ross County	-	-	-	-	-	-
Falkirk v Morton	0-1/4-1	3-1/1-1	-	1-0/1-0	1-1/0-1	0-3/3-1
Inverness CT v Dundee United	4-0/0-0/1-2	1-1/1-1	1-0/2-1/3-0	2-2/2-3	-	0-1/1-0
Partick v Alloa	-	-	-	-	-	-
Queen of Sth v Dunfermline	-	-	-	-	2-2/0-1	0-0/0-0

Ladbrokes League One

	2012-13	2013-14	2014-15	2015-16	2016-17	2017-18
Arbroath v Raith	-	-	-	-	-	1-2/1-1
Dumbarton v East Fife	-	-	-	-	-	-
Montrose v Airdrieonians	-	-	-	-	-	-
Stenhousemuir v Forfar	0-4/2-0	1-1/4-1	0-2/1-3	2-2/2-1	-	-
Stranraer v Brechin	0-2/3-2	3-0/1-2	2-2/0-2	1-0/2-0	0-1/2-0	-

Ladbrokes League Two

	2012-13	2013-14	2014-15	2015-16	2016-17	2017-18
Albion v Edinburgh City	-	-	-	-	-	-
Clyde v Berwick	2-1/2-1	1-0/3-3	3-3/0-3	1-1/2-1	3-2/1-1	0-0/1-2
Elgin v Peterhead	2-0/0-3	2-4/2-3	-	-	-	0-2/0-1
Queens Park v Annan	2-2/2-2	2-5/0-1	0-0/2-0	0-1/1-3	-	-
Stirling v Cowdenbeath	-	-	-	-	1-2/0-3	1-0/2-2

Monday April 22, 2019

Championship

	2012-13	2013-14	2014-15	2015-16	2016-17	2017-18
Aston Villa v Millwall	-	-	-	-	-	0-0
Blackburn v Bolton	1-2	4-1	1-0	0-0	-	-
Brentford v Leeds	-	-	2-0	1-1	2-0	3-1
Derby v QPR	-	1-0	-	1-0	1-0	2-0
Hull v Sheffield United	-	-	-	-	-	1-0
Ipswich v Swansea	-	-	-	-	-	-
Nottm Forest v Middlesbrough	0-0	2-2	2-1	1-2	-	2-1
Reading v West Brom	3-2	-	-	-	-	-
Rotherham v Birmingham	-	-	0-1	0-0	1-1	-
Sheffield Weds v Bristol City	2-3	-	-	2-0	3-2	0-0
Stoke v Norwich	1-0	0-1	-	3-1	-	-
Wigan v Preston	-	-	-	-	0-0	-

League One

	2012-13	2013-14	2014-15	2015-16	2016-17	2017-18
Blackpool v Fleetwood Town	-	-	-	1-0	-	2-1
Bradford v Gillingham	0-1	1-1	1-1	1-2	2-2	1-0
Bristol Rovers v Rochdale	2-1	1-2	-	-	2-2	3-2
Charlton v Scunthorpe	-	-	-	-	2-1	0-1
Doncaster v Accrington	-	-	-	-	2-2	-
Luton v AFC Wimbledon	-	-	0-1	2-0	-	-
Peterborough v Sunderland	-	-	-	-	-	-
Plymouth v Barnsley	-	-	-	-	-	-
Portsmouth v Coventry	2-0	-	-	-	-	-
Shrewsbury v Oxford	-	-	2-0	-	2-0	3-2
Southend v Burton	0-1	1-0	0-0	3-1	-	-
Wycombe v Walsall	-	-	-	-	-	-

League Two

	2012-13	2013-14	2014-15	2015-16	2016-17	2017-18
Bury v Northampton	-	1-1	2-1	-	3-0	2-3
Crawley Town v Notts County	0-0	1-0	2-0	0-1	1-3	0-1
Forest Green v Cambridge U	1-1	3-2	-	-	-	5-2
Grimsby v Carlisle	-	-	-	-	2-2	0-1
Lincoln v Tranmere	-	-	-	1-0	2-1	-
Macclesfield v Newport County	1-1	-	-	-	-	-
MK Dons v Port Vale	-	3-0	1-0	-	0-1	-
Morecambe v Cheltenham	0-0	0-1	0-0	-	1-2	2-1
Oldham v Mansfield	-	-	-	-	-	-
Stevenage v Exeter	-	-	1-0	0-2	0-2	3-1
Swindon v Crewe	4-1	5-0	2-0	4-3	-	4-3
Yeovil v Colchester	3-1	-	0-1	-	2-1	0-1

Results cover matches from Premier League to National League and Scottish Premiership to Scottish League Two

National League

	2012-13	2013-14	2014-15	2015-16	2016-17	2017-18
Aldershot v Havant & W	-	-	-	-	-	-
Barnet v Bromley	-	-	-	-	-	-
Barrow v Hartlepool	-	-	-	-	-	1-2
Braintree v Dag & Red	-	-	-	-	3-2	-
Chesterfield v Boreham Wood	-	-	-	-	-	-
Eastleigh v Maidenhead	-	3-2	-	-	-	2-2
Ebbsfleet v Dover	-	0-2	-	-	-	2-1
Halifax v Wrexham	-	3-2	2-2	2-0	-	0-0
Harrogate T v Gateshead	-	-	-	-	-	-
Salford City v Fylde	-	-	-	-	-	-
Solihull Moors v Leyton Orient	-	-	-	-	-	1-0
Sutton Utd v Maidstone	-	-	-	0-2	2-2	1-3

Saturday April 27, 2019

Premier League

	2012-13	2013-14	2014-15	2015-16	2016-17	2017-18
Brighton v Newcastle	-	-	-	-	1-2	1-0
Burnley v Man City	-	-	1-0	-	1-2	1-1
Crystal Palace v Everton	-	0-0	0-1	0-0	0-1	2-2
Fulham v Cardiff	-	1-2	1-1	2-1	2-2	1-1
Leicester v Arsenal	-	-	1-1	2-5	0-0	3-1
Liverpool v Huddersfield	-	-	-	-	-	3-0
Man United v Chelsea	0-1	0-0	1-1	0-0	2-0	2-1
Southampton v Bournemouth	-	-	-	2-0	0-0	2-1
Tottenham v West Ham	3-1	0-3	2-2	4-1	3-2	1-1
Watford v Wolves	2-1	-	0-1	-	-	-

Championship

	2012-13	2013-14	2014-15	2015-16	2016-17	2017-18
Birmingham v Wigan	-	0-1	3-1	-	0-1	-
Bolton v Brentford	-	-	3-1	1-1	-	0-3
Bristol City v Derby	0-2	-	-	2-3	1-1	4-1
Leeds v Aston Villa	-	-	-	-	2-0	1-1
Middlesbrough v Reading	-	3-0	0-1	2-1	-	2-1
Millwall v Stoke	-	-	-	-	-	-
Norwich v Blackburn	-	-	3-1	-	2-2	-
Preston v Sheffield Weds	-	-	-	1-0	1-1	1-0
QPR v Nottm Forest	-	5-2	-	1-2	2-0	2-5
Sheffield United v Ipswich	-	-	-	-	-	1-0
Swansea v Hull	-	1-1	3-1	-	0-2	-
West Brom v Rotherham	-	-	-	-	-	-

League One

	2012-13	2013-14	2014-15	2015-16	2016-17	2017-18
Accrington v Plymouth	1-1	1-1	1-0	2-1	0-1	-
AFC Wimbledon v Wycombe	2-2	1-0	0-0	1-1	-	-
Barnsley v Blackpool	1-1	2-0	-	4-2	-	-
Burton v Luton	-	-	1-0	-	-	-
Coventry v Shrewsbury	0-1	0-0	-	3-0	0-0	-
Fleetwood Town v Bristol Rovers	0-3	3-1	-	-	3-1	2-0
Gillingham v Charlton	-	-	-	-	1-1	1-0
Oxford v Doncaster	-	-	-	-	-	1-0
Rochdale v Southend	4-2	0-3	-	4-1	3-0	0-0
Scunthorpe v Bradford	-	-	1-1	0-2	3-2	1-1
Sunderland v Portsmouth	-	-	-	-	-	-
Walsall v Peterborough	-	2-0	0-0	2-0	2-0	1-1

League Two

	2012-13	2013-14	2014-15	2015-16	2016-17	2017-18
Cambridge U v Morecambe	-	-	1-2	7-0	1-2	0-0
Carlisle v Crawley Town	0-2	1-1	-	3-1	3-1	2-2
Cheltenham v Swindon	-	-	-	-	-	2-1
Colchester v MK Dons	0-2	3-1	0-1	-	-	-
Crewe v Forest Green	-	-	-	-	-	3-1
Exeter v Oldham	-	-	-	-	-	-
Mansfield v Stevenage	-	-	1-0	2-1	1-2	1-0
Newport County v Lincoln	2-1	-	-	-	-	0-0

Results cover matches from Premier League to National League and Scottish Premiership to Scottish League Two

	2012-13	2013-14	2014-15	2015-16	2016-17	2017-18
Northampton v Yeovil	-	-	-	2-0	-	-
Notts County v Grimsby	-	-	-	-	2-2	0-0
Port Vale v Macclesfield	-	-	-	-	-	-
Tranmere v Bury	3-0	-	0-1	-	-	-

National League

	2012-13	2013-14	2014-15	2015-16	2016-17	2017-18
Boreham Wood v Eastleigh	-	0-3	-	1-1	0-1	1-0
Bromley v Ebbsfleet	-	0-0	1-2	-	-	4-2
Dag & Red v Solihull Moors	-	-	-	-	4-4	1-3
Dover v Sutton Utd	-	0-1	-	-	3-1	0-1
Fylde v Halifax	-	-	-	-	-	2-0
Gateshead v Barrow	0-1	-	-	1-1	4-1	1-2
Hartlepool v Salford City	-	-	-	-	-	-
Havant & W v Barnet	-	-	-	-	-	-
Leyton Orient v Braintree	-	-	-	-	-	-
Maidenhead v Chesterfield	-	-	-	-	-	-
Maidstone v Aldershot	-	-	-	-	0-2	1-1
Wrexham v Harrogate T	-	-	-	-	-	-

Ladbrokes Championship

	2012-13	2013-14	2014-15	2015-16	2016-17	2017-18
Alloa v Inverness CT	-	-	-	-	-	-
Dundee United v Falkirk	-	-	-	-	1-0/1-1	3-0/1-0
Dunfermline v Morton	2-2/1-4	-	1-2/0-4	-	2-1/3-1	1-1/0-0
Partick v Ayr	-	-	-	-	-	-
Ross County v Queen of Sth	-	-	-	-	-	-

Ladbrokes League One

	2012-13	2013-14	2014-15	2015-16	2016-17	2017-18
Airdrieonians v Arbroath	-	2-1/2-0	-	-	-	1-1/0-0
Dumbarton v Stranraer	-	-	-	-	-	-
Forfar v Montrose	-	-	-	-	1-3/0-0	-
Raith v Brechin	-	-	-	-	-	-
Stenhousemuir v East Fife	3-0/2-1	1-1/1-1	-	-	0-1/3-1	-

Ladbrokes League Two

	2012-13	2013-14	2014-15	2015-16	2016-17	2017-18
Annan v Cowdenbeath	-	-	-	-	2-0/1-0	1-0/1-1
Berwick v Albion	-	2-1/3-1	1-1/0-2	-	-	-
Clyde v Queens Park	0-3/2-3	3-0/1-2	0-2/2-0	0-2/0-1	-	-
Edinburgh City v Elgin	-	-	-	-	1-2/3-0	0-3/4-0
Peterhead v Stirling	2-2/0-0	3-1/0-4	1-1/2-1	-	-	2-4/4-3

Saturday May 4, 2019

Premier League

	2012-13	2013-14	2014-15	2015-16	2016-17	2017-18
Arsenal v Brighton	-	-	-	-	-	2-0
Bournemouth v Tottenham	-	-	-	1-5	0-0	1-4
Cardiff v Crystal Palace	2-1	0-3	-	-	-	-
Chelsea v Watford	-	-	-	2-2	4-3	4-2
Everton v Burnley	-	-	1-0	-	3-1	0-1
Huddersfield v Man United	-	-	-	-	-	2-1
Man City v Leicester	-	-	2-0	1-3	2-1	5-1
Newcastle v Liverpool	0-6	2-2	1-0	2-0	-	1-1
West Ham v Southampton	4-1	3-1	1-3	2-1	0-3	3-0
Wolves v Fulham	-	-	3-0	3-2	4-4	2-0

League One

	2012-13	2013-14	2014-15	2015-16	2016-17	2017-18
Blackpool v Gillingham	-	-	-	1-0	-	1-1
Bradford v AFC Wimbledon	5-1	-	-	-	3-0	0-4
Bristol Rovers v Barnsley	-	-	-	-	-	-
Charlton v Rochdale	-	-	-	-	0-1	2-1
Doncaster v Coventry	1-4	-	2-0	2-0	-	-
Luton v Oxford	-	-	2-0	2-2	-	-
Peterborough v Burton	-	-	-	0-1	-	-
Plymouth v Scunthorpe	-	0-2	-	-	-	0-4
Portsmouth v Accrington	-	1-0	2-3	0-0	2-0	-
Shrewsbury v Walsall	1-0	0-1	-	1-3	1-1	2-0
Southend v Sunderland	-	-	-	-	-	-
Wycombe v Fleetwood Town	1-0	1-1	-	-	-	-

Results cover matches from Premier League to National League and Scottish Premiership to Scottish League Two

League Two						
Bury v Port Vale	-	-	-	1-0	4-1	-
Crawley Town v Tranmere	2-5	2-0	-	-	-	-
Forest Green v Exeter	-	-	-	-	-	1-3
Grimsby v Crewe	-	-	-	-	0-2	1-0
Lincoln v Colchester	-	-	-	-	-	2-1
Macclesfield v Cambridge U	2-1	0-1	-	-	-	-
MK Dons v Mansfield	-	-	-	-	-	-
Morecambe v Newport County	-	4-1	3-2	1-2	0-1	2-1
Oldham v Northampton	-	-	-	-	0-0	5-1
Stevenage v Cheltenham	-	-	5-1	-	2-1	4-1
Swindon v Notts County	0-0	2-0	3-0	-	-	1-0
Yeovil v Carlisle	1-3	-	-	0-0	0-2	0-1
Ladbrokes Championship						
Ayr v Alloa	0-0/0-2	-	-	-	-	3-3/1-2
Falkirk v Ross County	-	-	-	-	-	-
Inverness CT v Dunfermline	-	-	-	-	-	1-0/2-2
Morton v Dundee United	-	-	-	-	0-0/1-1	0-2/1-1
Queen of Sth v Partick	-	-	-	-	-	-
Ladbrokes League One						
Arbroath v Dumbarton	-	-	-	-	-	-
Brechin v Stenhousemuir	7-2/1-2	0-1/1-3	1-0/2-1	1-2/1-0	2-1/2-2	-
East Fife v Forfar	3-0/1-2	1-3/2-1	-	-	-	3-0/1-2
Montrose v Raith	-	-	-	-	-	-
Stranraer v Airdrieonians	-	3-1/1-1	1-0/1-0	1-3/4-0	1-2/2-1	3-1/3-2
Ladbrokes League Two						
Albion v Annan	-	2-0/0-2	2-1/2-0	-	-	-
Cowdenbeath v Clyde	-	-	-	-	1-0/1-0	0-3/1-0
Elgin v Berwick	3-1/1-2	2-0/1-3	2-1/3-3	4-1/1-0	6-0/2-2	5-1/3-0
Queens Park v Peterhead	0-0/0-3	0-5/0-2	-	-	0-0/2-0	-
Stirling v Edinburgh City	-	-	-	-	1-1/1-0	2-0/2-2
Sunday May 5, 2019						
Championship						
Aston Villa v Norwich	1-1	4-1	-	2-0	2-0	4-2
Blackburn v Swansea	-	-	-	-	-	-
Brentford v Preston	1-0	1-0	-	2-1	5-0	1-1
Derby v West Brom	-	-	-	-	-	-
Hull v Bristol City	0-0	-	-	4-0	-	2-3
Ipswich v Leeds	3-0	1-2	4-1	2-1	1-1	1-0
Nottm Forest v Bolton	1-1	3-0	4-1	3-0	-	3-2
Reading v Birmingham	-	2-0	0-1	0-2	0-0	0-2
Rotherham v Middlesbrough	-	-	0-3	1-0	-	-
Sheffield Weds v QPR	-	3-0	-	1-1	1-0	1-1
Stoke v Sheffield United	-	-	-	-	-	-
Wigan v Millwall	-	0-1	0-0	2-2	-	-
Sunday May 12, 2019						
Premier League						
Brighton v Man City	-	-	-	-	-	0-2
Burnley v Arsenal	-	-	0-1	-	0-1	0-1
Crystal Palace v Bournemouth	-	-	-	1-2	1-1	2-2
Fulham v Newcastle	2-1	1-0	-	-	1-0	-
Leicester v Chelsea	-	-	1-3	2-1	0-3	1-2
Liverpool v Wolves	-	-	-	-	-	-
Man United v Cardiff	-	2-0	-	-	-	-
Southampton v Huddersfield	-	-	-	-	-	1-1
Tottenham v Everton	2-2	1-0	2-1	0-0	3-2	4-0
Watford v West Ham	-	-	-	2-0	1-1	2-0

Results cover matches from Premier League to National League and Scottish Premiership to Scottish League Two

WINNERS & LOSERS 2017-18

Premier League

Champions	Manchester City
Champions League	Manchester United
	Tottenham
	Liverpool
Europa League	Chelsea
	Arsenal
	Burnley
Relegated	Swansea
	Stoke
	West Brom

Championship

Champions	Wolves
Promoted	Cardiff
Playoff winners	Fulham
Relegated	Barnsley
	Burton
	Sunderland

League One

Champions	Wigan
Promoted	Blackburn
Playoff winners	Rotherham
Relegated	Oldham
	Northampton
	MK Dons
	Bury

League Two

Champions	Accrington
Promoted	Luton
	Wycombe
Playoff winners	Coventry
Relegated	Barnet
	Chesterfield

National League

Champions	Macclesfield
Playoff winners	Tranmere
Relegated	Woking
	Torquay
	Chester
	Guiseley

National League North

Champions	Salford City
Playoff winners	Harrogate
Relegated	Gainsborough
	Tamworth
	North Ferriby

National League South

Champions	Havant & W
Playoff winners	Braintree
Relegated	Poole Town
	Whitehawk
	Bognor Regis

Community Shield

Winners	Arsenal
Beaten finalists	Chelsea

FA Cup

Winners	Chelsea
Beaten finalists	Manchester United

League Cup

Winners	Manchester City
Beaten finalists	Arsenal

Football League Trophy

Winners	Lincoln
Beaten finalists	Shrewsbury

FA Trophy

Winners	Brackley
Beaten finalists	Bromley

Sunderland suffered the ignominy of successive relegations into League One

Motherwell were unlucky enough to bump into Celtic in two cup finals last season...

Scottish Premiership

Champions	Celtic
Europa League	Aberdeen
	Rangers
	Hibernian
Relegated	Partick Thistle
	Ross County

Scottish Championship

Champions	St Mirren
Promoted	Livingston
Relegated	Dumbarton
	Brechin

Scottish League One

Champions	Ayr United
Promoted	Alloa
Relegated	Queen's Park
	Albion Rovers

Scottish League Two

Champions	Montrose
Promoted	Stenhousemuir

Scottish Cup

Winners	Celtic
Beaten finalists	Motherwell

Scottish League Cup

Winners	Celtic
Beaten finalists	Motherwell

Scottish Challenge Cup

Winners	Inverness
Beaten finalists	Dumbarton

Champions League

Winners	Real Madrid
Beaten finalists	Liverpool

Europa League

Winners	Atletico Madrid
Beaten finalists	Marseille

Uefa Super Cup

Winners	Real Madrid
Beaten finalists	Manchester United

Fifa Club World Cup

Winners	Real Madrid
Beaten finalists	Gremio

2018 Fifa World Cup

Winners	France
Beaten finalists	Croatia

Ashley Barnes' Burnley smashed expectations in the Premier League

Premier League

Burnley	+22.47	Crystal Palace	-1.94
Man City	+7.72	Chelsea	-2.53
Man Utd	+5.31	Leicester	-4.98
West Brom	+4.75	Liverpool	-5.60
Newcastle	+3.36	West Ham	-6.71
Bournemouth	+2.63	Everton	-6.96
Watford	+2.07	Brighton	-7.26
Huddersfield	+1.90	Arsenal	-8.92
Swansea	+1.65	Stoke	-15.82
Tottenham	-1.29	Southampton	-22.60

Championship

Cardiff	+15.36	Sheff Wed	-2.95
Wolves	+13.35	Leeds	-3.55
Ipswich	+10.57	Birmingham	-4.22
Fulham	+8.07	QPR	-4.78
Aston Villa	+7.80	Bristol City	-5.08
Preston	+4.22	Norwich	-6.21
Millwall	+3.14	Brentford	-6.67
Nottm Forest	+2.74	Bolton	-8.47
Sheff Utd	+2.67	Reading	-13.37
Derby	+1.94	Barnsley	-14.30
Burton	+1.83	Sunderland	-14.80
Middlesbrough	-1.08	Hull	-19.28

All profit & loss figures calculated to a £1 level stake at best bookmakers' odds published in the Racing Post on match day

League One

Shrewsbury	+23.58	Portsmouth	-1.40
Plymouth	+19.34	Northampton	-2.40
Wigan	+14.70	Oxford Utd	-2.61
Gillingham	+9.30	Peterborough	-3.54
Blackburn	+8.91	AFC Wimbledon	-5.41
Rotherham	+8.00	Oldham	-6.55
Charlton	+4.92	Bristol Rovers	-6.94
Southend	+4.43	Walsall	-7.29
Bradford	+2.08	Doncaster	-12.43
Scunthorpe	+1.26	MK Dons	-13.27
Blackpool	+0.92	Rochdale	-16.72
Fleetwood	+0.40	Bury	-20.45

League Two

Accrington	+26.99	Lincoln	-2.79
Exeter	+15.69	Mansfield	-3.22
Swindon	+9.41	Yeovil	-4.11
Crewe	+8.27	Grimsby	-4.32
Crawley	+8.21	Carlisle	-4.56
Wycombe	+6.91	Cambridge Utd	-5.29
Coventry	+5.11	Stevenage	-7.53
Notts County	+3.14	Barnet	-11.20
Forest Green	-0.15	Chesterfield	-12.85
Colchester	-2.03	Morecambe	-13.10
Luton	-2.24	Cheltenham	-13.10
Newport County	-2.49	Port Vale	-14.58

National League

Macclesfield	+20.14
Bromley	+9.68
Sutton Utd	+8.81
AFC Fylde	+4.18
Dover	+2.77
Maidenhead	+2.57
Boreham Wood	+2.13
Solihull Moors	+0.31
Aldershot	-0.09
Eastleigh	-1.35
Wrexham	-2.52
Ebbsfleet	-2.66
Dag & Red	-3.00
Tranmere	-3.20
Leyton Orient	-4.89
Halifax	-5.64
Woking	-5.87
Hartlepool	-6.06
Maidstone	-8.34
Torquay	-10.15
Chester	-10.60
Barrow	-15.03
Gateshead	-18.18
Guiseley	-19.18

Scottish Premiership

Kilmarnock	+21.72
Aberdeen	+8.72
Hibernian	+5.19
St Johnstone	+2.63
Hamilton	+2.15
Hearts	-1.74
Dundee	-2.10
Motherwell	-2.53
Rangers	-2.96
Celtic	-6.25
Partick	-16.50
Ross County	-21.75

Scottish Championship

St Mirren	+13.39
Livingston	+5.76
Queen of Sth	+0.06
Dundee Utd	-0.15
Inverness CT	-1.06
Dunfermline	-3.65
Morton	-3.71
Falkirk	-4.37
Dumbarton	-12.35
Brechin	-36.00

Scottish League One

Stranraer	+19.05
Forfar	+11.10
Alloa	+4.81
Ayr	+4.19
Arbroath	+3.39
East Fife	+0.62
Raith	-0.16
Albion	-6.62
Airdrieonians	-9.55
Queen's Park	-13.55

Scottish League Two

Montrose	+22.56
Peterhead	+4.39
Clyde	+2.62
Stirling	+1.45
Stenhousemuir	+0.74
Berwick	-0.25
Elgin City	-0.62
Annan	-6.27
Edinburgh City	-14.58
Cowdenbeath	-19.87

SOCCERBASE.COM

Italian Serie A

Sampdoria	+15.27
Sassuolo	+11.05
Napoli	+4.18
Juventus	+4.11
Roma	+2.22
Lazio	+1.94
Udinese	+1.04
Fiorentina	+0.99
Cagliari	-0.27
Verona	-0.56
Milan	-4.20
Inter	-4.87
Torino	-5.16
Crotone	-6.13
Genoa	-7.07
Atalanta	-7.07
Bologna	-8.64
Benevento	-8.97
Chievo	-12.55
SPAL	-18.21

Spanish La Liga

Real Betis	+35.92
Villarreal	+12.18
Alaves	+11.37
Espanyol	+8.92
Girona	+8.50
Getafe	+8.48
Levante	+6.10
Valencia	+4.42
Atl Madrid	+1.41
Eibar	-0.13
Barcelona	-0.51
Leganes	-1.01
Sevilla	-4.90
Celta Vigo	-7.10
Sociedad	-8.34
Real Madrid	-9.42
Ath Bilbao	-13.28
Malaga	-17.01
Deportivo	-20.24
Las Palmas	-22.56

German Bundesliga

Stuttgart	+19.85
Schalke	+5.43
Hoffenheim	+4.25
B Munich	+2.56
RB Leipzig	+1.06
E Frankfurt	+1.06
Hertha Berlin	+0.83
Hannover	-0.62
Mgladbach	-1.69
W Bremen	-3.51
Augsburg	-4.60
B Leverkusen	-4.66
Mainz	-5.38
B Dortmund	-9.06
Hamburg	-9.38
Freiburg	-10.23
Cologne	-12.60
Wolfsburg	-18.27

French Ligue 1

Rennes	+17.85
Strasbourg	+11.20
Lyon	+8.45
Amiens	+4.07
Bordeaux	+0.33
Marseille	-0.02
Nantes	-1.23
St-Etienne	-2.65
Paris St-G	-3.24
Monaco	-3.77
Nice	-3.98
Metz	-5.60
Guingamp	-5.61
Caen	-6.20
Dijon	-6.35
Troyes	-7.45
Montpellier	-8.28
Lille	-8.92
Toulouse	-14.55
Angers	-15.72

Multiple bets

Selections	2	3	4	5	6	7
Doubles	1	3	6	10	15	21
Trebles		1	4	10	20	35
Fourfolds			1	5	15	35
Fivefolds				1	6	21
Sixfolds					1	7
Sevenfolds						1
Full cover	3	7	15	31	63	127

Patent (3 selections, 7 bets) 3 singles, 3 doubles, 1 treble

Trixie (3 selections, 4 bets) 3 doubles, 1 treble

Yankee (4 selections, 11 bets) 6 doubles, 4 trebles, 1 four-fold

Lucky 15 (4 selections, 15 bets) 4 singles,
6 doubles, 4 trebles,
1 four-fold

Canadian (5 selections, 26 bets) 10 doubles,
10 trebles, 5 four-folds,
1 five-fold

Lucky 31 (5 selections, 31 bets) 5 singles,
10 doubles, 10 trebles,
5 four-folds, 1 five-fold

Heinz (6 selections, 57 bets) 15 doubles,
20 trebles, 15 four-folds,
6 five-folds, 1 six-fold

Lucky 63 (6 selections, 63 bets) 6 singles, 15 doubles,
20 trebles, 15 four-folds,
6 five-folds, 1 six-fold

**Super Heinz
(7 selections, 120 bets)**
21 doubles, 35 trebles,
35 four-folds, 21 five-folds,
7 six-folds, 1 seven-fold

Goliath (8 selections, 247 bets) 28 doubles,
56 trebles, 70 four-folds,
56 five-folds, 28 six-folds,
8 seven-folds, 1 eight-fold

INDEX OF TEAMS

Index of teams **255**

Odds conversion

Odds-on As %	Decimal	Fractional	Odds-against Decimal	As %
50.00%	2.00	Evens	2.00	50.00%
52.38%	1.91	11-10	2.10	47.62%
54.55%	1.83	6-5	2.20	45.45%
55.56%	1.80	5-4	2.25	44.44%
57.89%	1.73	11-8	2.38	42.11%
60.00%	1.67	6-4	2.50	40.00%
61.90%	1.62	13-8	2.63	38.10%
63.64%	1.57	7-4	2.75	36.36%
65.22%	1.53	15-8	2.88	34.78%
66.67%	1.50	2-1	3.00	33.33%
69.23%	1.44	9-4	3.25	30.77%
71.43%	1.40	5-2	3.50	28.57%
72.22%	1.38	13-5	3.60	27.78%
73.33%	1.36	11-4	3.75	26.67%
73.68%	1.36	14-5	3.80	26.32%
75.00%	1.33	3-1	4.00	25.00%
76.92%	1.30	10-3	4.33	23.08%
77.78%	1.29	7-2	4.50	22.22%
80.00%	1.25	4-1	5.00	20.00%
81.82%	1.22	9-2	5.50	18.18%
83.33%	1.20	5-1	6.00	16.67%
84.62%	1.18	11-2	6.50	15.38%
85.71%	1.17	6-1	7.00	14.29%
86.67%	1.15	13-2	7.50	13.33%
87.50%	1.14	7-1	8.00	12.50%
88.24%	1.13	15-2	8.50	11.76%
88.89%	1.13	8-1	9.00	11.11%

Correct scores 2017-18

	Prem	Chmp	Lg1	Lg2	NL	ScPr	ScCh	Sc1	Sc2
1-0	44	57	59	58	53	17	16	11	20
2-0	27	47	47	39	35	21	9	20	7
2-1	32	51	47	46	44	20	12	17	11
3-0	15	20	20	17	14	11	7	12	14
3-1	13	25	25	37	20	5	11	5	5
3-2	4	10	13	14	20	6	6	5	9
4-0	9	6	4	5	10	4	4	1	3
4-1	11	9	8	13	7	5	6	1	2
4-2	1	3	3	1	7	0	2	2	0
4-3	2	1	1	5	1	0	0	0	1
0-0	32	49	41	46	51	18	18	6	9
1-1	45	65	74	67	68	27	17	14	24
2-2	19	27	26	24	35	10	8	14	8
3-3	3	6	7	6	7	0	1	1	1
4-4	0	0	1	0	2	0	0	0	0
0-1	23	42	51	48	50	20	18	8	14
0-2	15	29	19	22	35	13	10	8	10
1-2	24	37	42	43	41	20	6	16	8
0-3	12	15	15	11	6	5	7	2	7
1-3	5	18	14	9	13	9	7	3	9
2-3	11	7	11	12	10	2	3	10	7
0-4	7	5	6	3	6	2	2	2	1
1-4	7	2	5	6	5	4	2	5	3
2-4	1	5	3	3	1	1	0	0	2
3-4	0	3	1	2	1	1	0	2	0
Other	18	13	9	15	10	7	8	15	5

Home/draw/away percentages 2017-18

	Prem	Chmp	Lg1	Lg2	NL	ScPr	ScCh	Sc1	Sc2
Home	46	43	42	44	40	41	43	44	41
Draw	26	27	27	26	30	25	24	19	23
Away	28	30	31	30	31	35	33	37	36

Unders & overs percentages 2017-18

	Prem	Chmp	Lg1	Lg2	NL	ScPr	ScCh	Sc1	Sc2
<1.5	26	27	27	28	28	24	29	14	24
>1.5	74	73	73	72	72	76	71	86	76
<2.5	49	52	53	51	53	51	49	37	47
>2.5	51	48	47	49	47	49	51	63	53
<3.5	71	75	75	72	72	75	67	63	69
>3.5	29	25	25	28	28	25	33	37	31
<4.5	85	89	89	86	87	89	84	77	83
>4.5	15	11	11	14	13	11	16	23	17

Ante-post odds of recent champions

Premier League	Best odds
2017-18 Manchester City	19-10
2016-17 Chelsea	13-2
2015-16 Leicester	5,000-1

Championship	Best odds
2017-18 Wolves	12-1
2016-17 Newcastle	15-8
2015-16 Burnley	14-1

League One	Best odds
2017-18 Wigan	8-1
2016-17 Sheffield United	6-1
2015-16 Wigan	7-1

League Two	Best odds
2017-18 Accrington	25-1
2016-17 Portsmouth	9-2
2015-16 Northampton	14-1

National League	Best odds
2017-18 Macclesfield	28-1
2016-17 Lincoln	16-1
2015-16 Cheltenham	11-1

Scottish Premiership	Best odds
2017-18 Celtic	1-9
2016-17 Celtic	1-3
2015-16 Celtic	1-33

Scottish Championship	Best odds
2017-18 St Mirren	4-1
2016-17 Hibernian	5-4
2015-16 Rangers	4-5

Scottish League One	Best odds
2017-18 Ayr	11-4
2016-17 Livingston	11-2
2015-16 Dunfermline	9-2

Scottish League Two	Best odds
2017-18 Montrose	14-1
2016-17 Arbroath	6-1
2015-16 East Fife	13-2

Asian handicaps

Conceding handicap			Receiving handicap	
Result of bet	Result of game	Handicap	Result of game	Result of bet
Win	Win	0	Win	Win
No bet	Draw	Scratch	Draw	No bet
Lose	Lose		Lose	Lose
Win	Win	0,0.5	Win	Win
Lose half	Draw	0.25	Draw	Win half
Lose	Lose		Lose	Lose
Win	Win	0.5	Win	Win
Lose	Draw		Draw	Win
Lose	Lose		Lose	Lose
Win	Win by 2+	0.5,1	Lose by 2+	Lose
Win half	Win by 1	0.75	Lose by 1	Lose half
Lose	Draw		Draw	Win
Lose	Lose		Win	Win
Win	Win by 2+	1	Lose by 2+	Lose
Return stake	Win by 1		Lose by 1	Return stake
Lose	Draw		Draw	Win
Lose	Lose		Win	Win